JUDGMENT AND MERCY

JUDGMENT AND MERCY

THE TURBULENT LIFE AND TIMES OF THE JUDGE WHO CONDEMNED THE ROSENBERGS

MARTIN J. SIEGEL

THREE HILLS
AN IMPRINT OF CORNELL UNIVERSITY PRESS
Ithaca and London

First published 2023 by Cornell University Press

Printed in the United States of America

Library of Congress Cataloging-in-Publication Data

Names: Siegel, Martin J., 1966– author.
Title: Judgment and mercy : the turbulent life and times of the judge who condemned the Rosenbergs / Martin J. Siegel.
Description: Ithaca : Three Hills, an imprint of Cornell University Press, 2023. | Includes bibliographical references and index.
Identifiers: LCCN 2022034159 (print) | LCCN 2022034160 (ebook) | ISBN 9781501768521 (hardcover) | ISBN 9781501768538 (pdf) | ISBN 9781501768545 (epub)
Subjects: LCSH: Kaufman, Irving R. (Irving Robert), 1910–1992. | Judges—United States—Biography.
Classification: LCC KF373.K397 S54 2023 (print) | LCC KF373.K397 (ebook) | DDC 347.73/0234 [B]—dc23/eng/20221019
LC record available at https://lccn.loc.gov/2022034159
LC ebook record available at https://lccn.loc.gov/2022034160

To my parents—my greatest teachers,

Bettina—my greatest love,

and Lily and Asher—my greatest joys

And I, my head encircled by error, said:
"Master, what is this I hear, and what people
Are these so overcome by pain?"

And he said to me: "This miserable state is borne
By the wretched souls of those who lived
Without disgrace yet without praise."

Dante Alighieri, *Inferno*

Contents

Acknowledgments

This book has been in the making since 1994, when I tentatively and intermittently began researching Judge Kaufman's life for what I hoped might eventually become a biography, so there have been many to thank along the way.

Judge Kaufman's papers are housed at the Library of Congress, and I'm indebted to staff at the Manuscript Reading Room who assisted me on several visits, especially Alex LoBianco. The National Archives and Records Administration maintains the files of federal legal cases, and I benefited greatly from the assistance of several dedicated NARA archivists, including Pamela J. Anderson, Kelly McAnnaney, Trina Yeckley, Chris Gushman, Carey Stumm, Martin McGann, Richard Gelbke, and Allen Fisher.

Archivists and other experts at seven presidential libraries and many other collections were also responsive and helpful in guiding my research and providing copies, including particularly Hailey Philbin at the Kennedy Presidential Library; Danielle Clark and Meghan Lee-Parker at the Nixon Presidential Library; Beth Calleros at the Reagan Presidential Library; Sarah Patton and Diana Sykes at the Hoover Institution; Mary Person at Harvard Law School; Patrice Kane and Rev. Msgr. Professor Thomas Shelley at Fordham; Elizabeth Haluska-Rausch and Elizabeth Hilkin at the University of Texas Law School; Larry Sheldon, Patrick Raftery, and Barbara Davis at the New Rochelle Public Library; Lisette Matano at Georgetown; Ann Causey at the University of Virginia; Lynn Catanese at the Hagley Museum and Library; Elizabeth Hyman at the American Jewish Historical Society; Nancy Lyon at Yale; Melinda Wallington at Rochester; Kristen Nyitray at Stony Brook; Yvette Toledo at the New Hampshire State Department; Christa Cleeton at Princeton; Elisha Neely at Cornell; David Favaloro at the Lower East Side Tenement Museum; Julia Rodriguez at DeWitt Clinton High School;

Richard Collins at the American Bar Association; and Danielle Nista at New York University.

I owe further thanks to others who provided access to materials not otherwise available to the public. Chief among these is John Kaufman, Judge Kaufman's grandson, and his wife Laura, who graciously opened their home to me for several days so I could review and duplicate Kaufman family files, photos, and correspondence. A close second is Gerard Pelisson, who doggedly tracked down records relating to Judge Kaufman in old files at DeWitt Clinton High School. Thanks also to an old colleague, David Kennedy, an Assistant US Attorney in the Southern District of New York, who furnished copies of newsletters from that office during the 1930s; Alexander Wohl, who provided copies of documents used in his excellent biography of Justice Tom Clark; and Robert Cox, who connected me to primary sources knowledgeable about desegregation in New Rochelle.

Many people also deserve credit for assisting my research more directly. I worked with several fine student researchers, including Yasmeen Waheed, Caleb Kaufman (no relation to Judge Kaufman), Shalina Chatlani, Brendan Keenan, Sophie Jacobson, Aaron Shuchman, and Evan Siegel. Arthur Feldman permitted me to use his Westlaw subscription. Professional genealogist Barbara Sontz and freelance researchers Jon Taylor, Thera Webb, and Eduard Medrano were of great help as well. I made extensive use of several libraries in Houston and am especially obliged to Mary Lowery at Rice University's Fondren Library, whom I pestered repeatedly and who always cheerfully responded.

I'm grateful for my editors at Cornell University Press—Michael McGandy, Emily Andrew, and Clare Jones—for their belief in this book and their wise guidance in improving and completing it. Two old and generous friends read drafts of the manuscript and provided valuable advice and feedback: Professor Tim Schroer at the University of West Georgia and Professor Tracy Thomas at the University of Akron School of Law. I'm thankful also to Professor Rachel Toor of Eastern Washington University, who helped guide my proposal for academic presses, gratis, and offered encouragement and amusement just when both were in especially short supply. I can't name every person with whom I discussed the book over the years, but a few who went above and beyond in lending their ears, batting around ideas, and tendering moral support were Daphna Boros, Lance Hosey, Sue Heilbronner, Michael Cohen, Dan Elias, Dave Watkins, Daniel Shuchman, Ken Hughes, Professor Reuel Schiller, my brothers Charles and David Siegel, and my father and retired professor of history Stanley Siegel. Dan Elias, the Watkins-Lorenson family, and Pete Levitas merit special recognition for the mitzvah of hosting me during research trips.

Finally, the greatest thanks of all are due my family. During the years I spent working on this book at home, my children Lily and Asher not only tolerated their father's new and odd presence around the house during the workday but also kept me afloat with laughter, much-needed coffee breaks, and constant love and diversion. My wife Bettina lent her superb writing and editing skills to the manuscript and made innumerable key suggestions. Much more importantly, she provided steadfast support for this unorthodox turn in my career and, better still, unfailing love and emotional ballast. I could not have completed this project (or done much else) without her.

JUDGMENT AND MERCY

Prologue
The Funeral

On a freezing February morning in 1992, I left the tiny apartment I shared with an architect and his girlfriend near Washington Square and headed uptown. I was on a sad and surreal errand—my boss's funeral. He was a federal appellate judge, on the bench for forty years, and for the past six months I'd been one of his two law clerks. Just out of law school, we analyzed cases for him, recommended how to rule, and wrote first drafts of the court's opinions. Heady stuff for twenty-somethings still reeling from bar exams. But now we were filing past NYPD officers into the Moorish opulence of the Park Avenue Synagogue. We tiptoed around the dignitaries—former heads of the CIA and FBI, other judges, media bigwigs—and found seats in back.

I don't remember much of the service; mostly I was people watching. Then came the moment no one there will ever forget. The rabbi, a white-haired eminence, was winding up a soft-spoken eulogy when out of nowhere someone behind me bellowed: "*He murdered the Rosenbergs! Let him rot in hell!*" For a split second it felt as if a bomb had detonated. The elderly grandees gasped, ducked, lurched. I recovered in time to turn around and see an old, shabby figure calmly stride out of the sanctuary. The rabbi, a seasoned pro, recovered and went on.

After the service, out there on Madison Avenue, two or three people were parading in a little circle holding signs, picketing in the icy cold. I was dumbstruck. Protesting a dead man from the grainy, gray-and-white yesteryear of the McCarthy era? I was twenty-five, and to me they might as well have been screaming "Remember the *Maine*!" I couldn't believe actual living people still cared—still hated the man enough to find and infiltrate his funeral and hound him one last time, literally into the grave. Justice Felix Frankfurter once said that being forgotten "is the fate of all but very, very few judges." At least my old boss, Irving Robert Kaufman, was one of the few.[1]

In 1951, Kaufman wrangled to get the trial of Julius and Ethel Rosenberg, charged with stealing the "secret" of the atomic bomb and handing it to the monstrous Joseph Stalin. He was forty, one of the youngest federal judges in America and only sixteen months in office. During the trial, he often intervened in ways that helped the government. Upstairs in his chambers, he conducted secret, *ex parte* meetings with prosecutors, including the infamous Roy Cohn. No one knows what they discussed. Once jurors convicted, he deftly advertised his anguish over the sentence and alluded to solitary soul-searching in his empty, dimly lit synagogue. "I shall approach my task with deep humility," he'd written the president on his appointment, "for to judge man is almost a divine prerogative." Now the hour for judgment had come.[2]

But his lonely meditations didn't end in mercy. Instead, he condemned the young couple to die in the electric chair in Sing Sing and blasted them for nothing less than igniting the Korean War. "Who knows but that millions more of innocent people may pay the price of your treason," he thundered before a spellbound Manhattan courtroom. Carried out two years later despite a frenzied push for clemency that united Picasso and the pope, the death sentences convulsed America and ratcheted up Cold War tensions. By then, bomb threats had driven Kaufman and his family from their luxurious Park Avenue apartment.

The septuagenarian zealots stalking his memorial service were missing something, though. In the years that followed the Rosenberg case, the hanging judge became something few who didn't know him predicted: a progressive stalwart. He was the first federal judge to desegregate a school north of the Mason-Dixon Line. After President John F. Kennedy elevated him to the appellate bench—the United States Court of Appeals for the Second Circuit, then the second most important federal court in America—his opinions modernized the insanity defense, improved juvenile justice, reformed Attica-era prisons, and shielded conscientious objectors from the jungles of Vietnam. The grateful son of immigrants, he freed "the man without a country" stranded on Ellis Island and halted Richard Nixon's deportation of John Lennon on bogus drug charges. In a decision called the *Brown v. Board of Education* of human rights law, he breathed life into a vague, dusty statute from 1789 and permitted victims to bring their foreign torturers to justice in American courtrooms. His greatest mark was on the First Amendment, as he championed the press and free speech in the Pentagon Papers case, a landmark libel suit against *60 Minutes*, and other pathbreaking decisions. Floyd Abrams, then perhaps America's leading First Amendment lawyer, labeled Kaufman "one of the most eloquent articulators of the underlying meaning" of that constitutional guarantee; "his rulings reflected an abiding belief in the significance of free expression for everybody." Again and again, civil liberties lawyers would think of the martyred Rosenbergs and blanch on learning Kaufman was one of the three judges assigned to decide their appeal—only to turn ecstatic when he ruled in their favor. Grace withheld from the Rosenbergs overflowed toward others: the weak, the excluded, the unpopular.[3]

So the fierce, living passion aroused that day by the old, dead Irving Kaufman poses a riddle about judicial schizophrenia: How did the man responsible for two of the most infamous executions in American history become one of the most illustrious liberal jurists of his time? The question is what two historians called the "enigma" of the Rosenbergs' judge—a figure typically but wrongly caricatured as nothing more than a minor, bloodthirsty supporting cast member in the morality play of McCarthyism.[4]

Kaufman's clamorous send-off also reflected the wages of an extraordinarily tumultuous judicial life, one produced by a superheated energy and frantic ambition. "My entire career has been one dominated by a sense of urgency," he confided to a family member. In his first four decades, he rose from nothing to national hero. Most people thought the Rosenbergs got what they deserved, and newspapers and congressmen hailed his courage in defying communist bullying and lunatic death threats. Little seemed to block his path to the "Jewish seat" on the Supreme Court.

But gradually, over the second forty years, the terror of atomic annihilation and the red-baiting dissipated, and a deferred and scornful howl went up over what had happened to the Rosenbergs. In the 1970s, the couple's orphaned sons came of age and led a new generation's crusade to expose the government's asserted "frame-up" of their parents, charges made all too plausible by the stream of official lies in Vietnam and Watergate. When FBI records revealed Kaufman's private dealings with the prosecution, it was suddenly 1953 again. Dogged by new threats and strident protesters, denounced in print and faced with calls for impeachment, he lived under siege. His haunting by the eternally young couple bubbled to the surface in defensive outbursts to people he hardly knew and in a relentless, decades-long, secret campaign to counter and muzzle critics. I saw it in the sad, creased, oxidized-brown index cards I found on his desk in 1991 quoting praise from the Rosenbergs' lawyer almost a half century earlier.[5]

Life in this pressure cooker exacted its bitter toll. One of Kaufman's sons was in the synagogue that morning to say farewell. But two were absent. They'd predeceased Kaufman after decades of substance abuse, paternal haranguing, and in one case, mental illness. Dominated by the husband she'd married at nineteen, Kaufman's wife Helen suffered her own travails—alcoholism, anorexia, and attempted suicide. Misery shadowed the family's gilded lives among New York's Jewish elite, and few in the know chalked it up to coincidence.

For most who do it, judging offers one of life's quieter, cloistered pursuits. "By and large, judges lead unspectacular lives," wrote one profiler of the revered Judge Learned Hand in 1946. "Their careers, like broad plateaus, are unmarked by gullies and hills." For Kaufman, however, the judicial calling formed a backdrop to heartache and collateral damage. What began as dazzling and precocious self-made success, a sprint toward the summit of legal power, ended largely in self-inflicted tragedy. Just as the letter writers and funeral pickets wanted.

This book ignores much of Kaufman's jurisprudence, though he wrote important decisions in antitrust, copyright, civil procedure, and other fields. It also moves quickly through his lifelong work in the technical world of court reform, though as his friend Justice Thurgood Marshall once said, "no one can point to any forward movement in judicial administration in the last twenty-five years that Judge Kaufman wasn't either the leader of or had a hand in." Instead, this account aims to illuminate and explain the curious path from Sing Sing in 1953 to progressive champion in 1992, a period when political and judicial liberalism also experienced great evolution, and when judges increasingly came to be seen as willing political actors.

Mirroring and sometimes propelling this transition, Kaufman began as a Trumanesque "tough liberal," firmly statist and anticommunist. Anyone could see the large patches of want and inequality in society, and like others of his political persuasion he thought government and courts should address them. As a man who began empty-handed but gained wealth and power through law and government, he had great faith in, and gratitude toward, America. By the end, though, his liberalism had morphed into something different. He consistently supported the broadest and newest conceptions of individual rights and civil liberties, making him an unlikely partisan for dissidents and outcasts. Early confidence in the government's capacity to bring about badly needed change and deference to its stances on national security and law enforcement gave way to skepticism and endorsement of litigants fighting the power of the state. And he was frank and unapologetic about the judge's duty to formulate and implement social policy at a time of growing backlash against the idea.[6]

Finally, beyond the larger forces, lurks the man. Despite judges' importance, our system seeks to anonymize them, from uniform black robes to Delphic pronouncements in legalese. Yet temperament and inner life are among the key forces that contribute to judicial outcomes, though almost all the attention usually goes to ideology or political background. As one legal philosopher said famously long ago, "There is no guarantee of justice except the personality of the judge." Or as Kaufman himself put it, "Justice is administered by human beings." And Kaufman the man defiantly refused to recede into bureaucratic obscurity.[7]

Judges, especially appellate ones, are usually thought of as reactive, dispassionate, reserved, Olympian, contemplative. For better and worse, Kaufman was the opposite: active, hyperenergetic, combative, consumed with image, power hungry. At a bantamweight five feet, four inches, he disappeared into his leather-backed chair, leaving a head barely visible above the bench. His deep, loud, gravelly, heavily accented New York voice had to do the work, and it never failed to make itself heard. In court, the fleshy face with its broad and mashed-up nose and curled-down lower lip often formed what Roy Cohn called an "intimidating leer." Until gray emerged victorious in his sixties, his hair was thick and black and slicked back. He placed great stock in appearances—looking British and thinking Yiddish—and his dark three-piece suit was always well-tailored, with cufflinks and pocket square to boot.[8]

To those squirming under his thumb—clerks, secretaries, lawyers who didn't measure up—he was tyrannical, a grenade waiting to explode. One ex-clerk I called said simply, "That was the worst year of my life, and I don't want to talk about it." Another cried in the bathroom so often that, when Kaufman learned where she was, he decided she must be drinking too much water and ordered it banned from chambers. As for her co-clerk, Kaufman raised himself up on tiptoes and shouted in his face so rabidly that the clerk thought to himself, *I think I'm going to hit this guy*, and wondered if that was a federal crime. That was when Kaufman was eighty, after a triple bypass and a year from death. Before I even started, I heard about the time he got a call from security downstairs, after which he quietly put on his coat and left the office. A few minutes later, a marshal called back and was astonished that one of the clerks picked up the phone. "Didn't the judge tell you about the bomb threat?" the man asked. Of course he hadn't—Kaufman had wanted them to keep grinding. Was the story true? Who knows. The point is, it was believable. "Fundamentally, he was not a nice person," an earlier clerk acknowledged.[9]

Yet Dr. Jekyll was there, too—always. To friends and peers he was affectionate and dependable. A few clerks adroitly navigated the tantrums and emerged close confidantes, with a powerful and eager backer in their corner. His eye could twinkle as he charmed listeners with jokes delivered with "the polish of a Catskills comedian," as one former clerk put it. Gregarious and charismatic when he thought it was worth the effort, he could and did seize the spotlight in rooms full of more prominent people. Burt Neuborne, a renowned constitutional litigator and law professor who often appeared before Kaufman, found him conscientious and "crackling smart." Leonard Garment, White House counsel and eminent voice of reason in the Nixon administration, thought Kaufman "one of the handful of truly interesting men I have known," thanks to "high intelligence, large ambitions, clearly defined goals, plus tenacity, energy, a feel for public policy, and a guerilla-fighter's capacity to survive in the swamps of politics in government and in the law. I've known many men and women who may score higher on tests of sweetness and light," Garment allowed, "but none of these people—however commendable their lives—have ever really engaged my interest." In 1977, a reporter assigned to profile Kaufman found herself defeated and eventually gave up, telling her editor, "I could not come to terms with all the ambivalent feelings Irving Kaufman provoked. A man with a devouring passion for publicity. And one also who calls up a kind of sympathy for the raw nerves, the warmth, that are also a part of him. This is the stuff from which novels are made, not *Times Magazine* pieces." Or as one anonymous lawyer summarized Kaufman for a guide to the federal judiciary, "He's courageous, outspoken, opinionated, articulate, usually right, and not much loved."[10]

Memoranda between judges at the Second Circuit were addressed to recipients using their initials. Kaufman was "IRK." Everyone agreed it fit him perfectly.

CHAPTER 1

Isidore Mortem

In 1902, an Englishman traveling in King Carol's Bucharest came across crowds of homeless Jews languishing on the outskirts of the city. "Whole colonies of these outcasts are relegated to wait their turn for relief," he wrote, "or to take breathing time for some further flight to an unknown world outside, which, at worst, cannot be so cold and pitiless as their own inhospitable country." Tzvi Hersch bar Schloma and his wife Ruchel might have been among them.[1]

They'd fled Galicia, Austria-Hungary's backwater, for Romania for most of the reasons people leave bad for slightly better. Where they came from—a town of three thousand called Jagielnica, land now in western Ukraine—centuries of Jews had cycled through poverty and pogroms. They lived near the center of town in a cluster of wooden huts with threshing floors and tar paper roofs. The two main factories, one for bricks and one for tobacco, wouldn't hire Jews. The Galician parliament had new and harsher antisemitic voices, and the ancient curse of blood libel reappeared in 1882 when a Jewish couple was condemned to death for murdering a Christian girl. Only later was the verdict set aside in Vienna. Catholic hard-liners proclaimed a boycott of Jewish businesses in 1893, and pogroms erupted five years later. Tzvi and Ruchel decided to get out.[2]

But Romania was just a way station. Two of their children were born there, but they aimed to keep moving. "Suddenly America had flashed upon our consciousness and fanned our dormant souls to flames of consuming ambition," wrote Marcus Ravage, who left Romania for America in 1900. "All my relatives and all our neighbors—in fact, everybody who was anybody—had either gone or was going to New York." And so Tzvi and Ruchel and their two toddlers followed in the summer of 1903.[3]

Traveling first to Liverpool, where giant liners disgorged raw materials and tourists from America in exchange for bewildered emigrants, they boarded the SS *Campania*, one of Cunard's finest vessels, for New York. There was little luxury in steerage, however, where they pitched and swayed across the Atlantic with a thousand others. When their ship steamed into New York, Tzvi and Ruchel had all of forty-two dollars—not much, but more than many others belowdecks. Once Tzvi denied being an anarchist or a polygamist, they were admitted to the United States. After processing at Ellis Island, names duly anglicized to Herman and Rose Kaufman, the family inevitably followed the multitudes to the Lower East Side—what Henry James called "a Jewry that had burst all bounds." Streets suffocated with drays and pushcarts on both sides, while peddlers hawked everything imaginable, from cabbages to clothing. Homes weren't much better; one examination found most sleeping three or more to a room.[4]

The Kaufmans—usually pronounced "cowfman" by the locals, not "coughman"—landed in a five-story brick tenement on Division Street with sixteen other families. Soon there were three more children: Rebecca in 1904, Abraham in 1906, and Isidore on June 24, 1910. The street was dominated by an el track and the looming, gargantuan entrance to the Manhattan Bridge, opened only a few months earlier. Down below, slivers of light escaped from gaps in the train track, dotting the street here and there, and cinders occasionally fluttered down and came to rest on the heads of passersby.[5]

Nine of the families in the Kaufmans' building were headed by tailors, and their street was the center of the garment trade. Despite their address, the Kaufmans didn't live by clothes. Herman worked as a tinsmith, then a meter tester for the gas company, and at some point on the docks. Unlike many immigrant women, Rose didn't work. One of their daughters later said Herman forbade it, though he earned only two dollars a day reading meters.[6]

Like most newcomers, the Kaufmans sought out the familiar and joined the *Landsmanschaft* for new arrivals from Jagielnica. These benevolent societies provided everything from help during hard times to cemetery plots to comfort in cafés frequented by members. As *Galitzianers*, the Kaufmans hugged the bottom of their new home's totem pole, which placed even Russians and other Poles higher. To say nothing of the Germans, who formed a Jewish aristocracy far above Division Street tinsmiths. Hence a Galician girl complained to the Yiddish socialist newspaper the *Forward* that her coworker had told her "the *Galitzianer* are inhuman savages." (The *Forward* pronounced him "an idiot.") As the writer Joseph Roth summarized, "The Frankfurt Jew despises the Berlin Jew, the Berlin Jew despises the Viennese Jew, the Viennese Jew despises the Warsaw Jew. Then there are the Jews from all the way back in Galicia . . . the lowest of all Jews." One Lower East Sider recalled that a neighborhood settlement house packed children "on a bus, and we would ride all the way up Fifth Avenue. We would see where all the German Jews lived with the goyim." Isidore Kaufman would live there too, in a grand Upper East Side apartment house, and he might first have glimpsed his later surroundings from the window of one of those envy-stricken buses.[7]

For all the newcomers' perceived backwardness, however, Old World ways were fading. Some Jews abandoned their faith altogether, choosing new creeds like socialism or anarchism, while others more quietly and gradually shed the shtetl rituals. The Kaufmans seem to have epitomized this evolution, with the older children hewing close to orthodoxy while the younger siblings born in America adopted what Abraham Kaufman's son called a "revolving door" Judaism—synagogue attendance twice a year on high holidays. Isidore, the youngest, would gravitate to upscale Reform and Conservative synagogues and later called his Jewish education "scanty."[8]

If his Jewish learning was sparse, no one neglected the secular kind. Immigrant families jammed libraries and settlement house classes, desperate to learn. But their focus was the sons. The writer and critic Alfred Kazin remembered his parents working "in a rage to put us above their level; they had married to make *us* possible. We were the only conceivable end to all their striving; we were their America." And the sons responded with zeal. In his autobiography, Morris Raphael Cohen described such boys as personifying "a force that was more than the force of any single individual. It was as if a great dam had broken and the force of water accumulated over many years had been let loose." To

Irving Howe, this drive among the Jewish sons caused "precocity . . . a neurotic need for perfection"—in other words, Isidore Kaufman.[9]

Hundreds of thousands of families lived this familiar history in the twentieth century. Doctors, lawyers, scientists, professors, entrepreneurs, artists, entertainers, financiers—their ranks swelled with second-generation American Jews. But if the story is nothing new, few families embodied it more completely than the Kaufmans. Family lore, told two and three generations on, held that Rose sat her boys down one day and gave them an order. "You're going to be a doctor," she commanded Ben. Turning to Abraham, she said, "You're going to be a dentist." And to Isidore: "You like to talk a lot, so you're going to be a lawyer." Incredibly, these instructions were followed to the letter. Ben's son Herb, himself a prominent surgeon, conjured up what must have happened. "Someone looked around and said education is the only way out of here."[10]

So Kaufman began racing through the public schools of New York City. When he was seven, the family left the Lower East Side for West 111th Street, one block north of Central Park. The street boasted rows of new buildings with white façades and names meant to conjure European elegance, like "The Charles," and "Isabelle." But Harlem was fast becoming its own ghetto. A government survey found families "were crowded together in dark, ill-smelling apartments, and were unable to find better quarters." The war was on, exacerbating a citywide housing shortage. Seven-year-old Isidore saw the news and bought war savings stamps to help the young men fighting in France. Harlem was a center of cigar making, and Herman began making and selling humidors and moisteners.[11]

At twelve, Kaufman enrolled at DeWitt Clinton High School, an all-boys school. Located then at Fifty-Ninth Street and Tenth Avenue—soon it would move to the Bronx—it was surrounded by choking factories and eyesore tenements. One graduate remembered "a very tough block. . . . The cops would walk in threes, one with his back turned to guard the rear." But the school itself was a five-story, Flemish Renaissance-style temple boasting murals and gold plasterwork, a lunchroom for eight hundred, a well-stocked library, and a gym with running tracks and showers. Kaufman's older brothers had gone there, and he'd been impressed. "I saw what it did for them," he remembered more than a half century later. Ben called the school "David Clinton" because the student body was three-fourths Jewish. Nonetheless, every slice of life in the burgeoning city was represented—African Americans, Irish

Americans who spurned the city's Catholic schools for one reason or another, and newly arrived Italian Americans. Graduates included Fats Waller, Burt Lancaster, Stan Lee, Nathanael West, Neil Simon, James Baldwin, Ralph Lauren, Lionel Trilling, and many more—a sort of twentieth-century who's who.

In a history of Clinton, former teachers Gerard Pelisson and James Garvey wrote that the values taught to Kaufman in the 1920s "were those of mainstream Protestantism . . . democracy, laissez-faire capitalism, civic concern, propriety and self-reliance. The Clinton student who had not been born into these mores was encouraged to think and act as if he had been, especially if he wanted to arrive in the front ranks of society." Rigorous academics meshed with attention to home life. "Old and patched clothes may be worn neatly just as a new suit may look disorderly. Anyone of us can afford soap and water even though we may not be able to afford a new suit frequently," the *Clinton News* instructed. The exhortations worked. One photo of the French squad, which Kaufman captained in 1925, shows him and the others staring gravely back at the camera, suit jackets smartly buttoned, ties and pocket squares in place, hair perfectly combed and slicked.[12]

At home, Kaufman studied the piano. "People who had mostly lived in poverty and ignorance at home now had a piano or a violin

FIGURE 1. The DeWitt Clinton High School French squad in 1925. Kaufman is second from the left in the bottom row. *DeWitt Clinton High School.*

in the house," Abraham Cahan noted in his classic novel of ghetto life, *The Rise of David Levinsky*, "with a son or daughter to play it." Kaufman's brothers were the better musicians, though. Ben accompanied silent movies on the piano, while Al played drums with Sammy Kaye's band and entertained diners at the famous Concord Hotel. Kaufman worked in the Catskills, too. The pay was meager, but there were fresh air and lots of girls around, and he was likely glad to have the work.[13]

Only sixteen but finished with high school, Kaufman now had to pick a college. For most in his shoes, that was easy—City College beckoned. Tuition-free and nearly 90 percent Jewish, CCNY was said to stand for "College of the Circumcised Citizens of New York." Ben had enrolled at Fordham, however, because he figured his odds of admission to medical school would improve if he was from a Catholic school rather than just another Jew from CCNY. So his youngest brother followed suit. Since Fordham Law School had just increased its admission requirement to two years of college work, Kaufman and 383 others enrolled in a two-year program the school had designed for prelaw students.[14]

Fordham's old, main undergraduate campus was and remains at bucolic Rose Hill in the Bronx. But in 1914, its law school moved into the glorious, neo-Gothic Woolworth Building downtown, opposite City Hall and the courthouses. Other programs quickly followed, and "downtown Fordham" was born. At sixty stories, the Woolworth was then the tallest skyscraper in the world. Each day, Kaufman passed through a stunning marble lobby of mosaics, stained glass, and murals celebrating "Commerce" and "Labor." As at Clinton, grandiose surroundings pointed him onward and upward. In the Bronx, Fordham was a traditional college, all white and all male. Its boys were mostly Irish, and virtually all were Catholic. And judging from the 1928 *Maroon*, the Fordham yearbook, it was an insular place. That year's volume included ugly parodies of Jews and African Americans. In an undergraduate stab at comedy, a Jewish cartoon character with a beard and a hooked nose tells a story about Charles "Linboigh" in a mash-up of Yiddishized English: "Dey tought he vuz on'y a kid, mebbe, bout he shud 'em!"[15]

Downtown, though, a different Fordham was taking shape, one more in tune with the rapid changes cascading through the city. Jews, African Americans, and women—strivers all—learned side by side, closer to home and part-time jobs. Classes were also scheduled at flexible hours or at night. Kaufman joined Tau Epsilon Phi, a fraternity formed a few years earlier by Jews at Columbia excluded by the older societies.[16]

His first year in college proved difficult. Kaufman's grades were all Cs, except for a D in French and a B in public speaking. Besides the usual liberal arts curriculum, Fordham mandated theology courses like Epistemology, Cosmology and Ontology, and Principles of Natural Religion. These were thought salutary even for the Jewish students; as one Jesuit father wrote, the school was turning many "from a scoffer of religion to an interested spectator and well-wisher." Kaufman's struggles may have reflected the challenges of competing with older classmates or perhaps simply the transition to more difficult work. There were also the pressures of the age. College boys were suddenly killing themselves in alarmingly high numbers—fourteen alone in the first two months of 1927. At NYU, students formed an "anti-suicide club." Grasping for answers, one minister fingered overwork and Bolshevism, while a rabbi deplored "card parties, dances, jazz and cheap movies." When one of the suicides happened at Fordham, the school was faulted for neglecting its "humanistic, imaginative" ethos and "becoming more and more like great business institutions."[17]

Then, in the middle of Kaufman's first year, death hit closer to home when his father died of lung cancer. Watching his father weaken, and then the loss itself, must have jolted the sixteen-year-old. Nothing is known of his real relationship with his father other than a stock, bland tribute in *Current Biography* in 1953: "He [Kaufman] has spoken of the 'understanding, love and wise guidance' he received from his parents, now deceased, as the strongest influence on his life." Kaufman may have regarded his father with the faint embarrassment the second generation sometimes reserved for their greenhorn forebearers. Or he might have seen his father's journey from Galician shtetl to modest American success as a worthy model for his own, more ambitious self-manufacture just under way. In any case, losing his father surely knocked Kaufman off his stride precisely when he was struggling to adjust to harder work and different surroundings. He and his mother and sister Rebecca were taken in by his oldest sister, Sarah, and her husband, who lived in a tidy, two-story duplex in Borough Park, Brooklyn. The mostly Jewish neighborhood was a clear improvement over Harlem. Instead of overcrowded apartments, there were single-family houses. Instead of the deafening and jumbled street life, there were quiet gardens. Instead of Yiddish, English. The family did well enough to have a live-in maid.[18]

At school, things improved somewhat in Kaufman's second year, including As in American history and a theology course. The latter was due largely to a 99 on his final exam—an event described colorfully in a later *Saturday Evening Post* profile: "Kaufman enrolled at Fordham University at the age of fifteen and immediately impressed the Catholic fathers who taught him. When the final grades for a difficult course in Christian doctrine were announced, the Murphys and O'Briens drew down 75's and 80's, but Irving Kaufman rated 99, the highest in the class. Thereafter, his classmates took to calling him 'Pope Kaufman.'" Much about this—presumably confided to the reporter by the subject himself—is hyperbole. Kaufman entered Fordham at sixteen, not fifteen, and the grades he received in his first year make it doubtful he immediately impressed anyone. On at least one exam, though, he'd outscored the Catholics—and in theology, no less.[19]

Having completed his prelaw work, Kaufman filled out the brief law school application in June 1928. Its only substantive question asked why he wanted to study law and gave all of three lines to answer. Kaufman wrote, "So that I may become acquainted with the wonderful workings of the law, and carry out these teachings in such a manner that I may be an asset to my community." He elaborated on a later form for admission to the bar: "Since early youth I aspired to become a lawyer because the practice of the law symbolized to me the dispensation of justice to everyone; to me, the lawyer was the object of profound respect and admiration. I wanted a profession as a career, and my choice of the law is attributable both to my sense of fitness and qualification for that profession, and its honorable traditions." A few weeks later, he was admitted to Fordham Law School, with studies to begin in September. Tuition was $200 per year.[20]

Like the prelaw program, Fordham Law School was in the Woolworth Building. Enrollment was surging, continuing a pattern that began with returning World War I veterans, and the facilities were overwhelmed. Half the students were the children of immigrants, many going to school part-time, and the school welcomed African Americans and women—the latter first admitted to plug the hole left by soldiers shipped overseas. Jews made up almost a third of the classes in Kaufman's afternoon sessions and, by most accounts, felt right at home.[21]

When attending lectures, he sat in the same new chair screwed to the floor in every course. Men wore jackets and ties, as at Clinton. Called on to "recite," he had to stand and deliver a summary of the case under discussion and submit to a grilling by the professor, fielding questions as best he could. "Every course," he wrote a half century later, "in some small measure, seemed to promote one's advocacy skills through that delightful professorial technique known as the Socratic method." Classes covered standard subjects: contracts, criminal law, property, and so on. First years also took jurisprudence—a subject not then offered by most other schools. Father John X. Pyne's course stressed the linkage between Catholic thought and ideas of natural law undergirding America's founding documents. It was the law school's way of injecting Catholicism into the classroom and answering the more popular theory then sweeping the academy: legal realism. Realists sought to show that, despite the abstract and high-sounding rhetoric in judicial opinions, judges actually decided cases based on political and personal preferences shaped by society and all its inequities. They looked to social science and empiricism as the best means for explaining how laws and rules came about and what they meant. Not surprisingly, this was anathema to the Jesuits at Fordham, believers in immutable, God-given law as the cornerstone of American justice.[22]

Kaufman's grades were unexceptional. He averaged a low B every year, with a smattering of As and Cs here and there. Today's grade inflation might make this record look worse than it actually was, since As were rare then. Yet he was not among the ten graduates who could boast of finishing cum laude. As with Kaufman's college record, though, later accounts would greatly exaggerate his law school performance. Articles, including one by a dogged young *Newsday* reporter named Robert Caro, routinely said he "ranked at the top of his graduating class" or was its "top man." Kaufman himself was likely the cause of this embellishment. Early on, he wrote and told others he was the best student in his class. One résumé he prepared in 1940 said he was "ranked at the top of his graduating class"; he said the same to FBI background investigators in 1947. Yet Kaufman *was* at a disadvantage. The furious dash through school that led him into college at sixteen and law school at eighteen forced him, as before, to compete against older rivals. When an earlier FBI background investigator called the school, the registrar volunteered "that she thought [Kaufman] must have been very clever inasmuch as he completed a law course before he was twenty-one years of age."[23]

Outside the Woolworth Building, law students also learned by watching and doing. Kaufman had only to cross the street and slip quietly into the courtrooms of the federal building. He sat in the back, taking it in. It was there, he said later, that he first saw the commanding, black-robed judges and resolved to become one.[24]

Kaufman finished his educational race and reached the tape in June 1931. Because his twenty-first birthday fell eight days after commencement, he couldn't graduate with his class, and his degree wasn't officially conferred until October. The bar exam posed a greater hurdle; applicants had to be twenty-one, so Kaufman would have to wait several months to start practicing law. Finding this patently unacceptable, he did what he would do throughout his life when confronted with roadblocks—he furiously worked the problem behind the scenes. As the *Saturday Evening Post* explained, "Much distressed, [Kaufman] urged an attorney friend to petition the New York State Court of Appeals to waive the age requirement in his case. The attorney called informally on the late Chief Judge Cuthbert Pound, who duly considered the petition. 'Tell the young man to slow down a bit,' the chief judge said finally. 'A few months wait will do him good.' The following October Kaufman was allowed to take his examination and passed promptly."[25]

The end of school warranted another change, too. He decided during his third year to become Irving rather than Isidore. Isidore must have struck him as unprofessional or too Jewish or too Old World or just embarrassing somehow, so he went to the courthouse, wrote up the necessary forms, and emerged as Irving. In his papers to the court, he said he had been known as Irving by friends and later business associates since childhood. Kaufman had never had a middle name, but now he made one up: Robert. To a lifelong Anglophile, this may have connoted a sort of aristocratic gravity. The change wasn't something he told others later in life. It appears nowhere in print, and his grandsons, who knew him well, were completely unaware. But he was far from alone in seeking this sort of Americanization. All his siblings except Ben did the same. Abraham became Al, Sarah became Shirley, and Rebecca was Beatrice or Beatty. Kaufman had shed poverty and the Lower East Side. He had rocketed through school and was on the precipice of a new life. Now he ditched Isidore and became Irving Robert Kaufman, *IRK*.[26]

Chapter 2

Demon Boy Prosecutor

Prospects for graduates like Kaufman were bleak in 1931. The Depression was in full swing, and he was an average student from an average school. And there was a deeper problem: the doors of many law offices were closed to Jewish applicants. The elite bar was horrified by the influx of what establishment titan George Wickersham called the "pestiferous horde" of Eastern European newcomers lacking "the faintest comprehension of the nature of our institutions, or their history and development." So it tightened admissions requirements and politely declined job inquiries. Two out of every three Jewish lawyers in the city practiced alone, and those who could find jobs with existing firms were almost invariably hired by other Jews.[1]

Kaufman was one of the latter. In his last year at Fordham, he found a clerkship with a Manhattan lawyer named Louis Rosenberg—no relation to the couple so central to his later life. He knew Rosenberg's eldest son Herbert at Fordham Law, and Herbert also joined the firm after graduation. Kaufman remained a clerk until he passed the bar exam and obtained his license in 1932. On his bar application, which required applicants to give their "plans for the immediate future," Kaufman declared his intention to stay with Rosenberg long enough to acquire necessary experience. Then, he said, "as soon as I feel that in justice to myself and my future clients I have become sufficiently qualified to assume the responsibilities which an attorney is called upon to, I will engage in the practice of law in my own behalf." After Kaufman's bar admission, Rosenberg paid him all of twenty-five dollars a week.[2]

Rosenberg had arrived from Budapest as a child in 1886. While at NYU Law School, he became a tenement inspector charged with scouring ramshackle buildings for trash, broken windows, and poor ventilation, and taking complaints from the tenants in their native Yiddish. But soon he was representing some of the same miscreant landlords he'd previously targeted, as well as subcontractors, architects, and construction firms. So great was his mastery of the field that his family called him "Lien Law Louie," after the property liens contractors used to guarantee payment. Louis Nizer, one of the country's most famous courtroom advocates, thought Rosenberg "an outstanding lawyer." Better still, Rosenberg's practice led naturally to wheeling and dealing in real estate, which made him a wealthy man. He specialized particularly in the new parking garages starting to rise in Manhattan for the automobiles just beginning to jam city streets.[3]

Rosenberg's home life befitted a successful lawyer and minor real estate mogul. He was firmly an "allrightnik"—the immigrant or immigrant's son who makes it in America and ditches the ghetto for the Upper West Side. Home on Central Park West was an eighteen-story, neo-Renaissance palace with a pink marble lobby and vast apartments. Kaufman's new boss stood before him as all he might attain if the practice of law smiled on him as it had on Louis Rosenberg.[4]

Before long, Kaufman was the office's "managing attorney"—an impressive title that, back then, referred mostly to office administration. Over time Kaufman tackled motions, briefs, and eventually trials. And clients began asking for him. As Rosenberg said at the time, Kaufman was blessed with "a good legal mind," the ability "to dissect and digest legal problems easily," and the "mentality and will necessary to the attainment of success." His demeanor impressed, too; Kaufman "is always pleasant, punctual, and willing to work," Rosenberg allowed.[5]

Construction lawsuits and scofflaw landlords couldn't hold Kaufman's attention, however, and he began to think of higher things. This wasn't a complete surprise around Rosenberg's office; in a reference supporting Kaufman's bar application, one lawyer there had thought him "molded by humanitarian and idealistic considerations rather than by business principles." His target was the United States Attorney's Office.[6]

The crusading prosecutor lionized for incorruptibility and selfless public service is a type known everywhere, but it might have reached an apex in New York in the 1930s. The city had already celebrated several such men in Kaufman's short lifetime: Charles Whitman, a district attorney who unearthed rotten links between police and organized crime and rose to the governorship; Samuel Seabury, an old-fashioned pillar of rectitude who dethroned the corrupt and flamboyant mayor Jimmy Walker; and Ferdinand Pecora, counsel to a Senate banking committee who highlighted the Wall Street chicanery leading to the crash of 1929. Above all, there was another young man like Kaufman just beginning to make a name for himself in the US Attorney's Office: Thomas E. Dewey. Dewey's takedown of the gangster Waxey Gordon—"If the revenue laws break down, disband your Army, sink your Navy, fire your President and have anarchy," he memorably convinced jurors—made him a national hero. He became known as the "baby prosecutor," his tender age belied only by a thin mustache.[7]

The US Attorney in Manhattan was and remains the nation's second-most-important federal prosecutor, behind only the attorney general. The office's hard-won autonomy from the Justice Department in Washington gave rise to its nickname, the "Sovereign District of New York." Those who filled the position before Kaufman's first days in practice went on to scale the mountaintop of law and politics, filling the governorship, cabinet posts, and high judgeships. Beneath the US Attorney worked the cream of New York's newly minted lawyers—"a corps d'elite," explained Milton Gould, who chronicled that era of the New York bar, "young, zealous, educated to the point of snobbery." They were there to perfect their craft and begin building reputations. "For the younger men, especially," said the US Attorney in 1933, "there is the satisfaction of not being obliged to wait interminably behind a shingle for work that is slow in coming. It is here in plenty." Government service particularly attracted Jewish lawyers in the early thirties, since the Depression and persistent bias made jobs at law firms so hard to come by. Top Jewish graduates from the Ivies were pouring into Washington to staff the New Deal, but for Fordham graduates, New York was usually the ceiling.[8]

If its reputation and the rapid ascent of men like Dewey drew Kaufman to the US Attorney's Office, how was an applicant from a lesser school with average grades supposed to get in? Luckily, it was an unusually good time to hail from Fordham. Franklin Roosevelt's new US Attorney, Martin Conboy, was a major Catholic lay leader decorated by Pope

Pius himself, and his chief assistant had actually gone to Fordham. Politics also helped. Republicans had run the office for twelve long years, and now it was the other party's turn. A feud between New York's Democratic machine, Tammany Hall, and Roosevelt had cooled by 1934, and Tammany influence likely greased the wheels for Kaufman's hiring. Real estate men like Louis Rosenberg were often politically connected, and his family built ties to New York's Tammanyite senator, Robert F. Wagner. Kaufman's FBI background report noted that Wagner had "sponsored him for appointment." However he arranged it, Rosenberg had an especially powerful motive to promote his managing attorney's career: the young man was soon to be his son-in-law.[9]

When Kaufman first met her, Rosenberg's youngest child, Helen, must have struck him as everything he wasn't. Kaufman had known typical immigrant privation, while Helen's girlhood memories were of Central Park West and rides around town in a Stutz Bearcat. Like the fictional Marjorie Morningstar, also born in 1916, she looked out over the city and could revel in "the spacious view of the green park and the skyscrapers . . . a sense of luxury each day when she awoke." That sense was heightened by the cook, chambermaid, laundress, and nannies who catered to her and her siblings; the family's summer home on the Jersey shore; and vacations to Caracas and Trinidad.[10]

Of necessity, Kaufman had been serious and driven, consumed with education. Helen was vivacious and fun but not much of a student, failing to finish a two-year normal school that trained kindergarten teachers. Her lack of more serious education contrasted not only with her brothers, both Columbia men, but even her mother, a Hunter graduate. A great-niece thought Helen's family wrongly dismissed her as "not that smart," perhaps unduly limiting her potential. Or Helen may simply have imagined little more for herself than she saw in her mother, a wealthy homemaker. "Helen absolutely worshipped her mother and father," her daughter-in-law reported. She cut out dozens of little poems from the women's pages of newspapers with romantic and marital advice and glued them into a gold-embossed, monogrammed bankbook her father gave her, such as,

> To knit, to sew, to spin,
> Was once a girl's enjoyment,
> But now to fix, and catch a beau
> Is all of her employment.

and

> **Feminist**
> If there ever comes a time
> When a lover's kiss
> Simply leaves me cold,
> Or connubial bliss
> Is a little frayed,
> And a manly stride
> Or a rumbling bass
> I can't abide—
> I hope the gods will take their cue
> And renovate my point of view.[11]

Over the years, profiles of Kaufman told the same story of how he chose to court Helen, who was only fourteen or fifteen when they met. As one newspaper put it,

> Louis Rosenberg had a daughter, a pretty, blue-eyed brunette named Helen. Every once in a while Helen would traipse through the office to see her father. Kaufman always said hello to her, and goodbye, only those words and no more.
>
> In an informal moment, Kaufman once confided that he knew immediately this was the girl he wanted to marry. While he worked for Louis Rosenberg, he made no overt move lest somebody think he was trying to get in good with the boss. When he won a government job as a prosecutor, his first private action was to phone Helen Rosenberg for a date.[12]

In reality, Kaufman probably had more contact with Helen before they started dating than he let on to journalists. Rosenberg told FBI agents checking Kaufman's background that Kaufman had frequently visited his home, meaning that Kaufman probably knew Helen better than a "hello" in the office. And dating her may have preceded his new job as a federal prosecutor, not the other way around. One family member thought the marriage had essentially been "arranged" between Kaufman and his onetime boss. As a family friend remembered, "Louis got him the job after he married Helen." The friend's timing is off—they didn't marry until the following year—but Kaufman's relationship with Helen, perhaps even hints or promises of marriage, may have helped him get the federal position rather than coincidentally postdated it.[13]

Kaufman joined the US Attorney's Office in early 1935. His new workplace was "Mullett's Monstrosity"—a giant specimen of French Second Empire kitsch dating to 1878 and nicknamed for its hated architect. It was a blasphemous, triangular wedding cake of columns, balconies, domes, and mansard roofs. Inside, the absence of air conditioning forced the windows open during the summer, bringing in the city's dust and din. Throngs awaiting naturalization crowded the corridors, as did lawyers and their clients. The place was so frenzied that judges had been forced to move their chambers across the street into the Woolworth Building, where Kaufman had gone to school.[14]

The US Attorney and his assistants occupied three floors in the ancient structure. Every irregular corner of the office offered reminders of a dim and distant past. Remains of a primitive, interoffice "speaking tube" system installed by Elihu Root, US Attorney in the 1880s and later secretary of state, could still be seen, as could a records room under the north dome rumored to have been where prisoners were hanged. "Probably no congeries of offices was ever shoved into more uncomfortable and drearier surroundings," one reporter observed. In these archaic quarters, Conboy's fifty assistants were hard at work on the government's legal business. "Every young and ambitious lawyer is willing to devote to his work, if need be, all the hours he can spare from sleep," the boss observed. "When the law offices of lower Manhattan close," one newspaper profile reported, "that of the nation here practically begins another day. There is a hum of activity to midnight and often the rooms are busy until dawn." Camaraderie eased the burden, though; Assistants also golfed, played cards, and drank together.[15]

At first, Kaufman's job was to support the more experienced prosecutors. In one case seemingly plagiarized from Dashiell Hammett, a private detective named Noel Scaffa deftly recovered $185,000 in diamond jewelry stolen from the Miami Biltmore room of a Follies dancer, Margaret Hawkesworth Bell. The case took a twist when investigators determined that Scaffa had secretly worked with gamblers to recover the jewels and pocket a tidy profit from Lloyds. Kaufman and others secured his conviction. Other early cases targeted a serial swindler hyped by postal inspectors as America's "super confidence man"; sailors who caused a melee aboard a luxury liner by attacking crewmen from a rival union; and Samuel Roth, whose name would eventually grace one of the most important First Amendment decisions of the twentieth century.[16]

FIGURE 2. Kaufman began work as an Assistant US Attorney in 1935 in the federal post office and courthouse built in 1878 known as "Mullet's Monstrosity." *Wikimedia Commons.*

Roth started with serious literary ambitions but ended up peddling pornography with titles like *Kate's Secret Tryst.* Kaufman appeared at his arraignment and declared the inventory the "filthiest he had ever seen." At trial, Roth's defense lawyer tried to humanize him by having his daughter Adelaide dramatically run into court and embrace her mother, who'd also been charged. The ham-handed stratagem backfired when Kaufman put her on the stand, had her admit she was studying acting, and established that she'd written shipping orders for some of the material—proving the Roths had stooped to enlisting their children in the crime. She later scorned Kaufman as her "ambitious little opponent" possessed of special zeal, she believed, out of abhorrence at her father's antisemitic writings (though Roth was himself Jewish). It wouldn't be the last time Kaufman was accused of bending over backward to punish a coreligionist. Roth was convicted, served time, eventually resumed his old trade, and then gave his name to the 1957 Supreme Court decision that greatly loosened obscenity laws. For Kaufman, a First Amendment

FIGURE 3. In 1936, the US Attorney's Office moved to a new federal courthouse in Foley Square designed by Cass Gilbert, where Kaufman would also preside as a judge and which still stands. *Brandon Saglam.*

champion on the bench, the irony of helping to jail a man for selling books and pictures wouldn't be apparent for several decades.[17]

The Roth case gave Kaufman his first taste of publicity as a crime fighter, and his first dose of responsibility for a high-profile case. And 1936 brought other changes. Federal prosecutors left Mullett's Monstrosity for a new, thirty-story courthouse a few blocks away in an old slum rechristened "Foley Square," after a Tammany saloon-keeper. The building by celebrated architect Cass Gilbert effected an awkward marriage between skyscraper and traditional federal-style courthouse, complete with portico and four-story Corinthian columns, but its gold-leafed pyramid and lantern still decorate the city's skyline. Inside, white-veined marble and spacious wood-paneled and air-conditioned courtrooms made the proceedings as dignified and quiet as they'd previously been deafening and oppressive. Kaufman and the other assistants moved into ample quarters with new furniture and the latest-model telephones. Kaufman also had a new boss: Lamar Hardy, a dapper and courtly southerner who had played football at Vanderbilt with the famous sportswriter Grantland Rice.[18]

There was momentous change outside the office, too, when he married Helen after a seven-month engagement. The rabbi at Congregation B'Nai Jeshurun officiated, and the ceremony likely took place at the beautiful and imposing synagogue on Eighty-Eighth Street near West End Avenue. The Rosenberg family's old and prosperous synagogue was a long way from the tiny storefront *minyan* for downtrodden Galitzianers the groom probably knew as a boy. Not long after the wedding, the couple moved into a new apartment in a white, art deco high-rise on West Ninety-Sixth Street, half a block from Central Park. A family photo captioned "1st apartment" shows a well-appointed living room with wall-to-wall carpeting, deco torchieres, sleek upholstered furniture, and a crystal service set. The location and accoutrements suggest a lifestyle safely beyond the $150 Kaufman received from Washington every month, as did their membership in a country club in leafy Mount Vernon, just north of the city. Helen had always known luxury, and her father duly supplemented the couple's resources.[19]

As Kaufman was finishing with the Roth prosecution in October 1936, lawyers for large insurance companies like Prudential and New York Life rode downtown to Foley Square to talk to James J. Doran, New York City's chief postal inspector. "Something's fishy here," one began, as they laid out evidence of questionable claims for payments on policies for disability insurance. Kaufman was assigned to the case and quickly set up a task force with Frank Shea, one of Doran's veterans and a local legend. Shea was a former altar boy, now in his sixties, with white hair parted near the middle in the old-fashioned style, a bushy white mustache, and sharp blue eyes. "No man with that face would ever lie," prosecutors routinely told jurors. Years before, he'd captured "Gentleman George" Chapman, the gangster labeled America's first "Public Enemy Number 1," after a deadly shootout.[20]

Before long, they zeroed in on a lawyer, Joseph Weiss. A surprising number of Weiss's clients had obtained disability policies and then turned up ill. Soon, a detective dressed as a telephone repairman went to Weiss's basement and diverted phone lines to a room where Shea was listening. As calls came in, operators yelled "record!" and turntables with new RCA Victor records spun into action, preserving every word. At the end of each day, the discs were put into sleeves, carefully labeled, and ferried downtown. Eventually, Kaufman had six thousand of them.[21]

What he heard was astonishing. Sometimes the exchanges were cryptic, or in Hungarian or Yiddish, but slowly a vast fraud came into focus. First, "chasers" working for Weiss enlisted people willing to buy disability policies. Next, crooked doctors fed them black coffee and pink digitalis pills, elevating the heart rate, and had them run up and down stairs or walk the Brooklyn Bridge. Then, they checked into hospitals, where the doctors administered electrocardiograms recording the irregular cardiac findings. The paper trail complete, Weiss reentered the picture and filed for coverage for heart disease. The men had been "doped like race-horses," Hardy told the press, and had reaped tens of millions in bogus payouts.[22]

Once Kaufman had the recordings, he set about getting confessions. A reporter described Shea's interviews with Weiss's accomplices, no doubt embellishing:

> "I've been dying for months," a stooge would groan, tottering to a chair.
>
> And Shea, soothingly: "Perhaps a little music will make you feel better. I've got a new record I'll play on my phonograph."
>
> Then the inspector would turn on a transcription. In a moment, his caller stiffened into perfect health, shrieked: "That's my voice! How'd you get this?"[23]

When the arrests began in May 1937, it was front page news; "Health Insurance Racket Bared," ran a typical headline. Guilty pleas led to threats against the stool pigeons Kaufman needed, however,

FIGURE 4. Assistant US Attorneys Kaufman and Gregory Noonan, later his law partner and a federal district judge, listen to phonographs of wiretapped conversations in the disability insurance racket case, 1938. *Associated Press.*

endangering the prosecution. "We know that a car full of gunmen was cruising around, looking for a chance to shoot down at least one of the defendants, a government witness," he told a reporter sensationally. And Kaufman himself was threatened. "When Federal officers closed in," he said later, "the ring was desperate. They had a sweet racket and wouldn't stop at murder."[24]

Weiss was the first of many to face trial, and his lawyer was one of the most formidable of the age–Lloyd Paul Stryker. "With a head that would have looked well over a Roman toga, the vocabulary of an eighteenth century essayist and the timing of a trapeze artist," one obituarist wrote, "he never disappointed his audience–whether his clients won or lost." True to form, Stryker's opening statement colorfully called a cooperating cardiologist so corrupt that jurors shouldn't believe him even if it only "involved whether a yellow dog was to be killed or not." His client Weiss, on the other hand, had put himself through school by working in a factory, and a "man that has worked with heavy hammers, with an anvil, the forge, has not quite the background for a cheap fraudulent thief." By comparison, Hardy's opening statement for the government was bland and lackluster.[25]

Kaufman examined the first government witness, a policyholder. "I took the pills," the man recounted, "and my heart began jumping around like a grasshopper. I screamed in pretended agony until the nurse jammed me with the hypo needle." Asked if he had any real pain, the witness seemed offended and pounded his chest: "I'm proud of my health!" He filed twenty or thirty false claims, and the checks came rolling in, endorsed by Weiss. Then government aides wheeled in giant filing cabinets with meticulously organized records and a black phonograph, and the jury heard the man's voice and Weiss coaching him. This touched off a key battle in the case: whether the intercepted conversations could be admitted into evidence. Stryker tried to bully his rookie opponent, until eventually Kaufman had had enough: "I refrained from interrupting Mr. Stryker when he was making his beautiful speech about wiretapping, and I submit that I now have a right to state my [argument]." No trial in the city yet had featured phonographs playing criminals' private talks, and witnesses and spectators alike—even Weiss—crowded around the black machine in wonder during recesses.

For his part, Stryker tried to show policyholders genuinely could have had heart disease, or that their doctors might have been innocently mistaken. Kaufman ridiculed him for the resulting medical tutorial, laughing that "while I am quite ready to admit that this is very enlightening, and I really enjoy it, and I am learning an awful lot, still I do not think it has anything to do with this case." Stryker portrayed Weiss as a successful lawyer unknowingly surrounded by con men, but the façade dissolved under the drip-drip-drip of Kaufman's cross-examination. He exposed Weiss's fishy practices: having clients change their names to get new policies, sending claimants to preselected doctors, and dictating the contents of medical reports. When Weiss pleaded forgetfulness, Kaufman asked if he wanted to hear the matter discussed in his own voice. At this, Weiss repeatedly winced, knowing what would happen if the black phonograph machine cranked up again. Eventually Stryker exploded, demanding a mistrial over Kaufman's "threatening and very impolite method of cross-examination," but the judge coolly overruled him.

After seven weeks of trial, four hundred exhibits, and five thousand pages of testimony, all that remained were closing statements. Going first, Stryker claimed it was the government that had conspired, working hand in glove with greedy insurance companies. Kaufman's witnesses were liars, he asserted, boasting that he'd "sent a bucket down into this dirty, framed-up case, and I have brought it up and shown it to you. Can you too stand the smell of the perjury?"

Then Kaufman stood before the jury—jet black hair perfectly slicked back, conservative dark suit, pin holding the knot of his tie just over the collar of a pressed white shirt, immaculately folded pocket square. He looked like a cherubic and well-off college freshman. He'd once considered growing a Dewey-like mustache to confer some gravitas, but Helen and others had talked him out of it; now he might have wished he'd gone through with it. "The courtroom was in tears when [Stryker] finished," one article said years later. How would his novice adversary respond? Wisely, Kaufman turned his youth to his advantage:

> I have the misfortune of having to follow such an eloquent speaker as Mr. Stryker. I cannot hope to match his eloquence and his rhetorical [powers], I cannot hope to be able to play upon your emotions and to pull at your heart strings the way Mr. Stryker [has]. . . . After all, I am a babe in arms in the law. Mr. Stryker was practicing law probably before I was born. But I say that in a case of this kind not all the Strykers . . . not all the oratory, not all the eloquence can change the facts and the evidence on my side, and . . . make 1 and 1 3, it still equals 2.

Kaufman reminded jurors that everything his much-maligned witnesses had said "was corroborated by these little black discs, which they would not dare question." That "nice American boy," Weiss, had used Hungarian to cover his tracks, unaware that what he said, "even in Hungarian, would be recorded." What an "awful miscarriage of justice" it would be, Kaufman finished, if the small fries who admitted their guilt were convicted while the higher-ups went free. "What a premium would be put on the maxim of the underworld, 'Keep your mouth shut.' "[26]

A day later, he and Stryker and everyone else reassembled to hear the jury's verdict: the junior prosecutor and his phonograph had bested Stryker's speechifying. Public accolades followed, with the Associated Press offering the ultimate comparison: "In a startling parallel to the sensational vice-ring and racket-smashing investigations of [Thomas Dewey] . . . another bright young law college graduate, 28 year-old," had won an impressive legal victory. The piece noted Kaufman's police protection and how, like Dewey, he'd "ignored personal threats." Kaufman was "seven years younger than Dewey," readers learned, and occupied "the same post where Dewey began his spectacular rise." Kaufman himself explained the case's significance:

> "As a direct result of the investigation disability claims dropped more than 50 per cent," Kaufman said. "One big company alone reported a $9,000,000 decrease in claims over the previous year." Claimants with "bad" hearts and other health-crippling afflictions suddenly decided they felt better all at once. "Some of the cures," said Kaufman with a twinkle, "were really remarkable."[27]

Yet while Kaufman was basking in praise, Weiss quietly went about appealing his case all the way to the Supreme Court, which decided that the Federal Communications Act of 1934 precluded the government's use of the wiretapped calls. What seemed like a terrible defeat happily proved short-lived, however. When the case came back to New York, all the fight went out of Weiss. He decided another trial was too risky, even without the stacks of records and the black phonograph. Weiss caved and pleaded guilty, though by then Kaufman was barely paying attention. He was consumed with another case—an even bigger and more spectacular fraud.[28]

McKesson & Robbins was an old and venerable drug firm. Founded in 1833, it supplied medicines to clipper ships and sometimes took payment in California gold dust. By 1926, internal squabbling and poor management had led it to the auction block. The man who bought it for $1 million was a short, pudgy, bald doctor with an owlish face and horn-rimmed glasses named F. Donald Coster.

Coster headed Girard & Co., a smaller drug company in Fairfield, Connecticut. And since the purchase, McKesson had thrived. Where prior leaders were weak and conflicted, Coster moved boldly. To secure better deals on raw materials, he hired lawyers abroad and smashed the iodine monopoly in Chile, the bismuth trust in Bolivia, the combination that set quinine prices in Amsterdam. Then he conceived a daring plan to reinvent the whole pharmaceutical industry by consolidating with regional wholesalers and independent druggists. Both were being squeezed by the rapidly growing chains like Walgreen's, and a merger would create economies of scale. By 1937, McKesson distributed fifty thousand products to thirty thousand retailers and manufactured much of what it sold. With $155 million in sales (almost $3 billion in today's dollars), it had a net worth of $88 million.[29]

Not surprisingly, the man responsible for this resurrection was hailed as a business genius. According to his entry in *Who's Who*, Coster had a PhD from the University of Heidelberg and had practiced medicine in New York. As his biographer wrote, Coster "was not only president; he was the company. His board of directors . . . had been brought to heel by the impact of his driving ambition, the brilliance of his ideas, and, of course, the fat dividends on their investments." His management style was imperious. Underlings called him "the Duke," while he referred to them as "maggots." "If you asked him one question, he'd get sore, and if you asked him two he'd fire you," remembered one frightened subordinate.[30]

His home life in Fairfield was opulent. He bought an Italianate mansion on seven acres of gardens and supplemented those accommodations with a 123-foot yacht. Money compensated for his lack of established social connections, and he bought his way into the Lotos Club and the New York Yacht Club. Politicians, bank presidents, and local gentry often joined him for cocktails. "After a couple of highballs, he wasn't a bad guy," said one. Yet he was strangely aloof. His basement fit a hundred partygoers but was never used; nor did he frequent his rarefied clubs. When he went to the city, he declined social invitations and returned home as soon as possible. He even tended to walk a bit ahead of colleagues on the street. "We guessed that the great man was just absorbed in thought," one acquaintance said.[31]

Coster also dabbled in politics. Like many successful businessmen of the day, he regarded Roosevelt's New Deal as a ruinous folly. He wrote angry letters to the White House and supported politicians useful to McKesson. In 1937, Republicans were on the hunt for a businessman to bear their standard—a search that would culminate in Wendell Wilkie. Before fixing on Wilkie, they visited Coster at his Connecticut home. "Dr. Coster, we think you should be a candidate for President of the United States," a bank president announced in Coster's library. Coster had received a telegram from California Republicans with the same plea. He demurred, assuring them he was flattered and citing unspecified personal considerations.[32]

Given all this, the news that hit the city's pavement on December 7, 1938, was startling. A federal judge in Connecticut had appointed temporary receivers to examine allegations of falsified records in McKesson's "crude drug" department—a unit that bought and sold extracts and compounds used in medicines and cosmetic products. The next day brought news that investigators working for the newly created

Securities and Exchange Commission were also investigating, and a federal grand jury was soon impaneled. Kaufman's experience with the complex disability racket made him a natural fit to lead the case.[33]

He soon realized he should start at the top. The government issued a warrant for Coster's arrest, and as a freezing dawn broke the next morning, Kaufman was on a train to Connecticut. By the time he boarded, strange doubts had started to swirl in New York. On the hunch of an old state investigator who'd seen the news and Coster's photo, detectives were beginning to pull dusty case files from long-forgotten crimes committed decades earlier.[34]

Arriving in Fairfield, Kaufman went to Coster's house, the most luxurious he'd ever seen. Twenty reporters and photographers packed into the library to capture the scene. As he entered, Coster had what one of the reporters called a "stricken, blind look that glazed his eyes." He wore a bathrobe over his clothes and seemed tired, leaning on his psychiatrist for support. On a table was a framed quotation from Harriett Beecher Stowe: "When you get into a tight place and everything goes against you till it seems as if you couldn't hold on a minute longer, never give up then, for that is just the place and time the tide will turn." Coster's lawyer announced his client would waive the customary reading of the arrest warrants, and the US marshal turned to Coster and said, "You are now formally under arrest." Coster just sat motionless and put his hand over his eyes. People were about to leave when Kaufman turned to Coster's lawyer and made a surprising demand: his client would have to be fingerprinted.[35]

The procedure made little sense for Coster. He was widely known, and this wasn't, say, an unsolved burglary. Roused from his stupor, Coster angrily objected, but Kaufman threatened to drag him to the nearest federal courthouse if he preferred. Coster whispered to his lawyer, and they disappeared into another room. Twenty minutes later, they glumly summoned Kaufman. "This is testy," Coster muttered, as he hesitantly offered his hand. Back in Manhattan, Kaufman reflected on the bizarre scene. "That man has a weird look in his eye," he told Greg Noonan, one of Hardy's deputies. "He'll either die a natural death or kill himself before this is over."[36]

Meanwhile, in the records room of a Lower East Side police station, hours of searching yielded a file filled with crimes committed by a fugitive years ago, as well as his fingerprints. The prints Kaufman had captured were taken to police headquarters, and just before midnight, officials summoned reporters for a stupefying announcement: Dr. F. Donald

Coster of McKesson & Robbins wasn't F. Donald Coster at all. He was Philip Musica, a twice-convicted swindler who had vanished almost two decades earlier only to resurface now, somehow, as the acclaimed president of one of America's leading corporations. The next morning, the news was on front pages all over America.[37]

Utterly unknown today, Musica is one of the most remarkable tricksters in the history of a city with more than its share. "Nothing in local criminal history quite compares with it," the *Times* said after three hundred years of local criminal history, and the statement remains true after eighty-five more. As the paper's legendary city desk man, Meyer Berger, put it, "the whole story out-fictionizes fiction."[38]

The studious son of Neapolitans with a store near the East River docks, Musica joined the family business at sixteen and quickly devised a competitive edge: he convinced customs officers to understate the weight of the mortadellas and salamis arriving from Italy, paid less in import duties, undersold rival stores, and split the difference with crooked officers. Profits soared, and the Musicas bought a mansion in Brooklyn while young Philip frequented Delmonico's and befriended the Great Caruso. In 1909, however, someone blew the whistle, and Philip went to the state reformatory at Elmira. He served five and a half months until his sentence was mysteriously commuted by President Taft. When his early days were closely reexamined in 1938, no one could say how he managed to arrange a presidential pardon.[39]

Back in the city, Musica hit on another importing scam: human hair shipped from overseas and sold for eighty dollars a pound to construct women's elaborate coiffures. Founding the "United States Hair Company," he dispatched his mother to banks to obtain loans secured by nonexistent inventory. When suspicions aroused by a forged bill of lading led bank officers to seize Musica's crates, all they found was worthless barbershop clippings and newspaper. Days later, private detectives located the entire family on a steamer about to leave New Orleans for Honduras. As they were being led away, Philip dramatically brandished a revolver and declared "I'll kill myself before I get there!" Detectives wrestled the gun away from him, and he quickly regained his composure. They weren't fleeing at all, he said confidently, they'd always just wanted to see Central America. For the first time but not the last, he made the front pages of New York newspapers.

This time Musica went to the Tombs, where he began a rewarding career as a snitch. His first mark, Hans Schmidt, was a minister accused of murdering and dismembering his girlfriend. At Musica's suggestion, Schmidt tried to evade guilt by feigning mental illness, but then Musica switched sides and exposed Schmidt's ruse, leading to the minister's execution. This not unpopular result earned Musica his freedom, and he became a full-time investigator for New York's attorney general, under the name William Johnson. Assigned to the "poultry war" murder of a prominent kosher-chicken dealer, Musica conjured an affidavit from an old friend in the Tombs fingering Joseph Cohen, an innocent man who also ended up on death row. Musica's most sensational case involved William Randolph Hearst, whose newspapers had enthusiastically publicized Musica's frauds. Producing statements from chauffeurs and doormen, Musica claimed Hearst had conspired during World War I with Bolo Pasha, a wealthy French adventurer and German agent. While the claim tarnished Hearst, Musica was eventually the bigger loser. During hearings after the war, a Hearst-friendly senator unmasked "Johnson" and demanded to know how an aliased convict was working for New York law enforcement. The lawyer in charge stammered that he "became convinced that [Musica] had repented of his sins," calling him "a beautiful Christian spirit." Only Pasha came off worse in the embarrassing affair when the French shot him for treason.[40]

The Hearst debacle received wide publicity, rendering "William Johnson" as unsuitable for continued use as "Philip Musica." After the hearings, Musica "came into our office, grabbed his hat and coat and disappeared," his old boss told reporters. It was a good time to run, since authorities were in the process of discovering that Joseph Cohen, once only seven minutes from execution, had been framed. Musica was indicted for suborning perjury, but the case languished for some reason—another puzzle no one could explain later—and the missing defendant quietly took yet another identity: Frank Costa, head of the Adelphi Pharmaceutical Manufacturing Co. in Brooklyn. Adelphi sold hair tonics, mouthwash, and furniture polish—anything with high alcohol content that bootleggers could turn into cheap whiskey during Prohibition. Then he founded Girard & Co.; changed Costa to Coster; installed his brothers George and Robert as corporate officers under the last name "Dietrich"; and had a third brother, Arthur, become "George Varnard" of the fictitious outside firm W. W. Smith & Co., supposedly a broker. Flush with large sums from bootlegging, he was poised to conquer McKesson. After the purchase, he installed the "Dietrich" brothers as officers.[41]

Once in control, Musica homed in on the crude drug department, supposedly run from a Canadian subsidiary. On paper, the division bought natural oils and extracts used in drugs, held them as inventory, then resold them to foreign buyers at a profit. Musica made a habit of dazzling colleagues by murmuring knowingly about exotic ingredients like oil of juniper and benzoin of Siam, and McKesson's bankers and board members were suitably impressed. And why not? The unit's books showed growing profits, inventory, and accounts receivable.[42]

In fact, it was all a sham, buttressed by counterfeit purchase orders, made-up invoices, and other documents created using different typewriters and mailed back and forth between Fairfield and dummy offices in Canada and Brooklyn. This charade of record-keeping was mostly for McKesson's accountants at Price Waterhouse. Musica understood that auditors only examined the records given to them and never inspected stated inventory to see if what appeared on paper actually existed in warehouses. Nor did they call listed customers to see if they were really doing business with McKesson. Yet some things might have been obvious just from the records. The volume of ketone musk listed in McKesson's Canadian warehouses exceeded what could possibly be derived from all the Himalayan musk deer in Asia. The records said vanilla beans had been shipped in two-hundred-pound bags, though in reality vanilla beans were packed in tins. And the Musicas' phony routing orders sometimes moved products overseas "by truck."[43]

The unraveling started in 1937, when McKesson's treasurer, Julian Thompson, noticed that money from the crude drug department was being pumped back into the unit instead of financing the parent company, as with other divisions. Inquiries to Musica were deflected, but Thompson kept digging. When contacted, listed British customers had never heard of McKesson. Dun & Bradstreet reports had been forged. Finally, Thompson dropped in on the Brooklyn office of W. W. Smith & Co., Varnard's fake firm, and found it empty except for a secretary and one person, Arthur Musica, who seemed to be drunk. Thompson alerted McKesson's board and Musica's ruse was up.[44]

The day after Kaufman's fingerprinting unmasked Musica, Kaufman filed additional charges in New York, which necessitated Musica's rearraignment. Rather than travel back to Fairfield, Kaufman arranged for prosecutors in Connecticut to do the job. At a few minutes after noon on December 16, 1938, they were entering his house. This time, Musica had resolved that things would end differently. He'd woken up early that morning and sullenly declined breakfast in favor of a stiff drink, something he never did. After wandering around in his bathrobe with a vacant and distracted look, Musica headed up to the bathroom and closed the door. As federal agents and his own attorneys were crossing the threshold, he put a pistol to his ear and fired. A suicide note absolved his brothers and claimed, "As God is my judge I am the victim of Wall Street plunder and blackmail in a struggle for honest existence. Oh merciful God, bring the truth to light."[45]

As if fulfilling Coster's dying wish, Kaufman would spend all of 1939 and much of 1940 bringing the truth to light. The drama may have lost its lead, but there was still much to investigate. Had others at McKesson committed crimes? How much money had Musica embezzled, and where was it? Since Musica had supplied bootleggers for years and insinuated himself into Connecticut politics, were politicians or gamblers also involved? The case took on even greater urgency at the Justice Department because Attorney General Homer Cummings and his top lieutenant, Brien McMahon, were both from Connecticut. "Nothing in the files of the Department of Justice can compare with this case," McMahon said, and he personally supervised Kaufman and beat back his rivals—Dewey at the district attorney's office, and New York attorney general John J. Bennett.[46]

The surviving Musica brothers had no serious defense and quickly pleaded guilty, turning the spotlight on other McKesson officers. Three grand juries heard from hundreds of witnesses over several months. By one account, Kaufman and his colleagues reviewed over a million pieces of correspondence. It was the largest case ever handled by post office inspectors. But for all his investigative tenacity, Kaufman suffered setback after setback. The Musicas had destroyed incriminating records. One of Kaufman's star witnesses, company treasurer Julian Thompson, caught the flu and died. After all the probing, his case boiled down to three company officers: Horace Merwin, a Bridgeport banker and McKesson director; Rowley Phillips, a Waterbury investment banker and also a McKesson director; and John McGloon, McKesson's former comptroller and vice president. The goal was to show they had abetted Musica's frauds.[47]

On the appointed morning in March 1940, Kaufman strode to the lectern in the new, high-ceilinged courtroom. He nodded to jurors who, like the jurors in all his cases, were probably wondering how a boy his age could have gotten a law license. His theme was simple: however canny and devious he may have been, Philip Musica couldn't have carried off such a monumental swindle without help. "He was no banker; he was no accountant. As a matter of fact he was a small-timer with a very unsavory reputation. He couldn't have gotten to first base without the front and prestige of these men," Kaufman said, pointing at the well-dressed Connecticut bankers at the defendants' table. "We will show that the thing that put this over was the front and prestige and financial chicanery supplied to Coster by some of these individuals." He spoke for two hours, tracing Musica's astounding criminal odyssey and showing what the defendants knew.[48]

Like Joseph Weiss, Musica's associates spared no expense in their choice of lawyers, retaining George Medalie, US Attorney in the 1920s and Dewey's chief patron, and Harold Corbin, a respected trial veteran. Looking back decades later, Kaufman recalled the two administering "daily lessons, impressing upon me what a floundering neophyte I was." They described a very different Philip Musica—a "wizard" responsible for "the greatest deception in business and finance in the world's history," one that had even deceived Price Waterhouse, "the Tiffany of accountants." How could Kaufman expect normal, genteel men of business like the defendants to have seen through him when his "methods were so clever, so diabolically clever, that no one would have expected it?"[49]

Kaufman's main witness was George Musica, who testified for six days. He implicated McGloon, especially, because McGloon had helped create dummy accounts and a slush fund for politicians. George also detailed Phillips's and Merwin's role in selling $1 million in stock in the crude drug subsidiary, falsely promising investors it would manufacture in Canada. But George didn't help by continuing to maintain his brother's honesty and, asked to name those aware of Philip's fraud, admitting, "I can't swear that anyone else knew it."[50]

The defense strategy was simple and direct: put the accused on the stand to explain that, like everyone else, they'd been duped by McKesson's secretive president. McGloon went first and stressed that he could hardly check every last report that crossed his desk. Then Phillips testified. He was hale and cheerful, with his wife and children in court. "You forgot the most important member of the family," Corbin chided as he described his background: "My granddaughter," he said laughing, "she's only 9 months." As for knowing about Musica's misdeeds, he'd relied on Thompson, he said—a handy explanation, since Thompson, like Musica, wouldn't be testifying anytime soon. Besides, Price Waterhouse had found the books in order, and "they are tops among accounting firms."[51]

Kaufman's cross-examination got off to a raucous start. "Primarily, you are a stock salesman?" he asked. "I am a broker and an investment banker, and that is not the same thing," Phillips responded, aggrieved. "Aren't you like a shoe salesman who can find a shoe to fit—" Now Corbin was shouting and interrupting: "I don't care if he does represent the government, it's our government as well as his." When the theatrics died down, Kaufman found Phillips a frustrating man to corner. Phillips's letters suggested he had known that public statements about the Canadian division were false, but he said he hadn't read or didn't recall them. "What kind of director were you?" Kaufman asked sarcastically, but little seemed to stick to the chipper financier, despite eleven days on the stand. "Coster lied to us to the end," he maintained.[52]

Last was Merwin, who also described having "the utmost faith in Mr. Coster. He was a most unusual man and had shown remarkable progress in the management of the company." Kaufman exposed Merwin's manipulation of the value of McKesson's goodwill for purposes of selling stock in the Canadian entity, raising it on paper to increase the stock's book value and then lowering it back to one dollar after the sale. "And you consider yourself a conservative banker?" Kaufman asked incredulously. As he left the witness stand after six days, Merwin, a good-looking and genial leader of Bridgeport society who'd enlisted local clergy to vouch for his character, wasn't much damaged either.[53]

Final arguments to the jury reprised each side's initial themes. Medalie reiterated that Musica was a one-of-a-kind genius acting on his own. Corbin stressed Phillips's all-American roots; his "character was built stone by stone over the years in a small Connecticut town. You can't get away with a new tie on Sunday in a town like that without somebody talking about it." When his moment came, Kaufman again portrayed Musica as a small-time grifter unable to manage gigantic corporate frauds without the help of the respectable men accused. "By your verdict in this case you will say whether people are to have confidence in corporations and directors of corporations."[54]

In the end, though, Kaufman's case, which had largely dwindled to the dubious stock offering, seemed like a sideline when measured against the historic fraud. One observer thought Kaufman "was depending more upon sheer tonnage of evidence than damaging proof that the men were any more than victims of a criminal genius. The government's case contained more holes than a wheel of Emmentaler cheese." Jurors agreed, acquitting the Bridgeport bankers after twenty minutes. And they acquitted McGloon, too, except for the least important count against him—signing a false financial statement filed with the SEC. Jurors couldn't let *everyone* walk, and as an actual McKesson officer, McGloon was the handiest target. The judge praised Kaufman to the jurors, commending his "splendid and excellent and unusual service," and the easygoing Phillips told reporters he had "nothing but respect for Mr. Kaufman." Five days later, McGloon received a year and a day in prison. Arthur Musica got three years, George Musica two and a half, and Robert Musica one and a half. The McKesson case was finished.[55]

Although his painstaking case flopped, Kaufman's work had an impact. The Securities and Exchange Act was only six years old when he prosecuted McGloon, and his conviction was the first under the new law for filing false reports. That mundane requirement would become a critical tool by which the government protects investors and ensures fair and competitive markets. The case is also a watershed in the history of accounting. Accountants can no longer shrug their shoulders and claim checking inventory isn't their problem. Standards issued by the American Institute of Accountants in 1941 required practitioners to eyeball the client's stock and confirm the actual existence of accounts receivable. There were also calls for more responsibility from corporate directors, and more ethics training in business. It even resonated overseas. "This type of crime flourishes only on democratic soil," one Nazi German paper sneered, adding that the US "should not preach morals when there is a rotten smell at home."[56]

At McKesson, the scandal dented profits, but the company quickly recovered, since the essentials of its national drug distribution business had never been involved. After all the inquiries and post hoc forensic accounting, it was eventually determined that Musica had embezzled approximately $3.2 million. No one could say for sure where the money went, and for years afterward trespassers snooped around his Fairfield property, shovels in hand. It remains part of Musica lore, along with the deeper question of what drove the strange man to such bizarre feats of criminality. For some, the mystery extended to whether Musica was even dead. Tales circulated among McKesson employees of sightings in South America, where Musica had supposedly assumed yet another identity and amassed another fortune.[57]

Finally, the case had a major impact on Kaufman. He played a central role in unmasking the key villain through his sharp insistence on fingerprinting Musica, just as his meticulous preparation for trial revealed much that was not previously known about the fraud. He secured the confessions, cooperation, and convictions of Musica's main accomplices. And while he couldn't nail the slippery, amiable Connecticut bankers, his valiant effort and partial success with McGloon must have given pause to corporate insiders who had once assumed their shadiest dealings would remain hidden from view.

Above all, the case cemented his reputation as a comer. When he quit the US Attorney's Office two months after the trial, every newspaper in New York carried the news and highlighted his work bringing down Musica. The *World Telegram* called him "an outstanding cross-examiner" and described how he'd unmasked the McKesson trickster. The *Sun* marveled at the staggering number of witnesses questioned, bank accounts reviewed, and so on. The *Herald Tribune* stressed his youth and gushed that he "was opposed by some of the most prominent attorneys in New York, most of them old enough to be his father." In Bridgeport, McKesson's home base, the *Sunday Herald*'s headline was simply "Brilliant District Atty. Uncovered Coster-Musica." A later profile called him "the demon boy-prosecutor." After only five years in government and at an age when most lawyers were just finding their sea legs, he had fashioned himself into the latest prosecutor-hero in a city that especially celebrated the type. "I can assure you that my service in that office proved to be the turning point in my professional life," Kaufman wrote his nephew forty years later. Now the challenge was to husband his hard-won capital until he could use it.[58]

CHAPTER 3

A Dream Come True

Kaufman's departure from the government made perfect sense. Success in private practice would help burnish his résumé for the bench, and he would also need the patronage of political types, who were easier to court outside government. Above all, there was a growing family to provide for, unless he wanted to live forever on Lien Law Louie's money. He and Helen had had a son in 1939, whom they named Robert by repurposing Kaufman's own invented middle name. They called him Bobby or sometimes "Bobbichka." In 1941, Helen was pregnant again, this time possibly with twins, and her anxiety was running high.

That summer, Kaufman traveled to a mineral bath resort in Mount Clemens, Michigan, known as "Bath City" and wrote daily letters to Helen at her parents' summer home in New Jersey. She signed hers "Helen, Bobby,? and??," referring to the as yet unnamed additions to the family. "If it has to be, dear," he wrote back, "you and I will be very happy and I'm sure they wouldn't starve." She worried about the delivery, but Kaufman assured her that his brother Ben, the doctor, believed twins were "much easier on the patient." Ben also offered comfort about Helen's own obstetrician, who could apparently be off-putting. His "manner [was] just that of the gentile," her husband relayed: "Typical frankness—whatever is on his mind is on his tongue. . . . But, he has exceptional ability." "All my love to you, my handsome son and! and!! or shall I say $, $$." That October, Helen gave birth to twin boys, Richard ("Dicky") and James ("Jimmy"), and the family moved to a larger apartment on Seventy-Seventh Street overlooking the Natural History Museum and Central Park.[1]

Kaufman's trip to Mount Clemens was on his doctor's orders. He'd developed gout, and the disease gave rise to arthritis and stabbing pains in joints all over his body. Even walking was a trial. The disease also kept him out of the armed forces, though as a husband and father over thirty he likely wouldn't have been drafted anyway. Soaking in the black, buoyant mineral water helped the pain, and Kaufman wrote of his relief and also his fear the torment would return:

> You have no idea how apprehensive I am of the aches and pains I get. I ask myself each time "is it starting all over again," "must I go through all this again," "when will I once again be a perfectly normal human being." Thank the good God that it looks like I may once again go back to a normal life. I really must admit Helen, that I had just about despaired of everything—office, life. It really was hell—constant torturing pain, cares, sleepless nights, on yours and everybody else's nerves and an object of sympathy.[2]

While the baths eased his symptoms, attacks of gout would come and go for the rest of his life. They might also have intensified a lifelong hypochondria. His nephew Roger, Ben's son, remembered that Kaufman "was always complaining about something," leaving Ben to play some combination of soothing family doctor and wise older brother. Ben learned to tell Kaufman that his perceived aches and pains were actually a *positive* sign that his lungs or eyes or something else were at least working and would soon get better. Kaufman would appear out of the blue at Ben's home in a working-class Brooklyn neighborhood to be examined for this or that new ailment, real or imagined, while a crowd gathered outside to gawk at his expensive car.[3]

Kaufman went back to Bath City the following summer, 1942, and his daily letters from both visits provide a glimpse into the early years of his and Helen's marriage. He was the boy from the ghetto, much closer to the Old World and her father despite the generation gap. He delighted in embarrassing her with his Yiddish. "Der place she is very luffly," he wrote, mimicking the resort's heavily Jewish clientele. "Huge mamelas vit big bellies . . . Adolph Hitler should only show up here and I guarantee he wouldn't live 5 minutes." He befriended a fellow guest—"a goy—how's that—[with] millions, I'm told"—and joked about talking to him mainly "to counterbalance that fine Yiddish accent I'm picking up." He referred to a "grubber yunk"—a coarse or grubby young man—and added: "If my little Wellesley girl does not know what that means, consult counsel Rosenberg—he'll tell you." Helen never went to Wellesley, but the joke fit her status as the more refined, upper-crust member of their twosome.[4]

Kaufman missed Helen and the children terribly—"I'm getting so fed up with this lonesome existence I could scream"—and showered her with pet nicknames like "little perpetual motion." Their love and closeness after five years of marriage were real, but darker strains were there too. She was often depressed, whether from concerns about having twins or more prosaic difficulties like troubles with household help. And while loving, his attitude toward her was sometimes infantilizing. He thought she still needed parental coddling ("Tell your mother . . . I was also pleased to see her following my orders to take care of little Helen"); he commanded her to rest during the pregnancy, though she'd been through one before ("Helen dear, I've come to the conclusion that your working days are over for the time being. You must get rest and more rest. You have no idea how important that is"); and he carped about her spending ("I suggest you take a bank holiday"), though on other occasions he acknowledged she was "a sensible girl and I don't have to tell you how to use money." As time went on, Helen's frailty and Kaufman's domineering manner would both increase.

Now that he was out of government, Kaufman's private practice took off. He joined a small firm with a rotating cast of more senior partners. There was Kenneth Simpson, a Republican elected to Congress who died suddenly weeks later; Dave Brady, with whom Kaufman's falling out led to litigation; Eddie Eagan, a Rhodes Scholar and still the only Olympic gold medalist in both the summer and winter games, ejected from the firm because he spent most of his time running New York's boxing commission; and Greg Noonan, Kaufman's old supervisor at the US Attorney's Office.[5]

Despite the partnership upheavals, Kaufman's practice thrived. In one case, he represented men caught up in a vast operation to steal Ford parts from Michigan factories. The Galveston mobster Sam Maceo, charged with drug trafficking in New York, was also a client, as was a lieutenant colonel who profited from selling barges that should have gone to the government for free. Still in his early thirties, Kaufman "had trouble convincing his first clients that he was mature enough to handle their large affairs," the *Saturday Evening Post* later reported. "Meeting the problem head on, Kaufman adopted a rather fatherly attitude toward the clients, tending to scold them whenever he felt they needed it." Gradually, the firm's clients came to include a roster of significant corporations with reliable repeat business, such as the Safeway grocery store chain, one of the largest manufacturers of women's coats, and a subsidiary of the Swiss chemical company Ciba. For his part, Kaufman increasingly focused on representing a handful of men very much like himself, only older: Jews raised in immigrant poverty whose talent and indomitable will led to success at a remarkably early age, and who soon became titans in their fields.[6]

One of these was J. Meyer Schine, a Latvian-Jewish immigrant who started by buying a nickelodeon in Gloversville, New York, and ended with nationwide chains of theaters and hotels. Another was Henry Garfinkle, a hustling newsboy who went from a single newsstand in the Staten Island ferry building to America's largest seller and distributor of magazines and newspapers. Larger still was Sam Newhouse, another self-made media tycoon who eventually owned several major dailies, television stations, Random House, the Condé Nast group of magazines, and the *New Yorker*. Newhouse was a workaholic with few close friends, but as one biographer wrote, those who penetrated his inner circle "were mostly men much like himself—short, Jewish, born of immigrant parents, self-made . . . people with whom he could feel comfortable, in whose similar backgrounds he could sense an almost immediate kinship. These men happened as well to be younger than he was, and they treated him accordingly." Kaufman fit this profile perfectly.[7]

Kaufman's most important client wasn't Newhouse or Garfinkle, though—it was "Mr. Television," Milton Berle. When the two met in the mid-1940s, Berle was already Broadway's highest-paid comic and a national presence in nightclubs, radio programs, and movies. But after 1948, that looked like nothing. That year, he took a chance on an untested medium and convinced ABC and NBC to let him produce and star in a live comedy hour modeled on his old vaudeville performances. Soon he was America's "Uncle Miltie," credited for the rise in TV ownership from 136,000 sets in 1947 to 700,000 by the end of 1948.[8]

Beginning in 1945, it was the rare month that didn't include hundreds or thousands in fees from Berle. The entertainer and his on-again, off-again wife Joyce were spendthrifts, with Berle a regular at the racetrack and Joyce a compulsive shopper, so they arranged for Kaufman to

FIGURE 5. The comedian Milton Berle, *right*, with Kaufman in 1944, became Kaufman's best-known client and a useful tool in helping Kaufman court powerful figures in Washington. *Kaufman Family Photo Collection.*

handle their finances. "If Joyce and I were to end up with any money," Berle wrote, "the only solution was that my income not come straight to me. It went instead to Irving R. Kaufman, the lawyer who handled my money." It was no easy task, as Berle just went around his careful young attorney by using IOUs with bookies, while Joyce shopped on credit. Kaufman also likely had a hand in Berle's many contracts with clubs, theaters, and broadcasters. And he seems to have overseen both sides of a contract between Berle's business entity and the William Morris talent agency, also Kaufman's client. He even dealt with landlords. A *Daily News* story in 1946 recounted Berle's battle to avoid eviction and referred to Kaufman as "the high-priced legal talent at his elbow." " 'Milton's been harassed,' his attorney, Irving Kaufman, broke in. 'He's spent thousands of dollars fixing up the place, and he's been in tenterhooks ever since his lease expired last September and Fleischman wouldn't renew it.' " For Kaufman, the case must have seemed like a more glamorous version of his father-in-law's real estate docket.[9]

By 1947, Kaufman earned $56,000, twice what his partner Noonan made. This was rich for the day, especially considering Kaufman was still under forty; but he appears to have gilded the lily again when talking himself up to journalists. One later profile reported that "before Kaufman was thirty-five years old, he was netting more than $100,000 annually," which was a serious exaggeration. More important than the specific figures, however, is the fact that Kaufman achieved his goal of establishing a successful and profitable law practice—and in very short order, as always.[10]

Yet a lucrative practice wasn't what Kaufman wanted. So even as he toiled at his office in an elegant skyscraper on Wall Street, he worked just as assiduously to lay the groundwork for what he'd coveted since first wandering into Mullett's Monstrosity and watching in fascination as men in black robes choreographed their courtrooms.

During Kaufman's first years in private practice, this meant doing his part to support the Roosevelt administration and the war effort. In January 1941, he authored an opinion piece for the *Journal and American* that advocated giving "Great Britain all aid short of war, and short of undermining our own defense. . . . The hope for democracy and the continuation of our way of life is the defeat of those who seek to crush it." His isolationist counterpart on the other side of the page urged America to turn inward, perfect "Christian civilization," and forswear "scrubbing the ears of the 'Great Unwashed' of Europe, Africa and Asia."[11]

More tangibly, Kaufman volunteered as a government appeals agent for Draft Board 29 in Manhattan, which met at a public school a few blocks from his family's old apartment in Harlem. Draft boards had to fill manpower quotas while also assessing claims of exemption based on conscientious objection, family obligations, essential civilian jobs, and so on. Inductees could appeal the board's decisions, and Kaufman's responsibility was to represent the government's interests before an appellate board. He did the job well and evenhandedly; as a colleague told the FBI, Kaufman willingly "listen[ed] to both sides of the arguments. . . . He has not been inclined to run 'rough shod' over [draftees'] claims for deferment in favor of the government's demand for men." His service ended in 1944, when a new rule required agents to be older than thirty-eight, because men that age were now being drafted.[12]

Kaufman took on a different sort of volunteer assignment for the Association of the Bar of the City of New York, in 1943. State judge Thomas Aurelio was accused of conspiring with the powerful gangster Frank Costello, and the bar wanted to investigate. Kaufman assisted a lawyer leading the probe—a man who would figure prominently in his later career. Harold Medina was the son of a Mexican immigrant whose pugnacious spirit was honed by unrelenting bullying from classmates during the Spanish-American War. He became a Columbia law professor and earned riches from a popular bar review class Kaufman himself took in 1931. A dapper character sporting a bushy mustache, horn-rimmed glasses, and a pipe—an expert in everything from Latin verse to sailing to entomology—Medina was outgoing and shamelessly egotistical. Their investigation ended abruptly, however, when District Attorney Frank Hogan snatched control of it, which may have been just as well, since the charges were eventually dropped.[13]

Volunteer work in the public interest was one way for Kaufman to advance his judicial ambitions, but he was also working a more time-honored angle: cultivating powerful patrons. Objects of Kaufman's offers of congratulations, requests for signed photographs, or solicitations of career advice included Robert Patterson, judge in the Weiss case and later Roosevelt's secretary of war; John Knox, chief judge of the district; Julian Mack, a highly regarded judge and the second Jew to serve on the Second Circuit; and even his old foe in the Musica case, George Medalie, recently appointed to New York's highest court by his former assistant and now governor, Tom Dewey. Kaufman's campaign must have made headway; he listed Medalie and Patterson as "social intimates" when applying to a private club in 1944.[14]

Yet these important men hardly rated compared to Kaufman's two prime targets. When Kaufman first worked with the FBI as a prosecutor in the late 1930s, J. Edgar Hoover was the incorruptible hero of gangster wars and dramatic shoot-outs and vanquished "public enemies" like Bonnie and Clyde. Books and movies celebrated his fearless, clean-cut crime-fighters, and boys slept in G-man pajamas. True, even then Hoover gave off "an undercurrent of feeling that somehow he [was] doing something to undermine the citadel of liberty," as the *New Yorker* put it in a 1937 profile. He'd helped craft the Red Scare of 1919–20, when scores of immigrants, socialists, and unionists were rounded up and held on flimsy charges or deported, but he'd succeeded in mostly obscuring his part in the operation. Kaufman was either unaware or unconcerned. Personal traits may also have drawn them together. Both were undersized scrappers. Both were insecure about diplomas from lower-ranked schools (Hoover attended George Washington University). And both were particularly keen and successful publicity hounds and press manipulators.[15]

In 1941, Kaufman began a lifelong campaign of Hoover adoration, writing initially to compliment him on a favorable column by Damon Runyon. He used the star power of Milton Berle, inviting Hoover and others to parties with Berle as well as the Washington opening of the comedian's show, "Spring in Brazil." As the men became closer in the late 1940s, Kaufman and his family repeatedly dropped in on FBI headquarters, leading to cute but odd correspondence between Hoover and Kaufman's sons ("Dear Mr. Hoover, are you having a nice time in Washington? We are having a nice time in camp"). In a 1949 letter, Kaufman passed along an editorial noting Hoover's twenty-fifth anniversary at the FBI, titled "We're Lucky We've Got Him." And he added his own extra dollop, which he often repeated in later correspondence: "In my opinion, you are the greatest public servant of our time."[16]

Determined as it was, Kaufman's courtship of Hoover paled in comparison to his wooing of Tom Clark, who became his most important patron. The affable Texan came to Washington in 1937 as a Department of Justice lawyer and met Kaufman soon after. When Clark became attorney general in 1945, Berle wrote him saying "Irving Kaufman had talked so much about your character and personality within recent weeks that I was just about getting ready to find a part for you in my new show." Clark's work sometimes brought him to New York, and Kaufman arranged for theater tickets. At holidays, or for no reason at all, he sent gifts—a humidor, a suit, a crate of Florida oranges. "It was indeed a blessed day when some years back my path crossed yours," Kaufman wrote, "for since that day I have known nothing but happiness and pride in that friendship. . . . You are a truly great man and a kind man."[17]

And Kaufman made sure reporters knew he and the attorney general were close. According to a *Daily Mirror* item in 1946, someone anonymously used an employee complaint box to advise the attorney general, "You are no longer an obscure Texas lawyer. You have become a public figure. You should acquire dignity. Toward that end I would suggest that you stop wearing those atrocious bow ties." Clark then "summoned a party named J. Edgar Hoover," who duly unmasked the complainer: "Your son, Ramsey!" It was Kaufman who passed along this light-hearted tale.

> The inside stuff on this case of sheer, unadulterated villainy has just been forwarded by the Attorney General through Mr. Irving R. Kaufman, who used to be an Assistant A.G. . . . "The scoundrel has been brought to book, as we say in Department of Justice circles," said Mr. Kaufman, who is sojourning a couple of upholstered cells away from me at the Roney Plaza [Hotel, in Miami Beach]. "If ever there was a case of brazen knavery this is it."[18]

Kaufman also used his ties with Clark when representing defendants fighting the Justice Department. In 1944, the government indicted the Coat Corporation of America for fraudulently understating profits earned from military contracts. One company officer, Charles Davis, was active in Democratic circles. A month after Clark became attorney general, Kaufman obtained dismissal of all but one count of the indictment, and his clients paid only modest penalties. In a 1972 book, a retired lobbyist who happened to work at the company at the time, Robert Winter-Berger, charged that Clark and Kaufman had fixed the case:

> Rumor spread through Washington that Truman would appoint Tom Clark as the U.S. Attorney General. As these rumors reached New York, Charlie Davis told me that Clark himself had telephoned Irving Kaufman and said "You can stop worrying now." . . .
>
> About two weeks [after the plea agreement], on a stifling day, Al Davis and I saw Tom Clark himself enter the large showroom of A. Davis & Sons. . . . I watched him cross the room and accept a suitcase that was given to him by Charlie Davis, and he walked out with it. After he left, Charlie told me, in a bragging fashion, that the suitcase contained $250,000 in cash.[19]

Rumors of financial corruption dogged Clark before he joined the Supreme Court in 1949, and there is no way to know if Winter-Berger's claim is true. Clark's leading biographer doubts it, and the notion of an attorney general traveling around with suitcases of cash seems ridiculous. Nor would Kaufman have jeopardized his carefully tended judicial aspirations—to say nothing of his law license and personal liberty—with such a risky and criminal scheme. Moreover, Winter-Berger's larger credibility collapsed when accusations he leveled against Gerald Ford in the same book were closely examined by the Senate and almost resulted in perjury charges.[20]

A second case that raised eyebrows involved the Schine theater chain, which Kaufman defended against charges of antitrust violations. In 1948, the lead prosecutor, Philip Marcus, was summoned to a meeting by his boss and found Kaufman waiting for him. After the pleasantries, Kaufman calmly turned to Marcus's supervisor and said Marcus was biased and should be removed. Marcus was flabbergasted—a defense lawyer telling federal prosecutors how to staff their cases? Kaufman then secretly negotiated over his head with higher-ups, sometimes including Clark himself, and the final settlement was so lenient that Marcus became convinced Kaufman had somehow finagled special treatment. In a later departmental investigation, he charged Clark with knuckling under because of Kaufman's fund-raising for Democrats and perhaps Schine's own donations. Other DOJ lawyers strenuously disagreed, however. In the end, nothing was found to suggest political influence or improper collusion, and the inquiry died. Kaufman had simply done what all good defense lawyers do: use connections or any other tool to win his case.[21]

Beyond ingratiating himself with useful older men, Kaufman volunteered for more direct political involvement in 1946 and became finance director of New York's Democratic Party. As it happened, antipathy to Truman, fatigue with years of Democratic dominance, and satisfaction with Dewey's stint as governor led to a wipeout. Nonetheless, state party chairman Paul Fitzpatrick thanked Kaufman for "the very fine job you turned in on what was a most difficult assignment. Not many fellows would have stood up under the pounding you had to take."[22]

Kaufman didn't have to wait long to see whether that pounding paid off. A Southern District judge resigned two weeks after the election, and news reports mentioned Kaufman among the contenders. He was called one of Tammany's choices—which wasn't ideal, since the White House's on-again, off-again feud with the machine was back on. Kaufman quickly went to work on Bob Hannegan, the Democratic Party's national chairman and also US postmaster general, while local party stalwarts Fitzpatrick and Bronx Democratic boss Ed Flynn agreed to recommend him for the post.[23]

Meanwhile, Clark directed the FBI to conduct a background check on Kaufman, a customary step for potential nominees. The results were disappointing. Old friends and colleagues offered praise but also allowed that Kaufman could be "too aggressive, and as a result has irritated some of his associates." Interviewees repeatedly noted Kaufman's political calculation—how he was "very careful concerning the people that he associates with." The report summarized: "Is regarded by former associates as industrious, honest, loyal and conservative; a good lawyer but not outstanding in either trial or appellate work; is not a student of the law; is aggressive, shrewd, ambitious and politically wise."

Even more damning reviews came from judges who'd seen him in action. The chief judge, John Knox, whom Kaufman had courted with visits and letters, said Kaufman "had displayed a good deal of legal ability and considerable energy. He was active and aggressive and is personally likeable." Yet Knox wouldn't endorse him. To Knox, Kaufman "had a tendency to display self-satisfaction . . . [was] over aggressive and would be inclined to be impatient in conducting a courtroom." Two other judges said the same. Kaufman suffered from a "lack of objectivity" and likely wouldn't have the necessary "judicial temperament and approach." He was "a little young for the position and . . . does not have the maturity required." All believed there were far more qualified candidates.[24]

The bar association Kaufman had aided in the Aurelio investigation was also unenthusiastic, forcing Kaufman into spin mode with Clark: "I can only say that anything you might have heard is attributable to persons who would undoubtedly do anything to accomplish their end. Such is not my creed—and my friendship, regard and respect for you excel any other consideration. I only hope the feeling is mutual for then I shall have attained something which can more than take the place of any ambition which might be frustrated." Clark responded with a brief letter noting simply that his view of his protégé hadn't changed.[25]

And true to his word, Clark initially ignored the lukewarm evaluations and obtained Truman's approval for Kaufman's nomination—the final necessary step. He then phoned the president's executive clerk to ask him to send Kaufman's name over to the Senate for confirmation. That same day, however, the nomination struck a hidden iceberg, and Clark had a change of heart. The attorney general's assistant called the White House back, reversed the instructions, and said not to transmit Kaufman's nomination after all. The organized bar had gotten to Clark or perhaps Truman himself in the nick of time and managed to convince them to discount party considerations. They had their own selection: Kaufman's old boss in the Aurelio affair, Harold Medina.

At fifty-nine, Medina was significantly older than the typical appointee, and he lacked Kaufman's political pull. But he was universally beloved and respected by lawyers in the city, and they went to bat for him. Bar leaders even lied to Clark about Medina's religion, claiming he was Jewish when in fact Medina was Episcopalian, and thereby appeased a key Democratic bloc. The newspapers also gushed at the surprising absence of "politics in this appointment, which is a matter for acclaim." Indeed, politics were so irrelevant to the choice that Clark cluelessly announced Medina's nomination the same day New York Democrats gathered for a dinner to honor Flynn, leaving the politicos dumbfounded by the White House's snub. "'Mr. Truman wants to be elected President again, doesn't he,' was their only question," one newsman reported.[26]

Although defeat had arrived at the last minute, Kaufman squelched any bitterness. The day after Clark announced Medina's nomination, Kaufman sent him a handwritten note: "All I can say is that I thank you from the bottom of my heart." And Hannegan's deputy Gael Sullivan wrote Kaufman: "All your friends are let down that a more kind fate did not finger you for the Federal Judgeship—but there is no chronic gloom—we are still moving aggressively forward in your interests."[27]

Sullivan's confidence was justified. Judges often fall short in their first tries at appointment, and Kaufman had at least demonstrated support in Democratic circles and at the top of the Justice Department. All he needed was the additional legal seasoning demanded by the organized bar, and he was only thirty-six. Once again, Clark interceded. In 1947, he made Kaufman a special assistant to examine Washington lobbying. The previous year, Congress had passed a new law requiring lobbyists to register and disclose the sources and amounts of their funding and expenditures, but few had actually complied. When Truman was forced to swallow a Republican bill loosening wartime rent controls in 1947, he blamed the "real estate lobby," and the time was ripe for a crackdown. Kaufman took an office at "Main Justice" in Washington and began weekly commutes to DC.[28]

Despite all Kaufman had done to butter up Hoover, his arrival wasn't warmly greeted by the FBI. That was due in part to Jerome Doyle, a former colleague of Kaufman's in the US Attorney's Office, who now worked for the Bureau. Doyle told his superiors he'd once had to evaluate a case Kaufman wanted to prosecute and concluded that, even if Kaufman won a conviction, it wouldn't stand up on appeal. According to Doyle, Kaufman "very frankly" admitted that "all he wanted to do was to prosecute the case in the trial court and get the publicity prior to the time he resigned. Kaufman indicated he did not care what became of the government's case on appeal, since he would be gone and wouldn't have to worry about it." "Some 'addition' to the D of J!" Deputy Director Edward Tamm added in his memo to Hoover. "It is quite apparent in the course of my interview with Kaufman," another official wrote after an initial meeting, "that he intends to make a big thing of his new assignment and that he will probably engage in fishing expeditions or any other tactics which will result in publicizing not only the Federal Regulation of Lobbying Act, but particularly the man who has been designated by the Attorney General to administer that Act."[29]

Kaufman's main work consisted of calling in large corporations, trade associations, and unions and informing them that their government expected them to register and file the necessary reports. Most had maintained that the law only applied to organizations whose "principal purpose" was lobbying, and they conveniently denied that this was their main goal. But Kaufman proved persuasive. "You can't be a good prosecutor and a nice guy, too," he told a reporter, explaining his willingness to browbeat. "Their spirit in most cases is one of cooperation," he testified to a Senate committee; "in most cases there seems to be agreement over the fact that, well, they were not sure what they ought to do, but in view of the fact that the Department of Justice feels that there should be compliance, they will comply."[30]

There were a few holdouts, though. The National Association of Manufacturers sued, claiming the statute was unconstitutional and triggering years of litigation. And criminal cases were also in the works. Kaufman convened a grand jury, and his assistants soon obtained indictments. They first targeted the United States Savings and Loan League, which represented the mortgage banks, an integral part of Truman's nemesis, the real estate lobby. The second indictment alleged that a colorful lobbyist and commodities trader, Frank W. Moore, conspired with agricultural commissioners in Texas and Georgia and a New York banker to lobby for measures benefiting their private trading. Moore was known for entertaining congressmen at lavish affairs at the Mayflower Hotel while boasting, "I never have to bribe anyone . . . I just show them how to make a little money."[31]

In July 1948, Kaufman decided he'd had enough of traveling back and forth to Washington, and perhaps of the town itself. "It's a jungle there," he told Roy Cohn a few years later, and "all you'll get is aggravation and misery." Kaufman told Clark he intended to resign and drafted a report summarizing his unit's progress and recommending amendments to strengthen the lobbying law and eliminate the "principal purpose" requirement. Clark then created a permanent task force to enforce the statute, staffed by Kaufman's hires. Overall, the assignment was an almost perfect success. Registration under the law skyrocketed, giving "a documented if admittedly partial picture of the Washington lobby front," one observer wrote at the time. The press and others paying attention got at least a glimpse into the seamy world of influence peddling. In 1954, the Supreme Court also rejected the National Association of Manufacturers' constitutional challenge and upheld the law.[32]

The lobbying position achieved Kaufman's personal goals, too. The *Herald Tribune* called him an "efficient young New York prosecutor," while the influential syndicated columnist Drew Pearson lauded his laborious investigative work. A *New York Post* profile describing his "hush-hush job of national importance" was titled simply "The Boy Prosecutor Grows Up." A 1951 book on lobbying enthused, "To his great credit Kaufman did not engage in headline hunting. Instead, he went quietly to work and with noticeable results." But the FBI's fear that Kaufman would promote himself along with the newly potent lobbying law also proved justified; news stories' details about the unit's work and their verbatim quotation of Kaufman's correspondence left little doubt where journalists got their information.[33]

In only one respect was Kaufman's performance wanting: actual criminal prosecutions. In 1949, months after his departure, a district judge quietly dismissed the indictment of the United States Savings and Loan League. The case against Moore met the same fate. A former Missouri congressman was also acquitted in a prosecution called "shamefully weak" by the *Washington Post*. Kaufman wasn't entirely responsible for these losses; it was hard to prove what lobbyists did in their hideaways, and trial judges seemed determined to apply the law narrowly. The embarrassing outcomes may also have vindicated Jerome Doyle's warning, though: Kaufman may again have focused more on the headlines generated by the indictments than the possibility of dismissals later, when he would be long gone.

While harrying lobbyists in Washington, Kaufman lost out on a second judicial opening in New York. But his dejection lifted when Truman confounded everyone by winning the 1948 election, guaranteeing four more years of Democratic judicial appointments. "The people demonstrated that despite the newspapers, radio, polls, etc., they could not be fooled," he exulted to Clark, adding that "there is nothing greater that a human being could possess on this earth than your true friendship and loyalty." Kaufman had again fundraised during the campaign, which earned thanks from the very top. "I have heard of the generous way in which you expressed confidence in my leadership and want you to know of my heartfelt appreciation," Truman wrote.[34]

Nor did Kaufman's advocacy for the administration end on Election Day. Three weeks later he appeared on a nationally syndicated radio show to argue for a stricter lobbying law. In May 1949, he helped promote the administration's civil rights program through a dinner he organized for the ecumenical group Interfaith in Action, featuring Berle and Rhode Island senator Howard McGrath as keynote speakers. The evening was carried on ABC radio stations, and Kaufman prepared an advance draft of McGrath's speech. Revolted by vicious mob attacks on returning Black veterans, Truman had directed more vigorous Justice Department enforcement of civil rights; executive orders desegregating the military and curtailing discrimination in federal employment; and a commission that published a landmark report, *To Secure These Rights*, advocating the end of segregation along with other changes. He then proposed enactment of a new civil rights law codifying the commission's recommendations.[35]

Kaufman's speech for McGrath was an eloquent plea for the imperative to advance civil rights, as McGrath had introduced Truman's proposed bill in the Senate. "Let us see just what is involved," Kaufman wrote, continuing,

> I have proposed that no man should be denied equal justice because of his color—that the threat of lynching be forever erased from this land. I have proposed that no man shall be denied a voice in choosing his rulers because he cannot pay a tax or because he cannot pass a rigged literacy test. I have proposed in this land devoted to the free enterprise system that the most basic enterprise of earning a living at any trade shall not be barred to any man because of race or creed or national origin. Surely these are basic *human* rights. Surely they are the foundations of the dignity

FIGURE 6. Kaufman (*right*), with his chief patron during the 1940s, Attorney General Tom Clark (*second from right*). *Kaufman Family Photo Collection.*

> of the human personality, and they must be preferred over the arid principle of states' rights—or to be more accurate, the principle of states wrongs. After all, what rights are involved in our opponents' program—the right to prevent people from voting because of their color—the right to prevent people from finding jobs because of their faith. If these were not wrongs—instead of states' rights—this issue never would have arisen.

McGrath more or less stuck to Kaufman's script but, notably, left out his caustic attack on states' rights, which he probably deemed too extreme. A decade would elapse before Kaufman himself would be in a position to do something about the injustice he had McGrath denounce on the radio.[36]

On July 19, 1949, Supreme Court Justice Frank Murphy died in his sleep, and Clark and McGrath were immediately rumored as successors. Within two weeks, Truman named Clark to Murphy's seat and

FIGURE 7. Kaufman idealized FBI director J. Edgar Hoover, who also promoted his career. Hoover is shown in a 1959 photo he inscribed to Kaufman. *Max Munn Autrey.*

nominated McGrath for Clark's old job as attorney general. In a role reversal Kaufman must have relished, he was able to facilitate *their* nominations by arranging for the national chairman of the Anti-Defamation League to telegraph Senator Pat McCarran of Nevada, chairman of the

Judiciary Committee, urging confirmation. And two days after Truman announced the Clark and McGrath appointments, he signed a bill creating twenty-seven new lower court judgeships, including four in Manhattan. After two false starts, Kaufman's best shot at a judicial appointment had finally arrived.[37]

This time, both the bench and the bar were on board. What the FBI heard was glowing. One DOJ lawyer noted Kaufman's "great capacity for work" and called him "an inspiration to the men working with him" in the lobbying unit. In New York, FBI agents heard about his "quick mind" and "broad experience" and how he "conducted himself in a gentlemanly fashion at all times." The judges, too, had come around. In fact, they sounded almost remorseful. One, probably Knox, recalled previously saying Kaufman was too aggressive. Now he discounted that "as an example of [Kaufman's] combative spirit developed in practice, and [said] that this was not a trait which would prevent him from recommending the applicant for a judicial appointment." Another convert "recalled that in 1947 he'd ventured the opinion that the applicant was too young for a position on the federal bench but now [he] believes that Kaufman is matured and rounded out and suitable for a judicial position."[38]

Kaufman's political support hadn't waned, either. The White House delegated the selections to Fitzpatrick, still the state party chairman, and he continued to back Kaufman. Other party honchos chimed in, such as New York state judge Albert Cohn, father of Roy and a Flynn protégé, and Defense Secretary Louis Johnson, whom Kaufman had gotten to know during the 1948 campaign. Even unions got involved; at word of Kaufman's possible selection, one leader telegraphed the White House: "Thirty thousand members of the Utility Workers Union of America CIO in New York City hail the naming of Irving Kaufman."[39]

On October 15, 1949, Truman installed Kaufman on the Southern District bench using a "recess appointment," since the Senate was out of session. Kaufman would then have to be confirmed when the Senate reconvened. "It is difficult to find words to adequately express my gratitude to you," he wrote the president in thanks. "My burning desire is to be a credit to you, my country and my family." "I am sure you will make a good judge and that is all I ask," Truman replied. At the same time, Truman appointed Kaufman's law partner Greg Noonan to the same court, an extraordinary success for what was essentially a two-man firm. And of course, there was Clark to thank. Writing as the new justice's "pupil," Kaufman asked for "charity in great measure when reviewing my work."[40]

At about this time, Kaufman drafted remarks addressing his "friends" that he likely delivered at a reception celebrating his swearing in or some similar event. The document remained in his files until his death. "When the President of the United States appointed me to the Federal Bench," he wrote, "my dream came true—the dream of every young lawyer. My highest aspirations and ambitions suddenly have been realized, and believe me, I could not ask for more." He overflowed with an ardent patriotism, telling his audience, "This can only happen in America . . . [which] thank GOD retains" democratic principles. Above all, he touched on personal circumstances that, in the coming years, he would almost never mention in public again.

> As I look around, my mind goes back to my early youth, the son of immigrants, and I promise you and all my other friends that I shall endeavor, and hope to be privileged to make it a lot easier for those who are now struggling like I did 20 years ago. Only in such a fashion can I reward the faith placed in me by this great distinction. . . .
>
> In the very same chambers where I shall now preside, immigrants come every day to swear allegiance to our nation and to be accepted as full-fledged citizens of our country. I know that my father and mother were naturalized in this very building, and as I will administer this duty—this very happy duty—of administering the oath of citizenship to those who will come before me, I shall never forget how fortunate we are.[41]

CHAPTER 4

At Home on the Bench and Park Avenue

On November 1, 1949, dozens of visitors gathered in Room 506 of the Foley Square courthouse, one of the building's massive ceremonial courtrooms. Unable to squeeze in, many more packed the corridors outside. Never had the federal trial court in Manhattan sworn in four judges at once, and family members, friends, and well-wishers from the bar appeared in force. The latest additions made up fully a quarter of the newly expanded court. At two o'clock, the existing judges filed in and took their seats. John Knox, their chief, rose to administer the oaths of office. Kindly and considerate and a ferociously hard worker in his thirty-first year on the court, he was universally beloved. After the clerk read out Kaufman's recess commission signed by President Truman, Kaufman recited the oath in the well of the courtroom, right hand raised. Behind him, one of the older judges, Alfred Coxe, whispered, "he looks just like a choir boy."[1]

Years later, Kaufman recalled his intimidation at starting life on the federal court. Although some news reports wrongly described him as the youngest federal judge in America—that was J. Skelly Wright, named to the district court in New Orleans at the same time—the thirty-nine-year-old Kaufman was still plenty green. And now he was to preside in the same building as Knox and the legendary Learned Hand, a thought that "was enough to make me feel like Gulliver among the Brobdingnagians."[2]

Hand, uniquely, inspired terror and awe. By then Hand was the regular recipient of paeans recognizing him not simply as America's greatest living judge, but the greatest in the entire English-speaking world. Five years before, his instantly classic and widely reprinted speech on "I Am an American Day," "The Spirit of Liberty," made him famous to millions with no reason to know of his hundreds and hundreds of decisions elucidating every corner of the law in sharp and vivid prose, and, as a consequence of those decisions, his top reputation among lawyers. "The philosopher judge . . . the only possible successor to the mantle of Holmes," went one typical ode. Now Kaufman was nominally his peer.[3]

Nonetheless, he had to begin. He hired Norman Beier, a Columbia Law School graduate who learned of the job from a friend—Roy Cohn—as his first law clerk and got to work. In court, the new judge was strikingly decisive despite his judicial inexperience. One early clerk recalled him as a "dynamo"—a sort of ruthless "businessman" of judicial work. He briskly sliced through lawyers' arguments, stalling tactics, unpreparedness, and confusion to identify the roadblock, decide the key issue, and move the case. He rarely brooded over decisions, the clerk recalled, but "knew how to come to conclusions." To Leonard Sand, who clerked for Kaufman in 1952–53 and became a trial judge himself, Kaufman was a "superb" courtroom manager able "to cut through sham and focus on the real substance of the controversy." "All discovery or procedural motions were decided immediately from the bench," Sand remembered.[4]

Word soon got around that lawyers had better be prepared. If one fumbled with his notes or paused for a long time while examining a witness, Kaufman cut in and announced "I assume you have no more questions." He meant it as an order, not a question. Lawyers who became repetitive or discursive were told to keep moving. Witnesses who rambled or tried to dodge the question were politely but firmly steered back to the subject at hand. Excuses weren't tolerated. Once, when a junior lawyer appeared at a pretrial conference, Kaufman scheduled the trial for the following day. When the lawyer protested that his more experienced colleague wasn't available, Kaufman squinted down at him and asked, "You're a lawyer, aren't you?" He was, the man admitted, but he'd never tried a case. "Well, tomorrow you're going to learn."[5]

Another way to move the cases was to jawbone lawyers into settlements and plea agreements. While some judges see this as beyond their role or beneath their dignity, Kaufman was a master at it. He dug into the facts and quickly saw the weak points that could frighten counsel and their clients into forgoing a trial, adding that he "wouldn't look kindly" on their arguments if the lawsuit staggered forward. In one case, Kaufman asked counsel for the defendant, an insurance company, whether he had been touch with the company's president. The lawyer said he had, but it was complicated because the man was based in London. Seeing an opening, Kaufman ordered the president to appear in his court the next day. The lawyer howled at such a patently unreasonable demand, but the order stood. The case settled that afternoon.[6]

Kaufman's efficiency and strong command of the courtroom had its drawbacks, though. He was quick—often too quick—to interject with his own questions to witnesses. "I thought when I became a judge that I would just sit back and hear the plaintiff's case, the defendant's case, and then decide," he confided to Sand, as if unaware that, temperamentally, he couldn't sit back under almost any circumstances. "But what I do is, in my mind, try the case for the plaintiff and try the case for the defendant." This happened out loud more than he seems to have realized. There was also a sternness from the bench that, consciously or not, he may have fallen back on in part to compensate for his youth. One clerk recalled "a certain bullying quality," though Kaufman could also be convivial if the lawyers bantered with the appropriate deference. To another clerk he called to mind "a little general." As Caro wrote for *Newsday*, lawyers and recalcitrant witnesses heard "his tongue crack . . . like a whiplash."[7]

The obsession with efficiency governed life in Kaufman's chambers on the nineteenth floor of the courthouse even more than in his courtroom. He arrived most mornings around nine, and woe to the law clerk not already hard at work. Once there, he stayed until five or six, the door to his office usually closed to the outside world. A few judges ate lunch together in the special judges' cafeteria on the twenty-sixth floor, but Kaufman rarely joined them. Unless he had to leave to dine with a friend or attend a bar meeting, he usually continued working and ate an American cheese or cream cheese and jelly sandwich at his desk. After lunch he smoked one cigar.

The work usually continued after Kaufman left Foley Square and headed uptown. An early libel case exemplified the habit and led to a tremulous encounter with Hand:

> I was a young district court judge having been on the court for about one year when I encountered Judge Hand in the public elevator at about 7 p.m. The judge's [elevator] car was shut down

> for the evening. Hand was almost eighty years old, and there he stood with his cousin Augustus, and I believe my dear friend Harold Medina was there too. As I entered with my briefcase, Judge Learned Hand's voice boomed over the passengers, "Young man, what are you doing with that briefcase? How many times have I told you not to take any work home with you?" I was overawed of course, being in the presence of these most distinguished judges—and particularly the great Hand. I responded somewhat hesitantly "Well, I have had a difficult motion under consideration for more than a month now and I am determined to decide it tonight."

Kaufman then explained that the plaintiffs were Neiman Marcus saleswomen accused of being " 'ladies of the evening' who were moonlighting by selling themselves instead of the store's merchandise," and that he was stumped by whether so large a group, 382 women, could be defamed collectively. "By this time we were on the lobby floor and as I was about to leave the elevator, Judge Hand's voice rumbled over all the passengers, 'Give me the address of the store,' he said, 'and I will give you the answer.' "[8]

In the evenings, Kaufman would often call back into the office to make sure his clerks hadn't followed him out the door a few minutes later. Clerks even got calls at night as questions and ideas popped into his head. They were also expected to work with him on Saturdays, sometimes at his apartment, sometimes in chambers, and sometimes by phone. He "worked as hard as hell and wanted his clerks to work as hard as hell," said Robert Haft (1954–55). "I can always count on Kaufman being in his office on the holidays," a friend wrote him after a Veterans Day phone call from chambers. Andrew Hartzell (1953–54) made the mistake of planning to move to a new apartment on Long Island over Columbus Day weekend. He called into chambers, nervously, to make sure all was well, and was stunned to find Kaufman in the office and steaming. He was soon on the receiving end of a tirade about a draft he had finished on Friday, and Kaufman ordered him into the office immediately. Only extended pleading and distance spared him.[9]

Clerks were charged with reading the lawyers' motion papers, recommending how to decide, and writing up drafts of orders or longer opinions for Kaufman's review. They also wrote first drafts of the legal instructions he read to juries. Drafts in hand, Kaufman spread out files and law books on his conference table and burrowed into the cases. He tended to home in on a case's facts more than the legal principles.

Good trial judges had to be "obsessed with the facts," he wrote once; "academic sagacity, no matter how sharp, is simply not enough." His editing of clerks' drafts was usually modest unless he disagreed with a recommendation. But speed was essential. His trusted secretary from private practice who followed him to the courthouse, Anna Strasser, started pestering clerks for their drafts within two or three days of the argument in court. Clerks might have to pull all-nighters, but nothing lingered. Kaufman's desk had a buzzer he used to summon clerks, and they learned on their first day in chambers to drop whatever they were doing and run to the inner sanctum when it sounded. Some started to hear the terrifying noise in their sleep.[10]

Yet despite the clerks' long hours, their boss was rarely satisfied. He would often belittle them at high volume. Clerks from Harvard were sarcastically called "Harvard," and drafts deemed inadequate were thrown back at them with "I know more than you do and I went to Fordham!" Donald Zoeller worked as Kaufman's bailiff from 1954 to 1958, while he was a night student at Fordham, and then as his law clerk in 1958–59. Once, he promised Kaufman to write two drafts of an opinion, each reaching the opposite result, to see which was more persuasive. After spending most of the night in chambers working on one of the drafts, which proved unexpectedly hard, he tried explaining the delay to Kaufman the following morning only to hear "I don't care about the one you've been working on—*where's the other one?!*" Once or twice a year, Kaufman would explode at something Zoeller had done and fire him. Gradually, Zoeller learned that the way to deal with these eruptions was just to wait them out. When Kaufman next buzzed him in, he would slump into the chair next to Kaufman's desk instead of standing at attention as usual. Kaufman dissolved at this show of submission, asking, "Don, what am I going to do with you?" and shaking his head. Zoeller came to think Kaufman just wanted—maybe *needed*—to watch clerks at his desk tremble, physically shake, at his dominance.[11]

Other clerks never learned Zoeller's lesson and stayed fired, like one hired in 1952 only to be cashiered a few months later and replaced by Sand. The experience drove him out of the law altogether, and he ended up producing soap operas. Two other clerks quit later in the 1950s, and Kaufman responded by calling up former clerks to see if they could be persuaded to come back for a few months. None wanted to, having already graduated from the IRK boot camp. So they called the clerks who'd just quit, told them they didn't want to make a permanent enemy of Kaufman, and cajoled them into returning. This became a routine.

One of the clerks who quit and came back lamented that he'd been "rejected by the army for nerves—and now look where I am!" At least the abuse usually declined as a clerk's year progressed and Kaufman became more comfortable relying on the clerk's work. At about that time Kaufman would begin bragging at how much better the clerk's performance had become thanks to his training in chambers the last few months. "I'm glad I taught you so much," he told one.[12]

For all this, real training *did* accompany the pain. When lawyers at a trial were selecting jurors, Kaufman told Sand to pay attention. "Don't just sit there and be a spectator. Ask yourself, who would I want and who would I challenge?" Although he demanded that clerks produce their drafts as fast as possible, he also told Haft to come downstairs from chambers to watch trials, so he'd know what to do himself when the time came. His intense focus on facts and thorough review of language foreshadowed the meticulous pretrial and drafting work clerks would soon encounter in practice. Kaufman saw his law clerks as "unmolded clay," one said, and it was his job to "make them into lawyers."[13]

Kaufman also provided help getting the next job. When the US Attorney, Irving Saypol, was dragging his feet on hiring Beier because Tammany boss Carmine DeSapio hadn't signed off, Kaufman exploded and told Saypol to come to his chambers immediately. If he didn't, Kaufman threatened, he'd call DeSapio himself and tell him not to make Saypol a state judge—the next job Saypol wanted. Minutes later, Saypol was swearing in Beier as a federal prosecutor in Kaufman's chambers. In 1953, Sand also wanted to be an Assistant US Attorney, but he couldn't get an answer from Saypol's successor, Ed Lumbard. With a white-shoe Republican like Lumbard now in office, Kaufman knew more subtlety was needed. Telling Sand, "everybody likes to feed the full belly," he advised securing offers from law firms and then pressuring Lumbard by pretending he was about to take one. Like Beier, Sand was hired. In 1955, Kaufman chose Frances Bernstein as his clerk, long before hiring women for the position was common. His willingness to buck tradition "opened doors that might otherwise have remained closed," she said.[14]

Most of Kaufman's district court clerks were therefore grateful for the experience and believed it had been invaluable preparation despite treatment that ranged from sarcasm and impatience to shouting and humiliation. Hartzell remembered visiting chambers after his clerkship ended. He wanted to tell Kaufman that, while it had been a hard year, he now appreciated everything he'd learned. Before he could finish the thought, Kaufman was dragging him out of his office into the clerks' room, where Hartzell saw his successor cowering over his typewriter. "See!" Kaufman yelled at the younger man, "listen to Hartzell! He'll tell you how good it is when you're under the big gun!"[15]

A few months after taking the bench, Kaufman made another dramatic break and left the Upper West Side for an apartment on Park Avenue, where he and Helen would live for the rest of their lives. Park Avenue had been a hard nut to crack for even wealthy Jewish buyers—many owners and co-op boards simply wouldn't take them—but the Kaufmans' building had been an exception since opening in 1929. Occupying the entire block on the east side of the avenue between Ninety-Third and Ninety-Fourth Streets, 1185 Park housed 165 apartments on fifteen floors. Doormen in crisp, dark uniforms with silver whistles watched over Venetian gothic archways of elegant white stone. Past this black-gated entrance lay a circular drive and a well-tended garden courtyard at the building's center, "like you might expect at the palace of European royalty," as one apartment guide put it.[16]

The Kaufmans took a thirty-eight-hundred-square-foot "classic eight" on the fifth floor. An elevator operated by a liveried and white-gloved attendant opened only to their apartment and one other. Inside, a large entrance gallery led to an oversize living room with a working fireplace. Long hallways connected an equally spacious dining room, kitchen, and four bedrooms. In a red-carpeted study, a plush couch and ample wooden desk accompanied bookshelves holding a full set of federal case reporters and other volumes ferried uptown by his law clerks. Presidents, justices, and other luminaries looked out from signed photos. The Kaufmans employed a maid, a cook, and for some years also a nanny, and the apartment had bedrooms for live-in help off the kitchen.[17]

The family's step up in lifestyle, notwithstanding the pay cut that came with Kaufman's new job, largely owed to Helen's share of the family's parking garage empire. "Parking lots are better than oil," Kaufman once gushed to a friend; "cars come in and they go out but they never stop." Yet he was also ambivalent. As cash businesses, garages could be converted into tools or shelters for crime or money laundering if a rogue employee put his mind to it. Fearing scandal, Kaufman wanted to sell the garages, but his relatives balked. The garages would put generations of Kaufman and Rosenberg children through college, and most had no interest in interrupting the gravy train.[18]

More than just a physical move, Kaufman's transition to Park Avenue confirmed his arrival in the upper reaches of New York Jewish society. As Alfred Kazin put it, "The West Side as a whole was ethnic territory, foreign, 'Jew land,' the cheaper side of town and the last stand of all exiles, refugees, proscribed and displaced persons." Across the park was different, the cradle of New York's WASP establishment. Some couldn't accept what the neighborhood represented, regardless of their means. Kaufman's client Henry Garfinkle thought "Park Avenue was a dirty word. It was simply too hoity-toity." Kaufman had no such qualms, even if his more limited resources consigned him to less desirable precincts farther north, only two blocks south of East Harlem. "On our Park Avenue the men wore fedoras and left the house each day with a clean white cotton handkerchief in their breast pocket. The women wore hats with veils and Chanel suits and tight corsets," wrote Anne Roiphe, who grew up in Kaufman's building, part of a wealthy Jewish family. "They lunched at the Plaza, they drank martinis after five o'clock, and on Saturdays they hopped in their cars and played a round of golf at their clubs in Westchester or New Jersey." Nothing better captured how Kaufman and his ilk were seen on Park Avenue than the nickname conferred on the newcomers by their more established, German-Jewish brethren. To the earlier arrivals, the pushy *Ostjuden* suddenly joining the fanciest Reform synagogue in town, Emanu-El, founded by German Jews in 1845, were "the Emanu-elbowers."[19]

Kaufman's social circle was populated largely by such *arrivistes*, that is, men essentially like himself. He and they had "repolished themselves," as one of Kaufman's clerks put it. He became personally close to certain clients, especially Newhouse and Berle. David Sarnoff and Lew Rosenstiel became two more of Kaufman's rags-to-fantastic-riches friends. Sarnoff was a first-generation Russian-Jewish immigrant who virtually invented the modern radio and television industries and rose to command RCA and NBC. Having become a brigadier general serving in a vital communications post after D-Day, he was called simply "the General," even by his family. Rosenstiel spent Prohibition buying shuttered distilleries so that, by the 1950s, his company Schenley rivaled Seagram. Yet his millions couldn't cleanse a reputation for shadiness, fed by a 1929 indictment for bootlegging and friendships with organized crime figures like Meyer Lansky. And his serial marriages and contested divorces didn't help. One ex-wife divorced Rosenstiel and married Walter Annenberg, yet another enormously wealthy media figure Kaufman befriended. Both men were virulent anticommunists who, like Kaufman, venerated J. Edgar Hoover.[20]

The best snapshot of Kaufman's social circle might be the guest list to his son Bobby's bar mitzvah in 1952. At one table, the Sarnoffs joined Roosevelt adviser and power-broker Sam Rosenman and the Newhouses. At another, Tom Dodd, Kaufman's friend from the Justice Department and soon to serve in Congress from Connecticut, sat next to Brigadier General Julius Klein, commander of the Jewish War Veterans of the United States of America, who helped broker payments from West Germany to Holocaust victims. Other guests included old clients Berle, Garfinkle, and J. Meyer Schine; the Rosenstiels and Cohns; Abe Feinberg, a key Democratic donor; Ed Weisl, a New York lawyer, Paramount Pictures board member, and close friend to Lyndon Johnson; Harry Cohn, the founder of Columbia Pictures; Irving Geist, a clothing maker and celebrated wartime philanthropist decorated by Truman; and the gossip columnist Leonard Lyons. As a clerk put it, Kaufman seemed to know "everyone who was important."[21]

The group's home away from home was the City Athletic Club, where Kaufman went most Sundays. The men-only sanctuary was founded in 1908 as an alternative for well-to-do Jews shut out of exclusive preserves like the University Club and the New York Athletic Club. After swimming or other exercise in the morning, Kaufman and his sons would have lunch in the restaurant or grill room—jackets required—and chat with whatever *Macher* from government or commerce wandered by. Now-archaic rituals abounded, like "Father and Son Night," which Kaufman organized in 1950, enlisting Berle to perform again. In the biggest city in America, the Jews who made it to Park Avenue inhabited a very small world.[22]

The Kaufmans' three boys attended elementary school at the Riverdale Country School, a select private academy along the Hudson and a world away from DeWitt Clinton, where boys had been exhorted to bathe. In June, they were off to summer camp by a bucolic lake in the New Hampshire mountains. At home, the paterfamilias unwound with a good after-dinner cigar—always and only his second of the day—and a good read. He didn't "like gangster shows or detective stories," one profile detailed, and "he does not cry at the movies. For relaxation give him a historical novel, preferably about the renaissance period, and perhaps a scotch highball. He is not an enthusiastic drinker." On weekends there were outings to the park with a family dog, Yankees games with his sons, and "he will even attend a rodeo, which he detests. He always scrambles the family's Sunday morning eggs."[23]

FIGURE 8. The Kaufman family, approximately 1950. *Kaufman Family Photo Collection.*

Kaufman's attendance at the Park Avenue Synagogue was spotty, and when he did go he had his driver let him off a few blocks away so he would appear to be walking to services like the devout Jews who refuse to drive on the Sabbath. His religious literacy was limited; "I must confess that the Bible has not been the strongest part of my education," he wrote one friend. Asked in 1972 to give a short Bible reading at an American Bar Association prayer breakfast, he had to ask the chancellor of the Jewish Theological Seminary and then his rabbi at the Park Avenue Synagogue for appropriate verses. Yet his faith in God was real. As he enthused to a friend after a trip to Colorado, "The beauty of this country is breathtaking. I don't know what would become of all atheists if they could visit here. This magnificence can only be explained by a belief in the Almighty." Looking back on his years at Fordham when accepting an award from the university, he cited as one of his lessons there "how everything—yes everything—is affected by one's love of the Almighty." Through the years, his correspondence was peppered with thanks to God for important friendships, career successes, and so on.[24]

There was the occasional expedition to Grossinger's, the famed Jewish resort in the Catskills, where Kaufman played golf, and a Christmas tree lit up the family's apartment over the holidays, though they were usually out of town at the time. The family spent New Year's in Florida at the lavish Boca Raton Hotel, owned by the Schines. In the summers, California beckoned. Before the introduction of more reliable air conditioning, activity in the courthouse slowed when the temperature rose, and the Kaufmans often headed west for a month or so, flying separately from the children in case a plane went down. Federal judges can arrange to hear limited numbers of cases in other courts, and Kaufman would sometime sit in the trial or appellate courts based in Los Angeles and San Francisco. The family would ensconce itself in the Beverly Hills Hotel, famous pink home to the Rat Pack and other Hollywood royalty as well as Kaufman's friends Berle and Sarnoff. While there, Kaufman could kibitz with Hollywood buddies Harry Cohn; Louis Mayer, cofounder of MGM Studios; Charles Vidor, a director married to Harry Warner's daughter; Armand Deutsch, heir to the Sears Roebuck fortune and a Hollywood producer; and others. They were people like him and his Park Avenue cohort except for their unusual line of work and proximity to a different ocean. He also befriended Ben Thau, then a vice president and later head of MGM, who introduced Kaufman to a minor actor then running the Screen Actors Guild: Ronald Reagan. All in all, it was a pretty nice life.[25]

Although Kaufman began work on the bench under a recess appointment in 1949, he wasn't actually confirmed by the Senate until April 1950. Knox swore him in again—this time alone and with life tenure under Article III of the Constitution—and the Rosenstiels held a dinner to celebrate. Six weeks later, a nondescript and unknown biochemist appeared at 10:45 at night in a suddenly mobbed Philadelphia courtroom and heard an FBI agent accuse him of spying for Soviet Russia. Harry Gold owed his arrest to Klaus Fuchs, a German physicist living in London and Gold's partner in espionage. Fuchs had fled Nazism, joined the Manhattan Project, and passed much of what he learned about the atomic bomb to the Soviets. After the FBI visited Fuchs in his English jail cell, Washington officials predicted more arrests. Kaufman's life was about to change.[26]

The FBI's hunt for traitors had its origins in Project Venona, the successful American effort to crack Russia's code during World War II. Intercepted messages described a conspiracy by American spies working for the Soviets to acquire information related to "Enormous," Russian code for the bomb. Then, in September 1949, the USSR detonated an atomic explosion that signaled the end of America's nuclear monopoly. Although Truman told the nation this had long been expected, hardliners like Richard Nixon claimed it could only have happened through the theft of American secrets.[27]

Gold led the FBI to David Greenglass, a twenty-eight-year-old machinist who had occupied low-level positions at the military's facility at Los Alamos, New Mexico, where the bomb was engineered and produced. Then, early on June 16, they came for Greenglass's brother-in-law and former business partner, Julius Rosenberg. When Julius opened the door of the four-room apartment he shared with his wife Ethel and their two little boys on the Lower East Side, he was in his undershirt, shaving cream slathered all over his face. Calmly refusing the agents' request to search his apartment, he finished his shave and agreed to accompany them downtown.[28]

A few weeks later the FBI arrested Abraham Brothman, a chemical engineer known as "the Penguin," and his assistant Miriam Moskowitz. They weren't charged with espionage, just working with Gold to lie to a grand jury, but the newspapers made clear they were believed to be members of the rapidly metastasizing spy ring. While Gold and Greenglass were busy cooperating and Julius Rosenberg was maintaining his innocence, Brothman and Moskowitz became the first accused members of the conspiracy to demand a trial. They would get their wish before Kaufman.[29]

Defiant as they were, Brothman and Moskowitz knew the climate could hardly have been worse for a courtroom showdown. The Truman administration, triumphant only eighteen months earlier, was on the defensive over communism. The 1948 election victory, which Kaufman had supported through fundraising, marked the surprising success of a certain brand of tough liberalism. The president and political supporters like Americans for Democratic Action had prevailed on two fronts. To the right, they battled Republicans they accused of secretly plotting to reverse the New Deal. To the left, they confronted Henry Wallace's Progressives, whom they charged with coddling communists. An ADA petition during the campaign extolled "fighting liberalism" and "militant liberalism" and denounced Wallace for indulging totalitarians at the same time it praised Truman for embracing "the most liberal platform ever adopted by a major party in America." Some left-leaning intellectuals made the same case. Sidney Hook called for liberalism to "toughen its fiber" for combat on all sides, and Arthur Schlesinger urged liberals to reclaim America's "activist tradition" while spurning communists.[30]

This fighting liberalism was unabashedly statist, its benefits to be facilitated or perhaps even directly conferred by a powerful national government. In a speech late in the campaign, Truman had declared forthrightly, "We believe that the people are entitled to prosperity, to health, to education, to social security. We believe that it is the function of government to see to it that the people have these advantages." Governmental power was also necessary to finally begin cleansing America of her original sin. "The extension of civil rights today means not protection of the people against the Government," Truman said, "but protection of the people *by* the Government." Truman's "Fair Deal," proposed in early 1949, advocated national health care, action on civil rights, substantial aid for housing, and other domestic proposals aimed at accelerating and spreading the growing postwar prosperity. In his landmark manifesto *The Vital Center*, published that same year, Schlesinger quoted Kaufman's beloved Hoover in arguing for improved domestic counterespionage. But he also stressed that greater government power "may often be an essential part of society's attack on evils of want and injustice." America was at war with international communism at home and abroad, and boldly deploying government to improve society and advance human rights would win that war by illustrating American superiority.[31]

By 1950, however, the prospects for victory seemed to darken. America's wartime alliance with Stalin had given way to a series of never-ending skirmishes and flashpoints: the Greek civil war in 1947, Czechoslovakia's communist takeover in 1948, the Berlin airlift in 1948–49, and the abrupt and shocking "loss" of China to Mao and the Reds in 1949. Then, on June 24, 1950, North Korean troops stormed south across the thirty-eighth parallel and the United States was suddenly and unexpectedly in a shooting war with communists in Asia—one made much harder and bloodier by Chinese intervention after Thanksgiving. It was widely believed the North Koreans and Chinese were merely proxies for Moscow, and that World War III was just around the corner.

At home, Americans heard constantly that a communist fifth column was boring away from within. In House hearings, former communists exposed moles in government and hidden Reds outside. Whittaker Chambers's testimony there led to Alger Hiss's perjury trial in 1950 before Samuel Kaufman, another Southern District judge with whom Irving was often confused. Hiss's eventual conviction and disgrace confirmed for many that America's foreign policy establishment was rife with traitors. Hollywood, too, seemed to have been penetrated, as well-known entertainers were hauled in to "name names" or take the Fifth.

Tom Clark, then still attorney general, responded with a program to identify undesirables based largely on their affiliation with ninety groups placed on an "Attorney General's list of subversive organizations." Millions of federal workers were examined for disloyalty, thousands faced formal charges, and many of these resigned or were fired. In February 1950, Wisconsin senator Joe McCarthy raised the temperature even further by claiming to have a list of "card-carrying communists" in the State Department and urging Secretary of State Dean Acheson to phone him at his hotel to find out who they were. His opportunistic fear-mongering would only intensify over the following months. States carried out their own mini-purges, and powerful organizations outside government like the Chamber of Commerce and the American Bar Association did their part to smoke out communists in unions, businesses, and the professions. Universities harassed and sacked leftish faculty members, while newspapers and columnists stoked the panic. After the Korean War broke out, Hearst columnist Westbrook Pegler wrote that members of the American Communist Party should simply be executed—"the only sensible and courageous way to deal with communists in our midst."[32]

All this anxiety may have run highest among New Yorkers, the very people who would judge Brothman and Moskowitz, and later the Rosenbergs. In 1949 in Peekskill, only forty miles outside the city, riots fomented by the American Legion broke out at a concert for the Civil Rights Congress, one of the left-wing groups on Clark's list. Veterans stoned attendees' cars, and one person was stabbed. In the city, the United States prosecuted the leaders of the American Communist Party for violating the Smith Act, which made it a crime to advocate the violent overthrow of the government or to belong to a group that did. Called the "Battle of Foley Square"—the courthouse was often picketed and resembled an armed camp—the tedious, months-long trial often degenerated into farce as defense lawyers gave party-line speeches and goaded prosecutors and the court with insults and raised voices. Although the presiding judge, Harold Medina, seemed unable to corral the proceedings, the jury convicted and Medina imposed maximum five-year sentences on all but one defendant. As the *Washington Post* recognized, the case left many with "mixed feelings" about whether the prosecution hadn't actually "brought us closer to what we dread"—America's own suppression of free thought.[33]

Then, throughout 1950, came the spy arrests in New York and increasingly ominous pronouncements by Hoover and Attorney General McGrath about hidden Russian agents. Affirming the communist leaders' convictions that year, Learned Hand summarized the public's fear that disaster could descend at any moment: "Any border fray, any diplomatic incident, any difference in construction of the modus vivendi . . . might prove a spark in the tinder-box, and lead to war. We do not understand how one could ask for a more probable danger, unless we must wait till the actual eve of hostilities." Fantastical illustrations showing Manhattan obliterated by atomic implosion were popular; the New York Civil Defense Commission distributed almost a million copies of a pamphlet titled "You and the Atomic Bomb," with the city in ruins on the cover. E. B. White captured New Yorkers' edginess in his famous description of the city at midcentury, *Here Is New York*, written in 1948. It was "something people don't speak much about but that is in everyone's mind": "The city, for the first time in its long history, is destructible. A single flight of planes no bigger than a wedge of geese can quickly end this island fantasy, burn the towers, crumble the bridges, turn the underground passages into lethal chambers, cremate the millions. The intimation of mortality is part of New York now: in the sound of jets overhead, in the black headlines of the latest edition."[34]

The man preparing to prosecute Brothman and Moskowitz was Irving Saypol, the United States Attorney himself. He was forty-seven, yet another product of the Lower East Side—a "stocky New Yorker with a firm chin," as *Time* lauded. His young aide Roy Cohn was less charitable, calling Saypol "the very epitome of vanity. Obsequious to his superiors, contemptuous of those under him, wrongheaded, supercilious." With his old-fashioned glasses and grandiloquent speaking style, the Brooklyn Law School graduate came off as something of a throwback. His participation in the Hiss perjury trial and the case against Communist Party leaders before Medina earned him *Time*'s moniker "the nation's number 1 legal hunter of top Communists."[35]

Kaufman and Saypol were friendly, if not especially close. But Kaufman thought enough of him—or perhaps whoever occupied his office—to do him an extraordinary personal favor a few months before trial. Saypol had a relative stationed in Europe whose "parents [were] terribly disturbed over an affair of the heart which this young man is having with a girl, and they are fearful he is going to marry her." Kaufman reached out to his friend Louis Johnson, now secretary of defense. Perhaps the lovestruck soldier could be transferred? "If this request is out of order," Kaufman hastened to add, "please disregard this communication. If, however, it is in order, in the interest of the boy and the family, I would appreciate it if you would have a proper officer in your Department examine into the facts and take whatever steps are proper." While it's hard to see how asking the secretary of defense to reassign an enlisted soldier for personal reasons would ever be "in order," Johnson "immediately had an investigation made . . . and steps are now being taken to have this transfer accomplished," he wrote Kaufman. In Germany, the major in charge waffled until his superior wrote him: "I am enclosing a little memorandum that I received after a conference with the people in the Secretary of Defense Office that are interested in this case. Need I say more?" He didn't, and the transfer took place. This link between judge and prosecutor wasn't disclosed to the Brothman-Moskowitz defense.[36]

Cohn assisted Saypol at trial. The soon-to-be infamous lawyer-fixer was then just a twenty-three-year-old wunderkind, unknown to all but upper-crust Jewish Manhattan, the clubhouse pols around his father Al, and gossip columnists like Lyons. The Park Avenue circle pegged him as the first Jewish president—he could recite the preamble to the Constitution at five—but Roiphe's mother also thought him the sort of boy who would keep a snake as a pet and feed it live mice. He had uncanny parallels to Kaufman, though he'd grown up wealthy. Both had been "antsy to get my life moving toward the real world," as Cohn put it. Both completed programs that combined college and law school—in Cohn's case, at Columbia. Both had finished school before twenty-one and been required to kill time before taking the bar exam. And both quickly joined the US Attorney's Office. "He would indict somebody," a colleague recalled, "issue a press release, indict him again, issue another press release. . . . Roy was the object of derision in the office as a publicity hound." Derision or no, it was clear to everyone that the strange and precocious kid with the droopy eyelids and friends in high places was skyrocketing upward.[37]

It was Cohn who later called the Brothman-Moskowitz case "a dry run of the upcoming Rosenberg trial," a sort of lab that allowed the prosecutors to test some of the witnesses and themes they were thinking of using if Julius and Ethel still refused to confess. Trial began on November 9, 1950, with the testimony of Elizabeth Bentley, a confessed agent dubbed the "Red Spy Queen." At earlier trials and appearances before the House Un-American Activities Committee, the Vassar graduate cut a striking figure as she exposed communists in mostly low places, or sometimes simply repeated hearsay about who was and wasn't a party member. She recounted cloak-and-dagger meetings in cars and on dark street corners to collect plans from Brothman for her Soviet handler.

Nonetheless, Gold was the government's star witness. He described furtive late-night get-togethers with Brothman, stolen blueprints for synthetic rubber, and the lies they had told grand jurors. Foreshadowing the Rosenberg trial, Kaufman often jumped in to help Saypol. "We were in reality facing two prosecutors," Moskowitz thought. The defendants' lawyer landed some blows in cross-examination, including the fact that much of the technical information involved was already public. Gold also admitted fabricating florid stories about a beautiful wife and twins, which he persisted with long past the point of needing a cover story for spying. Brothman and Moskowitz didn't capitalize on these openings by testifying themselves, however. They were hamstrung by trying to conceal something besides espionage: their extramarital affair. Rather than wreck Brothman's family, they "sat mute and unblinking as dummies in a waxworks," as *Time* put it. The jury quickly convicted.[38]

Sentencing hardly went better. As Moskowitz saw it, Kaufman was "imperious, unreachable, coldly outside the community of mere mortals, unresponsive to doubt and draped in the majesty of the robes of his office. The mahogany of his bench, burnished to a soft patina, was like an impregnable fortress." Kaufman ordered the maximum penalty—seven years for Brothman and two for Moskowitz—and lamented that he couldn't give more:

> What I do not understand and simply cannot fathom is why people seek to undermine the country which gave them every opportunity—opportunity for education, opportunity for livelihood, yes, and an opportunity for a fair trial such as they have received here. . . .
>
> The parents of these defendants came to America seeking a haven from oppression, so that these defendants—their children—could be brought up in a wholesome atmosphere, an atmosphere which recognized that God had created a human being, the greatest thing which God has ever done.[39]

With the dry run finished, the stage was set for the main event.

CHAPTER 5

The Trial of the Century

Calling the Rosenberg case "the trial of the century," a description first but imprecisely attributed to J. Edgar Hoover, was probably hyperbolic. Before it ended, the twentieth century saw innumerable trials of the century, from the 1907 trial of Harry Thaw for shooting celebrity architect Stanford White to the O. J. Simpson carnival almost nine decades later. "Every time I turn around there's a new trial of the century," the criminal defense lawyer F. Lee Bailey once quipped.[1]

But the larger point is hard to deny. The Rosenberg case deeply divided Americans, inflamed Cold War passions all over the world, and still rates among the most controversial episodes in American law. The day after it ended, the *Herald Tribune* called it "one of the most dramatic proceedings of its kind ever held in the country." For decades after the couple's executions, Americans continued to write the president or the attorney general or their congressmen asking for information about the case—anything that might explain what had happened and why. Even the Rosenbergs' lawyer conceded the point when he should have been arguing just the opposite, trying to minimize the damage. As he told jurors, they had witnessed "one of the most moving dramas that any human being could concoct. . . . Playwrights and movie script writers could do a lot with a case like this."[2]

Kaufman knew he could too. Certain of the career-making possibilities of high-profile trials from his days as a prosecutor, he could see the case's obvious potential. So he called Cohn to have him contact Dave Sweeney, a clerk of the court. Then, unlike now, cases ready for trial rotated to judges new to the litigation. As Cohn recounted,

> He wanted the case as much as he wanted the judgeship—and when Irving wants something he doesn't stop, he doesn't leave you alone until you do what he wants.
>
> We were vacationing in Florida, during the Christmas season of 1950. Irving and his wife were in Boca Raton, I was in Palm Beach. We might as well have been in the same room. I think he called me fifty times a day. Call Dave Sweeney, call Dave Sweeney, call Dave Sweeney. If you don't call him some other judge is liable to put pressure on him. Everybody wants this case, you've got to get to it, Roy, call Dave Sweeney. So all right, already, I'll call Dave Sweeney. As soon as I said that, Irving called me so many times I couldn't get through to Dave Sweeney! Make this point, make that point, don't forget this that and the other thing.

Mainly, Kaufman told him to stress the Brothman-Moskowitz trial, saying "the Rosenberg case is really a follow-up, so it would be a waste of taxpayer's money to have a new judge, who is not aware of these issues." When Sweeney relented, Kaufman changed his tune entirely and coyly pretended he rued the difficult task ahead. "Well," Cohn recalled Kaufman saying, "you've really put me in the soup now, my friend. Whatever I do I'm sure to be criticized. There's no way to be popular in a case this fraught with emotion and political overtones. But it's my duty. When you take this job you must accept the consequences." Cohn called it one of "the phoniest conversations of the 20th century."[3]

While Cohn's lifetime of lying puts his credibility in question, his account of the Sweeney call rings true and perfectly captures Kaufman's modus operandi. Kaufman *would* incessantly noodge and pester subordinates like Cohn until he got what he wanted. Beier and Sand also thought it likely Kaufman finagled the assignment. For the government's part, the most junior member of the Rosenberg prosecution team, James Kilsheimer, recalled the government's pleasure at the outcome. Kaufman was a "law and order man" with "guts," they thought, and wouldn't shrink from the death penalty. If anything, FBI officials feared that his pro-government bent might lead him overboard and endanger the case on appeal.[4]

The Rosenbergs were represented by Emmanuel "Manny" Bloch and his father Alexander. Technically, Alexander was Ethel's lawyer, while Manny was Julius's, but there was no real distinction. Alexander was seventy-four and best known for representing bakeries and furriers; it was his first criminal case. Manny was forty-nine and did almost all the speaking in court for both defendants. He had represented prominent communists in other cases with political dimensions and was therefore a natural choice for this one. The defense team was outgunned by the government's manpower, resources, and knowledge of the facts. Plus, the case had made them pariahs. A young associate who helped the defense at trial, Gloria Agrin, recalled years later that they "couldn't even get a lawyer to come in to assist us at the trial. Bloch and I were isolated. Left-wing lawyers walked across the street when they saw us coming—they didn't want to be tarred by the spy brush. Bloch was working without a fee. Both of us went broke. We lost our shirts."[5]

What the Rosenbergs badly needed was someone able to scratch out wins in tough cases by any means possible—like the savvy and grizzled courtroom veterans Kaufman had once battled, a Stryker or a Medalie. Or perhaps what Cohn would become when representing the mob. Instead, they had the courtly and clueless Blochs. Faced with blunt and barely professional hostility from Saypol and Cohn, they usually offered obsequiousness. Only days after the trial ended, the *Herald Tribune* called their performance "half-hearted and unconvincing," while even the National Committee to Reopen the Rosenberg Case, a group formed years later to exonerate the pair, decried it as a "horribly sloppy job." Beier watched the trial from start to finish and gradually became convinced that their ineptitude could only be explained by a desire to produce martyrs for international communism. No less an authority than a former member of the party's central committee agreed. He thought Bloch ended up with the job because "he was not one of the very competent Party lawyers and the whole idea was that they should not win their case."[6]

Once in charge, Kaufman scheduled trial for March 1951. Beforehand, he held a pretrial conference to inform the defense lawyers of his social connections to Cohn. As in the Brothman-Moskowitz case, he said nothing about intervening for Saypol with the secretary of defense. According to Cohn—no transcript of the hearing exists—Kaufman said he and Cohn weren't close, which wasn't accurate; that Helen and Dora Cohn were friends; and that he knew Cohn's father, which was true of every federal judge. Cohn recognized that the conference was a formality; "nobody was going to ask him to recuse," since under the law the decision was his to make, and he would simply deny the request.[7]

Then, as trial approached, Kaufman began holding secret, back-channel discussions with the prosecution team, something he continued throughout the trial. Beier recalled his law school friend Cohn meeting with Kaufman in chambers every afternoon. The clerk who replaced Beier later in 1951 similarly remembered Cohn always being in chambers—a practice he thought would now be "looked askance at." Charles Stillman, who clerked in the late 1950s, reported the same thing during a major trial he worked on: Kaufman conducting regular meetings with prosecutors to talk about the case, strategize, and preview upcoming testimony or trouble spots. An FBI memo created during the Rosenberg trial reflected other contacts between Kaufman and the prosecution. It quotes Ray Wherty, a senior Justice Department lawyer, saying he knew Kaufman would impose the death penalty "if he doesn't change his mind," indicating that someone on the government's side had been talking to Kaufman. A month before trial, the head of DOJ's Criminal Division, James McInerny, similarly told Gordon Dean, chairman of the Atomic Energy Commission (AEC), that he had spoken to Kaufman and learned he was "prepared to impose [the death penalty] if the evidence warrants."[8]

Not surprisingly, the most colorful account of Kaufman's secret meetings with the government comes from the prosecutor who took part in them:

> Before, during and after the trial, the prosecution team—particularly Irving Saypol and I—were in constant communication with Judge Kaufman. I mean private, or what lawyers call *ex parte* communication, without the presence of the defense lawyers. Not that the defense attorneys weren't aware that we were talking to the judge; no lawyer worth his salt wasn't aware in those days that prosecutors talked privately to judges about cases. There were a few exceptions, a few judges who would never speak *ex parte*, but most of them did and most of them did it without a thought, it was normal.

When they weren't meeting in person, Cohn reported using the phone in the courtroom to call Kaufman, though "Kaufman was always wary of wiretaps, not by the commies, but by the government, and he was probably right to worry."[9]

FIGURE 9. Julius and Ethel Rosenberg after the jury's guilty verdict, 1951. *Library of Congress.*

It was gray and desolate on the morning of Tuesday, March 6, 1951, when Kaufman briskly followed his bailiff into the courthouse's largest, ceremonial courtroom and onto the bench. Getting his first look at the man who would decide his fate, Julius Rosenberg whispered to Bloch that he saw a cross between a rabbinical student and a drill sergeant. Those peering at Ethel saw a tiny woman, no more than five feet tall, calm, with a red bodice supplying what one reporter called "the brightest dab of color in the great chestnut-paneled chamber." If Ethel was composed, Julius, with large glasses and a thin mustache, looked pale and drummed nervously on the defense's heavy oak table. To the *New York Times* reporter covering the trial, "an undefinable tenseness pervaded the courtroom."[10]

The clerk read the indictment—a jumble of legalese that boiled down to the government's accusation that Julius and Ethel, David Greenglass, a radar expert named Morton Sobell, and their absent Soviet handler Anatoli Yakovlev had conspired to violate the 1917 Espionage Act during wartime by transmitting national security information to the USSR. It didn't matter that Russia had been an American ally during the war; the law covered information given to any "foreign power."

Attention then turned to selecting a jury from among the three hundred people called in for the job. The process was remarkable mostly for the absurdly long list of groups and publications Judge Kaufman read to them to determine political bias—over 150 in all. Most were on Clark's list of subversive organizations. Several potential jurors expressed opposition to capital punishment and were immediately excused, though Kaufman reiterated that he was the one who would decide any sentence.

As the hours ground on and selection continued, Manny Bloch hit what would become a recurring note throughout the case: that no one should get the strange idea that communism was on trial. When a potential juror confessed that he couldn't give the same credence to testimony from a communist as from someone else, Bloch rose to "dissipate any misimpression . . . that the question of membership in the Communist Party is involved." Puzzled, Kaufman asked whether Bloch wouldn't want to know if a juror was biased against his clients. It was a sensible question. As one writer put it after the trial, how was a potential juror supposed to keep an open mind when "almost every newspaper, magazine, television or radio commentator, church sermon, employer's speech, government spokesman, had done so much to fill his mind with fear and loathing of anything connected with communism?"[11]

Mostly the lawyers just bet on intangible hunches, as attorneys selecting juries always do. Cohn admitted wanting to exclude housewives but said it was for fear they would "get nervous because no one is feeding the kids" when the trial ran late—not, of course, because mothers might naturally sympathize with Ethel and her two little boys. The tactic worked; only one woman made it on the jury. The defense, meanwhile, was "looking for iconoclasts, people who could stand up to the influence of the times," said Agrin. They were happy with the woman and with the only Black juror. Jews were wild cards. Would they see the defendants as persecuted coreligionists, or want to punish two new Judases? It was hard to predict, so both sides stayed away, and none ended up on the jury, a stark oddity in New York that would later fuel criticism of the trial.[12]

Eventually, the lawyers settled on a jury of largely male, largely white, low-level professionals. There was a caterer, three auditors, a bar owner, an accountant, an estimator, and no Reds from the Lower East Side. Five lived in the suburbs. The foreman was Vincent Lebonitte, a thirty-year-old who'd served under Patton, graduated Fordham like Kaufman, and now worked at Macy's. All in all, they were a jury of the Rosenbergs's "peers" in the legal sense but no other. "Jury satisfactory all around," Kaufman pronounced when the parties said they would lodge no further challenges, and the jurors settled into their green leather swivel chairs.[13]

Next were opening statements, and Kaufman urged the lawyers to keep them short. Saypol went first, and people strained to hear him as he read from the script Cohn had written. The Rosenbergs were traitors who "dedicated themselves to the destruction of our country," he explained. They "worshiped" Soviet Russia and so transmitted "this one weapon, that might well hold the key to the survival of this nation and means the peace of the world, the atomic bomb." When Saypol mentioned the Rosenbergs' allegiance to world communism, their feet shifted nervously under the table, and Bloch stood to object. "The charge here is espionage," Kaufman responded. "It is not that the defendants are members of the Communist Party or that they had any interest in communism." On the other hand, if Saypol wanted to prove they were communists as part of "establishing a motive for what they were doing," Kaufman promised to rule on that later. One of the jurors would later tell reporter Ted Morgan, who wrote an article about the jury for *Esquire* in 1975, that despite this admonition and several more like it during the trial, "I started to get the impression that communism *was* on trial. . . . That doesn't necessarily mean they were spies. But after all, the communists were out to overthrow the government."[14]

If Saypol's opening was incendiary, Manny Bloch's sounded like he'd only met his client a day or so before. The defense team knew little more about the case than did the jury, he admitted sheepishly, so rather than preview his case, Bloch simply asked for a "fair shake in the American way." He sounded strangely disconnected from his client and said legalistically that Julius "has pleaded not guilty to this indictment." The whole thing lasted only a few minutes. Ironically, his aged father did a better job for Ethel, warning jurors "not to condemn her because her brother is a self-confessed traitor" who, along with his wife, wanted to "transfer and lighten their burden of responsibility." He noted Ethel's role as "basically a housewife and nothing more," and as a mother to two little children. Then he, too, sat down.[15]

With opening statements over, Kaufman turned and faced the apprehensive jurors. "We have a task before us, you and I, together. While we might be irritable and uncomfortable on occasion, yet I am sure we are all good citizens and we are going to grit our teeth and do our respective jobs. So just be calm and be relaxed and be attentive."[16]

Saypol's first witness hardly seemed to match the moment. Max Elitcher was a boyish-looking man with stooped shoulders and massive glasses. Kaufman had to beg him to speak up. He couldn't take the pressure of testifying at all, Elitcher confessed, but for the help of a psychiatrist he saw for "personality problems." Elitcher detailed meetings throughout the 1940s when Julius and Sobell pestered him for anything he could take from his job at the Navy's Bureau of Ordinance. He relayed that Julius had described speaking to the famous Elizabeth Bentley. And he sensationally described joining Sobell in a secretive rendezvous with Julius to deliver a can of 35 mm film. Despite the many witnesses to come, he supplied the government's only direct proof against Sobell.[17]

Next up was the prosecution's star performer, David Greenglass—the man at the center of the drama. He was twenty-nine and heavyset, with a puggish face topped off by wavy black hair. One of the AEC officials who knew him from Los Alamos called him a "moonfaced, happy little guy [with] no intellectual depth whatsoever." His eerie smile would hardly leave his face as he told his grim tale of national and family betrayal. "Are you aware that you are smiling?" Bloch asked him during cross-examination, as David admitted knowing that his spying could earn him the death penalty. "Not very," he replied, and for a second the grin departed his face. Then it returned. No matter—the jury was mesmerized, as at a car wreck. "Here was a brother sending his sister to the gallows to save his own skin. . . . We studied him real sharply," one of the jurors recalled years later. So did Ethel, turning paler and paler—"almost snow pale" at one point, until she just covered her face with her hands.[18]

Under Cohn's questioning, David recounted his days as a machinist at Los Alamos from 1944 to 1946 and then described Julius's interest in information from the facility. David demurred at first, but eventually gave in when his wife Ruth repeated Ethel and Julius's argument that, after all, Russia was an ally and deserved the aid. First, David supplied the names of the scientists there, and other less crucial facts. But soon attention focused on "sketches on the lens mold," a critical component of the atom bomb, "and how they were used in experiments." With that hanging in the air, Cohn asked to recess for the weekend. "Well, it sort of goes against the grain of my Scotch soul," Kaufman answered regretfully, but he agreed, and the trial ended for the week.

The following Monday morning, Cohn brandished Government Exhibit 2, a sketch of the lens mold. David agreed it was identical to the one he'd delivered to Julius in 1945, but his notes about the device were indecipherable: "Julius came to the house and received the information, and my wife, in [a] passing remark that the handwriting would be bad and would need interpretation, and Julius said there was nothing to worry about *as Ethel would type it up, retype the information*." Kaufman immediately caught the significance of the testimony and asked the court reporter to repeat it for the jurors. Or Cohn may have tipped him off beforehand. A few minutes later, David described Ruth's noticing that Ethel looked tired, "and Ethel remarked that she was tired between the child and staying up late at night, keeping—typing over notes that Julius had brought her." Thus was Ethel placed in the conspiracy as its stenographer. From the witness stand, David never looked at her.[19]

Next, David explained Julius's plan to retrieve information from Los Alamos. Ruth emerged from the kitchen holding one side of a Jell-O box while Julius held the other half. Ruth would move to Albuquerque, keep her half of the box, and a courier would present the other when he arrived. "Oh, that is very clever," David gushed. All lawyers like a reenactment, so Cohn had David cut a new Jell-O box "just as he remembers it was cut on that night." In June 1945, the courier—Harry Gold—arrived with the Jell-O box fragment and whispered, "Julius sent me." David gave him more lens mold sketches and a list of possible recruits, while Gold handed over $500.[20]

In the middle of this blockbuster testimony, David was excused so that Walter Koski, a Johns Hopkins professor who'd known David at Los Alamos, could testify. The government's witness list included eminences famous for their work on the Manhattan Project, like Robert Oppenheimer and General Leslie Groves, but Saypol produced the unknown Koski. Koski vouched for the accuracy of Greenglass's descriptions of the lens mold and agreed it would help any government that got it. Under cross-examination, he conceded that David's drawings were only rough sketches. Kaufman then interjected: "You say it does, however, set forth the important principle involved, is that correct?" After Saypol got another turn at questioning, Bloch again got Koski to admit that David's drawing lacked necessary "precision," but Kaufman closed in for the kill: "While there might have been some other details that might also have been of some use to a foreign nation . . . the substance of your testimony, as I understand it, was that there was sufficient [information] . . . to reveal to an expert [what] was going on at Los Alamos?" "Yes, your Honor," Koski answered.[21]

With Koski finished, Cohn produced David's sketches and had him testify that Ethel was there when he gave them to Julius in September 1945. What happened next was one of the trial's strangest and most pivotal moments. After Cohn offered the sketches into evidence, Bloch leapt to his feet, objected, and asked that the sketches be impounded "so that it remains secret to the Court, the jury and counsel." Even Saypol was flabbergasted, calling it "a rather strange request coming from the defendants," since the Constitution requires public evidence and open trials. "If I had said it," Saypol observed, "there might have been some criticism." Kaufman went him one better: "As a matter of fact there might have been some question on appeal. I welcome the suggestion coming from the defense because it removes the question completely."

Thinking he knew how to keep the information under wraps, Kaufman asked the defendants to simply stipulate that the information involved was secret. Bloch helpfully consented, saying he was doing so "as an American citizen and as someone who owes his allegiance to this country." Sobell's lawyer refused, however. Annoyed, Kaufman decided to clear the courtroom of spectators, but when reporters objected, he let them stay, trusting to their "good taste and your good judgment on the matter of publishing portions of this testimony." Thus, incredibly, Kaufman exiled ordinary people but not the ones there precisely to tell the whole world what was happening. And predictably enough, the *Times* described Greenglass's sketch fairly completely the next morning. "The Solomonic decision by Irving Kaufman was out of the Marx brothers," as Cohn put it. Yet while incomprehensible today, Kaufman's move fit in well with the times. Reporters so unpatriotic or adversarial that they might disclose military secrets were inconceivable to Kaufman and most others in his position then.[22]

According to Agrin, Bloch's move was an attempt "to show the court—we are just as patriotic as the others. He was trying to avoid the death sentence by lifting the stigma of treason. It was a courtroom decision, made on the spur of the moment." But seconding the government's claim that Greenglass's sketch was a vital secret instead of an uneducated machinist's useless doodling backfired spectacularly. As the courtroom was cleared, at least one juror thought, "this must be really important." Sobell considered Bloch's concession nothing less than a "betrayal." Agrin blamed it on the defense team's inability to find a scientific expert willing to help them; "for all we knew, [a lens mold] was part of a camera," she recalled.[23]

With the courtroom's oak benches empty, David finished his testimony by describing Julius's reaction to his sketch: "'This is very good. We ought to have this typed up immediately.' . . . Ethel did the typing and Ruth and Julius and Ethel did the correction of the grammar." The handwritten notes were burned in a frying pan, their ashes flushed down the drain. Julius also told David how he left microfilm or messages for the Russians in a movie theater's alcove, or would meet them "at some lonely spot in Long Island." They repaid him and Ethel with wristwatches and a mahogany console table. And Julius boasted of passing along other, non-atomic military and technical information to the Soviets.

Talking through a heavy cold, Bloch began his cross-examination by forcing David to admit several small infractions, like taking money from Julius to cover debts but keeping it instead, and violating his army oath. David recounted early doubts over his espionage but, under Kaufman's questioning, said he hadn't communicated his hesitation to Julius because he "had a kind of hero-worship there and I did not want my hero to fail." As cross-examination wore on, Kaufman's temperature rose. Again and again he chastised Bloch for interrupting and asking "clumsy" questions. "Mr. Bloch is a very impatient young man, and he wants his answer fast," Kaufman mocked. Bloch, older than Kaufman, simply gave thanks for being called young.

More important were Kaufman's efforts to protect David. When Bloch tried to show David had lied to the FBI, Kaufman took over:

BLOCH: You didn't lie about a single question during that five and a half hour interval?

GREENGLASS: No, as a matter of fact I volunteered information.
KAUFMAN: He didn't say it was a five and a half hour interview.... Be careful about that. He said he was only questioned for about an hour.
BLOCH: But the interval was from two to 7:30.
KAUFMAN: I don't like the implication.

Later, while Bloch tried to show David hadn't had a lawyer during his first FBI interview, Kaufman hastened in: "Did they tell you that you could have counsel?" "Oh, yes," David replied. Bloch elicited that David hadn't mentioned getting $1,000 from Julius. "But you had told them about it?" Kaufman asked, and David agreed. When David explained his omission of certain particulars from FBI statements, Kaufman helpfully added: "It wasn't your intention at that time to give every minute detail?" And on the all-important question of what David told the FBI about Ethel, Bloch elicited that David couldn't remember what he said to the government about Ethel at first. Before this could sink in, however, Kaufman interrupted again and got David to say he hadn't "conscientiously" withheld anything.[24]

In fact, David had said nothing about Ethel typing Julius's notes or otherwise actively supporting the conspiracy, either in his first statements to the FBI or before the grand jury. He changed his story immediately before the trial under prodding from Cohn, who needed to bolster the prosecution's case against Ethel. Since the rules then didn't give the Rosenbergs automatic access to David's grand jury testimony, and they failed to ask Kaufman to order it, they couldn't show the jury the inconsistency that might have saved Ethel's life.[25]

As Bloch tried to resume—"Now let me ask you, so that there will be complete clarification here"—Kaufman, incredibly, cut him off again: "I think you are taking much too long with this subject matter. I haven't interrupted you." Bloch surely wanted to scream. They broke for lunch, and Kaufman asked him to speed it up even more. When Bloch didn't, Kaufman chastised him further, as if oblivious that Bloch's clients were on trial for their lives. Toward the end of the cross-examination, Bloch sought to cast doubt on David's education and technical abilities, but again, Kaufman proved a stout adversary:

BLOCH: Did you fail in your subjects?
COHN: I would now object to that, your Honor....
KAUFMAN: Before you answer that question, let me ask you: These sketches that are in evidence, are they the product of your own

mind? By that, I mean, were you helped by anybody on the outside in drawing those sketches?

GREENGLASS: Nobody else, just myself.

KAUFMAN: Did anybody tell you to change any line here or change any line there?

GREENGLASS: Nobody told me anything like that.

David admitted failing every class he took at Brooklyn Polytech and never even taking calculus, nuclear physics, and other seemingly relevant courses, but Kaufman rescued him once more, noting that no witness had said such classes were necessary.[26]

Yet if Kaufman vented his spleen with Bloch and often intervened to protect David, Bloch generally managed to cover what he wanted to. He simply couldn't gain traction or plant any plausible explanation for why a man would condemn his sister, other than that he was telling the awful, inescapable truth. Kaufman felt the same way. He told a law clerk three years later that it was David's willingness to implicate his own sister that ultimately convinced him of the Rosenbergs' guilt. "What boy would testify against his sister if it wasn't true?" he'd asked.[27]

David's wife Ruth testified next. As if describing a starlet, the *Times* called her "a tall, buxom and self-possessed brunette." Yet behind the superficial confidence lurked a bone-deep anxiety. Like Ethel, she had two small children to consider, and Saypol could indict her for capital espionage at any moment.[28]

She offered her own version of how Julius and Ethel led her into the conspiracy: "If all nations had the information," Julius told her, "then one nation couldn't use the bomb as a threat against another." She repeated the account of Julius telling David not to worry over his messy handwriting because Ethel would retype the notes, and described her own conversation with Ethel, who said "she had been typing." As with David's account, this crucial testimony diverged from her grand jury testimony, where she said *she* had actually written up David's information. This jibed with information from Venona that the Russians received handwritten, not typed, notes. The Greenglasses rationalized their typing fantasy because they were certain Ethel was involved regardless of the absence of solid evidence. "I know she had to know," Ruth declared later; "I know there are husbands and wives where they never know what they are doing. But this was not the case with them." As David finally acknowledged in 2001, Ruth was more involved than Ethel, but he told prosecutors he would clam up if they went after her, and she was never charged.

Ruth also described Gold's visit to Albuquerque; the Jell-O box meeting; Ethel showing her the console table, which had a hidden lamp to create microfilm; and Julius's arrival with $1,000 and instructions to flee after Gold was arrested. Ruth protested that they had a ten-day-old infant, but Julius helpfully offered that "babies are born on the ocean and on trains every day." Julius gave David another $4,000 wrapped in brown paper, which they hid in the fireplace. The plan was to run to Mexico and all meet up, but only Sobell actually made it there. Overall, Ruth struck observers as a bizarre mash-up of ordinary housewife, conscientious mother, and international spy. She didn't have compunctions about keeping the $5,000, either. "It was out of the Russians' pocket, and I had plenty of headaches."[29]

Alexander Bloch, rather than Manny, rose to cross-examine her, but as usual he had to battle the judge as well as a hostile witness. Bloch suggested Ruth was "confused" and "excited"—none too subtly invoking feminine stereotypes. Kaufman came to her rescue: "Now Mr. Bloch, I think she hasn't been excited." When Bloch persisted, urging her to calm down, Kaufman bristled, "She has been a calm witness. Let's not be too solicitous." Bloch pointed out how Ruth had kept no notes but somehow "remembered every detail from memory," but Kaufman interjected: "She remembered. I don't know about 'every detail.' I think that question is objectionable." When Bloch suggested her testimony had been memorized because it tracked her statement to the FBI verbatim, Kaufman sustained the government's objection and mocked, "I don't know exactly what the point is. If the witness has left out something, Mr. Bloch would say that the witness didn't repeat the story accurately. And the witness repeats it accurately, and apparently that isn't any good."[30]

On the trial's eighth day—Thursday, March 15—there was a diversion. That morning, the *Times* ran a front page story reporting the FBI's arrest of William Perl, a Columbia physics instructor, charged with lying during the grand jury's investigation of the Rosenbergs. Although the indictment had been sealed by another judge, Saypol took it to Kaufman during the trial, who signed a warrant for Perl's immediate arrest. The need to hurry wasn't apparent, since Perl had testified months earlier. Saypol was quoted in the article saying Perl would corroborate the Greenglasses' story, but he never took the stand in the Rosenberg case. Seen as a blatant publicity stunt by Saypol and Hoover, and an effort to bias jurors with outside information about an ever-widening spy plot, the arrest drew sharp criticism. Kaufman seems to have overlooked the possibility of tainting the jury with the incendiary news and making the trial at least appear to be less fair. In the end, nothing came of it because Bloch chose to complain off the record rather than seek a formal mistrial—yet another tactical error. Despite his mysteriously accelerated arrest, Perl didn't face trial for another two years, likely because the government hoped the Rosenbergs would finally cooperate and provide better evidence against him. Nonetheless, he was convicted and imprisoned.[31]

The government's remaining witnesses went quickly. Harry Gold described his job as courier, and Bloch fumbled again by failing to confront him with the lies about his personal life he had admitted telling at the Brothman-Moskowitz trial. Unknown to Bloch, Gold's story, too, had evolved while preparing with Cohn; at trial, he recounted arriving in Albuquerque and telling David "I come from Julius," whereas he'd originally told FBI agents the phrase was "Greetings from Ben." The Rosenbergs' family doctor testified that Julius had asked him about shots needed to travel to Mexico, claiming a friend had to go. Two Manhattan Project officials testified that "the Russians were much interested in what we were doing," and authenticated David's sketch. One said it "demonstrate[d] substantially and with substantial accuracy the principle involved in the 1945 atomic bomb" and would permit a foreign expert to perceive "what the actual construction of the bomb was." Elizabeth Bentley went last, lending her celebrity to the proceedings and explaining how the American Communist Party operated. She also confirmed coordinating on the phone with someone named Julius to pick up items for the Russians; this dovetailed with Elitcher's testimony that Julius told him he had spoken to Bentley.

As with the Greenglasses, Kaufman often intervened to help these witnesses. For example, when Bloch asked one of the government officials whether David's notes represented a "complete description of the bomb," Kaufman simply cut in and answered for him: "I don't think it was offered on the theory that it represented a complete" description. When Bentley admitted not knowing Gold, Kaufman interjected and helpfully asked whether it was "the policy of those engaged in this kind of work not to talk very much about the others that are engaged in similar kind of work." Then the government rested.[32]

There was no point delaying, so Bloch's first witness was his client. Wearing a gray double-breasted suit and floral necktie, Julius made his way to the stand. "He certainly looks like a spy," a woman whispered in back. The stakes couldn't have been higher, but Bloch's dubious strategy boiled down to little more than going through the allegations made by Greenglass and others, asking if the claims were true, and eliciting rote denials.[33]

And Julius denied virtually everything—talking to Ruth about approaching David for information, knowing where David was stationed, knowing what Los Alamos was, giving Ruth money to travel to New Mexico, and telling David to flee. "No" to seeing sketches or notes, knowing the workings of the bomb, knowing any Russians, cutting up Jell-O boxes or having Ethel type up notes. Kaufman interrupted frequently, often reiterating prosecution witness testimony. Sometimes, his questions seemed intended to give Julius one last chance to explain himself, as when he asked whether "anybody at all discussed with you the atom bomb." Julius said no. Kaufman also deferred to Bloch on occasion, retracting questions when Bloch said he would come to it.

Asked by Kaufman about the relative merits of the Russian and American systems, Julius equivocated. "There are merits in both systems," he allowed, though he was "heartily in favor of our Constitution and Bill of Rights and I owe my allegiance to my country at all times." Yet it was true he also thought the Soviets had "improved the lot of the underdog there," and was glad the USSR had "contributed a major share in destroying the Hitler beast who killed six million of my coreligionists." For a trial with such Jewish overtones, this was one of the only explicit references to anything Jewish. Bloch calling Greenglass a "schnook" in summation was another.[34]

As Bloch and occasionally Kaufman continued exploring Julius's political views, they eventually arrived at the question the defense had feared from the beginning: what to say when asked about communism. "Did you ever belong to any group that discussed the system of Russia?" Kaufman asked. Faced with bad options, Julius and Ethel chose the worst: taking the Fifth. This was tantamount to admitting party affiliation without the ability to explain or minimize. As Cohn put it, "Any chance they had went down the drain with these answers, you could see it on the faces of the jurors." At least one juror confirmed the point years later: "To me," he recalled, taking the Fifth "meant they were hiding something, even if it was their constitutional privilege." It had been the Rosenbergs' decision. Although Manny advocated it on principle, his father railed against the damage it would cause. The Rosenbergs pointed out that other defendants, like Alger Hiss, had stayed away from the Fifth but reaped no benefit at all, and they desperately wanted to avoid having to implicate old friends. In the middle of Julius's testimony, the trial broke for the long Easter weekend.[35]

Saypol cross-examined on Monday morning, and his questions about Julius's associations forced repeated reassertions of the Fifth. Eventually, Kaufman had to order him to change subjects. The US Attorney mocked Julius's statement that the Soviets had helped the underdog, asking if he read it in the *Daily Worker* or "the Wall Street Journal, perhaps." "No, I don't read the Wall Street Journal," Julius deadpanned. Again, Kaufman stepped in, asking Julius whether he discussed things like the Soviet and American systems and whether Russia should "share in all our secrets" after bearing the brunt of the war. After testifying that he hadn't revealed David's plan to steal parts from the army, Julius insisted that "when a man is in trouble, the one thing his family should do is stick by the man, regardless of the trouble he is in." If only his in-laws agreed.[36]

Soon it was Ethel's turn. "She regards everything with a beatific gaze," an observer noticed, "but her oval mouth is pursed and pinched, and there is a certain care with which she selects her words, suggesting reluctance rather than hesitancy." Bloch led her through a description of her family and education and, more important, had her explain that the children were at a temporary shelter in the Bronx and hadn't seen their parents since the arrest. She was just a housewife, saddled with the "cooking, washing, cleaning, darning, scrubbing." Kaufman asked whether Julius was dismissed from the army for Communist Party membership, which prompted her to join her husband in taking the Fifth. He asked what her views were of the US having "any weapon" Russia lacked. When Ethel said she had none, he asked again: "Your mind was a blank on the subject?" "Absolutely." Kaufman even asked if she had any Jell-O boxes in her apartment. Yes, she admitted, they ate Jell-O.

Ethel's testimony largely mimicked Julius's. The elder Bloch proceeded tediously through the Greenglasses' allegations, and she denied them until Kaufman began losing patience. "Are you taking up every conversation she supposedly had with Julius. . . . I don't want you to get the impression I am rushing you, but I don't want you to overtry a case, Mr. Bloch." The greatest drama came with her description of confronting Ruth after David's arrest. Ethel had asked Ruth if she and David were "really mixed up in this horrible mess" and pledged to support them no matter what. Ruth had then "flared up and said 'What are you asking such silly questions for. . . . We are going to fight this case because we are not guilty.'"

Saypol approached Ethel much as he had Julius, focusing on communist affiliations that forced her into repeatedly taking the Fifth. On other points, her inability to give clear denials and use of phrases like "I may have" seemed wishy-washy. Then Saypol pointed out that she'd covered certain topics during Bloch's questioning but had taken the Fifth in the grand jury, suggesting she'd hoped to avoid prosecution and then changed tack once she was on trial. "You weren't taking any chances," Saypol asked knowingly, "isn't that it?" When Ethel couldn't reconstruct her thinking in the grand jury, Kaufman responded, "In your own interest, I think you ought to think about it and see if you can give us some reason." Bloch tried to salvage things, having Ethel point out that she had only been in the grand jury because of a subpoena, but Kaufman just reemphasized Saypol's attack: "The point is, you answered these questions at the trial and refused to on the ground that it would tend to incriminate you before the grand jury." Saypol closed by drawing out her loathing of the baby brother who was now imperiling her life. It would be "pretty unnatural" if her feelings hadn't changed, she declared—and at last she'd said something the jurors could easily understand.[37]

After Ethel, the defense rested. The Rosenbergs hadn't made a good impression. "I never saw any two people so devoid of any emotion," one juror remembered. "They were stone faced. You couldn't help but notice it." Between the two, Ethel may actually have fared worse, though the case against her was much thinner. A juror later described her as "steel, stony, tight-lipped"—the "mastermind" who somehow controlled her "more human" husband, though there wasn't a scrap of evidence for this. Sobell didn't testify.[38]

For rebuttal, the government called the Rosenbergs' part-time housekeeper, who said Ethel told her the console table had been given to Julius from a friend and had been hidden away in a closet at one point. Saypol also called Ben Schneider, a photographer who testified that the Rosenbergs and their "unruly" children had visited his shop near the courthouse and ordered three dozen passport photos for use, they said, in an upcoming trip to France. When Bloch wondered how he could possibly remember the Rosenbergs out of all his customers, Kaufman cut in yet again: "Is it fair to say that you never got more than three on any Saturday?" Although their time on the stand was brief, these two witnesses impressed the jury because they "were little bystanders with no axe to grind," as one juror remembered. With that, the government also rested.[39]

Alexander Bloch then rose "reluctantly" to ask for something he knew would trigger Kaufman's wrath—a mistrial due to "the frequent questioning by the Court." Kaufman responded that the defense lawyers hadn't objected at the time, when he might have stopped his interruptions, and called the request "purely an afterthought" asserted to facilitate an appeal. That was the end of Bloch's motion.[40]

All that remained of the two-week spectacle were the lawyers' closing arguments. As Ethel was led in that morning, someone blurted out, "Look at her smiling, the bitch! I wonder if she'll smile while she's hanging." Other events had sometimes knocked the case off the front pages. Tennessee senator Estes Kefauver's committee on organized crime had taken its road show to New York and held hearings upstairs in the courthouse during the trial. During recesses in the hearings, senators sometimes wandered downstairs, and one afternoon Kaufman arranged for New Hampshire's Charles Tobey to meet the jurors before they scattered for the day. "We could use people like you upstairs," Senator Tobey told them solemnly. One juror thought the whole episode stank, believing "the connection between the gangsters and the Rosenbergs, all of them taking the Fifth Amendment, was impressed upon the jury." There had been other diversions, too—the execution of the "lonely hearts killers," the CCNY basketball point-shaving scandal. Now the trial was ending, though, and the country turned its attention to Kaufman's courtroom and awaited the finale.[41]

Manny Bloch went first and began by thanking Kaufman for treating him and his co-counsel "with the utmost courtesy," and for extending "the privileges that we expect as lawyers, and despite any disagreements we may have had with the Court on questions of law, we feel the trial has been conducted and we hope we have contributed our share, with that dignity and decorum that befits an American trial." Bloch may have said this because he thought it was required or to seem patriotic before the jury or to curry favor with the man who might sentence his clients or because he sincerely meant it. Whatever his reason, the effect was far greater than he intended. The statement would be used against the Rosenbergs in every future judicial opinion in the case—and there were many. And Kaufman and his defenders would cite it long after the Rosenbergs were gone as the ultimate refutation of almost any sort of criticism of the trial. This was the quote on the old and finger-wrinkled index card on Kaufman's desk, gathering dust when I saw it in 1991. Cohn called Bloch's statement "one of the biggest favors" Bloch inadvertently did for the government. "So thanks, Manny," Cohn added, "wherever you are."

Bloch urged the jury to focus on the crime at hand—espionage—rather than the Rosenbergs' beliefs: "If you want to convict these defendants because you think that they are communists and you don't like communism . . . then, ladies and gentlemen, I can sit down now and there is absolutely no use in my talking." What the case boiled down to, he argued, was simply "whether or not the Greenglasses were telling the truth or whether the Rosenbergs were telling the truth." And there was no way one could believe David Greenglass: "He is the lowest of the lowest animals that I have ever seen. . . . I wonder whether in anything you have read or in anything that you have experienced, you have ever come across a man, who comes around to bury his own sister and smiles. Tell me, is this the kind of man you are going to believe?"

Having likened David to an animal, Bloch supplied his motive: he "was willing to bury his sister and his brother-in-law to save his wife." Decades later, this was confirmed by Greenglass himself in an interview with *New York Times* reporter Sam Roberts: "I told them the story and left [Ethel] out of it, right? But my wife put her in it. So what am I gonna do, call my wife a liar? My wife is my wife. I mean, I don't sleep with my sister, you know? There's more to it than sex, you understand. . . . You make a life with somebody. In my generation, that's the way I would go. My wife is more important to me than my sister."

As Bloch spun it, Rosenberg was a "clay pigeon" ripe for shooting by the Greenglasses—"a guy who was very open and expressed his views about the United States and the Soviet Union, which may have been alright when the Soviet Union and the United States were allies, but today it is anathema. . . . Is this your concept of a racketeer . . . a man who lived in a Knickerbocker Village apartment at $45 a month . . . whose wife did the scrubbing and cleaning?" Ethel the washerwoman was contrasted with Ruth, "who came in here all dolled up, arrogant, smart, cute, eager-beaver, like a phonograph record." He dealt with the evidence, too—the Jell-O box, the console table, the passport photos—trying to poke holes where he could. He ended by linking acquittal with patriotism, which was no easy sell in light of the charges. "With this climate, with this hullabaloo about this case, I have got enough confidence in twelve American jurors to believe that they will . . . bring in an honest verdict." When they decided the Rosenbergs were innocent, he finished, they would "show to the world that in America a man can get a fair trial." Incredibly, there was no separate summation for Ethel, against whom the evidence was weakest.[42]

Saypol got his turn after lunch and was soon off on a tangent, attacking Sobell's lawyer by implying he was a communist. Kaufman quickly shut him down. According to Cohn, he'd warned Kaufman this was coming in one of their *ex parte* meetings, and Kaufman had pledged to "take care of it. We're not going to have a mistrial here." Duly upbraided, Saypol turned to the evidence. The Rosenbergs "stole the most important scientific secrets ever known to mankind from this country and delivered them to the Soviet Union," he charged, after "infect[ing] Ruth and David Greenglass with the poison of Communist ideology." David may not be likable, but he had exposed himself to the death penalty by confessing, and it was absurd to think he would do that "to satisfy a business grudge," as Julius had claimed, referring to their squabbling after going into business together after the war. Hadn't Gold corroborated much of David's story—Gold, of whom Bloch hadn't dared ask a single question? And what about the other evidence: Elitcher, the Jell-O box, questions about vaccinations for Mexico? Against all this, the Rosenbergs offered only themselves—they "who plainly have the greatest motive in the world for lying." Often, his imagery was colorful. Ethel "sat at that typewriter and struck the keys, blow by blow, against her own country in the interests of the Soviets." It was wrong to imply the defendants were "on trial for being communists," Saypol concluded. Their crime was far worse: serving "a foreign party which today seeks to wipe us off the face of the earth."[43]

With the lawyers finally finished, all that remained was for Kaufman to read his legal instructions, or "jury charge," to the jurors, telling them the law necessary to guide their deliberations. It would take an hour to read. As was customary, the courtroom doors were closed and locked, and absolute silence descended. He began by extending thanks for performing "one of the most sacred duties of citizenship" and covered the basics of their task. "Justice in your hands is like a child in the hands of its parents," he said. "Just as a child will be warped in a home of bickering and wrangling—so will justice be thwarted in a jury room of heat, bickering and wrangling. Just as the child can be guided by discussion and reasoning so can you mete out justice by discussion and reasoning among yourselves." From there he explained the 1917 statute, summarized each side's factual claims, and reiterated "most strenuously" that Communist Party membership was relevant only to show the defendants' motive. More generally, he cautioned, jurors shouldn't give his questions or statements during the trial undue weight. He assured them he had no view of the defendants' guilt or innocence, and if they'd "formed any such impression you must put it out of your mind and utterly disregard it." Finally, he reminded jurors not to draw conclusions from the Rosenbergs' use of the Fifth Amendment or consider their possible punishment.[44]

So girded, the jury retired at 4:53 in the afternoon. On their first vote, one or two voted to acquit. As deliberations proceeded, only one juror, forty-eight-year-old James Gibbons, continued to hold out against convicting Ethel. While Gibbons didn't think she was innocent, he simply recoiled from playing any part in ushering her toward the electric chair. He had kids of his own, and "the idea that a mother with two children could be put to death was revolting to him," Morgan reported. So at 10:55 p.m., the jury sent out a note explaining that "one of the jurors has some doubt in his mind as to whether he can recommend leniency for one of the defendants." Kaufman's response was to reread the portion of his instructions telling the jury that he alone was responsible for sentencing, but he added that they could recommend a particular sentence for his consideration. Ironically, other jurors explained to the holdout that Ethel probably wouldn't get the death penalty. Still, Kaufman's instruction didn't clinch it, and after midnight, the jury headed to the Knickerbocker Hotel in midtown.

By morning, the other jurors had had enough. One juror told the lone holdout, James Gibbons, "Look possibly this woman that you want to save will someday be a part of a conspiracy to transmit secret information to a foreign power that would result in your own doom and the destruction of your wife and your children." As Morgan recounts, "it did not take long that morning for Gibbons to give in. He felt the relief that a man feels who has been defending an unpopular point of view against uneven odds. Now that it was over, he recalls, 'I felt like Pontius Pilate washing his hands.'"[45]

At 11:00 a.m. on March 29, the jurors filed into the courtroom to announce their verdict. Julius and Ethel clasped hands under the table while Sobell pursed his lips. The foreman Lebonitte stood, fixed his blue eyes on Kaufman, and said simply, "We the jury find Julius Rosenberg guilty as charged. We the jury find Ethel Rosenberg guilty as charged. We the jury find Morton Sobell guilty as charged." Julius remained impassive while Ethel nodded her head slightly in disbelief and then looked at the floor in despair. Despite the inquiry during deliberations, the jury didn't recommend sentences to Kaufman. After Lebonitte finished, Kaufman thanked the jurors and seconded their conclusion: "My own opinion is that your verdict is a correct verdict. I must say that as an individual I cannot be happy because it is a sad day for America. The thought that citizens of our country would lend themselves to the destruction of their own country by the most destructive weapon known to man is so shocking that I can't find words to describe this loathsome offense." He set sentencing for the following week, then took the opportunity to publicly commend the "splendid job" done by Hoover and the FBI.

To the reporters outside, Bloch lamented that his clients' "chances in this kind of climate were minimal." Indeed, the same day as the verdict, Ohio senator John Bricker proposed that Congress investigate federal judges handling cases involving communists in light of their supposed lenience. "I do not believe the courts of our country are sacred cows," he said. Presumably Kaufman wasn't on his list.[46]

Did Kaufman give the Rosenbergs a fair trial? No and yes. No because he seems to have prejudged the case and believed in the Rosenbergs' guilt from the outset. And that belief infected the trial. In 1957, Kaufman addressed the FBI's graduating class of new agents and cautioned them against convincing themselves of a suspect's guilt: "Neither you nor I nor any man can 'know' that a person is guilty until a duly appointed jury has rendered its verdict." In 1951, however, Kaufman treated the Rosenbergs as if he knew they were guilty. Yet the trial was fair in the larger sense that Kaufman didn't fundamentally change the Rosenbergs' defense or the outcome of the case. They were convicted by the persuasive evidence against them, the temper of the times, and their lawyers' anemic response to the government's legal onslaught—not because of Kaufman.[47]

Most of Kaufman's management of the trial was legally proper. Although critics soon claimed the government had targeted the Rosenbergs because they were communists, Kaufman's handling of that issue obeyed the operative legal rules. Establishing a defendant's motive is a standard basis for introducing evidence at a criminal trial, and Saypol was correctly allowed to show why the Rosenbergs had committed espionage. Kaufman frequently and properly reminded the jury that communism wasn't on trial, and that evidence of the Rosenbergs' political views was only proper to show their motive. When Kaufman thought

Saypol was overdoing it during his cross-examination of Ethel, he ordered him to move on. In upholding the convictions, the court of appeals acknowledged the possibility that Kaufman's warnings to the jury were "no more than an empty ritual without any practical effect on the jurors." But the admonitions resonated with at least one of them, who recalled that Kaufman was "constantly telling us that communism was not a factor. He harped on this, and I tried to dispel it from my mind." In any event, since evidence of the Rosenbergs' party membership was admissible, there was nothing more Kaufman could do than caution the jury, which he did repeatedly.[48]

Kaufman was also correct in his framing of the law to the jury. Along with deciding whether to admit or exclude particular evidence, formulating the legal instructions to the jury is the trial judge's most important task. There have been no serious or lasting critiques of how Kaufman interpreted the key legal principles governing the case against the Rosenbergs and communicated them to the jury.

Still, while Kaufman got much right in overseeing the trial, his apparent prejudgment of the Rosenbergs' guilt led him into two serious errors. First, he was far too eager to intervene in the trial in ways that almost always transparently helped the prosecution. Whether interrupting to directly cross-examine Julius and Ethel, rehabilitating Greenglass when Bloch obtained concessions, bolstering a government scientist's qualifications, or belittling Bloch in front of jurors, Kaufman's intrusions often colored pivotal moments in the trial. While judges may question witnesses to clarify the facts, they can go too far, and convictions have been overturned based on a judge's one-sided interjections. Ironically, one such case occurred in 1970, when Kaufman was on the appellate panel. The trial judge in that case had repeatedly interrupted the defense lawyer to question his client's version of events but was "far more patient and moderate" with the government's key witness and helped him "unfold his story." As the court of appeals concluded, a "trial judge's responsibility to assist the jury in understanding the evidence . . . must not be so zealously pursued as to give the jury the impression of partisanship." Everything written in this unknown case in 1970 about the theft of wristwatch movements could be said of Kaufman's conduct in 1951.[49]

Most contemporary analysts of the trial agree that Kaufman displayed partiality. To the historian Daniel Yergin, Kaufman was "consistently hard on the defense lawyers [and] much more sympathetic to the prosecution." Ronald Radosh and Joyce Milton, authors of what many consider the most evenhanded deep dive into the case, write that "Kaufman's belief in the defendants' guilt had been evident throughout the trial." But there is room for disagreement. In their appeal, the Rosenbergs highlighted nearly a hundred instances of Kaufman's interferences. Yet the court of appeals found he "stayed well inside the discretion allowed him," concluding, "In general, we can find no purpose in the judge's questioning except that of clarification." One of the three judges who heard the appeal, Jerome Frank, actually *advocated* judicial questioning in his book *Courts on Trial* because he distrusted the "fighting method of conducting trials" practiced by lawyers hired to be partial. This may be why he described the Rosenbergs' trial in private correspondence as "more fair than many in which convictions have been affirmed." On the Supreme Court, Justice Hugo Black thought Kaufman's interventions had been biased and unfair, but no other justice agreed.[50]

And there is retroactive support for Frank's conclusion in Morgan's interviews with jurors. To them, Morgan wrote, "the black-robed judge sitting on his high bench was a figure of absolute authority. They viewed him with . . . well, reverence is not too strong a word." One went as far as to say "Kaufman's running of the trial verged on perfection. He bent over backward to give both sides a chance." And of course Kaufman did decide in the Rosenbergs' favor on occasion—sustaining some of their objections, denying some of Saypol's, giving them access to Elitcher's grand jury minutes, and otherwise ruling for both sides. Beier, far from a reflexive defender of his old boss, thought Kaufman's active role in the trial wasn't intended to shape the result but was simply Kaufman being Kaufman—how he ran every trial. Once a star prosecutor, he needed to show he was better than the poor slob the government was paying to do the job now.[51]

Whatever reasonable differences of opinion might exist over Kaufman's conduct vanish when it comes to his second major lapse, however: his secret contacts with the prosecution. Any meetings Kaufman held with Cohn and Saypol before and during the trial—as distinct from after conviction—would have been highly improper. Over sixty years earlier, a leading scholar whose lectures would help form the basis for legal codes of ethics wrote,

> Another plain duty of counsel is to present everything in the cause to the court openly in the course of the public discharge of its duties. It is not often, indeed, that gentlemen of the Bar so forget

> themselves as to attempt to exert privately an influence upon the judge, to seek private interviews, or take occasional opportunities of accidental or social meetings to make *ex parte* statements, or to endeavor to impress their views. They know that such conduct is wrong in itself and has a tendency to impair confidence in the administration of justice, which ought not only to be pure but unsuspected.[52]

The first national code of ethics for lawyers, promulgated by the American Bar Association in 1908, provided that "a lawyer should not communicate or argue privately with the Judge as to the merits of any pending cause." The ABA's nonbinding *Canons of Judicial Ethics*, formulated sixteen years later after work by a committee chaired by Chief Justice Taft, contained a similar rule. A major work on legal ethics published two years after the Rosenberg trial likewise held that "a lawyer may not informally discuss a case with the judge without the other lawyer's presence, nor should the judge permit this." That rule came from a committee that included some of the New York bar's leading lights, including Judge Seabury, J. Edward Lumbard, John W. Davis, and Joseph Proskauer. They knew the norms and habits of New York's federal courts and wouldn't have lightly forbidden a practice thought harmless or routine. At least two of America's foremost experts in legal ethics have also condemned Kaufman's conduct. New York University Law School professor Stephen Gillers commented that Kaufman's *ex parte* communications "violated judicial ethics rules and due process guarantees as understood at the time as well as today," while Monroe Freedman wrote that Kaufman committed "extremely serious judicial misconduct." Judicial decisions before 1951 also unequivocally condemned private meetings between the judge and counsel for one side.[53]

Nonetheless, Cohn may have been right that Kaufman wasn't the only judge who privately spoke to prosecutors. Like Cohn, former clerk Charles Stillman recalled other judges doing so behind the backs of the defense. On the other hand, the junior prosecutor on the Rosenberg team, James Kilsheimer, disagreed with the notion that secret contacts were standard operating procedure. And Stillman noted that many judges would never have talked to a prosecutor out of the presence of defense counsel, citing the highly regarded Ed Weinfeld in particular. He also thought defense lawyers would have been "pissed off" had they known, in contrast to Cohn's breezy assertion that any good defense lawyer would have understood it was happening. "It was not right," Stillman concluded.[54]

Knowing whether or how Kaufman's *ex parte* conversations affected the Rosenbergs' trial is impossible. He and Cohn and Saypol may have kept their discussions to the sorts of housekeeping or logistical details that plague any trial. Or Cohn may be right that Kaufman mostly babysat and refereed the prosecution team's internal squabbling. Or it may have gone further. Kaufman may have suggested trial strategies or handy solutions to evidentiary problems. He may have intimated how to arrange things to avoid legal objections, or telegraphed coming rulings. In the one specific instance Cohn mentions—Saypol's personal attack on Sobell's lawyer during summations—Kaufman's advance knowledge may have headed off a mistrial. Interestingly, Julius suspected the *ex parte* contacts, musing in a letter from prison that "the possibility exists that [Kaufman] was acquainted beforehand with the important points the prosecution was going to establish. How else can you account for the many times" he intervened proactively to help the government? Whatever their substance, backstage meetings with prosecutors would have placed Kaufman firmly on the government's team despite his fundamental obligation to remain neutral.[55]

In betraying this basic duty, Kaufman was likely driven by a tangled complex of motives. He was a creature of federal law enforcement and its highest leaders, such as Hoover and Clark, and even in private practice he gravitated to former prosecutors as law partners. One law clerk from that era was struck by how much Kaufman still wanted to be "one of the boys" with the prosecutors, though he'd graduated and moved on to a different branch of government. Another observed how he "glorified" the US Attorney's Office and that one of the key administrators in the office then, Silvio Mollo, was in chambers "every other day." On the bench for only sixteen months when he tried the Rosenbergs, Kaufman hadn't yet acquired the distance and detachment necessary to see himself as something more than a gear in the state's machinery for convicting people.[56]

And convicting the Rosenbergs, to Kaufman, was undoubtedly a right and just outcome worth coaxing along from the bench. Stillman thought Kaufman went into criminal cases believing the government was usually right, the defendant had probably done what he was accused of, and "we have to convict this guy." That feeling would only have intensified in a high-profile case that raised issues of war and peace. An FBI memo written days after the Rosenbergs' execution recounted Kaufman telling Bureau officials that, all along, he had suspected the government had more information on the Rosenbergs than it could risk revealing in open court. Thus, he didn't see their trial as a vehicle for uncovering the truth and determining what happened, but as the necessary rigmarole to be completed so guilty and dangerous spies could be punished.[57]

Then there were personal considerations. If a conviction was expected and even vital for national security, acquittal would represent failure. The stench of that failure might attach chiefly to the prosecutors, who would be attacked as bunglers, and even jurors, who would be called dupes. But some would inevitably reach the judge, potentially crippling prospects for advancement. After all, Judge Samuel Kaufman, who had somehow let the jury deadlock without convicting Alger Hiss in his first perjury trial, faced scorn from politicians and citizens whose misunderstanding of the process led them to blame him for the disappointing result. By contrast, Medina had reaped national fame, an adoring biography, and rapid promotion after top communist leaders were convicted on his watch. Kaufman knew this history well. Its effect on him may have been subtle, even subconscious, but it would have been hard for him to tune it out entirely. He hadn't realized his life's ambition in nearly record time in order to watch the whole project crash and burn while communist agents walked free from his courtroom.[58]

Finally, there were even deeper motives at work—the same considerations he faced as he began to grapple with the task of pronouncing sentence. What did he think of the Rosenbergs and others like them who had forsworn the American way of life in obeisance to the alien doctrine of Marxism? How grave was the crime of giving military secrets to the USSR? What message did he want their trial and punishment to send to Americans and the wider world? He gave himself a week to mull their fate.

Chapter 6

Worse Than Murder

Sentencing the Rosenbergs was the act that would come to define Kaufman. Their own recklessness led them to the dock. Saypol and Cohn prosecuted them. Twelve ordinary New Yorkers convicted them. Now the moment was entirely his. "In no other judicial function is the judge more alone," he declared years later. The law he had to apply, the 1917 Espionage Act, posed an unusually stark choice. It didn't allow for life in prison. Instead, the maximum term was thirty years, and the Rosenbergs would be eligible for parole in only ten. Or Kaufman could order them to die.[1]

He was apparently leaning toward execution for at least Julius even before the convictions. Both the diary of AEC chief Gordon Dean and the FBI memo quoting Ray Wherty at the Justice Department recorded as much, though their information was secondhand. Cohn also wrote in his autobiography that "Kaufman told me *before* the trial started that he was going to sentence Julius Rosenberg to death." And tell-all *New York Post* columnist Leonard Lyons, who was close to Cohn and Kaufman, wrote two days after the verdict that "courtroom observers" thought Julius would "get the extreme penalty next week." Other columnists retailed similar rumors of death sentences as leverage to get the defendants to "crack under the strain and talk out loud to save their hides," as one delicately put it.[2]

Despite these hints, Kaufman hadn't fully decided what to do when the trial ended. So he began canvassing others. Now that the trial was over, the ethical rules prohibiting *ex parte* or secret meetings with one side or the other no longer applied, and he could talk to whomever he wanted.[3]

First, there were the government's views to consider, as in any criminal case. According to Cohn, Kaufman called him from a phone booth near the Park Avenue Synagogue and "said he was concerned about a possible public opinion backlash if he sentenced a woman to the electric chair, particularly a mother with two young children." In response, Cohn reiterated Ethel's work to recruit David and called her the spy ring's "mastermind"—a claim for which there was no proof at all. On the other hand, a contemporaneous FBI memo describes Cohn telling the head of the FBI's New York office that Kaufman "personally favored" sentencing both Julius and Ethel to death and that Cohn had tried to convince Kaufman to spare Ethel—the opposite of the version in his autobiography—because of the "possibility that she would talk and additional prosecutions could be had on the basis of her evidence."[4]

Opinions were equally muddled in Washington. Kaufman asked for Saypol's view on April 4, the day before sentencing, and Saypol recommended death for both Julius and Ethel. Kaufman asked whether officials at DOJ felt the same way, and Saypol said he didn't know. Incredibly, he hadn't bothered to ask. When Kaufman told him to sound out his superiors, Saypol immediately flew to Washington, where he found "there were differences all around" among top DOJ officials. He flew home to New York and, as it happened, ran into Kaufman at a dinner. "Upon narrating to him the Washington division I was then asked by the judge to refrain from making any recommendation for punishment the next day in the course of my closing statement at sentence." Like Cohn, however, Saypol gave a different version of this years later, in a private conversation with Beier. By then, Saypol was a state court judge, and Beier happened to appear in his courtroom on a routine matter. Saypol waved Beier up to the bench and, apropos of nothing, whispered confessionally that he'd actually only wanted Julius to die. To Beier, the encounter felt like a belated and misdirected bid for forgiveness.[5]

There was also Hoover to consider. Afraid of a hostile "psychological reaction" to executing a mother of small children and cognizant of her more minor role in the affair, the FBI chief wanted to spare Ethel, though perversely he thought the more minor figure Sobell deserved the ultimate punishment. Deputy Attorney General Peyton Ford agreed with Hoover that death for Ethel would only be counterproductive. Hoover sent a memo conveying his views to Attorney General McGrath, and they were passed along to Kaufman somehow, perhaps through Saypol or Cohn.[6]

Kaufman also sounded out other judges, according to an FBI memo quoting Cohn. He talked to Jerome Frank, who would end up being one of the three appellate judges assigned to hear the case later in the year. Frank told him he opposed capital punishment on principle but suggested he talk to his colleague Ed Weinfeld. The FBI memo records Weinfeld telling Kaufman he favored death for all three defendants, though Weinfeld's biographer doubts this because Weinfeld later criticized the executions and was himself a lenient sentencer. Learned Hand also favored the death penalty, if Kaufman is to be believed. James Zirin, a New York lawyer, recounts a dinner party decades later where the hostess pointedly asked Kaufman "how he could justify the Rosenberg death penalty. There was stunned silence in the room. 'I consulted with Learned Hand and other judges in the courthouse before I did it,' he said in a tone of solemnity. 'They all agreed it was the right thing to do.'" Kaufman's claim is plausible, considering that Hand recommended him for elevation to the court of appeals ten years later. Saying every last colleague he spoke to agreed with him, on the other hand, was probably an exaggeration contrived to repulse a sudden social ambush, or perhaps a case of remembering what he wanted to rather than what actually occurred.[7]

What had to have been Kaufman's most difficult meeting took place the day before sentencing. Ethel's mother Tessie Greenglass had asked for an audience, and Kaufman agreed. "You're just putting yourself through the ringer," a sympathetic colleague told him, urging him to back out. "She's entitled to see me," Kaufman said with a sigh. "David has done a terrible thing," Tessie was reported to have told Kaufman, "but the prophets say that one who sins and confesses should be blessed." As for Ethel, her mother told Kaufman of their impoverished lives in the ghetto and broke down in sobs after admitting she hadn't seen her daughter in prison because Ethel forbade it.[8]

Then there were the views of ordinary Americans. "If Judge Kaufman decides on the death penalty," one article noted before the sentencing—passing on information Kaufman or Cohn must have provided—"his verdict will be in line with the majority opinion expressed in hundreds of letters he has received in the last few days." These letters were transmitted to the FBI so agents could inspect them for anything favorable to communists.[9]

In the end, though, gathering other people's thoughts couldn't resolve Kaufman's quandary. He had no choice but to search within. As the *Saturday Evening Post* profile of him in 1953 dramatically described,

> Kaufman wanted time to think and the week was running out. On several afternoons, he went alone to the Park Avenue Synagogue to sit and meditate in the dimly lighted temple. In the evening he came home with no appetite for food. His young sons, back from school, found him glum and unresponsive at the dinner table. After dinner the worried judge went to his study. There was nothing more in the trial record than he already knew. But he returned again and again to the record and was still bent over it when his family went to sleep.

Newspapers told their readers Kaufman had slept only ten hours all week.[10]

Because these accounts came from Kaufman himself, their objectivity is questionable. Overstating the heroic loneliness of his duty would have been a natural temptation. Yet it is still true and hardly surprising that the sentencing pushed Kaufman to his limit. While not unusual then in the state courts, death sentences were extremely rare in the federal system, and no recently appointed district judge would have thought much about capital sentencing before taking the bench, or done much to prepare for the brutal soul-searching required. "In formulating and pronouncing the sentence I was subjected to a terrible ordeal, one that I hope and pray I shall never have to go through again," he wrote Attorney General McGrath a few days after it was over. That was likely an honest assessment.[11]

Saypol spoke first, and as he and Kaufman had agreed the previous day, said he would refrain from offering a recommendation because the sentence "lies solely within the discretion of the trial court. The prosecutor's function is fulfilled when he has completed the case and the verdict of the jury rendered." This was absurd and must have prompted amazement from anyone even dimly familiar with how the system really worked. Prosecutors almost always recommended specific sentences, and judges often adopted them to the letter.

Turning to the case, Saypol described the struggle against international communism as "the greatest issue of our age" and said, "A society that did not defend itself is not worthy of survival." Young American soldiers were "daily sacrificed in Korea in defense of our way of life," he added, while the Rosenbergs had "affected the lives, and perhaps the freedom, of whole generations of mankind. Any consideration of their personal interests necessarily involves a hardening of the heart toward the fate and suffering of countless other human beings."[12]

When it was his turn, Bloch began with yet another compliment for Kaufman, as if one last show of servility might save his clients. The court, he said, had "conducted itself as an American judge." Still, Bloch admitted that his hands were tied by the Rosenbergs' refusal to acknowledge any guilt, which he acknowledged made his task more difficult. Nevertheless, he tried. He noted that Moscow and Washington were wartime allies when most of the espionage occurred, but Kaufman quickly interrupted to point out that the conspiracy continued into the Cold War. Bloch then tried arguing that other nations would have rapidly obtained atomic weapons regardless of his clients. "Are you saying, Mr. Bloch," Kaufman asked patiently, "that because it was inevitable that Russia would eventually be able to develop the atomic bomb, therefore it was perfectly proper for any American citizen to turn over any information which would help them develop it much sooner?"

Met at every pass, Bloch soldiered on. He pointed out that Tokyo Rose and Axis Sally, who had worked for wartime enemies rather than allies like Soviet Russia, had gotten only ten to fifteen years, as if making radio broadcasts equated to atomic espionage. Then he conjured a future when the international atmosphere might not be so tense and lenient sentences might seem more appropriate. "You know, your honor, history turns. . . . Who knows that but tomorrow the Soviet Union and the United States may not find some accord and find the basis for resolving their differences." He ended with a plea personal to Kaufman: "I know you haven't been on the bench very long, but I know you have had a lot of experience in criminal law as a prosecutor, and I assume, a modicum of experience as a judge in criminal trials. I am going to ask you to say to yourself, in your own conscience, your Honor, whether or not these people were the type of people that ordinarily come before you in a criminal case." Bloch was right. To Kaufman, the Rosenbergs weren't the con men and pornographers he had once prosecuted; as he would soon make clear, they were much worse.[13]

After Julius and Ethel declined to address the court themselves, Kaufman finally had the floor. His voice was hoarse and faint, and people in the courtroom thought he was tired and worn. Staring up at the bench and focusing intently, Julius swayed back and forth on the balls of his feet. Ethel occasionally wrinkled her forehead in concentration, or perhaps foreboding.

Kaufman began with a half-truth that would only embarrass him when the full story emerged decades later. "Because of the seriousness of this case and the lack of precedence," he said, "I have refrained from asking the Government for a recommendation. The responsibility is so great that I believe the Court alone should assume this responsibility." Actually, Kaufman wanted and had sought the government's views but had instructed Saypol not to air them in court because of the Justice Department's internal disagreements. Knowing the death sentences would look harsher if they contradicted senior prosecutors' wishes, Kaufman neatly avoided the problem by pretending he was going it alone.

After noting the Espionage Act's wide disparity in permissible sentences, Kaufman moved on to the war against communism. Americans could "be under none of the delusions about the benignity of Soviet power that they might have been prior to World War II," he announced. "The nature of Russian terrorism is now self-evident. Idealism as a rationale dissolves." That such idealism might have been easier during the war, when Julius committed the atomic espionage, received no mention. Although America faced "a challenge to our very existence," Kaufman continued, the Rosenbergs had "made the choice of devoting themselves to the Russian ideology of denial of God, denial of the sanctity of the individual and aggression against free men everywhere instead of serving the cause of liberty and freedom." Then Kaufman launched into the portion of the sentence most would remember and quote: "I consider your crime worse than murder. . . . I believe your conduct in putting into the hands of the Russians the A-bomb years before our best scientists predicted Russia would perfect the bomb has already caused, in my opinion, the Communist aggression in Korea, with the resultant casualties exceeding 50,000 and who knows but that millions more of innocent people may pay the price of your treason." By now, no one in the courtroom could have entertained much doubt about what was coming, at least for Julius. Incredibly, the bells of St. Andrews Church next door to the courthouse were tolling noon.

Turning to Ethel, Kaufman acknowledged her husband as "the prime mover in this conspiracy" but described her as having "encouraged and assisted the cause. She was a mature woman—almost three years older than her husband and almost seven years older than her younger brother. She was a full-fledged partner in this crime." At this, Ethel's right hand gripped the chair in front of her, knuckles white. Worst of all, Kaufman piled on, she was a derelict mother. She and

Julius knew "they were sacrificing their own children, should their misdeeds be detected. . . . Love for their cause dominated their lives—it was even greater than their love for their children."

Now Kaufman reached the end, and his words came more slowly:

> What I am about to say is not easy for me. I have deliberated for hours, days and nights. I have carefully weighed the evidence. Every nerve, every fibre of my body has been taxed. I am just as human as are the people who have given me the power to impose sentence. I am convinced beyond any doubt of your guilt. I have searched the records—I have searched my conscience—to find some reason for mercy—for it is only human to be merciful and it is natural to try to spare lives. I am convinced, however, that I would violate the solemn and sacred trust that the people of this land have placed in my hands were I to show leniency to the defendants Rosenberg.
>
> It is not in my power, Julius and Ethel Rosenberg, to forgive you. Only the Lord can find mercy for what you have done.
>
> The sentence of the Court upon Julius and Ethel Rosenberg is, for the crime for which you have been convicted, you are hereby sentenced to the punishment of death, and it is ordered upon some day within the week beginning with Monday, May 21st, you shall be executed according to law.[14]

There was an audible gasp in the courtroom when Kaufman said the word "death," but the Rosenbergs barely flinched. One reporter saw Julius's jaw muscles tighten and Ethel's breathing quicken—that was it. Moments later Julius nodded to Ethel to leave, and four marshals escorted them out a side door. "How are you feeling?" he asked her in the hallway. "Fine. I'm alright as long as you are." Back inside, Kaufman sentenced Sobell to thirty years, explaining his comparative lenience by declaring ironically, "I cannot be moved by hysteria or motivated by a desire to do the popular thing." The Rosenbergs' accomplice simply stared out the window.[15]

After the hearing ended, Kaufman headed upstairs to chambers. The atmosphere in the small suite of offices was tense and suffocating—"funereal," as Kaufman's nephew, then in the eighth grade, remembered it. Kaufman's sister-in-law had brought the boy down to Foley Square for the historic event. Kaufman ushered in reporters and photographers and told them of his anguish and exhaustion.

Outside the courthouse, Bloch took Kaufman's word "hysteria" and used it against him. The Rosenbergs were victims of "political hysteria," he charged, and their sentence was the product of "extraneous political considerations." The couple would maintain their innocence, he declared, "as long as they breathe," which ended up being true. Reporters also descended on the tenement of Tessie Greenglass, who sobbed and said she'd "expected any sentence but not that." Somewhere else in New York, as Morgan wrote a quarter-century later, "the jurors who had convinced James Gibbons that the chance of a death sentence was remote must have felt rather sheepish." The next day, Greenglass received fifteen years.[16]

The case finally over, Kaufman set off for Palm Beach with Tom Dodd. Calling himself "the most exhausted man in the world," he told reporters he hoped to sleep "for four days in a boat." From Florida they sailed on to the Bahamas, and Kaufman landed a five-foot wahoo, which cheered him up. While he was fishing in the Atlantic, a letter from Hoover arrived in chambers. Despite Kaufman's having condemned two people to death and given a bombastic speech blaming them for the Korean War, Hoover commended the "restraint" shown by his "statements in imposing sentences on the accused. Even at this early hour the effect of this trial has been noted in the Communist underground ranks which have been stunned by your forthright action." Soon the communists and many others would regroup, however, and mount a desperate and ferocious campaign against the sentences and the judge who ordered them.[17]

Kaufman's death sentences were broadly popular at first. Even before sentencing, the *Herald Tribune* argued that "no penalty, no matter how severe, would be unjust." The *Los Angeles Times* agreed with Kaufman that the Rosenbergs' crimes dwarfed mere murder and that the world lived "under a siege of terrorism" orchestrated from Moscow; "in the jungle one must maintain constant vigilance in self-defense." Other editorial pages concurred. In February 1953, just after President Eisenhower denied clemency to the Rosenbergs, Gallup asked fifteen hundred people whether they approved of the sentences, and 76 percent did—a number that was surely even higher right after the trial.[18]

Most liberals initially went along, too. In his appellate opinion, Frank wrote that it was "impossible to say the community is shocked and outraged by such sentences"—"shock and outrage" being the legal test for a violation of constitutional due process. The ACLU found the death penalty "not so disproportionate to the severity of the crime as to amount to a denial of due process." Liberal historian, political consigliere, and all-around gadfly Arthur Schlesinger defended the sentences in much the same violent terms Kaufman had used to impose them. He labeled the Rosenbergs "professional spies, whose work may yet result in the murder of millions of Americans," and quoted a passage from Thomas Jefferson arguing that "traitors" should "get what they deserved." Max Lerner, the humanist writer and academic, said the sentences were "drastic, yet it is scarcely possible to challenge [their] justice."[19]

But "history turned," as Bloch had weakly predicted in his unsuccessful argument for mercy, and few now think the death sentences were just. In part, that shift was inevitable. Except for thirteen nerve-racking days in 1962, the atmosphere in early 1951 might have represented the height of American Cold War angst. Over time, the air raid sirens fell silent, the duck-and-cover drills stopped, and Americans warmed up to mutually assured destruction. They found it harder to remember or care much about a time when only we had the bomb. The Korean War ended, Stalin died, McCarthyism flamed out, and détente eventually replaced confrontation. Then, miraculously, the Soviet Union itself disappeared. Executing the Rosenbergs came to seem like an ancient and fanatical overreaction.

Nor did Kaufman's strident courtroom speech wear well over time. Blaming a luckless electrician and his wife for the Korean War was ludicrous, and his claim that they had imperiled the very existence of the United States was exaggerated verging on apocalyptic. Only a few years later, Kaufman's hyperbole was already being called "ridiculous" by people like Jonathan Root, a reporter who wrote a government-friendly book about the case. The Rosenbergs hadn't been convicted of treason, for which the Constitution requires heightened proof. Yet Kaufman fumed that the Rosenbergs were "traitors" whose deaths were crucial to "the preservation of our society." As Justice Frankfurter put it, the Rosenbergs had been "tried for conspiracy and sentenced for treason." According to Kaufman, the Rosenbergs hadn't simply wanted to aid a foreign country or balance the international scales—they had cooked up a "diabolical conspiracy to destroy a God-fearing nation." One recent writer rightly deemed Kaufman's hyperbole "an exemplar of 'the paranoid style' of American cold-war politics," echoing Richard Hofstadter's famous dissection of McCarthyite conspiracy theorists and their unhinged antecedents. The historian Stacy Schiff placed Kaufman's speech firmly in the frightened and wrathful tradition of New England's witch trials.[20]

Then there was the public advertisement of piety implicit in Kaufman's disclosure of long, tortured hours of soul-searching in the dimly lit pews of the Park Avenue Synagogue. Kaufman may have imbibed this from Medina, who had been vocal about the comfort he took from his deeply felt Christianity during the personally taxing trial of the communist leaders. In 1952, Medina gave a talk to the Church Club of New York describing the effect of his faith on his judging, and Kaufman kept a reprint of the speech in his files. But flaunting religion like this rubbed some the wrong way. As Frankfurter wrote Hand in 1958, "I despise a judge who feels God told him to impose a death sentence." Many others were similarly, if silently, disgusted.[21]

The fates of other spies also suggest Kaufman's sentences were disproportionate. People who gave the Soviets far more useful and important information—Klaus Fuchs, in particular, who spent only fourteen years in prison—received lesser penalties. None was even jailed for life, and one, Ruth Greenglass, was never jailed at all. True, Fuchs, Gold, Alfred Dean Slack, and the eleven party chiefs all received the harshest punishments allowed by applicable statutes. And most also cooperated with prosecutors after they were caught. But these differences can't fully rationalize the extreme novelty and severity of the death sentences. Greenglass couldn't be blamed when he said, years later, "Judging from what happened to the other people that were involved when I was arrested, I never thought anything like that would ever come about." Then there were the spies no one ever learned about. John Haynes and Harvey Klehr, scholars of Soviet espionage and hardly Rosenberg sympathizers, believe that if Kaufman and the public had known about the greater contribution of other spies revealed through Venona but kept secret, the Rosenbergs wouldn't have received the death penalty.[22]

In addition, Kaufman overvalued the material Julius and David transmitted to the Soviets. The government's scientific witnesses from Los Alamos testified generally that Greenglass's information was a closely guarded secret that conveyed key principles of the atomic bomb and would have been of interest to foreign governments. But they provided no specific information about what role it played in the USSR's effort to produce its own nuclear weapon. The government either didn't know or chose not to expose the information in court. Yet Kaufman based the sentences in part on his conclusion that the Rosenbergs gave the Russians the bomb "years before our best scientists predicted Russia would perfect" it. James R. Browning, an assistant to the attorney general who analyzed the Rosenbergs' clemency petition in 1953 and would later serve as a federal appellate judge, saw the missing link in Kaufman's reasoning. As he acknowledged in a memo, "the question of whether, in view of published scientific material and the progress of Russia's experimentation at that date, the supplying of the information involved did substantially aid Russia in developing an atomic bomb was not at issue at the trial and has not been determined on the record."[23]

Nor has more recent information validated Kaufman's view. Only a year after the executions, Leslie Groves, the general who oversaw the Manhattan Project, confirmed that the information Julius gave was of minor value (though Groves still supported the death sentences, since he considered the Rosenbergs traitors). James Beckerly, an AEC official who sat at the prosecution's table for a portion of the trial, said in 1954 that the United States should stop "kidding" itself "about atomic 'secrets.' The atom bomb and the hydrogen bomb were not stolen from us by spies." George Kristiakowsky, who directed the explosives division at Los Alamos, thought the value of David's sketch was "almost nil." Most analysts now believe Julius and David mainly corroborated Fuchs's more important information, which along with other pieces of the puzzle likely helped Moscow quicken its pace to the finish line. Not an insignificant contribution—but not all-important either. Yet Kaufman uncritically accepted the popular notion that there was a single grand "secret" to the atomic bomb reducible to a few pages of notes. As Philip Morrison, a theoretical physicist who worked on the explosive lenses at Los Alamos, put it in 1974, "It's just too much for one man to know. Too much for one book to tell. Too much to write on any piece of paper. Volumes of technical skill. Laboratories full of people. Factories, machinists, machines, all sorts of things. That's what it takes. It's an industry. Not a recipe."[24]

Kaufman also simply ignored the fact that Julius and David passed the atomic information to Soviet Russia when it was an American ally, and when Americans could have understandably regarded that country differently from how they did in 1951. Indeed, David specifically testified that Ruth convinced him to transmit information by saying "Julius and Ethel had told her that Russia was an ally and as such deserved this information." At sentencing, Kaufman correctly said that "the nature of Russian terrorism is now self-evident," but its obviousness during the war was the more pertinent question. Kaufman was surely right that ordinary citizens didn't have the privilege to decide for themselves what military information to give other countries, and that some of Julius's non-nuclear spying occurred after the war, when tensions between the United States and the USSR were rising. Regardless, the Soviets' status as a wartime ally, when the most important information was compromised, should at least have entered the moral calculus. Many Americans, including some who worked on the Manhattan Project, believed that atomic information should be made available to all countries, and the USSR in particular, to prevent any one from threatening world peace.

The Soviets' wartime status was also relevant under the 1917 Espionage Act. In 1970, Kaufman wrote James Bennett and offered the only extended discussion of the sentences found in his papers, and the only one that appears outside his oral and written rulings in 1951 and 1953. Bennett had directed federal prisons in 1953 and tried to get the Rosenbergs to confess shortly before the executions. Seventeen years later, he wrote in his memoir of "doubt[ing] that the imposition of the death penalty was justified." When he learned of Bennett's view, Kaufman wrote him a scolding letter he denoted as "Personal and Confidential" that claimed he'd effectively had no choice but to order death. Congress had included the death penalty in the 1917 law, Kaufman reasoned, so the penalty must have been intended for the most serious cases, and the Rosenbergs' offense was the most serious imaginable since they had disclosed "information on what was and is surely the most devastating weapon ever inflicted on mankind." "A judge," he wrote Bennett, "faced with the awesome responsibility of sentencing in a capital case, would be unworthy of the name if he permitted his personal views to sway his judgment of what conduct Congress meant to punish by death. Given the magnitude of the crime necessarily implied by the jury's verdict, there was, in reality, no room for discretion in the sentencing judge."[25]

Much about this justification is suspect. There is no evidence Kaufman opposed capital punishment in 1951, and more important, his bombastic remarks at sentencing reflected enthusiastic support for the executions, not the reluctance of someone whose hands were tied. Nor, as it happened, was Kaufman correct about Congress's intentions in 1917. The Espionage Act was passed two months after American entry into World War I and had been aimed at German spies and saboteurs as well as homegrown opponents of the war. Although the death penalty provision prompted little debate, the law's proponents likely wouldn't have viewed providing information to wartime allies like England and France in the same terms as transmitting it to Germany. "We all agree that a spy, whoever he may be, whether a citizen or an alien, who reveals military secrets *to an enemy* should be summarily and expeditiously disposed of," then-congressman Fiorello La Guardia said when debating the bill in the House. In 1944–45, the USSR wasn't an enemy. This was the view of Robert L. Stern, the solicitor general who represented the government in the Rosenberg case in the Supreme Court, as well as Assistant Attorney General Browning, author of the clemency memo. Browning wrote, "It is probable that Congress, in providing the death penalty, had particularly in mind the transmission of information to an enemy nation in time of war." While Kaufman's death sentences were technically permissible under the literal terms of the 1917 law, they flouted its most natural interpretation and historical context, despite his after-the-fact defense to Bennett.[26]

Suspicion that the Rosenbergs—and Ethel especially—received the death penalty in order to frighten them into confessing and cooperating has also soured views of Kaufman's sentences. Some in government had been thinking in those terms all along: Julius was supposed to confess to save Ethel, while Ethel was supposed to confess for the children. One week before trial, Saypol's deputy Myles Lane testified in Washington to a closed session of the Joint Congressional Committee on Atomic Energy and stressed that the electric chair was the only real leverage to get Julius to identify coconspirators and describe what he gave the Russians. At the same hearing, the AEC's Gordon Dean called Julius "a tough man [who] may not break, but his wife is in this too, and faces a 25 or 30 year sentence, and I think he might talk." Hoover wrote Attorney General McGrath that "proceeding against his wife might serve as a lever in this matter." Saypol waited a month after Julius's arrest to charge her and did so only as it became clear Julius was holding out. Had he caved, Ethel might have been spared altogether, like Ruth Greenglass. As trial approached and evidence against Ethel failed to materialize, Cohn pressured the Greenglasses into changing their accounts and implicating her as a typist.[27]

Kaufman's view of the lever strategy before sentencing isn't known. In the months after, however, he appeared to adopt the idea by emphasizing that pleas for mercy should be directed to the Rosenbergs, not him, because they could save their own lives by cooperating. "As you know," Hoover wrote a Justice Department official in early 1953, "Judge Kaufman indicated he would grant them clemency if they would make a full disclosure of their activities." In any case, the death sentences came to be seen as threats meant to coerce confession and cooperation, whatever Kaufman's original intentions. "Was this not their real crime?" the pro-Rosenberg polemicist John Wexley asked in 1955, referring to the couple's failure to name names. Leading constitutional scholar Alexander Bickel, who accepted the Rosenbergs' guilt, described the executions in 1966 as, "in effect, in retribution for their silence. This action is disgusting. There is no other word for it." More recently, condemnation of the lever strategy appeared in a 2015 New York City proclamation honoring "the life and memory" of Ethel on her one hundredth birthday. "How diabolical, how bestial, how utterly depraved!" she wrote of the lever strategy from prison. Most people now agree with her.[28]

Finally, special ignominy surrounds Ethel's execution. Testimony at trial provided scant evidence of her involvement in espionage. The Greenglasses told the jury that Ethel joined their meetings with Julius to recruit David and plan how they would pilfer information from Los Alamos, but according to them her only concrete action consisted of typing David's notes. Kaufman conceded her lesser role at sentencing but still imposed the same punishment. It was the electric chair for "encouragement" and transcribing handwriting—modest contributions to the Russian bomb by any measure. As Julius yelled at Bennett in Sing Sing, "Just imagine . . . my wife is awaiting a horrible end for having typed a few notes!"[29]

In the absence of much evidence about her at trial, Kaufman seems to have fallen back on a stereotype of the scheming, domineering wife who manipulates her weak and vacillating husband. Cohn wrote of telling Kaufman, "She's the older one, she's the one with the brains . . . she engineered the whole thing, she was the mastermind of the conspiracy." This fantasy may have originated with Ruth, who described Ethel in an interview before trial in the Yiddish newspaper the *Forward* as "the dominant person" in her marriage. Or perhaps it was rooted in Cohn's view of his own controlling mother. In *Angels in America*, playwright Tony Kushner has Cohn describe Ethel as "that sweet, unprepossessing woman [who] reminded us all of our little Jewish mamas." But Doris Cohn was no shrinking violet—and Rose Kaufman likely wasn't either, having managed transition to a new country and kept the family together when her husband died. Ethel's manly image may also have taken hold because of her steely composure at trial, disappointing those who expected an emotional breakdown. Then there were the descriptions of communist wives in books and movies—women who supposedly surpassed their husbands in fanatical and ingenious devotion to the cause. Hiss's accomplished, socialist wife had also been suspected of driving him into espionage. One *World-Telegram* article in 1953 called Ethel a "red spider" keen to "dominate a man."[30]

Or perhaps Kaufman simply overlooked Ethel when it came to sentencing. Her own lawyers did nothing to differentiate her from Julius when setting out the defense, treating the two as a unit, though the evidence against Julius was much stronger. Her putative counsel, the elder Bloch, didn't even bother to give a separate closing argument on her behalf. He might have used the occasion to home in on the skimpy evidence against her, or at least evoked some sympathy for the children. To the cynics who believed the party preferred the Rosenbergs as martyrs, especially the young mother, the Blochs' strange refusal to offer a separate and vigorous defense for Ethel tends to confirm the suspicion. Whether malevolent schemer or powerless wifely appendage, she couldn't seem to break free of her era's preconceptions.[31]

And now it's clear she didn't even type the notes. Greenglass's admission in the 1990s that he fabricated the story of Ethel typing in order to shield his wife obliterated the already flimsy argument for her execution. Aficionados of the case steeped in the arcana of Soviet archival materials and decrypted Venona cables still tirelessly debate her responsibility. Her supporters emphasize that the Soviets never gave her a code name, as they did for active agents like Julius, and that some Russian cables and files describe her as aware of Julius's work but not a direct participant. One KGB cable said, "Knows about her husband's work. . . . In view of delicate health does not work." As Sobell said in 2008, "She knew what he was doing, but what was she guilty of? Of being Julius's wife." Alexander Feklisov, one of Julius's Soviet handlers, said in the 1990s that Ethel "had nothing to do with this—she was completely innocent." An FBI memorandum drafted days after the executions that describes the Venona information likewise states only that she "knew of the extent of her husband's activities," not that she took part in them. But some facts point the other way. In taped conversations before his death, Nikita Khrushchev reportedly said that the Rosenbergs, *plural*, "provided very significant help in accelerating the production of our atomic bomb," though there are questions about the reliability of the transcripts. And a different Venona cable indicates that Julius and Ethel together recommended Ruth's recruitment into the espionage ring.[32]

Overall, the evidence is fragmentary, stale, and tantalizingly unresolved. The Rosenbergs' sons once wrote of the impossibility of proving "someone played no role in a secret conspiracy," and they're right. Still, with the revelation that Ethel went to her death in the electric chair on the strength of perjured testimony, revulsion at her sentence became almost universal. Even Radosh, a conservative-leaning soldier in the long wars over the case, concedes that Ethel's execution was "a miscarriage of justice."[33]

Of course, Kaufman lacked the benefit of Greenglass's and Sobell's belated admissions and never saw any Soviet files. Doubts aired in FBI meetings and high-level memos weren't presented to him in open court. But one drawback of the death penalty is its devastating finality, its elimination of any chance to bend to new information. Questionable as the sentences were originally, Kaufman assumed the risk they would look even worse after the fact. He lost the bet.

If personal ambition and a reflexive identification with the prosecution biased Kaufman during the Rosenberg trial, deeper forces were at work when it came to sentencing. Finding mercy for Soviet atomic spies would have been challenging in any courtroom in 1951, but Kaufman might have been the defendants' worst option. Few were as hardwired to view the Rosenbergs with greater contempt.

For one thing, Kaufman's antipathy to communism was especially intense. Some of this probably traced to his formative years at Fordham. Most Jews of Kaufman's ilk, Julius Rosenberg included, streamed into City College, where it wasn't hard to find party members and fellow travelers among students and faculty. At Fordham, the Jesuits were waging war on socialism in the name of God and natural law. A former dean of the law school, Francis Garvan, had served as an assistant attorney general during the Red Scare of 1919 and worked to deport anarchists like Emma Goldman. On campus, the tone was strongly anticommunist, whether in the school's unique, religiously influenced jurisprudence class or at public gatherings for commencement and other occasions. At such events, Catholic and other speakers vigorously denounced socialism as equal parts un-Christian and un-American.[34]

The influence of this thinking on Kaufman was apparent in a speech he gave in 1950 to thousands of New Yorkers in Central Park for "I Am an American Day," a celebration honoring newly naturalized citizens and those old enough to vote for the first time. As war loomed in 1940, Congress had proclaimed the new patriotic holiday to take place on the third Sunday of every May. Kaufman's address centered on America's divine origins and its superiority to the Godlessness in Moscow. The country's foundation "is the law of God," he explained, "and America is built, brick by brick, from the plan given to us by the greatest architect of human dignity." Communism, on the other hand, was atheism and ruination: "When man-made law departs from the law of God, the fundamental principles of morality are violated. We are observing with horror the waves of brutality and cruelty which are rolling over whole peoples. The enslavement of the person, the denial of human rights, the revelations of the human capacity for sin and misery, and also revelations of Godlessness." The speech could have come directly from one of Father Pyne's jurisprudence lectures. It perfectly foreshadowed Kaufman's condemnation of the Rosenbergs at sentencing as slaves to "the Russian ideology of denial of God," architects of a "diabolical conspiracy to destroy a God-fearing nation," and traitors for whom "only the Lord can find mercy."[35]

Kaufman was also inspired by Hoover. Some of his constant and unrestrained flattery of the most feared man in Washington was simple career advancement, but there was more to it than that. As the head of the FBI's New York office recognized in an internal memo, Kaufman was "a real admirer of the Director." And the director's obsession since his first days in government had been leftist subversion. The Communist Party was "a Trojan horse of disloyalty, coiled like a serpent in the very heart of America," he told *U.S. News & World Report* shortly after the Rosenbergs' indictment. A few months later, when Kaufman faced two people who seemed to prove Hoover's point, Kaufman was unlikely to feel sympathy. "How true it is that these false prophets come to us in sheep's clothing but are nothing more than ravening wolves," he wrote Hoover years afterward.[36]

Furthermore, there was the related menace from antisemites who had always seen communism as a Jewish plot to dominate the world. More and more Jews were on edge as McCarthyism intensified. Only three months before the spy trial, an unrelated Rosenberg–Anna–came to symbolize the tangle between Jews and communists and antisemites. She was a longtime Democratic labor expert nominated by Truman to serve as assistant secretary of defense. Murky charges of communist sympathies secretly spread by Gerald L. K. Smith, a pro-Nazi leader of the tiny Christian Nationalist Party, almost torpedoed her Senate confirmation. As Kaufman's clerk wrote in a draft speech in 1952, "The attack was remarkably simple and direct. She was a Jew and therefore a Communist and, ergo, a traitor. The attack came close to success." Tempests like this made a lot of people defensive. "I did resent very much the idea of associating Jews with a sympathy toward communism," Cohn said in 1979. "And I do admit that this is something that has always bothered me, and I've tried in every way I can to make it clear that the fact that my name is Cohn and the fact of my religion has nothing to do except perfect compatibility with my love for America and my dislike for communism." The playwright Arthur Miller wrote of "the anxiety in myself, to be candid about it, the worry and the chill of unquiet that there had been so many Jews noticeable in the left over the past decades. So I could understand the perhaps special need Jews could have, their very complicated desire to show that they too were patriotic Americans."[37]

Miller's trepidation foreshadowed one of the main lines of Kaufman criticism: that he bent over backward to demonstrate Jewish American loyalty by making an example of the Rosenbergs. Immediately after the sentencing, Yiddish newspapers attacked him on this ground. *Jewish Day* asked whether Kaufman feared "that, perhaps, if he were not to give them the death penalty, he would be suspected of not having done so because he is a Jew." Even a non-Jewish juror picked this up. "I felt good that this was strictly a Jewish show," he told Morgan, referring not only to Kaufman but the prosecutors and defendants. "It was Jew against Jew. It wasn't the Christians hanging the Jews. Any other judge would have been more lenient than Kaufman, but the Jews hated the Rosenbergs for the disgrace they had brought upon their race. Kaufman wanted to make an example of someone who had disgraced the Jewish people." Conversely, others like the *Daily Mirror* praised Kaufman as a fine exemplar of Jewish Americanism: "Some bigots will say the three spies are Jews and will denounce all Jews. They will forget to say that the judge, the prosecutor and his assistant who did such a magnificent job for America, are also Jews." No less an icon than Louis Brandeis shared this kind of thinking, writing years earlier that, "large as this country is, no Jew can behave badly without injuring each of us in the end. . . . Since the act of each becomes thus the concern of all, we must exact even from the lowliest the avoidance of things dishonorable; and we may properly brand the guilty as a traitor to the race."[38]

Whatever Kaufman's concern for appearances, he didn't have to manufacture his patriotic outrage. It was genuine. At his core, there was an inevitable revulsion for two people who had once been just like him but then spurned everything he stood for. Kaufman and the Rosenbergs had all been poor Jews on the Lower East Side—second-generation children of refugees from the dark, eastern lands. Julius was born in Kaufman's old neighborhood, Jewish Harlem, a few months after the Kaufmans arrived. For a while, their paths were the same—acclimating to America in an immigrant family, enduring privation, loosening religious strictures, passing through the city's public schools. In short, the second generation. But then the road forked.

Kaufman reached for and grasped the lifeline extended however inconsistently and grudgingly to Jews and other newcomers: success according to the well-established rules of the American game. With no regard at all for his religion or meager background, a Catholic university had generously taken him in and trained him. The government had hired him and sent him into court in the greatest city in the world to represent the American people. He had piled up money through law and business, and his family lived well on New York's most prestigious boulevard. He was welcomed into party politics and rewarded again with promotion to higher government office in the capital. And all this was just a prelude to realizing his ultimate ambition: a seat on the bench. "This can only happen in America," he had gushed after his appointment, and he was more or less right.

To the Rosenbergs, though, Kaufman's road was a mirage. Unlike most Jews, they hadn't yet made it out of the ghetto. The American dream they saw was a put-on invented by those at the top to mask widespread class exploitation, violence against racial minorities, and imperialism abroad. Outraged by local labor disputes, the Tom Mooney case, the Scottsboro boys, and other injustices, they had started down the other path trod by American Jews toward a different dream: a new system to serve the masses, not just the talented strivers. America was a "callous society," they wrote one another from prison, where so-called "honorable men" in power duped and suppressed the people. "World cartels, controlled by finance capital," ran the government and "appoint[ed] as errand boys such men as Saypol and Kaufman." In fact, to Julius, Kaufman and his ilk from Park Avenue and the City Athletic Club were nothing less than the *Judenrat*—the German word for the Jewish councils the Nazis formed to facilitate their genocide and a term Julius often used to pillory the established Jewish leadership and press. To the Rosenbergs, Kaufman's American dream was hollow and corrupt.[39]

The chasm between these two different outlooks was vast and all-encompassing. Whether Kaufman was fully conscious of it or not, this is what he meant when he charged the Rosenbergs at sentencing with wanting to destroy America. It was *his* America they wanted to end, the promised land Jews like him had searched out for millennia and finally found. In the end, this was Abe Brothman's and Miriam Moskowitz's and Julius Rosenberg's and Ethel Rosenberg's and Morton Sobell's true offense. "Judges are not saints," Kaufman himself wrote decades later, "and they are subject to influences they are not aware exist. For example, judges may allow their subconscious social prejudices to lead them."[40]

In 1952, as the Rosenbergs' executions were approaching, and Kaufman was under pressure to reduce their sentences, Helen wrote him a note to buck up his spirits. Though written twenty-one months after the trial, it exposes the thinking at work all along:

Irving Dear,

Don't let the commies get you down. Keep remembering—they are trying to undermine the safety of our country. *Where could we go from here?* Be strong, and just roll with the punches. We all love and admire you.

Where indeed? For Kaufman and all the other lucky Jews, there was nowhere left after America.[41]

Chapter 7

Immortality

Before long, Kaufman had finished chasing marlins in the Atlantic and was back in New York. He saw Milton Berle, who worried that his old lawyer hadn't yet shaken the careworn mien of a man who'd just issued America's most famous death sentences. "Be careful, Irving," he joked, "or you'll drop the world." Sometimes he was recognized by total strangers. It might have been his imagination, but taxi drivers now seemed unusually solicitous, and the box office clerk at Otto Preminger's hit *The Moon Is Blue* reached through the ticket window bars to congratulate him. Laudatory mail piled up in chambers, and some proposed he run for governor, a less far-fetched proposition than it might seem given past judges and prosecutors in New York who'd been nominated and sometimes won. His old fraternity, Tau Epsilon Phi, named him "Man of the Year," an award he acknowledged "might have been easier because General Ridgeway and Jackie Robinson are not TEP men."[1]

Things had generally been quiet since the sentencing, as Manny Bloch prepared the Rosenbergs' appeal to the Second Circuit. But in August, a small dissenting voice rose from the multitudes who had found no fault with the case and moved on. The *National Guardian* was a far left newsweekly with fifty thousand or so subscribers. Although notables like Norman Mailer, W. E.B. Du Bois, and Ring Lardner contributed to the magazine, its heated opposition to the Korean War shunted it far out of the mainstream. Crusading journalists James Aronson and William Reuben then began a series of articles on the case. "Is this the Dreyfus case of Cold War America?" the first article's headline asked. The magazine also published heartrending, if propaganda-rich, letters between Julius and Ethel. Aronson and Reuben argued that the pair were probably innocent, that they might have been victimized by a "political frame-up," and that the sentences were akin to lynching.[2]

One of the *Guardian*'s readers was a lawyer and academic who happened to live in the same apartments as the Rosenbergs but didn't know them. "No one was doing anything," Emily Alman thought, so she set up an organization to press for a new trial or clemency: the National Committee to Secure Justice in the Rosenberg Case. Reuben helped her get started, and the group, 125 strong, issued its first press release on January 3, 1952. "Grave doubt exists as to the guilt of Ethel and Julius Rosenberg," it claimed, and "beyond the fate of this family is the right of all people in this country to freedom of thought." The release also played up the Jewish angle, noting that Jewish and other newspapers had voiced "fear that the Rosenbergs were also victims of religious bigotry." In a separate statement, the committee's head, the Zionist writer Joseph Brainin, added that "the fact that judge and prosecutor both were Jewish has led to fears that they surrendered to the McCarthy-like hysteria of the day." Ironically, the Rosenbergs themselves mostly wanted to avoid claims of antisemitism, seeing that as a "tactical mistake" that diverted attention from their supposed political persecution. The committee never got the message. Its release asked readers to join and contribute money. Shortly after, its first advertisement appeared in the *Guardian* and listed prominent left-wing intellectuals as supporters, including Du Bois, Nelson Algren, and Herbert Aptheker.[3]

One week after Alman's first press release, a bailiff gaveled the Second Circuit to order, and Judges Jerome Frank, Harrie Chase, and Thomas Swan filed in to hear oral argument in the Rosenbergs' appeal. Frank was a nationally famous civil libertarian who had served in the New Deal and written pathbreaking works on psychology and the law. While not as liberal, Chase and Swan were highly esteemed and had served on the court for decades. If these three believed the Rosenbergs had been railroaded somehow, they were unlikely to have let public opprobrium or political pressure stand in the way of ruling in their favor. Six weeks later they issued an opinion affirming the verdict and sentences. Frank had been afraid the other two judges would ask him to write the opinion because he was Jewish, and for that or other reasons it worked out that way. "Since two of the defendants must be put to death if the judgments stand," he wrote, "it goes without saying that we have scrutinized the record with extraordinary care to see whether it contains any of the errors asserted on this appeal." None was found, and the judges deemed the trial fair in all respects.[4]

As for the sentences, trial judges had long enjoyed absolute discretion over sentencing as long as the penalty fell within the range set by the law, and the 1917 statute allowed for capital punishment. Frank was in the habit of soliciting advice from law professors and others he trusted, and one such memorandum urged him to wiggle around this rule because the sentences were unjust, "the patent result of a vindictive mind, or one woefully confused." The writer admitted his legal grounds for this were weak, and Frank had no interest in such creativity regardless. He did, however, coyly suggest in his written decision that the Supreme Court alter the precedent that removed sentences from appellate review. If his court *was* given such power, Frank hinted broadly in a footnote, "it might take into consideration the fact that the evidence of the Rosenbergs' activities after Germany's defeat (as well as of their earlier espionage activities) came almost entirely from accomplices." But first the Rosenbergs would have to ask the Supreme Court to change the law. Bloch began working on his petition to do just that.[5]

The Rosenberg committee was starting to make waves even before Frank's disappointing decision, which only added to the urgency. Chapters were forming all over America—soon they would be active in twenty-six cities—and tens of thousands of pamphlets and leaflets penned by Reuben were rolling off the presses. The committee also wrote and took out ads in newspapers and magazines. More and more people sent checks to keep the campaign going, and public rallies needed larger meeting spaces. One in New York in March drew over a thousand people who heard speakers remind them of Sacco and Vanzetti. In Washington, supporters began showing up unannounced at the Department of Justice and their representatives' offices carrying the committee's material and asking to talk to someone about the case. Protests and hostile newspaper pieces also began appearing in Europe.[6]

Meanwhile, Kaufman's Foley Square mailbag began to bulge. "Although as a Jew, you undoubtedly felt obliged to indicate no partiality in the Rosenberg case," one New Yorker wrote him, "this sentence can serve only to create a general association of traitor-Jew in the mind of Americans, and thus fan the fires of anti-Semitism." Another correspondent asked whether he could "claim to have mercy in your heart." The FBI checked its files but found no "identifiable subversive data" on the writers. The Bureau was also monitoring the committee through informants who secretly slipped into its meetings.[7]

The committee's efforts particularly roiled the Jewish community, where its energetic spadework and charges of antisemitism threatened to touch off internecine war. In Chicago, Temple Judea agreed to host a rally, but pressure from the ADL forced it to cancel suddenly, causing an uproar over free speech. Chicago was also home to Dr. G. George Fox, a Reform rabbi who took up the Rosenbergs' cause. He charged in the city's Jewish paper that Kaufman had "lean[ed] over backward in his desire to show that Jews condemn treason" and urged readers to write President Truman. "This is not primarily a Jewish case," Fox argued, "but unless we Jews show some interest, I fear nothing will be done. . . . The death of the Rosenbergs for treason, even though undeserved, will give our enemies a handle to a paddle which will never be out of use." In the Brooklyn *Jewish Examiner*, a different rabbi wrote that Kaufman's meditation in synagogue before the sentencing "was a pretty gesture. But he should have gone to the Talmud," where he "would have found that Jewish tradition has always been unalterably opposed to the death penalty." A third rabbi, the Orthodox Meyer Sharff from Williamsburg, took to appearing at Rosenberg committee rallies and declaring that "if Judge Kaufman really wanted to know what an honest Jew would have done, he need not have gone to a synagogue. He could have walked on any street in New York and asked any ten good Jews." In Los Angeles, the publisher of the *California Jewish Voice* wrote of "despis[ing] the cowardly Jewish judge" for emulating fascist and communist justice with such draconian sentencing. The committee quoted these articles in their flyers and disseminated copies at meetings.[8]

Faced with these attacks on Kaufman, major national Jewish groups returned fire. In May, an umbrella organization for the American Jewish Committee, the ADL, the American Jewish Congress, the Jewish War Veterans of the United States, and other groups issued a statement calling the Rosenberg committee "communist-inspired" and denouncing "unsupported charges that the religious ancestry of the defendants was a factor in this case." B'nai B'rith groups in Virginia and the Jewish War Veterans gave Kaufman citations. Julius Klein, as the veterans' group's leader and Kaufman's friend, wrote him in a public letter: "We despise equally those who would callously use the Rosenbergs to injure the Jews and those who would callously use the Jews to help the Rosenbergs."[9]

The mainstream press also joined in. In the *New York Post*, Max Lerner was starting to waffle on the sentences, now calling them "unprecedented and harsh," though still he believed crying antisemitism was "an insult to the overwhelming number of American Jews, who hate every form of totalitarianism, and it is a mockery of the millions of Jewish martyrs in Europe." *Time* called the issue of antisemitism a "diversion" and noted, along with most who favored the government, the obvious irony that prosecutors and judges behind the Iron Curtain *really were* murderously antisemitic—a fact never mentioned by the Rosenbergs' defenders. In November 1952, communist Czechoslovakia purged several high-ranking Jewish party members, quickly convened a show trial, and hanged them a few days later. Accusations that antisemitism lay behind the Rosenberg case stepped up as communists found themselves on the defensive over the real thing in Prague.[10]

Kaufman was stunned by his change in fortune. While he had been almost universally celebrated for his fortitude immediately after the trial, he was caught off guard by rising criticism the following year. And some of his own brethren were leading the charge, even if they weren't the Park Avenue sort. Tradition prevented judges from speaking out directly to explain their decisions or counter criticism, though no ethics rule precluded it. They addressed the public through their comments in open court and their published opinions. Beyond that, decorum and deeper notions of the limited role of the judiciary in a democratic society demanded that they remain well above the scrum where disappointed litigants, politicians, and copy-hungry reporters fought over court decisions. Judges were supposed to be secure in the knowledge their rulings were correct and blissfully unconcerned whether others agreed. But Kaufman was eager—temperamentally compelled, in fact—to do battle. Even a glowing magazine profile of him hinted at this elemental need, telling readers of his "gnawing desire to answer his critics." The article said nothing about his actually doing so; on the contrary, it depicted him as soldiering on "in silence." In reality, he didn't intend to meet his foes with silence. It was just that established practice forced him to find surrogates.[11]

At first, Kaufman likely operated through those few journalists already knee-deep in the trenches fighting the Rosenberg committee, like his friend Leonard Lyons and Oliver Pilat. One Saturday in November 1952, he invited the *Daily Mirror* columnist Victor Riesel, best known for exposing corruption in unions, and ADL executive Arnold

Forster to his Park Avenue study. Riesel, who described the meeting to the FBI's assistant director, Lou Nichols, found Kaufman outwardly "calm and collected" but "inwardly disturbed." Kaufman confessed feeling "terrific pressure in the Rosenberg case from Jewish sources. Several rabbis have been to see him. Members of his own synagogue are putting pressure on him. He is standing alone so far as the Rosenberg case is concerned." Kaufman proposed that Riesel call Nichols for "some angles to build up public opinion on behalf of the Judge's position." Riesel promised to help, suggesting he might start with the antisemitism in Czechoslovakia. For his part, Nichols thought the Bureau shouldn't take a position on Riesel's plans but told him "the best way he could help the Judge would be to document the communist connections with the committee."[12]

Weaponizing columnists wasn't Kaufman's only tool, however. There were levers to pull behind the scenes, too, as always. Nor for that matter were defensiveness and resolve his only reactions to the growing firestorm. He believed he had done his duty in condemning the Rosenbergs and was determined to stand by his decision to the end. But that didn't mean he necessarily wanted them dead—or that he craved eternal identification as the man responsible. One person could take the unpleasant problem off his hands by granting clemency. That would leave Kaufman with the best of all possible outcomes: praise for staunchly defending America without the burden of orphaning two children.

So, according to a former Justice Department lawyer, Kaufman called the White House and asked President Truman to commute the Rosenbergs' sentences. What he said went unrecorded, but the move would have been unusual, especially for such a blockbuster case. Judges mostly stay out of commutation or pardon requests, and the Rosenbergs hadn't even made one yet. Truman, in turn, called a former assistant, David K. Niles, a specialist in Zionism and Jewish affairs. Niles called Harvey Spear, an assistant to the attorney general, who described the result: "After I talked with David Niles and he discussed his views with President Truman, the president's answer to Judge Kaufman was that, if Judge Kaufman felt strongly enough to urge the president to commute the death sentences, then Judge Kaufman should commute the sentences himself." Truman and Democrats had long been under attack for caving to communists, and the president might have seen lenience for the Rosenbergs in 1952 as election year suicide. Or he may have resented Kaufman's request as a transparent effort to pass the buck. Regardless, he had no interest in solving Kaufman's problem for him. If Spear's account is accurate, Kaufman's call was virtually the only chink in the armor he constructed and wore for the rest of his life when it came to the Rosenbergs—the only hint of doubts or second thoughts outside of a brief and anomalous period a quarter century later when outside events mixed with grief over family tragedy to force a personal reckoning.[13]

If the Rosenbergs were unexpectedly gaining ground in the battle for public opinion, they were losing in court. In October, the Supreme Court refused to review their case, with only Hugo Black dissenting. Bloch asked the high court to reconsider and lost 8–1 again, though this time Frankfurter was moved to write a short, tortured opinion noting that Kaufman's sentences were "not within the power of this Court to revise." "Who will save the Rosenbergs from death?" Frankfurter's old friend Charles Burlingham wrote him mournfully; "we must not go back to the 16th Century." The Supreme Court defeat led Kaufman to reset the execution date for the week of January 12, 1953.[14]

Bloch wasn't finished, though. He tried returning to the trial court, Kaufman's court, with new arguments about the trial, but first he demanded Kaufman admit he was biased, recuse himself, and let another judge rule. One of Bloch's new grounds was Saypol's publicity stunt of indicting the Columbia instructor William Perl during trial. For appearances' sake only, Kaufman agreed to stand aside, and his colleague Sylvester Ryan denied the application. Reviewing Ryan's decision, the Second Circuit agreed with Bloch that Saypol's tactics in the Perl episode had been "wholly reprehensible." The court denied any relief, however, since Bloch hadn't asked for a mistrial at the time. This left the Rosenbergs with no choice but to go back to the only judge the appellate courts said could reduce their sentences. It was now December 1952, and somehow Bloch had to get through to the same man he'd accused of incurable bias in November. The executions were only two weeks away.[15]

Before he heard Bloch's legal arguments, Kaufman agreed to meet with Julius's mother and siblings in chambers on Christmas Eve. Leonard Sand, Kaufman's clerk, remembered how the somber occasion contrasted with the festive spirit that otherwise filled the courthouse for the holiday. Kaufman let the Rosenbergs do the talking. The government was out to get Julius and Ethel because they were "little people," they claimed; David was a liar, and the government had brought off a frame-up. Eventually Kaufman interrupted and repeated what he'd told Rabbi Rackman: the man they were there to save was master of his own fate. He could confess and save his own life. This didn't go over well—Kaufman later told the FBI his visitors reacted with "indignation"—and the Rosenbergs started yelling. "Look at me, look at my eyes, I want to see your face!" Sophie Rosenberg demanded. Kaufman was a father too, she sobbed—didn't he understand? Kaufman went home feeling like he'd been punched in the gut.[16]

Five days later, Bloch appeared in court to argue for reducing the sentences. Rosenberg supporters had turned out en masse, and some hissed at the new US Attorney Myles Lane and his assistant Kilsheimer as they passed in the hall. Bloch had often stumbled during trial, but now he launched into a passionate and eloquent presentation. "What is it about this case that has so aroused the world," he began, which was already too much for Kaufman. "I have frankly been hounded, pounded by vilification and by pressurists," Kaufman responded, "and I think you would be as resentful as I am if it came from the other side, so that I think it is not a mere accident that some people have been aroused in these countries." Bloch agreed Kaufman had been "subjected to pressures," but Kaufman cut in again, saying it had been "overwhelming" the last few days, "as if by someone whipping it up, knowing that this is coming on today, this barrage of telegrams that I received yesterday." It wouldn't matter, Kaufman vowed, "because when the day comes that we are subjected to pressures, I think you will agree with me that we might as well close the door to justice."

Bloch turned to his clients' curious obstinacy. They knew that "if they would only confess, they would save themselves," so why didn't they? "I have pondered that question," Kaufman interjected, adding that it could only be "the very thing that drove them into it, Mr. Bloch. I don't know the answer to that." Bloch then went through the evidence, Kaufman fencing with him every step. Eventually Bloch homed in on Kaufman himself. "There are some judges who find themselves in a horrible position of having to inflict death upon a defendant because it is mandatory," he offered sympathetically—to which the object of his concern agreed that the situation was "horrible and tragic" but that the outcome was "almost mandatory," since the 1917 law endorsed capital punishment even before there were such all-important secrets to steal. This notion that Congress had effectively removed his discretion prefigured his defensive letter to Bureau of Prisons chief James Bennett in 1970. Wrapping up, Bloch had nothing left to do but beg:

> BLOCH: Your honor, have a heart. Have compassion. I know you don't want to take away two lives uselessly, unnecessarily. God! These are parents. They have got two children. Believe me, your Honor, they love them the way you love your children. Please, think. Please, think. Please consult with your conscience. Please consult with your reason. Don't let the political clamor of the day get the better of your judgment. Please. This will remain with you and with me and with all of us. We have got to survive. We have got to live with ourselves. You have to look yourself in the mirror, your Honor. . . . I am appealing to you, and I would get on my knees—
>
> KAUFMAN: Please don't.
>
> BLOCH: I would get on my knees because I know you are human.
>
> KAUFMAN: You have kept this on a high level and I wish you would continue to do so.[17]

Kaufman went home late in the day and started writing. He was still at it after midnight, when he started feeling dizzy. He padded into the dark bedroom but never made it to bed, passing out and smashing his head on a door frame. A surgeon stitched him up later that morning, but Kaufman shrugged it off and kept working as the year turned to 1953, determined to answer the critics who had suddenly appeared from nowhere, and with his usual, manic efficiency. He was ready with a written opinion by January 2.[18]

"It would be, indeed, simple and less trying," Kaufman started, if he simply gave in and reduced the sentences, but this would violate his "solemn trust" from the American people. The defendants had exposed "millions of their countrymen to danger or death," Kaufman explained, and "throughout history the crimes of traitors stand as those most abhorred by people." Although his sentences were "in some respects unprecedented . . . times change and conditions change." (Ironically, applying the law to fit changing social circumstances would be central to his later jurisprudence and displease some of the very people who favored his decision now.) While it was true Fuchs and other spies received lesser punishment, they had cooperated or been sentenced under foreign law. Above all, the Rosenbergs had betrayed all they should have held most dear in the Jews' new homeland:

> The defendants were born in America, reared in America and educated in the public schools of America. They had lived their entire

> lives among us; they had all the advantages of our free institutions and had enjoyed the privileges of American citizenship. . . . [Yet] they chose the path of traitors and decided to abandon those who had nurtured and fed them in favor of a nation whose ideology was repugnant to everything we have learned, lived for and to which we have been dedicated. They knew well that the stakes were high and the consequences of failure were dire.

He finished—as he had in open court in 1951 and as Bloch had the week before—by turning the lens back on himself:

> I have meditated and reflected long and difficult hours over the sentence in this case. I have studied and re-studied the record and I have seen nothing nor has anything been presented to me to cause me to change the sentence originally imposed. I still feel that their crime was worse than murder. Nor have I seen any evidence that the defendants have experienced any remorse or repentance. Unfortunately, in its place this Court has been subjected to a mounting organized campaign of vilification, abuse and pressure. This Court, however, is not subject to such organized campaign and the pressures which have been brought to bear in this case, nor does it require such tactics to make it cognizant of the human tragedy involved.
>
> The application is denied.

After she got the dreadful news in Sing Sing, Ethel wrote Bloch: "It strikes me that Judge Irving R. Kaufman's immortality is at last assured."[19]

Confirmation of the death sentences hardened the battle lines formed the previous year. Mainstream editorial opinion and establishment figures supported him, while on the other side Rosenberg partisans stepped up their pickets and marches and vigils around the country, including just outside the White House. Overseas, American diplomats saw protests just beyond their embassies' gates. The *Chicago Daily News* became the first major outlet to come out for commutation, and Albert Einstein released an open letter to Truman urging clemency.[20]

Then, on January 7, the most important voice yet declared for mercy when Pope Pius XII's earlier request to the White House for clemency became public. "That a woman should wait in a 'death chamber' for the moment of execution is in itself an event as tragic as it is rare and is such as to arouse instinctively a sense of horror," he emphasized. Not one to forbear, even with the pope, Kaufman asked Cohn to intercede with New York's archbishop, the powerful Cardinal Francis Spellman. Cohn tried to explain that Spellman couldn't possibly help now that the pope's views were public, "but Irving was, as always, impervious to logic when he wanted a result. He said that Cardinal Spellman was privately in favor of capital punishment (which was true), and that Spellman could, in a respectful way, a carefully worded way, contradict the Pope." Though Cohn knew the mission was futile, "Irving could wear you down," so he tried and was, as expected, politely rebuffed. As a consolation prize, Spellman praised Kaufman after the executions in an address in Brussels that deplored Europe's attitude toward the case.[21]

The executions were now just ten days away, and Kaufman wasn't sure of his legal power to change the schedule while Bloch sought presidential clemency, so he consulted the prosecution in yet more *ex parte* discussions and pressured Kilsheimer to urge DOJ's pardon attorney to speed up his vetting for the president's review. Truman failed to act, however, and the newly inaugurated President Eisenhower denied clemency on February 11. The former Allied commander was unlikely to sympathize with spies or to shrink from executions that might deter them, and he believed the possibility of the Rosenbergs' early parole from prison would encourage more spying. Others in his nascent administration also saw clemency as weakness at a dangerous international moment. The Rosenbergs learned the news through a radio blared over prison loudspeakers.[22]

Now Bloch had precious little left to work with. Back before Kaufman and seeking more time to appeal Judge Ryan's decision to the Supreme Court, Bloch was harangued: "The harassment has stepped up both in temper and in tempo since the ruling of President Eisenhower. It is the most amazing thing, the way telegrams and telephone calls come into my chambers." Bloch adamantly denied blame for this, but Kaufman wasn't mollified. "You search your conscience and you will have the answer. The Committee to Secure Justice for the Rosenbergs has made misstatements in its pamphlets, and has circulated half-truths about this case." As for the executions, Kaufman claimed that stringing things out would only "increase the mental anguish of the defendants and possibly . . . raise false hopes." He set the date for three weeks later. "They are desperate and want to bury us quickly," Julius told Bloch.[23]

That same day, a man in Detroit penned Kaufman a note on hotel stationery with most of the letterhead cut off. "Concerning about the Rosenbergs case you better not kill them, if you do you are a marked man. I am not a Jew but my wife is, they remarked that if the Rosenbergs

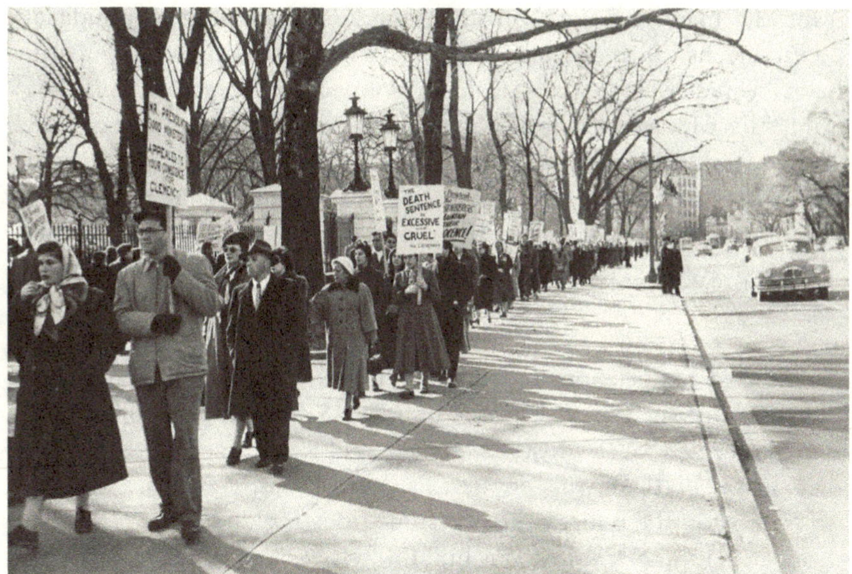

FIGURE 10. Pickets seeking clemency for the Rosenbergs march outside the White House, March 1953. People's World, Daily Worker, *and* Daily World *Photographs Collection, Tamiment Library and Robert F. Wagner Labor Archive, Elmer Holmes Bobst Library, New York University.*

die, they will get you. Watch your life. . . . I am telling you as a friend, they will get someone from your family. You are a Jew and went against your people." The crazy letter rattled Kaufman. He was used to getting pleas for mercy and didn't even read them anymore; he'd gotten around fifteen hundred by then. He'd even started to get phone calls at home, so he switched to an unlisted number. But this threat couldn't be ignored. Already busy reviewing Kaufman's mail, the FBI intensified its efforts but couldn't find the writer.[24]

Kaufman may have felt further delay was only cruel to the Rosenbergs, but his haste wasn't shared by the Second Circuit, which considered his refusal to reduce the sentences. "I would not want these people precluded from having their opportunity before the Supreme Court. I wouldn't want it on my conscience," Frank said in court. When Kilsheimer objected to further extensions, Learned Hand lost his patience: "People don't dispose of lives just because an attorney didn't make a point. . . . Your duty, Mr. Prosecutor, is to seek justice, not to act as a time-keeper." The court stayed the executions until the Supreme Court could rule. Kaufman was appalled; it was easy for Frank to look out for his conscience, but he wouldn't be the one besieged by phone calls and mail—and now, threats. Abandoning any lingering judicial neutrality, he called the head of the FBI's New York office, L. V. Boardman. "Unless the matter is pushed vigorously by the government," he said, "this whole case may hang over until Fall." Boardman replied that Kaufman's suggestion was better addressed to the lawyers who could do as he wanted, not FBI agents, so Kaufman dialed up Kilsheimer, treating the junior prosecutor like one of his law clerks. Kilsheimer got the message, hung up the phone, and wrote and called Main Justice in Washington asking them to expedite things.[25]

Bloch filed his petition asking the Supreme Court to reverse Ryan's decision, but the Court denied it on May 25 after an acrimonious internal process that saw Justices Douglas and Jackson switch their votes in a bizarre battle of wills. Aware this meant the case was coming back to New York, the police quietly resumed posting an armed officer in front of Kaufman's apartment building. Back on the bench to set yet another execution date, Kaufman rejected the defense request to wait until July—"I cannot remember, Mr. Bloch, any case in our American courts receiving the care and attention at all judicial levels that this case has received"—and chose the week of June 15. Kaufman also met with Hoover and "generally discussed" the case, though it isn't known what was covered. Considering that the case was ongoing, and he knew he would be getting further applications with the government on the other side, the meeting was one more improper encounter.[26]

Almost immediately, there were new motions to deny. One arguing a defect in the indictment was pressed by a pacifist Nashville lawyer, Fyke Farmer, who'd appeared in New York out of the blue offering unsolicited help. Bloch felt obligated to present the point but his heart wasn't in it. After a ten-minute recess, Kaufman summarily denied it. Then, on June 8, Bloch; Malcolm Sharp, a University of Chicago law professor; and John Finerty, an old leftist combatant who'd tried and failed to save Sacco and Vanzetti, brought a motion based on new evidence, including proof that the Rosenbergs' console table—not produced at trial and suddenly located in plain sight at Julius's mother's apartment—wasn't a special device for copying microfilm but just a garden-variety item from Macy's. This time Kaufman recessed for fifteen minutes, came back, and read out a thirty-minute oral opinion rejecting the motion. "While perhaps delaying my decision might give rise to better form," he conceded, "it would not change the substance of the opinion which I am about to render." Nobel laureate and Manhattan Project official

Harold Urey, who believed the Rosenbergs' importance to the Soviet atomic effort had been exaggerated, was in court and lashed out to a reporter: "Now that I've seen what goes on in there, I see not Irving Kaufman but McCarthy. . . . The judge's bias is so obvious." Nonetheless, the Second Circuit affirmed Kaufman two days later, and Bloch and his new co-counsel trudged back to the Supreme Court for a third time.[27]

Defeats in court only threw gas on the increasingly frantic public campaign. Forty American cities now had their own committees. Altogether, they distributed six million leaflets and pamphlets and purchased forty thousand lines of advertising. In New York, two thousand people appeared for a program at Carnegie Hall, while a rally in the Triborough Stadium drew ten thousand. A "clemency float" trundled around the city, and someone pressed a flyer into the hands of an impressionable seventh grader who'd recently moved from Dallas and whose later, erratic Marxism was traced in some small part to the handbill: Lee Harvey Oswald. On May 28, the *Washington Post* essentially endorsed clemency, writing that it was "no criticism of Judge Irving R. Kaufman . . . to suggest that the value of this case to the international communist propaganda would have been far less if the milder penalty had been imposed." The White House received thousands of letters on the case every day, including one from Arthur Miller pleading that the executions defiled America's otherwise "humane justice." His play on Broadway at the time about the madness of the Salem witch trials, *The Crucible*, had come to be seen as a metaphor for the Rosenberg case and McCarthyism in general, though actually he'd written it years before anyone knew of the couple. In Boston, a Mrs. Buckman of Dorchester assured readers of the *Jewish Advocate* that it wasn't too late to contact the president: "In the cowboy films the children see, new evidence brought up the last minute saves the victim as the noose slips over his head." Overseas, the moderate French newspaper *Le Figaro* printed copies of the Rosenbergs' letters, while in London protests looked as if they might mar the new young queen's coronation. American diplomats tried haplessly to contain the damage they feared the case was doing to America's image.[28]

The campaign's increased activity brought increased anxiety for Kaufman. June 18 couldn't come fast enough. Bags of mail seeking mercy and even uninvited visitors to chambers were one thing—everyone was used to that by now—but the threats kept ramping up. Someone who spoke with a foreign accent phoned Lien Law Louie's office and told the secretary who answered, "I want him to know that he is going to have the pleasure of having his daughter and grandchildren blown up." A week or so later, a caller told police a bomb was in Kaufman's apartment. Officers combed the place but found nothing.

Understandably rattled, Kaufman called in the FBI. "His judgment was not too good when it came to members of his family," Kaufman admitted, and "a man could be bumped off six times by the time he got hold of the police." Plus, the NYPD officer outside had a troubling tendency to wander off. Hoover got the hint and decreed round-the-clock FBI protection. Two agents stayed with the family in the apartment at all times, ate with them, and generally kept the family in view—"with sensible exceptions." Another agent took Kaufman to work, accompanied him all day, and drove him home. Still others saw the boys to and from school. At first Kaufman chafed against such blanket coverage, but eventually he warmed to his protectors. They were imposing men—one had played football with the Los Angeles Rams—and would start up impromptu games of catch with the boys in the grassy Park Avenue median.[29]

The Rosenbergs' encounter with federal agents just then was less copacetic. On June 5, Bennett visited them in Sing Sing to ask if they had anything to say. In Julius's telling, Bennett implored: "Sure Judge Kaufman has made a terrible blunder with this outrageous sentence and he has the bull by the tail and he can't let go. That's right, Julius, he needs you to help him change this sentence and you can do this by telling all you know"—to which Julius said he wouldn't "bail [Kaufman] out for his mistake." Ethel was equally scornful. In a statement for the outside world, they said they had been offered a "deal" to save themselves but would never "help to purify the foul record of a fraudulent conviction and a barbaric sentence" with bogus confessions. "If we are executed, it will be murder of innocent people and the shame will be on the Government of the United States."[30]

Fyke Farmer was dispirited by Bloch's lackluster presentation of his argument about the indictment; still, the quixotic Tennessean wasn't about to give up. On Saturday, June 13, he reappeared in New York with a brand new claim: the Rosenbergs had been prosecuted under the wrong law, the 1917 Espionage Act, instead of a newer law that took precedence, the 1946 Atomic Energy Act, which precluded a death sentence unless a jury recommended it after finding that the spying had injured the United States. Bloch and Sharp and Finnerty were in Washington making separate arguments to Justice Douglas and knew nothing of Farmer's self-appointed mission. Farmer's habeas corpus petition could be presented to *any* judge, not just Kaufman, so he approached one he knew personally in New York: Edward Dimmock. Dimmock just turned pale and phoned Kaufman, who said Farmer should give his petition to Kilsheimer and Sand. As he handed it over, Farmer instructed Sand to focus his legal research for Kaufman on the precedent that helped the Rosenbergs, not cases unfavorable to their cause, as if Sand was *his* clerk. Sand was dumbfounded. That same Saturday, a man called the police precinct at East 104th Street and said a bomb would detonate in Kaufman's apartment within the hour. Policemen scouring the apartment again found nothing.[31]

Seething at being fobbed off on Kilsheimer and Sand, two neophytes half his age, Farmer found Kaufman's home address the next morning in a news article about the bomb threat and headed uptown to deliver his petition. Under standing orders, the doorman refused to let Farmer near the elevators, and Kaufman was out anyway. As it happened, he was with Cohn, probably at the City Athletic Club, since it was Sunday. So Farmer set out to reach Sand again and finally tracked him down at his Bronx apartment at nine thirty that night. Sand was amazed at the sudden nocturnal appearance of this Southern lawyer who, as far as he could tell, had no business in the case at all but hadn't hesitated to tell him how to do his work. He just shook his head and promised to call Kaufman.[32]

The next morning, Kaufman released a brief order denying Farmer's application. He had communicated with Bloch in Washington, and the Rosenbergs' lawyer had disavowed Farmer's rogue effort, so Kaufman labeled Farmer and another lawyer helping him, Daniel Marshall, "intruders and interlopers" with no legal standing to argue for the doomed couple. Nor did he think their argument had merit anyway.[33]

That same day, completely unaware of Farmer's work on her behalf, Ethel sat alone in her cell and wrote a remarkable letter to President Eisenhower. Unlike her notes to Julius and Bloch, strident and full of dogma, this showed she wanted to live and would do almost anything to make it happen. Anything except call back Bennett and tell the government what she knew. Her letter requested the attention of "the affectionate grandfather, the sensitive artist, the devoutly religious man": "I ask this man, whose name is one with glory, what glory there is that is greater than the offering to God, of a simple act of compassion? Take counsel with your good wife . . . with the mother of your only son; her heart which understands my grief so well, and my longing to see my sons grow to manhood like her own. . . . Her heart must plead my cause with grace and with felicity!"[34]

Not at all discouraged by Kaufman's rebuff, Farmer and Marshall took the midnight train to Washington and asked to see Justice Douglas. The Court's term had just ended, but Douglas agreed to stay the executions until the full Court could hear the case during its new term in the fall. Delirious and stunned, Farmer and Marshall exulted. "Intruders and interlopers are we? We're all-American interlopers, that's what we are." They couldn't have known that Chief Justice Vinson had already met secretly with Justice Jackson and the new attorney general, Herbert Brownell, and agreed to call the Court back into session to vacate any stay. Kaufman, then, wasn't the only judge secretly colluding with prosecutors, and he was happy when Kilsheimer told him of the meeting. Meanwhile, in New York, twenty-two police officers and detectives descended on 1185 Park yet again to search for bombs. Kaufman, Helen, and the boys were now staying with the Rosenstiels in Connecticut; the NYPD posted four more officers outside anyway.

Farmer and Marshall's unexpected triumph was short-lived. At noon on Friday, June 19, the justices convened and orally rejected Farmer's petition, 6–3. In a separate opinion, Jackson, like Frankfurter before him, was careful to point out that the Court shouldn't "be construed as indorsing the wisdom or appropriateness to this case of a death sentence," which was solely Kaufman's handiwork. Douglas, Black, and Frankfurter dissented, and by the time the justices stopped talking and filed out, Bloch had to be consoled by the other lawyers. He was sobbing.[35]

This final act in the Supreme Court set off a mad scramble in Washington and New York to find something—anything—to stave off the inevitable. Earlier that week, Bloch had submitted a second pitch for clemency to Eisenhower. Unlike Ethel's moving plea for mercy, which may never have made it to the president, this request reemphasized the couple's innocence and reeked of their usual self-righteousness. "The guilt, if we die, will be America's," they lectured. Eisenhower responded with a statement again denying clemency and reviving Kaufman's specter of "tens of millions of innocent people all over the world" vaporized in an atomic war made more likely by the Rosenbergs. Leniency would just convince the communists America was soft, he told a friend in a letter. He'd also imbibed Cohn's and Kaufman's baseless notions about Ethel, writing his son that "in this instance it is the woman who is the strong and recalcitrant character, the man who is the weak one. She has obviously been the leader in everything they did in the spy ring." Inside the White House, the shades were drawn to block the view of the pickets shuffling by outside.[36]

At Foley Square, Kaufman sat waiting tensely for the onslaught of last-minute maneuvers. At some point, he left the courthouse and was photographed by newsmen out on the street with his trademark frown, the dapper suit and a light, summer Panama hat on his head. In the afternoon, he was back in chambers when the lawyers started appearing. First, two attorneys allied with Bloch handed him a new petition based on the 1946 law; Kaufman scribbled "denied" across the top, and they raced out to find appellate judges who might intervene. A little later in the afternoon, other counsel showed up to urge postponing the executions, scheduled for 11:00 p.m., until after the Jewish Sabbath. Kaufman interrupted in a low voice to say he too had "considerable concern" about the issue but had already been reassured by Brownell that the sentences wouldn't be carried out on the Sabbath. The lawyers left thinking they'd bought the Rosenbergs another day, at least. In reality, Kaufman and Brownell had solved the problem by *moving up* the executions to 8:00 p.m., a few minutes before sundown. When he learned this on Friday afternoon, Sing Sing's Jewish chaplain, Rabbi Irving Koslowe, called Kaufman to ask him to delay the executions until Saturday night. Kaufman said he'd talked to B'nai B'rith, which agreed "it would be a *shanda* [shame] for Jews to be executed on the sabbath, so he set the time" to avoid it. But Eisenhower wanted the executions to proceed that day, he told Koslowe. Brownell may well have told Kaufman that, and the president's urgency would have been understandable, given the worldwide uproar. Or it may simply have been Kaufman who wanted it over—the endless, repetitive petitions; the deluge of letters; the bomb threats. He ended Koslowe's call with a dictate: "Rabbi, you do your job. I'll do mine."

At 7:15, with only forty-five minutes left, the last lawyer filed in. It was Marshall, who had rushed back from Washington to make one last, desperate pitch: the Supreme Court may have vacated Douglas's stay, but the portion of his order instructing the lower courts to consider Farmer's argument about the 1946 law still stood. They met across Kaufman's desk in his chambers. Marshall tried to navigate through the intricacies of his position as Kaufman told him to "get along with your argument" since the executions were only minutes away. At this, Marshall implored him to call the prison and issue a stay of execution so he could finish, saying it would be "terrible if I could convince your honor that you should grant the application and it would be too late." Fingering his wristwatch, Kaufman said he had dealt with this argument a week ago. Marshall rejoined that it was Kaufman's last chance to rectify a terrible miscarriage of justice. "It is unfair to put that kind of burden on a judge," Kaufman replied steadily. "It's difficult enough. I am aware of the tragedy involved." Then he looked at Marshall and said only, "Your petition is denied."[37]

Fifteen minutes after 8:00 p.m., his secretary Anna Strasser came into his office and handed him a note. Sing Sing had called to say the Rosenbergs were dead. They'd beaten the Sabbath by fifteen minutes. To the end, the FBI futilely maintained a command post at the prison with agents, stenographers, and open telephone lines if either Julius or Ethel finally caved. One question on the FBI's thirteen-page list for Julius said it all: "Was your wife cognizant of your activities?" That, as she was about to be executed for masterminding the whole plot. As for the government's strategy of prosecuting her to get Julius to talk, William Rogers, deputy attorney general at the time, told Sam Roberts ruefully, "She called our bluff."[38]

In Union Square, five thousand assembled for a final rally timed to coincide with the executions. Told the Rosenbergs had entered the execution chamber right before 8:00 p.m., the crowd "showed signs of mass hysteria," as one reporter put it, but then police cut the electricity to the loudspeakers "to avoid trouble," and a few minutes later the marchers dispersed somberly. In that evening's performance of *The Crucible*, some theatergoers stood and bowed their heads for a few minutes as the character John Proctor was being killed with heavy stones. No one applauded when the play ended. Pickets at the White House lowered their signs and trudged away as some government supporters honked their horns at them and called them bums. Crowds in Paris rioted at the Place de la Concorde and a teenager was shot, while Italians massed in front of the American embassy and shouted "Assassins! Assassins!" Kaufman and two FBI escorts took the judges' elevator down to the garage in the innards of the Foley Square courthouse and got into an FBI car. Then the car pulled onto the darkening city streets and headed north for Lew Rosenstiel's estate in Connecticut, where his family was waiting.[39]

CHAPTER 8

Beaten by the Harvards

A few days after the Rosenbergs died at Sing Sing, Kaufman confronted the mountains of mail on his desk and started with a thank-you note to his in-laws for their birthday gift. He'd just turned forty-three. "Of course, you know the last few weeks have been rather hectic," he confided, "and I have been in a state of exhaustion since last Friday." That state would last a while. Months later, he wrote Clark of going through checkup after checkup with doctors, but all they could tell him was that he was "having a 'reaction' to the aftermath of the strain . . . and 'you'd better get away.'" To Hoover, he complained of "the mental unrest experienced by all the Kaufmans as a result of the organized harassment to which we have been subjected over the many months." Unlike Clark or his in-laws, however, there was something the director could do to ease his mind. Once Kaufman returned to work, two FBI officials stopped in to see him in chambers. According to the resulting memo,

> They gave him information, in general terms, indicating that Julius Rosenberg was an important Russian agent and that we had information from unimpeachable sources to so indicate, which information did not come out at the trial; that the same sources reflected that Ethel Rosenberg knew of the extent of her

husband's activities. Judge Kaufman said all along that he felt we had additional information, not brought out at the trial, and that he was very appreciative of the fact that the Director thought enough of him to brief him on this. Judge Kaufman was told that the nature of our information was not known to more than half a dozen people; consequently, it should be held confidential. He promised to do this.[1]

Kaufman thus became one of the very few Americans privy to the existence of the Venona intercepts, though presumably he wasn't given the details or told the United States had actually broken the Soviets' wartime code. Shortly before he died, Cohn boasted to Alan Dershowitz that he'd also known about the intercepts and told Kaufman about them *before* the trial, and that the two had therefore plotted to obtain the convictions. "Irving was in on everything," Dershowitz remembered Cohn saying. "He knew about the secret intercepts and that we couldn't use them." Although Cohn's story could be true, considering his closeness to and *ex parte* communications with Kaufman, it is otherwise unclear when or to what extent Cohn learned of Venona. It seems more likely that the contemporaneous FBI memorandum accurately records when Kaufman first became aware of the intercepts. Notably, too, the FBI indicated only that Ethel knew of the espionage—not that she participated. Still, the FBI's secret assurance undoubtedly bolstered Kaufman's certainty in the correctness of his cause as he battled critics for the next forty years.[2]

Kaufman planned to keep his FBI bodyguards for ten days after the executions, particularly covering the period when the Rosenberg family would be "sitting shiva"—conducting the communal seven-day Jewish mourning period. "Jewish people become very emotional at such a time," he informed the agents. Then, on June 28, Walter Winchell mentioned on his national radio show that the FBI was still guarding Kaufman, and he was embarrassed. He suggested the FBI limit itself to taking him to and from work, ensuring his safety when he was outside the heavily guarded courthouse and his doorman-protected building.

Beyond driving, Kaufman started looking to the FBI for other personal services. Out of town once to give a speech, he asked agents to call his housekeeper to check on his children. The head of the New York office delicately recommended responding that this was "somewhat out of our line." Usually though, the FBI proved accommodating. It agreed to send an agent to the Connecticut boarding school where Kaufman's oldest son Bobby was studying "to see how the youngster is progressing," given "the kid's intense interest in the Bureau." (The visits were discontinued after one semester.) For decades, the FBI also acted as travel agent and tour guide when the Kaufmans left home—services not generally extended to other judges. Agents met the family at airports, shepherded them to hotels and meetings, and escorted them to the local sights. "How delightful it is for us to have the friendly hand of an Agent extended to us as we descend from a plane in some distant part of the United States," Kaufman wrote Lou Nichols in 1957; "it is like a member of your family being there to greet you."[3]

Kaufman's personal relationship with Hoover deepened, too, greased by a never-ending stream of flattery. "One thing which has emerged from the Army-McCarthy hearings," Kaufman wrote him, seemingly oblivious to widespread public revulsion over the episode, "is the fact that all decent Americans hold Edgar Hoover and the FBI in very high esteem." A piece Hoover authored about juvenile crime prompted, "Believe me each of my teenagers will not only read your warning but spread the gospel. Once again you have demonstrated your devotion to the youngsters of America." He worried Hoover might retire, saying, "I just don't want to think about the F.B.I. without you." And he became a one-man ad agency, handing out copies of the Hoover hagiography *The FBI Story* to people he ran across, like the governor of Illinois. Vacationing with Cohn in Havana in 1957, he surprised FBI agents there by whipping a copy of the book out of his briefcase and "proudly exhibit[ing] the dedicatory paragraph from the Director appearing on the flyleaf." Eventually, he was calling Hoover so often on the Bureau's private line from the New York office to Washington that his use of it had to be restricted.[4]

Kaufman also ran interference for Hoover, even when the director himself demurred. In 1953, Hoover complained to Kaufman that Kaufman's friend Julius Klein had helped an FBI critic, Max Lowenthal, avoid testifying at Senator William Jenner's subcommittee on internal security. After writing a book questioning the FBI's respect for civil liberties, Lowenthal had been branded by some as a communist sympathizer. Kaufman summoned Klein and "literally tore him apart" on Hoover's behalf, as an FBI memo quoting Cohn put it, until Klein begged to go to Washington to apologize to Hoover personally. Less gravely, a sketch on Jack Paar's *Tonight Show* in 1958 poked fun at bumbling FBI agents stalking a harmless Russian "spy" in Greenwich Village. Hoover himself told Kaufman to forget it, but Kaufman couldn't resist raising the matter with his friend David Sarnoff, the head of NBC, who promptly began asking subordinates how his network could have allowed mockery of the FBI. "I am getting a little sick and tired of these snide remarks, supposedly humorous, heaping ridicule on the FBI and on you," Kaufman wrote the director. "I am familiar with this tactic and know it for what it is. . . . It spreads disrespect for the law by causing people to laugh at the FBI—the greatest law enforcement agency the world has ever known."[5]

In addition to standing up for Hoover, there was his own handiwork to defend. When the *Times* reported on a law review article that didn't criticize Kaufman but did decry the rushed proceedings in the Supreme Court—the headline was "Spies Were Cheated, Law Students Hold"— Kaufman promptly wrote publisher Arthur Hays Sulzberger admonishing that "more care should have been taken in reporting, so that those who fan the fire of communist propaganda would not have additional fuel." A talkative and undisciplined David Greenglass might supply such fuel, too, Kaufman thought. When Cohn planned for David to testify before McCarthy's committee, Kaufman proposed interceding with the attorney general behind Cohn's back. "Greenglass might have a bad day," he told the FBI; "he might not look good." David never appeared. Kaufman also prodded former clerks Beier and Sand to write an article in the *American Bar Association Journal* praising him for ensuring a fair trial despite "constant vilification," and he persuaded the venerable journalist Herbert Bayard Swope to write a letter to the *Times* contesting a pro-Rosenberg speech by Urey.[6]

In 1955, the playwright John Wexley published a polemic, *The Judgment of Julius and Ethel and Rosenberg,* which claimed the couple had been framed. Wexley called Kaufman "a perfidious little Tartuffe" while comparing Julius to Jesus Christ. Worse still, someone mailed a flyer for the book to Kaufman at home with a letter saying he should be the one "facing the electric chair for the murder of this unfortunate, friendless, guiltless couple." Another letter threatened to "finish you by remote control."

Wexley's screed led Kaufman to ask the FBI "if the time had not come to get some good substantial writer to do the authentic book on the Rosenbergs." Although Kaufman opened his files to the selected candidate, Jim Bishop, the project stalled when government lawyers couldn't agree on declassifying trial exhibits. Kaufman then tried to get Hoover to ask the anticommunist British journalist and author Rebecca West to do the job but was rejected. He had to settle for an article rebutting Wexley in *Look* that relied heavily on a lengthy internal DOJ report reviewing the case. "As you know, I have not uttered a word—as indeed I should not—in answer to these horribly concocted Communist charges concerning my conduct in the trial," he wrote Brownell, "although I must confess on occasions it was rather difficult to remain silent." Brownell was probably bemused by this dubious account of resigned forbearance.[7]

The case moved from the court of public opinion back to Kaufman's actual courtroom in 1956, when Morton Sobell filed new motions to overturn his conviction based on how Mexican authorities had roughed him up and handed him over to the Feds. As before, Kaufman violated ethics rules and spoke *ex parte* to the government about Sobell's application. Kilsheimer, now in private practice, also got involved, and Kaufman told him he would deny the motions without a hearing. His written opinion fairly bristled with frustration: "An effort has been made to lay to rest with finality baseless contentions and accusations which have been repeated not primarily to aid the petitioner but rather to embarrass and injure our courts and country."[8]

There were also subtler ways to make the case. To put the lie to the idea that he'd condemned the Rosenbergs for their political beliefs instead of their spying, Kaufman gave several speeches highlighting the duty of the bar to represent communists despite their unpopularity. The need was real enough; government employees, teachers, and others in the crosshairs of loyalty boards often found themselves desperate for counsel after being shunned by established lawyers fearful of guilt by association. "I have become increasingly disturbed," Kaufman noted in one address in 1954, by "evidence that in our sincere and urgent national effort to combat the Soviet ideology which today threatens our world, some of our political conservatives unwittingly are leaning toward dangerous radicalism in their attitude toward the Constitution and in their search for quick cure-alls." The bar's cowardice, the Army-McCarthy hearings, proposals to limit use of the Fifth Amendment, and some senators' hurried willingness to approve far-reaching constitutional amendments were all symptoms of a "constitutional illiteracy" lawyers should strenuously resist, Kaufman argued. In other speeches during the 1950s, Kaufman frequently urged modernization of law enforcement tactics, strict observance of defendants' constitutional rights, upholding free expression, and even the updating of commercial law as tools to rebut Soviet criticism of the American system.[9]

Yet his allusion to McCarthy's unsavory tactics didn't cause Kaufman to shun the man himself. Robert Haft, law clerk in 1954, recalled being buried in law books one day and hearing a gruff voice say "I'd like to see Judge Kaufman please." He looked up to see the infamous red-baiter in the flesh. Astonished and dismayed—Haft called himself a classic "Bronx liberal"—he ushered the surprise guest into Kaufman's office. For the next half hour, he overheard animated conversation and laughter from inside as cigar smoke wafted under the door and out into chambers.[10]

Kaufman similarly met and corresponded with the era's other exemplar of anticommunism, Richard Nixon, swapping copies of speeches and articles and relaying views from the like-minded Sarnoff. When Nixon (typically) bemoaned the disloyalty of the Ivy League crowd, Kaufman agreed that "the Communists, by clever and insidious methods, have made a distinct effort to impress the intellectuals." But he had more faith in higher education than the vice president. Proposing a poll of college professors to resolve the matter, Kaufman offered hopefully, "I like to think that they [the communists] have failed. . . . I believe a poll would show that by and large this group is a very discerning one."[11]

Certain rulings were also useful in rebutting charges of anticommunist fanaticism. Ignatz Mezei entered the United States illegally but lived quietly in Buffalo until leaving to visit his dying mother in Romania. Returning in 1950, he was mysteriously stopped at Ellis Island. No one would tell him why, but it was easy enough to guess from questions the immigration officers asked, including, "Were you ever a member of a communist organization?" After months in limbo, Mezei wrote the federal court in New York in anguish: "Let me go free. I did not kill anybody, I did not steal anybody, I did not make any crime." Kaufman got the assignment and quickly saw the basic question at issue: "The man apparently has no place to go. Is the government justified in keeping him at Ellis Island, perhaps indefinitely?" The United States maintained that the Constitution gives the president almost total power over aliens, but "I do not agree," Kaufman wrote. The Constitution applied everywhere in America, he explained, including its entry points, and the Fifth Amendment guarantees due process of law to all "persons," not merely citizens. "The government sounds a grim warning that releasing this alien from detention will bring a flood of enemy agents, spies, saboteurs, madmen, homicidal maniacs and lepers down upon us," Kaufman commented sarcastically, but he wasn't cowed. He ordered Mezei freed.[12]

The government appealed, and the case reached the Supreme Court. Disappointing Kaufman's joking entreaty in 1949 that he go easy on his protégé's work, Clark and a bare majority of four other justices reversed him. If the president wanted to bar an alien deemed a security threat, Clark wrote, no hearing or judicial review was necessary. In dissent, Justice Jackson warned that denying Mezei due process risked re-creating Nazi Germany's "protective custody"—a euphemism for packing nonpersons off to concentration camps without trial. It was a form of despotism Jackson knew well after his stint leading Allied prosecutors in Nuremberg. He simply rejected the notion that giving Mezei and others like him hearings "would menace the security of this country. No one can make me believe that we are that far gone." After almost seventy years, the Court's opinion exalting the president's near-absolute power over aliens remains relevant and has been cited in recent cases involving Guantanamo detainees and terrorism suspects. Jackson's dissent, which seconded Kaufman's view, likewise remains a stirring objection to abandoning certain classes of people to the mercy of the state.[13]

And so Mezei headed back to Ellis Island in 1953. "What means 'security risk'?" he asked when reporters stopped him. "I have only my own two hands. What did I do all my life but work? If I could find out what they have against me, I would at least make sure they knew the truth." On Ellis Island, guards called him "a nice man" and looked forward to his repairs of recreation hall furniture. "How does it feel to be going back to the island, maybe forever?" one reporter asked. Mezei started to answer but choked up and began sobbing. All he could manage was "It is like going to death." His case hadn't gone unnoticed, though. Liberal groups pressured the Justice Department, while newspapers ran sympathetic stories with headlines like "Man without a Country." In 1954, with plans in the works to close the storied facility, Mezei was quietly shipped back to Manhattan and released "pending further consideration of his case." That was government-speak for trying to save face. No further consideration of his case actually occurred, and Mezei lived unobtrusively in Buffalo until heading to Budapest to die in the 1970s.[14]

For his part, Kaufman earned praise from those who saw his decision as proof of his basic fairness. "Irving R. Kaufman, radical one day, reactionary the next?" asked one glowing piece. In other asylum cases in the 1950s, he tended to side against the government, though there were isolated exceptions. It was the one area where his promise to ease the way for others "struggling like I did 20 years ago"—"my mind goes back to my early youth, *the son of immigrants*"—was redeemed not later but immediately.[15]

More than a source of renown or a cause to defend, the Rosenberg case was supposed to vault Kaufman up the judicial ladder. As always, he didn't tarry. Only a month after the executions, Cohn called Nichols at home to tell him that "several individuals have been urging [Kaufman's] appointment" to the Second Circuit, where there were two vacancies. Nichols dryly intuited that "while Cohn did not ask, obviously both Kaufman and Cohn want the Director to say something about Kaufman's availability." Over the next several years, Kaufman would jockey for elevation, though his odds as a Democrat seeking appointment from a Republican president would ordinarily have been slim. He had unusual bipartisan support, though, and came within a hairsbreadth of winning the prize. His campaign culminated in a pitched battle in 1958 that was more than a competition between judicial rivals. It was more like a clash of civilizations.[16]

First, however, there were two undercards. A Second Circuit opening arose in 1955 when a judge only briefly on that court, John Marshall Harlan, joined the Supreme Court. Newspapers were quickly advocating for Kaufman's promotion, with the *Herald Tribune*, *World-Telegram*, and *Daily Mirror* editorializing on his behalf. He'd taken "a beating manfully in the atom-spy case and never faltered," the latter argued. Kaufman's secretary Anna Strasser sent the *World-Telegram* piece to Justice Clark's secretary as if on her own initiative, and Nichols got a copy anonymously. "Since it advocates Judge Kaufman for appointment to the Circuit Court of Appeals," Nichols wrote Hoover's number two and close personal companion Clyde Tolson dryly, "it is obvious that Irving sent it." Regardless, Brownell chose the US Attorney in Manhattan and a white-shoe Republican, J. Edward Lumbard.[17]

In January 1957, Jerome Frank, the civil libertarian who'd affirmed Kaufman in the Rosenberg case, died suddenly, giving Kaufman another chance. This time, with longer tenure on the trial court and the newspapers in his corner, he knew he could press harder. "Irving Kaufman is making a determined bid for this appointment," Nichols noted, as other contenders also began maneuvering. Kaufman's main champion in the Senate was New Hampshire's Styles Bridges, a fervently anticommunist Republican who saw Kaufman's elevation as "deserved recognition of exemplary conduct under heavy attack," as one newspaper put it. Bridges had defended McCarthy, one of only twenty-two against censure, and liberals derisively dubbed him "the senator from yesterday." Still, he mattered in the Republican caucus, and Kaufman had carefully cultivated him with private dinners in New York, meetings in Washington, and frequent mailings of his latest speech or opinion. Rosenstiel's lobbyist may also have gotten to him. Sometime earlier, the senator claimed to have extracted a commitment from Brownell to appoint Kaufman if a "Democratic vacancy" arose, and Frank had been a Democrat. Senator Estes Kefauver of Tennessee, also a Kaufman ally, reported receiving the same pledge. The new Republican senator from New York, Jacob Javits—yet another overachieving, undersized Jewish dynamo from the tenements—joined in, too. He'd known Kaufman for years from legal and political circles as well as the City Athletic Club. Kaufman even had help in the House, less important when it came to judicial appointments. Manny Celler, a liberal Democrat from Brooklyn, was overseeing an administration-backed effort to create new judgeships to cope with rising caseloads across the country, and he warned Brownell "that unless Irving was appointed" there would be no bill.[18]

More telling still were the Kaufman supporters outside officialdom, men just like him who badly wanted to see one of their own rewarded. There was Sidney Weinberg, a man from the Jewish slums with no college education who rose from a janitor's assistant at Goldman Sachs to head of the firm. He began working on Eisenhower. Philip Klutznick was a Chicago housing developer and Democratic fund-raiser who served as national president of B'nai B'rith. Kaufman would be a tribute to the judiciary, Klutznick argued, and "what is of equal importance to me is that he will also be a credit to our people wherever he sits." This hinted at what was really happening: Kaufman was good for the Jews. No one pressed this case more fervently than Julius Klein, one more Horatio Alger figure supporting Kaufman. Klein had been decorated for bravery in the Pacific, led the national Jewish veterans' organization, negotiated West German reparations to Holocaust survivors, and become a wealthy Republican lobbyist with friends in both parties. "We are all proud of Judge Kaufman," he wrote Eisenhower, "not only because he is a great jurist but for his courage in sending the Rosenberg traitors to the electric chair. I was one of many loyal Americans of Jewish faith who urged you at that time not to show clemency to these people who betrayed our country." To Javits, he wrote more as a brother in arms: "Because of what Kaufman did in the Rosenberg case, we American Jews can walk erect on Main Streets in America. . . . My only interest in

Kaufman is a patriotic one. It means nothing to me, it means nothing to Klutznick. But it means a lot to our people."[19]

In February, the backstage wrangling spilled into rare public view with an article in the *Times*, "Big U.S. Court Job Hotly Contested." As the author reported, "One of the main arguments being used in favor of Judge Kaufman is that his promotion would constitute an expression of presidential and senatorial approval for his conduct of the Rosenberg trial." But the person who mattered most, Brownell, cared more about continuing to redress the judicial imbalance achieved during twenty years of Democratic dominance under Roosevelt and Truman, and the job went to a Republican, Leonard Moore, the US Attorney in Brooklyn. Sensitive to the politics involved, however, Brownell wrote Weinberg to say he shared a "high opinion" of Kaufman and hoped "we can include your friend in the list of those to be promoted" if Congress created new judgeships.[20]

The bill for new judges languished, but there were soon hints of a new possibility. "A little bird tells me that by mid-February there will probably be a vacancy on our court," Chief Judge Charles Clark of the Second Circuit wrote Kaufman, "and that you will be named to fill it. If this fowl is truthful I shall be quite happy, because I do know your capacity for good hard work and accomplishment and we shall utilize that quickly and extensively." Kaufman immediately forwarded this news to Javits, and Harold Medina soon announced his resignation. Moreover, Medina publicly touted Kaufman as his replacement in a highly unusual move, telling reporters, "I hope it comes true. I would be delighted because a better man could not be selected." A few weeks later, another *Times* piece announced "Kaufman Slated for Higher Bench." The article said Kaufman had been promised the appointment, noted Celler's threat to bottle up the judgeships bill unless that happened, and concluded with a description of the potential nominee: "Among lawyers here Judge Kaufman is regarded as ambitious, hard-working and exceptionally able as a trial judge. The only criticism heard has been that he has taken too active a part in seeking the promotion to the Second Circuit." Remarkably, Kaufman even sewed up approval from the New York Republican Party committee. And the anticommunist press resumed its clamor, none more colorfully than the *Daily News*: "Any judge whom the commies around the world hate as fiercely as they hate Judge Kaufman deserves promotion, in our opinion. Indeed, what's the matter with putting Old Rough-on-Reds on the Supreme Court someday?"[21]

The coronation was premature. More liberal journals like the *New Republic* and *National Guardian* objected to rewarding Kaufman for two executions, leading Kaufman to complain to Hoover that the slow pace of the appointment was encouraging opposition: "In the event that it should ultimately be blocked, it will be proclaimed as a great victory by the Communists, the pro-Communists, and their friends on the left." Kaufman had little to fear from liberal journalists, however, who had minimal influence on the Eisenhower Justice Department. A far more potent threat was just coalescing behind closed doors—three intellectual giants connected to an institution Kaufman could only associate with by hiring its graduates as law clerks. Felix Frankfurter, Learned Hand, and Henry Friendly all hailed from Harvard Law School. To Kaufman, then, they were "Harvards"—his half-derisive, half-envious term for clerks who studied there. The three men would now conspire to deny Kaufman a spot on the court of appeals.[22]

Frankfurter's loathing for Kaufman, first revealed by the historian Bruce Allen Murphy, ran deep, and he led the crusade. "I despise a judge who feels God told him to impose a death sentence—or any—and K is an ass-kisser to boot," he wrote Hand. Frankfurter understood that Kaufman's ambitions were hardly limited to Foley Square. "I am mean enough to try to stay here long enough so that K will be too old to succeed me!!" Hand lacked this venom but made his preferences clear enough when Kaufman went to his chambers to seek his endorsement. He arranged for his clerk to sit with him in his inner office so Kaufman would be too uncomfortable to ask. Frankfurter and Hand weren't simply against Kaufman, however. They were ardently for someone else, a man Frankfurter compared to Byron in letters and Mozart in music, someone so stupendous he was "one of those rare creatures whose talents and capabilities so far exceed those even of able men that in talking of him one must indulge in conscious understatement in order to avoid disbelief on the part of those who have not had intimate experience with his capacities."[23]

Born in a small city in western New York, Henry Friendly was much Kaufman wasn't. His prosperous family of German Jews had landed in America before the Civil War and boasted an ample house, maids, and an automobile for weekend rides in the country. Kaufman's parents had joined the Jagielnicians' shabby *Landsmanschaft* while Friendly's helped fund the local Reform temple. Like many of his kind, Friendly's father disdained his unwashed coreligionists teeming in the cities—people like the Kaufmans. Both boys entered college at sixteen, but Kaufman's humble destination was downtown Manhattan, while Friendly headed for Harvard Yard. Kaufman's grades were so middling that he later felt the need to embellish them. Friendly was a straight-A student who won prizes in history competitions and a prestigious fellowship to study in Europe. Then he earned what might have been the highest grades ever bestowed by Harvard Law School. While Kaufman came under the tutelage of Lien Law Louie, Frankfurter sent his student Friendly to clerk on the Supreme Court for Brandeis, who told Frankfurter never to give him another such apprentice: "If you do, I'll have nothing left to do." Kaufman sought advancement through courtroom pugilistics and fame in the newspapers while Friendly rejected teaching at Harvard and government service in favor of the staid world of corporate law. Even in private practice, the differences were telling; Kaufman represented new men and outsider tycoons while Friendly's clients were blue chip companies with railroad and bankruptcy issues. He became general counsel for Pan Am. Kaufman rose with Tammany backing through messy Democratic politics, while Friendly largely eschewed unseemly partisan pursuits.[24]

Friendly lacked strong Republican support, but Frankfurter and Hand promoted him to Brownell for the seat that ended up going to Moore. "It is merely that an old dog would like to see the kennel filled with the right sort of pup," Hand wrote. "The Second Circuit was once composed of Hough and the two Hands," Frankfurter pointed out. "Is it conceivable that a Moore or a Kaufman could contribute any such distinction to that court?" Then he added, parenthetically, "What a claim to a seat on that court that a man presided at a capital trial as he presumably should have presided!" After reading the *Times* piece on the battle over the Moore vacancy, Hand wrote Frankfurter: "Did you see today's *Times* and the reasons said to be put forward in Washington for moving up Kaufman? 'To show the President approved his decision to execute the Rosenbergs?' Oh, oh oh! How low can people get! I don't mean K; he didn't start that, I believe; but the Swine, the Swine, the Swine!!!"[25]

By 1958, after Moore had been seated and Medina quit, Friendly was Kaufman's only rival. And Friendly himself thought Kaufman already had "a lien" on the position. Hand did too, writing Frankfurter that Medina's successor was "settled—Irving Kaufman—a thoroughly competent lawyer, but interested primarily, if not completely, in the recognition of Irving Kaufman." In another letter the following month, he tried to reconcile Frankfurter to Kaufman's inevitable triumph:

> Don't feel too badly about Kaufman. He will be a serviceable circuit judge, has brains and enough law. I know, I know, he's too anxious for promotion, and he will be gunning for your place, if he isn't already. But Hells Bells, Felix, all government in all countries—except perhaps G.B.—goes to the lads, with some exceptions, who know how to make themselves important to those at the wheel. . . . The little cus, I.K., knows how to play both sides of the street. But, as I say, unless I am mistaken, he won't be so bad unless it comes to his own advancement.
>
> Good God! How immoral one gets when one comes to the end![26]

This comforted Frankfurter not at all, and the old justice began lobbying the new attorney general, Bill Rogers, not to "yield . . . to the pressures on behalf of Irving Kaufman's promotion." Although there was talk Medina's seat should be filled by a Jew, since Frank's death had left the court encompassing the city with America's largest Jewish population without Jewish representation, Frankfurter scorned looking "for a Jew or a non-Jew in the choice of judges." It was an interesting sentiment from the man who held the so-called Jewish seat on the Supreme Court. The entire scrum was souring Frankfurter on his exalted third branch: "Today is a bad day for me to feel too romantic about the judiciary," he wrote his and Hand's friend Charles Burlingham. "I refer to the political and other scheming by which Irving Kaufman is having himself put on the Court of Appeals."[27]

Friendly could hardly sit on the sidelines while his patrons were hard at work on his behalf. Although less politically connected and not a natural self-promoter, he set out to beat Kaufman at his own game. He enlisted friends to write or meet with New York's senators, furnishing them with letters from Frankfurter and Hand. Those outside New York were conscripted to write *their* senators, or any other senator they knew. The possibility that Congress might create additional judgeships let them claim, as one wrote his senator, that "Mr. Friendly's candidacy is in no way competitive with Judge Kaufman's promotion." As time elapsed and Kaufman wasn't nominated, Friendly knew his stock was rising. After the 1958 elections, he felt confident enough to arrange for a Boston lawyer he knew to meet with Kaufman's main Republican supporter, Styles Bridges. He even used a little Kaufmanesque flattery, telling Bridges his "victory is just one more piece of evidence of the great regard so deservedly held for you by your colleagues and by the country." Now the *Times* called Friendly "the leading candidate." As the capstone to the Harvards' campaign, Hand wrote Eisenhower directly recommending Friendly and adding that there hadn't been "more than two occasions during the long period that I have served as a judge" when he'd taken such a step. Soon after, the letter was reported in the *Times*, proving Kaufman wasn't the only one adept at exploiting the press.[28]

Seeing his prospects fade, Kaufman characteristically went on offense. According to Friendly's biographer David Dorsen, he used emissaries to propose to Friendly that he take Medina's seat while Friendly wait and take a spot on the court being created by the resignation of a judge from Connecticut. Knowing full well the Connecticut vacancy would be filled by someone from that state, Friendly scoffed, though he relayed the idea to the Justice Department in any case. There was also a last, defiant blast from Kaufman's allies. "The Kaufman recommendation stands," Javits said angrily, recognizing that his man's defeat reflected poorly on his own status. Editorials in the conservative *World-Telegram* blamed Friendly's ascent on "blind partisanship" and "political monkeyshines in the U.S. Attorney General's office," while Tom Dodd, Kaufman's old Justice Department friend newly elected to the Senate from Connecticut, argued the case on the Senate floor and in the press and correspondence to Eisenhower. "The Kaufman quarters are stirring up considerable trouble in the Senate Democratic leadership," Friendly wrote an associate.[29]

These sorties were too little, too late. Hand's letter had been of "decisive importance," according to Rogers's deputy. Eisenhower nominated Friendly, who gratefully enthused to Hand, "The amateurs can't win this kind of victory over the professionals without a *deus ex machina*—and I've always regarded you as a kind of *deus*. Here you were Zeus with the thunderbolt." Friendly was right; Kaufman had depended mostly on professional politicians, and Friendly hadn't. But Friendly's troops were far from "amateurs." Hand was an American legend, and Frankfurter had long had the ear of presidents and attorneys general. Other prominent friends had lobbied senators and Justice Department officials. They had used journalists as needed. Forced into an invisible political battle, Friendly had risen to the occasion and bested a more practiced foe. The *Herald Tribune* ascribed Kaufman's defeat to membership in the wrong political party and the fact that "his advocates were far more vocal in sponsoring his case than is usual in high bench appointments." Regardless, Frankfurter was ecstatic and lauded Rogers's "pertinacious courage in not yielding to the enormous pressure behind Irving Kaufman's greedy ambition. Why Kaufman should have such a drag with so many people of influence is beyond my understanding." Frankfurter didn't explain why Kaufman's ambition was "greedy" but Friendly's was somehow chaste. Hand had more sympathy, writing Frankfurter that he was sorry for Kaufman, "for he is reported to be absolutely crushed."[30]

Kaufman was gracious in defeat, conscious that while he might have failed again in 1959, his odds of eventually reaching the court were still high, and once there Friendly would be a colleague. "My prime interest," he wrote his victorious rival, "is that the Court of Appeals for this Circuit continue to maintain its traditional high standing. Your appointment assures this. I send you my congratulations and sincere wishes for a long and honorable career on this distinguished bench." The *Times* and the *Washington Post* praised the appointment as a rare example of apolitical merit selection. "Job sought the man," the *Post* proclaimed, unaware or ignoring that Friendly had also energetically sought the job. Kaufman also wrote a poignant letter to Hand, a judge he worshipped as did everyone, on the occasion of Hand's fiftieth year of judicial service. Alluding to his ambitions for elevation despite Hand's public support for his opponent, Kaufman explained, "It is presumptuous for a neophyte to tell the master that few have equaled his contributions to our craft but I know you will permit me to express this opinion. Perhaps, therefore, you will understand why so many aspire to serve the court which the revered 'Old Chief' has served so well."[31]

The game wasn't entirely over. Kaufman's Senate allies, Dodd especially, slow-walked Friendly's confirmation, mostly out of pique. As the months passed, Kaufman stayed quiet, but his chorus in the press felt no such restraint. Jim Bishop, then supposedly working on the Rosenberg book, wrote a syndicated column titled "The Judge Who Never Wavered." Describing Kaufman as "a short, handsome man with a gentle sense of humor," he argued that rejecting him amounted to, "in effect, telling the Soviet Union that their campaign of vituperation against Kaufman—that he was a poor judge of evidence and that the Rosenbergs were not guilty as charged—has paid off and that we will now punish him for them." Similar editorial sentiment appeared as far away as South Carolina. Kaufman booster William Randolph Hearst Jr. sent

Bishop's or another of his newspapers' columns to Nixon, accusingly, forcing the vice president to defend himself by reiterating that he had "always felt that men of Irving Kaufmann's [*sic*] courage should be recognized wherever possible" and that he would "continue to urge that Kaufmann be considered for the next appointment that comes up." In reality, Nixon had done little or no urging at all.[32]

In the end, Friendly's campaign triumphed where it began: with Frankfurter and Hand. Friendly's biographer writes that the two decided Frankfurter should see Lyndon Johnson, the Senate majority leader, who agreed to lean on Dodd and ensure confirmation in September 1959. Friendly's victory in the twenty-month fight was thereby official, and Kaufman's third try at elevation came to naught. He knew his odds would improve if a Democrat succeeded Ike, but there was no guarantee of that either. Moreover, the clock was ticking. He was approaching his fiftieth birthday, and he knew youth was an important consideration in any Supreme Court nomination—a prize he had no hope of unless he first made it to the court of appeals. If renown from the Rosenberg case and his formidable and bipartisan political support couldn't secure a spot on the Second Circuit, and if the Republicans won again in 1960 and continued to stymie his promotion, he would be in his mid-fifties before he could even take the second step on the three-rung ladder. And that would be too late.[33]

CHAPTER 9

Apalachin and the Little Rock of the North

Cold War espionage wasn't the only mid-century preoccupation to land in Kaufman's courtroom in the 1950s. Two other rising national concerns—the fast but subterranean spread of organized crime, and school desegregation—also came before him in historically significant cases. Along with the Rosenberg drama, they seemed to reaffirm Tocqueville's aphorism that, in America, all political controversies become legal ones.[1]

The first case started by chance on a gray November afternoon in 1957 in the tiny upstate town of Apalachin, New York. Ed Croswell was a taciturn police lifer there with cold eyes and an ulcer. Since his divorce, he'd bunked in state police barracks. "My hobby is police work," he told one reporter. When Croswell overheard that Joseph Barbara Sr. was renting several hotel rooms at a nearby motel, he decided to find out why. Barbara owned a local bottling plant but was secretly "the big mobster in our area," Croswell thought.

The next day, Croswell drove out to Barbara's mansion on a hill overlooking the Susquehanna River and saw men in suits "like the men in the rackets wear," complete with diamond belt buckles and gold watches. "It looked like a meeting of George Rafts." They were milling around an open barbecue pit and chewing steak sandwiches, and now they were eyeing Croswell, too. When Croswell saw all the cars parked behind Barbara's barn, he knew he'd stumbled on something extraordinary. He called for backup, drove back down the hill, and set up a roadblock. At the house, there was panic. Men scurried for their cars and started down toward Croswell. Others forgot their cars entirely and broke for the nearby woods, alligator loafers and all. One by one, the new Cadillacs and Lincolns came rolling down into Croswell's dragnet. He stopped each car and demanded registration. Meanwhile, it had started to rain, and Barbara's more adventurous guests were being fished out of the soggy woods. "Those city boys didn't have a chance," Croswell told the papers. "With their fancy shoes and their hats and coats snagging on tree branches, we could grab them easy."[2]

Apalachin's surprise visitors, sixty-three in all, were taken to a police station and interviewed. Who were they, and what were they doing in the sleepy town almost two hundred miles from New York City? Some knew they didn't have to talk and snapped that they wouldn't, but most were polite. They were there to visit their friend Barbara, who'd been very sick with heart disease, and they had no idea other men would be there too or that some sort of meeting was happening. "We gave them a rough time at the station house," Croswell allowed with a wink, "but we couldn't even make them commit disorderly conduct there." Since even a suspicious get-together isn't a crime, Croswell had nothing to charge them with. He didn't even have grounds to search Barbara's house. Hours later, he let them all go.[3]

Nonetheless, Croswell's coup made national news. The men were "the hard core of the underworld," one official said: Vito "King of the Rackets" Genovese, supposedly Frank Costello's heir as the head of the whole Mafia; Joseph "Olive Oil King" Profaci, whom the Kefauver Committee called "one of the top leaders of the Mafia"; Vincent Rao, a Lucky Luciano pal repeatedly arrested for homicide; Joseph "Joe Bananas" Bonanno, also fingered by Kefauver as an underworld power. And those were just some of the New Yorkers; men had come from Florida, Texas, California, and elsewhere. The episode set off a national frenzy to investigate the mob. Somehow, dozens and dozens of known criminals had convened with no one at all to bother them but a small-town cop who exposed them by accident. Hoover had long downplayed any danger from organized crime, claiming local gangs and local hoodlums were local matters, but now people wanted action. "The FBI has 1,000 or more agents in New York doing nothing but watching Reds and suspected Reds," the *Herald Tribune* noted. "But what is it doing to catch the Costellos, Anastasias, Genoveses, *et al.*, *ad nauseum* [*sic*]?"[4]

Five months after Apalachin, the Justice Department established a "Special Group on Organized Crime" with eighteen handpicked lawyers. Appearing before grand juries, the Apalachinites repeated their far-fetched tales of coincidentally bumping into one another at Barbara's place. That led DOJ to indict twenty-seven men in May 1959 for conspiracy to obstruct justice and impede federal investigations by repeatedly lying to grand juries and investigators. Yet while the Apalachin meeting seemed fishy, and the men involved seemed to be lying about it, the indictment required the government to prove something more: that the twenty-seven had worked together to obstruct justice. Considering how little the Feds actually knew about what went on before the meeting or inside Barbara's house, that wasn't going to be easy.

Speedy as ever, Kaufman ordered a pretrial conference with the government and defense lawyers within a week of receiving the case. In the months that followed, he decided ninety-five pretrial motions. One set of these concerned the press. Under pressure from Kaufman, three networks agreed to delay planned shows on the mob. Then he squashed a movie: "When I was informed that a movie called 'Inside the Mafia' dealing with a meeting at 'Apple lake' was about to be released, I contacted the distributor, and convinced him that civic duty was more important, at times, than profits." The lead prosecutor also sent a letter to eleven New York papers asking them to limit comment on the trial to the evidence admitted in court, and they agreed. "I am not sure the press would ever cooperate to this extent again," Kaufman wrote after the trial, and he was right—today, this kind of silencing would be unimaginable.[5]

The most important pretrial matter concerned the defendants' claim that Croswell lacked probable cause under the Fourth Amendment to stop and question them, since they'd done nothing more than gather socially. The officer himself told grand jurors he'd been "going out on a limb" and hadn't been sure his investigation was "entirely legal." "I held these fellows, but I had no basis for it," Croswell conceded. That was rare stuff from a policeman, but Kaufman found for the government anyway. The men hadn't been formally arrested and had voluntarily answered questions. Given the suspicious circumstances, Kaufman decided, Croswell was entitled to investigate, and time was precious. Indeed, allowing brief detentions would *protect* the rights of innocent bystanders and limit needless arrests, he wrote counterintuitively; otherwise, "instead of giving a person an opportunity to exculpate himself from any suspicion of wrongdoing, they will arrest him first and ask questions afterwards." The decision gratified those eager to see the accused mobsters get what they had coming—which was pretty much everyone—but drew flak from civil libertarians. The *Washington Post* called it "a most dangerous doctrine."[6]

Kaufman's decision jibed with a continued tendency to favor the prosecution during the years he remained a trial judge. He consistently ruled for the government and usually denied defendants' standard requests to gain access to government evidence, dismiss the indictments against them, or suppress evidence purportedly gathered in illegal searches. While defendants typically lose many more such motions than they win, Kaufman was usually unsympathetic even by ordinary standards. In one episode, he secretly lobbied DOJ and Hearst newspaper editors to statutorily reverse a Supreme Court decision ordering greater disclosure of prosecutors' evidence, writing Hoover (and quoting Learned Hand): "Our dangers do not lie in too little tenderness to the accused. Our procedure has been always haunted by the ghost of the innocent man convicted. It is an unreal dream. What we need to fear is the archaic formalism and the watery sentiment that obstructs, delays, and defeats the prosecution of crime."[7]

Preliminaries resolved, the actual trial was anticlimactic verging on boring. The prosecutors' long and meticulous case focused on proving Barbara had planned the meeting, which therefore couldn't have been a series of spontaneous sick calls from old friends, and that the defendants had given similar, ridiculous explanations for why they were there, suggesting a joint cover-up. Jurors heard the defendants in grand juries doing their best to weasel out of divulging why they had been in Apalachin. Sick calls on Barbara, a "pleasure trip," house hunting, animal hunting, brake trouble, delivering coats to a niece—the excuses kept coming. Receipts for flights, hotels, and advance orders of giant boxes of Wisconsin veal cutlets further proved that a large meeting had been planned in advance. The defendants didn't testify, limiting their strategy to trying but mostly failing to score points in cross-examination. The highlight of the trial might have been the appearance of a celebrity witness from Washington—the thirty-four-year-old Robert Kennedy—there to explain his investigation of criminal influence on organized labor as counsel to a Senate committee.[8]

On the whole, Kaufman intervened less frequently in the questioning of witnesses and gave no signs of overt partiality, as he had in the Rosenberg trial. He showed a lighter and defter touch and let the lawyers and witnesses do their jobs. This earned him no points with defense counsel, however. At the end of the trial, while the jury deliberated, Kaufman and the lawyers gathered informally in the robing room behind the bench. "All right boys," he said, "off the record, you gotta admit I gave you a fair trial." "Fair Trial?" one bellowed. "It was an abomination!" Kaufman turned bright red.[9]

And despite his in-court impartiality, Kaufman continued the dubious practice of conducting *ex parte* meetings with the prosecutors about the case. His clerk Charles Stillman recalled regular private meetings between Kaufman and the lead prosecutor throughout the trial. He wasn't present but assumed they went over the day's testimony, previewed upcoming evidence, strategized, and so on. Kaufman also dispatched Stillman to communicate with prosecutors now and then about logistical issues and to get copies of their write-ups summarizing witness testimony, a practice other clerks also remembered. This meant Kaufman was using the government's version of what witnesses and documents said when he reviewed the evidence before making a legal ruling or summarizing the evidence for the jury before deliberations. Apparently, Kaufman still didn't think such secret coziness with the prosecution was incompatible with a fair trial.[10]

When jurors returned to the courtroom at dusk on a cold December Saturday, the atmosphere was tense. Deliberations had dragged, and it was thought at least some of the men might get off. Yet the foreman repeatedly pronounced "guilty" until every defendant stood convicted. Kaufman commended jurors for ensuring grand juries wouldn't be "defied nor sneered at by any people who consider themselves above the law," and weeks later he doled out mostly maximum sentences: five years. And once again, plaudits flowed in for his meticulous care as a jurist and his ironclad resolve to protect the public. Newspapers everywhere quoted his remarks when sentencing the guilty "hoods," and the *Times* reprinted excerpts of his decision upholding Croswell's questioning. *Time* identified this ruling as "key to the Government's successful long-shot prosecution" and called the case the "biggest courtroom victory against organized crime since the conviction of Al Capone."[11]

Echoes of the Rosenberg case seemed even louder three months later when one of Kaufman's twin sons, Dick, then a freshman at Syracuse, received four menacing notes. "We're going to get you," "Your time is up," "We know you're there," and "We haven't forgotten you," the letters threatened. They might have been a prank by a fellow student—or they might have come from the Mafia. A "visibly upset" Kaufman issued a statement saying he was content to let the FBI and local authorities investigate the matter, and campus police began guarding Dick's dorm and accompanying him out at night. Newspapers covered the incident, and New York's Senator Kenneth Keating repeated their commendations of Kaufman on the Senate floor. "Helen and I console ourselves with the thought that this, too, will pass," Kaufman wrote wearily to a friend.[12]

Then the story unexpectedly changed. In November 1960, the Second Circuit reversed the convictions and issued a thorough and caustic rebuke of the prosecutions. The government hadn't proven any crime, Judges Lumbard, Friendly, and Clark held. Instead of a conspiracy, it was "just as likely that each one present decided for himself that it would be wiser not to discuss all that he knew." More deeply, the court scorned the notion of prosecuting so many men at once using the testimony of eighty-four witnesses and dozens of records of interviews and grand jury testimony all brought together under the leaky umbrella of conspiracy.

Lumbard did praise Kaufman for giving jurors "a careful summary of the evidence." As Stillman recalled, Kaufman called Lumbard or perhaps Clark and successfully lobbied for this after seeing a draft opinion. Nonetheless, the opinion contained muted criticism of Kaufman for letting the case get as far as it did. Clark was even harsher in a separate, concurring opinion, condemning the notion that new "crash methods" were required to fight organized crime. "We should have known better," he finished, "and a prosecution framed on such a doubtful basis should never have been initiated or allowed to proceed so far. For in America we still respect the dignity of the individual, and even an unsavory character is not to be imprisoned except on definite proof of specific crime." A different Clark—Tom—told Kaufman later that the Supreme Court likely would have reinstated the guilty verdicts if the Justice Department had only appealed, but for some reason prosecutors decided not to.[13]

The Apalachin reversals shocked all but those who had carefully followed the case and understood its ambitiousness. "Gangsterville, U.S.A. has cause for celebration," one paper editorialized in a typical piece. "To most Americans, however, the reversal is startling and depressing. That would include . . . Federal Judge Irving R. Kaufman." They were right about that. The day after the ruling, Kaufman ran into Lumbard's clerk and unloaded. The man remembered it decades later: "Judge Kaufman confronted me—whom he recognized as a clerk of Judge Lumbard's—in the courthouse elevator on the day after the ruling was announced to vent his displeasure. He did not—and could not—quarrel with the legal validity or rationale of the decision, but only with the outcome." Although upbraiding another judge's law clerk was déclassé, Kaufman couldn't stop himself. Nor could he admit he had been wrong. Writing a friend, he unconvincingly denied the Second Circuit had "cut him down" since it hadn't questioned his ruling on Croswell's roadblock or his instructions to the jury.[14]

Despite Kaufman's dismay, however, the Second Circuit's reversal and its veiled criticism of his work did little to dim his star. Most people and politicians reacted to the decision by saying Charles Clark had it exactly backward: if well-known mobsters like the Apalachinites could get away with holding a national convention and then blatantly lie about it under oath, new methods *were* needed to keep them in check. And only two weeks after the appellate decision, President-elect Kennedy announced he would name his brother attorney general. Robert Kennedy had been a persistent critic of his department's and Hoover's past dithering on the mob, and he sharply escalated the war. Assisted by new laws that made crossing state lines for gambling and extortion federal offenses, prosecutions and convictions rose all over the country, especially in New York. Important crime figures found themselves under surveillance or deported. The offensive continued over decades until, in the 1980s, Kaufman would rejoin the battle.[15]

If organized crime was carefully hidden, dependent on public trials and congressional hearings for exposure, the escalating revolt against Jim Crow was just the opposite. Its soldiers *wanted* attention—needed it as a weapon—but government and other institutions ranged from vehement hostility to more benign foot-dragging. That was especially true in the North, where it was easy to temporize and see the issue as an exclusively Southern problem. Paul Burgess Zuber was determined to change that.

It might have been the beatings Zuber took from a white gang called the "John Hancocks" when he was a Black boy in Harlem. It might have been the mortified look on the faces of the Brown University fraternity brothers who'd admitted him, sight unseen, and assumed from his name that he was Pennsylvania Dutch. During rush, his new friends burst into his dorm room and piled on his back, only to gasp in shock when they saw him full on. "I'll never forget the look on their faces," Zuber remembered. Or maybe it was the bleak reality of the city's Black ghettos seen as a Health Department worker while studying law at night. Whatever the cause, by 1957, Zuber was fairly convinced racism wasn't limited to Dixie. "Down home," the thirty-two-year-old would say in an affected Southern accent, "our bigots come in white sheets. Up here, they come in Brooks Brothers suits and ties."

Zuber was a charging bull of a man at six foot, three inches and 230 pounds. He had played football on a college scholarship and continued running through people on the gridiron in the army. "Meeting Mr. Zuber for the first time," a reporter wrote, "one gets the impression of a man uneasily packed into his suit." He was absolutely fearless, with a penetrating intelligence and a wicked sense of humor. And he shared more than a little in common with the federal judge who would decide his most famous case. Both started as outsiders with a racing, barely corralled ambition. Before thirty, Zuber had run unsuccessfully for the New York State Senate. Both enjoyed seeing their name in the newspaper and made sure it appeared there often. And both were congenitally impatient. "I'm a maverick," Zuber said proudly. Other descriptions soon to appear in print would include "battering ram" and "Sherman tank."[16]

Zuber came of age in a city that at least professed a full commitment to equality, and that plus his own self-assurance led him to feel that equality fully. "We are just as good as any white person in this country and in many instances better, so Charlie you had better learn to live with it," he wrote in New York's Black weekly, the *Amsterdam News*. Yet he saw the hollowness of the promise while at work for the city and at home in Harlem. Years had passed since the Supreme Court's decision in *Brown v. Board of Education* was supposed to end school segregation with "all deliberate speed," but Zuber saw segregated and dilapidated schools in Harlem, and no one seemed to be doing anything about it. Not the NAACP. Not the famous Black congressman from Harlem, Adam Clayton Powell Jr. And certainly not the white liberals who talked a good game while quietly sending their children to very different schools. So as soon as he passed the bar exam, he turned around and sued the same city he was working for.[17]

Zuber's case, in July 1957, made the front page of the *New York Times*. He claimed the city's strict zoning policy assigning Harlem children to their inferior, all-Black neighborhood schools amounted to segregation by race in violation of *Brown*. The novel suit from a newly minted lawyer no one had heard of raised eyebrows in some quarters, but Harlemites applauded. "Lawyers who lap at the public trough are rushing uptown and telling Negro people that Zuber does not know what he is doing," the *Amsterdam News* editorialized. "The only ones who are cheering young Mr. Zuber are the Negro masses whom he is trying to help." The case languished until Zuber orchestrated a student walkout. When truant officers came around, he got the court battle he wanted. Not only did the judge dismiss the truancy charges, she went on to find Harlem's schools segregated and inferior. "The Constitution requires equality," she wrote, "not palliatives." Her ruling had no effect beyond dismissing the truancy prosecutions; it didn't order integration or mandate better education. But it made news and energized activists to work even harder. The board eventually altered its zoning policy to allow parents of Black and Puerto Rican children greater leeway to transfer their children to other schools.[18]

Zuber's victory put him on the map, and in 1960 he got a call from a well-heeled suburb northeast of the city in leafy Westchester County. Norman Rockwell, Lou Gehrig, and Douglas Fairbanks had made their homes in New Rochelle, and a song from *How to Succeed in Business without Really Trying* included the lyrics "New Rochelle, New Rochelle, that's the place where the mansion will be." More than prosperous, the town of seventy-six thousand was famously welcoming. Jewish, Italian, and Irish immigrants found refuge from the city and created a multiethnic community rare for suburbia. "When contrasted to the country-club exclusiveness of some other Westchester suburbs," one observer wrote in 1960, "New Rochelle is a veritable bastion of brotherhood."[19]

The brotherhood extended to African Americans, sixteen thousand of whom called New Rochelle home. They ranged from Giants' star Willie Mays to professionals and small businessmen to blue collar laborers. Many women found domestic work in the households of neighboring Scarsdale and Mamaroneck. "We had a vibrant, incredible Black community," Linda Tarrant Reid, a girl in the late 1950s, remembered. "It was wonderful. . . . It was like 'Leave it to Beaver.' It was so idyllic." But there were limits. Older African Americans quietly observed an unstated but well understood color line when it came to the jobs they should apply for and where to sit in restaurants and movie theaters. Horizons often shrank to the familiar and accepted. When Marilyn Littman taught sixth grade to Black children in New Rochelle in 1954 and asked the girls in her class what they wanted to be when they grew up, most said "maids."[20]

New Rochelle's well-regarded high school educated students of all races, as did the town's two junior highs. The schools hired Black teachers and the appointed school board usually included one African

American. The town had even been held up as a national model. After *Brown* in 1954, administrators from Washington, DC, and Baltimore visited the high school to see how integration was done. Some of New Rochelle's twelve elementary schools were also diverse, but by 1960 one was badly imbalanced. The Lincoln School had 454 Black children and only 29 whites. Built in 1898, it was now falling apart—literally. A piece of the outside masonry had recently dislodged and crashed to pieces on the school's playground. Many parents whose children attended Lincoln under a mandatory, inflexible zoning rule similar to New York City's also thought the education lagged, thanks to poorer teachers and softer curriculum, and a group had complained to the school board in 1949. One Lincoln graduate recalled years later that his teachers had "asked only a low level of performance. They used to have us sing *Old Black Joe* and *Swanee River* at assemblies. You had to go to high school to find out how much you didn't know."[21]

In 1957, the board retained Dan Dodson, a well-known professor of education and "human relations" at NYU. He and other experts proposed redrawing the zoning lines, more flexibility in school assignments, and rebuilding Lincoln in the same location after merging with another school. Its student body would then be only 71 percent Black. Dodson's plan went nowhere, however, hardening Black suspicion. Two years later, the NAACP led pickets and boycotts, one involving two hundred children. Yet as was true throughout the North, Lincoln's Black parents were hardly monolithic. Many frowned on disrupting school to make a political point, and others simply wanted a more modern facility on the same spot. There were also muffled, worried discussions about the kind of reception their children might get in other, whiter schools. Hoping to placate both sides, the board ordered a bond election for a new, smaller Lincoln. The new school would have been just as Black, however, and the idea only increased tensions. Despite opposition from civil rights groups and even the Elks, the measure passed by a 3–1 margin, with even many Lincoln-area voters approving.[22]

Defeat at the polls left the local NAACP demoralized and ready to move on, but a few had only begun to fight. Convinced her daughter Leslie was floundering at Lincoln, Hallie Taylor telephoned Paul Zuber. "He gave us strength and courage that we could take on anything in the world," Taylor said years later, "and we did." Without telling the NAACP, Zuber designed a campaign that looked a lot like his war in Harlem. First, the Taylors and other parents took twelve children out of Lincoln and set up private tutoring. Then the boycotting mothers started showing up at white elementary schools to register their children—demands that were politely if nervously refused. Once, they pulled up to a white elementary school, and children playing outside dropped their toys and ran inside to tell the principal "the Black kids are coming!" At the nearly all-white Roosevelt school in the nicest part of town, Zuber and his foot soldiers encountered an unusual obstacle: Dr. Barbara Mason, the district's only African American principal. The face-off between Black parents demanding integration and a Black principal saying "no" was irresistible to reporters. A photo of Zuber and the parents crowded into the little Roosevelt front office confronting Mason made the front page of the *Times*. Mason was quoted saying she "completely believed" in the board's neighborhood school policy, while New Rochelle schools superintendent Herbert Clish added that he didn't "believe in playing God and sorting people according to race, color and creed." Zuber replied that what the board really feared was African Americans moving into white neighborhoods.[23]

The following week, Zuber borrowed the imagery of sit-ins at Southern lunch counters and led twenty-three parents and children with folding chairs to the conspicuously new and white Ward school, where they were ticketed for trespassing and disorderly conduct. Again, the *Times* put the story on page one. Despite the good press, though, Zuber's strategy was sputtering. He seized on the fact that an African diplomat lived in New Rochelle and telegrammed the president of Ghana asking that his representative withdraw his children from Roosevelt. The novel tactic backfired when Ambassador Alex Quaisson-Sackey politely declined to take part in the boycott. If discrimination existed in New Rochelle, he added, "then I don't know about it." An NAACP leader was quoted calling Zuber's protests "ridiculous" and saying most African Americans opposed them. Zuber himself did further damage by saying the widely respected Mason was "using her position to subjugate members of her own race" and calling her the "Aunt Jemima of Uncle Tom's cabin."[24]

Running out of options, Zuber began preparing a federal lawsuit. Moreover, he liked the courtroom. "Demonstrations are for babies," he told *Life* somewhat oddly, having organized so many. "You can go out there and march up and down with placards and sing *We Shall Overcome* till you fall down. The other side comes out and yells 'Two, Four, Six, Eight, We don't wanna integrate! . . . a Mexican standoff. But in court only one man can talk at a time and one man in front of a judge is just

FIGURE 11. Paul Zuber, the plaintiffs' lawyer in the New Rochelle desegregation lawsuit (*tall man, left center, looking at police officer*), leads parents and students in an attempt to register at a predominantly white elementary school, September 1960. *Morris Warman.*

as big as a whole damn school board." He filed suit in federal court on October 20, 1960.[25]

Zuber wanted a judge instead of a demonstration, and Kaufman was it. Zuber's complaint was unusual. He wasn't pleading that New Rochelle's segregation stemmed from racist laws or forced separation, as in the South. It claimed only that the Lincoln school zone was overwhelmingly Black and that "application of the 'neighborhood school' policy to such areas invariably results in segregated schools." This idea was widely referred to as *de facto* segregation—segregation in fact—as distinct from the old and more familiar *de jure* segregation, or segregation directly imposed by law. To Zuber, one was as unconstitutional as the other, since both gave rise to single-race schools. Because innumerable Northern and Western communities had both a Black part of town and neighborhood schools, acceptance of Zuber's basic theory would require a broad restructuring of education across the country.[26]

The first hearing in the case was called to address Zuber's request for an emergency order permitting Lincoln students to register elsewhere. New Rochelle's counsel Murray Fuerst vehemently denied the existence of segregation, since no school was entirely single-race and, technically, no part of town was off-limits to African Americans. "Our friend Willie Mays" lived in a white neighborhood, Fuerst boasted, "and we have Negroes living within the entire city of New Rochelle, and we are proud of it." Fuerst was mainly incensed that Zuber's antics were tarnishing New Rochelle's reputation: "This isn't Alabama and this isn't Arkansas, this isn't Georgia, and your Honor knows it." Kaufman denied Zuber's request, unwilling to upend schools in the middle of the year, but with typical dispatch he scheduled trial for only three weeks later. In the days that followed, he balanced his other work with nighttime reading on school desegregation, from key court decisions to nonlegal material. "I have done a lot of educating myself in the past few weeks," he told the lawyers when they reconvened for trial. "I have done a lot of reading."[27]

Zuber's case began with Bertha White, a teacher and activist who had reviewed board minutes going back to 1930. She explained how the board gerrymandered the lines of Lincoln's zone to return some African Americans who'd moved away. At the same time, it transferred a different, white enclave out of the zone, which resulted in some neighbors sending their children to different elementary schools, depending on their race. White also revealed that the board had quietly let white families transfer children out of the Lincoln zone despite the neighborhood assignments rule. Dodson testified that the board's plan for a new and smaller Lincoln would further limit the school's white population; that integration had improved school performance in Washington, DC; and that transferring students was feasible. "You can stall for years waiting for people to make up their mind," Dodson said of recalcitrant board members, and Kaufman agreed, adding that Zuber's clients only wanted "some start made on this question." Zuber's last witness was Clish, the superintendent. When Clish claimed the racial composition of a school wasn't important—only its educational quality—Kaufman was incredulous, responding that America had come "a long way from *Plessey v. Ferguson* which enunciated the separate but equal doctrine." Most important, Zuber showed that student achievement scores were lower at Lincoln, and even Clish had to grudgingly concede that the school's single-race status might bear some of the blame.[28]

New Rochelle's leadoff witness was Seth Low, a lawyer and president of the board during Dodson's study and the bond referendum. Low was no reactionary; he'd joined the Urban League and publicly condemned the board for past steps cementing an all-Black Lincoln. Now, though, he swore New Rochelle had done all it could—that transfers of whites had stopped in 1949, that the neighborhood school policy enabled children to go home for lunch, and that busing students was too expensive. Couldn't the board do *anything* to "bring about a better balance?" Kaufman wondered. Low promised they had thought of everything but could find no workable solutions, and that treating anyone differently based on race by allowing them to transfer would compromise "equal treatment for all." "But by not treating some group differently, you can also violate a basic constitutional provision," Kaufman mused. Low claimed segregation wasn't involved because Lincoln families had "the perfect privilege to go to any school in the city." "You mean the privilege to pick up bag and baggage and move?" Kaufman asked icily. "Mr. Low aren't you suggesting the impossible?"[29]

Things only worsened for the defense when Low opined that Black children underachieved not because of poor schools, but because their parents couldn't give them the same opportunities as whites and hadn't gone to college. "Let me ask you this, sir," Zuber fumed. "I am a Negro. My father works in the Post Office. He did not finish high school. My mother finished high school. I went to Brown University. Does this fit into your generality as far as Negroes achieving only because of the college background of their parents?" Low called Zuber "a fine exception." Later Zuber reinforced the point by asking a different witness: "Did you ever hear of the Lower East Side in the city of New York? And the number of judges sitting on both the federal and state bench, who emanated from the Lower East Side, which was considered the slum?" The trial record doesn't reflect whether Kaufman was stifling a smile.[30]

New Rochelle's lawyer, Julius Weiss, also offered former and current Lincoln principals who testified that the teachers, facilities, and instruction there matched those at other schools ("We had a film strip machine. We had a tape recorder.") and that lower scores weren't Lincoln's fault. Kaufman interjected, "Then you think that a program or doctrine of separate but equal is alright?" Like Low, one former principal suggested Lincoln's families could simply move if need be. "Well, now, are the Negroes able to purchase homes all over New Rochelle?" Kaufman asked. He himself had moved within New Rochelle, the white principal protested, and doing so was "the American dream." "It is wonderful when you can afford it," Kaufman shot back.[31]

Finally, Barbara Mason took the stand. The respected Black educator should have been Weiss's star witness, given her outspoken support for neighborhood schools. But even she ended up bolstering Zuber's case when she told Kaufman she fully favored integration and agreed that rebuilding Lincoln in the same location would only perpetuate an all-Black school. She also admitted integration would never come without discarding the existing assignment system. Mason stood firm only on her opposition to transferring students out of Lincoln because of their race. "As a Negro," she explained, "I do not want to be given treatment, whether it is preferential treatment or whether it is treatment that is worse, than treatment given other people. I want the same treatment, and I think this is the way most Negroes feel." Zuber found this color-blindness disingenuous. "Have you heard the Board of Education laud and glory the fact that you are their only Negro principal?" he asked. Mason claimed she hadn't.[32]

With testimony finished, Zuber and Weiss appeared for final argument two weeks later. "The only rule of eligibility for school children in New Rochelle is residence," Weiss argued, "and Negroes and whites are treated alike on that basis." He urged Kaufman to remember that "once pigmentation alone is made the basis of government action, we embark on dangerous and uncharted seas." Zuber's argument stressed the board's culpability for keeping Lincoln all-Black–moving the zoning lines, transferring white students, ignoring Dodson's plan, and proposing a smaller Lincoln. Given this evidence of conscious discrimination, Zuber no longer had to rely on the untested theory of de facto segregation. Moreover, the suggestion of some defense witnesses that New Rochelle's Black children were doomed to fail ignored "all the reasons why immigrants escaped and left Europe, and all of the reasons why people have come from all over the world to this country, because they have always felt and we have always been taught that it is not how much money you have or how high an education your mother and father have, that that opportunity is available for you as long as you want it, and you should have the opportunity to get it." Kaufman knew exactly what he was talking about.[33]

Decades later, Marc Cherno, one of Kaufman's clerks at the time, remembered the New Rochelle case as one that "worried" Kaufman, one he bore down on to make sure he got it right. In fact, he'd tried to avoid deciding it altogether. Throughout the trial, he conducted regular, off-the-record conferences with the lawyers in his chambers, trying to jawbone them into settlement. When that failed, an opinion became unavoidable, and it came on January 24, 1961. Kaufman's decision ran to forty-eight pages and exhaustively described New Rochelle's sorry history of keeping Lincoln entirely Black, excoriated the board for shirking its legal and moral duty to desegregate, and paved the way for change. In the process, it made history.[34]

First, Kaufman laid out the factual background of the Lincoln dispute and the board's conduct in painstaking detail, denouncing it for hiring experts and preparing reports while taking "no action whatsoever to alter the racial imbalance in the Lincoln School. It has met the problem with mere words, barren of meaning, for they were never followed by deeds." New Rochelle stalled even though *Brown*, Kaufman wrote, "heralded a new epoch in the quest for equality of the individual," and compliance "was not to be less forthright in the North than in the South."

Turning to the law, Kaufman rejected the board's central legal argument that the Supreme Court had outlawed only formally segregated systems like those in the South. "Constitutional rights are determined by realities, not by labels or semantics." *Brown* had been premised on the damage segregation did to "the educational and mental development of the minority group children," and that was happening in New Rochelle, too. Nor were neighborhood schools automatically "sacrosanct" or permissible "as an instrument to confine Negroes" in a gerrymandered zone. To the claim that Black students shouldn't get special treatment, Kaufman responded that "the Constitution is not this color-blind. . . . There are instances where it is not only justified, but necessary, to provide for such allegedly 'unequal treatment' in order to achieve the equality guaranteed by the Constitution." Then he finished: "Men of good will, such as the individual members of the Board submit they are, could have solved and still can solve the problem by exercising the judgment and understanding for which they presumably were chosen. . . . The Board cannot relieve itself of this responsibility by giving the community whatever result might gratify the impulse of the moment." Rather than prescribe a specific solution, he gave the board three months to present a desegregation plan.[35]

Kaufman's ruling brought jubilation to Lincoln Avenue. Some burst into tears. Five of the plaintiffs met across the street from the school to celebrate, and as cars drove by drivers stuck their hands out the window and made the V sign for victory. Hallie Taylor, the mother who'd stubbornly refused to accept the bond referendum as the end of the matter, proclaimed the decision "a step forward for the whole North. I am so elated. I am so very, very happy that I don't know what to do." With what proved to be only modest hyperbole, Zuber told reporters his victory would have "tremendous impact on practically every Northern city where segregation is practiced on a wholesale basis by officials who mouth support for integration." The *Amsterdam News* celebrated his triumph with the headline "Zuber Fought Alone." But just as some African Americans had chafed at comparing New Rochelle to Little Rock, some were ambivalent now. "The school has been very nice," one said. "There should be more talk about the good education it provides and not so much talk about what color people are."[36]

Northern newspapers treated Kaufman's opinion as an important corrective to any recent gloating over troubles down South. "What's sauce for the goose is sauce for the gander," the *Daily News* proclaimed. The *Boston Globe* thought "benefits of value to the whole nation should accrue" from the case, which would reassure Southerners that "the courts' effort to end discriminatory practices is nationwide, and not just aimed exclusively at their region." In the South, editors either indulged in schadenfreude or painted the decision as a dangerous extension of *Brown* by targeting schools that were only segregated by virtue of residential patterns. "Far from drawing any amusement from it by reason of its discomfiture of Northern school officials," one editorial commented, "Southerners should be alarmed at it."[37]

Though they should have seen it coming, Weiss and his clients were stunned by the decision, unable to accept that New Rochelle's transparent good faith and long-standing image of progressivism hadn't carried the day. At the next school board meeting, two hundred impassioned residents heard the head of the local NAACP intone gravely, "You asked our grandfathers to wait. You asked our fathers to wait. You asked us to wait. You're now asking our children to wait. We don't want to wait any longer." Supporters of the status quo were out in force, too. One claimed, "Negroes never had it so good as in New Rochelle." The board voted 6–3 to appeal Kaufman's ruling.[38]

The decision to keep fighting inflamed things further. Zuber went on the radio and vowed to rain lawsuits down on towns across Westchester County. In New Rochelle, 105 Lincoln students boycotted classes. On the other side, Clish threatened to prosecute the boycotters for truancy and had the children questioned like criminals. And it became clear that not all those unhappy with Kaufman's decision were well-meaning liberals like Seth Low. One of these wrote into the *New Rochelle Standard-Star*, calling it "frightening that a community of higher type Negroes can be swept under by thoughtless propaganda." Black parents were insulted on the streets while their children got hectoring telephone calls. A menacing letter signed "KKK" arrived at the home of one of the boycott's organizers, and a threat to blow up Lincoln required police to search the building. Once again, Kaufman was also the object of threats. One letter called him a "stinking kike n----- lover," and another said he should be tarred and feathered.[39]

Forced to submit a plan, New Rochelle did so "under protest" and proposed that all elementary school students be allowed to transfer to non-neighborhood schools, but only if they got approval from school personnel and reapplied every year. To Kaufman, this was simply "a palliative to the court—he wanted a plan, well, here it is—without any substantial thought or concern having gone into it." When a board member suggested during a follow-up hearing that students' psyches be considered before approving a transfer, Kaufman asked sarcastically, "Are you going to test the child or his emotional stability now?" Then the witness let slip that he didn't think Lincoln was actually segregated at all, and Kaufman shut him down: "I wish we wouldn't have any more of that. . . . The Court has spoken." Board president Merryle Rukeyser fared little better. When he described Lincoln students' right to transfer as "preferential treatment," Kaufman asked, "Do you think that this is a pleasure for these children to be transferred? Do you think it is anything delightful?"[40]

Kaufman responded to the board's recalcitrance by writing the new attorney general, Robert Kennedy, to "invite" the Justice Department to propose ways to desegregate Lincoln. The government responded with a brief labeling the board's plan "defective" and offering "guidelines" for desegregation, including unencumbered voluntary transfers from Lincoln and publication of the numbers of vacancies in other schools so parents could choose their destinations. Board members who'd voted against appealing also filed their own, more sweeping plan, advocating mandatory transfers and Lincoln's closure. Zuber and the plaintiffs supported this minority plan.[41]

When Kaufman issued his decision on May 31, he was scalding. "Respect for the law is a hallmark of our society," he wrote. "Yet the majority members of the Board have clearly manifested a continuation of their attitude of arrogance." Despite his vehemence, however, the plan Kaufman formulated was less sweeping than the minority board members' plan endorsed by Zuber. Instead, he essentially adopted the Justice Department's proposal. Students would be permitted to transfer without school approval: "The Constitution does not provide that only academically superior or emotionally well-adjusted Negroes are to have an opportunity to secure an education free from officially-created segregation." Nor would there be annual reapplications; students could remain at their new schools. Kaufman ordered the board to disclose vacancies in the district's elementary schools and permit parents to rank four preferred destinations, though it needn't transport children to any school and could limit the number of transfers based on class size. Nor would further delay be tolerated; imminent deadlines were set so children could elect transfers in time to start the new year in only three months. "Seven years have passed since the Supreme Court's historic decision in *Brown*," Kaufman wrote, frustration fairly leaping off the page, and "it is time now to get down to the serious business of integration."[42]

Forceful as it was, Kaufman's determination changed few minds in New Rochelle. The board appealed as planned, and Rukeyser kept insisting to the press that his town was already integrated. Even the supposedly all-white elementary schools had "a sprinkling of Orientals," he reminded people. Another blow-up occurred when the board sent transfer applications to Lincoln parents identifying only 375 vacant seats in other schools. At trial, Clish had testified that 940 such vacancies existed. Zuber was immediately back in court, charging bad faith and wondering where the extra 565 seats had gone. "I will not stand for these six people, constituting themselves a super Supreme Court, to sit in judgment on the proprieties of my holding," Kaufman lectured the lawyers, referring to the board majority. His ruling must be carried out "meticulously," he warned. "No one is above the law."[43]

The legal battle finally ended when the Second Circuit upheld Kaufman's decisions shortly before New Rochelle's children returned to class. In a short opinion, the court agreed that the evidence supported Kaufman's finding of intentional discrimination and that his remedial order was "noteworthy for its moderation." Leonard Moore, the judge Eisenhower appointed instead of Kaufman in 1957, dissented by alluding ominously to European fascism: "If Federal courts undertake the operation, directly or indirectly, of the public schools, what will be the end result? Recent history has noted other government operations originally justified because business improved and the trains ran on time."[44]

Triumphant after *Taylor*, Zuber became even more strident. "The North ain't seen nothing yet," he boasted to one reporter, and stepped up his particularly harsh denunciation of the "Madison Avenue type of segregationist—suave, sophisticated and subtle." He had little use for potential allies, telling *Life*, "Of course we get support from white liberals, but it tends to fade off when they realize integration could also get to *their* street." And relations with the NAACP continued to sour. "The way he prepares his cases gives the methodical, painstaking NAACP lawyers ulcers," the Black journalist Louis Lomax wrote in 1962. "My approach is not the organization approach," Zuber shrugged. He was in the vanguard of a new surge of Black activism, tired of compromise and caution. A "crisis is developing," Lomax warned in *The Negro Revolt*; "the Negro masses are demanding action, immediately, and leadership organizations are being circumvented when they hesitate or stand in the way."[45]

Thus Zuber found himself racing from city to city, but the meetings with Black parents were always the same. They wanted to know if he could get them what he'd gotten the Taylors in New Rochelle. He filed suits in Chicago, Newark, and Harlem again, and Newark and New York City switched to open-enrollment high schools. Englewood, New Jersey, also had a 95 percent Black elementary school named for Abraham Lincoln, and when Zuber succeeded there, too, the *Herald Tribune* dubbed him "Mr. Desegregation."[46]

After Englewood, though, Zuber seemed to lose his way. He threw his hat in the ring for Congress against Adam Clayton Powell Jr. but later withdrew. In 1963, only thirty-six, he announced his retirement from desegregation work. Paid all of $4,300 by the NAACP for the New Rochelle case, he was exhausted and almost broke. "I had to close my office or be put out," he told Lomax, "and how the hell would it look for the man who cracked school segregation in the North to be put out because he couldn't pay his rent?" Plus, he'd grown resentful. "I've had a thick skin for six years, but now the brickbats bother me." "Please no, Paul," the *Amsterdam News* begged.[47]

Yet he couldn't stay retired, either. Six weeks after his announcement he appeared before Kaufman for a follow-up hearing in *Taylor* and referred to coming "out from my self-imposed retirement." "What do you mean, you are coming out of retirement?" Kaufman asked, not having heard. "You are not the kind who ever retires." And Kaufman was right. Only three months later Zuber filed suit again in New York City for his own daughter, saying "if the best elementary school in the city is Hunter College Elementary School, somebody in this city is going to have to explain to me in court why my daughter and other Negro and Puerto Rican children cannot go there." In 1964, he announced he would enter the Republican presidential primary in New Hampshire in order to raise the issue of civil rights—a stunt that earned little press and soon fizzled. Two years later, a state appellate court publicly censured him for "intimidating" a trial judge in a criminal case, and his law license was suspended at the behest of an all-white panel in a place where he had few friends: Westchester County. In 1969, he was jailed for failure to pay an earlier libel judgment to a policeman he accused of planting drugs on his client. Black churches had to pitch in to raise the money to get him released.[48]

By then he'd really had enough. The following year Zuber left the law and the city for good and accepted a teaching position at Rensselaer Polytechnic Institute. "I won't be wearing a beard and I'll have a short haircut," he joked, "but we will have a new technique and a new approach to urban studies." Stunning all who knew him, he embraced a life much closer to Vermont than Harlem and never left. So complete was his departure that the *Amsterdam News* later ran a story asking "Whatever Happened to Paul Zuber?" and quoted him saying "It's a quiet academic life." He had decided that change through litigation, case by hard-fought case, wasn't the answer anymore: "The fight to improve the lives of Blacks in this country has moved out of the court. Progress today can only come from the use of political and economic clout." In 1987, only sixty years old, he tragically died of a sudden heart attack.[49]

Kaufman's order in the New Rochelle case was the first by a federal court to desegregate a Northern school. A handful of other systems had started integrating voluntarily, and parents and the NAACP were aggressively pushing integration before many city councils and school boards, but no Northern federal judge had yet ordered measures of the kind being glacially set in place—and often violently resisted—in the South. Even in cities like New York, Boston, and Chicago, white resistance and flight to the suburbs produced much slower and choppier integration than optimists expected after the victory in *Brown*.[50]

That Kaufman agreed with the arguments of the brash and energetic Zuber, a man in whom he could have seen some echo of himself, wasn't surprising. New Yorkers are "tolerant not only from disposition but from necessity," E. B. White wrote. "The city has to be tolerant, otherwise it would explode in a radioactive cloud of hate and rancor and bigotry." All his life, Kaufman had absorbed New York's cosmopolitanism, and in 1949 he had spoken eloquently in favor of equal rights when drafting Attorney General McGrath's speech advocating President

Truman's civil rights bill—more pointedly, in fact, than McGrath preferred. As someone who had learned side by side with African Americans at Clinton and Fordham, he was unlikely to downplay or discount steps by the New Rochelle board that separated Black from white. His approach to the case also expressly reflected a deep-seated loathing of semantics over realities, form over substance. He had no objection to neighborhood schools but refused to pretend they were always colorblind or allow that policy to cover for a legacy of more odious segregation. And his always active personality simply disdained the excuses of people like Seth Low, who had the best of intentions but threw up their hands and said there was nothing they could do. *Do something, get started already* was always Kaufman's answer to any problem.[51]

His endorsement of the Justice Department's desegregation plan also signaled another factor at work in both the New Rochelle and Apalachin cases: his trust in the federal government. By 1961, the executive branch was ramping up the battle against mobsters and, however slowly and tentatively, turning against segregation. Kaufman's inclination toward the powerful liberal state naturally led him to help. Where his superiors on the court of appeals saw an overreaching prosecution, Kaufman saw a righteous cause. Conversely, when the government proposed a milder form of desegregation than that advocated by pro-integration school board members and the complaining parents themselves, he thought the government's caution represented the wiser approach. Never mind that the United States hadn't even been a party to the case until Kaufman invited it to comment after the trial. In both cases, supporting the federal government's stab at problem-solving seemed right to Kaufman, as it generally did to most Americans.

Finally, desegregating Lincoln perfectly served Kaufman's ambition to rise through the judicial ranks. After the *Brown* decision, ending Jim Crow in schools represented the wave of the future, and the New Rochelle case offered Kaufman an enviable opening to plant himself at its leading edge. For a Northern liberal operating at the outset of a new, energetic Democratic administration, the case presented a sort of personal godsend, and Kaufman's thorough and progressive response to it took full advantage.

The *Taylor* decision ignited efforts at desegregation throughout the North and West. These were both voluntarily undertaken by school boards—Kaufman's ruling "jogged white minds all over the North," *Time* gushed—and prodded by dozens of lawsuits in cities from Philadelphia to San Francisco. One authority on Northern desegregation, Thomas

J. Sugrue, calculates that by late 1962 there were NAACP-assisted challenges to segregation in sixty-nine cities in fifteen Northern and Western states. Progress occurred in a growing number of districts through a variety of measures: busing, permissive transfers, open enrollment, new district lines, the "Princeton Plan" merging elementary schools, and others. Gradually the numbers of students learning with children of other races grew significantly compared to the days before *Brown* and *Taylor*. But that momentum would stall and then reverse in later years. By then, much of Kaufman's legacy would be under an assault led by his personal friend Chief Justice Warren Burger.[52]

Today, New Rochelle's public schools are considerably more diverse than in 1960, and none of its seven elementary schools is majority white. Still, some are badly imbalanced, just as before. Three have non-white student bodies of over 80 percent, though the largest minority group at these schools is now Hispanic. And one is only 7 percent white and 89 percent Hispanic and Black—numbers disturbingly reminiscent of Lincoln six decades earlier. In 1986, New Rochelle erected a bronze plaque reading, "On this site stood Lincoln School, the first segregated school in the North to be closed by a court order. This tablet honors all who participated in this struggle for equality in education and commemorates the twenty-fifth anniversary of the landmark *Taylor v. Board of Education of New Rochelle* decision of 1961, a milestone in the search for unity in the midst of our diversity."[53]

CHAPTER 10

Elevation and Descent

On a clear and temperate summer evening in 1960, Kaufman and Helen strode into David Sarnoff's opulent townhouse off Park Avenue for Kaufman's fiftieth birthday party. His best friends were waiting for him. To Tom Clark, who came up from Washington, he mused in a letter the next day, "As I become a venerable old man of fifty, I reflect over the years that have passed. . . . We go through life achieving successes, meeting new people, but that our friendship has endured all these years is an indication of a genuine bond. For this I am grateful to the Almighty."[1]

He felt gratitude again a few months later when voters narrowly chose Kennedy over Nixon. Better still, the new Democratic Congress finally moved on Celler's bill creating new federal judgeships. The party's prolonged gamble—that they would triumph in 1960 and then fill the new positions rather than gifting them to Eisenhower—hit pay dirt. The new administration suddenly had seventy-three new benches to fill, a 23 percent increase in the judiciary. The Second Circuit was slated to grow by half again, from six to nine judges, and Kaufman was finally poised for promotion. Many years later, ironically, he deplored the effort to cut backlogs by adding new appellate judges, claiming this only lowered a court's prestige and compromised its collegiality. He had no such qualms in 1961.[2]

This time, all the pieces were in place. New York's Republican senators Javits and Keating had backed him before and hadn't changed their minds. The new attorney general, Robert Kennedy, knew Kaufman from the Apalachin and New Rochelle cases. If the court of appeals thought Kaufman had been too tough on Joseph Barbara's out-of-town guests, that wouldn't put off the president's brother, who'd made the crusade against organized crime a signature issue. And Kaufman resolved not to be sidelined again by the Harvard crowd. Frankfurter was a lost cause, but Kaufman's extended courtship of Learned Hand finally bore fruit in early 1961. The living legend had supported Friendly in 1958 but now, at eighty-nine and a few months short of death, he relented. He wrote President Kennedy that he'd "come to know Judge Kaufman well since he has been a district judge, and I assure you that he is a man of most exceptional capacity. He has an admirable mind, and is most anxious to discharge his duties without prejudice or favor, and is extraordinarily diligent." "Thank you, thank you so much," Kaufman effused in response. "I am deeply touched by your warm words, more so when they come from one whom I have admired and revered." He later wrote contacts at DOJ asking them to find and send him the original of Hand's letter.[3]

With these bases covered and no apparent opposition, the Kennedys approved Kaufman's nomination and announced it in September 1961. The press was typically favorable. The *Herald Tribune* called him "an uncompromising perfectionist" but said he was nonetheless "known also as a man of tender compassion and before he sentenced the Rosenbergs he spent a day of meditation in a synagogue." Senate confirmation was equally uneventful, and rapid. Even relatively noncontroversial judicial confirmations now typically take several months; then they were often accomplished in days. Kaufman's hearing before a subcommittee of the Judiciary Committee occurred five days after public announcement of the nomination and consisted of Javits, Dodd, and Keating lavishing praise on the nominee for a few minutes. Kaufman had been "afraid that some of his Communist 'friends' might appear at the hearing and give him some trouble," as he told the FBI, but nothing of the sort materialized. Asked if he had anything to say, Kaufman thanked the senators and added, "I have always told lawyers that when you are winning your case, you ought to keep your mouth shut, and so I would like to follow that admonition." Then he boarded the train back to New York to make it home for Yom Kippur, "one of my few religious observances." The full Senate confirmed him unanimously two days later. In all, the constitutional process of "advice and consent" took one week.[4]

A few days after his Senate confirmation he was sworn in at Foley Square as Javits, Dodd, Sarnoff, and two hundred others looked on. The other two newly created judgeships were filled later that year by Thurgood Marshall, the famed NAACP litigator, and Paul Hays, leader of New York's Liberal Party, whose appointment followed his organization's support of Kennedy in the election. To his frequent correspondents in the FBI, Kaufman expressed gratitude to their leader: "He feels that his rise to this appointment is directly attributable to the guidance and direction given to him as a Judge through the years by Mr. Hoover."[5]

The Kennedy administration wasn't especially ideological in choosing judges; as Deputy Attorney General Nicholas Katzenbach later put it, a typical appointee should be "a careful liberal, a good technician, liberal yet cautious." Kaufman more or less fit the mold, though his work in the 1950s marked him more as a tough liberal than a timid or cautious one—someone closer to the president who first appointed him: "Give 'em Hell Harry." Kaufman's political work and resulting advancement had occurred under the wings of Truman favorites in the 1940s, men like Tom Clark and Bob Hannegan, and so far he'd perfectly exemplified Truman's brand of anticommunist but progressive, statist liberalism while on the bench.[6]

After the Rosenberg trial, there was no questioning his zeal toward communists. In more conventional criminal cases, he was thoroughly pro-government to the point of secretly conferring with prosecutors and doling out maximum sentences. In 1962, he wrote Hoover to heap praise on yet another of the director's speeches on crime and communism and condemned a "concept of the system which so frequently favors the accused over the accuser . . . those little niceties which so often tip the scales against the public." And he resented those who thought protecting the country against communists made them hard-hearted: "Those of us who have stood up to this menace have been pigeon-holed as rightists or extremists, while, for some strange reason, those who went to the other extreme were considered men of heart or compassion." Yet Kaufman also fully embraced his patrons' faith in government action to bring about social progress. Beyond using the power of his office to compel integration, he worked actively for the improvement of judicial administration and argued that the reforms he proposed were necessary to advance civil rights, ensure due process, and thereby demonstrate to the world that American justice was superior to its facsimile behind the Iron Curtain. Only in immigration cases had his vision of an open and welcome Americanism led him to part company with the government.[7]

Yet if Kaufman's judicial liberalism mirrored the political liberalism of the late 1940s and 1950s, both were changing, drifting away from the state and toward the individual. Through the 1960s and 1970s, political liberalism began to strike some more as a cacophonous campaign for particularized individual rights or special interests than the effort to make government serve the broad American middle, as epitomized by Roosevelt's New Deal and Truman's Fair Deal. Racial minorities and women stepped forward to claim long-promised civil rights. Young people demanded the right to dissent, experiment with new lifestyles, and avoid death in combat in faraway jungles. Disadvantaged people appeared from the shadows to reap new government benefits promised by the Great Society. And a new wave of activists noisily demanded redress for injuries inflicted by corporations on consumers and the environment; motivated by Ralph Nader and others, they formed countless public interest organizations and saturated the courts with lawsuits against government agencies and private companies. To liberals, these claims were righteous and long overdue. To many in what Richard Nixon famously labeled the "silent majority," they seemed to hack away at the pilings propping up civilized society. Conservatives connected them to the frightful chaos on display when inner cities rioted and policemen clubbed and gassed protesters in Chicago in 1968. "It was as if the historical temperature in America went up every month," Norman Mailer wrote that year. "At different heats, the oils of separate psyches were loosened—different good Americans began to fry."[8]

Under Chief Justice Earl Warren, judicial liberalism was undergoing a similar metamorphosis. When Kaufman was a young lawyer, judicial liberals favored the state over claims by individual businessmen and companies who argued that economic reforms—Progressive Era laws protecting workers and New Deal measures to revive the economy—violated their "freedom of contract." By slowing government-led social and economic progress in the name of a bygone, nineteenth-century conception of individual liberty, the Roosevelt-era Court lost legitimacy until new appointments changed its character. But now, in a sort of reversal, liberals saw the individual as king, and his constitutional and statutory rights against the state were expanding rapidly. While Kaufman was on the district court, and accelerating after he joined the Second Circuit, the Warren Court was revolutionizing constitutional law and civil liberties in favor of justice for the individual. And not just well-placed individuals but the downtrodden, the accused, the dissident.

Hence in *Brown* and later decisions, the Warren Court sought to dismantle government-sponsored segregation and achieve legal equality for African Americans and other racial minorities. In criminal law, the Court bolstered the rights of suspects and defendants against law enforcement with decisions restricting age-old investigative and prosecutorial practices used by police and district attorneys. These included the famous *Gideon v. Wainwright*, commanding local governments to provide counsel to every indigent person charged with a felony, and *Miranda v. Arizona*, requiring police to notify arrested suspects of their rights to remain silent and see a lawyer. In *New York Times v. Sullivan*, the brethren freed journalists and other critics of government from the threat of retaliation by vengeful public officials in the form of libel suits. In *Baker v. Carr* and later cases, the Court required legislative districts to contain roughly the same number of voters so that everyone's vote counts equally, ending blatant gerrymandering that favored powerful rural interests. In *Griswold v. Connecticut*, the justices recognized that a woman's privacy under the Constitution includes the right to use contraception. In *Engel v. Vitale*, the Court sided with parents who objected to their children reciting a government-crafted prayer in public schools. As Justice William Brennan, the Warren Court's pivotal thinker and architect, wrote in 1965: "Law is again coming alive as a living process responsive to changing human needs. The shift is to justice and away from fine-spun technicalities and abstract rules."[9]

The question, then, for any judge joining a circuit court in 1961 was whether to join and even advance the Supreme Court's individual rights revolution, or to try to thwart it. At the outset, as a product of the old liberalism, Kaufman was hesitant. In an *Atlantic* article he wrote in 1963 titled "The Supreme Court and Its Critics," he wondered whether the "the specter of the early New Deal Court, hopelessly out of tune with the spirit of the times, should make us seriously ponder the questions raised when an appointive federal body attempts either to gauge and give force to popular sentiment or affirmatively to lead that sentiment along lines thought more in accord with fundamental constitutional verities." When it came to segregation and grossly rigged legislative districts, Kaufman acknowledged that the other branches of government had failed. Those were also areas essential to self-government. He was more skeptical of the Supreme Court's willingness to outlaw prayer in school and rewrite police procedure. As he concluded,

> It is always pleasing to have our problems solved for us. Indeed, many of the Court's opinions effectuate substantive solutions with which few can quarrel. But as Justice Harlan has warned, we should be wary of relying upon the Court to settle all our vexing problems, particularly questions which are more properly within the province of the legislative or executive branch of government; of shirking our duties as citizens to resolve the problems which beset society at the ballot box and of acting as spectators as to the actions of a judiciary which is appointed for life.[10]

When he took his seat on the Second Circuit, Kaufman became the thirty-fifth judge in the court's 160-year history. His appointment also marked a small milestone in the Jewish history of New York. Four other Jews had reached the court before him, but Kaufman was the first drawn from the descendants of the millions and millions of Eastern Europeans who began arriving in the 1880s. By 1961, they were by far the largest and dominant segment of Jews in the city, having swamped the older and smaller German and Sephardic communities. This enormous wave had washed over and changed most aspects of life in New York, and law was no exception. Kaufman's appointment heralded his tribe's arrival at the gates of the city's highest legal citadel. They had gone from brazen, customary exclusion from the best law schools and law firms to a place literally above both: a high stone tower filled with gold leaf and marble whose occupants dispensed justice while looking down on New York. And among the millions, Kaufman was their first representative there. Improbably and despite the obstacles, they had risen high—and through his congenital impatience and overbearing willpower, he had risen highest.[11]

The court itself was generally thought to be the second most distinguished and important in the United States after the Supreme Court. It had the largest docket and covered America's biggest and most commercially vital city. In ability, its judges had often been ranked *above* their nine bosses in Washington by lawyers and academics. Over time, its distinction as the second most important court passed to the District of Columbia Circuit because of the mushrooming volume and rising stakes of that court's governmental cases and the promotion of some of its judges to the Supreme Court. When Kaufman joined it, though, the

Second Circuit still enjoyed a reputation for preeminence. Hand died a few weeks before Kaufman took his seat, and Kaufman inherited both his chambers and some furniture, including a beautiful Shaker-style standing desk. Few clerks completed their years without hearing that they were in the presence of totems from the bygone master.[12]

Kaufman, Marshall, and Hays joined Charles Clark and five recent Eisenhower appointees. Three were the New Yorkers who had edged out Kaufman in the 1950s: Lumbard, Moore, and Friendly. The two other active judges were from the circuit's two smaller states, Connecticut and Vermont. Several other judges, including the ageless and cheerful Medina, continued to hear appeals as senior judges. Kaufman was particularly friendly with Clark, Medina, Lumbard, and Marshall, whose jokes and garrulous storytelling Kaufman treasured. Far more than even Kaufman, Marshall was an outsider to New York's Ivy League, Wall Street legal establishment, and Kaufman immediately recognized a kindred spirit.[13]

Then as now, the Second Circuit heard appeals in panels of three judges, with one presiding. Each month, these trios get twenty or so cases to decide. Boxes with the transcribed proceedings in the district court and the parties' legal briefs then begin appearing in chambers. Appellate courts don't hear from witnesses, find facts, or redo trials; their decisions are based on the "cold record" given to them and usually involve untangling and deciding disputed questions of law. The Second Circuit's main courtroom somehow imparts both intimacy and majesty—a long, rectangular space enrobed in dark wood paneling interrupted by arched windows looking north over the city. Carved pilasters evoke classical grandeur while intricate gold trim and painted red rosettes highlight a ceiling twenty-two feet above navy-and-gold carpeting. Counsel there typically unfold elaborate legal arguments in conversational tones. "There is no feeling in the room of excitement and importance, or momentous decisions in the making," one observer wrote near the time of Kaufman's appointment. "To the outsider, the atmosphere is completely relaxed and unhurried." Not that Kaufman felt relaxed as he adjusted to his new job. "Indeed, I would say that it is far more difficult and time consuming than being a trial judge," he wrote an acquaintance.[14]

In chambers, law clerks toiled in the shadows of filing cabinets and teetering stacks of paper in a small outer office. Longtime secretary Anna Strasser used a middle workspace, telephone and typewriter at hand, while Kaufman was back behind a closed door in the vast interior office the architect Cass Gilbert designed for judges. He sat in a massive leather chair behind a heavy wooden desk in a room carpeted in deep, imperial crimson. Each morning, a law clerk made sure the desk had newly sharpened pencils waiting for use in editing draft orders and opinions. Behind him were windows with views all the way to midtown's skyscrapers. Dark wooden bookshelves filled with case reporters and other volumes lined the walls, and a gargantuan wooden conference table swallowed up the middle of the room. An American flag on a gold flagpole sat motionless in the corner.

Clerks began the evaluation of each appeal by reading the record produced in the trial court, digesting the parties' briefs, and researching the applicable law. Then they drafted "bench memos" summarizing the case for Kaufman and recommending how he should rule. He insisted these be short and crisp, just a few pages. "Voting memos" circulated to other judges before oral argument indicating how Kaufman would vote were usually only a paragraph or two, but he made sure they were sufficiently clear that on at least one occasion they received extraordinary praise. Kaufman had been on the court four years when Thomas Swan, a Connecticut judge then in his thirty-ninth year on the Second Circuit, wrote him a note: "I am sure it will please you to know that, in my opinion, your memoranda are better than those of any judge I have ever sat with except Learned Hand. His were equally helpful but no better!"[15]

After the lawyers gave brief oral arguments—usually just ten or fifteen minutes for each side, interrupted by the judges' questions—it fell to the clerks to prepare the first drafts of Kaufman's appellate opinions. This was true for almost all judges, though a few holdouts, including Hand and Friendly, insisted on writing their own. Former clerks have conflicting memories of the degree to which Kaufman edited and revised draft opinions. Some remembered him poring over drafts and hashing through picayune details. He wanted Latin and literary allusions and berated clerks for not matching the erudite references to Socrates and Blackstone he thought clerks were packing into Friendly's opinions, apparently unaware Friendly did all the writing himself. So Kaufman's opinions duly mentioned Seneca and Alexander Pope and Lord Melbourne. "Drive me to the dictionary!" he admonished, and clerks responded with words like "apodictic," "tessara," "ambagious," "amphibolic," and "pasquinading." Other clerks remembered little intervention, with one calling Kaufman "a big picture guy." Another sarcastically said Kaufman would "change a comma and add a few silly phrases, and all of a sudden it was brilliant. If he spent an hour polishing our work and turning it into his kind of prose, from the piece of drek that we gave him, then . . . it was terrific." In reality, most appeals presented routine issues, and in these clerks had freer rein. But the harder cases received Kaufman's serious attention. Jack Auspitz remembered wheeling in carts of books and documents for Kaufman's review. In the mornings, Kaufman would come in and say, "I was up last night and thought of the answer and here it is," handing Auspitz a piece of paper. "Usually those were wrong," Auspitz laughed, "like everyone's midnight thoughts."[16]

The first paragraph of his opinions became a Kaufman calling card. He wanted it to be "eye-catching," one clerk said, and to introduce the case by placing it in some larger legal or historical context. This practice had mixed success, sometimes feeling clunky and forced. Occasionally, though, it captured a case's greater meaning with style and pith. It also drew mixed reviews. Judge José Cabranes, then on the district court in Connecticut, liked the device, while Second Circuit Judge Lawrence Pierce thought Kaufman's introductions deployed "strikingly expressive prose that in many ways placed the legal and factual issues in quite sharp focus." On the other hand, Jon O. Newman, another later addition to the court of appeals, panned it as an "affectation."[17]

Kaufman's often tortured relationship with his clerks continued on as before. "Law clerks are like wild horses," he actually told Jon Lindsey, who clerked in 1975–76; "until you break them they're no good to anybody." The newly graduated assistants still hailed mostly from Harvard and Columbia, and occasionally Yale or Stanford. Ironically, Fordham graduates never got a shot at the prestigious position. This was sometimes ascribed to Kaufman's embarrassment over his own humble academic origins and status as an outsider—a way to compensate for past blots on his pedigree. Perhaps. But his colleagues hired from comparable schools, with the crème de la crème—the valedictorians and law review editors—usually finding their way to Friendly.

Expectations remained high. "He was a very demanding boss," Jerrold Ganzfried recalled. "You knew there could be no mistakes. And there were none." As always, the work had to be done as fast as possible, sometimes faster. "I am sure you know by now that when I get a job to do, I like to do it yesterday," Kaufman wrote another judge. Every opinion from one sitting had to be finished before the next began the following month. Nor were clerks' duties confined to judicial work. They were also expected to think up and write op-ed pieces as well as more technical articles for law reviews. They were amateur speechwriters, preparing remarks several times a year for bar functions, testimonial dinners, legal education programs, and the like, as well as managers of Kaufman's work on endless committees. Sometimes these assignments verged on the surreal, as when Kaufman asked Dan Kelly to draft his "Memories of Thurgood Marshall on the Second Circuit" without supplying any memories for Kelly to recount. Kelly had to scavenge news clippings for material.

IRK's buzzer still ruled clerks' days and haunted their sleep. "It was like you were on an electric chair and that was an electric shock you were getting and you had to go into his office," Richard Abt, who clerked in 1971–72, recalled. Now that Kaufman had two clerks (the number would later rise to three), he used different signals for his different clerks, with his favorite at the moment getting one buzz and the other two. This could change over time, depending on the merry-go-round of who was up and who was down. Kaufman continued to play favorites among his clerks, sometimes shifting assignments between them or having one, humiliatingly, check another's work. The clerk in the doghouse was often just ignored altogether.

As before, new clerks were lambasted as shockingly ignorant and unprepared. When one presented his first draft opinion, Kaufman began reading and then threw the pages on the floor and exploded. "What do they teach you boys at Harvard?! This is crap!" Mortified, the clerk slunk back to his cubbyhole and called a predecessor who often handled such things. "I think I ought to leave," he confided. The old clerk scoffed and told him he had gotten off easy. "When I gave him my first opinion, he said 'this is *shit*!'" The old clerk advised selecting some unimportant language in the first paragraph and changing it—minor tweaking only—and handing it back in. Like clockwork, Kaufman called the new draft "a big improvement." Abt remembered similar treatment. "He would call you an idiot, say you couldn't write, 'How did you get on the *Harvard Law Review*?'—personal attacks on your intelligence and, in my case, my work ethic." Or if there was some particular foible or quirk, Kaufman would pick at that. "He had this incredible ability to zero in on somebody's insecurities or weaknesses and keep drilling at them," one clerk said. Kaufman once assigned Peter Kreindler, there in 1971–72, an emergency application in a complex case scheduled for argument the following day. Kreindler stayed up until four in the morning writing a bench memo and then collapsed on the office couch. "If you were any good, you would have finished earlier and you could have gone home to sleep" was all Kaufman said the next morning. To Kreindler, that "typified" Kaufman. "He generally had an inferiority complex . . . and was always putting you down to make himself feel better."

Kaufman's insecurity led him to blame clerks in weird ways. He ordered Michael Tabak, in chambers in 1975–76, to send an angry letter to a colleague that Tabak thought was unbecoming. Unable to talk Kaufman out of it, he dropped it in the mailbox. The next morning, Kaufman asked if he'd mailed the letter. When Tabak said he had, Kaufman erupted. "Why the hell did you mail that letter? You're supposed to protect me from myself!" A different clerk who'd drafted a decision the Supreme Court voted to review faced Kaufman's wrath for exposing him to the potential embarrassment of high court reversal. "I haven't been reversed in years. It's all your fault—why'd I listen to you?" As it happened, the Supreme Court ended up affirming. When Kaufman sat on a panel with Friendly, clerks worked especially hard, since he feared humiliation next to the court's intellectual giant. "He was terrified of Friendly," Richard Friedman remembered, once describing a morning he was scheduled to hear cases with Friendly as "the most important day of the year." In this, at least, Kaufman wasn't alone; another judge circulating his first draft opinion to Friendly wrote of feeling "like a high school student submitting a math paper to Einstein."

Clerks' hours were still long, regardless of when they physically departed the courthouse. Kaufman would often leave at five, using a back door to make sure the clerks wouldn't see him go, and soon enough he would call back into chambers to make sure they were still grinding away. Or he'd call their homes, dispense with preliminaries like "hello," and start barking orders rapid-fire. If he'd told a clerk to do something important, he might call back a few minutes later and harangue, "Well, have you done it yet?"

Sometimes these directives included household errands, though Kaufman was hardly the only judge in his day to indulge in the personal use of staff. One clerk remembered changing the tires on Kaufman's car, adding, "We were his serfs." Before departing for Europe, Kaufman once left instructions for clerks that included a grocery list, so the returning travelers wouldn't face an empty refrigerator. Strangest of all may have been Tom Dahdouh's experience in 1987; Kaufman took him to Van Cleef & Arpels to buy jewelry for Helen, and Dahdouh found himself a prop in Kaufman's bargaining for a discount. "My clerk here is horrified by this price," he told the salesperson, and to Dahdouh's amazement it worked—the store lowered the price.

Attempts at respite rarely succeeded. Most of Kaufman's clerks over the years were Jewish, but he resisted their missing even a day or two for the high holidays. When he realized one Orthodox clerk was slipping off to the stairwell three times a day to pray, Kaufman ordered a fellow clerk to go get him. "There's an authority even higher than you," that clerk grumbled, and refused. Even the most unavoidable personal absences proved difficult to arrange. In 1965, Michael Rosen and his wife made plans to travel to Miami to pick up a baby girl they were adopting. Nervously, he told Kaufman well in advance that he'd have to be gone over a Thursday and Friday. But as the weekend approached there was little understanding. "Why do you have to go?" Kaufman carped repeatedly. "*Can't your wife do it?*" When Rosen stressed the event's obvious importance to his young family, Kaufman just asked, "But do you have to be gone so long?" Another clerk mentioned that his wife was pregnant only to be told he couldn't be working hard enough if that was true. It seemed like it had to be a joke but the clerk wasn't entirely sure. In screening law students for future clerkships, Tabak flatly refused to submit a Yale Law School friend's résumé to Kaufman because his friend was newly married. The would-be applicant was furious, but Tabak responded simply, "I'm telling you, your marriage won't survive the year."

All this kept clerks quitting in unusually high numbers, while others were fired. These never-quite-surprising departures prompted Kaufman to call his best friend Simon Rifkind, a former district judge and celebrated lawyer to clients as diverse as Jackie Onassis, Justice William O. Douglas (himself a tyrant to law clerks), and General Motors. Several former Kaufman clerks practiced at Rifkind's blue chip firm—Paul, Weiss, Rifkind, Wharton & Garrison—and Rifkind or an underling would send over an associate to replace the clerk who'd fled. Those clerks who gutted it out sometimes drew on special stubbornness or past experiences, such as a dictatorial parent, to get by. When Kaufman returned one of his drafts with a cutting remark, Kelly stormed into his office, crumpled up the paper, and threw it down on Kaufman's desk. As if that wasn't bad enough, the ball of paper bounced up and hit Kaufman. There was stunned silence for a moment, but Kaufman didn't say anything. He didn't bring it up later, either. "Early on," Kelly concluded, "you had to take him on."

Yet for all the misery it was also still true that, for many clerks, the experience improved as the year went on and Kaufman softened. After a few months on the job, Robert Gorman found that his relationship with Kaufman became "affectionate." Kaufman would buzz him in to try out canned Borscht Belt jokes in foreign dialects rendered surprisingly well, and the two would laugh together. A later clerk, Lee Levine, recalled occasional sessions during the year when Kaufman, full of bonhomie and virtually performing, would call him and his co-clerks into his inner office and recount stories from his early years. Over the course of the year, Kaufman typically grew fonder of his clerks' work and attributed the real or imagined improvement to his own tutelage. "That was an illusion he had, another product of his insecurity," one clerk said. Compliments may have been rare, but they weren't nonexistent. "Will you undertake your usual thorough preparation for me?" he asked one clerk in a memo. When a clerk spotted another judge's error or determined that the panel's proposed decision was wrong for some reason, Kaufman was happy to give him credit in memos to colleagues. This once happened to Ganzfried, who wasn't praised for it directly but then ran into someone outside chambers who knew Kaufman and said, "Oh, you must be the brilliant clerk from Stanford the judge was telling us about."

After the job was over, Kaufman was willing to promote the careers of his favorite clerks, taking pride in and credit for their accomplishments. He invited them to Second Circuit conferences and other events, seating them next to important people, and wrangled junior places for them on prestigious court and bar committees. Auspitz recalled a "constant parade" of ex-clerks in chambers to discuss job prospects. In his own case, he decided to seek appointment as the attorney general of American Samoa, a federal position he coveted for its dramatic change of pace. Instead it went to a Republican, which was understandable, since it was the Nixon administration doling out patronage. When Kaufman learned of the episode, he erupted. "You should've come to me! I would have gone to work for you!" Needing a backup plan, Auspitz went to Paul Weiss. As it happened, he'd let his hair grow longer in keeping with the fashion then, and one morning he walked into his office to find an envelope with no return address on his desk. Inside was an unsigned note, but Auspitz recognized the handwriting immediately. "Get a haircut," Kaufman had written, and enclosed a $5 bill.[18]

Kaufman's domineering manner usually bred successful results at the courthouse. If he chose the stick over the carrot, at least the stick kept his chambers running tightly on schedule and yielded generally well-received opinions, articles, and newspaper coverage. When he applied more or less the same methods at home, the results were very different.

The first and most immediate target of Kaufman's need for control was Helen. She'd never been ambitious or independent, moving from her parents' Central Park West aerie to her new home with her husband at age twenty. She was especially close to her mother, who still phoned from across the park when skies darkened to make sure Helen was wearing her rain boots. Helen did have some power over the family purse, since much of their money originated from Lien Law Louie, but she wasn't the type to exploit her leverage or conserve. Mitzi Newhouse, Sam's wife, was once scandalized to run into the Kaufmans' eldest son Bob buying socks at Saks Fifth Avenue. Fantastically wealthy herself, dressed by Givenchy and Dior, she spread the story around the Upper East Side that "the judge's son buys his socks at Saks."

Lacking the life experience or native fortitude to resist, Helen didn't. Kaufman's outsize personality fully dominated Apartment 5A. Family dinners on Friday nights were formal events beginning with canapés served by staff in the living room before meals on fine china, followed by finger bowls. A buzzer under the carpet under the dining table allowed Helen to buzz in maids to clear the table, much as Kaufman buzzed in clerks down at Foley Square. Kaufman was always served first and always held forth. "Irving would pontificate," their daughter-in-law Maxine Berman recalled; "It wasn't a normal family conversation, 'Hi, what did you do? How was your week?' It was him telling us about the world and his week," though he rarely discussed cases. Helen was treated "like the village idiot," Berman said. "Everything had to be his way." She could be in the middle of a sentence, but if Kaufman wanted to talk it was "Helen, I'm trying to say something, you need to be quiet." Conversations revolved around Kaufman's preoccupations—law, politics, news—and little else. "Irving was not a man of broad interests," remembered Rosalind Rosenberg, a history professor at Columbia and Barnard who married Helen's nephew. Her own in-laws, Helen's brother Irwin and wife Doris, were more worldly, sampling the city's cultural offerings at plays, concerts, or lectures almost nightly. To Rosenberg, it seemed Kaufman and other family members were dismissive of Helen, as if "she wasn't that smart," though some thought she was. Just as his clerks' work usually wasn't good enough the first time, the same was true around the house. Kaufman "probably belittled her" when she failed to meet expectations, Rosenberg thought, which would have been often. It wasn't that he didn't love her; by all accounts he did, though neither was terribly demonstrative about it. Berman rarely saw hugging or kissing among any of the Kaufmans, parents or children. It was just that his inborn perfectionism and censoriousness spared no one, least of all those closest at hand.

And so Helen broke down. This could have been due to the pressure to satisfy her seldom satisfied husband, or something else. She started "self-medicating," as one grandchild put it. This meant drinking too much, to the point that it was sometimes noticeable by the time the staff cleared the dinner table. "She had to have her glasses of wine, and she couldn't handle them," Berman said. Cigarettes were a less dramatic addiction. Sometime in the 1950s Helen got a nose job, which may have kicked off her use and eventual abuse of painkillers. She also developed anorexia, an affliction endured for years, if not the rest of her life. More than once she addressed these ailments by leaving home and entering a residential treatment facility or mental hospital of some kind. She was also under the care of a psychiatrist in the city.

But lasting stability was hard to find, and Helen's condition deteriorated to the point that suicide came to seem reasonable. She downed fistfuls of sleeping pills or other drugs in repeated attempts to kill herself. On one of these occasions, with Kaufman out at a dinner, she managed to call her daughter-in-law after swallowing the pills. Berman could tell something was off and rushed over to Park Avenue, assuming Helen had overdosed. When she arrived, Helen was unresponsive—"she was just gone." Berman phoned for help, and Helen was taken out of the building in the service elevators to avoid awkward encounters with neighbors. "Nobody ever said 'thank you' or appreciated that I obviously cared enough or felt responsible enough to do that," Berman added. Other times, Kaufman was there when Helen was falling apart. But he had no idea how to comfort her or help her regain her bearings. Clueless and floundering, he would call her brother Irwin. "Irwin, you have to come up here and deal with her," he would plead, at sea when it came to his own wife. And Irwin would always come.[19]

However bad it was for Helen under Kaufman's thumb, it was worse for his sons. With Helen, he might not have been able to help himself. With his sons, his naturally dictatorial manner joined with a conscious decision that his job as their father required riding them until they showed the sort of drive and success he'd shown himself. And if the results of that strategy were disappointing, the objects of his disappointment must be informed and even greater pressure applied. He "did a job on all his sons," a grandson said.[20]

His philosophy of child-rearing might have been inadvertently captured in an exchange during the New Rochelle desegregation trial, when a board member was asked a softball question: whether "it would be an advantage or disadvantage for all people to be in good homes and have parents with a rich cultural background." "Certainly," said the board member without thinking, but then Kaufman surprised everyone by interjecting "It might not be." After all, look where deprivation had gotten him. He didn't want his kids to have it too easy, either. In this he was like other second-generation fathers of his circle who'd made it to Park Avenue. Kaufman's friend Sam Newhouse was so tough on his son—his expectations so great, his giant shoes so hard to fill, his humiliations so calculating—that young Si considered suicide.[21]

Then there was simply Kaufman's stature. When the boys were young, the FBI had invaded their home and guarded their father with guns, as if he was the most important man in America, which the blaring newspaper headlines seemed to suggest he was. They rarely had a friend who didn't know precisely who their father was and what he had done. They met Truman in the White House, Hoover in FBI headquarters, the ambassador to the Court of St. James's in London, and a Supreme Court justice in their own home. Many assumed their father would join his friend Tom Clark in Washington. At college, a server in Kaufman's son's dining hall explained how her daughter, a Catholic schoolgirl in the city, had been told by the nuns that his father was the greatest judge in America and would be the country's next Supreme Court justice. It probably wasn't the first time he or his brothers had heard that. At the Plaza's Palm Court and the fabled 21 Club, maître d's greeted the family with a knowing "Good evening, judge." "We hope we will make you as proud of us as we are of you," two of his sons telegraphed when he was nominated for the Second Circuit. The shadow the Kaufman boys grew under was long.[22]

Academically, the boys struggled to reach their father's lofty goals. After elementary school at Riverdale in the Bronx, Bob was packed off to boarding school in Connecticut at fourteen, and later the Wilbraham Academy in western Massachusetts for high school. "We're not sure as yet whether Bobby likes the idea of going away to school," Kaufman wrote Clark, "but as parents we know it is best for him and that someday he will be grateful to us." At Wilbraham, Bob had to give a five-minute oration to his classmates and chose the FBI as his topic, leading Kaufman to mail a copy of the laudatory speech to Hoover with a revelatory cover letter. "Being a difficult task master," he told Hoover,

"I have written to Bobby and told him he could have done better." Strasser also saw the taskmaster in action and tried to run interference. When Kaufman scrawled messages like "These marks are unacceptable" on his sons' report cards, she would go back to him with a gently admonishing "You can't say that!" Jim, who suffered from a mild form of epilepsy, stayed in New York and graduated from Riverdale.[23]

Bob enrolled at the University of Virginia but soon dropped out and came home, an indifferent student pining for a girlfriend he'd left behind in New York. He bounced around and ended up at Syracuse, writing his parents dutifully, "We are grinding this semester and believe it or not I haven't had a date yet. It really doesn't bother me as it used to. It isn't as important as the work is and I only wish I had realized that sooner." Two years younger, one twin, Dick, also enrolled at Syracuse, while the other, Jim, started at the University of Pennsylvania. But Kaufman didn't like Jim's focus on the wrestling team at Penn and had him transfer to the University of Oklahoma, probably on the advice of his close friend there, Tenth Circuit Judge Alfred Murrah. Although degrees from Syracuse and Oklahoma shouldn't have been shameful, they did little to appease their recipients' father. Kaufman "went out of his way to denigrate their accomplishments," Jim's son John said. Nor did it help that chambers were stocked with Harvard and Columbia men, or that two of the boys' cousins—Kaufman's oldest brother Ben's sons Herb and Roger—made it to Princeton. Herb then attended Harvard Medical School and became a renowned ophthalmologist. Roger remembered Kaufman always browbeating his boys—"Why can't you be like Herb and Roger?" Clerks were equally useful props. One of Kaufman's sons appeared in chambers while Charles Stillman was there, and Kaufman began haranguing him. "Why can't you be like Charlie?" he implored. "He's responsible, he goes to school at night, he's a married man."[24]

Kaufman tried to steer his children toward law—he'd pointed Bob toward the University of Virginia because of its highly regarded law school, while Jim took some classes at the law school at Oklahoma—but none followed through. In this, at least, they were defiant. He later admitted they'd been right, writing his in-laws: "Ninety-nine percent of the battle is won when our children make their own choices on careers—and are happy with them." But his sons still needed his connections. Kaufman knew Sidney Solomon, CEO of the department store chain Abraham & Straus, and soon Bob was in a training program there. Then Kaufman's friendship with Gus Levy, head of Goldman Sachs, led Bob to the firm's commercial paper department. Personable and well-liked by clients and colleagues, Bob took to the job and did well. Yet he hardly escaped his background; "Everyone knew who his dad was at Goldman," an old friend of his there remembered. Jim also spurned law for a slot in the research department at Goldman's competitor, Lazard Frères.[25]

Soon after starting careers, Bob and Jim started families. Bob married a woman he met in the A&S training program—Berman. "When I met him, he was a spoiled brat," she said frankly, recalling a New Year's Eve when Bob pulled up in a rental limousine. Kaufman soon got her a job in advertising at *Glamour*, owned by Sam Newhouse, and rarely let her forget it. "I kept them from firing you," he would say ominously. One of Bob's groomsmen was a fun-loving pilot he'd befriended in basic training: Fred Trump Jr., elder brother of the forty-fifth president. Trump and his wife Linda remained friends with Bob and Maxine through the years, often joining them at galas and benefits as Maxine witnessed Trump slowly "drinking himself to death."

Relations with the in-laws were prickly. Annoyed that the middle-class Bermans hadn't hosted an affair in their Massachusetts hometown to introduce the groom-to-be to family and friends ("like Irving would've gone to a party at my house"), Kaufman canceled a planned rehearsal dinner in New York at the last minute. As guests circulated and ate hors d'oeuvres at the wedding reception on the roof of the St. Regis, the headwaiter approached Maxine's father and whispered, "The judge is ready to have lunch." "This isn't the judge's wedding," Mr. Berman replied icily. "This is my wedding, and we'll have lunch when I'm ready." Overall, Maxine was convinced Kaufman frowned on her less affluent, less connected family. On the other hand, Jim married a woman whose background—Manhattan upbringing, the Dalton School, Sarah Lawrence—was more acceptable. Both couples settled on the Upper East Side, the better to use the family-owned garage on Eighty-Seventh Street.[26]

Yet for all the appearance of getting on with prosperous and socially well-placed lives, the boys were beginning to show signs of having inherited their parents' afflictions. Short like his father, Bob felt the need or was pressured to use elevator shoes to compensate. When Berman found them among Bob's things when they moved in together, she threw them out. Far worse, he followed his mother into prolonged substance abuse, probably including cocaine. Despite his job at Goldman, they were soon regularly going to Kaufman and Helen for money. According to Berman, the Kaufmans said they had been told that $3,000 was the limit of what they could give at any one time without tax consequences, so that's what the young couple got. When Berman became pregnant with the couple's third child a few years later, Bob came to his parents in despair, scared to death he couldn't afford another round of private school and college tuition. More even than Bob, the equally sociable Jim inherited a fixation on status and showiness. His dark tan, precise tailoring, and carefully folded pocket square proclaimed his affluence. Soon, his drug problem surpassed his older brother's. Like Helen, he became addicted to painkillers. Demerol, originally prescribed for migraines, slowly began to wreck his life.[27]

None was as troubled as Dick. A glimpse of his stormy relationship with his parents appears in a letter he wrote home from Syracuse in 1961 after some unspecified incident: "I realize how foolish I was and how much I hurt you. . . . I was aware of the fact that our relationship was not as it should have been but there was only one person to blame and that was myself. . . . I wish that we were less of a problem [and] that you wouldn't have to spend all these sleepless nights." The next year, his life went off the rails, as documented in FBI memos:

> Dick attempted to run away with a young female student at the University. At that time [he] contacted Roy Cohn, who at one time had been a good friend of Judge Kaufman. However, of late, there seems to be bad blood between Judge Kaufman and Roy Cohn. Because of this, Roy Cohn advised Judge Kaufman's son that he was of age and he should not go home to his father if he did not want to. Judge Kaufman hired private detectives to locate his son, and finally after locating him, inveigled him to go home. It was after this incident that Judge Kaufman took his son to a psychiatrist and it was decided that he needed treatment. He was placed in the Institute of Living and has been there since that time.

At first, Dick did well at the institute, a well-appointed residential facility in Hartford dating to 1822. But then he fled that facility, too, this time with *two* women. One was the wife of "a prominent Wall street broker." Kaufman called the FBI because "he does not know where to turn for assistance, he cannot think clearly, and he has always considered the Director his closest friend, especially at a time of need such as this." Despite this plea, agents told Kaufman the matter was outside FBI jurisdiction. All was resolved when Dick called Cohn again, and Cohn reversed himself and advised Dick to call home. "Arrangements were then made to return the son to the Institute. Judge Kaufman stated that the son had fallen in love with a young divorcee who was also at the same Institute. He stated that the authorities at the Institute are not permitting the return of the girl."[28]

Dick's worsening mental illness, his brothers' problems with drugs and money, Helen's descent into substance abuse and attempted suicide—Kaufman's family was slipping perilously out of his control. And he was a man who badly needed control—domination, really—and who'd succeeded in establishing it over the small but important universe of his professional life.

Kaufman's niece Rosalind Rosenberg traced the family's fissures to the weeks in 1953 when FBI agents occupied their apartment and everyone involved, most of all Kaufman, could see they'd run up against a superior force, a danger from which his status and power and remarkable force of will couldn't necessarily protect them. "It destroyed the twins," she said of Kaufman's two younger sons, whose conditions would sharply deteriorate as time passed. Perhaps understandably, the death threats and guards and vilification created a permanent sense of a family under siege. "How do you have a normal childhood when your father is trying the Rosenbergs and there's FBI all over the house?" Berman asked. And like many people under extreme pressure, Kaufman reacted by tightening the screws even further. A downward spiral that would end in even greater heartache had begun.[29]

CHAPTER 11

The Forgotten Man

After Roy Cohn told Dick Kaufman he was a man now and didn't have to go home or back to Syracuse if he didn't want to, Cohn's relationship with his old mentor seems to have soured for good. In later years Cohn became a celebrity mob lawyer and eventually a defendant himself—stuff Kaufman wanted nothing to do with. When Kaufman heard in 1962 that Hoover had attended the wedding of the daughter of Cohn's close friend George Sokolsky, the McCarthyite columnist, he feared Sokolsky was bad-mouthing him to the director. He had been trying to reach Hoover for days but received no response. "Judge Kaufman then stated that he may be letting his imagination run away with him but he was concerned about the fact that he could not get through to the Director," the head of the New York office recorded. Over the next few years, Hoover and Kaufman slowly drifted apart, too. There was never an overt break, and Kaufman continued to pen fawning letters whenever the FBI cracked a big case. He also kept his portrait of Hoover on the wall in chambers. Yet they weren't as close. "I don't remember a period in the last ten years when so much time has elapsed between our visits," Kaufman wrote him plaintively in 1963.[1]

The growing estrangement mirrored Kaufman's slow evolution away from law enforcement now that he was on the court of appeals. Fittingly, one of the first examples involved his and Hoover's old obsession:

communism. Haled before the House Un-American Activities Committee, the folk singer Pete Seeger adamantly refused to address "my associations, my philosophical or religious beliefs or my political beliefs" and was duly convicted of contempt of Congress. The trial judge politely declined his offer to sing "Wasn't That a Time" before sentencing. Kaufman wrote for the court overturning the conviction because the indictment was technically deficient. He also made a broader point, echoing his recent speeches on lawyers' duty to represent communists: "We are not inclined to dismiss lightly claims of constitutional stature because they are asserted by one who may appear unworthy of sympathy. Once we embark upon shortcuts by creating a category of 'obviously guilty' whose rights are denied, we run the risk that the circle of the unprotected will grow." Freed to keep performing, Seeger became an icon to civil rights and Vietnam protesters, a Grammy winner, and a performer at President Obama's first inauguration.[2]

Over the next few years, Kaufman authored several other opinions against the government in criminal cases. Sometimes federal agents were too aggressive in searching or questioning suspects. Sometimes trial judges made mistakes, such as failing to give a required instruction to jurors that would have helped the defendant. In most of these cases, the decisions were unanimous. Kaufman was generally in the middle of the road in criminal cases. Then and now, the vast majority of convictions are affirmed, even by judges with liberal leanings, and Kaufman was no exception. In general, he tried to look past form to the substance of whether a defendant got a fair trial. For example, he upheld a drug dealer's conviction despite a single reference at trial to a question asked during an improper interrogation, lest the court "transform a meaningful expression of concern for the rights of the individual into a meaningless mechanism for the obstruction of justice." And he didn't require prosecutors to make a confidential informant available for cross-examination because his role was minor and the facts formed "a mosaic which, when looked at as a whole," showed a fair trial.[3]

Occasionally, the criminal appeals Kaufman heard sounded strange echoes from his past. In 1965, the full court decided an espionage case dimly reminiscent of 1951: the conviction of seaman Nelson Drummond for passing classified documents to Soviet handlers for $24,000. In a careful opinion, Kaufman rejected Drummond's challenge to the admissibility of his confession, given before the FBI permitted access to a lawyer, and his claim that, like the Rosenbergs, he had really been tried for treason instead of espionage. Drummond was the first African

American caught spying for the Russians, and his case offered a useful reminder to Kaufman's critics that Soviet intelligence operations were real and ongoing.[4]

A later case dove deeper into Kaufman's history, all the way back to his Brooklyn adolescence. The Borough Park neighborhood where Kaufman lived after his father's death began as a Jewish refuge from the Lower East Side and largely stayed that way. In the 1970s, it birthed the Jewish Defense League, a motley troupe devoted to the provocative idea that "if the Jew is kicked, he will kick back." Its leader was a young and charismatic rabbi with a law degree, Meir Kahane, whose knack for press coverage Kaufman might have admired. "We're frightened," Kahane fulminated, "so we're out to change the traditional image of the Jew as a patsy." As the writer Leon Wieseltier, an early member, observed, Kahane recruited "the Jews from the provinces, the not-so-prosperous Jews, the Jews with accents, the Jews in yarmulkes." Initially focused on local muggings and cemetery desecrations, the JDL pushed post-Holocaust angst and revenge-seeking in neighborhoods full of survivors and their descendants. Then there was "the class resentment of the lower-middle-class Jews in semidetached houses for the genteel Jews in buildings with doormen," as Wieseltier put it. Predictably, the Jewish establishment denounced the group as thugs inimical to the Jewish tradition. To Kahane, these court Jews were defined by the "be nice, Irving" mentality and the never-ending quest for "respectability." As a man who had named himself Irving, who wanted respectability more than anything and eagerly joined the establishment, and who wouldn't think of living in a building without a doorman, Kaufman seemed the very person Kahane was talking about.[5]

Before long, the JDL shifted from protecting old Jews in Brooklyn to the plight of Soviet Jewry. They disrupted a Russian pianist's concert at Carnegie Hall, bombed a Soviet trade office, and fired shots into the USSR's mission to the United Nations. On January 26, 1972, a smoke bomb went off in the midtown offices of a Jewish promoter who brought Russian acts like the Bolshoi Ballet to the United States. His accountant, also Jewish, suffocated. The JDL denied responsibility for this stunt gone awry, but no one was fooled. Three members were indicted for the young woman's murder.[6]

One of the men charged was a Borough Parker named Sheldon Seigel, and the lawyer he persuaded to take his case also grew up in the neighborhood—a then-unknown Harvard Law professor named Alan Dershowitz. Goaded by local and Jewish solidarity, Dershowitz reluctantly signed on, only to learn his client was a secret government informant pressured into selling out his friends by yet another son of Borough Park, New York City detective Santo Parola. Although Parola had assured Seigel he would never be outed, the government had no case without him. Federal prosecutors blithely reneged on Parola's promise and granted Seigel immunity for his part in the bombing in order to compel his public testimony. If he still refused, he could be jailed for contempt of court. Dreading identification as the neighborhood turncoat more than prison, Seigel begged Dershowitz to find a way out. The only hope was the law professor's discovery that the FBI had illegally tapped Seigel's phone and destroyed the recordings. If Dershowitz could show Seigel's agreement to testify stemmed from the government's illegal evidence-gathering, Seigel might walk. The trial judge rejected this gambit, but Dershowitz immediately appealed.

Once in the Second Circuit, Dershowitz hoped to avoid Kaufman. As someone charged with extra harshness toward his coreligionists in the Rosenberg case, Kaufman might repeat himself in a matter "involving the most notorious Jewish organization in the world. I was hoping for a panel of non-Jewish judges who could more easily remove themselves from the emotional component of the case." Still, one of the judges he got was Kaufman. Told of Kaufman's acerbic way with counsel, Dershowitz vowed to be ready and headed to the library to research his record. He was pleasantly surprised by what he found: a judge willing to free guilty defendants when the government broke the rules. "My reading of Judge Kaufman's court of appeals opinions gave me some encouragement. He was not a government man. . . . He was prepared—at least on occasion—to free obviously guilty criminals in order to enforce the principles of the Constitution." Dershowitz's spirits rose further at the argument when Kaufman homed in on the FBI's destruction of the wiretapping recordings—a fact barely covered in his brief.[7]

Two weeks later, Kaufman issued a startling opinion upbraiding his old ally, the FBI. Because agents had violated federal law by destroying the tapes, the government could never show Seigel's recruitment as an informant hadn't begun with his identification as a JDL bomber on the illegally recorded phone calls. Prosecutors stressed the FBI's supposed good faith about what the tapes would have showed, but Kaufman was skeptical: "Indeed, the government's good faith did not prevent illegal wiretapping." In later decisions, too, Kaufman would consistently enforce the wiretapping laws, recognizing their potential for abuse. "We can never acquiesce in a principle that condones lawlessness by law enforcers in the name of a just end."[8]

In Seigel and his ilk, Kaufman saw a familiar type. They too spurned the American dream, just like the Rosenbergs, though they'd fled in the opposite direction, toward militant Jewish nationalism. But Kaufman had no more use for the JDL's insular, Borough Park worldview than he had for Soviet-inspired communism. It was just that, by 1973, his fidelity to the Constitution exceeded his loathing of misguided *Landsmen* with a grudge against Park Avenue.

If Drummond and Seigel summoned old memories, Charles Freeman might have reminded him of more current difficulties at home. Freeman was a thirty-five-year-old heroin addict, also battered in the boxing ring, who suffered from seizures and hallucinations. Nabbed in a petty drug sting, he'd pleaded insanity but was convicted anyway. On appeal, his legal aid lawyers challenged the way federal courts defined mental illness for purposes of fixing criminal responsibility.[9]

That definition stretched back to Tudor England and the eighteenth century's "wild beast test," which freed a defendant if he "doth not know what he is doing, no more than an infant, than a brute or a wild beast." When a Scottish schizophrenic named Daniel M'Naghten shot the prime minister's private secretary in 1843, a jury acquitted based on a more enlightened definition of mental illness. But Queen Victoria, herself the target of assassination plots, summoned the judges of the House of Lords to reconsider. Their response became the "M'Naghten rule," which restored the traditional requirement that defendants prove their inability to distinguish right from wrong in order to be acquitted as criminally insane. The rule persisted in American courts despite decades of criticism. In 1929, Justice Benjamin Cardozo told New York's Academy of Medicine that the rule had "little relation to the truths of mental life" and "palters with reality," while Frankfurter called it "a sham." Nonetheless, the Supreme Court repeatedly ducked the issue, and only two lower federal courts and a few states abandoned M'Naghten for more up-to-date definitions of mental illness. Freeman lost in the trial court because he admitted, in effect, that he knew right from wrong—that is, that he understood he had been selling heroin and that doing so was illegal.[10]

Freeman's appellate lawyer was a twenty-six-year-old newbie at the Legal Aid Society whose boss tossed him the file and said "go change the law on insanity." Will Hellerstein thought the odds of that were so long that he didn't even lead with the issue in his brief. At argument, Kaufman began by asking Hellerstein whether he'd read a recent article in the Columbia alumni bulletin speculating that, if the test were liberalized, even well-heeled defendants in antitrust cases could claim insanity. Caught unawares, Hellerstein stalled and said he was a Harvard man and didn't read magazines from Columbia. The rest of the argument wasn't much easier, and Hellerstein wasn't exactly upbeat when he left the courthouse.[11]

He was in for a surprise. By the time Kaufman contemplated the life of Charles Freeman in 1965, he'd acquired his own bitterly earned understanding of mental illness, thanks to what one of his grandchildren called Helen's "demons." Nine years earlier, he'd written Lou Nichols at the FBI and commented, "Unfortunately, we are so slow in recognizing that mental sickness must be treated and cured just like any other sickness and while it may not carry the dramatic possibility of contagion as do other illnesses, it does carry with it the potentiality of wreaking great havoc." He knew that havoc firsthand, and he saw Freeman's appeal as an opportunity, he wrote later, "to test the strength of Victor Hugo's remark that there is nothing as powerful as an idea whose time has come." Nor did he hesitate to put that idea into practice. As Hellerstein put it, "You know the judge, when he wanted to do something, he did it."[12]

Kaufman's opinion began by recognizing that defining mental illness only as the inability to distinguish right from wrong stranded people like Freeman, who at least partially knew the difference but still couldn't control themselves. As a result, those with no true moral responsibility for their crimes were punished, which was barbarous. They also received no psychiatric care in prison, which was dangerous. Furthermore, psychiatrists complained that making them assess someone's sanity based only on the cognitive appreciation of right and wrong effectively required "professional perjury," as one put it. Above all, ignoring relevant and important scientific knowledge offended Kaufman's sense that that courts existed to render society's fair and correct judgment of the criminal. "Few areas of modern American culture—from the personnel offices of our giant corporations to the pages of our mass circulation magazines—have been untouched by the psychiatric revolution. In this setting, a test which depends vitally on notions already discredited when M'Naghten was adopted can no longer be blandly accepted as representing the 'moral sense of the community.' "

To solve the problem, Kaufman looked to a recent provision of the American Law Institute's Model Penal Code: "A person is not responsible for criminal conduct if at the time of such conduct as a result of mental disease or defect he lacks substantial capacity either to appreciate the wrongfulness of his conduct or to conform his conduct to the requirements of law." This new definition covered those with "substantial"—not just any, but also not necessarily total—inability to abide by the law rather than simply people who couldn't tell right from wrong. "Drawing upon the past," Kaufman concluded, "the law must serve—and traditionally has served—the needs of the present. The outrage of a frightened Queen has for too long caused us to forego the expert guidance that modern psychiatry is able to provide."[13]

Freeman was hailed as an important reform in all quarters, with the *New York Times* covering it on the front page and *Time* lauding Kaufman's opinion as "lucid" and "replete with psychiatric, legal and historical scholarship." Herbert Wechsler, then the ALI's director and one of the twentieth century's most influential legal scholars, wrote to say it would "rank in the most distinguished of judicial contributions to the rational humanization of our penal law"—perhaps not surprising praise since Kaufman had adopted the ALI's definition. Within a few years, all other federal courts of appeals also abandoned M'Naghten for one or another version of the ALI test, and states began changing their standards too. Warren Burger, then a judge on the DC Circuit, also wrote to commend Kaufman's "fine piece of work" and quoted the comedian Jimmy Durante in a postscript, leading Kaufman to respond somewhat insensitively: "I am all for Jimmy Durante becoming a member of this Court. . . . Can't you just hear him saying 'All dis bizness about the nuts is for the squirrels.' Now that we have got it all down to a mouthful of words, let us see what happens."[14]

While Kaufman's decisions in appeals from federal convictions generally put him in the middle of the spectrum, his liberalism stood out in another kind of criminal case: petitions from inmates languishing in state prisons who claimed their convictions violated the Constitution and wanted federal judges to set them free using the ancient and "great writ" of habeas corpus.

In Kaufman's first years on the Second Circuit, the Supreme Court was busy revising precedent in ways that benefited criminal defendants. Decisions expansively interpreted the Fourth, Fifth, and Sixth Amendments to limit the use of coerced confessions, exclude growing categories of illegally seized evidence, broaden suspects' right to counsel, ensure the voluntariness of guilty pleas, and more. While reforming federal criminal justice was one thing, the Court then went further and allowed *state* prisoners to claim the new protections through habeas corpus petitions to federal district court. Judges were instructed to hold evidentiary hearings and overturn convictions obtained in violation of the Constitution. In an article for the *Atlantic*, Kaufman called this new approach "almost revolutionary" and pinpointed its salient feature: "The institutional imperatives of federalism, which had traditionally dictated deference to the states in our system of dual sovereignty, have become subordinated to the moral imperatives of the Constitution."[15]

Elevating those moral imperatives over the old deference to police had its critics. Violent crime was slowly increasing, and conservative politicians like Barry Goldwater, the 1964 Republican presidential nominee, vilified Warren for "needlessly pampering" dangerous lawbreakers. Richard Nixon would do the same in 1968, with greater success. "Impeach Earl Warren" appeared on billboards and bumper stickers while the chief justice, usually loath to dignify criticism, wearily responded that constitutional rights "can never be compromised by shortcuts," and that "thinking people" knew the rise in crime was due to social factors, not court decisions. On the Court, Frankfurter and John Marshall Harlan, a New Yorker who had served on the Second Circuit for one year before Eisenhower promoted him, led the opposition and frequently dissented from rulings that expanded state defendants' rights and means of redress. Harlan was a mentor and old friend to Lumbard and Friendly, and they and Eisenhower's other New York appointee to the Second Circuit, Leonard Moore, mirrored his approach on the court of appeals. By contrast, the court's older and newer judges, including Kaufman, were more liberal and, by Kaufman's lights, more faithful to the Supreme Court's recent commands.[16]

Consequently, in two cases in 1963 and 1964, Kaufman voided the state conviction of a prisoner who claimed the judge bullied him into pleading guilty during an off-the-record conversation, and extended *Gideon v. Wainwright*, which guaranteed court-appointed lawyers to the indigent, to state prisoners who had pleaded guilty before the *Gideon* decision. He acknowledged the "deeply disturbing" prospect of having to revisit old state trials in these cases but saw no choice. Friendly and Lumbard dissented, with the *Times* proclaiming of the latter case, "Court Ruling May Free Thousands of Convicts."[17]

A case at the sunset of the Warren Court in 1969, *Ross v. McMann*, prompted the sharpest clash between Kaufman and the Eisenhower trio. A majority of the full court voted to grant evidentiary hearings to state prisoners who claimed their guilty pleas were tainted because their lawyers hadn't challenged prosecutors' plans to use their coerced confessions at trial. Faced with illegally obtained evidence, they argued, they'd had no choice but to plead guilty. Lumbard, Moore, and Friendly dissented acidly, each writing separate opinions. Lumbard urged that the guilty pleas were informed bargains that couldn't be reneged on years later and that, practically, retrials would be impossible. He closed with a broader *cri de cœur*: "I wish to be counted among those who do not think federal judges were ever meant to review every state criminal proceeding, or that there is any basis for supposing that they can reach a more just result than the state court judges. We would be well advised not to arrogate so much ultimate power to ourselves, as has been done by federal decisions the past six years, in the name of safeguarding constitutional rights, and to be chary of exercising such power except in the most compelling circumstances."

Separately, Friendly and Kaufman wrote opinions attacking each other. Friendly maintained the petitioners' pleas had been " 'voluntary' in the ordinary use of language" and that they might have pleaded guilty anyway, regardless of the tainted confessions. He added, "Men who first confess and then, on the advice of counsel, plead guilty to serious crimes, do so because they are." Kaufman's rejoinder was equally spirited and illustrated his evolution. "Notwithstanding the caustic tones" of Friendly's dissent, he began, the majority had not become "an ally of criminals, devoid of all interest in the community's safety and living insensitively in its ivory tower." Friendly's emphasis on the petitioners' supposed guilt was "gratuitous and irrelevant to the issue before us: whether the state procedures" were constitutional. What Friendly et al. really disliked was simply the price of progress: "Although our decisions may encourage some prisoners to file petitions wholly devoid of merit, the short answer to this is that most advances in the law have been subject to abuse. But, if this were to deter courts from doing what should be done, the law would remain stagnant."[18]

Ross typified Kaufman's view in major habeas appeals. He was willing to apply and extend the Warren Court's newly expanded constitutional protections to old state convictions despite the disruption of long-settled outcomes. Nor would he get sidetracked by the petitioner's guilt or innocence, noting in one opinion, "We cannot tolerate the debasement of the judicial process by preoccupation with a correct result." And he was dismissive of dire warnings that criminals would soon be running wild on city streets. Perhaps above all, Kaufman also correctly recognized that state and local police and prosecutors wouldn't independently change old and unfair practices. "The federal courts have been required to act," he wrote in 1965, "because the states have simply failed to meet their constitutional obligations." Until that changed, Kaufman believed, energetic federal supervision was both inevitable and justified. This view was fully in character. Friendly, Lumbard, and others weren't blind to the deficiency of particular state and local practices, they just denied federal responsibility or power to fix them. Kaufman saw the problem and, as always, wanted to do something about it.[19]

This spirit extended to prisons. Roy Schuster exhibited more textbook mental illness when he committed his crime than Charles Freeman had. In the 1920s, Schuster was a tap dancer on a par, he later claimed modestly, with Fred Astaire. Touring in Milwaukee, he met a pretty dancer and settled down. Then the Depression set in, his salary plunged, and life at home soured. Schuster's wife left and he responded by turning up the gas in his apartment and trying to kill himself. Later, at his wife's lawyer's office, he pulled a revolver and started shooting, killing his wife and wounding her lawyer. He fled into the street but his timing was poor; a police parade had just been postponed, and hundreds of officers were milling around. Schuster was quickly caught, convicted, and sentenced to twenty-five years to life. At trial, he'd claimed temporary mental "panic" and unawareness of what he was doing, while the state maintained he was perfectly sane. Before long, those positions would reverse.[20]

Schuster thrived behind bars. The furies that drove him to attempted suicide and murder passed. He starred in a prison show with Robert Gooding, a band leader convicted of having five wives. Schuster danced while Gooding crooned, "I suppose you wonder why all women fall for me." But Schuster started complaining about corruption at the prison and ignored clear warnings to hush. In 1941, after a single rigged interview with the prison doctor, he was shipped to the state mental hospital at Dannemora, declared insane.[21]

There, incredibly, he languished for twenty-eight years, trying time and again to convince a host of seemingly uninterested New York penal, medical, and judicial officers that the summary transfer had violated his rights and that he had no business being locked away in an asylum.

"Schuster, I can't find anything wrong with you," he claimed the hospital's doctor said when he arrived, but it didn't matter. In 1944, 1950, and 1960, state judges denied his habeas petitions. He would have become eligible for parole in 1948, but inmates committed to Dannemora were never paroled, out of misguided fear for public safety. In 1961, Governor Nelson Rockefeller turned down a request for executive intercession. In 1962, Schuster lost in state court again. All the while, he received no psychiatric care, though he was supposedly ill. Everyone agreed he behaved well and wasn't dangerous. Still, he was often confined to a straight-back chair for hours on end, and other inmates were kicked and beaten for minor infractions. "Although called a 'hospital,'" one New York court soberly recognized, Dannemora "was essentially a prison with facilities for controlling psychotic convicts . . . men living without hope, sitting day in and day out in a big room looking at each other."[22]

In 1963, the state ordered a hearing, but the state psychiatrist said Schuster was incurably paranoid. Perversely, Schuster's stubborn insistence that he'd been wronged and was actually sane became the very basis for his confinement. Perhaps there *had* been prison corruption back in 1941, as Schuster claimed, but the prison's psychiatrist decided that anyone who thought they'd actually been punished for complaining about it had to be delusional. Schuster was barely allowed to speak at the hearing and was denied yet again. Finally, he petitioned a federal court. This time, he had energetic ACLU lawyers in his corner and a doctor who testified he was perfectly sane. He still lost.[23]

Unlike the phalanx of state and federal judges who did nothing for Roy Schuster, Kaufman had no trouble seeing, as he wrote, the "forgotten man in a mental institution which has nothing to offer him," and the "terrifying possibility that the transferred prisoner may not be mentally ill at all." The state argued that Schuster's removal to Dannemora was unimportant, merely the substitution of one kind of detention for another, but Kaufman recognized the obvious difference: "Confined with those who are insane, told repeatedly that he too is insane and indeed treated as insane, it does not take much for a man to question his own sanity and in the end to succumb to some mental aberration." In reality, Schuster had been "marooned and forsaken," and possibly robbed of two decades of freedom, since he might have been paroled in 1948. In legal terms, Kaufman decided that the cursory way Schuster had been committed in 1941 violated his constitutional right to equal protection under the law because far greater procedural safeguards had been given civilians facing involuntary commitment to mental hospitals. Kaufman's decision therefore ordered that criminally convicted prisoners receive these protections too, including a jury trial on their sanity, regular evaluation after commitment, and other measures. Schuster was to get his hearing within sixty days. Moore, allergic to almost any intrusion into state criminal justice decision making, dissented.[24]

Kaufman expected his decision would quickly end Schuster's nightmare. The man was plainly well and harmless; he would be transferred back to a normal prison and paroled in a few weeks. And Kaufman was pleased with his opinion, drafted after much back-and-forth with his clerk Jack Auspitz. When *Times* publisher Punch Sulzberger sent him a copy of the paper's favorable coverage, Kaufman thanked him but couldn't help noting how "unfortunate" it was that a previous edition had only carried a shorter version, since "it was a decision of some importance and already has become the subject of much discussion by bench and bar." The following year, the DC Circuit adopted his reasoning and also required parallel safeguards for civil and criminal commitment. As time went on, other courts took different routes to ensure more robust review before someone could simply be shuttled from a prison to a mental hospital.[25]

Bizarrely, though, the Schuster case was far from over. Rather than hold his hearing within sixty days, Dannemora officials dickered with him over where it would be held and found other reasons for delay. Then Schuster was suddenly and unilaterally declared cured and transferred to a regular prison. Though this was what he'd wanted, he was incensed. The hearing had been his chance to show he was sane and that his transfer to Dannemora had been a cruel fraud, and now they had taken that from him, too. A few months later, he filed into a parole hearing for the first time since 1948, but instead of cooperating, he demanded immediate and unconditional release, not the usual five-year period of supervision by parole officers. They had conspired in his detention all these years, he explained, and were "not morally fit to supervise anyone, certainly not me." Nor did he bother feigning contrition for his long-ago murder, claiming his only crime had actually been "coming home and catching my wife for the sixth time in the act of adultery and kicking her out instead of shooting her which is the usual practice." When he *did* shoot her, he allowed, he was just "a young fellow" who "finally blew my top. I hadn't done anything wrong, why should I be penalized?" Parole was denied, as it was again in 1973 and 1974, though frustrated state officials eventually offered the most minimally restrictive post-release oversight as a way to get rid of him once and for all. But still Schuster said no, vowing to die behind bars if necessary. And he went back to federal court.[26]

This time, Kaufman was merciless. His clerk, Michael Tabak, told him they were stuck, given Schuster's rejection of the legally prescribed conditions of parole. Kaufman wasn't hearing it. "I don't care what you have to come up with, we have to find a way to let this guy out. He's not staying in jail at all." Stumped, Tabak called Louis Pollak, his old law professor at Penn. Soon to be a district judge in his own right, Pollak came up with the answer: Schuster would be deemed "constructively paroled" in 1969, meaning that any five-year oversight period had already expired. There was no precedent, exactly, for "constructive parole," but Pollack's device did the trick. For good measure, Kaufman blasted the state's "total callousness to the ordinary decency due every human" and its "Tartuffian self-righteousness. . . . We can no longer sit by and permit the State to continue toying with Roy Schuster's freedom."[27]

Three days later, on September 26, 1975, Schuster walked out of Green Haven penitentiary with prison-issued clothes and forty dollars in cash. Seventy years old, frail and down to 108 pounds, he'd last seen New York City in the Depression. "From what I can gather it has changed quite a bit," he said tentatively, "for the worse." As for the future, tap dancing was out, and anyway "I'm more of the retiring type now. I'm not looking for glamour." But still he felt cheated. "I would feel good if I knew I had been completely exonerated, not of the crime of murder, but that I was crazy." Kaufman hadn't done that, but at least he'd been willing to look past dubious psychiatric reports and the ever-present temptation to defer to prison administrators and free a man who, however stubborn and remorseless, had been thrown away and forgotten by the state.[28]

The Attica prison revolt and its savage suppression in 1971 claimed forty-three lives. Packed into decaying and overcrowded buildings, stuffed into tiny cells, permitted only weekly showers, barely paid for forced labor, fed on sixty-three cents a day, deprived of meaningful education and drug programs, sick from poor medical care, and subject to constant racial harassment, the mostly young and minority inmates seethed and then blew. As the state commission formed to investigate the uprising concluded, "The only way to salvage meaning out of the otherwise senseless killings at Attica is to learn from this experience that our Atticas are failures."[29]

Kaufman already knew that, and after Attica he became even less indulgent of state prison officials. Earlier decisions had been mixed. He'd struck down Clinton State Prison's infamous "strip cell," where prisoners disciplined for infractions huddled naked in winter, ate from a bowl on the concrete floor, and were prevented from sleeping. On the other hand, he voided a trial judge's ruling limiting solitary confinement to fifteen days in the case of Martin Sostre, a longtime prison activist. Although Kaufman condemned the practice, he doubted it was uniformly "cruel *and unusual*" under the Constitution because most prisons used it, and its use and effects varied from case to case. To this day, no court has invalidated solitary confinement across the board, despite its well-documented harmfulness.[30]

After Attica, though, Kaufman hoped judges were "confident enough of their role as guardians of basic rights to recognize that human dignity demands more than mere freedom from a bestial, subhuman existence." He certainly was. In a 1972 speech at Fordham, he commended decisions ordering better diets, more exercise, and mental health treatment, and predicted more judicial intervention in prisons if states continued to lag. The *Daily News* praised him for avoiding "the wishful thinking and slobbering sentimentality the subject too often evokes." Better still, the editor of the *Stafford Sunblaze*, published by federal inmates in Arizona, wrote with congratulations and an offer of a subscription.[31]

His subsequent decisions almost always sided with inmates. When the court considered an appeal that presented the mirror image of *Schuster*—did inmates who became mentally ill in prison and were sent to mental hospitals deserve protections before being returned to prison?—Kaufman dissented from the majority's decision denying the patients due process. He believed the facts showed "an almost sadistic propensity" by state psychiatrists and administrators to retaliate against difficult patients who broke the rules by shunting them back to regular prisons. In another case, Kaufman found that a raft of deficient medical procedures in prison constituted cruel and unusual punishment.[32]

Other decisions faulted prison discipline. When an inmate was transferred to a facility farther from home in retaliation for protesting limits on his jailhouse lawyering, Kaufman referenced 1971: "One scarcely needs to be reminded of the sad events at Attica prison three years ago to understand the explosive potential flowing from the lamentable conditions which confront many prisoners." Prisons could quickly transfer men to avoid riots, Kaufman conceded, but not to exact vengeance, and not without a hearing. In a different case, he protested a decision transferring inmates to punishment cells without due process.[33]

Finally, the court confronted conditions at a grossly overcrowded federal jail attached to the courthouse in Manhattan, the Metropolitan Correctional Center, or "MCC," which held people charged with crimes but not yet tried. Such pretrial detainees were still presumed innocent and therefore had greater rights. Kaufman criticized aspects of the lower court's order for failing "to reserve the judge's awesome power and authority for matters of substance, not to be diminished by triflings," but he upheld the more serious changes. These included limits on the number of inmates in a room and greater access to reading material, mail, and counsel. Most importantly, he upheld the district judge's order ending automatic body cavity searches of all inmates after every meeting with a visitor, finding them "degrading and humiliating."[34]

The MCC case, decided in 1979, completed Kaufman's transformation from the man willing to condemn a young mother to death on scant evidence to the man so acutely concerned for the welfare of common prisoners that he zealously safeguarded their magazines and sleeping space. Almost thirty years separate the two men, and the earlier judge might not have recognized the later.

Kaufman also made important contributions to the modernization and liberalization of criminal law off the bench. In 1966, Chief Justice Warren chose him to lead a previously dormant committee of federal judges charged with examining the jury system. Not surprisingly, its lassitude was soon a thing of the past. In most districts, clerks used the antiquated "key man" system to pick so-called blue-ribbon juries. That is, they privately asked well-connected friends and associates to serve, and bring their buddies with them. One court relied heavily on rosters from local Harvard and Yale clubs. Whole social groups—minorities, women, poor people—were often left out. As a result, federal juries were "predominantly middle-aged, middle class and middle minded," Kaufman wrote. The Johnson administration had promoted a bill to choose jurors from voter rolls as part of its civil rights program, but it died in a Senate filibuster. Kaufman and clerk Robert Freedman helped draft a more flexible substitute, and Kaufman testified before Congress to promote it. In 1968, Congress passed Kaufman's bill, one of the most significant reforms in the history of federal jury selection. Newspapers celebrated the overdue change, and a colleague on his committee praised Kaufman as its "chief architect" and the "virtual father of the present system."[35]

Criminal sentencing was another area of interest, perhaps understandably after the events of 1951–53. As the Second Circuit's chief judge in the 1970s, Kaufman created a committee to address irrational differences in sentences imposed by different judges for the same crime. Often these disparities seemed to turn on the defendant's race, means, location, and quality of counsel. The *Times*, which had uncovered substantial variances in a 1972 study, rewarded Kaufman's initiative with a front page article and editorial. His committee formulated a pilot project to supply trial judges with "benchmark" sentences for particular crimes, with any divergences requiring explanation. Defense counsel would also now take more of a hand in preparing presentence reports, the court would hold sentencing conferences, and judges would explain the grounds for their sentencing decisions. The aim was "greater openness, fairness and certainty," Kaufman said. All but one district court in the circuit agreed to use the new system, which prefigured federal legislation in 1984 establishing mandatory sentencing guidelines throughout the country. Ultimately, those guidelines would be praised for increasing uniformity but denounced for leading to unnecessarily harsh and rigid outcomes, particularly in drug cases that disproportionately penalized African Americans.[36]

Kaufman's most important extrajudicial contribution to criminal law involved juvenile justice—a field he first encountered in two cases challenging harsh and irrational aspects of New York's system. The first of these, in 1971, struck down the state's "wayward minor" statute, a 1923 law that allowed judges to incarcerate anyone between sixteen and twenty-one found to be "morally depraved" or even "in danger of becoming morally depraved," whatever that meant. Teens were shut away in adult prisons for up to three years for disobeying social workers, running away from home, premarital sex, and other perceived lapses that weren't crimes. Finding the term "morally depraved" to be unconstitutionally vague, Kaufman invalidated the law and freed two hundred minors. "The law permitted punishment as if they were criminals," he told *Time*, adding, "The state will simply have to find different ways to treat these youths. Foster homes, halfway houses—but not penal institutions."

The second case, in 1974, remedied an equally flagrant injustice: a state law consigning minors to prison terms for misdemeanors like shoplifting, parole violations, and loitering that were much longer than the maximums imposed on adults. Originally, the children had been sent to reform schools for indeterminate terms of special rehabilitation. Then the state closed the schools and simply dumped the occupants in adult prisons without reducing the sentences.[37]

Shortly before the 1971 case, Kaufman agreed to chair a committee to study the juvenile justice system, widely thought to be a failure given skyrocketing rates of juvenile crime, mishandled cases of parental abuse, and gross underfunding and inattention. The project originated with the Institute for Judicial Administration at NYU Law School, where Kaufman somehow found time to serve as president and executive committee chairman. In 1973, the American Bar Association joined the effort, which became the "IJA-ABA Joint Commission on Juvenile Justice Standards." Thirty-five eminent judges, lawyers, psychiatrists, sociologists, juvenile and family court officials, and penologists ultimately served as commissioners, with over two hundred more performing research and other roles. For five years, Kaufman chaired periodic three-day sessions to review and debate volumes of standards governing one or another topic prepared by an academic expert and then vetted by "drafting committees." The commission then revised and approved twenty-three volumes of standards.[38]

The standards embodied wide-ranging reforms to be implemented by state legislatures and courts, since federal law rarely affected minors. In criminal cases, first offenders would be diverted out of the justice system. There would be less pretrial detention and more basic due process, such as probable cause hearings, counsel, and six-member juries. The goal was to professionalize juvenile proceedings, curtailing some of the judges' previous wide and paternalistic discretion. Juvenile court judges would now have to give reasons for their dispositions and use fixed sentences, never longer than two years, based on the crime and the child's history. When incarcerated, minors should receive the educational and vocational services always promised but rarely implemented, though the most violent sixteen- and seventeen-year-olds could be transferred to adult courts and prisons. The standards also proposed eliminating "status offenses" of the sort Kaufman struck down in his 1971 decision—truancy, morals violations, and the like—handing such issues to new community-based youth agencies for crisis intervention, therapy, and job training. The commission also delineated the rights of children aside from their parents, such as to medical care and the ability to work, and specified children's rights in school. In a front page story quoting Kaufman at length, the *Times* praised all these measures as "radical changes."[39]

The first step in getting the standards into statute books was adoption by the full ABA, which demanded much lobbying on Kaufman's part. "During the last seven years," he said in a speech to the organization's House of Delegates, "I have devoted more time to this project than to any other endeavor in almost thirty years as a federal judge." An association of juvenile court judges offered the strongest opposition, but as they were the mainstays of the current system, their hostility had been expected. In 1979 and 1980, the House approved twenty volumes of the standards. The volume withdrawing juvenile court jurisdiction over noncriminal "status offenses" was narrowly defeated, however, while two others finalized later were never submitted for approval (relating to school discipline and student rights, and parental abuse and separation proceedings). By then, the project was out of funding. Still, Kaufman was "exultant" with what was almost a total triumph, a decade in the making. "For the first time now, you have a model for a juvenile justice system," he crowed justifiably.[40]

In the ensuing decades, however, the standards, intended as a full and comprehensive guide with interdependent parts, languished. They were instead adopted piecemeal by certain states, while complementary recommendations were ignored. The Reagan administration withdrew federal support from a planned effort to lobby state governments, and budget cuts, along with a general toughening of attitudes toward crime in the 1980s and 1990s, limited acceptance of the standards' more socially liberal provisions. Contrary to the commission's recommendation, children were transferred to adult courts at younger and younger ages.

Nevertheless, some state courts effectively implemented the standards through supervisory judicial decisions. Trends promoted by the standards and increasingly accepted by states included greater counsel for minors, sentencing reforms, and more lenient and community-based incarceration. As two commentators wrote in 2014, "although the project did not precipitate a juvenile justice 'revolution,' the inherent validity of the standards have greatly contributed to the development of juvenile justice."[41]

Chapter 12

Hippieland

One day in 1969, Simon Rifkind stood before an audience of lawyers who belonged to the American Jewish Committee and heaped scorn on the Age of Aquarius.

"Our generation, currently in command, is on the defensive," he started. "It admits its guilt, often and loudly. It confesses its hypocrisy; it acknowledges its lack of integrity; it acknowledges that it has utterly failed, that it has made no contribution, that it has lived in utter darkness. Only the young rebels, it is asserted, have glimpsed the light." This disgusted him. After all, he noted, his generation had beaten the Depression and fascism, ended segregation, cured disease, and sent men to the moon. "Have the principles we have lived by really proved so utterly faulty?" Then he turned to America's youth. Many were "earnest, intelligent, well-informed, thoughtful," he conceded, probably thinking of the clean-cut associates at his law firm. But there were also the other kind: "the exhibitionists, the impudent loudmouths, the stone-throwers, the window-smashers." They had brought on "a period of foolishness like in the days of the Children's Crusade in the Thirteenth Century. *Now it is time to stop the nonsense.*" By this he meant the ceaseless attacks on institutions; the flirtation with violence; the "life of the scavenger pigeon . . . that is, to sleep where you pause, to feed on the bread others have labored to produce, and to practice none of the arts of civilization except the art of self-indulgence." He ended defiantly: "I do not believe that the way to paradise is through the jungle of Hippieland."[1]

Ten years younger than his eminent friend, Kaufman might have been expected to agree. He could only have been dumbstruck by young adults who thoroughly rejected a system he'd worked so perfectly. In a letter to New York's master builder Robert Moses, he panned the " 'youth must be served' vogue"—though he simultaneously couldn't resist touting Fordham students' good sense in choosing himself for an award as proof that "the 'generation gap' did not prevent the young rebels from picking this old guy." Certainly Kaufman didn't know any hippies; his sons were too old and busy beavering away in finance, while his career-minded young law clerks were as far from the counterculture as possible. And he wondered how their problems got to federal court; "I have now been at it for 22 years," he wrote Grace Mayes, wife of the magazine editor and writer Herbert Mayes, "and I must say that we never before were required to deal with possible constitutional violations because of restraints on the length of hair or the publication of a school newspaper, etc." Yet despite all this, when their cases showed up, Kaufman saw only the principles—not the off-putting litigants or their crunchy public-interest lawyers. And the hippies almost invariably won his vote.[2]

No cause animated Hippieland like Vietnam, and like most judges of his time, Kaufman repeatedly confronted cases arising out of the divisive war. The most famous of these concerned a man whose views about war predated the morass in Southeast Asia, though the significance of his case was magnified by it.

Dan Seeger had been raised a devout Catholic in a politically conservative home during the patriotic upsurge of World War II. Two uncles were priests and he'd been educated by nuns, but he "dropped out of Roman Catholicism" in college and started reading Thoreau and Dewey and Gandhi. Once Seeger's student deferment from the draft expired in 1957, he got a form for conscientious objectors and saw the question "Do you believe in a Supreme Being?" Under federal law, only those with "a relation to a Supreme Being involving duties superior to those arising from any human relation" qualified for conscientious objection. The form had boxes to check for "yes" and "no," but Seeger added a third labeled "please see attached pages" and included what he later called "an eight-page essay on the knowability and unknowability of God, but [which] claimed to have a religious sort of concern for peace and non-violence."

This attempt to duck the problem failed, however, and Seeger was ordered to report for duty. Instead, a friend told him about the Quakers, and Seeger made his way to their small office over a barbershop on Third Avenue. He became a test case for their belief that pacifists who were agnostic or atheist deserved the same treatment as more traditional believers. Although they recruited an accomplished lawyer and established a defense fund, they lost the first round when the district judge gave Seeger a year and a day in prison. The case then moved upstairs, and like other civil libertarians over the next few years who knew Kaufman only from the Rosenberg saga, Seeger "was not thrilled at all to find him on my case." That quickly changed, he admitted. "Judge Kaufman wrote an opinion that astounded everybody."

That opinion began with first principles the Warren Court had only recently confirmed in decisions striking down school prayer and burdens on employment: the government had to be neutral toward religion and couldn't favor one sect over another. Yet the Selective Service law inherently preferred theistic religions to faiths like "Buddhism, Taoism, Ethical Culture and Secular Humanism [that] do not teach a belief in the existence of a Supreme Being." Given Seeger's long missive to the draft board, there was no denying his spirituality, even if he was agnostic. And as Kaufman recognized, Seeger's brand of college-inspired faith was more and more common: "For many in today's 'skeptical generation,' just as for Daniel Seeger, the stern and moral voice of conscience occupies that hallowed place in the hearts and minds of men which was traditionally reserved for the commandments of God." The law therefore violated the constitutional guarantee of equal protection of the law by discriminating among faiths and disadvantaging draftees like Seeger.

Although his ruling extended protection to an agnostic, Kaufman closed with the same muscular use of God as in his Rosenberg denunciations. He might also have wanted to inoculate himself politically for helping out draft-dodging atheists, a point noticed by *Time* ("Lest its ruling be considered antireligious, the court took care to point out . . ."). "Dedication to the freedom of the individual," Kaufman wrote, "of which our Bill of Rights is the most eloquent expression, is in large measure the result of the nation's religious heritage. Indeed, we here respect the right of Daniel Seeger to believe what he will largely because of the conviction that every individual is a child of God; and that Man, created in the image of his Maker, is endowed for that reason with human dignity." Thus Kaufman deftly credited the deity when relieving Seeger and others like him of the obligation to believe in one.[3]

The opinion was widely noticed—"you made every newspaper in the country," one colleague gushed—including in his favorite place: page one of the *Times*. The outcome "seems to us humane and enlightened reason as well as sound constitutional law," the editors added a few days later. New York City's Unitarian Universalists gave Kaufman their Thomas Jefferson Award "for conspicuous service in the cause of religious liberty." Meanwhile Seeger "trott[ed] around to all the studios," as he put it, and appeared on television talk shows with Basil Rathbone and Phyllis Diller. A unanimous Supreme Court upheld Kaufman but on more technical grounds and dodged the constitutional question he had decided. Seeger thought the opinion "forced" and nowhere near Kaufman's "brilliant and wonderful decision." Congress eventually removed all reference to a "Supreme Being" in the law, and the military's official guidance now says that "beliefs which qualify a registrant for CO status may be religious in nature, but don't have to be."[4]

Issued in January 1964, Kaufman's *Seeger* decision had little immediate impact. But five weeks after the Supreme Court affirmed him the next year, approximately twenty thousand marchers thronged the Washington Monument, where the last speaker, from a little-known group called Students for a Democratic Society, closed by pledging to "build a movement that will find ways to support the increasing numbers of young men who are unwilling to and will not fight in Vietnam." And so they did. Conscientious objection soared over the next few years until, by 1972, more men were exempted than inducted. Many fit themselves into the broader definition of conscience endorsed by Kaufman. As for Seeger, who went on to a long career promoting nonviolence and social justice, he wrote in 2017 that "to this day, I still meet people who, when they've learned my name, exclaim that my case was the reason they did not have to go to Vietnam, or to jail, or to Canada."[5]

Kaufman faced more draft-related cases as the war progressed, and he routinely sided against the government he had once favored heavily in national security matters. He approved late-blooming claims of pacifism asserted just before induction, though the military and some other judges tended to see these declarations as just a convenient way to dodge service. The Supreme Court later reversed him and upheld regulations making it harder for men who didn't announce their objections after first being ordered to report. Kaufman was similarly willing to expand habeas corpus beyond convicted criminals to a naval reservist who sought release from the "custody" of military service. Dissenting, Friendly called this "civil interference with the military." When two Second Circuit colleagues upheld a draftee's conviction for refusing to report despite his claim of suffering from LSD flashbacks—he had a supporting letter from a psychologist but lacked required documentation from a "doctor of medicine"—Kaufman dissented and claimed the army was so flouting "common sense and sound public policy as to be wholly unreasonable." It was 1972, and Kaufman added a plaintive note: "We are told in the press that the war hopefully is drawing to a close (and with it the draft, the press optimistically adds), holding out the hope that cases of this type will not long continue to vex our judicial system."[6]

Kaufman's solicitude went beyond servicemen to protesters. As the war escalated, it careened into America's schools. In 1969, Charles James was teaching eleventh-graders near the city of Elmira, New York. When Vietnam opponents declared two "moratorium days," James, a Quaker like Seeger, tied some black silk from J. C. Penny around his sleeve before going to school. It seemed "a very small way to protest," he said. Deciding James had injected politics into class, though James himself made clear his act was religious rather than political and that he was simply "against killing," the school board fired him. Job-like misery ensued. He was blackballed from other teaching positions and ended up on food stamps. His wife, herself a Quaker, began to doubt whether the sacrifice was worth it. There were dirty looks in town and denunciations on local radio. "I just assumed that I had some kind of right to express my conscience," he remembered later, sadly, after years of ostracism and privation. Ironically, few students had even understood James's act; people in Elmira mostly supported the war, and students assumed protests were limited to the unpatriotic hippies on TV.[7]

Susan Russo also taught high school in upstate New York in 1969. While Charles James didn't see his protest as political, Russo looked at America and decided she couldn't abide the pledge of allegiance students recited in her class every morning. The line "and liberty and justice for all" struck her as obvious hypocrisy. Rather than mouth falsehoods, she faced the flag silently, arms at her side. Unlike in Elmira, though, students at Russo's high school had started to speak out about the war, and the school board tried to defuse tension by allowing objectors to sit during the pledge. It had to backtrack, however, when 350 people appeared at a school board meeting with a petition reading

"You Don't Stand for the Flag!!! We won't stand for the Budget!!!" In this atmosphere, Russo stood little chance; nonconforming students had to be managed somehow, but teachers could just be fired. "I never assumed that it would bother anyone," she said of her mute protest. Like James, she was fired, then blackballed.[8]

The James and Russo appeals reached the Second Circuit within a few months of each other in 1972. In both cases, the same elderly, unsympathetic district judge issued terse decisions upholding the terminations. Only three years earlier, the Supreme Court had decided that Des Moines high school students couldn't be suspended for wearing black armbands to protest Vietnam—the same symbol worn by Charles James. As for the pledge, an even more famous case decided during World War II had ordered states to stop forcing Seventh-day Adventist children to recite it while saluting the flag with a stiff-armed gesture many thought akin to what was happening in Hitler's Germany. Did these decisions protect teachers, or only students? No court of appeals had spoken yet.[9]

James's lawyer was Burt Neuborne, then a young New York Civil Liberties Union lawyer who would go on to be the ACLU's national legal director and a renowned constitutional litigator. He recognized that teachers presented a harder case than students. Their protests and symbols were likely to influence students more than speech from classmates. And personally, Neuborne didn't like the idea of teachers brainwashing captive kids. Before he took the case, he went to Elmira and interviewed ten of James's students until he satisfied himself that they hadn't felt pressured. As expected, New York argued in both cases that armbands and pledge boycotts communicated an antiwar message despite teachers' obligation to stay neutral and cover all sides of political topics.[10]

At argument, Neuborne found Kaufman "annoyed at everybody," a familiar posture. He immediately voiced the Achilles' heel in James's case, asking, "You don't really think that teachers and students are the same here?" Neuborne was ready. He emphasized the fact-specific, contextual nature of the problem and admitted that teachers' freedom of speech could be restricted if they coerced students. The school district's lawyer lacked Neuborne's dexterity, and Kaufman let him have it. He was furious at the ordeal James was enduring over such mild-mannered dissent. "And the principal did this to the family," Kaufman asked incredulously, "knowing it would have this effect?" When Kaufman asked whether the school would fire James if he wore a black tie instead of an armband, and the district's lawyer enthusiastically answered "yes," Kaufman looked like he might laugh. Eventually he swiveled around behind the bench and stopped listening.[11]

Kaufman wrote both decisions for unanimous panels, and both vindicated teachers' freedom of expression as long as they didn't disrupt order or learning. Schools couldn't "arbitrarily censor a teacher's speech merely because they do not agree with the teacher's political philosophies or leanings," Kaufman held in *James*. In *Russo*, he was more eloquent:

> Patriotism, particularly at a time when that virtuous quality appears much maligned, should not be the object of derision. But patriotism that is forced is a false patriotism just as loyalty that is coerced is the very antithesis of loyalty. . . .
>
> To compel a person to speak what is not in his mind offends the very principles of tolerance and understanding which for so long have been the foundation of our great land.

The decisions weren't absolute. Both stressed that the teachers hadn't caused a disturbance or tried to indoctrinate students; that schools retained broad power to ensure order, shape curriculum, and inculcate patriotism; and that older students were involved. In *Russo*, Kaufman felt compelled to add "we do not share her views." Nevertheless, unpopular speech like Russo's was protected, too. Ruth Bader Ginsburg, then a Columbia Law School professor, wrote Kaufman to say she considered *James* a "shining example of how the good judge thinks and acts."[12]

James and Russo eventually received awards of back pay and, after more bruising litigation, finally went back to teaching at different schools. But for James, especially, the damage couldn't be undone. His wife eventually left him, and "his family just disintegrated," Neuborne remembered; "it was tragic." Even the Quakers shunned him, thinking he'd made something of an idol out of the black armband. And the patriotic ire continued. "I thought he was a Communist three years ago," one woman in Elmira told a reporter, "and I still say he is, no matter what the court says." Russo got a letter calling her "a dog. One our country can do without." She resurfaced, though, when pro athletes starting kneeling during the national anthem in 2016. "These are quiet and personal protests over what is still not right in this country," she reaffirmed four decades after her own battle, "and if we don't know that now, then we are blind."[13]

There was only one thing Kaufman wouldn't do for Vietnam opponents and that was end the war itself. Throughout the conflict, soldiers brought lawsuits urging courts to declare the war or specific offensives illegal because Congress hadn't declared war, as required by the Constitution. Kaufman declined the invitation. "Judges, deficient in military knowledge, lacking vital information upon which to assess the nature of battlefield decisions, and sitting thousands of miles from the field of action," couldn't evaluate facts best left to political leaders and military commanders, he wrote in one opinion. Neuborne, who argued these cases too, gave Kaufman credit for not simply dismissing the soldiers' arguments out of hand. Kaufman was "more troubled than I think he expected to be," Neuborne recalled. In 1973, Neuborne did manage to convince a district judge in Brooklyn to enjoin the unauthorized bombing of Cambodia, but the Second Circuit blocked the ruling two days later. Neuborne then flew to Yakima, Washington, to try to persuade Justice Douglas to undo the Second Circuit's order. In the middle of his argument, Douglas asked if Neuborne remembered what had happened twenty years before. By this Douglas meant the Rosenberg case, when he had enjoined the executions Kaufman ordered only to be reversed by his colleagues the next day. Once again, as in June 1953, Douglas issued an injunction and was almost immediately countermanded by the full Court. The bombing, like the executions, proceeded.[14]

The source of Kaufman's hostility to the government in Vietnam-era cases is murky. It fit his growing liberalism but also recalled his stint as an appeal agent for a draft board in World War II, when he had been praised for his fairness and refusal to "run 'rough shod'" over young men's claims for exemption. Some federal judges began dropping the traditional mask of judicial inscrutability as the casualties mounted. A district judge in Kaufman's circuit, John Curtin in Buffalo, gave a speech charging the war with turning "all our best ideals to dust. . . . Let us think less of losing a war and more about human life." This was nothing compared to Kaufman's colleague on the Fourth Circuit, J. Braxton Craven, who publicly denounced Vietnam as "a monstrous, muddleheaded, pridefully aggressive, immorally jingoistic crime against humanity." Kaufman was more circumspect. Years later he wrote simply that "every American citizen had his or her own view on the war in Vietnam [and] judges were no exception."[15]

Kaufman might have eschewed public comment on the war, but more personal reckoning was unavoidable. In the late 1950s and 1960s, his children and law clerks were of age to be drafted, and Kaufman had to either act or refrain from acting on their behalf. Although the federal courts had a general rule that serving as a law clerk didn't qualify eligible men for deferments, Kaufman decided otherwise. Through the years, he repeatedly wrote draft boards to postpone or prevent his clerks' military service, claiming they were essential federal personnel despite the larger policy. When it came to his son Bob, Maxine Berman, his wife, recalled Kaufman asking his old friend Senator Tom Dodd to intervene and maneuver Bob out of the basic training he'd begun. Dodd "got Bobby out," she said, and Kaufman's oldest son was "thrilled" to be back in civvies. When Dodd was later investigated for violating tax laws, Bob and Berman "were really afraid that there were going to be some papers that would show that he got Bobby out of the army." No document confirms Berman's story, but Kaufman did have a history of asking Dodd for special favors. In 1964, Dodd lobbied the State Department and Immigration Service to grant a waiver allowing a Finnish nurse who was helping his nephew Herb in his academic research to stay in the country. The effort required multiple contacts and enlistment of another senator's help, but it proved successful, though Dodd had warned that such waivers presented "the toughest cases" at the State Department. Herb later married the nurse. Contending with the draft wasn't needed for the twins, who were medically exempt. Whether Kaufman skirted any rules in guiding his son and law clerks away from military service can't be known; at the least, he seems to have obtained special treatment as a result of his unique position. Above all, he clearly didn't see going to Vietnam as essential or worthwhile—a position many Americans came to share.[16]

The year after his decision desegregating New Rochelle schools, Kaufman addressed lawyers in Connecticut and spoke of their professional brethren twelve hundred miles away. Two weeks before, it had taken three thousand federal troops to register James Meredith for classes at Ole Miss over the die-hard resistance of the governor and most of the state's political and legal establishment. The ensuing riot killed two people. To Kaufman, the debacle in Mississippi represented the same kind of failure as when unpopular criminal defendants and communists couldn't find lawyers. Whatever their views on integration, he argued, attorneys were duty-bound to serve "a cause well beyond the merely personal—it is the cause of equal justice for all and of fidelity to law. . . . The bloodshed and injuries stemming from that grave controversy might well have been avoided if these leaders of the bar, the Governor among them, had learned the lesson I have tried to emphasize."[17]

As events in Mississippi illustrated, Vietnam wasn't the only source of strife in the hippie years. The drive to right the wrongs of entrenched discrimination accelerated, and litigation over schools, housing programs, employment, and other issues regularly reached the Second Circuit. Often such cases turned on access to federal court in the first place, before charges of bias could even be considered, and with a few early exceptions Kaufman was generous in opening the courthouse doors. When poor Black residents of Westchester County sued federal agencies for awarding grants for new sewers and parks to a wealthy, mostly white town, a majority of the full Second Circuit found that the plaintiffs were barred from federal court because they hadn't suffered a legally cognizable injury. They didn't live in the town that received the grants, hadn't been denied housing there, and didn't claim they should have gotten the money. With three other judges, Kaufman dissented. It was enough, they wrote, that the plaintiffs claimed the town practiced discriminatory zoning, and that the grants would perpetuate it by shoring up the town.

The willingness to order vigorous remedies for civil rights violations was another litmus test of judicial support for equal justice, and Kaufman stood out here too. In Norwalk, Connecticut, the school board decided to voluntarily integrate by closing three schools in Black and Puerto Rican neighborhoods and busing 775 minority students to white schools. On the other hand, only 39 white children were bused. The superintendent blamed this disparity on the Black part of town being "a little dangerous"; as the district judge put it, the board just wanted to avoid "the apprehensions of a white child regarding attendance at a school in an undesirable neighborhood." In fact, white fears ran so rampant after rioting in New Haven and other Connecticut cities in the summer of 1967 that police had to suspend skyrocketing gun sales. African Americans had wearied of bearing the brunt of integration, however. Many now asked why their children couldn't attend an integrated school in *their* neighborhood—why their children were always the ones on the bus. Kaufman dissented from a decision upholding Norwalk's plan and pointed out that white fear of attending school in Black neighborhoods wasn't a valid basis for any plan of integration. He praised the board for undertaking desegregation voluntarily but thought the town was "legitimizing the very racial misunderstandings it seeks to eradicate."[18]

Job discrimination presented judges with similar choices over how far to go to correct past unfairness. Some endorsed the tool of setting aside specific numbers of positions for minority workers who had been excluded in the past—quotas, in other words—while others saw this as "reverse discrimination" against whites, who might be individually blameless for earlier bias. Kaufman was in the first camp, in keeping with his preference for robust tools to bring about change. In a case where the Second Circuit reversed a district court order requiring New York to promote one minority correctional officer to sergeant for every three whites promoted, Kaufman joined a dissent from the full court's refusal to take up the case. Unlike some of his colleagues, he was under no illusions that equality could be achieved without a vigorous federal role. The legacy of slavery and discrimination remained America's "national agony," he said in a speech in 1976, and after two centuries the country had still "failed to eradicate completely the inequality on which the Union was built."[19]

Yet Kaufman's progressivism in racial discrimination cases didn't entirely preclude thinking along ethnic lines in a way common to many of his generation. John Garvey clerked for Kaufman in 1974–75 and went on to become a law professor and president of Catholic University. His work and manner impressed Kaufman, who then clumsily extolled him as an example to other Irish Catholic clerks. "Why can't you be more like that other Irish Catholic?" Kaufman asked Dan Kelly, referring to Garvey. Bruce Kraus clerked for Kaufman in 1979–80 and once accompanied him to lunch in the judges' private dining room. As Friendly approached their table, Kaufman announced "I want you to meet my half-Chinese, half-Jewish law clerk." To Kraus, it seemed like Kaufman was smirking. "Today, you'd call it a micro-aggression," Kraus said. "It was a humiliation, the kind of thing you have to smile your way through. It's the kind of thing that really stays with you for a long time. He's challenging your identity, your self-respect."[20]

When it came to cases about race, the contending parties at least agreed that the Constitution protected racial minorities. What about poor people? Both groups were uniquely "on the outskirts of hope," as President Johnson said in 1964 when introducing his War on Poverty, and their membership overlapped. Lawyers were called to enlist in Johnson's crusade by Attorney General Robert Kennedy, who urged them to fill the unmet legal needs of the economically disadvantaged and even "develop new kinds of legal rights." The administration created the Legal Services Program to fund groups assisting the poor, and "poverty lawyers" emerged to represent welfare recipients, tenants, low-wage workers, and others—just as similar groups had formed in earlier periods to press the causes of racial and religious minorities. In the legal academy, Professor Charles Reich at Yale argued that welfare payments, Social Security and Medicare benefits, housing vouchers, and the like were akin to more traditional forms of property and deserved the same legal protection. Others proposed interpreting the constitutional guarantees of equal protection of the law and due process to forbid discrimination against poor people.[21]

Amid this ferment, the Warren and early Burger Courts issued decisions striking down rules that handicapped the poor by charging exorbitant fees for necessary government services and arbitrarily withdrawing welfare benefits without due process. States could no longer try to ward off poor people from moving in by delaying welfare and medical care to new arrivals. Some believed a majority of the justices might soon declare that the Constitution required government to guarantee some basic level of sustenance to its poorest citizens.[22]

Kaufman entered this fray with gusto and issued opinions advocating expansive constitutional protection for the poor. Usually, his rationale was to prevent discrimination against the indigent under the Fourteenth Amendment's Equal Protection Clause, as when he declined to dismiss an impoverished ex-felon's attack on the five-dollar fee Connecticut charged to restore his voting rights after leaving prison. In a later case, Kaufman held that a landlord couldn't refuse to rent to welfare recipients.[23]

Even more ambitious was Kaufman's dissent from a 1971 decision upholding New York's law permitting local school districts to require elementary school children to pay for textbooks, though the state admitted this left poorer students "sitting bookless" next to their wealthier classmates. In one case, a child was threatened with an F because he didn't have the book, and when he tried to share one with classmates he was told to draw pictures by himself instead. Insisting New York had to treat its charges equally, Kaufman likened its insensitivity to poverty to racial segregation and quoted *Brown v. Board of Education* at length: "The enduring lesson [schoolchildren] are thus taught . . . is that wealth breeds favored treatment while disadvantage leads on to still greater handicaps." It was spoken like a kid from Jewish Harlem, schooled for free or nearly in magnificent halls of learning like DeWitt Clinton and the Woolworth Building. Followed to its logical conclusion, Kaufman's opinion sketched a constitutional right of poor children to the same educational assets enjoyed by rich ones—comparable facilities, equally good teachers, and so on. He wasn't alone in this regard; a few other pathbreaking judges around the country were coming to the same conclusion. If adopted, their view might bring about greater equity and far-reaching improvement to public schools. The Supreme Court granted review in the New York textbook case but then dismissed the appeal when the town where the plaintiffs lived approved a tax to buy books for everyone.[24]

Discrimination against poor people was one thing, but Kaufman went further. New York's welfare laws required recipients to reimburse the state for their support payments if they owned real estate or received payouts from personal injury awards or life insurance policies. The Constitution wasn't a tool to eradicate income inequality, Judge Marvin Frankel wrote in approving the law, but Kaufman took a different view. To him, "a largely overlooked aspect of personal liberty" was at stake: "one's right to be an independent individual, not compelled to rely on government for the right to exist." Paradoxically, he thought, New York made welfare recipients *more* dependent on government by forcing them to pay restitution, making it harder to escape welfare altogether. "It may be true," Kaufman concluded in his dissent, "that the Constitution does not impose an affirmative obligation on the state to create the circumstances in which people will become independent and self-supporting. But I do suggest that it does prohibit the State from placing obstacles in the path of efforts to become independent of welfare bounty or to maintain the independence already achieved." Had Kaufman's concept of a right to financial self-sufficiency prevailed, it could well have forced a comprehensive retooling of state social service efforts and other laws to better meet the needs of poor Americans.[25]

Conscientious objectors, war protesters, African Americans tired of the raw deal of prejudice, poor people stiffed by businesses and government—all fared well before Kaufman. "Things are changing so fast that nobody seems to be quite as confident or dogmatic as he used to be about his ideas and prejudices," he said in that whirlwind year, 1968. The comment nicely encapsulated his ongoing progression from the special harshness of 1950–51 to a greater sympathy with the outsiders of Hippieland. While demonstrators and poverty activists were far removed from convicted spies and perjurers, they shared an alienation from the society and government so hospitable to Kaufman and other second-generation Jewish winners. The difference was that, by

1968 and certainly after, the institutions and arrangements underlying Kaufman's early confidence in government and the establishment—the liberal statist consensus he'd personified as a Truman Democrat—seemed to be disintegrating. Societal pillars like law enforcement, universities, the architects of foreign and military policy, and the imperial presidency itself faced embarrassing exposure as brutal, hollow, incompetent, and two-faced. Some attacks could be waved away as naïve or nihilist or cannily self-interested, but others had self-evident heft and made clear Kaufman was living in a different world and might reasonably respond accordingly. Important, too, was the fact that people like Dan Seeger, Susan Russo, and Charles James sat safely outside the personal blind spot that enveloped the Rosenbergs and Abraham Brothman and Miriam Moskowitz—the immutable characteristics of birth and background that made them more than just traitors to America but traitors to Kaufman himself.[26]

Nonetheless, one oppressed minority found no relief amid this timely jettisoning of dogmas and preconceptions. Clive Michael Boutilier left his family's small farm in Canada for New York at twenty-one. Nine years later he applied for citizenship, which required him to disclose an arrest for sodomy. Unaware that this admission threatened not only his hopes to become a citizen but even his staying on in America, he soon found himself fielding questions about his sex life. When he'd first entered the country in 1955, people "afflicted with psychopathic personality" were legally barred, and that term was a euphemism for gay people and other "sex perverts." In practice, the law was toothless because it was usually easy to deny or conceal previous same-sex activity, but for some reason Boutilier was expansively honest. The interrogation—"I am an officer of the Immigration and Naturalization Service and I desire to question you under oath regarding your homosexual activities"—was intentionally humiliating, forcing Boutilier to recount his encounters in vivid detail and answer inquiries like "what do you mean by orgasm" and "what do you mean by ejaculate." Boutilier had been preyed on by an older man at fourteen and had sex with men three or four times a year starting around sixteen, though he'd also occasionally had sex with women. In the United States, he'd lived for years with a man. All this was enough for the government to declare he'd been a "psychopathic personality" in Canada before 1955 and to order him deported.[27]

When Boutilier's appeal reached the Second Circuit in 1966, *Time* called it "The Case of the Elusive Euphemism." The legal struggle for gay rights was in its infancy but slowly gaining steam. "The United

States is moving toward détente, if not a peace treaty, with its homosexuals," the *Times* wrote the following year. Vice squad officers still trolled parks and restrooms looking for furtive men to arrest while their colleagues raided gay bars. Stonewall was three years off. The American Psychiatric Association classified homosexuality as a mental illness, and gays were stripped of government jobs, flushed from the military, and barred from entire professions like teaching. On the other hand, educated and affluent Americans and progressive religious denominations showed increasing acceptance. Some employers, like the City of New York, no longer considered homosexuality a firing offense. A handful of states were considering repealing antiquated sodomy laws, as proposed by the American Law Institute, and more and more activists and organizations manned the barricades for equality. "Homosexuals in many instances are boldly challenging the right of others to make them second class citizens," the *Wall Street Journal* recognized, and Boutilier joined the vanguard of those no longer willing to keep quiet. He'd made a life in New York and resolved to stay, though he also moved back in with his mother and abandoned sex altogether, a psychologist observed, "because of the annoyance and disgust with the problems these activities have brought him."[28]

Boutilier turned to Blanch Freedman, a lawyer who'd defended accused communists in immigration cases. Her law partner was none other than Gloria Agrin, the young associate who helped the Blochs during the Rosenberg trial. For all the new directness of gay rights advocates, Freedman's strategy was cautious. She stressed Boutilier's stable home life, his continuous employment, his clean police record except for the one arrest, and his honesty with investigators. And she emphasized his experiences with women, going as far as to label him heterosexual. Two psychiatrists confirmed he wasn't mentally ill, though one acknowledged Boutilier was "beginning treatment" for a "psychosexual disorder," that is, sex with men. Freedman also cited Kinsey, who'd found that 37 percent of adult men reported at least one same-sex experience. One third of all male immigrants couldn't be psychopaths, could they? The law was too vague, and Boutilier was really being punished for more recent homosexual acts in the United States, not his ambiguous status in 1955. The brief on the other side was equally thorough. "We knew it was a test type of case," remembered one of the government's lawyers, "and we briefed it accordingly."[29]

Despite Kaufman's growing sympathy for the marginalized, gay equality was simply too much for him in 1966. He began the opinion with a paragraph that condescended to the young people Rifkind later attacked more vehemently:

> Although a relatively young segment of contemporary society prides itself on its readiness to cast off conventional and tested disciplines and to experiment with nonconformance and the unorthodox merely to act out its contempt for traditional values, certain areas of conduct continue to be as controversial in modern and beau monde circles as they were in bygone and more staid eras. Homosexual behavior, despite Sigmund Freud and other noted authors, remains such a fervently debated issue that too often emotions on both sides obscure reason. But, the craft of judging requires a personal detachment—as far as it is humanly possible—so that issues which are apt to overwhelm the emotions may be approached in the dispassionate manner fitting for a judicial determination.

The reference to Freud was a nod to gay rights, since an accompanying footnote quoted the famous doctor's 1935 "Letter to an American Mother" calling homosexuality "no vice, no degradation." Kaufman also cited Kinsey. But that was it. After parsing the legislative history of the applicable provision, he held that "Congress utilized the phrase 'psychopathic personality' not as a medical or psychiatric formulation but as a legal term of art designed to preclude the admission of homosexual aliens into the United States." Nor was the statute defeated by its vagueness. "It is not our function to sit in judgment on Congress' wisdom in enacting the law," he concluded, washing his hands of the ugly result. Surprisingly, Leonard Moore, Kaufman's frequent opposite in civil liberties cases, dissented. Moore believed Congress couldn't have wanted to keep out so many valued immigrants, and he had to have been startled when his opinion was quoted in *Playboy*, of all places.[30]

Kaufman's decision was legally defensible; in fact, it was the most straightforward outcome given the law at the time and the basic requirement that judges enforce it, like it or not. Still, the legal debate wasn't black and white. His reliance on somewhat ambiguous Senate committee reports and Congress's clarification, only *after* Boutilier's case began, that it intended a blanket exclusion of gays has been criticized by a leading expert in statutory construction. Beyond the technicalities, Kaufman's special solicitude for immigrants and his increasing willingness to take bold stances for civil and human rights deserted him, though admittedly the latter was a quality more pronounced in later years. In later years, too, Kaufman would encounter more and more mental illness and tragic dysfunction in his own family—qualities wrongly and grotesquely attributed to Boutilier but which clearly colored how others saw his case. That also might have softened Kaufman's regard for the Canadian immigrant and led him to look for creative ways to rule in his favor had his appeal come along later.[31]

With financial and legal support from nascent gay rights groups and the ACLU, Boutilier continued on to the Supreme Court. There he was opposed, ironically, by Thurgood Marshall, no longer Kaufman's colleague on the Second Circuit but now the solicitor general representing the government in the high court. Boutilier lost in Washington, too, with the era's namesake liberal champion, Earl Warren, joining Kaufman in voting against him.[32]

The American Psychological Association finally dropped homosexuality as a mental illness in 1973, but Congress didn't repeal the restriction on gay immigrants until 1990. These changes came too late for Boutilier—a man undone by prejudice and his own sweet, naïve honesty. Just before he was sent back to Canada, Boutilier stepped off a New York City sidewalk and was hit by a car. Some thought it a suicide attempt. Left tragically brain damaged, he lived out his days cared for by family and in group homes for the disabled and died in 2003. But neither time nor infirmity erased Boutilier's painful awareness of the "affliction" that had uprooted him and sent him searching for "treatment." Late in his life, when a niece referred to another family member who was gay, Boutilier asked her, "He has the problem too, doesn't he?"[33]

If Boutilier was a nobody whose battle to stay in the United States was largely invisible, the reverse was true of one of Hippieland's most famous ambassadors: the Englishman who'd taken up residence in New York City but asked his generation to "imagine there's no countries." On December 12, 1971, John Lennon played a benefit in Ann Arbor for John Sinclair, an avant-garde poet. Sinclair was serving ten years for giving two joints to an undercover cop—"ten for two," it was called—and his imprisonment had become a minor cause for the Woodstock set. Wearing "Free John Now" T-shirts, Lennon and his wife Yoko Ono joined Allen Ginsburg, Stevie Wonder, and Bob Seger onstage before fifteen thousand fans and several undercover police officers. "If he had been a soldier man," Lennon sang after 3:00 a.m. in a haze of marijuana smoke, "Shooting gooks in Vietnam / If he was the CIA / Selling dope and making hay / He'd be free, they'd let him be / Breathing air like you and me." "Lennon formerly with group known as the Beatles," an FBI agent summarizing the event helpfully noted.[34]

Lennon had vague plans to tour the country in 1972 playing concerts to drum up youth votes against President Nixon, since the voting age had dropped to eighteen a few months earlier. Deciding Lennon was dangerous, the FBI began watching him. Agents openly trailed him and tapped his phones. But like the administration's similar job at the Watergate Hotel, there was more than a little Keystone Cops about the effort. One FBI memo listed his residence as "Saint Regis Hotel, One Fifty Bank Street," though the St. Regis is in midtown and Lennon lived at *105* Bank Street in the Village. Lennon's face was one of the most famous in the world; still, the New York office asked Washington to forward a "photo of subject." Another memo dutifully cataloged a left-wing political meeting that featured a parrot who occasionally interjected with "Right on!" The Bureau wasn't living up to Kaufman's early idolatry.[35]

More ominously, conservative South Carolina senator Strom Thurmond wrote Attorney General John Mitchell obliquely suggesting they avoid "many headaches" by simply removing Lennon, a United Kingdom citizen in America on a temporary visa. On cue from the White House, the INS promptly moved to deport him and Yoko. The pretext was Lennon's 1968 guilty plea in London for stashing hash. American law made aliens convicted of illegal possession of "narcotic drugs or marijuana" excludable unless the INS temporarily waived the rule, as it previously had for Lennon. Now the INS told him to leave.

Lennon's resourceful lawyer, Leon Wildes, had little hope of averting deportation. But he discovered that British law seemed to allow conviction of people caught with drugs unknowingly—if drugs were found in their home, or if they didn't know the substance was an illegal drug at all—and this might not satisfy American standards for legitimate criminal convictions. He also battled in the court of public opinion. "There are grounds for suspicion that Mr. Lennon is being considered persona non grata because of his unconventional views and radical statements," the *Times* editorialized, while the *Los Angeles Times* asked "where is the threat?" A committee of artists and celebrities including Fred Astaire, Saul Bellow, Leonard Bernstein, and Jasper Johns rallied to the cause, as did New York's mayor John Lindsay. Bob Dylan wrote the INS, saying simply, "This country's got plenty of room and space. Let John and Yoko stay!"[36]

At the hearing before the immigration judge, Lennon virtually begged for lenience: "I don't know if there is any mercy to plead for because we are not in a Federal Court but if there is any, I'd like it please for both of us and our child." His fervent desire to stay appeared in lyrics from his 1972 song "New York City": "Well nobody came to bug us / Hustle us or shove us / So we decided to make it our home / If the Man wants to shove us out / We gonna jump and shout / The Statue of Liberty said, 'Come!'" He lost anyway. At a press conference Wildes scheduled for April Fool's Day, John and Yoko pulled out white handkerchiefs and declared them the flag of a new, "conceptual country, NUTOPIA. . . . Nutopia has no land, no boundaries, no passports, only people." As Nutopian ambassadors, they asked for diplomatic immunity from deportation. Then John blew his nose in his handkerchief.[37]

Kaufman had first learned of the Beatles nine years earlier when his in-laws gave him an album. "I look forward with much anticipation to the summer months so that I can explore the world of the Beatles—or perhaps at least one of them," he wrote in thanks. Now one of them was before him—and Kaufman loved it. As one clerk put it, Kaufman never met a celebrity "he didn't have some fondness for." By the time the appeal reached the Second Circuit, it was 1975 and Nixon was gone. A separate federal lawsuit Wildes filed also uncovered the Strom Thurmond letter and other evidence suggesting the INS had targeted Lennon for his political activities. How to do the right thing, though? As his clerk that year, Jon Lindsey, remembered, "You can't just say, 'Oh well, I love his music, he gets to stay.' But it would be an obvious injustice if he gets thrown out. We had to come up with something that would lead to the right result for Lennon but wouldn't open the door to hordes of drug addicts." Lindsey's co-clerk Brian Schwartz took Wildes's argument about the British criminal process and had the idea to focus on "*mens rea*," the guilty knowledge necessary for conviction in the United States. Since the British law Lennon had pleaded guilty to violating allowed convictions for even accidental possession, it ran afoul of the basic American *mens rea* requirement. That would do the trick for Lennon without risking help for other druggies, since the British law was so unique. Kaufman liked the idea and touted it to the other, equally cautious judges. "The one thing you could always count on IRK for," Schwartz recalled, "he always sympathized with immigrants."[38]

Kaufman's opinion featured an arid exploration of *mens rea*, but then he turned to the government's conduct—"a brief word on Lennon's contention that he was singled out for deportation because of his political activities and beliefs." That issue was not directly before the court, Kaufman noted, but "we do not take his claim lightly. . . . The courts will not condone selective deportation based upon secret political grounds." And the immigrants' son ended with a moving tribute to Lennon and others who wanted nothing more than a life in America: "If, in our two hundred years of independence, we have in some measure realized our ideals, it is in large part because we have always found a place for those committed to the spirit of liberty and willing to help implement it. Lennon's four-year battle to remain in our country is testimony to his faith in this American dream."[39]

The decision came out two days before Lennon's thirty-fifth birthday and, in a happy coincidence, the day his son Sean was born. He called it "a great birthday gift from America for me, Yoko and the baby." Wildes, a Jew, needled his client that, despite Lennon's well-publicized support for the Northern Irish struggle against Britain, the two judges voting for him, Kaufman and Murray Gurfein, were Jewish, while the only Irish American judge on the panel, William Mulligan, had dissented. The next year, the INS granted Lennon permanent residency in the United States. He vowed to devote himself to "wife, kids, and a job, the same as everybody else," and by then he was staying home and raising his new baby boy. "This is the best place to bring up a Eurasian child," Lennon added. "This city is cosmopolitan. Everywhere else, there's only one flavor." As a one-off mostly useful only to Lennon, Kaufman's decision had little lasting impact on American law. But it was undoubtedly his greatest service yet to Hippieland. Still, he wasn't exactly a resident. At the same time he was vindicating Lennon, he was relentlessly badgering Schwartz to shave his beard.[40]

CHAPTER 13

The Most Cherished Tenet

If the courtroom is law's theater, judges' chambers are backstage—quiet refuges where jurists and their clerks unwind and work unbothered. Lawyers rarely enter, and usually only in great emergencies. Yet Kaufman's chambers had already hosted lawyers arguing one of the most significant cases in American history. That had been on June 19, 1953, when the Rosenbergs' attorneys sat across his desk and tried to stave off electrocutions then only hours away. Now, eighteen years later to the day, lawyers in a case of similar gravity headed up to the twenty-fourth floor. And like the first time, this one involved national security and the espionage laws. June 19, 1971, was a Saturday, and that was the day Kaufman first confronted the Pentagon Papers.

Earlier that afternoon, Judge Murray Gurfein issued an opinion allowing the *New York Times* to publish news stories about and excerpts of Defense Department documents from what became known as the Pentagon Papers: a forty-seven-volume opus dissecting the origins of America's involvement in Vietnam and its conduct of the war until 1968. Johnson's secretary of defense, Robert McNamara, had commissioned the in-house study, and Daniel Ellsberg, one of its authors, had leaked portions to the *Times*. Although the volumes were designated "Top Secret," much of their content was already public in the form of old news articles and official memoirs. Nonetheless, the United States claimed describing them in print would reveal important facts damaging to American alliances and secret negotiations to withdraw from Vietnam. Privately, Nixon and Mitchell fumed at their liberal "enemies" in the media.[1]

The previous Tuesday, June 15, Gurfein had ordered the *Times* to temporarily halt its series—there had been three installments so far—until he could decide whether publication violated the same law that netted the Rosenbergs: the 1917 Espionage Act. Yet it was generally agreed that, if the First Amendment meant anything, it prohibited the government or a judge from directly telling a newspaper it couldn't run a story—what the law calls a "prior restraint." And as far as anyone could tell, Gurfein's temporary order was the first time a federal judge had stopped the presses in such a case.

At a hearing Friday, however, government witnesses couldn't persuade Gurfein that resuming the series would cause anything worse than embarrassment. Nor did he think the 1917 law applied to journalists openly writing articles, as opposed to spies covertly selling secrets. He was ready to allow publication but continued his original, temporary blackout order long enough for the government to ask the court of appeals to enter a similar one. Incredibly, Gurfein had been a judge for all of one week; this was his very first case on the bench.[2]

That Saturday Kaufman *was* the court of appeals—the one judge on weekend duty to consider the United States' application. With the lawyers sitting in his office, Kaufman heard a brief argument and then adjourned to write up a short opinion. He decided to continue Gurfein's original order temporarily prohibiting publication until a full panel of the court could decide the appeal on Monday, though he said he wasn't tipping his hand as to how he would ultimately vote. One historian has accused Kaufman of being "defensive and apologetic" in issuing the injunction, and "creating a misleading impression that his hands were tied." In reality, though, almost every judge in America would have done the same thing. Kaufman was right that, without another short and temporary prohibition, the *Times* would have resumed publishing and potentially exposed information the whole court of appeals might think should remain secret. The *Times*' counsel James Goodale, who knew Kaufman personally and liked him, was "really stunned" by the ruling. Still, he thought he understood it. Kaufman was an outsider on the court, "a public figure in a way that his peers were not," and making doubly sure he was including them was the "only way he could get along with the boys on the bench."[3]

After signing his order, Kaufman dove deeper into the case. What he read left him unimpressed. Publication had been prevented for nearly a week, he wrote his fellow judges on Monday morning, and "this unprecedented and dangerous restraint has been premised entirely upon the government's mere assertion that public security would be endangered by publication." This although Gurfein hadn't found "so much as a remote and speculative danger to the national interest, much less a 'clear and present' one." He urged his colleagues to hear the case immediately, and Friendly, then chief judge, set argument for Tuesday. The DC Circuit would hear a separate, essentially identical appeal involving the *Washington Post* at the same time. To avoid any conflict, Kaufman sold shares of the *Post* his broker had coincidentally purchased days earlier.[4]

In its brief, the United States argued that the Constitution allowed prior restraints on publication of material harmful to national security and that courts should defer to the executive branch's assessment of when such damage would occur. The *Times*' submission centered on a nonconstitutional position favored by the paper's lead counsel, Yale Law School professor Alexander Bickel. Bickel doubted the courts would buy a simple argument that the First Amendment precluded censorship of articles revealing secret government documents, so he argued more technically that publication couldn't be enjoined because no federal statute specifically authorized it. Although the case later became a free speech icon, the paper's brief at this stage barely invoked the First Amendment at all.[5]

All eight judges constituting the full court convened on Tuesday at 2:00 p.m.—the first time it ever bypassed its usual three-member panels and heard a case initially together. Fifty reporters crammed into the spectators' benches, while hundreds of other people were turned away. Someone hissed as the government's lawyers entered. Kaufman asked the first question, interrupting the US Attorney Whitney North Seymour to inquire why the Espionage Act covered mailing but not publication. Seymour cited the government's inherent powers, not the statute only. If the material was stolen "from a government office or agency," Kaufman inquired, "the newspaper under no conditions has any right to publish them?" No, Seymour admitted, the *Times*' illegal possession was only "a weight in the scales." As the argument unfolded, Kaufman led the court's skeptics in probing the US Attorney, who attacked the newspaper for claiming for itself the power to determine the national interest and concluded that the government had shown that disclosure would "plainly imperil the military and foreign affairs of the United States."

Bickel gave the *Times*' argument, and Kaufman sympathized with his client despite the advocate. A Romanian immigrant and former Frankfurter clerk, the brilliant and urbane professor was, like his old boss, politically liberal but philosophically opposed to judges like Kaufman decreeing social reform. This conservative bent got him frequently mentioned for the Supreme Court after Nixon's election, though the president actually had little interest in appointing either Jews or Ivy League intellectuals. More directly, Bickel had clerked for Frankfurter in that year so pivotal to Kaufman, 1953, and shared his old employer's dim view of the Rosenberg sentences, calling them "a ghastly and shameful episode" in a 1966 book review.

Yet for all his erudition, Bickel wasn't used to the cut and thrust of arguing in court. Kaufman offered help where he could, asking at one point, "It would be all wrong to make a broad injunction against all of the documents, wouldn't it?" Bickel said the government hadn't persuaded Gurfein *any* were harmful. As in his brief, he often shied away from the First Amendment and was sometimes hard to follow. To co-counsel Floyd Abrams, "he seemed beaten." It was left to the ACLU's Norman Dorsen, given only five minutes at the lectern, to passionately champion free speech and urge a much stricter test for prior restraints.[6]

After the argument, Kaufman called the *Times* and wanted to talk about Bickel's underwhelming performance. Whatever the Second Circuit decided, the case was almost certainly headed to the Supreme Court, and Kaufman believed the newspaper's lawyer had made a mistake by not stressing the First Amendment. It's unclear whom he called; Goodale heard about it but wasn't on the phone. The move couldn't have been more typical—a back-channel bid to fix a problem and yet another breach in the traditional barrier separating judges from litigants. And because it happened before the Second Circuit issued its decision, the call was also an *ex parte* communication in violation of the rules of legal ethics. Just as in 1951. Goodale wasn't surprised by the call "because Kaufman was a *New York Times* lover and he loved being part of the action," but he was still appalled. "I said to myself, 'that's totally improper. What the hell is IRK doing?' *What the hell?* Irving has a tendency to do things like that. I wasn't surprised, but I said to myself 'Jesus he shouldn't have done that.'" At least Kaufman wasn't the only one on his court eager to sway the justices. Friendly sent a memorandum supporting the government's position to Justice Harlan, apparently hoping to influence the Supreme Court in what his biographer calls an "arguably unethical action."[7]

The Second Circuit's deliberations have been called "a bitter battle," a "violent argument," and in one judge's view "possibly the 'most emotional' conference of his period of service" on the court. The next day, Kaufman wrote another memo to his colleagues reiterating his opposition to any more censorship. "My law clerk spent most of last night and the night before examining each of the references cited by the government to portions of the papers that the government believes are harmful. . . . I found nothing which would remotely justify a prior restraint." Whether the *Times* had improperly acquired the papers and ignored their "Top Secret" label didn't matter; "the rules that govern a GS-15 [government employee] do not govern the *New York Times*." Moreover, he was sure past reporting on the war had already affected American "diplomacy and military operations far greater than would anything contained in these papers."[8]

But Kaufman didn't have the votes. While Wilfred Feinberg and the newly appointed James Oakes agreed with him, four more conservative judges—Friendly, Lumbard, Hays, and Connecticut's Joseph Smith—favored the government. That left Walter Mansfield, a Nixon appointee who'd replaced Leonard Moore and had barely been there a month. So the court issued a precise, compromise order: halt all publication for two more days so the government could designate specific documents for Gurfein's evaluation. Then Gurfein had nine days to decide whether they "pose[d] such grave and immediate danger to the security of the United States as to warrant their publication being enjoined." Anything not designated could be published immediately. Unwilling to extend censorship even one more hour, Kaufman, Feinberg and Oakes dissented. By agreement, no judge wrote an opinion, so as to speed the case to its next stop: the Supreme Court.[9]

Rather than return to Gurfein, however, the *Times* chose immediate appeal—a decision made easier by the government's simultaneous appeal of the *Washington Post*'s victory in the DC Circuit. The rest is well known constitutional history. One week later, the justices ruled 6–3 approving publication. Although each justice wrote a separate opinion, Justice Potter Stewart's formulation requiring proof of "direct, immediate, and irreparable damage to our Nation or its people" effectively stands as the Court's test for a prior restraint. The standard is stringent, close to if not quite as demanding as what the *Times* had asked for, and no federal court has successfully imposed a prior restraint in the last half-century.[10]

Kaufman's role in the Pentagon Papers case was relatively minor, but at least he could take satisfaction in ending up on the right side of the famous controversy. On the other hand, Friendly's biographer reports that the judge's grandson asked him years later about an article saying he'd voted "the wrong way," to which Friendly replied that he thought the *Times* was "obviously right" but felt it was "up to the Supreme Court to make that decision." This seems more than a little disingenuous considering his attempts to persuade Harlan to delay publication.[11]

Twenty years earlier, Kaufman had condemned the Rosenbergs for arrogating to themselves the decision to transmit atomic information to the Russians, even if the USSR was then an ally. Now, when the government accused the *Times* of a similar sort of arrogance—claiming it could decide for itself whether disclosing secret documents threatened the nation—Kaufman was far less credulous. The two cases differed greatly, of course, but it's also true that after two decades on the bench and all the accompanying political and social change, Kaufman was simply less willing to swallow government protestations of national security. Nor did he still believe other interests so easily trumped the public's right to know, as when he had leaned on newspapers and television producers to hold off on shows and stories about the Mafia before and during the Apalachin trial in order to guarantee an untainted jury. The individual right to receive information and the press's freedom to disseminate it were beginning to trump the once paramount needs of the state.

The fight over publishing the Pentagon Papers was dramatic and important, in part because of its novelty, but a more common threat to the press was emerging at the same time: attempts to make reporters cough up their sources and background materials. Once rare, subpoenas to reporters from prosecutors, grand juries, and civil litigants had ramped up in recent years, and in 1972 Goodale helped bring a case to the Supreme Court challenging the practice. He and others argued that the names of reporters' confidential sources were privileged and shouldn't have to be disclosed unless the sources' information was directly relevant to the investigation and couldn't be obtained some other way. They lost, however, 5–4. In a vague concurrence, Justice Powell suggested journalists could still seek judicial protection on a case-by-case basis if prosecutors had no serious need for the information, and that the duty to assist law enforcement had to be balanced with freedom of speech. The decision, *Branzburg v. Hayes*, didn't say what would happen if the subpoena came from private lawyers seeking information in a civil lawsuit rather than grand jurors probing a crime.[12]

Kaufman faced that question only six months later in a vast class action brought by Black home-buyers in Chicago against real estate agents and lenders they accused of housing discrimination. The plaintiffs took testimony from a sympathetic journalist, Alfred Balk, who'd written "Confessions of a Block-Buster" in the *Saturday Evening Post.* Presented as a first-person tell-all from the pseudonymous agent "Norris Vitchek," Balk's piece was astonishingly candid in describing "Vitchek's" lucrative playbook: scare middle-class whites in older Chicago neighborhoods into thinking African Americans were moving in, buy up their homes at a loss, and resell to Black buyers at much higher prices. When the plaintiffs' lawyers asked Balk to name "Vitchek," he balked.

And Kaufman upheld him. Acknowledging that the rules were "at best ambiguous," he noted that state laws in New York and Illinois favored protecting journalists; that no criminal investigation was involved, unlike in *Branzburg*; and that the plaintiffs could identify Balk's real estate agent in other ways. Forced disclosure would endanger the important practice of confidential reporting and thereby "threaten freedom of the press and the public's need to be informed." At the same time, however, he made clear the privilege wasn't absolute; judges should weigh the importance of the information in each case, its availability from other sources, and the effect on press freedom. In later years, other federal courts cited and adopted Kaufman's approach, enabling journalists to protect their sources in many federal civil cases, though different judges have rejected any sort of journalistic immunity.[13]

Frank admissions of block-busting were sensational, but nothing could match Kaufman's next reporter's privilege case. Anthony Herbert was the Korean War's most decorated enlisted man—twenty-two medals in all. Then he duplicated the performance in Vietnam, where a general called him "one of the best, if not the best combat commander in the whole goddamned Army." Herbert irritated the brass, though. "I had made all the wrong enemies, and I had swaggered more than a little, and I hadn't given a damn about telling people what I thought," he wrote. Cited for a litany of sham offenses, he was relieved and sent home, his dream of a general's stars ruined. Characteristically, Herbert fought back, charging he had actually been cashiered for notifying his superiors of war crimes. And what he described was horrific. There was the "St. Valentine's Day massacre" on February 14, 1969, where Herbert saw a Vietnamese policeman, overseen by an American adviser, slit a woman's throat while her wailing baby clung to her legs. Fifteen other detainees were shot down in cold blood. "I felt myself go empty, something drained from me in that moment that I have yet to replace," Herbert wrote. He also accused American military intelligence officers of using the infamous "water cure"—tying rags over suspects' faces and pouring water down their throats—and beating and using electric shocks on girls and women.[14]

Interviews in *Life* and *Playboy* and appearances on *The Dick Cavett Show* soon followed. Cavett introduced him as "one of America's great war heroes . . . [and] also one of its war victims." Congress wanted to hear from him, and the McGovern campaign announced he would advise the candidate. Newspapers throughout the country trumpeted his cause and denounced the army for destroying the career of one of America's finest warriors. In 1973, he published an autobiography titled, simply, *Soldier*. It presented its hero as a by-the-book but compassionate chief usually found "ass in the grass" with his troops—the kind of man who, forced to salute a general's pet duck, returned one night to wring its neck and turn it into sandwiches. Best of all, *Soldier* crackled with remembered confrontations in perfect army-speak, like when Herbert's supervisor exploded at his report of detainee abuse: "'What the hell did you expect, Herbert? Cigarettes? Candy? Flowers?' . . . 'Goddamn it, man this is war. W-A-R! And if you can't stomach it, then get the hell out.'"[15]

Despite his celebrity, however, no one was shocked when the army denied Herbert's charges and cleared his superiors. Certain this was just the latest Vietnam cover-up, Barry Lando, a CBS producer who admired Herbert, set out to prove the army wrong. He and a researcher talked to 120 people in and out of uniform who'd known Herbert, but to Lando's amazement, "one after another refuted many of Herbert's claims." The result was a *60 Minutes* segment that all but accused Herbert of fraud. Host Mike Wallace showed that Herbert's commander was in Hawaii on February 14, 1969, and couldn't have received a report about any massacre, as Herbert claimed. Men named in *Soldier* contradicted various stories in the book, while Herbert himself seemed evasive. In fact, Herbert couldn't prove he'd reported any atrocities at all until long after his dismissal, once other efforts to restore his command had failed. Some of his men even volunteered that, as Wallace put it, Herbert "could be brutal with captured enemy prisoners himself," and had beaten some. As one critic wrote, "Herbert had walked into his interview a heroic figure. He walked out a wreck."[16]

In response, Herbert sued Lando, Wallace, and CBS for $44 million. As the case progressed, Lando revealed his notes, drafts, memos to Wallace, and outtakes. But he drew the line at questions about his editorial thought process—why he'd followed some leads and not others, opinions about his sources' truthfulness, his brainstorming with Wallace, and why he'd left out facts favorable to Herbert. "Do we really have to turn over everything we said to each other?" Lando and Wallace asked their lawyer, Floyd Abrams, who'd worked with Bickel in the Pentagon Papers case. Abrams, in turn, asserted that these innermost editorial judgments and conversations were privileged from disclosure in a libel case. It was an untested argument cobbled together from other First Amendment decisions protecting other editorial prerogatives—such as one freeing newspapers from having to print replies to their stories—and the district judge rejected it completely.

Kaufman, on the other hand, saw the concept as essential to freedom of the press. To him, "judicial review of the editor's thought processes . . . unquestionably puts a freeze on the free interchange of ideas within the newsroom." Fearing libel suits, journalists might self-censor and shy away "from the creative verbal testing, probing, and discussion of hypotheses and alternatives which are the *sine qua non* of responsible journalism." Herbert had already uncovered "what Lando knew, saw, said and wrote," and that was enough for a jury to decide whether Lando had acted with the "actual malice" necessary to prove libel by knowingly making false statements about Herbert or acting with reckless disregard for the truth. Thomas Meskill, a recent Nixon appointee from Connecticut, dissented, calling it "remarkable on its face" that someone suing a reporter for libel couldn't ask him what he was thinking when he prepared the story.[17]

Having filed a brief supporting CBS, the *Times* hailed Kaufman's decision on the front page, editorializing the next day that it freed journalists from "a dangerous strain on the creative process." The *Washington Post* also cheered Kaufman's ruling while acknowledging that "what looks to us like a guarantee of the personal space to do our job increasingly looks to others like a structure of special privileges, perks and exemptions that put the press beyond the reach of normal obligations and restraints." Abrams, in the Supreme Court that morning to argue a different case, brandished the *Times* article celebrating his victory to his opposing counsel, the legendary "Man to See" in Washington, Edward Bennett Williams. "They're gonna have your ass up here next year," Williams growled.[18]

Williams was right. When the Supreme Court heard Herbert's appeal months later, it agreed that Kaufman's new privilege amounted to unwarranted special treatment and nixed it. A person's reputation also mattered, the justices held, and if the prospect of exposing a reporter's mind-set "discourages the publication of erroneous information known to be false or probably false, this . . . does not abridge either freedom of speech or of the press." Three justices dissented, although two (Brennan and Marshall) advocated a more limited privilege than Kaufman, and the third (Stewart) voted on another ground.[19]

Kaufman responded with an unrepentant speech weeks later. "Recently and with greater frequency," he began, "it appears that the courts are wielding the cutting edge against the press." The debate in *Herbert* wasn't over, he suggested, but had merely "shifted to another forum." He urged Congress and state legislatures to write his privilege into the statute books. In a later article, he called his Supreme Court reversal "press harassment." As it happened, *Herbert* and other rulings like *Branzburg* did prompt most states to enact qualified privileges protecting reporters from compelled disclosure of confidential sources and other information, and a few of the laws extend as far as Kaufman's rejected privilege to protect all unpublished information processed and formulated by journalists in the course of their work. Many federal courts still refuse to safeguard reporters' sources or deliberations, however.[20]

Years later, a second Kaufman opinion found that none of the statements in the *60 Minutes* broadcast evinced the necessary "actual malice" to libel Herbert, even if some included minor inaccuracies. Herbert became a practicing psychologist, often working with prisoners. In 2005, the *Los Angeles Times* obtained declassified documents verifying his claims that military intelligence officers had abused Vietnamese prisoners, though the records shed no light on when Herbert blew the whistle or whether that was why he'd been dismissed. "While the Army was working energetically to discredit Herbert," the paper reported, "military investigators were uncovering torture and mistreatment that went well beyond what he described."[21]

The Pentagon Papers and *Herbert* cases illustrated Kaufman's core belief that, as he wrote in another opinion, "in a society which takes seriously the principle that government rests upon the consent of the governed, freedom of the press must be the most cherished tenet." Often, as in *Herbert*, this freedom was tested in libel suits. In another case argued by Abrams for the *New York Times*, Kaufman reversed a libel judgment against the paper for reporting charges made by the Audubon Society that certain scientists advocated using the pesticide DDT because of financial ties to Big Agriculture. Reporters themselves weren't required to determine the truth or falsity of such accusations, he held; they need only accurately describe them. The decision originated what later cases called "the neutral reportage privilege," which received a mixed reception by other judges. Some courts have adopted it, while others believe the stringent "actual malice" standard does enough to protect the press. Kaufman also wrote and spoke about libel suits, believing their mere possibility chilled speech and proposing alternative remedies for defamation, like the right to obtain a retraction.[22]

Beyond libel, Kaufman worked to shield journalists from a more unusual threat: the copyright laws. In 1979, the *Nation* published "The Ford Memoirs—Behind the Nixon Pardon," an article based on a purloined copy of the ex-president's autobiography obtained before its release. Ruling against the publisher Harper & Row, Kaufman rejected broad assertions of what could be copyrighted, such as accounts of Ford's thoughts and impressions, as conflicting with the First Amendment's goal of fostering uninhibited political discourse. But his nine bosses in Washington disagreed again. Copyright wouldn't mean very much if a magazine could just steal whole quotes and passages from a forthcoming book, six justices decided, whether the topic was politics or something else.[23]

While New York's status as America's media mecca ensured regular litigation involving the press, there were other First Amendment claimants, too. Politicians, for instance. In one case, Kaufman joined colleagues in holding that an antitax group couldn't be fined for campaign reporting violations tied to its criticism of a congressman because its brochure didn't expressly call for his electoral defeat. But Kaufman went farther, suggesting any limits on campaign contributions and advocacy were unconstitutional: "It is incongruous to compel defendants to convince a court that they have not dared to 'expressly advocate' the defeat of a candidate for public office. I had always believed that such advocacy was to be applauded in a representative democracy." Not until authoring a *Times* op-ed in 1988 did he begin to rethink the value of regulating political spending as a means of preserving democracy. In a second case, Kaufman held that the same reporting laws couldn't be applied to the Communist Party USA because its donors, like other unpopular political minorities, had a First Amendment right to contribute anonymously. This despite his old view of communists as a Godless fifth column. In 1985, he struck down a Connecticut rule limiting a political party's primary to previously enrolled members. Under the First Amendment, he held, state Republicans could choose their candidates however they wanted. This time, the Supreme Court affirmed him.[24]

Less organized claimants also benefited from Kaufman's expansive view of free speech. When Port Authority officials threatened to arrest six antiwar protesters who simply wanted to distribute leaflets to passing travelers, Kaufman ruled they could stay. Years later, he went as far as suggesting that a homeowners' association might have a right to leave its brochures in residents' mailboxes, violating a postal service regulation. When the dispute reached the Supreme Court, however, a majority held that mailboxes aren't "public forums" open to messengers looking to avoid postage.[25]

Kaufman also decided that high schoolers should be free to express themselves. In one case, he required school officials to facilitate student publication of a school newspaper. In another, he reversed discipline for a satire titled "Hard Times," which mocked school lunches and gleefully endorsed masturbation, because it had been produced and distributed after school. "While these activities are certainly the proper subjects of parental discipline," he wrote, they couldn't be regulated off campus. Only one student lawsuit was too much even for Kaufman. He rejected a boy's claim that calling his teacher a "prick" somehow enjoyed constitutional protection. His clerk that year, Bruce Kraus, penned a voting memo in rhyme, "with apologies to Frost":

> Students have, we have held, as a general rule,
> The right of free speech in a public high school.
> But protection has never been thought to extend
> To expression whose purpose is but to offend.
> Such words do not aid the transmission of views;
> They are uttered entirely to shock and abuse.
> The "bon mot" in question—we need not repeat it—
> Is an expletive Antonio should well have deleted.[26]

When it came to harder stuff than "Hard Times," Kaufman was equally protective. In *Stanley v. Georgia*, the Warren Court had established a right to view pornography at home as long as the consumer wasn't marketing or selling it. Brooklynite Frank Dellapia *had* exchanged what he called "real stag films" for a little money and some pornographic photos, but to Kaufman, this seemed more like private association with other consenting adults than real commerce. He wanted Dellapia's conviction overturned, though he told his clerks to avoid announcing some kind of freestanding right to obtain pornography. What resulted was what one clerk called a "mushy way to get to the result": a so-called right to "the privacy of confidential communication or the privacy of being let alone if the communication does not harm others." The opinion may have been analytically loose, but it concluded powerfully: "The most fundamental premise of our constitutional scheme may be that every adult bears the freedom to nurture or neglect his own moral and intellectual growth. In a democracy one is free to work out one's own salvation in one's own way. If there is a justification for this premise, it is the faith—or the calculation—that to relinquish freedom of self-development would be to abandon most that is valuable about living." Quite a change from the man who once imprisoned one of America's most notorious pornographers, Samuel Roth, in the 1930s.[27]

Kaufman's many First Amendment opinions led some to question whether the Second Circuit had an unwritten rule barring consideration of free speech appeals without him on the panel. Abrams, a repeat performer in the circuit's free speech cases, began hearing opposing counsel "wonder out loud to him" about it. And some of Kaufman's colleagues doubted Kaufman's constant appearance on such panels was entirely coincidental. One judge mused that the circuit executive in control when Kaufman was chief judge in the 1970s may have steered the cases his way. As chief judge, Kaufman could assign whatever opinions he wanted to himself. Nor did he want anyone else adding their two cents. Shortly after joining the court in 1979, Judge Jon O. Newman thought he would write a concurrence in a First Amendment case, but Kaufman, also on the panel, tried to talk him out of it. Kaufman said the court had a long tradition of avoiding separate opinions in free speech appeals. After consulting another judge and learning that this was hogwash—no such tradition existed—he went ahead and wrote his concurrence.[28]

It was precisely because Kaufman "never met [a First Amendment claim] he didn't like," as Newman put it, that one of the very few exceptions stood out. Michael Selzer taught at Brooklyn College and agreed to debrief the CIA upon returning from a trip to Europe. This was a standard request made to legions of American businessmen, teachers, and other travelers—an inexpensive way to learn what was happening overseas. When word got out at the college, however, he was flayed for covertly "spying" for the government under the guise of academic research. Denied tenure, Selzer won $580,000 from a jury for violation of his First Amendment right to speak to whomever he wanted, government agents included. On appeal, the Second Circuit overturned the verdict on a technical point and granted a new trial. Kaufman, however, wanted Selzer's case thrown out altogether. The First Amendment wasn't absolute, he pointed out, and should yield if someone's speech or association caused too much disruption. "Brooklyn College was seeking a teacher and a scholar," he wrote, "not an espionage agent."[29]

Selzer was a minor case, but it graphically illustrated Kaufman's ideological journey. Once, he had believed fervently and without reservation in the work of American law enforcement and intelligence. He thought every American was morally obligated to help his government, and he would have regarded someone like Selzer as a run-of-the-mill patriot. By 1980, a professor who conducted a brief, harmless phone call with the CIA was "an espionage agent" subject to discipline for upsetting colleagues.

This remarkable turnabout didn't go unnoticed. Sidney Hook was a philosopher and public intellectual who began as a Marxist but migrated steadily rightward. In 1965, Kaufman importuned him to write a defense of the Rosenberg trial. Hook was interested but begged off years later after investigating Kaufman's wider record and uncovering what struck him as "an ultra-ritualistic liberal stance." He decided Kaufman's First Amendment jurisprudence "was more harmful to the prospects of a free society than the injustices he suffered at the hands of his Communist tormenters." In an article seemingly apropos of nothing nine years after the *Selzer* case, he attacked Kaufman as desperate for expiation for the Rosenberg executions and asserted that, despite his opinion siding with Selzer's colleagues, "the members of the department whom he unjustly sustained never forgave him for the sentence he passed on the Rosenbergs." On that, at least, Hook was probably right.[30]

At the same time Kaufman was protecting the press, he was energetically courting it. This was nothing new. In the 1930s, he promoted himself to reporters and won glowing coverage as the "demon boy prosecutor." In the 1940s, he represented publishing heavyweights like Sam Newhouse and Henry Garfinkle, as well as media magnets like Milton Berle, and befriended NBC owner David Sarnoff. In the 1950s, he used connections with columnists like Leonard Lyons, George Sokolsky, and Jim Bishop to land glowing profiles and urge his promotion to higher courts. By the 1970s, though, those columnists and the newspapers that published them were disappearing, and his attention focused on the *Times*. As Lee Levine, a law clerk in 1979–80, described it, "You would have thought, by that stage, 'Who the hell cares? Been there, done that.' [But] there *had* to be a *New York Times Magazine* article with his byline. He *had* to make sure the *Times* knew he had written this opinion that they ought to be writing about. It struck me as incredible then, and it strikes me as incredible now, that he cared about all that so much."[31]

Kaufman began courting the paper in the 1950s, if not before, sending copies of his opinions and speeches and making sure publisher Arthur Hays Sulzberger received anything positive said or written about the Rosenberg case. He also laid on the flattery, as when he wrote Sulzberger on the *Times*' hundredth anniversary ("this paper . . . is as much a part of American life as is the Constitution and the Bill of Rights"), and later on his retirement ("During your administration . . . it has risen to a point where all concede it to be the greatest newspaper in the world"). When Arthur Ochs "Punch" Sulzberger took over in 1963, Kaufman zeroed in on the younger dynast. The origin of their friendship is murky but may have been greased by the marriage of Kaufman's second law clerk, Leonard Sand, with whom he remained atypically close, to Punch's cousin. Punch socialized with Kaufman, occasionally inviting him to the vast family estate in Connecticut and society functions like the Gridiron Dinner in Washington. Kaufman reciprocated when hosting important events at 1185 Park, such as a 1976 dinner for England's lord chief justice. Kaufman also wined and dined A. M. Rosenthal, the paper's executive editor.[32]

It helped that Kaufman led a highly regarded effort to balance press freedoms with the accused's right to a fair trial. His committee's report in 1968, adopted by the judicial conference, protected defendants' confidentiality in some ways but stopped short of more draconian proposals, such as allowing judges to prohibit publication and punish reporters for disobedience. This won plaudits from the *Times*, which called it a "satisfactory accommodation," and other outlets.[33]

Once tight with those running the *Times*, Kaufman constantly bombarded its reporters. Tom Goldstein, who covered legal affairs, had to field Kaufman's constant calls because his boss on the metro desk, Sidney Schanberg, refused to. Craig Whitney handled the federal courthouse and sometimes saw Kaufman in the hall. He could come across as "smarmy" and "unctuous," Whitney remembered, as if it was "a little too obvious he was looking for coverage." Max Frankel, in charge of the editorial page, recalled that Kaufman "was always elaborately warm and full of praise and tended to empathize with threats to First Amendment freedoms, a fellow warrior so to speak, and of course he always managed to stress his relationship with Punch." Linda Greenhouse's usual beat was the Supreme Court, but that didn't protect her from the Kaufman treatment. Before long she became convinced "all the editors on the news side were terrified of Judge Kaufman because of his relationship with Punch Sulzberger." No one "would ever say 'Excuse me, this speech that Judge Kaufman is making tonight in some social club doesn't merit coverage in the *New York Times*.' They covered everything. It was just a joke among the staff. Literally every time this guy made a speech, it would be covered. You could have some Nobel Laureate down the block giving a speech and the *Times* wouldn't cover it. There was something very, very bizarre."[34]

And so *Times* articles cropped up on a Kaufman speech on courtroom decorum, a Kaufman talk on taking minor cases out of the federal courts, a Kaufman legal article on judicial writing, Kaufman after-dinner remarks on poorly trained counsel, a Kaufman program bringing high school students to the courthouse, a Kaufman award given by Fordham, Kaufman's role in producing a guide for legal affairs reporters, Kaufman's anniversaries as a judge, and so on. When he became chief judge of the circuit in 1973—an automatic handover dictated by seniority—the *Times* covered it with two separate stories. There were also reports on his labors in the vineyards of courthouse administration—pieces on rising caseloads, plans to shrink them, the court's calendar, and the like. Sometimes, no speech or writing was even needed. In 1974, the paper ran a piece titled "A Day in U.S. Circuit Court: From Trademarks to Prisoner Rights to Sex Bias." It featured Kaufman's photo and described a typical morning's cases, as well as some of the court's logistical challenges. These fluff pieces supplemented coverage of Kaufman's legitimately newsworthy work, such as opinions in important cases and reforms he helped spearhead in jury selection, sentencing, and other areas. "No other judge enjoyed such coverage," Goldstein observed, adding, "When Kaufman was involved in an event, normal news judgments were suspended." And not only would he harangue reporters "seeking favorable coverage of himself," Goldstein said, "he would sometimes be very upset that other people got favorable coverage. 'Why did you do a 'Man in the News' on X? Why not on me?'"[35]

Beyond the volume, there was also the slant. Reporters repeatedly ran up against special rules where Kaufman was concerned. In 1977, a young freelance journalist, Dorothy Rabinowitz, agreed to write a comprehensive *Times Magazine* profile of Kaufman, warts and all. At first, she didn't know about his friendship with Punch—then she met her subject and started hearing about it "every five minutes." Rabinowitz ultimately threw in the towel, and an article on Kaufman in a legal magazine quoted her blaming the *Times*: "I came to understand that there were some things one could not say. The editors were all lovely. I withdrew the article before they were put in the position of not behaving well." Writing Rosenthal privately, Rabinowitz claimed she'd been misquoted and simply meant there were things about Kaufman she couldn't come to grips with as a writer, not that she'd been muzzled. For whatever reason, the project wasn't reassigned, and the piece wasn't written. In chambers, the rumor was that Kaufman had succeeded in killing it.[36]

That same year, Goldstein tried to cover the fact that a hundred law professors had signed a letter sharply critical of Kaufman's behavior in the Rosenberg case. Editors didn't overtly bury the story, but they "kept on coming back to [Goldstein] with new questions" despite his effort to convince them that it was "extremely unusual for 100 law professors to agree on anything." Goldstein's story never ran either, though a reference to the letter eventually appeared in a different *Times* piece.[37]

Greenhouse also came to believe Kaufman couldn't be covered honestly at the *Times*: "All the reporters knew what game was afoot with Judge Kaufman." In 1983, the paper assigned her a "Man in the News" profile of him following his appointment to lead a presidential commission on organized crime, but Greenhouse agreed to the job only if it appeared without her byline. "The paper's not going to let me tell the truth," she told her editor, "and I don't want my byline on an untruthful story." In thirty years as a reporter, it was the only time she ever made such a request. And though the profile was almost entirely laudatory—"I mean, people couldn't pay for the 'Man in the News' I wrote," she said—it did contain some negative notes: that Kaufman had tried to extend his time as chief judge, criticism over the Rosenberg case, and the fact that several clerks had quit because Kaufman was a "stern taskmaster." Furious, Kaufman called Punch. According to Greenhouse's boss, Peter Millones, Punch tried to persuade Kaufman "to relax because it made him look good. But of course Kaufman can't relax." Kaufman then penned a three-page letter minutely detailing his complaints, especially that Greenhouse had ignored his "many landmark opinions of the past 15 years" (tellingly, he named only free speech cases), in favor of "ancient history." He quoted from the twenty-two-year-old Learned Hand letter advocating his promotion and accused Greenhouse of "poor judgment." Perhaps because of Greenhouse's protest, later coverage of Kaufman's work on the organized crime commission by other reporters contained more direct criticism.[38]

More than the object of copious and friendly coverage, Kaufman had a further role at the *Times*: contributor. Year after year, he browbeat clerks to draft articles for the paper, often letting them decide what to write about as long as it had a shot at publication. Frankel, head of the editorial page, hated the endless solicitations and more or less despised Kaufman as "a self-promoting pest to be avoided if at all possible and to be tolerated only because of his special relationship with the boss." Although he found most of what Kaufman submitted "uninteresting or self-promoting," the pieces ran anyway. From 1972 to 1990, Kaufman averaged more than one op-ed per year. "Having a *Times* op-ed was like the height of joy for him," former clerk Richard Friedman said. Topics included free speech, church-state conflicts, the qualities necessary in a good judge, the insanity defense, juvenile justice, criminal law, international human rights, and more. Goldstein, who discussed Kaufman's relationship with the *Times* in a 1985 book on journalistic ethics, found this frequency "extraordinary." But there was more. Kaufman also dominated the *Times Magazine*, publishing twelve articles there from 1966 to 1987. Goldstein calculated that, from 1979 to 1984, Kaufman was the magazine's "most consistent and frequent nonjournalist contributor." And even that wasn't enough. Not content merely with authorship, he once lobbied Rosenthal to make one of his pieces the cover story.[39]

There were other perks from Sulzberger's friendship, too. As head of a national committee of federal judges, Kaufman convinced Sulzberger of the need to increase judicial salaries and benefits in order to retain judges tempted by greater rewards in private practice. At Kaufman's direction, Punch ordered up a favorable *Times* editorial on the topic in 1980 and wrote a letter to eighty-five other publishers asking them to do likewise. He had "become convinced of this problem," he wrote his counterparts around the country, and "agreed to help my old friend, Judge Irving Kaufman." Then he dutifully reported back to Kaufman as publishers responded and agreed to pitch in. Sulzberger also contributed to Kaufman's pet causes in other ways, such as directing the New York Times Foundation to donate funds to the Institute of Judicial Administration.[40]

Not surprisingly, the sustained adoration Kaufman received from America's leading newspaper gave rise to grousing at the courthouse. "I see Irving has a front page ad in the paper this morning," one Second Circuit judge grumbled to a colleague over breakfast, referring to a *Times* piece on one of Kaufman's free speech rulings. Lawyers were aware, too. "He seems to have a special relationship with the *New York Times*, which often gives him space for his articles and also usually gives him favorable coverage," read one comment from an attorney in a compendium on federal judges. Even ordinary readers noticed. "Dear Mr. Rosenthal," a Queens subscriber wrote in 1983, "I cannot do without the *Times* every day, but I can do without such exhaustive coverage of Judge Irving Kaufman. I'm beginning to get the impression that Judge Kaufman is either a 'sacred cow,' or he's playing the *Times* like an organ. He seems to be an awful publicity hound." Rosenthal forwarded the letter to Sulzberger, saying "We sure have some smart readers. Would you care to reply to this one?" And Punch did, writing the man that he was Kaufman's "personal friend" and that his paper's coverage was "warranted by the flow of news. He is, after all, a senior judge of the Court of Appeals, and is active in a great many First Amendment decisions that are of particular interest to us and the readers of the *New York Times*."[41]

For someone else, all these links to the *Times* might have prompted soul-searching about whether he should withdraw from hearing cases involving the paper, such as the 1977 libel appeal targeting its story on DDT. Federal law requires recusal where the judge's impartiality might reasonably be questioned. And ironically, Kaufman had served on an ABA committee that stiffened the financial conflict-of-interest rules. Yet his ties to and interest in the *Times*, while not financial, were surely closer than owning some shares of stock. Given lawyers' and the public's awareness of his unusual relationship with the paper—let alone the things they didn't know, like his offer of legal advice after the Pentagon Papers argument and his regular socializing with Sulzberger and Rosenthal—many might reasonably doubt his impartiality.[42]

In any case, Sulzberger's letter to his loyal reader in Queens making clear that part of the paper's focus on Kaufman stemmed from Kaufman's role in First Amendment decisions echoed the larger question hovering over the relationship: how much of it was it simply back-scratching? Goodale, the paper's counsel, insisted Sulzberger would never directly intervene in the content of news stories to please Kaufman or anyone else, and Frankel affirmed the publisher's honorable intentions: "Punch's tolerance of [Kaufman], I'm sure, was no kind of favor-seeking or hunt for judicial support. It was born of loyalty for some good deed in the distant past—some kind of legal advice or service that I never heard discussed directly."[43]

The reporters in the trenches weren't so sure. A quid pro quo couldn't be proved "in an evidentiary sense," Goldstein acknowledged, "but it is hard not to conclude that Kaufman's extraordinary access to the pages of the newspaper and the uncritical coverage given his activities [were] directly related to his court decisions dealing with press issues and his numerous public statements supporting the press." In fact, Kaufman would actually joke about such favor-trading when he called Goldstein. "Look at the decision I just wrote for you," he would say, wheedling for more coverage. Looking back, Goldstein thought, "I was a naïve young reporter, and I didn't understand that's how things worked. And they may not have worked that way generally, but it certainly worked that way with him." Greenhouse agreed. In her view, Kaufman "set out to cultivate the owner of the *New York Times*, and he did it by . . . issuing all these fabulous First Amendment decisions. And so it was mutually supportive because the *Times* publisher wanted those decisions, and Judge Kaufman wanted the *Times* to love him, or need him, or something, and so they had this symbiotic relationship."[44]

From the *Times*' perspective, any help was welcome in an increasingly hostile environment. At a conference Kaufman helped organize in 1976, for example, Rosenthal bemoaned judges willing to "act as censors" and claimed press freedom was more and more "endangered" by courts happy to issue subpoenas for reporters and newsrooms. Thus he was pleased when Kaufman publicly and repeatedly advocated "a better relationship between the press and the courts. We've just got to find a way to live together. They depend on us to safeguard the First Amendment, and we depend on them to report our decisions correctly." Kaufman also frequently arranged for *Times* officials like Goodale and Rosenthal to serve on legal committees and address lawyers and judges—speeches the paper then covered—further amplifying what sometimes seemed like a joint public relations campaign. Privately, Kaufman was even more explicit; as he wrote Bob Erburu, head of the *Los Angeles Times*' parent company and a friend, "A more natural alliance than the press and the judiciary is difficult to imagine; First Amendment and judicial freedoms are intimately related."[45]

On Kaufman's side of the equation, his preoccupation with the *Times* had both public and personal dimensions. He saw society's understanding of judges and law as "woefully inadequate" and genuinely considered it part of a judge's official duty to, as he put it, "demystify the law" by writing for laypeople. To that end, he went beyond the *Times* and also wrote for the *Atlantic Monthly*, the *Wall Street Journal*, and the *Los Angeles Times*, facilitated by his friendship with Erburu. Whitney, for one, believed Kaufman's siege of reporters served a purpose beyond simple self-aggrandizement: "He just wanted to be sure his rulings got the right kind of coverage and figured the *Times* was probably the place that would give him the best shot at that." Nor is it likely Kaufman's press-friendly decisions were just a crude bid for coverage. His professed belief in the central role of free speech in a democracy and its importance to fully realizing one's identity jibed fully with his support for civil liberties across the board and his migration away from prioritizing the needs of the state and toward the claims of the individual.[46]

Still, constant exposure in the *Times* scratched what Goodale called Kaufman's personal itch "to be part of the action." As Goodale saw it, something like "200 people were opinion-makers in New York, and unlike other judges, [Kaufman] was the one judge I can think of who really *was* part of the action, and that is fun and makes one feel important. And also, it gives him peer leverage with his other judges because the judges as a group were then very naïve about how New York worked, and how the press worked, and how the press covered the judiciary, and Irving knew and they didn't." Being a fixture in the country's leading newspaper was also one more balm for his chronic insecurity—the same never-ending self-doubt that made him belittle his Harvard-trained clerks, keep Learned Hand's praise on a note card in his breast pocket, and demand that his opinions sparkle with enough Latin and literary allusions to prove his erudition once and for all.[47]

Finally, at the end, the *Times* did him one last favor. Kaufman's obituary headline mentioned the Rosenbergs, as he knew it would. (The obituary itself quoted a law student saying Kaufman had told him as much during his clerkship interview.) But in the same breath, the paper nodded to his staunch service in the holy cause. "Judge Irving Kaufman, of Rosenberg Spy Trial and Free Press Rulings, Dies at 81," the headline read. Not long after, Greenhouse ran into Punch's son,

Arthur Ochs Sulzberger Jr., and kidded him about all the free time his father probably had now that Kaufman wasn't constantly calling: "So Arthur, what's your father doing these days now that Judge Kaufman's no longer alive?" Junior didn't miss a beat and imagined a ghostly harassment only Kaufman could conjure: "Oh, he still speaks to him every day."[48]

Chapter 14

Annus Horribilis

By 1977, almost a quarter century had passed since the deaths of Julius and Ethel Rosenberg made Kaufman a historical figure. Since then, he'd ascended to the second-highest court in America, which he now led as chief judge. It was an administrative position some judges saw as tedious and politely declined, but Kaufman embraced it as a vehicle for widely praised judicial reform. He'd become one of the country's preeminent jurists, known far beyond New York thanks to major cases and enthusiastic press coverage he'd helped engineer himself. And he'd doggedly earned a reputation as a champion of civil liberties, case by groundbreaking case, impressing even ardent liberals once disgusted with the infamous death sentences.

From the outside, at least, his personal life was also enviable. There was the prosperous lifestyle of Park Avenue, lavish international travel, and frequent shoulder-rubbing with celebrities from the worlds of power and media in New York, Washington, Hollywood—even London. Two of his three sons seemed to be making their ways on Wall Street and were married with young children doted on by their proud and involved grandparents.

But despite all this, the hard-won success of a lifetime, a single year would mark an unraveling of death and defeat, throwing Kaufman back on his heels and shaming him before the public just when he was at life's apex.

Two weeks after swamping Barry Goldwater in the 1964 election, Lyndon Johnson was casting around for an attorney general. He was on the phone with J. Edgar Hoover when Hoover proposed someone Johnson didn't know:

> There's another name you might want to keep in mind, Mr. President, and that's the name of this judge Irving Kaufman in New York. He's a Jew, and I don't think there's any Jew in the cabinet at the present time. . . . He's a very close friend of this man, head of RCA, Sarnoff, and also has very close connections with the more decent people in New York. I merely mention him because he's a man I would say is in his 40s, maybe 50 by this time, and has been an excellent judge, and is a Jew. I think his ambitions ultimately would be to go to the Supreme Court if ever that happened to be open for him.[1]

Johnson murmured but ignored Hoover's suggestion, and the job eventually went to Nick Katzenbach, the man already doing it since Robert Kennedy had left to run for the Senate. Kaufman claimed not to want the job anyway; Deke DeLoach, one of Hoover's close aides, recorded him admitting "that at one time he had wanted this nomination; however, now he would not take the job even if it were offered to him." Hoover had planted the deeper seed, though: Kaufman, a Jew, for the Supreme Court.[2]

Two chances had already come and gone in 1962. First, Charles Whittaker resigned in March after only five years on the Court. Ted Sorenson prepared a list for President Kennedy with nineteen possible replacements, but only four were federal judges. Friendly was one of these, but not Kaufman. Lists compiled by Robert Kennedy at the Justice Department, his deputy Byron White, and then-chief of the Office of Legal Counsel Katzenbach also left Kaufman out. Leading candidates were William H. Hastie, a Third Circuit judge who would have been the first Black justice; Arthur Goldberg, secretary of labor and a key supporter during the 1960 campaign; and Paul Freund, a Harvard Law School professor. But each had drawbacks, and the spotlight soon focused on White himself. He was young, a former football star and Rhodes Scholar—the consummate New Frontiersman—and he got the appointment.[3]

A better possibility materialized months later when Frankfurter suffered a stroke. This was the fabled and shimmering "Jewish seat," first occupied by Louis Brandeis in 1916. It was the place Kaufman always imagined filling and where friends and foes had always seen him if the stars aligned. Frankfurter had once vowed he would stay long enough so that Kaufman would be too old to succeed him, but his body betrayed him. Now Kaufman hurried to Washington to plead his case, as an FBI memo recorded:

> Judge Kaufman stated that he was in Washington to discuss any vacancy that might exist, should Frankfurter retire from the Bench, with Mr. Katzenbach and Joseph F. Dolan, Assistant Deputy Attorney General. Judge Kaufman stated that he has at least a 50–50 chance of being appointed to any vacancy that might occur. He indicated that Abraham Ribicoff, Secretary of Health, Education, and Welfare, appears to be out of the running and that while Arthur J. Goldberg, Secretary of Labor, would be a leading contender, it is felt that his chances of appointment have been lessened by the previous appointment of Byron R. White, formerly Deputy Attorney General of the Department of Justice. The Judge indicated that there were two University professors interested in the appointment. He did not identify them other than to say that one is a Harvard Professor.[4]

The professors Kaufman referred to were likely Freund and Edward Levi, dean of the University of Chicago Law School. Ribicoff, Goldberg, Freund, Levi—all were Jewish. When Katzenbach had mentioned Levi to Kennedy for White's seat in March but added that the president "wouldn't want to appoint two Jews to the Supreme Court," Kennedy had shot back, "Why the hell shouldn't I?" At a minimum, he needed one; aides told him Jewish Democrats and organizations wouldn't like a high court with no Jews at all. Kaufman also hoped he had an ally in Joe Dolan, a lawyer who had worked for him in private practice and the lobbying investigation in 1948. Now Dolan worked for Katzenbach, perfectly positioned to help his old boss. Dolan wearily fielded Kaufman's many requests to arrange a meeting with Kennedy at the White House, but it never happened. And neither he nor Katzenbach bent to Kaufman's lobbying or took him seriously as a potential justice. Kennedy had always planned to put Goldberg on the Court, and he quickly made it official once Frankfurter finally decided he had to quit.[5]

Since Goldberg was only fifty-four, Kaufman must have glumly assumed the Jewish seat was gone. Then Goldberg unexpectedly quit in July 1965 to become ambassador to the United Nations. Little could Kaufman or anyone outside Lyndon Johnson's inner circle have known that the president had finagled Goldberg's departure in a power play to replace him with Johnson's old confidante and lawyer, Abe Fortas. For a few midsummer days, though, Fortas successfully resisted the legendary Johnson treatment, and the open seat seemed suspended in midair, there for the taking.[6]

At least two of Kaufman's friends pitched him to Johnson. Connecticut senator Tom Dodd wrote the president, recommending Kaufman as "one of the outstanding jurists of this country." He enclosed a copy of the letter Learned Hand had written four years earlier endorsing Kaufman for the Second Circuit. Dodd had already tried and failed the previous August to introduce the two and had even raised the specter of Kaufman helping LBJ in the 1964 election, writing the president's top aide, Jack Valenti: "I am sure [Kaufman] can be very helpful in the coming campaign, as he has a large and very influential circle of friends both in New York City and on the West Coast . . . Gen. Sarnoff and also Sam Newhouse etc. etc." There is no evidence Kaufman did anything to promote Johnson's election in 1964, but one wonders whether Dodd, Kaufman's close friend, would have made this offer without some assurance or belief that Kaufman would follow through. This although, as a former prosecutor, Dodd knew full well that politicking by a federal judge would traduce judicial ethics rules and traditions. Kaufman's old friend the Democratic fundraiser Ed Weisl similarly wrote Johnson and listed Kaufman among several judges he recommended.[7]

Kaufman may have also hoped his old mentor and Johnson's fellow Texan Tom Clark would put in a good word. "From the top trial judges to the top circuit is an accomplishment seldom enjoyed by anyone," Clark had written Kaufman recently, congratulating him on fifteen years of judicial service. "May you make the third step!" Yet Clark apparently never spoke to Johnson. His son Ramsey was now Katzenbach's deputy and thus another person, like Dolan earlier, who was positioned to help. Ramsey never promoted Kaufman either, however. Instead he suggested Herbert Wechsler, the Columbia law professor and American Law Institute head who would later praise Kaufman's revision of the insanity defense.[8]

Worst of all, the new attorney general, Katzenbach, hadn't changed his mind. He was ambivalent about continuing the tradition of the

Jewish seat, asserting that most Jews thought an appointment based on religious identity was offensive. Yet he simultaneously acknowledged that it would be "undesirable for there to be no Jew on the Court for too long a period." "On balance," he told LBJ, "I think if you appoint a Jew he should be so outstanding as to be selected clearly on his own merits as an individual." As far as Katzenbach was concerned, that wasn't Kaufman. Four months earlier, he'd politely repelled a move by Weisl to have Kaufman made the chairman of a commission to study and revamp law enforcement. The administration needed someone "whose name and achievement have received greater national attention and recognition," Katzenbach wrote delicately. He felt the same way about the Supreme Court, telling Johnson there was no "present member of the court of appeals (except for Judge Friendly) who would be regarded as an exceptional appointment." He suggested Freund again, Friendly, and several others—most but not all Jewish. On July 28, these recommendations went by the wayside when Johnson finally won his war of attrition with Fortas and announced the appointment, Fortas looking on forlornly.[9]

There were two more vacancies in Johnson's term, but no outsider like Kaufman stood a chance. One seat went to Kaufman's former colleague on the Second Circuit, Thurgood Marshall, a historic move Johnson had long planned. The other went to Johnson's old friend and Austin political ally Homer Thornberry, a man of whom Johnson exclaimed, "I know goddamn well what he would do for the next 25 years!" Thornberry's nomination died when Senate opposition scuttled Johnson's appointment of Fortas to become chief justice in October 1968.[10]

Nixon, like Johnson, wanted someone whose decisions could be predicted for the next quarter century, but he felt no need to perpetuate the Jewish seat vacated when Fortas resigned under an ethical cloud in 1969. Jews mostly supported the other party, and Nixon wanted a Southerner who shared his view that the Warren Court had favored lawbreakers and endangered the public. "This country is going so far to the right you won't recognize it," his attorney general, John Mitchell, happily told one reporter. "When are you going to fill that Jewish seat on the Supreme Court?" Mitchell later joked with Nixon on the phone. "Well, how about after I die?" the president laughed. More seriously, he told Pat Buchanan that "as long as I'm sitting in this chair there's not going to be any Jew appointed to that Court, not because they're Jewish, because there's no Jew . . . that can be right on the criminal law issue. . . . They're all hung up on civil rights."[11]

Despite Nixon's stereotypes, some Jews did receive passing consideration from advisers for the four vacancies filled in 1969 and 1971, including Arlin Adams of the Third Circuit, Philadelphia District Attorney Arlen Specter, and Friendly. Kaufman may have hoped the Rosenberg case would boost his chances, since Nixon had risen in national politics by attacking Reds during the McCarthy era. At least one Nixon supporter in the media seemed to agree. In 1969, after Fortas's resignation, the *Chicago Tribune*'s longtime Washington man and Nixon friend Walter Trohan wrote that Kaufman "appears to be destined for a seat on the Supreme Court," citing his most famous case as something "liberals might pillory him for" but which "those who believe in sound law" applauded. Mitchell assembled 100 or perhaps 150 names—the list or lists seem to have vanished—and the *Times* wrote later that Kaufman's "name was one of those submitted for consideration by Mr. Nixon" for vacancies in 1971, though it didn't say who did the submitting. Smaller lists excluded him, though, and his liberal decisions in criminal and other cases would surely have disqualified him had it gotten more serious. The New Rochelle case would also have hurt; "I don't want a fellow who is going to go hog-wild with integration, de facto segregation," Nixon told aides at one point.[12]

One back-channel recommendation unexpectedly became public in 1974 when the press unearthed a 1971 letter to Mitchell from Elmer Bobst, a close friend Nixon called his "honorary father." Bobst had proposed Kaufman for the Supreme Court, but his letter made news for other reasons: it appeared to offer Mitchell a $100,000 campaign contribution in exchange for Federal Trade Commission approval of a merger Bobst wanted. As the *Times* reported, "Mr. Bobst recommended that Chief Judge Irving R. Kaufman . . . be considered to fill one of the vacancies on the Supreme Court. Mr. Bobst said that he had been 'approached' by Judge Kaufman several days previously." Kaufman felt it necessary to issue a statement distancing himself from the embarrassing mess: "I am, of course, totally unaware of Mr. Bobst's suggestion to the former Attorney General that consideration be given to my appointment to the Supreme Court. The context within which he made his recommendation is unfortunate, and as I have said unknown to me. I have met Mr. Bobst casually two or three times at an annual luncheon given by a mutual friend attended by about 60 people. But I was not aware he was initiating any proposal regarding my judicial status."[13]

Did Kaufman ask Bobst to mention his name to Mitchell or Nixon, as Bobst wrote and contrary to Kaufman's public statement? It would have been typical, another instance of using whatever tools were available instead of passively sitting around and hoping for a call from Washington. Nor would he have been alone in that kind of politicking, which had worked for Burger when he won the chief justice's job in 1969, and for others before him. During the period when Bobst wrote Mitchell, with two vacancies on the Court, Kaufman's clerk remembered a frenzy of activity in chambers as Kaufman worked the phones. One call went to his well-connected Republican friend Walter Annenberg, the wealthy media mogul and Nixon ambassador in London. But no amount of lobbying could turn him into a Gentile strict constructionist. The 1971 vacancies Bobst had written about went to a corporate lawyer and former ABA head, Lewis Powell, and a young, conservative Mitchell deputy, William Rehnquist.[14]

If Kaufman couldn't be appointed by Nixon, perhaps he could investigate him. In April 1973, as Watergate began to devour the presidency, a newly appointed attorney general, Elliot Richardson, bowed to calls for an independent prosecutor to probe the break-in and cover-up. For a few days, Richardson and his team focused on judges as possible special prosecutors, and the *Times* reported that "persons close to" Kaufman said he'd been asked to do the job but declined. In fact, Richardson's papers make no mention of Kaufman as a possibility. Lumbard, by then partially retired, and district judge Harold Tyler, who almost accepted, were seriously considered before Richardson settled on Harvard Law School professor Archibald Cox. Regardless, Kaufman released a statement two days after the *Times* article saying he "consider[ed] it inappropriate for a sitting judge to conduct this inquiry. Indeed, the Code of Judicial Conduct, which I helped draft, forbids such an assignment."[15]

Whatever Kaufman's despondency at failing to secure a spot on the Supreme Court, he made light of it when receiving an honorary degree from NYU in 1973, just after supposedly declining the Watergate job:

> You know, of course, that this award means a great deal to me, in part because it provides a perfect opportunity to update my Who's Who resume, an opportunity not generally afforded to a man my age. After all, I could hardly have asked the editors of that publication to note that I had been considered for the Supreme Court in 1971 but that the President determined that a non-judge *should* fill the vacancy; or that I was asked to be the Special Watergate Prosecutor in 1973 but that a non-Judge *had* to fill that position. It appears that we judges are not much good for anything except receiving honorary degrees and judging—and I'm afraid you can still get a strong argument on the last point.[16]

It was a boastful and only marginally accurate thing to say, even by the standards of after-dinner entertainment, since he received no real consideration from Nixon. It was also the only time Kaufman publicly alluded to missing out on his dream.

Another vacancy occurred in 1975 when Douglas resigned, and the *Times* again reported that Kaufman's name was one of many possible appointees submitted to the ABA. Kaufman was older than the ceiling President Ford had privately set for the next justice, however. Thus by 1977, when Jimmy Carter took office, his window had closed. Carter was to make no appointments to the Court in any case.[17]

Kaufman had sped toward his goal since the publicity of 1951, and that ambition had been bolstered by friends and news stories over the years saying he had a shot. Even enemies like Frankfurter feared he would succeed. And some of the motivation behind what he'd done after 1951—the bids for publicity, extensive extracurricular writing, and committee work; the attempts to see the attorney general or president whenever in Washington; the long train of flattery for Hoover and others; the cultivation of corporate and media titans like Sulzberger, Newhouse, and Annenberg—was to help position him for appointment, even as it also simply fed his deeper hunger for recognition. Now he had to face what C. S. Lewis called "the shortness of the tether," the internal voice whispering "too late now . . . not for me."[18]

Although everyone knew Kaufman was past consideration in 1981, when Ronald Reagan became president, the prolonged palpability of his yearning was still fodder for gentle mockery. During the campaign that year, Reagan pledged to name a woman to the Court—a promise he redeemed a few months into his first term when he appointed Sandra Day O'Connor to replace Potter Stewart. One day the topic came up at the judges' long communal dining table in the Second Circuit cafeteria, and Mulligan leaned over to the judge next to him but spoke loudly enough for everyone to hear: "Hey, did you hear Irving's wearing a dress?"[19]

It was one thing to aim high and fall short; there was no shame in that. But just as it was becoming certain in the mid-1970s that Kaufman would never "make the third step," as Clark had put it, something far worse began to happen: his old enemies reappeared to threaten what he already had.

For years, the Rosenberg controversy was manageable, if not completely quiet. Morton Sobell kept raining applications on the federal courts to reverse his conviction, and Kaufman kept poking back behind the scenes. In 1962, Sobell's longtime lawyer Marshall Perlin argued to a Second Circuit panel that a 1957 Supreme Court decision compelled reexamination of his conviction, and Thurgood Marshall initially seemed receptive. When Kaufman heard about it, he found Marshall and "raised hell," as he told the FBI, adding that he thought Marshall was "somewhat naive and certainly inexperienced on the bench." While Marshall had only been a judge for two years, he probably wasn't naïve about criminal cases after devoting years to defending African Americans on trial for their lives across the South. In any case, the court denied Sobell's application. Three years later, when Sobell's wife and supporters unsuccessfully applied for a pardon, Kaufman called the FBI to argue that "Sobell should serve his entire sentence"—a mean-spirited move far beyond his jurisdiction and sharply at odds with the compassion he otherwise showed for prisoners. Sobell wasn't released until 1969, paroled after serving over half his sentence.[20]

One of Sobell's last applications was based largely on allegations aired in Walter and Miriam Schneir's book, *Invitation to an Inquest*, first published in 1965. The Schneirs, left-leaning freelance science writers, plunged deeper into the case than previous analysts and charged the government with fabricating evidence to convict innocent people needed as scapegoats for Russia's development of the bomb. The book plumbed holes and discrepancies in the government's proof—most notably a registration card from Gold's stay at an Albuquerque hotel with an incorrect date stamp, said to be proof of FBI forgery—offered alternative explanations for seemingly damning evidence, and explored facts and experts' views developed after the trial that raised questions about the convictions.

Kaufman wanted to respond and thought of Sidney Hook. "I was also hoping that you could do a completely objective and non-partisan book on the Rosenberg case," he asked, but Hook kept stalling. Kaufman also got to work arranging a *Times* letter to the editor, and the FBI spun into action. "Steps have already been taken in New York and by various 'contacts' of ours to refute the book by the Schneirs," the third-ranking official at the FBI, Deke DeLoach, wrote, emphasizing that Catholic publications would help. An FBI agent in Chicago also helped to suppress a television show the Schneirs tried to arrange. When a producer who had "always been cooperative in the past with regard to Bureau matters" offered to turn the Schneirs down, the FBI asked him to do just that, "for no good would accrue from it."[21]

While most dismissed its conspiracy theory, *Invitation to an Inquest* was thorough and seemingly disinterested enough to darken the cloud over a case where, as Nathan Glazer put it in a *Times* review, the evidence was "more tenuous than one would wish to still all doubts." Alexander Bickel, the Yale Law School constitutional authority and *Times* lawyer in the Pentagon Papers case, panned the Schneirs in *Commentary* for their inability to explain why the Greenglasses would invent a capital crime and implicate themselves in it. But he also went out of his way to deride Kaufman: "There is first of all the death sentence, and secondly the death sentence, and thirdly the death sentence, and then again the death sentence." To Bickel, Kaufman's rationales were little more than an "unchecked onslaught of anxiety and mindless surmise . . . in the best traditions of some superstition-ridden tribe."[22]

Sobell's release coincided with a play based on *Invitation to an Inquest* by an unknown teacher and journeyman dramatist named Donald Freed, which secured a small run in Cleveland. Despite Freed's obscurity, *The United States vs. Julius and Ethel Rosenberg* took that city by storm, filling every seat even after winning six extra weeks. Consisting largely of actors reading portions of the trial transcript and the doomed couple's letters, the drama ended with silhouettes trooping toward a ghostly electric chair. The actor playing Kaufman gave his damning speech at sentencing, and even his old friend Milton Berle was heard cracking jokes in a "sound collage" in the lobby. Freed wasn't trying to be neutral; he happily admitted dispensing with an "inhuman objectivity" and made the Rosenbergs morally perfect martyrs. This tended to grate on reviewers who conceded the production's power but, in one case, confessed to leaving the theater "feeling that a very gross attempt had been made to sell me a bill of goods." Another dubbed it "Invitation to a Whitewash."[23]

Had attention stopped with the *Cleveland Plain Dealer*, even Kaufman might not have cared. Notice reached New York, however, where the *Times* covered it twice in seven days, and Kaufman started getting the old hate mail again. One correspondent included the play's program with an index card saying "You are a fine Jew. . . . I hope you and your family can sleep nights." Reaching Hoover directly, he complained that the *Times*' coverage was unprecedented and that he would arrange a letter to the editor. "How dare the drama critic encroach upon our system of justice," Hoover recorded in his memo of the call, "as he would resent it if [Kaufman] tried to tell him how to review a play. . . . Judge Kaufman said he could see this gaining momentum and coming into New York and Washington and he could see all these bleeding hearts who forget the facts. I commented it would be another Sacco-Vanzetti case. I told the judge I would get to work on it and let the Attorney General know about it also." That same evening, an agent was dispatched to the Cleveland playhouse to see it in person, resulting in a flurry of memos dissecting the play. Agents investigated Freed's background and, true to his word, Hoover promptly notified Mitchell.[24]

Even as he was setting all this in motion, Kaufman pretended to others that he was restrained by judicial decorum from fighting back. After Kaufman poured out his troubles to a dinner companion one evening, his acquaintance wrote the next day offering to respond on his behalf and asking for information about the case. "Of course, I understand the current interest in the Rosenberg case," Kaufman replied, "but I hasten to make clear I can neither inspire nor encourage any action concerning that or any other case over which I presided." Yet actually he was doing just that—but in secret—deploying more trusted soldiers like Hoover and Simon Rifkind. Nor was he consistent. Kaufman had opened his files to the sympathetic columnist Jim Bishop to write a pro-prosecution book in the late 1950s. And he was more than willing to divulge his thought process about specific cases in several published articles and occasionally in interviews—just not his most notorious one. Instead, he increasingly relied on Rifkind, his best friend and most devoted advocate in the court of public opinion.[25]

In the *Times* letter Kaufman arranged about Freed's play, Rifkind condemned the baseless floating of suspicions that the Rosenbergs were innocent. And he warned of riots: "Such expressions can only lend fuel to the fires of present day rebellion by violence which is afflicting our cities, our universities and other sensitive areas of our society. It constitutes another charge of vicious brutality leveled at a generation at which the present younger set has already learned to look with contempt." Overheated, yes, but Rifkind was on to something. Freed *was* a student demonstrator, antiwar activist, and Black Panther sympathizer. "As the war in Vietnam went on," he told an interviewer, "I began to realize that the murder of the Rosenbergs was not an aberration but simply part of a murderous pattern." He thought "Huey Newton, Bobby Seale and Eldridge Cleaver are the Julius and Ethel Rosenberg of today."[26]

Freed exemplified a new generation, the New Left, free of the ancient odor of Stalinism and galvanized by America's more recent sins. The novelist and critic D. Keith Mano spotted what had changed: "Julius and Ethel aren't on trial; the 1950s are." A few weeks after Freed sold out Cleveland—the play would conquer New York the following year, just as Kaufman feared—a small group of elderly women held a vigil marking the sixteenth anniversary of the executions in New York. The sad turnout and the participants' senescence boded ominously for keeping their flame alive, but they were about to get reinforcements.[27]

Motivation for these fresh troops started with an unlikely source: Otto Preminger. The liberal director and champion of blacklisted writers wanted to make a movie about the case and asked a famous trial lawyer, Louis Nizer, to write the screenplay. With his Hollywood connections, Kaufman learned of Preminger's project and told the FBI chief in Los Angeles that "probably the best way of controlling Preminger would be through the financial sources that he must utilize to put together such a picture." The FBI suggested enlisting a friendly Paramount vice president "to insure there will be no embarrassment to the Federal Government," presumably by squelching Preminger's funding, and continued to monitor the project. When it died, Hoover personally wrote Kaufman with the good news. Meanwhile, Nizer's labors became a book, *The Implosion Conspiracy*, released in 1973. More interested in dramatically re-creating the trial than dissecting the evidence, Nizer concluded that the government's proof adequately supported the guilty verdicts but that Kaufman's sentences went too far. Two people who deliberately avoided Nizer's book, however, even as it moved up the bestseller lists, were Michael and Robert Meeropol, originally Michael and Robert Rosenberg.[28]

A year after the executions, Abel Meeropol and his wife Anne took in and later adopted the Rosenberg boys. Like Kaufman, Meeropol was a Clinton High graduate and later a teacher at the school. He became a poet and a songwriter best known for his haunting anti-lynching hymn, "Strange Fruit." He was also a communist. By 1973, Michael was a thirty-year-old economics professor at a small college in Springfield, Massachusetts, and Robert was a twenty-six-year-old graduate student there. Beneath seventies-perfect long hair and mustaches, they were their parents' look-alikes. Michael drove an old Volvo with a "Don't Blame Me, I Voted for McGovern" bumper sticker, and both had young children of their own. Although they'd taken the name Meeropol and hidden their origins from all but spouses and closest friends, both believed they'd kept the faith through New Left and antiwar activism. For years, they'd quietly debated when and how to go public, but hearing about Nizer's book stirred an outrage that forced their hands. The lawyer quoted liberally from the Rosenbergs' prison letters, which the

Meeropols believed infringed their copyright. Worse, they thought Nizer had committed slander by echoing Kaufman's view at sentencing that their parents loved communism more than their own children. Their parents were their legacy, and Nizer had polluted it.

The brothers sued Nizer for $3 million in copyright violations and defamation and began doing interviews. And "once we were out in the open," Robert said, "we had no alternative but to reopen the case." Emily Alman, who'd founded the original committee to generate public opposition to the executions in 1951–53, reappeared and called a meeting. The old-timers convinced the sons that "growing awareness of our government's lies and dirty tricks in Vietnam and during the Watergate scandal increased the likelihood of public acceptance that our government might frame people for crimes they did not commit," as Robert put it years later. And with détente, few still feared Soviet aggression.[29]

So the Meeropols were in, and by early 1974 the ground was increasingly fertile. Besides Nizer's book, there had been E. L. Doctorow's searing fictionalization of the Rosenberg case, *The Book of Daniel*, centered on two lost and wounded children of executed spies. Doctorow told reporters he saw the case as "unfinished business." In the novel, Kaufman was Judge Hirsch, a man whose "most intimate professional secret [is] that he hopes to be appointed to the Supreme Court." In early 1974, two TV shows took up the case, one a dramatic reconstruction on the prestigious *ABC Theater* and the other a documentary for public television produced by Alvin Goldstein. Like Freed and the Schneirs, both emphasized weaknesses in the prosecution's case and the frightened public climate at the time. Although most reviewers noted the shows' bias, Kaufman couldn't let it pass. As usual, the FBI checked Goldstein's background for subversion, while Kaufman, described as "upset" in memos, urged taking "a stand with respect to this matter as it appears Goldstein and others are attempting to 'whittle away' at the Government's case." Once more, the public response came from Rifkind's pen. His *TV Guide* article, reprinted on several newspapers' op-ed pages, made the familiar points, including Learned Hand's support for Kaufman's promotion. It also lamented the Rosenbergs' new status as "folk heroes" being used as left-wing tools to discredit the American legal system. To Goldstein, that kind of answer from someone like Rifkind simply reeked of "that part of America that is represented today by Watergate."[30]

As the Meeropols ramped up public appearances, the newly formed "National Committee to Reopen the Rosenberg Case" took office space

FIGURE 12. Michael, *left*, and Robert Meeropol in front of the federal courthouse in Washington, DC, in 1975. *Associated Press.*

and began raising money. The committee mixed veterans who had held on to their outrage and new believers in their twenties and thirties. Letterhead "sponsors" included Harry Belafonte, Paul Robeson, Norman Mailer, and Pete Seeger—a man whose conviction Kaufman had overturned in 1962 but who showed little love for him now. At Robert's events, fellow red diaper babies told him their own parents had been innocent communists, too, and that they'd grown up fearful of being next on what they imagined was the government's political orphan list. Carnegie Hall hosted the group's coming-out party in June 1974. It was the twenty-first anniversary of the executions, and twenty-eight hundred paying contributors rallied to begin a nationwide drive for exoneration. Giant blow-ups of Picasso's famous drawings of Julius and Ethel stood as backdrops while the actors Rip Torn and Jane Alexander read some of their letters. "In the next year we are going to blow the lid on this case," Robert exhorted. In the *Times*, a lawyer and former prosecutor, someone who couldn't be dismissed as a New Left ranter, soberly reviewed the evidence, rebutted Rifkind's *TV Guide* article, and lashed Kaufman for having been "caught up in the fever of the times."[31]

More ominously, condemnation was moving from the television screen and the newspaper to Kaufman's actual day-to-day life. At the annual Legal Aid Society board meeting, a contingent of young lawyers who worked for the society got up and walked out as Kaufman rose to speak. "These well-orchestrated 'events' are disturbing and one is apt to believe that there is substantial support for such conduct," he wrote morosely to the prominent lawyer Arthur Liman. He enlisted a deputy US marshal to travel with him to speaking engagements. But the showman in him could also joke. When he received the Federal Bar Council's prestigious Learned Hand Medal and Rosenberg supporters gathered outside to protest, Kaufman began his speech by complimenting the master of ceremonies for not only greeting him in the ballroom but also lining up a crowd "in front of the hotel—*that* is thoughtfulness. They have the right to picket, just as you have the right to give me an award. But in all honesty, I must confess that the exercise of your right is more pleasurable to me." And when a prisoner wrote the tough-on-crime Leonard Moore to thank him, improbably, for the fairness of a sentence he had imposed, Kaufman asked Lumbard, who showed him the missive, "Do you suppose [Moore] could get some of the Rosenberg fans to write me a similar letter?"[32]

Over the next several months, the Meeropols left their jobs and traveled the country. Once introverts hiding their past, they now led rallies, spoke on college campuses, and appeared on television. They called Kaufman a murderer and tried to bait him into suing them for libel, though they harbored little real hope of a courtroom showdown. If Kaufman would only sue, they reasoned, they could subpoena his files. But of course Kaufman wasn't dumb enough to oblige. In 1975, the Meeropols published *We Are Your Sons*, an affecting collection of their parents' letters interspersed with an account of their own early lives. Their committee formed chapters in fourteen cities and claimed a ten-thousand-person mailing list. In that year's version of the courthouse rally on the anniversary of the executions, Michael used a bullhorn to shout up at Kaufman. "Though the signs and the theme of the demonstration were based on the demand that the FBI open their secret files," he wrote, "the magnet of Kaufman's presence up on the twenty-second floor of that building (I don't even know if he was there in fact but his presence was sensed) drew all of us. . . . It felt personally good to be down at Foley Square paying Kaufman and Saypol back a tiny percentage of the anguish they had caused our family."[33]

As the Rosenberg sons became public figures, people materialized from the ether with tantalizing and unconfirmable tidbits about the case. Robert was fundraising in California in the mid-1970s when Perlin told him there was a wealthy and powerful Jewish leader in San Diego who wanted to talk. When Robert went to his house—something that reminded him of *The Great Gatsby*—the man took him to his study and described a visit from Kaufman back in 1951. Kaufman had shown up then, before the trial, and said "let's take a walk." Once outside and alone, Kaufman had supposedly told the man not to worry about the case generating antisemitism or wrongful convictions; the government had shown him top secret information proving the Rosenbergs were spies, and he couldn't go into it any further. As time went on, though, the community leader decided it was wrong for a judge to get secret material from one side of a case. He'd felt bad all these years, he said, and just wanted Robert to know. Another call, years later, came from a man who said he was the son of an FBI agent Hoover had assigned to keep an eye on Roy Cohn during the trial. Even then, no one trusted Cohn. The caller, twelve or thirteen at the time, used to listen in when his dad played cards with other FBI agents. He heard his dad tell his poker buddies how, every day during the trial, he eavesdropped on Cohn calling Kaufman from a courthouse telephone and talking strategy. He also just thought Robert should know.[34]

Like a clumsy and slow-moving army chasing nimble guerrillas, Rifkind tried to keep up. He published letters and articles in the *Times*, the *Los Angeles Times*, and the *Honolulu Advertiser*, where Kaufman knew the publisher. To the usual arguments—Bloch's praise of the trial, the extensive appellate review, the rejection of Sobell's supposed new evidence in the 1960s—Rifkind now added a defense of the sentences. Whatever one's views of capital punishment, he wrote, Congress plainly contemplated death for serious espionage, and life imprisonment wasn't authorized. He claimed appellate courts had approved the death penalties, without mentioning that trial judges then enjoyed almost limitless discretion in sentencing. And he noted that two presidents had chosen not to halt the executions. But the dead couple's children were compelling and sympathetic and less than half their opponents' ages. They looked and sounded like the new generation. Lawyerly counterpoints weren't about to calm the storm. Headlines like "Rosenbergs' 'Trial' Goes on after 23 Years" (*Chicago Tribune*) and "The Rosenbergs Retried" (*Newsweek*) and "Rosenberg Defenders March Again" (*Washington Post*) spread like contagion. In Los Angeles, a rally for hundreds at the Santa Monica Civic Auditorium was disrupted by someone throwing a tear gas bomb. After what one reporter called the "essentially older, affluent

Jewish crowd" streamed outside, tearing and vomiting, the program resumed and Henry Fonda did an excerpt of his one-man play *Clarence Darrow*.[35]

Kaufman had also scheduled a trip to California—to speak at the Pomona College commencement in Claremont. After the mess in Santa Monica, college officials wondered what might happen if Kaufman showed up in person. When they delicately raised this with Kaufman, he elected to withdraw before he was announced as the day's attraction. Soon after, though, he decided to use the episode to publicly protest his growing ostracism. In "A Free Speech for the Class of 75" in the *Times Magazine*, he described the feared protests at Pomona as part of "a continuing pattern of harassment because of a trial I presided over more than 20 years ago, prior even to the birth of the vast majority of present university students. I felt it unfortunate, if not unfair, that these old issues should affect an invitation to speak today, for in the intervening years, I had written decisions in a wide range of cases that focused public interest—among them cases involving civil rights, school desegregation, prison reform, criminal insanity tests, conscientious objection, and freedom of expression." Decisions, in other words, most of the class of '75 would applaud. The article went on to critique "a new spirit of intolerance" on campus and advocate recommitment to the First Amendment's spirit of welcoming "conflicting beliefs and the right to express them." The First Amendment champion was reduced to pleading for his own right to be heard. Some of the letters to the editor were brutal. "The judge," one went, "having murdered the Eighth Amendment . . . throws himself on the mercy of the court of public opinion, on the grounds that the Class of '75 has violated his First Amendment rights. Three cheers for the Class of '75." The Pomona incident perfectly anticipated twenty-first-century battles over "cancel culture" and free speech on campus sparked by controversial conservative speakers who were heckled or disinvited. It also confirmed that Kaufman was fast becoming a pariah.[36]

That status bled into his social life. With glee, the Meeropols heard that "Kaufman couldn't even go to a party without people starting to argue with him about the Rosenberg case." James Zirin, a Manhattan lawyer, remembered an intimate dinner at the home of a partner whose wife, either oblivious or so upset that she didn't care, asked Kaufman how he could have condemned the Rosenbergs to die. "There was a stunned silence in the room" until Kaufman offered that he'd consulted with Learned Hand. Zirin also remembered dining with a client at Le Cirque one night when Kaufman entered. The posh temple of gastronomy and celebrity on the Upper East Side was one of Kaufman's favorites. As Kaufman passed by his table, Zirin overheard the man at the next table over tell his date, "That's Irving Kaufman, the judge who fried the Rosenbergs." Michael Meeropol received a letter from a man who "praised himself for spilling wine on Kaufman at a party and muttering under his breath, 'This is for Ethel and Julius.'" "You have no idea how many letters I've gotten from people who have confided in me little ways they've tried to be insulting to him," he said. In chambers, clerks were taught how to check the morning mail for bombs.[37]

If Rifkind couldn't quiet the criticism, there was little reason to think other and more Rifkinds might do the trick. Nevertheless, on the same day protesters demonstrated at Foley Square on the twenty-second anniversary of the executions, the current and seven past presidents of the Association of the Bar of the City of New York issued a statement meant to counteract the "rising crescendo of attacks" on Kaufman that "appear on the air, in print, and on picket signs which confront the judge at public dinners which he must attend." Because ethical canons prevented Kaufman from openly defending himself, the bar presidents claimed, it was their duty to speak for him lest the denunciations intensify "the present atmosphere of doubt about our institutions." They stressed the same points Rifkind always emphasized. For his part, Rifkind turned to a different bar group, the ABA, and convinced it to let him form a subcommittee to respond to the clamor. But neither development made much news, and it didn't surprise anyone that the established bar was rallying around the Second Circuit's chief judge.[38]

The New York City bar presidents' statement ended with the plaintive "hope that the present propaganda campaign will soon have run its course." In fact, the opposite was true. Thanks to several new developments—Hoover's death in 1972, less rigid positions taken by recent attorneys general, and amendments strengthening the Freedom of Information Act—the FBI's wall of silence started to crack. The Meeropols and a Smith College historian sued under FOIA and won, and the FBI started to disgorge documents in late 1975. It still redacted with abandon and held back most records, but the Meeropols finally had their first glimpse into the government's files on their parents' case. "Our idea [with the FOIA lawsuit] was, we're going to dig up dirt—we didn't know on who," Robert said. "We were going to focus on the juiciest stuff we got."[39]

The juiciest stuff was about the judge. As the Meeropols' lawyers and committee volunteers started reviewing the thirty thousand pages coughed up by the FBI, they stumbled on a couple that revealed Kaufman's private communications with the Bureau, and they stopped. "Forget everything," the lawyers said, just "read every document and pull out everything related to the name Kaufman." Michael was on a book and fundraising tour after publication of the paperback edition of *We Are Your Sons*, but his lawyers called and said, "Get your ass back to New York, we're going to have a press conference. This stuff is unbelievable."[40]

Buried in the stacks of paper were two FBI memos suggesting Kaufman's *ex parte* contacts with the government before trial, and that he'd decided on death before even hearing any evidence. There was also a 1975 letter from Saypol to Kelley recounting Kaufman's request after the trial that Saypol not recommend a particular sentence in open court. If believed, that put the lie to Kaufman's claim at sentencing that he hadn't asked the government for its views on the Rosenbergs' fate. Five memos written before the executions documented Kaufman's advice to prosecutors and his urging that they push the case to avoid further delays in carrying out the sentences. And twenty-three memos from 1956 right up to 1975 revealed his opposition to Sobell's applications—in one, he was quoted saying he would deny a motion before he'd even seen it—as well as his periodic maneuvers with the FBI to squelch and rebut public criticism. The memos weren't definitive; they were piecemeal and rife with hearsay. Yet they weren't easily dismissed either. Taken together, they depicted a judge who'd shed his impartiality and later become obsessed with muffling criticism in order to protect his reputation. The Rosenberg committee published the memos as a pamphlet titled *The Kaufman Papers*.[41]

The Meeropols held their press conference on June 10, 1976, and Perlin accused Kaufman of having defiled his oath of office. The *Times* and *Washington Post* followed up with descriptions of the FBI memos and Perlin's charge. Before the FBI's reluctant document dump, Kaufman had mostly been faulted for the draconian sentences. Even the Meeropols didn't "think that he had actually overstepped the boundaries of proper judicial conduct and legality," Robert wrote. But now that changed. A lawyer described in one news report as "a Kaufman watcher year after year" said, "It's a funny thing, Irving's always been afraid something was about to come out and really damage him, whether it was true or not. Sometimes you could catch that look on his face. '*When* is it going to happen?' So it's happened." Once accused only of cruelty, he was suddenly the face of corruption. And since the new campaign's animating idea was that the Rosenbergs had been framed, any hint of judicial misconduct or collusion with the prosecution threw gas on the fire.[42]

Perlin was essentially unknown. Soon, however, he had high-powered support from a colleague who had also helped with one of Sobell's petitions. Vern Countryman was a chain-smoking Montanan with a square jaw, an outdated crew cut, and a lifelong affinity for underdogs. His academic specialty at Harvard was bankruptcy and commercial law, but he was active in civil liberties issues and had gained attention in the 1950s as a public critic of Hoover and McCarthyism. His students called him "Stern Vern." Countryman began working on colleagues and, after a couple months, sent a six-page letter to the chairmen of the House and Senate Judiciary Committees asking them to investigate Kaufman. He acknowledged that the FBI memos raised rather than answered questions, but if they were true, he claimed, then Kaufman had engaged in "a shocking pattern of *ex parte* contacts" and efforts to stifle public discourse about the case "which would not be acceptable from a prosecuting attorney, much less from a judicial officer." One hundred and twelve law professors signed on, including several of Countryman's colleagues at Harvard and other stars of academia. One was Monroe Freedman, a preeminent authority on legal ethics who went even further than Countryman and publicly proposed that Congress consider impeaching Kaufman "for deliberately bringing about the deaths of two people by illegal and unethical abuse of judicial power."[43]

The law professors' broadside forced those in Kaufman's orbit to take sides. The ACLU asked Congress to investigate and more clearly outlaw *ex parte* communications, while the New York branch of the organization, more grateful for Kaufman's years of liberal rulings and stocked with lawyers who knew him personally, opposed the move on the ground that congressional investigations of judges threatened judicial independence. The ADL, to which Kaufman had belonged while in private practice and which had beaten back attacks in the 1950s that he was a self-hating Jew, also opposed the ACLU. And his friends at the *Times* came through with an editorial titled "Invitation to a Vendetta" that condemned the ACLU request as camouflage for reopening the case. "Judge Kaufman's record on the bench since [the Rosenberg case] has been exemplary," the piece noted. "Surely, after a quarter of a century, it is time to end the vendetta against him." The *Daily News* also used that word in deploring the "dirty, despicable vendetta against an outstanding jurist and an honorable man."[44]

More liberal outlets pounced, however, with Nat Hentoff of the *Village Voice* titling his piece "The Rosenberg Children Nail the Judge Who Made Them Orphans." "Judge Kaufman's Torment," blared the *New Republic*'s cover over a pen-and-ink drawing of Kaufman with a raven hovering nearby. The issue featured a piece by Countryman, "Out, Damned Spot," with a drawing of Lady Macbeth. The legal magazine *Juris Doctor* also put Kaufman on its cover, sepia Rosenbergs in the background, with the tagline "A Specter Is Haunting Irving Kaufman." The article described the FBI memos yet again and asked how Kaufman could continue to hear cases where Rifkind represented one of the litigants, as Kaufman did, since Rifkind was effectively his lawyer.[45]

Fiction piled on. A psychedelic novel published in 1977 by Robert Coover called *A Public Burning* reimagined the Rosenberg executions as a vast orgiastic carnival in Times Square narrated by Richard Nixon, who seduces Ethel Rosenberg and is sodomized by Uncle Sam. "Little Irving Kaufman" appears as a minor but recurring character—"the Boy Judge, a stubby Park Avenue Jew and Tammany Hall Democrat who looks a little like a groundhog himself with his plastered-down hair, thick bumpy nose, and damp beady eyes." At the climactic public electrocutions, Kaufman is cheered wildly but wonders whether "he and the Rosenbergs needed each other to fulfill themselves. . . . There were those who thanked him for putting the heat on them—but who has put the heat on whom?"[46]

Frustrated that nothing—not demonstrations, not articles, not even absurdist fiction—seemed to threaten any real consequences for Kaufman, the Rosenberg committee finally resorted to directly publishing several of the FBI memos in a full page "open letter" to him in his beloved Sunday *Times*. It was the twenty-fourth anniversary of the executions, June 1977. "You cannot remain silent," they admonished. "You must open your files." Anyone Kaufman knew who had somehow missed the hubbub or glossed over the details was now fully informed. Down at the courthouse at the annual demonstration that same week, the Meeropols and a hundred or so other protesters "raised the bullhorn until it faced the upper floors of the imposing courthouse and read sections of *The Kaufman Papers* to the lunchtime strollers, news media, and we hoped, Judge Kaufman," Michael wrote later. Then the exasperation boiled over and the Meeropols and Perlin went inside and phoned Kaufman's chambers, hoping, improbably, that he would actually talk to them. Instead, they got a law clerk. The clerk said "Judge Kaufman is a very busy man," and "you can't just walk off the street and see a federal appeals court judge." They gave their contact information and left.[47]

Despite the demand to speak in public or even on the phone, Kaufman didn't. He maintained his public stance that tradition and judicial ethics prevented a judge from defending himself. In one letter, he called himself "a 'sitting duck' who is not even permitted to quack." As always, though, his surrogates were hard at work—Rifkind; law professors and former clerks Arthur Leff and Robert Gorman; and Arnold Bauman, a former Southern District judge. They argued that the memos were hearsay and courthouse gossip ("piffle, mostly," Rifkind said); that Cohn (then) adamantly denied private meetings with Kaufman; that talking to prosecutors in private before sentencing was allowed and commonplace in 1951; that working with the FBI to arrange responses to books and plays about the case was only natural after years of harassment; and that Kaufman's overall career had been distinguished and progressive. In a private letter to Countryman, Rifkind added more personal views that the Meeropols were being used as a "recruiting device for the radical left" and that their parents were simply "spies who took and suffered the risks of their occupation." Justice Powell added his voice to the defense and praised Kaufman at a speech in New York for bearing a "shameful—and wholly unjustified—attack on his integrity as a judge with admirable courage and dignity."[48]

Kaufman's public silence was far from stoic indifference, however, as those who encountered him even glancingly soon learned. New clerks in the 1970s and 1980s were astonished to report for work and see yellowing index cards on his desk with typed quotations of Bloch's comments praising his running of the trial. He carried these around with him, along with quotations from the Learned Hand letter supporting his elevation, to whip out of his jacket pocket and read on the spot should the subject arise. And people who met with him for completely different reasons were surprised to have him bring up the case. The first time Kaufman invited the First Amendment specialist Floyd Abrams to discuss something in his chambers, Kaufman opened his desk drawer and pulled out a faded copy of Arthur Schlesinger's column from 1953 supporting the death sentences. Abrams was gobsmacked. It was "apropos of nothing at all that we were discussing," he recalled. "If one were looking for an example of the degree to which that case preoccupied him," that was it, Abrams added. Peter Vaira, a federal prosecutor

Kaufman first met in 1983, noted how Kaufman "always lapsed into" mentioning the case in "every conversation." Kaufman complained that Vaira couldn't possibly imagine the pressure the whole thing had put on him. Once, at Le Cirque, Kaufman saw Woody Allen. Annoyed by something the director had said or written about the Rosenbergs, Kaufman headed over to Allen's table for a confrontation. "I didn't like that comment you made about me," Kaufman started. Their exchange was cordial but pointed.[49]

Deeper anguish seeped into his letters to close friends. "The pressures on Helen, the children, and me have been quite difficult," he confided to the writer and ambassador Henry Taylor. He was particularly fulsome with Chief Justice Warren Burger. "You know what the Kaufmans have had to endure for 25 years by my failure to respond," he wrote Burger in 1976. Almost two years later, after the worst in 1977, he lamented, "Sometimes I wondered why a public official performing his duty—and no more—was forced to receive in silence for over 25 years malicious and reckless criticism, falsehoods, innuendos—all at an increasing rather than a diminishing pace—without the full-voiced responses of those who know better." With no thought of irony, he saw himself as the victim of a reconstituted McCarthyism. "The antagonists want controversy rather than a fair and objective consideration of the issue," he wrote Third Circuit judge John Biggs, "and much like Joe McCarthy, they hope to achieve their goal of confusion and disarray by the tactic of misleading publicity." Dan Kelly clerked for Kaufman in 1977 and saw him react to the pressure and the protests, the courthouse vigils and calls for investigation. "I know that bothered him," he said of one of the rallies in Foley Square. "Through the year, you just got the sense that it haunted him. It's just like one of those things that you don't bring up."[50]

At the beginning of 1977, the private life disrupted by the Rosenberg tumult was a good one—at least outwardly. Thanks to savings and investment from his years in private practice, Helen's family money, and continuous revenue from the family parking lots, the Kaufmans continued to live well. At Park Avenue, they still dined on china with crystal and finger bowls arranged by staff. On the town, they were regulars at the Plaza, 21, La Goulue, and Le Cirque. Sundays were still given over to the City Athletic Club, a fading stalwart hanging on in an era when men's clubs seemed increasingly fusty and Jews no longer needed a separate refuge. Kaufman's grandchildren now accompanied him and were silently horrified by the inexplicable, ancient rule that men had to swim naked. One grandson gasped on encountering his septuagenarian senior senator, Jacob Javits, in the buff. After a day at the club, the family often assembled for Sunday night dinner at the apartment.[51]

The Christmas holiday routine still centered on Boca, where Milton Berle occasionally popped in. Kaufman's grandson once walked in on Berle and his wife in one of the family suite's bedrooms, leading Berle to rage at his old lawyer, "Your little fucker fucked up my fucking!" Summers featured the familiar stay at the Beverly Hills Hotel, VIP studio tours, and a backstage visit to Disneyland. Helen ruled the Beverly Hills Tennis Club, where she learned from the onetime great Pancho Segura, instructor to the stars. "She has worn down a great many pros twice her size," Kaufman boasted. At night, they were wined and dined by old Hollywood friends like Armand Deutsch, Eddie Lasker, and Walter Annenberg. And they frequented more distant destinations like Hawaii, Acapulco, Europe, and Israel. Kaufman was a stickler for specific rooms in favorite hotels, like the Dorchester in London or the Kahala Hilton. When meeting coordinators and travel agents failed him, he went over their heads, once asking the ABA president himself to work on getting him a suite. In later years, there was often a Christmas cruise on the *Queen Elizabeth II*, which inevitably led to haggling with Cunard. "Our rooms if not luxurious will be close to it," he wrote one vice president. "After all, one does not leave a nine-room apartment on Park Avenue to travel second class."[52]

Judicial and legal conferences also provided extravagant travel opportunities, none tonier than the "Anglo-American Exchange," a quadrennial gathering of a few American judges, lawmakers, and attorneys selected by Chief Justice Burger with counterparts in Britain. Participants attended seminars and court sessions in London, New York, and Washington to learn more about the other side's legal systems. While these events included substantive sessions and no doubt increased attendees' grounding in comparative law, they also featured more than a little junketeering. In England, Kaufman enjoyed stays at the lavish country estate at Ditchley Park, a garden party at Buckingham Palace, lunches in Parliament, matches at Wimbledon, guided tours of Oxford and Cambridge, and dinners at the American embassy—usually followed by travel on the Continent and a stay at the Plaza Athénée in Paris. Perhaps not surprisingly, Kaufman particularly befriended Kenneth Diplock, a law lord criticized for establishing Northern Ireland's "Diplock courts." These were nonjury tribunals designed to deal more peremptorily with Irish Republican Army militants. When Lord Diplock appeared at the 1980 exchange in New York, Irish American activists and newspapers bitterly objected to hosting someone they saw as an architect of British repression. Kaufman could sympathize with the victim of that kind of unwanted publicity.[53]

Beyond the family, there was ample black-tie mingling with New York's and Washington's boldfaced names. "He was a social judge," Goodale remembered, or as an ex-clerk put it, "he could schmooze with the best of them." He and Helen were Lyndon Johnson's unlikely guests at a state dinner for the president of Chad, and President Ford's more expected guests at a dinner for federal judges at the White House. His Catholic connections arranged a private audience with Pope Paul VI in Rome, while his Jewish ones finagled a meeting with David Ben-Gurion in Israel. He was an annual fixture at the Gridiron Dinner in Washington and the Al Smith Dinner in New York. At home, the Kaufmans entertained other judges and lawyers and the rare former clerk who became a personal friend.[54]

The FBI willingly kept on as Kaufman's escort service and tour guide over the years. He'd even managed to extend the service to others, once arranging for an FBI car to surprise the Dodds at LaGuardia Airport after a delayed flight and ferry them to 21 so they wouldn't miss his and Helen's anniversary party. But a few months after Hoover's death in 1972, the new acting director, L. Patrick Gray, started looking into the practice. He was told Kaufman and a few others, like the head of the American Legion, received these "mutually beneficial . . . normal courtesies," which should continue "on a most selective basis." Kaufman himself asked if he would still get the old service with Hoover gone, and he cited a new menace: Arab terrorism. As one memo put it,

> After January 1, 1973, Judge Kaufman will be the Presiding Judge of the U.S. Second Circuit Court and as such, will be the ranking Jewish Judge in the US. There are no judges of Jewish extraction on the Supreme Court and he will be the only Jewish Chief Judge of the Circuit Courts in the U.S. This adds to his apprehension that he might be singled out for some retaliatory measures by the Arabs. Also, Judge Kaufman to this day continues to receive nasty and threatening letters concerning the Rosenberg case. It causes him considerable concern. Judge Kaufman has always been a great friend of the FBI and is most appreciative of everything that has been done for him.[55]

Gray probably didn't think Kaufman was on a PLO hit list, but he continued the "courtesies" anyway. FBI counsel eventually rebelled, however, noting that fetching notables at the airport violated government rules and could expose the agents to personal legal liability if they got into a wreck. Kaufman promptly asked for an exception, however, since the Rosenberg controversy had roared back and disturbing letters were picking up again. The lawyers still objected, arguing that since he was now accused of having had improper secret contacts with the FBI, resuming the old favors "could be interpreted as confirming his alleged 'cozy' relationship with the Department and the Bureau." Counsel also asked why, if Kaufman truly felt threatened, he only wanted drivers when he was outside New York, and why the FBI was involved at all when protecting judges was the US Marshals' job. In the end, Kaufman pulled out the old playbook—he found someone more powerful and went over his opponents' heads. Attorney General Griffin Bell overrode the lawyers and green-lighted maintaining the same service.[56]

As the Kaufmans lived their outwardly fortunate lives, however, the family scourges continued on with them. Helen's anorexia and alcoholism were ongoing, noticed wincingly by law clerks and others. Yet they also observed her kindness and what seemed like a special bond. "I think she was totally cowed, but she was sympathetic to our plight," one clerk said. To another she was "warm, forthright, unpretentious . . . everything Kaufman wasn't." She continued in the care of a psychiatrist, and in the heat of family arguments Kaufman sometimes snapped "Why don't you tell your shrink that?!" After one such quarrel, he repented with a note saying "truce, peace, shalom—armistice! The great cold war is over! Love?" Old couple bickering aside, they mostly seemed to get along in a loving and comfortable pattern befitting decades of marriage and, perhaps, the fact that Helen had never known any other life as an adult.[57]

If Helen managed to wrestle her demons to a draw, her three sons' troubles were gaining the upper hand. "As a man who has been in public life for over twenty-two years and as a parent," Kaufman wrote Ramsey Clark in 1965, "I know well the difficulties encountered by the sons of famous fathers." For all his understanding of the difficulties, however, he couldn't openly acknowledge them. Bob's and Jim's visible success in finance—the former at Goldman Sachs and the latter at Loeb Rhoades—hid festering struggles with drugs and mental illness. Bob's wife realized later that he was probably using cocaine. She saw the pressure at work combined with the drug use start to get to him. At

Goldman, he was too junior for partnership. Yet Kaufman went ahead and described him to others as a partner because, as the favorite son with what seemed like the brightest future, nothing less was tolerable. Something similar happened in Bob's personal life. He began an affair that he either couldn't or didn't want to hide. Everyone in the family knew about it. But Kaufman couldn't bring himself to acknowledge the blot on what had to be a perfect life.[58]

Jim's marriage also fractured as his addiction to prescription painkillers worsened. More than Bob, he was also addicted to the family obsession with status. He invented educational and other credentials he didn't have, trying to at least *appear* to be the man he thought his father expected. He told people he was an important Republican fund-raiser, though it wasn't true. His father would sometimes get into a taxi and

FIGURE 13. The Kaufman family in chambers after his swearing in as chief judge for the US Court of Appeals for the Second Circuit in 1973. *Kaufman Family Photo Collection.*

ask the driver, "Do you know who you have in your cab?" If the man seemed unimpressed on hearing the answer, Kaufman might whip out the Learned Hand letter or some article about himself or perhaps one he'd written for the *Times* and hand it up to the front seat for perusal while the cabbie tried to drive. Whatever bragging to taxi drivers said about Kaufman, at least the achievements he bragged about were his. Jim, outgoing and gregarious, also took to getting into taxis and asking, "Do you know who my father is?"

As before, Dick's mental illness was most acute, and he suffered the most. In and out of institutions earlier on, he held a job at an accountant's office. He was least able to care for himself and wasn't married. When the electric company cut off the electricity in his apartment for failure to pay, he simply ran an extension cord out to an outlet in the hall. Bob's wife thought her husband and Jim exploited their weaker brother's vulnerability, manipulating him into doing things for them that might have included drugs, or money from their parents. Eventually Dick was diagnosed with Munchausen syndrome, a mental illness that Jim's son John thought his own father might have suffered from as well. In John's view, the ailment was a way for the twins to win Kaufman's attention and unconditional love—love divorced from achievement or anyone else's opinion—and to get their outsized father's attention at last. They could become, however temporarily during one hospitalization or another, the center of things.[59]

Then, as all of Kaufman's children were faltering, 1977 struck its hardest blow. In April, a friend at Goldman Sachs offered Bob and Maxine free first class tickets to Peru, and they made an impulsive decision to go, leaving their children behind in New York. After touring Lima, they went on to Cuzco before a planned trek to Machu Picchu. As she slept one night, Maxine awoke to the sound of Bob choking. "My husband's dying!" she yelled into the hotel phone, but help came too late. Peruvian authorities ascribed his death to pulmonary edema, which American records linked to a heart attack. Maxine called Jim, who had to go to 1185 Park Avenue and break the unbearable news to Kaufman and Helen. Goldman's chairman called his client, the head of Continental Airlines, and the CEO's personal 727 was dispatched to bring Maxine and Bob's body home. He also called the State Department, which cut through red tape in Peru. Once back in New York, Maxine said she wanted an autopsy, but Kaufman told her it was too late—something she later came to question. "I don't think he wanted me to know what they might find," she said, referring to Bob's drug use. "I think Irving and Helen knew a lot more about that than I did."[60]

When Maxine returned from Peru, Kaufman took charge of sitting Bob's three children down along with her and telling them their father was gone. They'd been kept busy all day to keep them away from the papers, something Bob's son Steven puzzled at later: "As if I was reading the *Times* obituary section at age eleven." Unlike his two sisters, Steven took the news without tears, which seemed to trouble or annoy Kaufman. The family sat shiva in the Park Avenue apartment, and the notables came and went—Clark, Burger, Sulzberger, other judges, FBI people. Their host sat, dazed, on the expensive and old-fashioned living room furniture. The year would see him humiliated, but at least he was used to the rough-and-tumble of public criticism and had his time-honored way of dealing with it. Nothing had prepared him for this. "That was such a monumentally awful thing for the poor guy that it kind of knocked the stuffing out of him," his clerk Dan Kelly remembered. "To say 'day and night' is probably too much, but all of his meanness really changed a lot." Kaufman became "just a different person," Kelly recollected, who "kind of went into himself for a while."[61]

There was always work to bring him back. "When despair seems unbearable and the heart is on the edge of breaking, that is when men must summon hope and high resolve and one more stubborn affirmation of life," he wrote England's lord chief justice, letting him know he would attend that summer's Anglo-American exchange meeting in London. "Life must go on despite one's heartaches," he wrote another friend, adding, "I suppose the 'vendetta'—as the *New York Times* characterized it—that has been waged against me has, to some degree, conditioned me for the hardships. One must be philosophical over life's vicissitudes."[62]

Yet the pain remained, was there all the time. Those were "terrible days," his niece Rosalind Rosenberg recalled. "He was an extraordinary young man," Kaufman wrote to one of Bob's friends, "and as the months pass, our awareness of this increases. Mrs. Kaufman and I have tried to remember Hemingway's definition of courage, 'grace under pressure.'" In later years, clerks would get the message from Kaufman's longtime secretary that they were best off simply avoiding their boss, if possible, on the anniversary of Bob's death.[63]

More grace would be required in later years, though nothing could match the low of 1977. Relations with Maxine gradually became more distant. Although Kaufman was generous in treating Bob's children and other grandchildren to trips on the *QE2* and other vacations and paid for part of Steven's college education, Maxine came to feel they didn't support her as much as they could. "They told everyone I was a rich widow, ignoring the fact that I had three kids to raise, they were in private school and were going to need to go to college." But the rift wasn't total; when she remarried five years later, Kaufman attended the wedding.[64]

After Bob died, the twins' condition worsened. Dick's health deteriorated, and he shuttled in and out of hospitals for years. He died of complications related to Munchausen syndrome in 1991, only forty-nine years old, the second of Kaufman's sons to predecease him. Kaufman then flummoxed one of his clerks at the time, Daphna Boros, by ordering her to write Dick's death notice for the *Times*.

Jim's addiction torpedoed his marriage, which ended in 1982. At some point it also cost him a leg, owing to a hazy incident no one seemed to fully understand after the fact. He'd been alone in his apartment, high and unresponsive for days, and by the time he received treatment the limb couldn't be saved. He walked using an artificial leg for the rest of his life. To his son John, Jim was a loving and responsive father but a "fairly broken person."[65]

With his grandchildren, Kaufman was his usual mix of warmth and domination. He wanted and achieved a close relationship, cemented with Sunday dinners, high-end holiday travel, and regular phone calls. "You have created memories that will last for the rest of our lives," Steven gushed after one cruise. There were also loud echoes of the law clerk treatment, however. For one thing, he played favorites, just as in chambers. Steven was usually on top, as the oldest and Bob's son. Then it went back and forth as John got older. Pitted against each other and forced to battle for their famous grandfather's affection, Steven and John didn't grow up liking each other much. They became closer only after Kaufman was gone. And both believed he slighted Steven's two sisters. As girls, they seemed to be an "afterthought," John said, ranking at the bottom of Kaufman's pecking order.

Like clerks, his grandchildren were also expected to be on call in case Kaufman wanted them. If too much time passed between visits or phone calls, he let them have it. As a teenager, John once let two or three weeks elapse between touching base. When he did call and Kaufman exploded, he tried to explain that he had a lot on his mind with his parents' messy and public divorce, which had landed in one or another tabloid under the headline "Wall Street Biggie on Drugs, Says Wife." "Have you given any thought to how this is affecting *me*?" Kaufman asked. Stunned—was his grandfather really that solipsistic, comparing their respective misery?—John drifted away from his father's side of the family, which his other set of grandparents blamed on Kaufman. "It is difficult for me to believe that a wise man such as yourself can hold a grudge against a 15 year old boy for not returning a telephone call," John's mother's mother wrote. "Perhaps you have yet to accept the meaning of *unconditional* love for one close to you as I know John once was." "I really do think you ought to stop sermonizing," Kaufman responded testily. "I do not know of anyone who is anointed with the perfect formula for dealing with children or grandchildren." Grandparents shouldn't "push their attention and affection on a grandchild where it is rejected," he concluded. Preoccupied with appearances and still hoping to glue his son's family back together, Kaufman blamed John's mother for wanting the divorce and John for seeming to take his mother's side. After a couple of years, however, the estrangement passed, and their relationship resumed. Overall, John reflected decades later, he thought Kaufman had given him a lot to be mad about and a lot to be grateful for.[66]

That Kaufman's annus horribilis merged the personal hells of two separate families—Bob and Ethel were approximately the same age when they died—wasn't lost on either. Reeling from Bob's death, Kaufman lowered some kind of barrier and started musing out loud in chambers—not the sort of thing he usually did with his clerks. "He would occasionally get philosophical about life, and what we do, and God," Jerry Menikoff, one of his clerks in 1977, remembered. As Menikoff thought back to that time, he could hear Kaufman ruminating about the Rosenberg case in abstract, fatalistic terms, minus the familiar defensiveness. He "blamed his son's death on divine intervention based on the bad things he might have done relating to the case, or something like that." Wondering at how his life had turned out, Kaufman voiced a sense that "who knows but this is somehow fate rearing its ugly head," and that what had happened to Bob was "somehow related to what he had done years earlier." There was ethereal talk of "causation and higher beings."

Michael Meeropol also made the connection. When he learned of Bob's death, he "actually wanted to write [Kaufman] a letter noodging him to come clean, to tell us about what's in the documents and what's true and what's not true." So Meeropol sat down to write, and the letter he produced "included a sentence or two about the fact that 'I know you've recently suffered a tragedy, so you probably understand how I feel about my situation.'" Perhaps, he must have thought, the two might connect in some way, or at least both come to see some kind of tortured mutual legacy. His lawyer, Perlin, didn't like it. "Perlin persuaded me not to treat him like a human being, to take it out of that letter. And with twenty-twenty hindsight, I'm sorry I let Perlin talk me out of it because, not that I thought Kaufman had any real feelings, but I wanted to demonstrate to him that I had some feeling." Of course, Kaufman *did* have real feelings—had been overtaken by them, as anyone would be. But Meeropol, fated always to be the man outside in the street with the bullhorn calling Kaufman to account, would never see them.[67]

After 1977, the fever broke. Rifkind's ABA subcommittee finished its work in June that year and produced a 153-page defense brief for Kaufman and the prosecution. Some at the organization had bristled at Rifkind's showy press conference announcing the inquiry, though, and decided that releasing the report would make them look biased, as if they were simply protecting one of their own. Its board of governors quietly voted to shelve the report, which wasn't released until 1995.[68]

Aside from a meeting with some staffers, Congress ignored Countryman's letter and the other calls for investigations and impeachment. "Judge Kaufman is perceived as being a good judge," one congressional aide said, "and he's just a few years from retirement." Thousands did pack a rally in Union Square in June 1978 on the twenty-fifth anniversary—just as thousands had gathered there and trudged home in despair on execution day—but after that, attention waned. "Crowds at speaking engagements and receptions were dwindling," Robert Meeropol wrote later, "and my heart wasn't in it. Post-Watergate public support for a more open government and exposing abuses of power was fading. Reaganism was waiting in the wings. I felt that pursuing the reopening effort was becoming an exercise in futility."[69]

There were a few eruptions over the next decade, but more and more they smacked of repetition and lethargy. Kaufman's ordeal of ubiquitous pickets and public shaming was past. Much of what uproar there was originated with Ronald Radosh, a historian at the City University of New York. A left-winger slowly moving right, Radosh had joined the Rosenberg committee and then changed his mind after immersion in two hundred thousand pages of FBI documents. In coauthored articles in 1979 and a book in 1983, he argued persuasively that Julius had indeed led a spy ring but that Greenglass had lied about Ethel to save his wife. He offered little comfort to Kaufman, though, since he slammed the death sentences, branded the trial unfair, and joined the Rosenberg supporters' call for a public commission to investigate "one of the worst blots in the annals of American justice."[70]

The Schneirs then released an updated version of their book, and they and Radosh and his book's coauthor Joyce Milton met in a Manhattan auditorium for a public debate in 1983. It was the year of the thirtieth anniversary, and for one evening those on hand recaptured the passion of 1977. Many of the old and new players—Sobell, Julius Rosenberg's sister, Perlin, Michael Meeropol—came to hash through the case's nooks and crannies along with larger questions like the legacy of the Communist Party. There were cries of "Nobody on that jury was Jewish!" and "Left-wing McCarthyism!" Again, though, one of the few things everyone agreed on was the sentences. "The day the Rosenbergs were executed was a disgraceful day for America," Milton declared. The two sides also dueled in the *New York Review of Books*. At about the same time, Sidney Lumet's film of Doctorow's novel *Daniel* hit movie theaters. While Congress wasn't about to order the investigation many wanted, a subcommittee of the House Judiciary Committee did hear a few hours of testimony on the case from many of the old combatants in the context of debating capital punishment. All this generated new flurries of news articles, but it wasn't like before. The Foley Square demonstrators who reassembled each June attracted fewer and fewer diehards.[71]

A last blast occurred in 1988 when two books came out on Roy Cohn, Kaufman's old protégé-turned-friend-turned-nemesis. One was a posthumously released autobiography written with the journalist Sidney Zion, and the other was a more conventional biography by Nicholas von Hoffman. Like Rifkind but on his own, Cohn had vigorously defended the convictions and Kaufman over the years, appearing on television, in print, and at the House hearing on capital punishment. Whenever it came up, he steadfastly denied having had *ex parte* contacts with Kaufman despite the FBI memos. In his autobiography with Zion, though, he finally reversed himself and described his earlier stance as an effort "not to embarrass Kaufman." Now that the FBI documents unequivocally proved the defendants' guilt, he claimed, there was no point in keeping up appearances. Plus, the secret, in-trial discussions "were irrelevant to the outcome of the case," he asserted. *New York Magazine* excerpted the book and titled one section "The Judge, the Cardinal and the Pope." It gave an inside account of the sentencing, complete with Kaufman's and Cohn's discussions about the death penalty and

Kaufman's request to Cohn in 1953 that he get New York's Cardinal Spellman to publicly support the executions. By the end of his life, however, Cohn was widely despised and often disbelieved, thanks to a lifetime of malevolence and deceit. He had already been dead for two years when the books appeared, and it was a good bet that Kaufman hadn't mourned.[72]

As if having his erstwhile and original defender desert him in the end wasn't bad enough, even the FBI eventually had second thoughts. After the Bureau moved out of the Justice Department building in Washington and into its own headquarters in 1975, it reexamined the exhibits in the public tour and decided to drop the one on the Rosenberg case. Hoover wasn't around anymore to say no. "We felt that it was time to make some changes," an FBI spokesman said simply. Only Kaufman was left to soldier on.[73]

Chapter 15

Some Form of Justice

Kaufman's greatest liberal contribution began in the least likely place. Forty-six hundred miles from New York, in Ybycui, Paraguay, Dr. Joel Filártiga tended to the country's poorest peasants. Born to one of the old upper-class families, he spurned a comfortable practice in the capital for a makeshift clinic in the hinterland. There he treated Guarani-speaking cotton farmers whose grueling labor enriched plantation owners, shippers, bankers—everyone but themselves. They crowded into his clinic for everything from routine exams to serious surgery, though none had any money. So they paid in chickens or vegetables or by patching holes in Filártiga's roof.[1]

More than a selfless doctor, Filártiga was also an accomplished artist whose stark sketches documented local miseries. One critic called his art a "pure and unmasked encounter with psychic pain." To anyone who knew him, however, that pain was understandable.[2]

Since 1954, Paraguay had been ruled by General Alfredo Stroessner, as brutal a dictator as ever produced by Latin America's strongman politics. Stroessner's cartoonishly evil regime systematically squashed civil liberties, exterminated indigenous tribes, ran drugs to the United States, and shielded Nazi war criminals. A truth commission would eventually document over one hundred thousand victims of the general's bloodlust.[3]

Filártiga thought gangsters had stolen his beloved country, and he had opposed Stroessner since his student days. Over the years, this dissent led inexorably to harassment, imprisonment, and finally torture. Filártiga's trials included "the telephone," being struck on both ears simultaneously, and "the submarine"—submersion in water with jolts of electricity. Once he stood for seventy-six hours while soldiers beat him, music playing at ear-splitting volume to drown out his screams. The customary fate of troublemakers like Filártiga was described by Robert White, later the American ambassador there: "The usual four men dressed as civilians arriving in a Ford Falcon would take him away and he would never be heard from again." Filártiga avoided this only because his mother personally knew the president. Ironically, the family had originally supported Stroessner's rise to power.[4]

Despite persecution, Filártiga remained unbowed. He followed each release from prison with more opposition, which only brought more abuse. Years of this made him one of the government's most prominent antagonists. In 1976, he toured California, showing his sketches and speaking out against Stroessner. Back in Paraguay, his enemies noticed. Filártiga was working in Ybycui one morning shortly after his return when a messenger from the telephone office appeared to tell him his seventeen-year-old son had "suffered a tragedy" at their home in the capital. Joel and his wife raced to Asunción.[5]

Joelito was a bright, good-looking boy who helped at his father's clinic and planned to follow him into medicine. The night before, police rousted him out of bed after midnight and took him away. At four thirty in the morning, his older sister Dolly, asleep in another part of the house, heard pounding at the front door. She was escorted two doors over, to the home of police inspector Américo Norberto Peña-Irala, and shown Joelito's body on a bloody mattress. "What did you do to my brother?" she shrieked at Peña. "Here you have what you were looking for and deserved," he replied evenly. Ordered to remove her brother's body or see it tossed into the street, Dolly had it carried back to the family's home. There were signs of whipping, slashes, and burn marks. An aluminum wire for conducting electric current had been forced through Joelito's penis.[6]

The typical Paraguayan response to this sort of outrage was silence, since protest only invited further brutality. But Filártiga had never been typical. As a doctor and victim himself, he immediately saw the signs of torture on his son's battered body. He photographed Joelito and arranged for private autopsies. The authorities soon claimed Joelito had been caught with the daughter of Peña's girlfriend and killed by her husband, but few believed it.[7]

Although Stroessner controlled Paraguay's courts, Filártiga's wife sued Peña there anyway, keeping Filártiga himself in the background and counting on the pity due a grieving mother. Meanwhile, Filártiga found reporters willing to skirt government censorship. Not long after Joelito's death, on Good Friday, one tabloid's front page was filled with a photo of Joelito's battered body. Filártiga printed up five thousand postcards with the photo on one side and an anguished poem he'd written his dead son on the other. Then he had them handed out all over Asunción. People began praying at Joelito's grave as to a saint.

Stroessner soon hit back. Filártiga's wife and Dolly were briefly imprisoned. His lawyer was arrested, shackled to a wall, and disbarred. An emissary showed up to hint that Filártiga would be killed unless he dropped his case, while different messengers visited and offered to make Peña disappear if only the family would quiet down. Filártiga wanted justice, though, not vengeance, and with every court appearance and newspaper story, *Caso Filártiga* became a sensation in Paraguay.[8]

People around the world gradually started paying attention, too. In Congress, Representative Ed Koch and Senator Ted Kennedy denounced Stroessner's brutality and wondered why his government still got American weapons. Richard Alan White, an American academic and personal friend of Filártiga's, worked tirelessly to tell legislators and human rights groups about the hell in Paraguay and Filártiga's case specifically. Human rights groups produced reports highlighting conditions there, including Joelito's death, and sympathetic letters began pouring into Filártiga's home from the United States. In his campaign for the presidency, Jimmy Carter had vowed to make human rights a part of American foreign policy, and Robert White, now ambassador in Asunción, made a point of visiting the Filártigas to express solidarity. "Torturing kids just doesn't go down that well," he told Richard White privately, "even among some of the regime's top dogs."[9]

Yet while Filártiga could generate publicity, he couldn't manufacture justice. Stroessner's courts went through the motions but stymied the case. Through a fortuitous mistake, however, a better path opened. A letter intended for the Peña home came two houses down to the Filártigas instead. Opening it, Dolly realized Peña and his wife were in the United States. They had been quietly sent away to New York to "let the situation cool off," Peña told a friend. "When the letter from Peña was delivered to our house," Dolly remembered, "I decided that the only thing to do was to come to the United States to find him. I had no life in Paraguay." More than any other family member, Dolly had disintegrated after Joelito's murder. Pursuing Peña to New York restored a sense of purpose. "I wanted to have some form of justice," she testified later. She sought political asylum while she cleaned houses and washed dishes at a restaurant.[10]

Sniffing around Paraguayan expats, Dolly found Peña in Brooklyn. Richard White passed the information to contacts, who gave it to the INS, which arrested him as part of an anti-smuggling operation. Having overstayed a tourist visa—Peña had ostensibly come to America to visit Disneyland—he could elect to be deported rather than face prosecution in America, and he asked to leave for Paraguay immediately. Any hope of bringing him to justice in the United States was evaporating. Amnesty International knew about Peña's arrest from Richard White, and its executive director phoned a lawyer at the Center for Constitutional Rights—the CCR—in New York named Peter Weiss. "There is a notorious torturer sitting at the INS detention center at the former Brooklyn Navy yard in Brooklyn," Weiss was told; "You've got to keep him here and bring him to justice." "How are we going to do that?" Weiss asked. "That's your problem," the man said, and hung up.[11]

Weiss was particularly suited to the task. Once a refugee himself, he remembered being chased down the streets of Vienna as a boy by teenage thugs giddy with Jew hatred. He later served with American occupation forces in Germany and became fascinated by international law and its potential to bring order and justice to a world that, he knew personally, needed both. His trademark law practice paid the bills, but he devoted his spare time to the CCR.

When he got the call from Amnesty International about Peña, Weiss wasn't completely unprepared. Many years earlier, he'd run across an obscure statute enacted by the first Congress in 1789 and signed by George Washington as part of the law establishing the federal courts. It was called the "Alien Tort Statute," or ATS, and said simply, "The district courts shall have original jurisdiction of any civil action by an alien for a tort only, committed in violation of the law of nations or a treaty of the United States." Likely prompted by a Frenchman's assault on a French diplomat in Philadelphia in 1784, the law had rarely been cited since its passage, let alone applied to something like Joelito's case. Weiss was friends with the journalist Seymour Hersh, whose reporting helped uncover the My Lai massacre, and he had explored using the

ATS then to sue the army, going as far as traveling to Hanoi to talk to victims. But the project died.[12]

Now the time seemed ripe for Weiss to test the old law. His colleagues at the CCR weren't thrilled. Trying to get an American court to hear a case brought by one Paraguayan against another for events in Paraguay struck them as daft. Nor did anyone know what the ATS covered or what a "violation of the law of nations" was. Did it include torture? Yet no one had a better idea, and time was running out. An immigration judge had already ordered Peña deported, and he could be put on a flight home at any moment.

Overnight, Weiss and another CCR lawyer, Rhonda Copelon, banged out a short federal complaint. The next day, on a Friday afternoon, Copelon raced in a cab through rush hour traffic in Brooklyn to file it, beating the court's closing door by five minutes. It was April 6, 1979, three years to the day after the Filártigas had first sued in Paraguay. The American lawsuit was assigned to Judge Eugene Nickerson, who issued an order on Monday temporarily halting Peña's deportation. As he was leaving the bench, he stopped, turned back to the lawyers, and said, "interesting case." Improbably, *Caso Filártiga* had set down roots in the United States. Back in Asunción, someone left the severed head of a pig in the Filártigas' driveway.[13]

Weiss and Copelon were happy to get Nickerson. He was thought to be smart and liberal, and Weiss fondly remembered seeing him at antiwar demonstrations before he took the bench. But after hearing arguments in court, Nickerson dismissed the case. His language was sympathetic, and he agreed that torture offended international norms. "It was clear that he would have preferred to rule for us," Weiss remembered. Nickerson felt bound by two earlier Second Circuit decisions that had determined with little analysis that the ATS's phrase "law of nations" referred only to legal obligations between foreign states, not those owed by a state to its own citizens. One of the decisions tacitly carried special weight because it had been written by Judge Friendly, who dismissively called the statute "a kind of legal Lohengrin," after the mysterious knight from German mythology and Wagnerian opera. "No one seems to know whence it came." Although Peña was soon on a flight back to Paraguay, Weiss began planning an appeal.[14]

The brief he produced was painstakingly thorough. Weiss emphasized that the first Congress had wanted to strengthen the fledgling nation and bring uniformity to cases involving foreigners. Mainly,

FIGURE 14. Dolly Filártiga holds a photo of her brother Joelito Filártiga, in 1999. *Associated Press.*

though, he argued for expanding the traditional view that the law of nations only encompassed relations between states. Torture and political murder were outlawed by several postwar treaties, which now formed a global web protecting human rights. Even in 1789, the CCR noted, international law condemned some actions by individuals, not just states. Pirates, for example, were *hostes humanis generi*, enemies of all mankind, and thus could be "sent to the gibbet by the first into whose hands they fall," as one old authority put it. Friendly's view was simply "out of tune with the prevailing contemporary view that international law encompasses individual rights and duties," Weiss wrote, particularly considering the present administration's focus on human rights. Several eminent scholars of international law backed the Filártigas' position, and Amnesty International and other groups filed a supportive brief. On the other side, Paraguay warned that the CCR was proposing a dangerous precedent: if the Peñas of the world were suddenly targets of American justice, our own officials would soon be fair game in hostile foreign courtrooms.[15]

As so often happened in civil rights cases, few at the CCR were pleased when they learned Kaufman was on their panel. He was a law-and-order type, they thought, and they were aghast at the recent revelations about the Rosenberg case. Weiss was less worried. He accepted what he called "the common wisdom" that Kaufman was trying to rehabilitate himself by burnishing his liberal credentials. And what better way than putting some teeth into America's new commitment to human rights?[16]

"May it please the court, I'm Peter Weiss of the Center for Constitutional Rights appearing for appellant," Weiss began steadily. As a trademark lawyer more familiar with corporate deals, he had never stood at the lectern before the Second Circuit. Kaufman soon cut in, sarcasm in the gravelly, hammy voice: "You're able to do what Judge Friendly wasn't able to do?" Weiss explained the differences between the two cases. Soon Kaufman was on to something else: What did the State Department think? Weiss noted that Ambassador Robert White had told a Paraguayan newspaper that the case was properly before American courts. But an envoy's offhand remark to the foreign press wasn't good enough. Kaufman wanted to know why the department hadn't officially written the court.

> Weiss: I think there is a great deal of sympathetic interest on the part of many levels of the State Department in this case, and they're watching it with great interest, and why they haven't directly—

KAUFMAN: Doesn't that remind you of an opinion that begins by complimenting counsel and ends up with a decision against him?[17]

To Copelon, Kaufman came across as hostile, but she was off base. Having never seen him yell, she had no idea. That same afternoon, Kaufman arranged for the court to formally ask the State Department for its views. When she learned of it, the request made Copelon nervous; problems like Filártiga's could inevitably complicate foreign policy, and State Department bureaucrats might prefer to ignore them. Weiss was more confident. This was *Carter*'s State Department, after all, and the people he knew there were rooting for him. Either way, both lawyers fully understood the department's position would probably be decisive. "We said to ourselves, 'That brief is going to determine this case,'" Copelon recalled.[18]

In chambers, the appeal fell to Kaufman's new clerk Bruce Kraus, though he hadn't studied international law or even read a major appellate brief yet. While Kraus thought Nickerson's order had "please reverse me" all over it, he knew doing so raised the thorny question of what to do about Friendly's opinion. The irony was that Kraus was sure he would have preferred working for Friendly, whom he particularly admired. Still, he decided to recommend ruling for the Filártigas. Then, only three weeks after the argument, Iranian students overran the US Embassy in Tehran. As the hostage crisis dragged on, Kraus wondered whether it would harden the government's views or nudge officials analyzing the case to prize security over values. He was "hungry for conversation" about the issues but there was little of that with Kaufman, who rarely engaged unless and until he read a draft opinion and had some problem. Instead, Kraus felt a "deafening silence" that only heightened what he called the "terrifying responsibility" of coming to grips with the unique case.[19]

When the State Department brief finally arrived, Kraus could exhale. "*Phew*," he thought, "*OK fine, it's OK to do what's obviously the right thing.*" While there had been months of internal jockeying between old-school types in the department more comfortable with the Friendly approach and the new idealists focused on human rights, the idealists had mostly won out. The department filed a careful brief showing how international law had evolved in the twentieth century to embrace the individual's right to be free from torture, and how that right was so "clearly defined and universally" endorsed that it could be enforced by American courts without damaging the country's foreign relations.

"Absolutely amazing," Copelon told Weiss. "It could hardly be better if we'd written it ourselves."[20]

Kaufman's opinion for a unanimous panel agreed. American courts must "interpret international law not as it was in 1789," he observed, "but as it has evolved and exists among the nations of the world today." Because that law had come to prohibit torture, the Alien Tort Statute conferred federal jurisdiction "whenever an alleged torturer is found" in America. The opinion marshaled the UN resolutions and other treaties identified by Filártiga's supporters confirming that the prohibition of torture "is clear and unambiguous, and admits of no distinction between treatment of aliens and citizens."

What about Friendly's decision? Here, Kaufman lacked a free hand. Only the full court, consisting of all judges, could overrule decisions of prior three-member panels. So Friendly's opinion had to be distinguished and cabined somehow. Luckily that was easy, since the defendant's transgression in Friendly's case had been ordinary financial fraud—not violation of a basic human right like freedom from torture. Only the violation of key international treaties could be "an international law violation within the meaning of the statute," Kaufman wrote. Less persuasively, the decision claimed to be compatible with the tradition that the law of nations only reaches interactions between states because most governments had recently "made it their business" through their international accords to be concerned with other countries' human rights records. In reality, this clever lip service couldn't hide the fact that *Filártiga* essentially sought to bury the old, narrow view of international law espoused by Friendly.

The most memorable aspect of *Filártiga* was its closing. Mostly a technical exposition of international law and federal jurisdiction, the opinion ended with powerful and moving prose:

> Among the rights universally proclaimed by all nations, as we have noted, is the right to be free of physical torture. Indeed, for purposes of civil liability, the torturer has become like the pirate and slave trader before him *hostis humani generis*, an enemy of all mankind. Our holding today, giving effect to a jurisdictional provision enacted by our First Congress, is a small but important step in the fulfillment of the ageless dream to free all people from brutal violence.[21]

In a eulogy for the district judge in the Pentagon Papers case, Murray Gurfein, Kaufman said, "There are moments in a man's life in which the great themes that shape his career are captured and brought into focus." For Kaufman, at least as far as his life as an appellate judge was concerned, *Filártiga* was that moment. It combined forward thinking with a deep and basic sense of justice that triumphed over legalism.[22]

While the *Times* celebrated the decision, there wasn't much reaction elsewhere. Eager as always for more attention, Kaufman had Kraus's successor draft a piece for the *Times Magazine* four months later. It explicitly linked *Filártiga* to the liberal jurisprudence of the era: "The obligation of our courts to identify egregious violations of international law is in many ways analogous to the courts' traditional role in redressing deprivations of civil liberties that occur at home." To Kraus, also, the decision fit snugly in the school of the "living Constitution." Just as constitutional meaning wasn't frozen in 1789, nor was the content of the "law of nations" or the reach of the federal courts. As it happened, the *Times Magazine* article appeared just as Joel Filártiga was about to leave New York after a speaking tour of the United States. "It is hardly uncommon among those who in their hearts know what is right, but have pursued a career of opportunism," he told Richard White, when they discussed the piece. "As they approach the end of their life, often they seek redemption. Kaufman's eloquent defense of human rights is an attempt to save his soul."[23]

Back in district court, Paraguay simply stopped putting up a defense for Peña since he had returned to South America, and Nickerson awarded the full $10.4 million the Filártigas requested. As Dolly recognized, though, "from the beginning we knew we weren't going to get any money from Peña. He doesn't have any." Still, Nickerson understood the symbolic value of the figure, saying he wanted to "make clear the depth of the international revulsion against torture."[24]

By the time Nickerson ruled, which didn't happen until 1984, *Filártiga* was beginning to outgrow the Filártigas. Peña and Paraguay might seem inconsequential, but the new targets picked by emboldened human rights lawyers were much bigger. After longtime dictator Ferdinand Marcos was forced to flee the Philippines, ten thousand of his former victims sued him under the ATS. The Ninth Circuit agreed with Kaufman's reasoning in *Filártiga* and permitted the case to go forward, yielding judgments of over a billion dollars. Bosnian Muslims sued Radovan Karadžić, a Bosnian Serb commander, for rape, torture, and other crimes committed during the civil war in the former Yugoslavia. The Second Circuit reaffirmed *Filártiga*, answering other questions about cases under the ATS, and juries awarded massive sums in damages. Afterward, the jury foreman said, "I hope the world gets the message. What happened was reprehensible." Holocaust survivors and their heirs sued foreign governments, banks, and other companies under the ATS and other laws. Although many cases were dismissed, the effort led to approximately $10 billion in negotiated compensation for tens of thousands of victims and Holocaust-related charities. Villagers who were attacked, raped, and enslaved on a gas pipeline in the Burmese jungle sued the American and foreign corporations involved in building it and received millions after a favorable legal decision in the Ninth Circuit helped prod a settlement. Other cases arose from Argentina, Chile, Ethiopia, Haiti, Rwanda, and more.[25]

Often the plaintiffs in these cases couldn't collect money. But that wasn't the point, any more than it had been for the Filártigas. "They are a way of showing the world what happened," one lawyer said—truth commissions in miniature that sometimes also facilitated healing or catharsis for victims and witnesses. And they increased fear of exposure among people like Peña. In South Florida, home to so many from Latin America, people were suddenly on the lookout for reprehensible figures from their past. More generally, Kaufman's decision gave birth to a new wave of human rights activism here and abroad. Harold Koh, a preeminent authority in international law at Yale, wrote that "in *Filártiga*, human rights litigants and scholars finally found their *Brown v. Board of Education*." To Koh, the case was "seminal not just for what it held, but also for what it triggered": a growing cadre of attorneys and organizations with the know-how and determination to use domestic courts to promote international human rights, just as American civil rights lawyers had previously targeted racial and other forms of discrimination. Outside the United States, other countries used *Filártiga* as a model to expand their own courts' jurisdiction to hold human rights violators accountable. John Bellinger, a former legal adviser to the State Department, credits the ATS as reinvigorated by Kaufman as "the source of almost all significant human rights litigation in the United States and the world." Congress also stepped up to codify *Filártiga* in the Torture Victim Protection Act of 1991, which permits Americans or aliens to sue foreigners for torture or extrajudicial killing. Kaufman's Second Circuit colleague James Oakes called the law "a tribute to Irving Kaufman for all foreseeable time, long after most of the opinions of all of us and indeed of Irving's too, have faded into obscurity."[26]

In Paraguay, Stroessner's regime held out until 1988, when he was ousted in a coup. Former ambassador White traced the general's fall to Filártiga's defiance: "One man had faced them down, and the Paraguayan dictator and his official thugs would never recover. The regime would not fall for several years, but the countdown had begun." Long after their American lawsuit ended, Filártiga and Dolly and the rest of the family continued speaking out and working for people like those served by the clinic in Ybycui, where an elementary school is named for Joelito. And they were still risking their lives. On one occasion that must have refreshed bad memories, armed men wearing ski masks broke into the Filártigas' home in Asunción and held the family captive at gunpoint for two hours, eventually taking a safe full of cash and papers documenting agribusinesses' use of harmful pesticides. In 1991, HBO aired a movie based on Joelito's death and the family's struggle for justice starring the famed British actor Anthony Hopkins as Filártiga. When the real Filártiga saw the movie, *One Man's War*, it left him with mixed feelings. "The reality we lived through," he said, "was much more intense."[27]

Chapter 16

Keep the Beacon Burning

On April 10, 1980, over a thousand people paid seventy-five dollars each to fete Kaufman at the Waldorf Astoria. Organized by nineteen different bar associations, the dinner honored his three decades on the bench. His colleague Bill Mulligan roasted the guest of honor. Mulligan had wanted to turn down the gig, he joked, "until it was emphasized that the enthusiasm of the organized bar and the law schools with the imminent departure of Irving R. Kaufman as Chief Judge was so pronounced that a sellout crowd was expected here this evening." Known for his wit, Mulligan was funny and predictably complimentary, but he didn't bother sugarcoating Kaufman's less flattering qualities. "When speaking of the Chief Judge," he continued, "adjectives such as humble, reticent, self-effacing, do not come readily to mind or trippingly on the tongue. Nor should they. That is not his style. He is a mover of mountains, a man of broad vision, unbounded enthusiasm, and remarkable accomplishments." Kaufman wasn't afraid to "ruffle feathers," a characteristic Mulligan traced to his Jesuit education and that "native quality best captured in Homeric Greek expression: chutzpah." The lawyers roared knowingly, though one of them near the dais couldn't help noticing that the man of the hour "went back and forth from smiling to being furious," ultimately settling on a sort of forced, painful grin.[1]

A few weeks later, Kaufman was forced to surrender the chief judge's gavel, his since 1973. Federal law capped a chief's age at seventy, and Kaufman's time was nigh. Circuit chiefs handle a host of administrative duties and more generally serve as the public face of the court. They also assign judges to the panels of three that hear specific cases, and Kaufman used this prerogative to avoid sitting with Friendly, whose intellectual prowess put him on edge, as well as a few others he preferred to avoid. Perhaps he also sensed Friendly's disdain since, as Friendly's biographer reports, Friendly had come to loathe the Kaufman as a "showboat flush with self-importance." In a letter to his daughter, Friendly called Kaufman "my ambitious colleague, so well initialed as IRK." Just as Kaufman avoided sitting with Friendly, Friendly tried to do the same. When it came to other judges, one clerk recalled Kaufman instructing him to pair up two members of the court known to dislike each other, a directive he couldn't rationalize except for pure maliciousness. Overall, though, the chief judgeship was a role Kaufman was born to play. Judicial administration was Kaufman's "first love," he told Burger, and by most accounts he did it well.[2]

Being chief gave Kaufman a lab for experimentation. He insisted the court "clear" its cases—decide as many appeals as filed in a given year—and he used the judges' meetings every sixty days to brandish a list of unresolved appeals and interrogate the slowpokes. Although this peer pressure predated Kaufman, he applied it with special "rigor," Judge Newman recalled, and succeeded in "cowing" colleagues and thereby reducing delays. Kaufman also streamlined simpler appeals by issuing summary orders immediately after argument, though some judges thought this smacked of assembly-line justice. When he arrived for his first sitting with Kaufman, Judge George Pratt was taken aback when his more senior colleague began distributing copies of orders in the robing room behind the bench. Pratt explained that he preferred to wait to hear the lawyers' arguments before making up his mind, to which Kaufman pleasantly agreed. But as each argument concluded, Kaufman slyly slid the orders back across the bench, assuming Pratt's time for reflection was over.

More than browbeating, however, Kaufman genuinely innovated. His plan to expedite criminal appeals accelerated certain deadlines and resulted in the fastest average time for resolution in the country. Kaufman also created a "Civil Appeals Management Plan" deputizing the court's staff counsel to summon lawyers for settlement talks and clearing some appeals off the docket before the judges had to face them.

The program is still in place and has been widely imitated. Other bold ideas—a plan to stiffen requirements for admission to practice in the federal courts, "para-judges" to handle minor matters, lawyers "tithing" 10 percent of their time to assist the courts—fizzled but still reflected Kaufman's ceaseless, creative thinking about administrative reform. In 1985, former Harvard Law School dean Erwin Griswold wrote to tell Kaufman he was "perhaps the most important leader in the field of judicial administration."[3]

Time-limited as chief judge but unhappy relinquishing its power, Kaufman reverted to old habits. In 1931, he'd been too young to take the bar exam and sought a way around the rule by having a friend privately petition New York's chief judge. Five decades later, facing a different age-related rule he didn't like, he phoned Washington. He started with New York's senator Daniel Patrick Moynihan and "lobbied like crazy to get the law changed," the *Times*' Linda Greenhouse learned. He also approached the head of the Senate Judiciary Committee, Ted Kennedy, through his counsel Ken Feinberg, whom he invited to chambers for a sandwich. "He basically lobbied me to urge Senator Kennedy and the US Senate to change the law," Feinberg said. "He really leaned on me. . . . He just said, 'Look, I'd like to keep serving, I don't want to step down as chief, I'm enjoying this, I think I've brought a lot to the Second Circuit and I'd like to keep doing it.' It was just so self-serving—'I'm very important and I'm so good and I know I'm good, I'm gonna do this.' His self-promotion and ego were so raw, so unbounded, everybody was aghast at something like that."[4]

Moynihan dutifully introduced the bill Kaufman wanted, though Greenhouse was sure he "must have done that just to shut [Kaufman] up and never intended to, you know, actually do it." Regardless, the idea went nowhere and then embarrassed Kaufman when Greenhouse made it public in her 1983 profile. Kaufman angrily wrote her boss, claiming that extending the age limit had actually been Moynihan's idea and that he had "implored" the senator to withdraw the legislation. This version of events was, Greenhouse remembered, "total rot."[5]

Since the age limit stood, Kaufman had no choice but to hand the reins to the next in line, Judge Wilfred Feinberg (no relation to Kennedy's aide). Greenhouse attended the annual Second Circuit conference of judges and hundreds of lawyers in 1980, where Kaufman had to publicly acknowledge the transition. "It was just an amazing scene. He was so furious, and so ungracious." Etiquette called for him to toast Feinberg as the next chief, but Kaufman just stood there woodenly, "unable to express any graciousness. There was something so obviously off." For a time afterward, Kaufman took to referring to himself in writing as "Chief Judge Emeritus," a position that didn't actually exist in federal law. And he chafed at the "emeritus" part and became convinced his successor was disrespecting him. *He* had carefully sought advice from his elders when he was chief, he wrote Feinberg, "but from one friend to another, some of the younger people believe you deliberately avoid the courtesy of consultation with your predecessor. . . . Fortunately, we do not operate under the Russian system where a member of the hierarchy becomes a 'non-person.'" It seems doubtful new judges actually fretted about whether Kaufman was being consulted; he was closer to older colleagues like Medina and Lumbard, while many of the younger judges saw him as egotistical, stuffy, and formal—"someone to avoid," Pratt recalled. Kaufman must have thought invoking the newcomers would add weight. Perhaps, he suggested, "it would spare some hurt feelings" if he just skipped the circuit conference altogether that year.[6]

Surrendering the chief judgeship seemed to end an era for Kaufman. His most important patrons were gone now—Clark in 1977, and Hoover in '72. In 1971, Tom Dodd had collapsed from a heart attack after a fall from Senate grace that briefly threatened to ensnare Kaufman. Dodd had been censured by the Senate in 1967 for the personal use of campaign contributions collected at testimonial dinners. By 1969, he faced a protracted criminal investigation for evading taxes on over $100,000 of the rerouted money. In November that year, the Washington muckrakers Rowland Evans and Bob Novak suggested a "possible explanation" for why the Justice Department seemed reluctant to indict the senator: it was out of embarrassment that Kaufman and another federal judge had secretly advised Dodd on the legality of his campaign maneuvers. The columnists reported that, while Kaufman had been interviewed by IRS agents and denied giving Dodd legal advice, "the prospect of a federal appeals judge testifying in a tax evasion case is not a pretty one." Other Dodd files suggested Kaufman had helped plan one of the senator's testimonial dinners in Los Angeles, tapping Hollywood connections and introducing Dodd around. If true, that would have breached the canons of judicial ethics. Ultimately, prosecutors dropped the case, and Kaufman was spared having to defend himself or take a public role in an old friend's humiliation.[7]

A different columnist looking into Dodd, Jack Anderson, also stumbled on another old Kaufman friend who assisted Dodd's defense: the

Schenley liquor titan Lew Rosenstiel. Kaufman had once been so close to Rosenstiel that he'd decamped to his Connecticut estate on the night of the Rosenberg executions to escape the bomb threats. Over time, however, Rosenstiel became less useful. According to a 1967 memo to Anderson from coauthor Drew Pearson, Rosenstiel had given Kaufman "gifts of billfolds and jewelry. But hurriedly, approximately two years ago, Kaufman returned all of these gifts. I don't know the reason for the sudden decision. At any rate, he is very sensitive about his former connections with Rosenstiel." If the memo is accurate, the sensitivity undoubtedly grew from mushrooming public scrutiny. By 1971, a New York state commission on crime was investigating charges from Rosenstiel's bitterly estranged ex-wife that he had ties to organized crime. The committee considered Kaufman sufficiently informed to "invite" his testimony in Albany. Kaufman demurred, requesting a private call instead. "I have never had any relationship with Mr. Rosenstiel or any of his enterprises," he protested in a letter. "For a great many years my social contacts with him have been exceedingly rare." Publicly linking his name with the probe would be "grossly inappropriate," he cautioned. In the end, as in the Dodd case, Kaufman could breathe a sigh of relief. He wasn't required to testify, and Rosenstiel died in 1977—but not before Rosenstiel's lawyer Roy Cohn entered the dying man's hospital room and tricked him into signing a codicil making Cohn a trustee of his $40 million estate. The caper contributed to Cohn's embarrassing disbarment and revealed, yet again, Kaufman's constantly overlapping and double-backing social circle.[8]

Fully aware that Kaufman's ambitions for judicial reform extended beyond the circuit whose chiefdom he was yielding, Chief Justice Burger decided Kaufman should lead a larger crusade to combat the lousy treatment of federal judges by Congress, which routinely denied pay raises and was pondering new ways to discipline them. "The entire judiciary is edgy," the chief justice wrote, so he proposed "a hard hitting committee to 'develop the case' of our 700 colleagues" and shore up the judiciary's "independence, its dignity and its financial security." "The question is," Burger asked, "will one I. Kaufman chair this group?" Kaufman quickly agreed, and his new "Committee on the Judicial Branch" was formed with six judges, eventually growing to fourteen members.[9]

Interpreting his mandate broadly, Kaufman critiqued bills on judicial misconduct and opening internal court deliberations to public review. But his main focus was money. District judges earned $54,500 in 1980, and circuit judges made $3,000 more. While that didn't seem scandalously low, the runaway inflation of the 1970s had effectively inflicted a dramatic pay cut. And benefits for spouses and children were a pittance—just a few thousand a year, unless the judge had spent almost a lifetime on the bench—threatening to impoverish widows and limit college educations. In response, judges were quitting in far greater numbers. A few months after joyfully roasting Kaufman in 1980, Mulligan resigned and blamed the poor benefits, quipping, "You can live on the pay, but you can't die on it."

Kaufman went to work with his usual frenzy, repeatedly testifying, manufacturing reports to the full judiciary, working the phones with Congress, and prodding friends Sulzberger and Newhouse to apply media pressure. Years of arduous work yielded nothing, however; judges simply drew too little sympathy on the Hill, where salaries were also low but members didn't dare hike them for fear of voters. Improbably, the issue even united Ralph Nader and the Chamber of Commerce. Nader attacked the proposed raises at a time of "double-digit inflation" and high "rents and food bills," while the Chamber mocked judges for pleading poverty: "Watch out Mother Teresa, you've got competition!" Even Burger privately admitted to Kaufman that "we know salaries of our judges are absurdly low, but to millions of Americans they look like abundance." Still others were happy using judges' paychecks to punish them for unpopular rulings. "Let's face it," Kaufman wrote a friend, "Congress does not like federal judges. We are too independent, we try cases like Abscam, have jurisdiction over issues involving abortion and busing, etc., etc., etc."[10]

Kaufman often grumbled to friends about his prolonged labors on the committee, calling it "generally thankless." In reality, it was anything but. He received a torrent of grateful letters from judges and their families around the country, to say nothing of phone calls and buttonholing at judicial gatherings. Their stories revealed real anguish. "I have had to encroach upon my savings every year in order to educate my children and to maintain just a modest standard of living," read a typical missive. "Can this inequity be possible?" asked a different judge's widow. A third judge wrote of a son shot in the eye at close range with a fire hose by a drunken firefighter and tipped into "mental collapse." "He is totally dependent on me," the judge explained, noting that if he died, the boy would only get $1,450 a year. And the letters overflowed with appreciation, such as "I want you to know that I feel a great debt of gratitude to you for all that you have done," and "We are fortunate to have you as our advocate." Kaufman had become a minor hero to hundreds of federal judges throughout America. Happily well off, he didn't need a higher salary, and Helen didn't need greater survivors' benefits. He could have politely begged off of Burger's assignment. Instead, he gave years of spadework to the task of improving the lot of his colleagues because, as he replied to one thank-you note, "I love the judiciary too much to let it die from neglect and starvation." He resigned from the committee in 1983 only because an even bigger extrajudicial assignment came along.[11]

That assignment brought Kaufman back to his roots as the demon boy prosecutor and the man lauded for staring down the "hoods" of Apalachin. In 1978, Stamford, Connecticut, reporter Tony Dolan won a Pulitzer Prize for exposing mob-related municipal corruption. Later a speechwriter for President Reagan, Dolan convinced administration officials to take the fight national. Reagan's plan, announced in 1982, included a commission of "distinguished Americans . . . to undertake a region-by-region analysis of organized crime's influence, to analyze and debate the data it gathers, and to hold public hearings on its findings." Within a week, a small item in the *Times* disclosed that Kaufman had been "approached by administration officials" to head the body. Dolan had run into Kaufman in Bermuda, and they'd hit it off. Kaufman also knew Reagan distantly through California friends. For their part, Reagan and others in the White House admired Kaufman for enduring years of obloquy for standing up to the Reds.[12]

There was likely a further rationale. The administration wanted young conservatives on the bench and believed Kaufman's chairmanship would lead him to assume "senior status"—a form of quasi-retirement enabling judges to continue sitting while hearing fewer cases—handing the White House a seat to fill on the Second Circuit. Kaufman told Burger he would take senior status and presumably said or implied the same to the White House. In July 1983, his appointment was announced at a Rose Garden ceremony. Other commissioners were former Supreme Court justice Potter Stewart, South Carolina senator Strom Thurmond, New Jersey congressman Peter Rodino, two law professors, a crime reporter at *Reader's Digest*, police officials, prosecutors, and lawyers.[13]

The problems started almost immediately. Critics claimed installing a judge over an executive commission violated the separation of powers, and a court later agreed, though the ruling had no practical effect. Kaufman and Justice Department officials also squabbled over personnel. Within two months, the DOJ-selected choice for executive director, veteran prosecutor Peter Vaira, quit after finding Kaufman "irascible" and preoccupied with seeking a private plane, bodyguards, and a bigger travel budget. More substantively, Vaira favored more background work, while Kaufman struck him as more interested in flashy public hearings. Hitting back, Kaufman denounced Vaira as "a hot headed guy" with bad judgment. After two commissioners complained, DOJ blocked Kaufman's preferred replacement and brought in another experienced Mafia prosecutor, James Harmon. Above all, Kaufman antagonized the White House by refusing to resign his judgeship despite earlier hints or promises. "Crime Commission Bogs Down in Power Struggle," the *Times* reported, as DOJ officials anonymously carped that Kaufman's "personality contributed to the turmoil. He is widely known as a proud, independent man who is determined to get his own way."[14]

On top of all that, Kaufman was also losing his commissioners as months passed with little action. One labeled the experience "a sad waste of time." Kaufman asked Sam Skinner, a Chicago prosecutor and later a cabinet member, to smooth over relations with other panelists. "He was probably autocratic" and "tended to rub people the wrong way," Skinner recalled. "Because he'd been a judge for a long time, he was not used to collective [decision making]," Skinner thought. To Harmon, Kaufman admitted simply, "Jim, I've been a judge for 35 years. I'm not used to people talking back to me."[15]

Once in place, Harmon ably assembled a staff of lawyers, investigators, and assistants that grew to forty. He and Kaufman orchestrated public hearings in cities around the country that probed important but lesser-known aspects of organized crime, such as money laundering by groups as disparate as the Hell's Angels and Lockheed Aircraft, drug smuggling by previously obscure Asian gangs, and mob-controlled attorneys who secretly joined their clients in lawbreaking. Other sessions covered more familiar turf: drugs, dirty labor unions, and gambling. The hearings were often dramatic, with witnesses disguising themselves with black hoods and voice-scrambling machines. Higher-profile figures like Teamsters president Jackie Presser played what the *Chicago Tribune* called "a symphony of the Fifth," while shadowy cooperators spoke "of 'goons' and 'leg-breakers.'"[16]

Still, the catcalls continued. "Inquiry on Crime, a Year Old, Has Little to Show," a *Times* headline proclaimed. Disgruntled commissioners kept finding their way into print to say they were "reinvent[ing] the wheel," or "very disappointed in the way things are going." More seriously, civil libertarians objected to anonymous witnesses publicly fingering supposed gangsters who had no opportunity to respond. "I wonder if I am engaged in an utterly useless, frustrating experience that is doomed to fail," Kaufman mused to reporters, "or are we going to make some headway?"[17]

The commission's end products were a series of interim and final reports running the gamut from money laundering to drug smuggling to union corruption, and much in between. The volume on drugs was possibly "the most comprehensive report ever prepared by the government analyzing anti-drug strategies," according to the *Wall Street Journal*, and it proposed carrots (more education, counseling, and research) as well as sticks (more simple possession prosecutions and prisons). It also recommended drug testing for workers, however, which drew

To Judge Irving Kaufman
With appreciation and best wishes,

FIGURE 15. Kaufman presents President Reagan with reports of the President's Commission on Organized Crime, 1986. *White House photographer.*

fire from politicians and even several commissioners, who charged that they hadn't been told of the proposal in advance.[18]

More generally, ten of the nineteen commissioners released a separate statement blasting Kaufman's and Harmon's leadership of the entire project: "The true history of the [commission] is a saga of missed opportunity." They decried "poor management of time, money and staff" and a "rush-to-judgment" decision-making process. Skinner wasn't one of the irate majority, but looking back he understood the complaints. Kaufman had tried to run things "with an iron hand," he recalled, and was "probably troubled by the fact that they just didn't listen to what he had to say or go along with it." "Discord to the End," a *Times* piece headlined.[19]

Yet for all the friction and management flubs, Kaufman's commission scored some lasting successes. Congress agreed to make money laundering a specific federal crime, which Harmon called the commission's "greatest hit" and a "shot heard around the world," emulated by other countries. On drugs, Congress passed a bipartisan bill in 1986 that incorporated many of the body's recommendations, including greater funding for treatment and education. Increased prosecutions for possession and low-level dealing, longer prison terms, and greater use of random drug testing—all endorsed by the commission—became hallmarks of the nation's "war on drugs" during the 1980s and 1990s, with mixed and often inequitable results. Mobbed-up unions also came under assault by the Justice Department, as the commission proposed, eventually weakening organized crime's sway over organized labor.[20]

Vaira may have been right that Kaufman prioritized showy public hearings over original investigative work—likely an outgrowth of his memories of the televised Kefauver and McClellan hearings and his unquenchable thirst for the spotlight. And most of the information the commission highlighted in hearings and reports wasn't new; it had largely been excavated from older criminal cases, witnesses already tried and convicted, or dusty government records. One expert, Notre Dame law professor Robert Blakey, faulted the commission for failing to devise an overarching strategy for defeating organized crime and instead directing what "professionals in this business" viewed as "a publicity effort." But increasing public awareness had been part of the project's mandate, even if the know-it-alls shrugged. As Kaufman accurately put it, the commission "directed its searchlight on a few dark places, which will receive more attention than in the past."[21]

Kaufman's work on the commission capped decades of extrajudicial service that began almost as soon as he took office in 1949. "Almost from the day I went on the bench," he told a *Times* interviewer writing about his chairmanship, "I considered it terribly important to the system of justice for a judge not to view a case in microcosm, to understand that the case was part of a system of justice and how it was being administered." As his labors on the jury system, juvenile justice, judicial salaries, and other areas showed, Kaufman thought judges with expertise should unabashedly weigh in and "play the role of lions in the policymaking process, rather than lambs who withdraw to the safety and isolation of their chambers." And on a personal level, the diversions kept him fresh, energized, and interested. "Everyone asks the tired old question, 'How do you do so many things—judging, Chairman of the crime commission, speaking, writing,'" he wrote his sister-in-law. "I never told them but the answer is that all the extracurricular activities is my escape valve from 35 years of judging."[22]

Like his relationships with Tom Clark and J. Edgar Hoover in an earlier day, Kaufman's friendship with Warren Burger came with a hefty dose of flattery. As Kaufman's clerk in 1970 remembered, it was obvious Kaufman "wanted recognition by Warren Burger *a lot*." He stockpiled signed photos from the regal-looking chief. There was one for "the 'Burger Section' of my home library," which he unconvincingly blamed on Helen ("if I am to have peace at home I must accept my orders and request your autograph"). And there was one in chambers, which allowed him to joke to Burger that "a prerequisite for a clerkship with me will be that I observe the new fellow properly genuflect when his eyes (or *her* eyes) focus on the Great Chief." Burger sometimes sent along laudatory articles, which Kaufman duly praised. And Kaufman particularly acclaimed Burger's dissenting opinion in 1972 arguing for upholding the constitutionality of capital punishment. Not only were the "reasoning, logic, tone and writing . . . superb," he wrote Burger in a private note, but he "could not see any escape from your powerful argument." To be expected, perhaps, from a man vilified for imposing two death sentences.[23]

But neither the fawning nor a friendship built over years of collaborating on administrative projects could completely obscure something less cheerful for Kaufman: the Burger Court was slowly eviscerating much of his life's work. Looking back on his career after three decades on the bench, Kaufman told a reporter in 1980 that he and the judiciary had helped bring about "a kind of peaceful social revolution that has begun to eradicate some of the troubling inequities and contradictions in our social fabric." And he scoffed at the notion that this was beyond the purview of judges. "Of course, judges do make law," he'd written three years earlier. "They must. The vague commands of the equal protection clause or the First Amendment cannot be given life without rules made by judges."[24]

His superiors in Washington increasingly saw things differently, however. Burger's main appeal to Nixon had been his public criticism of the Warren Court's purportedly soft treatment of criminals. It was also expected that Burger and the five Republican appointees added during his years as chief, 1969 to 1986, would reorient constitutional law by favoring states' rights, pruning remedies for racial discrimination, endorsing government promotion of religion, and limiting press freedom. While the Burger Court's fulfillment of this wish list was far from consistent, it was also apparent that, in the words of Harvard Law School professor Abram Chayes, "the long summer of social reform that occupied the middle third of the century was drawing to a close." The Court would therefore repeatedly reject Kaufman's opinions and his judicial philosophy.[25]

In 1970, for example, the Court reversed the Second Circuit's decision in *McMann*, which had granted habeas hearings to state prisoners in order to reconsider guilty pleas entered after illegal pressure from police and prosecutors. Friendly, dissenting in 1970, and then Burger, writing for the majority, saw no need to protect confessed criminals, but later research would vindicate Kaufman. A 2015 report found that 15 percent of those exonerated through DNA testing and other methods had pleaded guilty beforehand. After *McMann*, the Burger Court continued limiting habeas corpus until Kaufman's vision of the federal courts as mostly open forums for people challenging unconstitutional conduct in state criminal systems dimmed considerably.[26]

The Burger Court similarly recoiled from supervising state prisons. In 1976, the justices reversed a Kaufman decision giving certain inmates the right to a hearing and other process before they could be punished by summary transfers to different institutions. Two years later, the Court narrowly voted to toss out Kaufman's decision upholding reforms to the federal jail in Manhattan, the MCC. Grossly overcrowded facilities, body cavity searches, and other restrictions weren't impermissible "punishment," the brethren held, just "discomforting." According to the clerk who worked on the MCC case, Kaufman had "tried to be very careful and very precise" in crafting a limited opinion that might evade high court review, but "it didn't work." In a 1987 opinion issued after Justice Rehnquist succeeded Burger as chief, the Court lowered the bar further and signaled endorsement of any prison condition that advanced legitimate penological goals, regardless of the effect on inmates. In dissent, Justice Brennan quoted Kaufman and endorsed a constitutional standard Kaufman had articulated in a 1985 decision extending more robust protection. But the votes weren't there.[27]

Kaufman's approach to crime and punishment also took hits from Congress. In March 1981, a psychotic loner obsessed with the actress Jodie Foster sprayed bullets at President Reagan. John Hinckley's startling acquittal by reason of insanity after weeks of conflicting psychiatric testimony enraged Americans who were sure the insanity defense was sport for doctors and "a "rich man's defense," as one senator claimed, since only the wealthy could hire the experts needed to prove it at trial. As bills proliferated in Congress, Kaufman took to his usual forum, the *Times*, to try to save his landmark *Freeman* decision, expanding the defense. In "The Insanity Plea on Trial," he warned against rushing changes in "an urge to punish one man." Congress ignored him, though, and completely nullified *Freeman*, reinstating the stricter, Victorian-era "M'Naghten rule." As a postscript, the Reagan administration publicly rejected Senator Moynihan's recommendation of a federal judgeship for Will Hellerstein, the lawyer who had argued *Freeman* to Kaufman almost two decades earlier. According to news accounts, Roy Cohn advised the administration that Hellerstein was a radical.[28]

Conservatives hoped Burger and the appointees after him would also take a different line on race, especially school desegregation. For years after Kaufman's New Rochelle decision, the Supreme Court stood with Black parents demanding concrete change, but then the winds shifted. President Nixon and other white politicians led a chorus of opposition to court-ordered busing, while angry white crowds bombed and stoned school buses in Pontiac, Michigan, and Boston. In 1974, the newly conservative Court struck down a desegregation plan in suburban Detroit. By the early 1990s, the justices held that desegregation orders could be terminated even if schools would revert to being all Black, and that districts needn't bother trying to counteract school resegregation brought about by "private choices" in housing. That such private outcomes were themselves compelled by age-old discriminatory lending, zoning, and development practices, as in New Rochelle, went unmentioned. Finally, in 2007, four justices agreed that students couldn't be assigned to different schools in order to boost diversity, while a fifth, Anthony Kennedy, left open the possibility that schools could consider race when confronting "the problem of *de facto* resegregation in schooling." Justice Kennedy retired in 2018, however, bringing ever closer the ahistorical color-blindness vigorously pushed by New Rochelle officials and rejected by Kaufman in 1961. At the same time, most Black and Hispanic children in America go to schools with few whites—a re-sorting by race at its worst in the region where Kaufman's decision initially had the most impact: the North.[29]

Kaufman had also argued that educational discrimination based on poverty was unconstitutional. In 1971, he dissented from a ruling upholding a New York law that charged the parents of elementary students for books. Two years later, however, a Supreme Court majority composed of the four new conservatives and Justice Stewart dashed Kaufman's and others' hopes of using the Constitution to force states to equalize educational funding for poor and wealthy students.[30]

The Burger Court never ruled on Kaufman's landmark holding in *Filártiga* that foreigners could sue their tormenters in American courts, but later justices did. At first, in 2004, the Court endorsed Kaufman's decision and subsequent holdings from other courts. Then, a trio of decisions beginning in 2013 effectively reversed *Filártiga* by barring actions based on activity outside the United States, precluding suit against foreign corporations, and likely limiting suit to three kinds of torts recognized in 1789: piracy, interfering with safe passage, and attacks on ambassadors. The question isn't "so much what is left of *Filártiga* today, at least in the United States," a dejected Peter Weiss, who argued the case, commented, "as what may be rediscovered at some time in the future."[31]

Burger and later justices were kinder to Kaufman in the field where he hoped to stand tallest—the First Amendment—but not much. Cases like *Herbert* exposed the Burger Court's stingier approach to press freedoms. The Court also eradicated what Kaufman had called "the privacy of confidential communication" in the obscenity prosecution of Frank Dellapia, the Brooklynite who mailed pornographic films to a California couple for $150. Instead, the justices denied any right to provide obscene material, even for free. In other respects, however, Kaufman's free speech absolutism well suited the increasingly conservative justices. The Rehnquist and Roberts Courts have rarely rejected First Amendment claims of any kind and have been particularly scornful of almost any restrictions on the raising and use of money in political campaigns, as was Kaufman. In 2021, the Court also affirmed Kaufman's opinion that off-campus speech by high school students, however vulgar, usually couldn't be restricted by school officials. On the other hand, Kaufman's last opinion was one of his very few *rejecting* a First Amendment claim—in this case from students who objected to a mandatory university fee that funded campus groups whose speech they disliked—and the Court eventually endorsed that position, too.[32]

Yet the First Amendment safeguards more than speech, and there Kaufman was completely out of step. Returning prayer to schools in whatever way possible was and remains a conservative dream, and Kaufman acted to thwart it. When a public high school in a small town near Albany rejected use of a classroom for student prayer, Kaufman upheld the decision, reasoning that approval would be an establishment of religion by signaling to "impressionable students . . . that the state has placed its imprimatur on a particular religious creed." In 1990, however, the Supreme Court effectively reversed him again, upholding the constitutionality of voluntary in-class prayer. This fit a still-ongoing pattern of greater approval of state support for religion. A friend of Kaufman's on the Third Circuit wrote to commiserate, asking "How could they be so wrong?!" The decision was "hard to fathom," Kaufman agreed.[33]

His frustration only increased when, ironically, he struck down a regulation as interfering with religion—a New York State Fair rule barring Hare Krishnas from approaching fairgoers—but the Supreme Court upheld the prohibition in a different case soon after. However he decided, he couldn't seem to please his chief—something Burger mocked at a judicial gathering in Washington. After dinner, Burger preceded Kaufman at the podium, leading Kaufman to joke that it was unusual for him to follow the chief, who usually capped off such occasions by speaking last. "I wish you'd follow me more often, Irving!" Burger interrupted to laughter.[34]

In fact, something did come between the two friends, though it probably wasn't Kaufman's doctrinal independence. In a tribute to Burger on his resignation in 1986, Kaufman noted that they had "often disagreed over the proper interpretation of the Constitution," but that he had "certainly never allowed our professional disputes to affect our warm friendship." It may have been a different story for Burger, though. Only a month earlier, Kaufman had written seeking a thaw after some sort of prolonged freeze, and he weakly invoked a mutual interest in appearances to make his case: "Don't you think it is about time, at this posture in our careers, that whatever nonsense caused the chasm become a relic of the past? Mature men look for ways to patch up, not tear down, very old relationships. Not to revert to the status quo ante only gives gossips the food and glee that nourishes them." While it is impossible to know what caused Burger's alienation—Kaufman's use of his chairmanship of the Committee on the Judicial Branch to try to speak for the whole judiciary is one candidate—his plea didn't have much effect. The pair corresponded infrequently and rarely saw each other after Burger's retirement.[35]

If it was reliably conservative in some areas like crime, race, and religion, the Burger Court was surprisingly liberal in others. It was the Burger Court, after all, that decided *Roe v. Wade* and a host of cases condemning gender discrimination as unconstitutional. But the 1980 elections accelerated the conservative drive to halt or roll back liberal precedents. Candidate Reagan pledged to name justices in tune with the "morals of the American majority," and the victorious president's new attorney general, William French Smith, assailed the courts for a multitude of sins: creating new constitutional rights to sexual privacy and abortion, imposing racial quotas on workplaces, and taking over prisons and housing projects. Liberal Harvard Law professor Laurence Tribe nervously labeled Smith's speech "somewhat Neanderthal."[36]

Slapped down repeatedly by the Burger Court, Kaufman still burned to fight back. He wanted to defend the new, individual-oriented liberalism he'd adopted along with his bold and activist way of judging. And unlike his colleagues, he could use the megaphone of the country's most important newspaper. Before the Reagan administration was a week old, Kaufman published a piece advising the new president on what he ought to look for in a jurist. While acknowledging the need to set aside personal views and accept that judicial lawmaking was "of an interstitial character" only, Kaufman stressed that "the highest form of the judge's craft involved the creation of an imaginative solution that sweeps away contradiction and ambiguity, advancing the law's true purpose within the bounds of precedent and reason. A judge should . . . not hesitate to strike out along new pathways that lead to the just result." This was a far cry from classic conservative judicial restraint. Cluelessly thinking his views might actually carry weight, he sent a copy of the piece directly to Reagan, boasting that it had received "quite a reception in legal and other circles."[37]

Later that year, Kaufman attacked one of the new conservative strategies for neutering liberal courts: bills to strip them of jurisdiction to decide certain politically controversial cases. By late 1981, more than thirty proposals were pending in Congress to deprive federal courts of the power to hear cases involving busing, abortion, and school prayer. Writing in the *Times Magazine*, Kaufman denounced the bills as an end run around the amendment process and a threat to the judiciary's power as the final arbiter of constitutional questions.[38]

After Reagan's reelection, and despite chairing the president's commission on organized crime, Kaufman only amplified his public opposition to the administration's conservative legal project. With Supreme Court vacancies looming, Kaufman cautioned in the *Times Magazine* against "employing the selection process solely to effect sweeping social change or to reverse an unpopular judicial decision." Given his own work effecting social change from the courthouse, this had to gall conservative readers finally enjoying their turn at the wheel.[39]

Simultaneously, Kaufman published a fervent defense of liberal judging in a law review article he titled "The Anatomy of Decisionmaking." Intended as a "selected reminiscence" to illuminate "the practical considerations that guide appellate judges," the wide-ranging article described his approach to the facts of cases, precedent, ambiguous statutes, and constitutional interpretation. He was unusually frank about the judge's role in making law and drawing on personal morality and the temper of the times when wrestling with ambiguous text or new circumstances. Law was "a vibrant and capacious vehicle for social advancement," he wrote, "capable of accommodating the variegated demands posed by an ever more sophisticated society." When judges face "decisional leeway," therefore, they should "recognize that our intuition, emotion and conscience are appropriate factors in the jurisprudential calculus."

This was candor "rarely seen in the scholarly pages of law reviews," the *Times* wrote, which was ironic, since the paper had refused to publish it. Abe Rosenthal had given Kaufman the rare thumbs down because the piece didn't address his decision-making process in the Rosenberg case, and as Rosenthal told the editor of the *Sunday Magazine*, "it will be difficult to run a piece for Judge Kaufman on judicial decisions without his most famous case being mentioned." Nonetheless, the *Times*' coverage of the article led the *Wall Street Journal* to respond with a scalding editorial titled "Tales Out of Court." The conservative organ called Kaufman's discussion "staggering only for its honesty" and a guilty plea "that he and other activist judges have been shooting from the hip" all along. These judges "may be sore at Kaufman for giving their game away," the editors speculated, but the "result of Kaufman-style judicial legislating is all too clear to the common man."[40]

Reagan's second term also featured a change at the Justice Department, and the new attorney general leaned even farther right than Smith. More of a social conservative, Ed Meese immediately began trumpeting a species of conservative legal thought less familiar than old-fashioned judicial restraint: originalism. Developed largely by Judge Robert Bork, Judge and later Justice Antonin Scalia, and certain law professors, originalism aims to effectuate the "original" understanding of the Constitution in 1787 (and after the Civil War) rather than a malleable "living Constitution" interpreted to address the perceived demands of modern life. Originalism "seeks to depoliticize the law," Meese claimed, by ignoring contemporary clamor and social fads and applying a constitutional meaning fixed in amber centuries ago. This was what Scalia meant when he called constitutional interpretation "a task sometimes better suited to the historian than the lawyer." After Meese took office, the Justice Department sought to advance their theory through Supreme Court appointments like Bork's and Scalia's and similar lower court selections, positions taken in court, and Meese's tireless public evangelism.[41]

For Kaufman, however, nothing could be more antithetical. He looked forward, not backward. He had wanted to modernize law, and through law to modernize America. As a creature of the most dynamic city and society in the world, he couldn't fathom making important decisions as if it was still the eighteenth century, and as if judges were nothing more than impotent, ivory tower historians. Constitutional provisions, he'd written in a 1976 case on housing discrimination, weren't "magical talismans, whose import is as immutable as the law of ancient Media and Persia. Rather, the words of the Constitution to a large extent derive their meaning from the perceived needs, desires and expectations of society."[42]

He also recognized, as he wrote in notes jotted for a speech, that "ambiguity is the hallmark of all decisionmaking." Originalism promised certainty and simplicity, but after a lifetime on the bench Kaufman thought that didn't exist. There were no easy answers, no dodging the hard work of marshaling *all* the decisional tools: the facts of the case, the text of the law, the draftsmen's purpose, previous judicial decisions, larger legal values, commentary from the academy, pertinent social factors, and the judge's own experiences and sense of morality. Only then could a judge achieve some approximation of appropriately individualized, case-by-case justice. "We must strain our hearts and minds to apply the most enlightened human spirit we can muster, and pray that our choices prove to be just ones," he said in a speech in 1980. Finally, Kaufman suspected the conservatives simply wanted doctrinal justification to eliminate specific and recent implied constitutional rights to personal autonomy and abortion access and had landed on a kind of ancestor worship as a means to this end.[43]

So he resumed his attack. In "What Did the Founding Fathers Intend?" in the *Times Magazine*, he lambasted originalism as a danger to "some of the greatest achievements of the Federal judiciary," meaning the decades of rulings expanding individual freedom and civil rights—some of which bore his name. One by one, he laid out the theory's biggest flaws. Ascertaining what the framers intended when crafting the Constitution's "grand yet cryptic phrases" is a "notoriously formidable task," given what Kaufman called "the paucity of materials," that is, limited historical information about what they thought. And who were "the framers" anyway—the delegates in Philadelphia in 1787, the multitudes who debated and ratified the Constitution, only the authors of *The Federalist Papers*? More deeply, there was the unavoidable fact that modern judges confront issues never pondered by Madison and others in his day. Kaufman conceded that *something* had to restrain judges, who couldn't just go around implementing their personal views, but he argued that more traditional guardrails, such as standing doctrine, adherence to precedent, and close attention to a case's specific facts did the job. In the end, judges have to live in the here and now. "Indeed, even if it were possible to decide hard cases on the basis of a strict interpretation of original intent, or originalism, that methodology would conflict with a judge's duty to apply the Constitution's underlying principles to changing circumstances."[44]

Kaufman didn't invent these critiques. Academics and justices skeptical of originalism, like William Brennan and John Paul Stevens, had voiced them earlier. But Kaufman's status and longevity in the public eye, his special entrée to the *Times*, and the coverage given his articles and speeches all combined to make him a conspicuous addition to the debate—a voice from the bench but uniquely addressed to laypeople. He kept up the assault in an acerbic *Times* op-ed for the Constitution's bicentennial that called originalism "specious" and highlighted an additional shortcoming: the framers themselves had understood that future generations would give content to the Constitution's vague and general phrases rather than perpetually look back for original meaning. It was the originalists who were undemocratic, Kaufman contended, by turning a blind eye to contemporary life and America's living citizens. "The Framers' legacy to modern times is the language and spirit of the Constitution, not the conflicting and dated conceptions . . . underneath that language. It is always a terrifying realization to learn that our fathers are no longer walking beside us. But we must be content that they provided us with general guidance."[45]

Kaufman may have jabbed at Meese in public but, as with Burger, he was privately solicitous. Three months after confirmation as attorney general in 1985, Meese was dining at 1185 Park Avenue with Punch Sulzberger, Abe Rosenthal, the Newhouses, and other Kaufman friends. "You have all the warm and kind characteristics that one searches for in a friend," Kaufman wrote Meese later. The dinners became annual occasions, leading Meese to call them "our best reason for coming to New York."[46]

This wooing reflected a vanished time Kaufman had known as a young Justice Department lawyer, when there were far fewer federal judges and they might drop in on the attorney general unannounced when in Washington. There was also his congenital and never-ending courtship of anyone in power. He had known or corresponded with every attorney general since Tom Clark in the forties, and he didn't see any reason to stop now just because he and Meese were such an ideological odd couple. There was something else, too, something more concrete. Kaufman badly wanted the Presidential Medal of Freedom, the country's highest civilian honor, and he knew Meese could help.

This was part and parcel of an ongoing quest for awards and tributes others at his station of life might have forgone as superfluous résumé padding. But for Kaufman, awards didn't lose their luster just because he lobbied for them. And as he neared the end of seven decades of life, they salved a nagging and peevish feeling of underappreciation. "I had thought that no one cared," he said at one award ceremony, while he told a law school dean that he believed his career "would be quickly forgotten."[47]

This gloom hardly lifted when other judges on the Second Circuit agreed in 1989 to install a bust in the Second Circuit courtroom of his old rival Henry Friendly, who had committed suicide three years earlier in despondency over declining health and the death of his wife.

Friendly joined Learned Hand as the only members of the court so honored. Judge Newman, who hatched the idea and secured the agreement of other judges, knew Kaufman wouldn't be enthusiastic, so he made sure he had plenty of yeses in hand before he made his approach. Seeing the campaign was unstoppable, Kaufman slyly proposed other living judges for busts, perhaps hoping to tie the project up with red tape or litter the courtroom with statuary, eventually including his own. Newman was a lunge ahead, however, and parried that only deceased judges would be considered. Kaufman was beaten.[48]

If immortality through sculpture was a long shot, there was always academia. While he received several honorary degrees over the years, it was affirmation from the Ivies he craved. Rifkind tried but failed to convince his alma mater Columbia to give Kaufman a degree. ("Such discourtesy will not go unrewarded," Rifkind vowed to Kaufman when the university failed even to respond to his request.) Kaufman met the same fate with Yale, despite personally importuning district judges in Connecticut, one of whom had been the university's general counsel.[49]

He had better luck at Harvard, though not in the form of a degree and not through his own string-pulling. Kaufman had known Walter Annenberg—media billionaire, Republican megadonor, and Nixon ambassador to the Court of St. James's—since the 1950s. And he'd known Annenberg's wife Lee even earlier, since her previous husband was Lou Rosenstiel. When in California, Kaufman and Helen socialized with the fantastically wealthy couple at Sunnylands, their vast estate in Rancho Mirage. One Saturday morning in 1989, Annenberg called Kaufman out of the blue to say he planned to give a million dollars to the recipient of Kaufman's choice in honor of his fortieth anniversary on the bench. Kaufman chose Harvard, and the law school established annual "Irving R. Kaufman Fellowships" to support graduates working in the public interest. Reporting on the fellowships, the *Harvard Crimson* dredged up the Rosenberg controversy but also quoted Alan Dershowitz calling Kaufman "an absolute saint compared to some of the people Harvard has named things after."[50]

As hard as it was to amass honors from top universities, however, the Medal of Freedom was something else entirely. So the old Kaufman came out and he worked even harder, spurred on no doubt by the fact that Friendly had received the medal from President Ford in 1977. Kaufman had tried in the Carter administration, cultivating Attorney General Griffin Bell and plotting with Rifkind about how to proceed. Aides talked Carter out of it, however, writing, "Although a highly talented judge, he has become a controversial figure. Indeed, demonstrators may protest the choice." Now he went to work on Meese. An unaddressed form letter in Meese's files, likely supplied by Kaufman and intended for supporters to send to the White House, stressed Kaufman's committee memberships, prolific writing, and First Amendment advocacy. And the letter made clear that what embarrassed Carter's staff was a selling point to Reagan: "With his valorous conduct during one of the most emotional trials in history, the Rosenberg case, he made an enormous contribution to the sanctity of the law and the impartiality of the courtroom: he refused to let the decision of a court and jury be unduly influenced by a propaganda campaign and political pressures organized by the outside."[51]

Kaufman's campaign failed in 1986, so he thanked Meese for his "valiant effort" and asked if there was "an anticipated date for the next go-round of the President's blessing." The next year, Meese, Dolan, and other Kaufman allies succeeded in persuading Reagan, but White House Counsel Arthur Culvahouse successfully objected because Kaufman was still a sitting judge, and Culvahouse had tried to prevent presidential approval or criticism of the judiciary, lest it be seen as interference. Meese and Dolan and Chief of Staff Howard Baker went back to Reagan, however, and got him to change his mind a second time. Meanwhile, Kaufman wrote the president to announce that he would take senior status. That circumvented Culvahouse's objection, though the resignation was only partial, and he would still be hearing cases. His quasi-retirement took effect on June 30, 1987, and Reagan wrote a letter awarding him the medal the very next day.[52]

Kaufman finally had the medal in sight, but the day after the White House publicly announced the award in September 1987, the *Washington Post* lifted the curtain with a front page story detailing everyone's lobbying, reversals, and disagreements. The paper claimed Meese had made "an explicit trade" of the honor in exchange for Kaufman's resignation so the administration could fill the vacancy with another conservative appointment to the Second Circuit late in Reagan's presidency. Meese was described dining at Kaufman's apartment and planting the suggestion of a medal if he agreed to go senior. Although Meese denied any trade had occurred, the *Post*'s account was accurate. In fact, Kaufman had agreed once before to take senior status in exchange for the medal, but feeling his old friend was being used, Rifkind had talked him out of it. As one of Kaufman's clerks at the time, Andrew Klein, put it, "It was a very sad chapter for all of us. . . . If you were a good liberal Democrat, you didn't want to be manipulated by Ed Meese." Kaufman had also had quadruple bypass surgery earlier that year, however, which probably contributed to the decision to go senior. He'd been recuperating at home for several weeks and might have used the leverage of a resignation he was contemplating anyway to his advantage with the White House.[53]

In any event, commentators were generally forgiving. Kaufman deserved the medal as much as some other recipients, one analyst wrote, observing that other presidents had also used it to pay political debts. "And besides, on a list that runs from Bear Bryant to Vladimir Horowitz, nobody is out of place." As it ended up, the entire episode was vintage Kaufman. He had badly wanted something, indefatigably lobbied for it in secret, marshaled powerful friends, and eventually won the prize—but then seen it tarnished by public exposure and controversy. Nothing came easy.[54]

In any case, the *Post*'s unwanted scrutiny couldn't mar the event itself. "All of us in public life have to ignore the gossip mongers," Kaufman wrote one White House aide. As Reagan entered the peach-walled Roosevelt Room across from the Oval Office, Kaufman, Helen, and his two grandsons stood waiting before a crowd of old friends on folding chairs. Towering over his honoree, the president gave an encomium that left no doubt Kaufman was being honored *because* of the Rosenberg case, not in spite of it. Reagan repeated Kaufman's account of conversations with Eisenhower, with the general-president telling the young judge that the chorus for clemency had been the greatest pressure he had ever faced, Normandy included, but that he had drawn strength from Kaufman's example and held firm. Reagan also applauded Kaufman's work on the Apalachin and New Rochelle cases and the crime commission. There was "one bureaucrat," Reagan joked, "who, when he stopped trying to get in the way, just threw up his hands and said that if we really wanted to eliminate organized crime in America, all we needed to do was provide [Kaufman] with the home phone numbers of the major mobsters."

Stepping to the lectern to accept, Kaufman said nothing at all about the famous case Reagan began with, and which he still held out hope wouldn't lead his obituary. And he was brief, his voice still powerful, as he thanked Meese, Helen, and others. "All my life," he finished, the volume suddenly rising, "I have sought to preserve and protect the core of our heritage." That core was the Constitution, he said, taking his right hand out of his suit jacket's front pocket and chopping it downward, "and so long as it guides the ship of state, we need not fear the rocks and shoals. And to that end, I have dedicated my heart and soul. And I take this award as confirmation, Mr. President, that in the eyes of my countrymen, I have helped keep the beacon burning."[55]

Epilogue

"I Can't Believe I'm Going to Die"

I first saw my new boss as he tottered toward me slowly across the waiting room at Kennedy Airport, tiny and immaculate in a blue business suit and his arm in a sling. He'd fallen during the annual vacation in California. It was summer 1991, and Kaufman and Helen had recently celebrated his eighty-first birthday. "Even though we've had some periods of rough sledding," Helen wrote in a card to him, "plus many happy ones, we have scaled Mt. Everest—fifty-five years. We are made of tough fiber." Yet he seemed anything but tough as he wobbled my way.[1]

My only prior encounter with him had been my interview the year before, where we'd unexpectedly hit it off. He said he liked Texans because he found them like New Yorkers—outspoken and direct. I had no idea his most important patron had been from Texas, and I'd probably only barely heard of Tom Clark then anyway, despite attending his alma mater. I did sense the cowed nervousness of Kaufman's clerks as they tiptoed around chambers on pins and needles. They explained that the judge was a difficult employer. But I wanted a clerkship on an appellate court and a year in the city, and my only other offer there was from a trial judge known to seek out impossibly technical patent lawsuits. The Rosenberg case gave me pause, naturally. I vaguely understood some people thought they were innocent and had been railroaded, but my knowledge of the case was minimal, and in any event that had all been a million years ago. Nor were my parents like those of some clerks—lefty New Yorkers who, as one put it, "couldn't believe I would clerk for this guy."[2]

My co-clerk Daphna Boros also came from Harvard Law School, though we hadn't known each other there. We signed on despite the career office's discouragement of clerkships with Kaufman. In fact, he'd had trouble recruiting there for years. In 1977, a Kaufman clerk had written his old classmate Susan Estrich, then the first woman leading the *Harvard Law Review* and later the first to manage a presidential campaign, trying to encourage applications. "I assume everyone is aware that Judge Kaufman is one of the leading liberal jurists in the United States," the clerk wrote. Since that wasn't the issue, he wanted to dispel any rumors that "the personal travail will prove too burdensome." In 1982, Kaufman himself wrote a Harvard Law School professor that he was "disturb[ed] to learn that able young people at Harvard prefer gossip to facts and reputation." Then, in 1986, three clerks from Harvard quit simultaneously—a middle finger perhaps unprecedented in the annals of clerks and federal judges. They'd decided that the only way to get Kaufman "to be nicer and just calm down" was by threatening to leave en masse, Andrew Klein remembered. Kaufman then exploded and yelled at them that they were fired—to which they declared they were quitting instead. Days later, however, Kaufman called Klein, who hadn't really wanted to leave in the first place, and convinced him to stay. "From that day forward, he was like an angel to me. He was like a different person." Still, the embarrassing mess made the *New York Post* and the *National Law Journal*.[3]

Was there a chance Kaufman's turnabout with Klein reflected a new self-awareness late in life? In correspondence, he took to describing himself as "compulsive." With his successor as chief judge, Wilfred Feinberg, he admitted he could "carry candor to a fault on occasions." But at least as far as clerks were concerned, Klein proved to be a one-off. In 1990, Wendy Leibowitz started the job but almost immediately regretted it. Kaufman fired her several times the first week, but her co-clerk told her to shake it off and take a walk around the block; the judge would forget. When Kaufman heard that a colleague's clerks had thrown their boss a birthday party, he told Leibowitz "*I* want a birthday party. Contact all my clerks and throw me a birthday party." She dodged the assignment by claiming she had no idea how to organize such a large event. Then Kaufman hit on a new project, telling her,

"Bring a legal pad, we're launching my autobiography." He'd thought a lot about telling his story, in fact, and had even been courted by a major literary agent before deciding he was too busy to move forward. In sessions with Leibowitz, he grilled her about the Rosenberg case—"what were they convicted of? Not treason, espionage!"—until she sat down and read the transcript. She remembered him saying something along the lines of, "Look, I'm the Rosenberg judge, and I want to clear my name." Before long, though, he fired Leibowitz for good, and the autobiography project died.[4]

Unlike Leibowitz or Klein or the many before them, however, I suffered little of the classic Kaufman treatment. Daphna had started two months earlier than I did and prepared a long orientation memo for me, advising, "Unfortunately, this clerkship has one rule: be perfect all the time, in every way, at home and at work, with no pause or rest at any time. Sounds impossible? It is, so the next best thing you can do is never take things personally. Keep a thick skin, and realize that the man you are working for is absolutely irrational. (After all, his initials aren't IRK for nothing.)" As it turned out, I hardly needed toughening up. He yelled a little, as I'd been warned, but mostly he was absent. Only once did he complete a week at the courthouse hearing oral argument, and when that was over he was palpably relieved at having made it through. He called Daphna and me into his office and joked around, the gregarious kibitzer on full view. Waving a finger at us and smiling, he asked if there was going to be a *shidduch*—a marriage. I now know this was standard; if one of his clerks was a woman (there were never two women), he assumed his clerks were dating. "No, judge," we laughed a little uneasily, "there's no wedding."[5]

Then he stopped coming in altogether, and as December became January we gradually understood he was ill. We didn't learn this from him, however, and we went right along with the work—drafting memos and opinions, keeping up with the cases and correspondence—as communication became less frequent. He had little or no input into what we were doing in his name, but it had largely been that way from the beginning of our time there. And it had been that way for years before, though some of his last clerks found him more engaged than others. Klein had sat around with his co-clerks puzzling over a massive insurance dispute they didn't understand when it hit them that, only a few months removed from the classroom, they were effectively one of three votes deciding a multimillion-dollar commercial controversy. He found the realization "really quite terrifying." In another sign of slippage,

Kaufman missed that his secretary at the time was using access to his finances to embezzle from him; by the time Helen noticed in 1987, the secretary had stolen $250,000.[6]

As the weeks elapsed and inquiries arrived from other judges, we feared disclosing Kaufman's illness and absence and understood that he didn't want anyone to know he wasn't coming in. We had little information to share, in any case. In hindsight, we should have stopped covering and covertly wielding the power reserved for presidential appointees and told the chief judge what was happening. But we feared Kaufman's wrath should he reappear, and we lacked the confidence to stick our necks out. And if I'm being honest, I should also admit that I didn't entirely dislike being an unsupervised, almost federal judge.

Our hesitance was also symptomatic of a larger protectiveness most Kaufman clerks felt—the notion that part of our job was to circle the wagons around our unpopular employer. Kaufman avidly promoted that idea. When he interviewed Leibowitz and she asked what quality he considered most important in a clerk, he responded "loyalty." Bruce Kraus described feeling "a deep ethical duty never to talk about how awful the judge was, because it was like an attorney-client privilege thing." Perversely, the pity we encountered from other judges' clerks also sometimes led us to downplay the job's lowlights in what felt like a species of Stockholm syndrome. For some, also, affection and sympathy mixed in. Kaufman "could be really charming and really disarming," Daphna recalled, "and as nasty and horrible as he was, there's no question that I always felt sort of sorry for him. It was almost as if you wanted to protect him from his own bad self. Because there was something there that was very needy and vulnerable." Whatever it was, it lingers in the bloodstream. Decades after his death, I was astonished—but also not—to hear more than one or two ex-clerks lower their voices or ask to go "off the record" before criticizing the man, as if he was still in the next room listening and might somehow inflict the old punishments.[7]

Then again, perhaps any chambers or office would have done as we did. As a lawyer, I've argued to silent octogenarian and nonagenarian judges obviously long past their primes, maybe not there at all, but still clinging to office because they could. As a US Senate staffer, I saw Strom Thurmond's aides guide him into and out of his seat and more or less do his job; he was reportedly determined to die a senator. The question of when and how to usher out elderly, life-tenured judges no longer up to their work is fruitlessly debated now and then, but there are no easy answers. Justifiably, still capable older judges object to mandatory retirement rules as ageist. They insist the problem, when it arises, is best solved through the discreet intervention of colleagues. Kaufman himself touched on this issue in a lecture in 1978, positing that "the problem can almost always be managed effectively in a personal and informal manner." After my experience with him, I wonder.[8]

On February 1, 1992, Kaufman died of pancreatic cancer. The nurse who tended to him later told us that, shortly before the end, he declared with a kind of wonder or bemusement fitting to someone with his lifetime of will and power, "I can't believe I'm going to die." Helen died in 2001. Once out of her husband's shadow, her grandson remembered, she underwent a sort of blossoming unusual for someone in her seventies. "She became her own person. She came into herself."[9]

Judge Jerome Frank, the liberal who wrote the Second Circuit's decision in the Rosenberg case, thought and wrote at length about the intersection of law and psychology. He questioned whether outsiders could ever truly understand the judicial mind, writing in 1930 that "the ultimately important influences in the decisions of any judge are the most obscure, and are the least discoverable—by anyone but the judge himself. They are tied up with intimate experience which no biographer, however sedulous, is likely to ferret out, and the emotional significance of which no one but the judge, or a psychologist in closest contact with him, could comprehend." At a 1995 symposium on judicial biography, participants half-seriously debated whether the genre should even exist. Trying to decode judicial behavior may be futile and entirely speculative, but Kaufman himself called his jurisprudence "an amalgam of external legal constraints and an internalized desire to respond to the world in which we live." Using this dichotomy, we can at least identify the external and internal forces behind Kaufman's transformation from Rosenberg executioner to one of the most significant progressive judges of his day.[10]

Externally, his evolution was a product of and mirrored the change in liberalism from the fighting, statist creed of his formative years to the expansion of individual rights in the 1960s and 1970s. Like many judges then and now, he began his career in the Department of Justice, used to taking his employer's good faith for granted. At first, government righteousness in the wars against communism and crime was so obvious to him that he colluded with prosecutors and began cases with the premise that, to quote one clerk, "We have to convict this guy." He'd also been a politically active Truman Democrat who understood that his team's fortunes depended on repulsing both communist accommodationists on the left and small-government conservatives on the right.

This paradigm faded, however, and as twentieth-century liberalism grew beyond simply trusting in government to spread prosperity and equality, Kaufman grew with it. Some of this shift was dictated by the Warren Court's constitutional revolution. As a judge on a lower court, Kaufman was bound to follow the justices' decisions whether he liked them or not; this was the greatest of the "external legal constraints" he referred to. Like all judges, Kaufman was routinely in the position of setting aside personal preferences and following existing law where it was unambiguous. He often quoted Justice Cardozo's formulation that a judge was no "knight-errant roaming at will in pursuit of his own ideal of beauty and goodness."[11]

Still, there were many novel cases over the course of his long judicial career where the result wasn't foreordained by precedent. In these, Kaufman reflected the contemporary liberal zeitgeist. As African Americans pushed forward with long-overdue claims of equality, he desegregated the New Rochelle schools. As a Democratic Congress liberalized immigration to the United States—before, in fact—he consistently ruled for asylum seekers. As the public fractured over the Vietnam War, he favored dissenters. As the Great Society confronted poverty, he endorsed a cutting-edge constitutional right to equal treatment for poor people. As reporters became more adversarial and political and other speakers became rawer and bolder, he sided with the press, the protesters, and the pornographers. In *Filártiga*, he approved and propelled the growing crusade for international human rights. Repeatedly, he extended the frontier of civil liberties against government authority by ordering recalcitrant officials to reform obsolete state and local laws and practices.

Moreover, decisions like these occurred against the backdrop of enormous social change. The government and society that had rewarded Kaufman so handsomely in his early life, and in which he therefore initially placed such reflexive faith and trust, buckled demonstrably as his judicial career advanced. Race riots, prison riots, assassinations, Vietnam, Watergate, economic shocks, cultural upheaval, the overall decline of authority—these forces and government failures tested many an establishmentarian and undoubtedly contributed to Kaufman's gradual transformation.

But recognizing that Kaufman reacted to social and political convulsion, and that he both followed and contributed to the dominant ideology of his time, still begs the question: *why?* Other judges bucked these trends and rejected Kaufman's core belief that, to quote the legal conservative and Kaufman critic Alexander Bickel, judges were "charged with a duty to act when majoritarian institutions do not." For this, internal explanations are needed.[12]

The leading one held that he was doing penance, "unconsciously trying to win favor among his persecutors by a show of ultra-liberalism," as Sidney Hook wrote. And Hook was being charitable; most thought Kaufman was acting quite consciously. Linda Greenhouse described "the received wisdom" about Kaufman: "After the Rosenberg executions, Irving Kaufman dedicated his life to trying to make sure that the first paragraph of his *New York Times* obituary would not be 'Judge Irving R. Kaufman, who sentenced the Rosenbergs to death.'" Even Joel Filártiga thought Kaufman ruled in his favor in order to "save his soul."[13]

The atonement theory is tempting and impossible to refute. Kaufman himself linked the Rosenberg case with his later jurisprudence in his *Times Magazine* article "A Free Speech for the Class of '75," calling it "unfair" that he had to cancel his commencement address at Pomona in light of his later liberal decisions. His tenacious lifelong battle to repel or even suppress criticism of the case—so unusual and inappropriate in any judge, let alone one so flamboyantly committed to free expression—confirms his bone-deep obsession with the controversy and its effect on his legacy. And it was also separately true that, as an egotist unable to master his insecurities or quench his thirst for public approval, Kaufman found deep fulfillment in the consistent praise he won from New York's and the nation's liberal establishment.[14]

But the expiation explanation also falters because it misses the early years. It begins in 1951 and so ignores Isidore, the immigrants' son whose mother sat him down in a tenement and told him to become a lawyer to escape poverty. It ignores the adolescent trained at Clinton High School and Downtown Fordham, grand sanctuaries of learning where he imbibed a tolerant Americanism side by side with New Yorkers of every kind. It ignores the young lawyer whose draft speech for Attorney General McGrath in 1949 condemned segregation and states' rights so vehemently that it had to be toned down. Well before Kaufman or anyone else had heard of Julius and Ethel Rosenberg, the newly appointed judge wrote that he saw his office as a way to try to "make it a lot easier for those who are now struggling like I did 20 years ago. Only in such a fashion can I reward the faith placed in me by this great distinction."[15]

This personal history focused Kaufman on *justice*, not simply laws or philosophies or systems. His clerk in 1975–76, Michael Tabak, recounted describing an appeal to Kaufman and identifying the key fact that, in Tabak's view, determined the outcome. Kaufman asked him about the other circumstances of the case, but Tabak breezily said they didn't matter. At this, Kaufman exclaimed "I'm not a legal automaton! I want to try to feel that I'm doing justice over here and I need to know what the facts are." As in the John Lennon and second Roy Schuster cases, Kaufman often made it clear what he wanted to do, what he believed the just outcome was, and then left it to his clerks to find the best route through the thicket of applicable laws and precedents. "At some moment three or more appellate judges may sense that 'justice' is not being done," he wrote of certain administrative law cases, though the passage applied to his outlook more generally. "At that point they may search for a peg on which to hang a decision."[16]

This isn't necessarily how the purists, the judge's judges, do it—a Henry Friendly, say. Some judges say and may even believe that their decisions shouldn't be swayed by the likely social consequences, only the cold dictates of the law on paper as previously set forth by others: legislatures, executives and agencies, and prior courts. Oliver Wendell Holmes famously described this idea of judging when he wrote that "if my fellow citizens want to go to hell, I will help them. It's my job." But a focus on justice has its defenders. Piero Calamandrei was an Italian legal scholar whose 1936 volume, *Eulogy of Lawyers*, still enjoys a cult following. Calamandrei wrote,

> It has been said that too much intelligence is harmful to a judge, but I do not subscribe to this. I do say, however, that the best judge is the one in whom a ready humanity prevails over a cautious intellectualism. A sense of justice, the innate quality bearing no relation to acquired legal techniques, which enables the judge after hearing the facts to feel which party is right, is as necessary to him as a good ear is to a musician; for, if this quality is wanting, no degree of intellectual pre-eminence will afford adequate compensation.

As time went on, Kaufman developed into a judge in whom a ready humanity won out.[17]

In his background and his resulting concentration on justice, as he understood it, Kaufman also typified a plentiful and much-noticed twentieth-century type: the Jewish American judge. Experienced or inherited memories of persecution and privation made most Jewish judges willing to take bold and novel stances to expand civil liberties. The model held from Brandeis to Ginsburg on the Supreme Court, and from Jerome Frank and David Bazelon to Stephen Reinhardt and Abner Mikva on the federal courts of appeals, plus many more. "Law became and remains an avenue of social mobility," Ginsburg said in a 2004 speech, and it also "became a bulwark against the kind of oppression Jews have encountered and survived throughout history. Jews in large numbers became lawyers in the United States, and some eventually became judges. The best of those lawyers and judges used the law not only for personal gain, but to secure justice for others." She might also have mentioned the effect of Jews' outsider status, at least during the first half of the century when lawyers like Kaufman came of age. Consequently, as one Kaufman clerk put it, "the cases that appealed to him were often 'little guy against the system' cases."[18]

The other internal force dictating his life as a judge was simply a feverishly active personality, unable to rest until the wish became fact. "But of course Kaufman can't relax," *Times* editor Peter Millones wrote in one memo. It was the quality that led him to graduate law school before twenty-one, achieve notoriety as a crime-fighter before thirty, and take the bench before forty. Every law clerk and anyone else at his disposal learned immediately that, as Roy Cohn put it, "When Irving wants something he doesn't stop, he doesn't leave you alone until you do what he wants."[19]

Thus "judicial restraint," the reigning conservative judicial philosophy of most of his years on the bench, was as foreign to Kaufman as any other kind of restraint. When it came to the cases before him, he was temperamentally compelled to act rather than forbear and assume some other cog in the system—the state legislature, prosecutors, the head of some agency—would do the right thing and fix the problem. This characteristic goaded Kaufman to reform old, stale doctrines, such as the "M'Naghten rule" version of the insanity defense and the notion that international law only reached conduct between sovereign states. It led him to order other governmental bodies and officials, like the New Rochelle school board and Dannemora State Hospital, to implement necessary change. "A Judge Who Likes Action" was the perfectly fitting headline of the 1983 *Times* profile from which Linda Greenhouse removed her byline.[20]

Yet this congenital restlessness inevitably clashed with the inherently passive, limited, and reactive nature of a job confined to examining a relatively small set of discrete legal disputes others happened to bring before him. It also contradicted the detached and reserved conception of the judicial role. One Kaufman colleague on the court of appeals described their job as one of "splendid isolation," but Kaufman expressly scorned judges becoming "monastic," and he was far from monk-like. Robert Gorman, a clerk who became a law professor, highlighted this contradiction in the first sentence of a biographical summary he prepared for Kaufman in 1966: "Irving Robert Kaufman is an activist by nature, and yet he [serves] as a member of that most contemplative society, the appellate judiciary." Carol Lam, a clerk two decades later who became a California state judge at a young age, wondered if Kaufman erred by taking the bench too early and might have thrived as a take-charge executive instead: "You're not running an agency, you can't make things happen in an operational sense. That can be limiting for certain types of personalities." Kaufman's desperate and ingrained need to move, to attack any problem and clear any roadblock, gave rise to impressive efficiency in the courtroom and great success as a judicial administrator and leader of extrajudicial groups like the commission to reform juvenile justice. But it also contributed to a dubious and lifelong tendency to try to evade inconvenient rules, from bar exam age minimums in 1930 to chief judge age ceilings in 1980, and much in between. And, more generally, it led him to strain against the cords binding all judges—even proactive ones like him—in America's democratic system, where people who run for office are supposed to wield the real power.[21]

In one sense, Kaufman lived a striking success story. Rising from Lower East Side rags to Upper East Side riches, from anonymity to the second-highest court in the land, he crafted a particularly impressive version of the classic American dream. As a judge, he was productively in tune with his times for most of his career, though he fell short of his goal of a seat on the Supreme Court. His most important appellate decisions improved life for many, expanded personal liberty, and infused justice with real compassion, while his deeply felt obligation to do still more through extrajudicial efforts added to that legacy. He used meaningful and significant work to persevere through and divert from family travails, and he reveled in the perks of high office and influential connections and great wealth—the conferences in London, dinners at Le Cirque, stays in Palm Beach and Beverly Hills, an award bestowed by the president. Had he actually completed an autobiography, he wouldn't have presented his life as tragic.

Yet from the outside peering in, his was also the familiar story of a man undone by his own inescapable flaws. Intense ambition and a special hostility to people who began as he had, but then spurned everything he stood for, led to ethical breaches and a fatal want of mercy in his most famous case. The eternally young, eternally sympathetic martyrs became shadows he could never outrun. By the 1970s, he was virtually their quarry. "If [the judge] ever consciously perpetrates an injustice," Kaufman said in a speech in 1958, "or fails to prevent an injustice, he will be haunted by it for the rest of his life." While he never publicly let on that he had caused an injustice—and almost certainly didn't think he had, even in the mournful, introspective depths of 1977—he was haunted nevertheless. The bomb threats and the letters and the stress helped corrode his family and private life. He was left to watch helplessly as his wife attempted suicide. Despite genuine love for his sons, he often seemed unable to grant them the same compassion and understanding present in his best opinions, exacerbating their ailments and damaging their lives. Today, the demon boy prosecutor's dazzling rise, the stature he won in the judiciary and New York society, the praise in the newspapers—all are forgotten. He is known for one thing only, just as he feared.[22]

Worse still, that thing made him a sort of Judas. Adam Eilenberg, who clerked for Kaufman in 1980–81, recounted traveling to Israel after the job and telling people on a kibbutz populated by hippieish Americans the identity of his former employer. "You clerked for Kaufman?" they asked him. "What a monster!" "It didn't improve my social life," Eilenberg added dryly. In his 2008 book *The Story of Yiddish*, the writer Neal Karlen muses on "what is a Jew" and writes, "Who can explain a tribe that holds to its chest Dr. Albert B. Sabin, inventor of the polio vaccine, but also has to count as its own Roy Cohn and Judge Irving Kaufman, who illegally conspired in chambers to convict Ethel and Julius Rosenberg, largely so that the case would go down as (good for the Jews)?" If Kaufman saw the Rosenbergs as bad for the Jews and acted accordingly—a gross oversimplification, but with its kernel of truth—great irony lies in the fact that, to people like Karlen, Kaufman himself now bears that stigma.[23]

But he was only human, and that accounted for all of the good and all of the bad. As he fully recognized,

> In the end, law is among the most human of all enterprises, and those who are appointed to decide questions of "law" must

contend with all the drama, confusion, failure and achievement that constitute the human experience. . . .

Our human qualities may cause us to make mistakes; after all, judges are not infallible. But these same human qualities may also prevent our making the worst error of all: creating a schism between a formalistic legal order and commonly held notions of social justice.[24]

NOTE ON SOURCES

I have generally inserted endnotes at the end of each paragraph or, less frequently, multiple paragraphs covering the same topic. Sources usually appear in each note in the order in which they are quoted or support the text.

Kaufman's papers are located in the Manuscript Division of the Library of Congress. The Finding Aid is at https://hdl.loc.gov.loc.mss/eadmss.ms011059. References to Kaufman's papers in the notes appear as "IRKP."

The FBI provided documents relating to Kaufman and other topics in response to multiple requests under the Freedom of Information Act. Unless otherwise indicated, cited FBI memoranda and correspondence, such as letters between Kaufman and J. Edgar Hoover, are on file with the author.

Files of cases adjudicated in the United States District Court for the Southern District of New York and the United States Court of Appeals for the Second Circuit are maintained by the National Archives and Records Administration.

Scraps was an intraoffice newsletter of the US Attorney's Office for the Southern District of New York; copies of issues produced in 1935–1940 were provided by that office.

Presidential libraries are denoted simply by the last name of the president followed by "Lib."—e.g., "Kennedy Lib."

Legal decisions, statutes, and law review articles are cited according to *The Bluebook: A Uniform System of Citation* (21st ed., Harvard Law Review Association, 2020).

In some cases, punctuation and capitalization of quotations have been edited for readability and clarity.

Abbreviations

General

HRK	Helen R. Kaufman
IRK	Irving R. Kaufman
NARA	National Archives and Records Administration
OFWA	on file with author
PCOC	President's Commission on Organized Crime
WH	White House

Archives and Collections

CCBP	Charles C. Burlingham Papers at the Harvard Law School Library
DPP	Drew Pearson Papers at the Lyndon B. Johnson Library
ELRP	Elliot L. Richardson Papers at the Library of Congress
EMP	Edwin Meese Papers at the Hoover Institution at Stanford University
FFP	Felix Frankfurter Papers at the Library of Congress
HBP	Herbert Brownell Jr. Papers at the Dwight D. Eisenhower Presidential Library
HJFP	Henry J. Friendly Papers at the Harvard Law School Library
HJMP	Howard J. McGrath Papers at the Harry S. Truman Presidential Library
HSBP	Henry Styles Bridges Papers at New Hampshire State Department–Division of Archives and Records Management
HSTP	Harry S. Truman Papers at the Harry S. Truman Presidential Library
JFKP	John F. Kennedy Papers at the John F. Kennedy Presidential Library
JKJP	Jacob K. Javits Papers at the Stony Brook University Library
KBKP	Kenneth B. Keating Papers at the University of Rochester
LAJP	Louis A. Johnson Papers at the University of Virginia Library
LHP	Learned Hand Papers at the Harvard Law School Library
NARA NY RF	Rosenberg case files at NARA, New York
NYTP	Papers of the *New York Times* at the New York Public Library

RMNP	Richard M. Nixon Papers at the Richard Nixon Presidential Library
SHP	Sidney Hook Papers at the Hoover Institution at Stanford University
TCCP	Tom C. Clark Papers at the Harry S. Truman Presidential Library
TCCP-UT	Tom C. Clark Papers at the University of Texas, Tarlton Law Library
TJDP	Thomas J. Dodd Papers at the University of Connecticut

Case Files

Bonanno SDNY	*United States v. Bonanno, et al.*, No. C 159–35 (SDNY)
Boutilier 2d Cir.	*Boutilier v. Immigration and Naturalization Service,* No. 429, Docket No. 30274 (2d Cir.)
Dellapia 2d Cir.	*U.S. v. Dellapia*, Docket No. 34858 (2d Cir.)
Filártiga SDNY	*Filártiga v. Peña-Irala*, No. 79 Civ. 917 (SDNY)
Filártiga 2d Cir.	*Filártiga v. Peña-Irala*, No. 79–6090 (2d Cir.)
Freeman 2d Cir.	*U.S. v. Charles Freeman*, No. 29688 (2d Cir.)
Herbert 2d Cir.	*Herbert v. Lando*, No. 77–7142 (2d Cir.)
James 2d Cir.	*Charles James v. Board of Education of Central District No. 1 of Towns of Addison*, No. 697, Docket 72-1109
Lennon 2d Cir.	*Lennon v. Immigration and Naturalization Service*, Docket 74-2189, No. 18 (2d Cir.)
Norwalk 2d Cir.	*Norwalk CORE v. Norwalk Bd. of Education*, Docket 33645, Case No. 135 (2d Cir.)
PP 2d Cir.	*U.S. v. New York Times*, Docket No. 71–1617 (2d Cir.)
Rosenberg SDNY	*U.S. v. Julius Rosenberg, et al.*, No. C. 134-245 (SDNY)
Russo 2d Cir.	*Russo v. Central School Dist. No. 1, Towns of Rush et al.*, No. 26, Docket 72-1303 (2d Cir.)
Schuster I 2d Cir.	*U.S. ex rel. Roy Schuster v. Herold*, No. 434, Docket 32194 (2d Cir.)
Schuster II 2d Cir.	*U.S. ex rel. Roy Schuster v. Vincent*, No. 79, Docket 75-2058 (2d Cir.)
Seeger 2d Cir.	*U.S. v. Peter Seeger*, No. 27, Docket 101 (2d Cir.)
Taylor SDNY	*Taylor v. Bd. of Education of the City School Dist. of the City of New Rochelle*, No. 60–4098 (SDNY)
Weiss SDNY	*U.S. v. Weiss, et al.*, No. C100-451 (SDNY)

Newspapers

CT	*Chicago Tribune*
LAT	*Los Angeles Times*
NRSS	*New Rochelle Standard-Star*
NYAN	*New York Amsterdam News*
NYDN	*New York Daily News*

NYHT	*New York Herald Tribune*
NYJA	*New York Journal-American*
NYLJ	*New York Law Journal*
NYP	*New York Post*
NYT	*New York Times*
NYWT	*New York World-Telegram*
WP	*Washington Post*
WSJ	*Wall Street Journal*

Reports

ABA Rosenberg	ABA Report of the Subcommittee on the Rosenberg Case, June 1977
FBI BR 1935	FBI report of background investigation of Kaufman, January 1935
FBI BR 1947	FBI report of background investigation of Kaufman, March 1947

Notes

Prologue

1. Felix Frankfurter to Charles Burlingham, February 14, 1958, box 5, folder 17, CCBP.

2. IRK to Truman, October 17, 1949, box 923, OF 208-I, HSTP.

3. Marilyn Berger, "Judge Irving Kaufman, of Rosenberg Spy Trial and Free-Press Rulings, Dies at 81," *NYT*, February 3, 1992 (quoting Abrams).

4. Radosh and Milton, *Rosenberg File*, 289.

5. IRK to Irwin Rosenberg, June 21, 1984, box 128, folder 18, IRKP.

6. *A Tribute to the Honorable Irving R. Kaufman*, 53 Ford. L. Rev. v (Oct. 1984) (quoting Thurgood Marshall).

7. Cardozo, *Judicial Process*, 12–13 (quoting Eugen Ehrlich); Causewell Vaughan, "Kaufman Marks 25th Year on U.S. Bench," *NYDN*, November 1, 1974.

8. Zion, *Autobiography*, 63.

9. Michael Swartz interview, October 9, 2020; Peter Kreindler interview, February 7, 2016.

10. Lee Levine interview, February 28, 2019; Burt Neuborne interview, June 12, 2019; Leonard Garment to IRK, November 21, 1989, box 116, folder 13, IRKP; Dorothy Rabinowitz to Rosenthal, November 3, 1977, box 22, folder 24, A. M. Rosenthal Papers, NYTP; *Almanac of the Federal Judiciary* (Upper Saddle River, NJ: Prentice Hall, 1990), 2nd Circuit-14.

1. Isidore Mortem

1. "The Case of Roumania," *American Hebrew*, December 26, 1902, 203.

2. Rachel Manekin, "Galicia," Yivo Encyclopedia of Jews in Eastern Europe, accessed November 11, 2021, www.yivoencyclopedia.org/article.aspx/Galicia; "Jagielnica," Encyclopedia of Jewish Communities in Poland, vol. 2, accessed November 11, 2021, www.jewishgen.org/Yizkor/pinkas_poland/pol2_00279.html; Piotr Wrobel, "The Jews of Galicia under Austrian-Polish Rule, 1869–1918," *Austrian History Yearbook* 25 (January 1994): 97–138, https://doi.org/10.1017/S0067237800006330.

3. United States Census, 1900, Leon Kaufman, OFWA. The 1905 New York census lists Sarah's and Benjamin's birthplaces as Russia, while Herman's 1908 naturalization petition lists them as Galicia, Austria. Later censuses identify them as being born in Romania, and Sarah's naturalization petition gives her birthplace as Bucharesti. Howe and Libo, *How We Lived*, 18.

4. Fox, *Transatlantic*, 331, 333; Howe, *World of Our Fathers*, 41, 397, 148; passenger manifest, SS *Campania*, July 19, 1903, OFWA; Henry James, *The American Scene*, in Hindus, *Old East Side*, 71–72.

5. Howe and Libo, *How We Lived*, 69; Katz and Frommer, *It Happened*, 6.

6. 1905 New York census, Herman Kaufman family, OFWA; John and Steven Kaufman interview, October 18, 2016; Ronald Hartman interview, November 28, 2016.

7. Find a Grave, Memorials, "Rose Swidower Kaufman" entry, accessed November 11, 2021, Findagrave.com/memorial/142778221/rose-kaufman (noting Kaufmans' membership in Jagulnicier Landsmanschaft); Metzker, *Bintel Brief*, 58–59; Wasserstein, *On the Eve*, 27 (quoting Joseph Roth); Kisseloff, *You Must Remember This*, 76.

8. Herbert Kaufman interview, September 9, 2016; Richard Kaufman interview, September 28, 2016; Rifkind, *One Man's World*, 3:527 (quoting IRK to Rifkind, November 15, 1985).

9. Kazin, *Walker*, 56; Morris Raphael Cohen, *A Dreamer's Journey*, in Hindus, *Old East Side*, 43; Sorin, *Howe*, 7.

10. Herbert Kaufman interview; John and Steven Kaufman interview.

11. Gurock, *Jews in Gotham*, 34; Gurock, *Jews of Harlem*, 161; Gurock, *When Harlem Was Jewish*, 29, 141; Herman Kaufman death certificate, February 24, 1927, OFWA; IRK New York State Bar Application, April, 8, 1932, OFWA (hereinafter cited as "IRK Bar Application").

12. Pelisson and Garvey, *Castle on the Parkway*, xii, 26, 30, 37–38, 46–48, 55; IRK note to clerk, box 119, folder 18, IRKP; Pelisson email, June 12, 2017; IRK Clinton photo, undated, OFWA.

13. Roger Kaufman interview, September 28, 2016; Richard Kaufman interview; Spence Toll interview, December 4, 2006; Cahan, *David Levinsky*, 391.

14. Gurock, *Jews in Gotham*, 48; Roger Kaufman interview; Kaczorowski, *School of Law*, 94.

15. Schroth, *Fordham*, 111–12; Gannon, *Up to the Present*, 161; Fordham *Maroon* (Fordham University, 1928), 359, 361.

16. Schroth, *Fordham*, 131; Thomas Shelley email, March 10, 2017; Kaczorowski, *School of Law*, 22; "Speech for Tau Epsilon Phi Dinner, October 18, 1951," box 30, folder 4, IRKP.

17. IRK Fordham University transcript, OFWA; Shelley, *Fordham*, 199; "Student Suicides Are Blamed on Slavic Influence," *Brooklyn Eagle*, February 7, 1927; "N.Y.U. Anti-suicide Club to Become National Move," *NYHT*, March 3, 1927; I. Montefiore Levy, "The Despair of Youth," *American Hebrew*, May 20, 1927, 48; "Student Suicides Are Blamed on Slavic Influence," *Brooklyn Eagle*, February 7, 1927, 4; Marjorie Dorman, "Year's First Student Suicide Deplored as Significant Attitude of College Today," *Brooklyn Eagle*, November 6, 1927.

18. Herman Kaufman death certificate; "Kaufman, Irving Robert," *Current Biography*, 1953 (New York: H. W. Wilson, 1953), 306.

19. Milton Lehman, "The Rosenberg Case: Judge Kaufman's Two Terrible Years," *Saturday Evening Post*, August 8, 1953, 84.

20. IRK application to Fordham Law School, June 18, 1928, OFWA; Kaczorowski, *School of Law*, 95.

21. Kaczorowski, *School of Law*, 35, 38, 60, 62, 73, 97; Schroth, *Fordham*, 174; Shelley, *Fordham*, 205.

22. IRK, *Advocacy as Craft—There Is More to Law School Than a "Paper Chase,"* 28 S.W. L. J. 495, 499 (Summer 1974); IRK Law Day Address at Fordham, May 1, 1958, OFWA; Shelley, *Fordham*, 205; Kaczorowski, *School of Law*, 26, 119, 144–47; IRK Fordham Law School transcript, OFWA (hereinafter cited as "IRK law school transcript").

23. "Brilliant District Atty. Uncovered Coster-Musica," *Bridgeport Sunday Herald*, June 16, 1940; Lehman, "Two Terrible Years," 84; Robert A. Caro, "Perfectionist Judge," *Newsday*, January 26, 1961; IRK, "Biographical Sketch of Irving R. Kaufman," box 49, TCCP; FBI BR 1947; FBI BR 1935.

24. Lehman, "Two Terrible Years," 84; IRK Bar Application.

25. Fordham Law School commencement booklet, June 16, 1931, OFWA; FBI BR 1935; Lehman, "Two Terrible Years," 84.

26. IRK law school transcript; IRK Bar Application.

2. Demon Boy Prosecutor

1. Kaczorowski, *School of Law*, 91, 111–13; Melvin F. Fagen, "The Status of Jewish Lawyers in New York City," *Jewish Social Studies* 1, no. 1 (January 1939): 84; Jerold S. Auerbach, "From Rags to Robes: The Legal Profession, Social Mobility and the American Jewish Experience," *American Jewish Historical Quarterly* 66, no. 2 (1976): 10, 104, 260.

2. IRK New York State Bar Application, April 8, 1932, OFWA (hereinafter cited as "IRK Bar Application"); FBI BR 1935, 4.

3. Rosalind Rosenberg interview, April 27, 2017; David Favaloro email, April 20, 2017, and attached educational materials regarding New York City Tenement House Department inspectors compiled by the Lower East Side Tenement Museum, New York, NY, OFWA; Nizer, *Implosion Conspiracy*, 35.

4. Description for 101 Central Park West, www.streeteasy.com/building/101-central-park-west-new_york, accessed November 12, 2021.

5. FBI BR 1935, 4–5.

6. IRK Bar Application.

7. Smith, *Dewey*, 139; C. Joseph Greaves, "How Prosecutors Brought Down Lucky Luciano," *American Bar Association Journal*, November 1, 2015, abajournal.com/magazine/article/how_prosecutors_brought_down_lucky_luciano.

8. Gould, *Witness*, 142; Martin Conboy, "A Salutation," *Scraps* 9, no. 2 (March 3, 1934): 1–2; "Gordon Convicted, to Serve 10 Years, Pay $80,000 Fine," *NYHT*, December 2, 1935.

9. LaCerra, *Roosevelt and Tammany Hall*; "List of Officials in O'Dwyer Administration," *NYHT*, January 2, 1946; FBI BR 1935, 4.

10. Maxine Berman interview, September 11, 2018; Herman Wouk, *Marjorie Morningstar* (New York: Doubleday, 1955), 4; Rosalind Rosenberg interview.

11. The normal school was the Harriette Melissa Mills School, affiliated with New York University. See Porter E. Sargent, *A Handbook of American Private Schools: An Annual Survey* (Cambridge, MA: Cosmos, 1922), 295. Rosalind Rosenberg interview. The clippings of poems appear in family files, OFWA.

12. Oliver Pilat, "The Judge in the A-Spy Case," *NYP*, January 11, 1953; Barbara Milz, "A Docket of Ideas in Bettering Justice," *Honolulu Advertiser*, January 22, 1970.

13. FBI BR 1935; Rosalind Rosenberg email, May 2, 2017; Berman interview.

14. Marcia Reiss, *Lost New York*, 61; Federal Bar Council, *Courthouses*, 32.

15. John Walker Harrington, "Conboy's Intention to Resign as U.S. Attorney before End of Term Follows Old Practice," *NYHT*, December 2, 1934, A3–5; *Scraps* 8, no. 9 (July 23, 1932): 2; "The Work of the Office, the Criminal Division, August 1935," *Scraps* 11, no. 8 (September 30, 1935): 28; Martin Conboy, "A Salutation," *Scraps* 9, no. 2 (March 3, 1934): 3.

16. The Scaffa case is reconstructed from contemporaneous news accounts in the *New York Times* from April 24 to September 17, 1935. The swindler was Leonard Weisman; his case is described in "Fraud Suspect Surrenders to End 6-Yr. Hunt," *NYHT*, August 16, 1935; "Weisman Held Guilty of Fraud; Gets 15 Years," *NYHT*, January 10, 1936; *U.S. v. Weisman*, 83 F.3d 470 (2d Cir. 1936). Accounts of the shipboard fight appear in news articles, including one from an unknown newspaper kept in Kaufman's private clipping file titled "Drawn Pistols Quell Battle on Ship at Sea," and "3 Held under Heavy Bail for Assault on the High Seas," *NYHT*, August 19, 1936.

17. Samuel Roth Papers, Butler Library, Columbia University, box 17, folders 2 and 5; FBI memos re Pauline Roth handwriting; Strub, *Obscenity Rules*, 50–67; "Roth and Wife Held Anew, Obscenity Charge Heard," *NYT*, September 4, 1936; "Roth and Wife Guilty on Vile Book Charges," *NYHT*, December 10, 1936; *Roth v. United States*, 354 U.S. 476 (1957).

18. Lewis Mumford, "The Sky Line," *New Yorker*, October 13, 1934, 59–60; "Federal Building Nearing the End," *NYT*, December 29, 1935; Federal Bar Council, *Courthouses*, 35–43; United States Court of Appeals for the Second Circuit website, accessed November 12, 2021, www.ca2.uscourts.gov/photos/slideshow.html.

19. IRK family photo, OFWA; Urban Research at the CUNY Graduate Center, "1943 Profile of the Central Park West, Manhattan Area, from the 1943 Market Analysis," 1940snewyork.com, accessed November 9, 2021; IRK application for membership in City Athletic Club, 1944, Center for Jewish History, American Jewish Historical Society, Collection I-533, Records of City Athletic Club, box 55, folder 3 (hereinafter cited as "IRK CAC App.").

20. George Carroll, "Wire-Tap Discs Bare Fraud Ring," *NYJA*, July 9, 1938; *Weiss* S.D.N.Y., Trial transcript (hereinafter cited as "WT") 2581; "Frank Shea Dead; Postal Inspector," *NYT*, April 27, 1941; "Chapman Is Caught by Police after 2-Year Hunt," *NYT*, January 19, 1925.

21. Roger D. Greene, "'Health Pirate' Insurance Fraud Rings Broken By U.S. Sleuths," *Rochester Democrat and Chronicle*, August 7, 1938; WT 560–84; *Weiss v. United States*, 308 U.S. 321 (1939); Carroll, "Wire-Tap Discs."

22. Roger D. Greene, "Insurance Racketeers Teach Heart Trouble," *Portland Sunday Telegram*, August 7, 1938; "Humans Doped Like Horses in Fake Injuries," *New York Evening Sun*, May 18, 1937; "One Confesses in Insurance Fraud Racket," *NYJA*, June 14, 1937; "39 Indicted by U.S. in Insurance Plot, 10 Doctors Named," *NYT*, July 31, 1937.

23. Carroll, "Wire-Tap Discs."

24. Greene, "'Health Pirate'"; "Suspects Guarded from Gang Threat," *NYT*, May 21, 1937.

25. "Lloyd Stryker, Attorney, Dead," *NYT*, June 22, 1955; "Lloyd Paul Stryker Dies, Noted Trial Lawyer Was 70," *NYHT*, June 22, 1955.

26. WT 87–94, 216–23, 275, 515, 1842–1929, 2473–583; Greene, "'Health Pirate'"; "Disks of Talks on Phone Used against Talkers," *NYHT*, January 14, 1938; Milton Lehman, "The Rosenberg Case: Judge Kaufman's Two Terrible Years," *Saturday Evening Post*, August 8, 1953, 84; Oliver Pilat, "The Boy Prosecutor Grows Up," *NYP*, November 21, 1947; IRK photos in "'Health Pirate"' and OFWA.

27. "2 Doctors Guilty in Insurance Plot," *NYT*, March 5, 1938; Carroll, "Wire-Tap Discs"; Greene, "'Health Pirate'"; Greene, "Insurance Racketeers Teach."

28. *Weiss*, 308 U.S. at 330.

29. Keats, *Magnificent Masquerade*, 85–101, 113–14, 118–19, 128–33, 153; Brief, *Accountancy*; Robert Shaplen, "Annals of Crime: The Metamorphosis of Philip Musica—II," *New Yorker*, October 29, 1955, 44, 81; "Coster's Dual Existence Unique in the Criminal History of City," *NYT*, December 16, 1938.

30. Keats, *Magnificent Masquerade*, 153; Shaplen, "Metamorphosis of Philip Musica—II," 44, 54.

31. "Drug House Faces Federal Inquiry," *NYT*, December 16, 1938; Keats, *Magnificent Masquerade*, 79–80, 101, 135–36, 155; Shaplen, "Metamorphosis of Philip Musica—II," 42–43; "Never Give Up Motto Hangs in Coster's Room," *NYHT*, December 17, 1938.

32. Keats, *Magnificent Masquerade*, 3–4.

33. "Exchange Halts Drug Stock Deals," *NYT*, December 7, 1938; "McKesson Drug Assets Short by $10,000,000," *NYHT*, December 9, 1938; Keats, *Magnificent Masquerade*, 175–190; "5 Agencies Act on $10,000,000 McKesson Loss," *NYHT*, December 10, 1938.

34. Shaplen, "Metamorphosis of Philip Musica—II," 68–73; Keats, *Magnificent Masquerade*, 175–190; "Drug House Faces Federal Inquiry"; "5 Agencies Act."

35. Keats, *Magnificent Masquerade*, 194–96; Shaplen, "Metamorphosis," 74. Accounts of Coster's arrest by Keats and Shaplen differ in some details, but Keats's account is followed here because he was present at the scene.

36. Shaplen, "Metamorphosis of Philip Musica—II," 77; Keats, *Magnificent Masquerade*, 195–96; Pilat, "Boy Prosecutor"; "Brilliant District Atty."; David J. Krajicek, "A Photo in Daily News Helps State Investigator Bring Down Con Man Whose Phony Products Made Him a Sweetheart of Wall Street," *NYDN*, June 21, 2014.

37. Keats, *Magnificent Masquerade*, 197–200; Shaplen, "Metamorphosis of Philip Musica—II," 77–78

38. "Coster's Dual Existence Unique"; Meyer Berger, "The Story of F. D. Coster (Musica): A Strange Human Record," *NYT*, December 25, 1938.

39. Riis, *Other Half*, 55; Keats, *Magnificent Masquerade*, 9–17; Robert Shaplen, "Annals of Crime: The Metamorphosis of Philip Musica—I," *New Yorker*,

October 22, 1955, 49–52; "Coster Is Philip Musica, Coster Aided U.S. in War Spy Hunt," *NYT*, December 17, 1938; "1913 Fingerprints Trap Drug Man as Ex-Convict," *NYHT*, December 16, 1938; "Musica Rose to Wealth after Two Convictions," *NYHT*, December 16, 1938; "Ex-Prosecutor Thinks Coster Had Protection," *NYHT*, December 31, 1938.

40. Shaplen, "Metamorphosis of Philip Musica—I," 52–62, 72–73; Keats, *Magnificent Masquerade*, 21–30, 48–53; "Coster Is Philip Musica"; "Coster Served as Investigator of Aliens in War," *NYHT*, December 17, 1938.

41. "Coster Aided U.S."; "Story of F. D. Coster (Musica)"; Keats, *Magnificent Masquerade*, 44–48, 54–57, 66–70, 77–78, 116–18; Shaplen, "Metamorphosis of Philip Musica—II," 44–51, 71–80; "Coster Kills Self; Officers at Door, Varnard, Two Dietrichs Exposed as His Brothers and Are Jailed," *NYHT*, December 17, 1938; "Three Seized in Coster Case Blackmailing," *NYHT*, December 28, 1938; "Strange Stories of the Musicas Is Unraveling," *NYT*, December 17, 1938; "Coster Revealed as Schultz Ally," *NYT*, January 27, 1939.

42. Keats, *Magnificent Masquerade*, 116–18; Shaplen, "Metamorphosis of Philip Musica—II," 50–51.

43. Shaplen, "Metamorphosis of Philip Musica—II," 50–51, 70–73; Keats, *Magnificent Masquerade*, 116–20; "Sea 'Trucks' Figure in Coster Inquiry," *NYT*, January 7, 1939.

44. Shaplen, "Metamorphosis of Philip Musica—II," 56–73; Keats, *Magnificent Masquerade*, 153–74; "McKesson Treasurer's Story of Coster's Rise in the Drug Field," *NYT*, December 15, 1938.

45. Keats, *Magnificent Masquerade*, 191–206; "Coster Kills Self, 'Never Give Up Motto,' Text of the Note Left by Coster," *NYT*, December 23, 1938.

46. "Dewey Finds Musicas Took 4 Million Cash," *NYHT*, December 20, 1938.

47. "Coster Guest List on Yacht Scanned," *NYT*, December 31, 1938; "50 Summoned in McKesson Inquiry by U.S.," *NYHT*, January 1, 1939; "Sea 'Trucks' "; "Murphy Drafts Plan to Protect Civil Liberties," *NYHT*, January 26, 1939; "U.S. Summons Three Bankers in Musica Case," *NYHT*, January 27, 1939; "Brilliant District Atty."; Keats, *Magnificent Masquerade*, 141–42, 223–28; Shaplen, "Metamorphosis of Philip Musica—II," 86; IRK, "The Grand Jury, Sword and Shield," *Atlantic Monthly*, April 1962, 54, 56; "Coster Burned Papers on Night before Suicide," *NYHT*, January 21, 1939; "J. F. Thompson, McKesson Firm Treasurer, Dies," *NYHT*, April 22, 1939.

48. "Five Go on Trial as Co-plotters in Musica Case," *NYHT*, March 8, 1940; "Two Portrayals of Musica Told at 5 Aids' [*sic*] Trial," *NYHT*, March 9, 1940; "Two Views Painted of Musica Fraud," *NYT*, March 9, 1940; "Five Defendants Duped by Coster, Counsel Declare," *Bridgeport Telegram*, March 9, 1940.

49. IRK speech draft commemorating thirtieth judicial anniversary, box 116, folder 12, IRKP; "Two Portrayals"; "Two Views."

50. Keats, *Magnificent Masquerade*, 232; "George Musica Tells of Banks' Drug Financing," *NYHT*, March 13, 1940; "How Coster Rose Told by Brother," *NYT*, March 13, 1940; "Vast Bootlegging Linked to Coster," *NYT*, March 14, 1940; "George Musica Blames Phillips in Drug Scandal," *NYHT*, March 13,

1940; "Coster 'Slushfund' Bared by Brother," *NYT*, March 15 1940; "Brother Thinks Others Knew of Musica Frauds," *NYHT*, March 16, 1940; "Coster's Schemes Termed No Secret," *NYT*, March 19, 1940; "'Pay-Off Man' Links Banker to Coster," *NYT*, March 23, 1940; "Coster Revealed as Helping Racket," *NYT*, March 26, 1940; "Official of Bank Asserts It Asked Favors of Coster," *NYHT*, March 26, 1940; "McKesson Drug Stockholder Is Heard at Trial," *NYHT*, March 27, 1940; "Stock Fraud Laid to Coster Bankers," *NYT*, March 27, 1940; "Bookkeeper Is Witness at McKesson Drug Trial," *NYHT*, March 28, 1940; "Coster's Looting in Canada Traced," *NYT*, April 9, 1940; "Coster Revealed as Trade Builder," *NYT*, April 10, 1940; "U.S. Rests Case against Five in McKesson Trial," *NYHT*, April 11, 1940.

51. "Court in Wrangle with Coster Aide," *NYT*, April 17, 1940; "Jenkins Pleads Guilty to Aiding in Coster Fraud," *NYHT*, April 18, 1940; "Pelley Asserts Drug Charges Aided Phillips," *NYHT*, April 19, 1940; "Phillips Tells of Banking Aid Given to Coster," *NYHT*, April 20, 1940; "Coster Covered Up Gifts to Two Parties," *NYT*, April 20, 1940; "Phillips Disputes Musica Charges," *NYT*, April 23, 1940; "Phillips Terms Coster Victim of Business Trend," *NYHT*, April 25, 1940; "Phillips Didn't Dream of Suspecting Coster," *NYHT*, April 27, 1940; Keats, *Magnificent Masquerade*, 234.

52. "Angry Arguments Stir Coster Trial," *NYT*, April 30, 1940; "Phillips Says He Tried to Get McKesson Audit," *NYHT*, April 30, 1940; "Assails Tad Jones at Coster Hearing," *NYT*, May 1, 1940; "Phillips' Letters Confront Him at M'Kesson Trial," *NYHT*, May 2, 1940; "Phillips Admits He Saw False Coster Report," *NYHT*, May 3, 1940; "Coster Convinced Bank, Says Merwin," *NYT*, May 7, 1940.

53. "Merwin Says He Advised against McKesson Plan," *NYHT*, May 8, 1940; "Merwin Defends Acts as Director," *NYT*, May 8, 1940; "M'Kesson Good Will Cut from $600,000 to $1," *NYHT*, May 9, 1940; Keats, *Magnificent Masquerade*, 233–34.

54. "Lawyers Sum Up in the Coster Trial," *NYT*, May 15, 1940; "Defense Counsel Close Arguments in M'Kesson Case," *Bridgeport Telegram*, May 16, 1940.

55. "Merwin Defends"; Keats, *Magnificent Masquerade*, 227, 235–36; "Lawyers Sum Up, Jury Gets Case of 3 Directors, M'Gloon Convicted in M'Kesson Fraud," *NYT*, May 18, 1940; "One Convicted, Two Freed in M'Kesson Case," *NYHT*, May 18, 1940; "Six Sentenced to 1 to 3 Years in Coster Fraud," *NYHT*, May 23, 1940; "7 Are Sentenced in M'Kesson Case," *NYT*, May 23, 1940; "Merwin, Phillips Acquitted, M'Gloon Guilty on Sec Count," *Bridgeport Telegram*, May 18, 1940.

56. "Coster 'Crime' Called One of a Democracy," *NYHT*, December 17, 1938; "Ethical Moral in McKesson Upset Is Seen," *NYHT*, December 18, 1938; George E. Sokolsky, "The Coster-Musica Case," *NYHT*, January 16, 1939.

57. Keats, *Magnificent Masquerade*, 213–14, 238–44; Shaplen, "Metamorphosis of Philip Musica–II," 82–85.

58. "Kaufman Resigns as Aid [*sic*] to Cahill," *NYWT*, June 13, 1940; "I. R. Kaufman Resigns," *New York Sun*, June 13, 1940; "Kaufman, Prosecutor, Takes

Law Partnership," *NYHT*, June 13, 1940; "Brilliant District Atty. Uncovered Coster-Musica," *Bridgeport Sunday Herald*, June 16, 1940; Pilat, "Boy Prosecutor"; IRK to Gerald Rosenberg, December 22, 1970, box 128, folder 17, IRKP.

3. A Dream Come True

1. IRK to HRK, August 1941 (hereinafter cited as "1941 Letters"), OFWA.

2. FBI BR 1947; Carl Zebrowski, "Your Number's Up!," America in WWII, December 2007, www.americainwwii.com/articles/your-numbers-up/; 1941 Letters.

3. IRK to Alfred R. Stern, December 3, 1982, box 126, folder 9, IRKP; Roger Kaufman interview, September 28, 2016.

4. 1941 Letters; IRK to HRK, August 1942, OFWA.

5. *Brady v. Noonan, Kaufman and Eagan*, N.Y. Sup. Ct., App. Div., 1st Dept. (1946); IRK to Eagan, October 1, 1948, box 128, folder 1, IRKP.

6. *Parts Mfg. Corp v. Lynch*, 129 F.2d 841, 843 (2d Cir. 1942); 1941 Letters; "A Colonel Flushes with Shame," *NYP*, April 27, 1944; Milton Lehman, "The Rosenberg Case: Judge Kaufman's Two Terrible Years," *Saturday Evening Post*, August 8, 1953, 84; Noonan, Kaufman & Eagan client ledgers, box 128, folder 1, IRKP.

7. "J. Meyer Schine, 78, Hotel Man, Dead," *NYT*, May 10, 1971; Meeker, *Newspaperman*, 49–50, 128, 179–80; "Henry Garfinkle, 80, Rose from Newsboy to Major Distributor," *NYT*, January 13, 1983; "Samuel I. Newhouse, Publisher, Dies at 84," *NYT*, August 30, 1979; IRK Remarks, Dedication of Newhouse Center, October 17, 1979, box 142, folder 4, IRKP; IRK to Collins Seitz, November 20, 1980, box 51, folder 7, IRKP.

8. Lawrence Van Gelder, "Milton Berle, TV's First Star as 'Uncle Miltie,' Dies at 93," *NYT*, March 28, 2002.

9. Berle and Frankel, *Milton Berle*, 241; Norma Abrams, "Bum's Rush from Apartment No Gag to Berle," *NYDN*, November 21, 1946.

10. Noonan, Kaufman & Eagan papers, box 128, folder 1, IRKP; Lehman, "Two Terrible Years," 84.

11. "Protector of Democracy? What Do You Think?," *New York Journal and American*, January 30, 1941.

12. Kennett, *G.I.*, 9–11; "1st Draft Boards Sworn in Speedily," *NYT*, October 19, 1940; Donald D. Stewart, "The Selective Service Appeal Board," *Southwestern Social Science Quarterly* 31, no. 1 (June 1950): 30–33; Selective Service to IRK, October 10, 1940, OFWA; FBI BR 1947.

13. "Aurelio Asks Time to Fight Disbarment," *NYHT*, October 19, 1943; Allen, *Tiger*, 258; "Harold Medina, U.S. Judge, Dies at 102," *NYT*, March 16, 1990; IRK address, "Special Session in Memory of the Honorable Harold R. Medina," box 79, folder 14, p. 37, IRKP; Daniel, *Judge Medina*; Robert Bird, "Hogan Named to Prosecute Aurelio Case," *NYHT*, October 22, 1943; Medina to IRK, October 21, 1943, OFWA; "Aurelio on Bench 'Tough' at Times," *NYT*, November 3, 1943.

14. Robert Patterson photograph, undated, inscribed to IRK, OFWA; Patterson to IRK, August 20, 1940, OFWA; George Medalie to IRK,

November 6, 1942, and December 3, 1945, OFWA; Knox to IRK, May 10, 1943, OFWA; IRK application for membership in City Athletic Club, 1944, Center for Jewish History, American Jewish Historical Society, Collection I-533, Records of City Athletic Club, box 55, folder 3 (hereinafter cited as "IRK CAC App.").

15. Jack Alexander, "The Director—II," *New Yorker*, October 2, 1937, 22–23; Gentry, *Hoover*, 65–105, 213.

16. IRK to Hoover, April 28, 1941; Hoover to IRK, May 2, 1941; Hoover to IRK, November 19, 1945; Hoover to IRK son [name redacted], July 12, 1948; IRK son [name redacted] to Hoover, July 8, 1948; Hoover to IRK son [name redacted], July 8, 1949; IRK son [name redacted] to Hoover, June 30, 1949; IRK to Hoover, May 11, 1949.

17. IRK-Clark correspondence, TCCP, box 49; Wohl, *Father, Son*, 78.

18. George Dixon, "Washington Scene," *Daily Mirror*, January 30, 1946.

19. IRK draft, "Tom Clark Lunch Remarks, August 10, 1970," box 77, folder 6, IRKP; Gronlund, *Tom C. Clark*, 88 (quoting Berle letter); Winter-Berger, *Washington Pay-Off*, 23–24.

20. Wohl, *Father, Son*, 420 n. 13, 432 n. 67.

21. Documents from the FBI's 1952 investigation of Clark appear in internal FBI memoranda provided to Mimi Clark Gronlund in response to a Freedom of Information Act request and provided to the author by Alexander Wohl. In particular, see FBI memo, SAC, WFO to Hoover, August 14, 1952 (containing affidavit of Phillip Marcus, August 13, 1952); FBI memo, A. Rosen to Ladd, November 3, 1952, 12–14; FBI Form 1, October 24, 1952, 4–5; FBI Form 1, October 8, 1952, 4; FBI memo, October 3, 1952, 149. The investigation is generally described in Gronlund, *Tom C. Clark*, 162–64, and Wohl, *Father, Son*, 151 and n. 67.

22. "Financial Managers," *New York Enquirer*, October 2, 1946; Paul E. Fitzpatrick to IRK, November 14, 1946, OFWA.

23. Allen, *Tiger*, 265–67; Warren Moscow, "Tammany to Lose More Patronage," *NYT*, November 26, 1946; "Opponents to Push Drive on Tammany," *NYT*, January 27, 1947; "Negro Favored as U.S. Judge in N.Y. District," *NYHT*, January 30, 1947; Hannegan to IRK, March 24, 1947, OFWA; Wohl, *Father, Son*, 75–77.

24. FBI BR 1947.

25. Memo excerpting Bar Association of the City of New York report re IRK, undated, box 49, TCCP; IRK to Clark, February 5, 1947, and Clark to IRK, February 10, 1947, box 49, TCCP.

26. "Superb Selection," *NYHT*, May 17, 1947; "A Judge Worth Waiting For," *NYT*, May 17, 1947; W.J.H. memo to Maurice Latta, April 7, 1947, box 923, OF 208-I, Truman Lib.; Clark to Truman, April 7, 1946, box 923, OF 208-I, Truman Lib.; "Medina Endorsed by Bar for Bench," *NYT*, May 14, 1947; "N.Y. Democrats Astonished by Medina Choice," *NYHT*, May 16, 1947; "Medina Is Named U.S. Judge Here," *NYT*, May 16, 1947; "Truman Flouts Leaders, Names Medina Judge," *NYHT*, May 16, 1947; Daniel, *Judge Medina*, 18–19.

27. IRK to Clark, May 16, 1947, box 49, TCCP; Gael Sullivan to IRK, May 19, 1947, OFWA; Daniel, *Judge Medina*, 22.

28. Schriftgiesser, *Lobbyists*, 86; "Text of Truman's Message to Congress on the Measure Continuing Modified Rent Controls," *NYT*, July 1, 1947; Drew Pearson, "Clark Quietly Probes 2 Senators," *WP*, June 5, 1948.

29. FBI memo, Tamm to Hoover, October 14, 1947; FBI memo, Coyne to Ladd, October 16, 1947. See also IRK to Hoover, December 11, 1947; FBI memo, Ladd to Tamm, April 21, 1948; FBI memo, Ladd to Tamm, April 24, 1948; FBI memo, Tamm to Hoover, April 26, 1948; FBI memo, Hoover to Quinn, April 26, 1948; Drew Pearson, "Sen. Thomas Defies Colleagues," *WP*, February 5, 1948.

30. Oliver Pilat, "The Boy Prosecutor Grows Up," *NYP*, November 21, 1947; *Hearings Before the Committee on Expenditures in the Executive Departments, United States Senate*, 80th Cong., 2nd Sess. (February 2, 17, 18, 23, and 25, 1948), 93; Anthony Leviero, "Intensive Inquiry on Lobbying Points to Criminal Action," *NYT*, December 26, 1947; "Lobbyists Comply on Supplying Data," *NYT*, April 19, 1948.

31. Drew Pearson, "Supreme Court Gets Lobby Case," *WP*, May 15, 1953; "U.S. Indicts 4 as Lobbyists for High Prices," *NYHT*, June 17, 1948; "Building-Loan Group Indicted as U.S. Lobbyist," *NYHT*, March 31, 1948.

32. Zion, *Autobiography*, 82; Clark to IRK, August 3, 1948, box 49, TCCP; IRK memo to Clark, July 29, 1948, box 49, TCCP; Schriftgiesser, *Lobbyists*, 101; "Lobby Investigation Is Made Permanent," *NYHT*, August 24, 1948; *United States v. Harriss*, 347 U.S. 612, 625 (1954).

33. "Looking into Lobbying," *NYHT*, December 27, 1947; "Clark Quietly Probes"; Pilat, "Boy Prosecutor"; "U.S. Begins Broad Probe of Lobbyists," *WP*, October 13, 1947; Schriftgiesser, *Lobbyists*, 99.

34. IRK to Clark, November 4, 1948, box 49, TCCP; Truman to IRK, November 12, 1948, OFWA.

35. Transcript of "Town Meeting," November 23, 1948 (New York: Town Hall, 1948), 8–10, 18; IRK to McGrath, May 3, 1949, box 6, HJMP.

36. Truman, *Years of Trial*, 214; Wohl, *Father, Son*, 82–93; Gronlund, *Tom C. Clark*, 106–12; IRK to McGrath, May 3, 1949, and attached drafts, box 6, HJMP.

37. "New Federal Judges," *NYT*, August 11, 1949, 22.

38. FBI Background Report on IRK, October 8, 1949, OFWA.

39. William Hassett memo to Clark, September 29, 1949 (attaching letter from Albert Cohn), box 924, OF 208-I, HSTP; Hassett to John Mullen, September 30, 1949, box 924, OF 208-I, HSTP; Patrick McGrath telegram to Truman, September 28, 1949, box 924, OF 208-I, HSTP; Goldman, *Picking Federal Judges*, 89–92; Peyton Ford memo to Donald Dawson, October 6, 1949, box 923, OF 208-I, HSTP.

40. McGrath to Truman, October 13 and 20, 1949, box 923, OF 208-I, HSTP; Donald Dawson telegram to IRK, October 21, 1949, box 923, OF 208-I, HSTP; IRK to Truman, October 17, 1949, and Truman to IRK, November 1, 1949, box 923, OF 208-I, HSTP; IRK to Clark, October 28, 1949, box B69, TCCP-UT.

41. IRK, "Draft–Extemporaneous Remarks," undated, box 29, folder 4, IRKP.

4. At Home on the Bench and Park Avenue

1. "Saypol, McGohey Aide, Made U.S. Attorney as Four New Judges Are Installed Here," *NYT*, November 2, 1949; "4 Sworn as Judges of District Court," *NYHT*, November 2, 1949; Burak, *History*, 13–16, 27–28; Milton Lehman, "The Rosenberg Case: Judge Kaufman's Two Terrible Years," *Saturday Evening Post*, August 8, 1953, 84; Second Circuit session honoring IRK's twenty-fifth year of judicial service, November 1, 1974, 23, OFWA.

2. Second Circuit session honoring IRK's twenty-fifth year, 23.

3. John P. Frank, "The Top U.S. Commercial Court," *Fortune*, January 1951, 111; Dillard, *Spirit of Liberty*, introduction.

4. Norman Beier interview, February 22, 2005; Second Circuit memorial service for IRK, Leonard Sand remarks, June 2, 1992, OFWA; Leonard Sand interview, January 10, 2007; Andrew Hartzell interview, November 30, 2006; Robert Haft interview, April 27, 2016.

5. Hartzell interview; Sand interview; Haft interview; Howard Weinrich interview, April 14, 2016.

6. Haft interview; Charles Stillman interview, November 29, 2006.

7. Sand interview; Donald Zoeller interview, April 20, 2016; Robert A. Caro, "Perfectionist Judge," *Newsday*, January 26, 1961; Zoeller interview; Beier interview; Spencer Toll interview, December 4, 2006.

8. *Neiman-Marcus v. Lait*, 13 F.R.D. 311 (S.D.N.Y. 1952); draft IRK speech, Learned Hand Medal 1974, box 70, folder 3, IRKP.

9. Haft interview; Alfred P. Murrah to IRK, November 12, 1968, box 70, note 8, IRKP; Hartzell interview; Robert Freedman interview, April 11, 2016; see also Stillman interview; Walsh, *Gift of Insecurity*, 147.

10. Rifkind, *One Man's World*, 3:13; Toll interview; Haft interview; Weinrich interview; Stillman interview; Haft interview; Hartzell interview, Beier interview.

11. Zoeller interview; Sand interview.

12. Zoeller interview; Sand interview; Stillman interview; Weinrich interview; Michael Rosen interview, April 28, 2016.

13. Sand interview; Haft interview; Toll interview.

14. Beier interview; Sand interview; Arnold H. Lubasch, "Ex-clerks to Honor Judge Kaufman," *NYT*, November 18, 1981.

15. Hartzell interview.

16. Lynch, *Manhattan Classic*, 79.

17. FBI BR 1947, 9 (Kaufman employed two maids and a "nurse").

18. Jack Auspitz interview, October 19, 2016; Rosalind Rosenberg interview, April 27, 2017.

19. Lederhendler, *New York Jews*, 51 (quoting Alfred Kazin); Meeker, *Newspaperman*, 123; Roiphe, *1185 Park*, 7; Birmingham, *"Rest of Us,"* 298.

20. Meeker, *Newspaperman*, 123; Haft interview; "David Sarnoff of RCA Is Dead; Visionary Broadcast Pioneer," *NYT*, December 13, 1971; Mitenbuler, *Bourbon Empire*, 213, 227, 242; Leonard Sloane, "Lewis Rosenstiel, Founder of Schenley Empire, Dies," *NYT*, January 22, 1976, 37; Beier interview; Robert D.

McFadden, "Lenore Annenberg, Philanthropist, Dies at 91," *NYT*, March 12, 2009.

21. Kaufman family papers, OFWA; IRK to Clark, March 5, 1952, box B69, TCCP-UT; Weinrich interview.

22. John and Steven Kaufman interview; "City Athletic Club Records," Historical Note, American Jewish Historical Society, accessed November 9, 2021, www.archives.cjh.org/repositories/3/resources/6014; interview with Anne Roiphe, American Jewish Committee Oral History Collection (January 1993), 4, https://digitalcollections.nypl.org/items/6a8691c0-02de-0131-ba52-58d385a7b928.

23. Oliver Pilat, "The Boy Prosecutor Grows Up," *NYP*, November 21, 1947; Oliver Pilat, "The Judge in A-Spy Case," *NYP*, January 11, 1953; Lehman, "Two Terrible Years," 86; IRK to Clark, February 4 and 8, 1954, box B69, TCCP-UT; Leonard Lyons, "The Lyons Den," *NYP*, June 16, 1953.

24. IRK to Nichols, July 12, 1955, OFWA; IRK to Abraham Feinberg, December 13, 1978, box 121, folder 2, IRKP; IRK speech on receiving award for thirty-five years of judicial service, box 122, folder 5, IRKP; IRK to Herbert Brownell, September 17, 1970, box 73, folder 9, IRKP; 1972 ABA prayer breakfast materials, box 36, folder 5, IRKP. As a law clerk, I heard the story of Kaufman's being dropped off near the synagogue, likely from IRK's driver at the time.

25. FBI memos, Malone to Hoover, July 30, 1953, and August 18, 1953; IRK to Armand S. Deutsch, July 13, 1983, box 49, folder 3, IRKP; HRK baby book for James Kaufman, OFWA; Ben Thau to IRK, June 27, 1955, and IRK to Thau, December 22, 1959, box 129, folder 17, IRKP; IRK to Reagan, January 30, 1981, box 128, folder 12, IRKP.

26. "Judge Kaufman Sworn In," *NYT*, April 12, 1950; Schneir and Schneir, *Invitation*, 70–71; "Philadelphian Seized as Spy Based on Data from Fuchs," *NYT*, May 24, 1950.

27. McCullough, *Truman*, 775–83; Kobrick, *Rosenberg Trial*, 1.

28. Radosh and Milton, *Rosenberg File*, 89; *Rosenberg* SDNY 1951 Trial Transcript 1562.

29. Harold Brown, "Chemist Held with Woman in Spy Case," *NYHT*, July 30, 1950, 1; Radosh and Milton, *Rosenberg File*, 153–55, 225–27; Schneir and Schneir, *Invitation*, 83–84.

30. Goldman, *Picking Federal Judges*, 163–73 (quoting Katzenbach at 163). The ADA petition, "An Appeal to the Liberals of America," appears attached to a letter from Harold Ickes to Sam Rosenman, October 14, 1948, www.trumanlibrary.org/whistlestop/study_collections/1948campaign/large/docs/documents/B26_13-11_02.jpg. Sidney Hook, *Heresy Yes, Conspiracy, No* (New York: John Day, 1953), in Fried, *McCarthyism*, 64–66; Schlesinger, *Vital Center*, 159, 149.

31. Harry Truman, Speech at Indianapolis, October 15, 1948, "The 1948 Election Campaign," www.trumanlibrary.org/whistlestop/study_collections/1948campaign/large/docs/; *To Secure These Rights*, Report of President's Committee on Civil Rights, October 29, 1947, 99, 101 (quoting Truman, my emphasis), accessed November 26, 2021, www.trumanlibrary.gov/library/to-secure-these-rights; United States House of Representatives (website), "Historical Highlights: President Harry S. Truman's Fair Deal Proposal to a Joint Session

of Congress, January 5, 1949," History, Art & Archives, accessed January 27, 2022, https://history.house.gov/Historical-Highlights/1901-1950/President-Harry-S--Truman-s-Fair-Deal-proposal-to-a-Joint-Session-of-Congress/; Schlesinger, *Vital Center*, 251; Brands, *Strange Death*, 67–82; Bell, *Liberal State on Trial*, 59, 126–27.

32. Richard Fried, *Nightmare in Red*, 64–104; Wohl, *Father, Son*, 117–18; Albert Fried, *McCarthyism*, 78 (excerpting McCarthy's interview following Wheeling speech); Neville, *Press*, 14 (quoting Pegler).

33. Richard Fried, *Nightmare in Red*, 97; Belknap, *American Political Trials*, 233–50; Belknap, *Cold War Political Justice*, 105; Kutler, *American Inquisition*, 153; "On 'Force and Violence,'" *WP*, October 23, 1949.

34. *United States v. Dennis*, 183 F.2d 201, 213 (2d Cir. 1950); *You and the Atomic Bomb*; White, *Here Is New York*, 50–51.

35. Zion, *Autobiography* 56, 61; "The Sheepdog," *Time*, July 23, 1951; "Justice Irving H. Saypol, 71, Dies, Rosenberg Spy-Trial Prosecutor," *NYT*, July 1, 1977; *225 Years*, 261–67.

36. Roiphe, *1185 Park*, 177; IRK to Louis Johnson, January 4, 1950, box 106, LAJP; Louis Johnson to IRK, January 14, 1950, box 106, LAJP; Memos and correspondence re transfer of Corp. Murray Zuckerman, January–February, 1950, box 106, LAJP; Louis Renfrow to IRK, March 29, 1950, box 106, LAJP.

37. von Hoffman, *Citizen Cohn*, 49–50, 70–78, 122; Roiphe, *1185 Park*, 124–26; Zion, *Autobiography*, 24–27, 30–32.

38. Thomas P. Ronan, "Brothman a Spy Says Miss Bentley," *NYT*, November 15, 1950; "Brothman Trial Told How Red Spies Work," *WP*, November 16, 1950; Thomas P. Ronan, "Soviet Gratitude to Spies Depicted," *NYT*, November 17, 1950; Moskowitz, *Phantom Spies*, 58–103, 77; Rebecca Mead, "Setting It Straight," *New Yorker*, November 29, 2010 (quoting *Time*); "Chemist, Woman Aide Guilty, Espionage Jury Here Finds," *NYT*, November 23, 1950.

39. Wexley, *Judgment*, 133; Edward Ranzal, "2 in Spy Case Get Maximum Penalty," *NYT*, November 29, 1950; Pilat, *Atom Spies*, 274; Moskowitz, *Phantom Spies*, 244–45.

5. The Trial of the Century

1. Peter Carlson, "(The Last) Trial of the Century!," *WP*, January 4, 1999 (quoting Bailey). Sources attributing the quote to Hoover include, e.g., Lori Clune, "Great Importance World-Wide: Presidential Decision-Making and the Executions of Julius and Ethel Rosenberg," *American Communist History* 10, no. 3 (2011): 263, and "Julius Rosenberg Was a Soviet Spy, Ethel's Case Is Murkier," *Economist*, June 26, 2021. Whether Hoover actually used the phrase is unclear, however, though he did call the larger Soviet atomic spying effort the "crime of the century." See J. Edgar Hoover, "The Crime of the Century," *Reader's Digest*, May 1, 1951, 149. In 2004, the Rosenberg case garnered 3 percent of the vote in a poll for the *Today Show* asking viewers to name the "trial of the century," with the O. J. Simpson trial winning. See "The Trial of the Century," MSNBC Poll, December 5, 2004, law2.umkc.edu/faculty/projects/ftrials/Todaysurvey.html.

2. "A Sad Day for America," *NYHT*, March 30, 1951; *Rosenberg* SDNY 1951 Trial Transcript (hereinafter cited as "RT") 2172–73.

3. Zion, *Autobiography*, 61–62. Former Kaufman clerks and Kilsheimer confirmed the power of prosecutors to essentially choose the judges for their cases given the rotating case system, as do other histories. See Charles Stillman interview, November 29, 2006; Leonard Sand interview, January 10, 2007; Robert Haft interview, April 27, 2016; James Kilsheimer interview, January 29 and March 1, 2007; Walsh, *Gift of Insecurity*, 150.

4. Norman Beier interview, February 22, 2005; Sand interview; Kilsheimer interview; Lamphere and Shachtman, *FBI-KGB War*, 211. On Cohn's questionable credibility see Geoffrey C. Ward, "Roy Cohn," *American Heritage*, July–August 1988; John C. Klotz, "Tainted Witness," *Newsday*, April 15, 1988 (specifically doubting Cohn's allegations about Kaufman). Von Hoffman writes that "later in life the gossip around New York was that Kaufman came to despise Roy," and Cohn may have wished to retaliate by slandering Kaufman. Von Hoffman, *Citizen Cohn*, 101. On the other hand, the fact that Cohn was dying when he completed his autobiography with Sidney Zion may have increased his truthfulness. More importantly, his account jibes with Kaufman's overall behavior and former clerks' accounts.

5. Daniel Yergin, "Victims of a Desperate Age," *New Times*, May 16, 1975, 23.

6. Sobell, *Doing Time*, 229; Ted Morgan, "The Rosenberg Jury," *Esquire*, May 1975, 108; Sam Roberts, "I Spy a Belated Confession," September 12, 2008, *NYT* podcast, MP3 audio, 5:30, cityroom.blogs.nytimes.com/2008/09/12/podcast-i-spy-a-belated-confession/; "'A Sad Day for America,'" *NYHT*, March 30, 1951; Beier interview; Radosh and Milton, *Rosenberg File*, 329.

7. Zion, *Autobiography*, 63.

8. Beier interview; Stillman interview; Spencer Toll interview, December 4, 2006; Radosh and Milton, *Rosenberg File*, 277; Gentry, *Hoover*, 422. A fourth clerk, Donald Zoeller, thought Kaufman likely conducted *ex parte* meetings with prosecutors, though he had no specific memory of it. See Zoeller interview, April 20, 2016. And Howard Weinrich, who clerked in 1957–58, recalled that prosecutors would draft daily summaries of what had happened in criminal trials and deliver them to chambers late the same day, though he didn't believe this practice biased him or Kaufman in the government's favor. Weinrich interview, April 14, 2016. Wherty's comment is memorialized in an FBI memo. See FBI memo, A. E. Belmont to Ladd, March 16, 1951, NARA NY RF, 10-9. Gordon Dean recorded the referenced conversation in his diary. See Radosh and Milton, *Rosenberg File*, 277.

9. Zion, *Autobiography*, 63–74.

10. Wexley, *Judgment*, 259; Meyer Berger, "3 Go to Trial Here as Atom Spies, War Crime Guilt Can Mean Death," *NYT*, March 7, 1951.

11. RT 28–59, 65, 130–31, 154; Wexley, *Judgment*, 261.

12. Morgan, "Rosenberg Jury," 108; Kilsheimer interview.

13. Morgan, "Rosenberg Jury," 108–9; RT 178.

14. Meyer Berger, "Theft of Atom Bomb Secrets in War Stressed at Spy Trial," *NYT*, March 8, 1951; von Hoffman, *Citizen Cohn*, 96; RT 227–30; Morgan, "Rosenberg Jury," 124 (emphasis mine).

15. RT 237–47.

16. RT 249.

17. RT 254–534; Meyer Berger, "Former College Classmate Accuses 2 on Trial as Spies," *NYT*, March 9, 1951.

18. Roberts, *Brother*, 286–88; RT 768; Blaine Littell, "Spy Asserts Rosenberg Warned Him to Flee after Fuchs Arrest," *NYHT*, March 14, 1951; Morgan, "Rosenberg Jury," 127; Meyer Berger, "Ex-sergeant Calls Sister a Member of Bomb Spy Ring," *NYT*, March 10, 1951; "Trial for Espionage," *NYT*, March 11, 1951.

19. RT 548–623 (emphasis mine); Radosh and Milton, *Rosenberg File*, 182–83; Berger, "Ex-sergeant."

20. RT 625–46.

21. RT 656–83; Berger, "Ex-sergeant"; Lamphere and Shachtman, *FBI-KGB War*, 213.

22. RT 700–720; William R. Conklin, "Atom Bomb Secret Described in Court," *NYT*, March 13/51; Zion, *Autobiography*, 73.

23. Morgan, "Rosenberg Jury," 127; Yergin, "Victims," 24; Sobell, *Doing Time*, 174.

24. RT 722–821.

25. *Sixty Minutes II* (*Sixty Minutes Wednesday*), season 5, episode 38, "The Traitor," produced by Jill Landes and Michael Rosenbaum, aired July 16, 2003, on CBS, youtube.com/watch?v=4zBOC5x3xbc; Roberts, *Brother*, 490–91; Sam Roberts, "Secret Grand Jury Testimony from Ethel Rosenberg's Brother Is Released," *NYT*, July 15, 2015; Schneir, *Final Verdict*, 87–114. Alan Dershowitz has also written that Cohn admitted to him that he "enhance[ed]" evidence, made Greenglass and others "improve" their stories, and effectively "framed" the Rosenbergs, whom he knew to be guilty based on intelligence information known to the government but not introduced at trial. See Alan M. Dershowitz, "Rosenbergs Were Guilty—and Framed," *LAT*, July 19, 1995; *Bully Coward Victim: The Story of Roy Cohn*, directed by Ivy Meeropol, aired 2019, on HBO.

26. RT 835, 871–75.

27. Haft interview.

28. William R. Conklin, "Greenglass' Wife Backs His Testimony on Theft of Atom Bomb Secrets," *NYT*, March 15, 1951; Radosh and Milton, *Rosenberg File*, 196; Root, *Betrayers*, 169.

29. RT 974–90, 1003–26; "Cold War Spy Testimony Revealed," *WP*, September 11, 2008; Roberts, *Brother*, 167–68, 298–99, 489–90; Radosh and Milton, *Rosenberg File*, 166–67; *Sixty Minutes II*, "The Traitor"; "My Friend, Yakovlev," *Time*, March 26, 1951.

30. Root, *Betrayers*, 172; RT 1036–1112.

31. "Columbia Teacher Arrested, Linked to 2 on Trial as Spies," *NYT*, March 15, 1951; Wexley, *Judgment*, 490; *United States v. Rosenberg*, 200 F.2d 666, 670 (2d Cir. 1952).

32. RT 1155–1201, 1236–41, 1299–1338, 1420–1512; William R. Conklin, "Admitted Spy, Gold Is Star U.S. Witness," *NYT*, March 16, 1951; "My Friend, Yakovlev"; Radosh and Milton, *Rosenberg File*, 160–62, 210; Root, *Betrayers*, 176, 178–79; Schneir and Schneir, *Invitation*, 271.

33. RT 1595; Blaine Littell, "Spy Defendant Denies Getting Data on Bomb," *NYHT*, March 22, 1951; Root, *Betrayers*, 185.

34. RT 1578-1651, 1600-1601, 2213.

35. RT 1602-3; Zion, *Autobiography*, 72; Morgan, "Rosenberg Jury," 127; Radosh and Milton, *Rosenberg File*, 236; Nizer, *Implosion Conspiracy*, 213.

36. RT 1615-1887; Blaine Littell, "Spy Defendant Won't Answer on Red Query," *NYHT*, March 23, 1951.

37. Root, *Betrayers*, 198; RT 1928-2085. In 1957, the Supreme Court outlawed questioning witnesses about the contradiction between taking the Fifth Amendment in a grand jury while testifying on the same subject at trial. See *Grunewald v. United States*, 353 U.S. 391, 415-24 (1957). Historians appear to disagree on whether Ethel officially joined the Communist Party. Compare Rhodes, *Dark Sun*, 134, with Sebba, *Ethel Rosenberg*, 42.

38. Morgan, "Rosenberg Jury," 127; Sobell, *Doing Time*, 217.

39. RT 2104-6, 2129-30; Morgan, "Rosenberg Jury," 128.

40. RT 2149-50.

41. Reppetto, *American Mafia*, 263; Sobell, *Doing Time*, 124; Morgan, "Rosenberg Jury," 127-28; Leonard Lyons, "The Lyons Den," *NYP*, March 19, 1951; Wexley, *Judgment*, 582, 591.

42. RT 2167-2238A; Zion, *Autobiography*, 73-74; Nizer, *Implosion Conspiracy*, 318; Roberts, *Brother*, 490.

43. RT 2267-313; Zion, *Autobiography*, 65.

44. RT 2337-67.

45. Morgan, "Rosenberg Jury," 128, 131; RT 2374-87; Nizer, *Implosion Conspiracy*, 359.

46. Blaine Littell, "All 3 Convicted as Atom Spies; May Get Death for Aid to Russia," *NYHT*, March 30, 1951; RT 2388-2400; "3 Convicted of Giving A-Secrets to Soviet," *WP*, March 30, 1951; "Bricker for Probe of Judges, Especially Those on Red Cases," *NYHT*, March 30, 1951.

47. IRK Address before FBI Graduation Exercises, June 6, 1957, OFWA.

48. Morgan, "Rosenberg Jury," 124; *Rosenberg*, 195 F.2d at 596.

49. *United States v. Filani*, 74 F.3d 378, 385 (2d Cir. 1996) (quoting Francis Bacon); *United States v. Grunberger*, 431 F.2d 1062 (2d Cir. 1970).

50. Yergin, "Victims," 23; Radosh and Milton, *Rosenberg File*, 287; Roberts, *Brother*, 370-71; *Rosenberg Case: Some Reflections on Federal Criminal Law*, 54 COLUM. L. REV. 219 n. 114 (Feb. 1954); *Rosenberg*, 195 F.2d at 593-94; Frank, *Courts on Trial*, 422; Parrish, *Supreme Court and the Rosenbergs*, 816 n. 34; Sharlitt, *Fatal Error*, 56.

51. Morgan, "Rosenberg Jury," 124; Beier interview.

52. Sharswood, *Essay on Professional Ethics*, 66; Pearce, *Rediscovering*, 245 n. 22.

53. Altman, *A.B.A.'s 1908 Canons of Ethics* (Cannon 3); ABA *Canons of Judicial Ethics (1924)*, Cannon 17; Martineau, *Enforcement*; Drinker, *Legal Ethics*, 73; Mary Reinholz, "Rosenberg Backers Say, 'Case Is Still Full of Holes,'" *Villager*, July 15-21, 2009; Monroe Freedman, "Another Look at the Rosenberg Case," *Newsday*, March 4, 1977; *Leber v. U.S ex rel. Fleming*, 170 F. 881 (9th Cir. 1909); *Root Refining Co. v. Universal Oil Products*, 169 F.2d 514, 541 (3d. Cir. 1938).

54. Stillman interview; Kilsheimer interview.

55. Meeropol, *Rosenberg Letters*, 585-86.

56. Toll interview; Haft interview.

57. Stillman interview; FBI memo, Belmont to Ladd, June 23, 1953.

58. Belknap, *American Political Trials*, 250–51; Belknap, *Cold War Political Justice*, 113; Bert Andrews, "Hiss Trial Judge Denounced in House Speech," *NYHT*, July 19, 1949; Daniel, *Judge Medina*.

6. Worse Than Murder

1. IRK, "Sentencing: The Judge's Problem," *Atlantic Monthly*, January 1960, 40.

2. Leonard Lyons, "The Lyons Den," *NYP*, April 1, 1951; Hy Gardner, "Early Bird on Broadway," *NYHT*, April 2, 1951; Zion, *Autobiography*, 74–75.

3. *Williams v. People of State of New York*, 337 U.S. 241, 250–51 (1949).

4. Zion, *Autobiography*, 74–75; FBI memo, Ladd to Hoover, April 3, 1951, NARA NY RF, box 10, folder 9.

5. Saypol to Clarence M. Kelley, March 13, 1975, NARA NY RF, box 10, folder 9; Norman Beier interview, February 22, 2005.

6. Radosh and Milton, *Rosenberg File*, 279–81; Gentry, *Hoover*, 424–25; *NOVA: Secrets, Lies, and Atomic Spies*, season 29, episode 13, aired February 5, 2002, on PBS; Douglas Martin, "Robert J. Lamphere, 83, Spy Chaser for the F.B.I., Dies," *NYT*, February 11, 2002 (Lamphere originally drafted Hoover's recommendation, sent to IRK).

7. FBI memo, February 3, 1951; Zirin, *Mother Court*, 90; William Nelson email, March 13, 2018.

8. Milton Lehman, "The Rosenberg Case: Judge Kaufman's Two Terrible Years," *Saturday Evening Post*, August 8, 1953, 84–86.

9. "4 Guilty Atom Spies to Hear Sentence Today," *CT*, April 5, 1951. Letters to Kaufman and their review by the FBI are detailed in FBI memos in 1953, OFWA, and NARA NY RF, box 10, folder 9.

10. Lehman, "Two Terrible Years," 84; William R. Conklin, "Atom Spy Couple Sentenced to Die, Aide Gets Thirty Years," *NYT*, April 6, 1951; Blaine Littell, "Death as Spy to Rosenberg and His Wife," *NYHT*, April 6, 1951; "Judge Sought Divine Guidance in Sending Rosenbergs to Chair," *Boston Globe*, April 6, 1951.

11. IRK to McGrath, April 19, 1951, HJMP, box 101.

12. *Rosenberg* SDNY 1951 Trial Transcript (hereinafter cited as "RT") 2427–32; Saypol to Kelley, March 13, 1975, NARA NY RF, box 10, folder 9.

13. RT 2432–47.

14. RT 2447–55.

15. Conklin, "Atom Spy Couple Sentenced"; Blaine Littell, "Death as Spy, Giving Atomic Data to Russia Altered Course of History, Kaufman Asserts," *WP*, April 6, 1951. The audible gasp was reported by Richard Kaufman, who attended the sentencing. See Richard Kaufman interview, September 28, 2016. The Rosenbergs' conversation is quoted in Neville, *Press*, 49.

16. Richard Kaufman interview; Conklin, "Atom Spy Couple Sentenced"; Littell, "Death as Spy"; Ted Morgan, "The Rosenberg Jury," *Esquire*, May 1975, 132; RT 2463–94.

17. "Judge Kaufman Resting," *NYT*, April 8, 1951; Lehman, "Two Terrible Years," 86; Hoover to IRK, April 6, 1951.

18. "A Sad Day for America," *NYHT*, March 30, 1951; "Death for the Atom Spies," *LAT*, April 6, 1951; "Traitors' End," *CT*, April 8, 1951; Neville, *Press*, 50–51; Gallup Poll, February 1953, Roper Center for Public Opinion Research, accessed May 24, 2018, https://ropercenter.cornell.edu/CFIDE/cf/action/ipoll.

19. *Rosenberg*, 195 F.2d at 609; ACLU statement, December 8, 1952, in ABA Rosenberg Rep., Appendices, 13A; Arthur Schlesinger Jr., "History of the Week," *NYP*, January 11, 1953; Lerner, *Unfinished Country*, 483.

20. Root, *Betrayers*, 292; Parrish, "Cold War Justice," 827; Neville, *Press*, 49; Stacy Schiff, "Anger: An American History," *NYT*, December 18, 2015. Frankfurter is quoted in Clune, *Executing the Rosenbergs*, 33–34.

21. Gunther, *Learned Hand*, 609–10; Harold R. Medina, "The Judge and His God," *Case and Comment* (November–December 1953), 12, in box 30, folder 2, IRKP; Frankfurter to Hand, January 25, 1958, LHP, box 105D, folder 23.

22. Radosh and Milton, *Rosenberg File*, 156; "Slack, Spy, Gets 15 Years," *NYT*, September 23, 1950; "Law Change Cited," *NYT*, October 22, 1949; Roberts, *Brother*, 504 (quoting Greenglass); Haynes and Klehr, *Venona*, 16.

23. James R. Browning memo to Herbert Brownell, February 5, 1953, in ABA Rosenberg Rep., Appendices, 68 (hereinafter cited as "Browning memo").

24. Schneir, *Final Verdict*, 156; Roberts, *Brother*, 416–18 (quoting Beckerly); *NOVA: Secrets, Lies, and Atomic Spies*; Radosh and Milton, *Rosenberg File*, 432–49; Daniel Yergin, "Victims of a Desperate Age," *New Times*, May 16, 1975, 25; Goldstein, *Unquiet Death* [unpaginated] (quoting Phillip Morrison). Even historians who stress the high value of the nuclear information conveyed by the Rosenberg network describe it as "valuable and practical confirmation of data [the KGB] was receiving from Klaus Fuchs and Ted Hall, the two major Soviet nuclear spies in the Manhattan Project." John Earl Haynes, Harvey Klehr, Allen M. Hornblum, Ronald Radosh, and Steven Usdin, "The New York Times Gets Greenglass Wrong," *Washington Examiner*, October 17, 2014.

25. Bennett, *I Chose Prison*, 170–71; IRK to Bennett, May 20, 1970, WH Official Files—Office Files, HBP, box 90, folder K.

26. Manz, *Civil Liberties in Wartime*, 1708; Stern, "Rosenberg Case in Perspective," 80; Browning memo, 67.

27. Roberts, *Brother*, 292–94; Radosh and Milton, *Rosenberg File*, 99, 147; Gentry, *Hoover*, 420–21.

28. FBI memo, Hoover to Charles B. Murray, January 14, 1953; Wexley, *Judgment*, 630; Alexander M. Bickel, "The Rosenberg Affair," *Commentary*, January 1966, 74; Meeropol, *Rosenberg Letters*, 591.

29. Meeropol, *Rosenberg Letters*, 688.

30. Zion, *Autobiography*, 75; Roberts, *Brother*, 278. Stereotypes of communist women are discussed in Olmsted, "Blond Queens," 78.

31. The Rosenbergs' clemency petition appears in Meeropol, *Rosenberg Letters*, lix. *See also* Brennan, *Popular Images*, 44; Miriam Schneir, "Mata Hari Was a Typist," *Ms.*, June 1979, 104. A recent biography of Ethel similarly concludes, "Both stereotypes of her as either a dutiful or domineering wife failed to take account of how she had struggled all her life to forge her own identity as a wife and mother but above all as herself, Ethel." Sebba, *Ethel Rosenberg*, 205.

32. Soviet cables referring to Ethel's role are excerpted in Haynes and Klehr, *In Denial*, 204, and *NOVA: Secrets, Lies, and Atomic Spies*. Notes of KGB files are cited in Roberts, *Brother*, 510. FBI memo, Belmont to Ladd, June 23, 1953. Those who view Ethel as more culpable ignore Greenglass's and Sobell's statements to the contrary, though in all other respects they accept the truth of the two men's accounts inculpating themselves, Julius, and others. Roberts, *Brother*, 506–10; Sam Roberts, "Figure in Rosenberg Case Admits to Soviet Spying," *NYT*, September 11, 2008; Alessandra Stanley, "KGB Agent Plays Down Atomic Role of Rosenbergs," *NYT*, March 16, 1997; Kevin Williamson, "New York Honors a Monster," *National Review*, September 30, 2015. Khrushchev is quoted in "Khrushchev's Secret Tapes," *Time*, October 1, 1990, but questions about the accuracy of the transcripts are discussed in Robert Meeropol, *Execution in the Family*, 204.

33. Michael Meeropol and Robert Meeropol, "The Meeropol Brothers: Exonerate our Mother, Ethel Rosenberg," *NYT*, August 10, 2015; Ronald Radosh, "Case Closed: The Rosenbergs Were Soviet Spies," *LAT*, September 17, 2008.

34. Kaczorowksi, *School of Law*, 50–57.

35. IRK, "I Am an American Day" speech, box 28, folder 4, IRKP.

36. "How Communists Operate: An Interview with J. Edgar Hoover," *U.S. News & World Report*, August 11, 1950; FBI memo, Laughlin to Belmont, March 17, 1952; IRK to Hoover, November 14, 1957; Yergin, "Victims," 23.

37. Raymond J. Blair, "Senators Clear Anna Rosenberg of Red Charges by 13-0 Vote," *NYHT*, December 15, 1950; IRK draft remarks for Richmond, VA, March 1952 (marked "not used"), box 28, folder 4, IRKP; von Hoffman, *Citizen Cohn*, 108 (quoting Cohn); Miller, "*The Crucible* and the Execution," 70.

38. Wexley, *Judgment*, 605 (quoting *Jewish Day* article); Morgan, "Rosenberg Jury," 124; "Orchestra of 8 Million," *Daily Mirror*, April 3, 1951; Louis D. Brandeis, "Our Richest Inheritance," in *The Menorah Treasury*, ed. Leo W. Schwarz (Philadelphia: Jewish Publication Society, 1964), 873.

39. Meeropol, *Rosenberg Letters*, 118, 476–81, 495, 520–23.

40. IRK, "I Like Being a Judge," *NYLJ*, April 11, 1980. The social and class gulf between Kaufman and the Rosenbergs was also emphasized by the historian Deborah Dash Moore in Moore, "Reconsidering the Rosenbergs," 21–22, 34.

41. HRK note to IRK, December 1952, ov 2, scrapbook vol. 2, IRKP (my emphasis).

7. Immortality

1. Milton Lehman, "The Rosenberg Case: Judge Kaufman's Two Terrible Years," *Saturday Evening Post*, August 8, 1953, 86; IRK, "Speech for Tau Epsilon Phi Dinner, October 18, 1951," box 30, folder 4, IRKP.

2. Neville, *Press*, 58–63; William Reuben, "Death: A Sentence 'Too Cruel and Too Horrible'—Unprecedented and Illegal in the Bargain," *National Guardian*, October 3, 1951; Clune, *Executing the Rosenbergs*, 36.

3. Radosh and Milton, *Rosenberg File*, 322–27; National Committee to Secure Justice in the Rosenberg Case press release, December 31, 1951, OFWA;

Meeropol, *Rosenberg Letters*, 466 (quoting letter from Julius to Bloch, November 10, 1952), 490 (Julius letter to Bloch, December 3, 1952).

4. *Rosenberg*, 195 F.3d at 590–603; Patricia Wald email, April 19, 2018.

5. Sarah Wald email, April 17, 2018. The quoted memorandum appears in Jerome Frank's papers. See memo to Jerome Frank, undated, Series V, box 105, folder 984, Jerome New Frank Papers, Yale University Library. Although the memo has been ascribed to Frank's clerk, see Parrish, "Cold War Justice," 815. Patricia Wald, his only law clerk at the time, identified it as one Frank either solicited or received. *Rosenberg*, 195 F.3d at 603–09 and n. 31.

6. Clune, *Executing the Rosenbergs*, 36; Report of the Committee on Un-American Activities, House of Representatives, *Trial by Treason: The National Committee to Secure Justice for the Rosenbergs and Morton Sobell*, August 25, 1956, 72–74 (hereinafter cited as "*Trial by Treason*").

7. FBI memo, Hoover to McInerny, April 1, 1952; FBI memo, John Harrington, June 3, 1952.

8. Sidney Ordower, "Rosenberg Case Rally Held Despite Cancelled Hall," *National Guardian*, February 13, 1952; G. George Fox, "'Let Justice Prevail,' Writer Asks, Calling on Community to Protest the Rosenbergs' Verdict," *Sentinel*, February 7, 1952; *Trial by Treason*, 95; S. Andhil Fineberg, "The Defense of Ethel and Julius Rosenberg, a Communist Attempt to Inject the Jewish Issue," American Jewish Committee paper, March 1952, www.ajcarchives.org/ajcarchive/DigitalArchive.aspx; Louis D. Gross, "He Should Have Gone to the Talmud," *Jewish Examiner*, March 14, 1952; Wexley, *Judgment*, 613–14 (quoting Meyer Sharff); Samuel B. Gach, "In the Know . . ., " *California Jewish Voice*, April 25, 1952.

9. Fineberg, *Rosenberg Case*, 69 (quoting Jewish organizations' statement); FBI memo, Laughlin to Belmont, March 17, 1942; Lehman, "Two Terrible Years," 87; Irving Spiegel, "Jersey Candidates Argue Civil Rights," *NYT*, October 19, 1952; "Rosenberg Judge Lauded for Stand," *NYT*, January 4, 1953.

10. Lerner, *Unfinished Country*, 485 (reprinting column dated June 19, 1952); "The Rosenberg Diversion," *Time*, December 1, 1952.

11. Lehman, "Two Terrible Years," 21. The Model Code of Judicial Conduct provides that "a judge may respond directly or through a third party to allegations in the media or elsewhere concerning the judge's conduct in a matter," though he may not comment publicly if doing so would "affect the outcome or impair the fairness of a matter pending or impending in any court." American Bar Association, *Model Code of Judicial Conduct*, Rule 2.10, americanbar.org/groups/professional_responsibility/publications/model_code_of_judicial_conduct/, accessed November 22, 2021.

12. FBI memo from Nichols to Tolson, November 24, 1952.

13. Spear's description of Kaufman's call to Truman appears in a letter to the editor of the *New York Times* following Kaufman's obituary. See Harvey M. Spear, "Kaufman Exceeded the Law in Death Sentence of Rosenbergs; Asked Truman to Act," *NYT*, February 12, 1992. His account is absent from standard histories of the Rosenberg case, and Spear died before he could be interviewed. Nor is there any mention of the phone call in Niles's papers or

other Truman Library collections, though one description of Niles claims he "put as little as possible in his files and stripped them annually in celebration of the New Year." Garrison Nelson and Sophie Scharlin-Pettee, "Mystery Man of the White House," Historytoday.com, April 12, 2018. Although two factual details in Spear's letter are mistaken (regarding timing and Niles's position), his account is believable. He was, as he wrote, an adviser to the attorney general at the time, and it seems incredible he would fabricate a forty-year-old conversation for no apparent reason. Moreover, Kaufman frequently contacted the Justice Department and the FBI about the Rosenberg case. And Kaufman felt he knew Truman well enough to call on him in the White House in 1950 and later in Kansas City.

14. *Rosenberg v. United States*, 344 U.S. 838 (1952); *Rosenberg v. United States*, 344 U.S. 889 (1952); Schneir and Schneir, *Invitation*, 179; Parrish, "Cold War Justice," 820 (quoting Burlingham letter to Frankfurter).

15. *United States v. Rosenberg*, 108 F. Supp. 796 (S.D.N.Y. 1952); *United States v. Rosenberg*, 200 F.2d 666 (1952).

16. Leonard Sand interview, January 10, 2007; Lehman, "Two Terrible Years," 87; Roberts, *Brother* 417; Root, *Betrayers*, 256; FBI memo, Hoover to McGranery, May 25, 1953.

17. Considine, *News to Me*, 168; Harold Brown, "Kaufman Hears 2¾-Hour Plea for Rosenbergs," *NYHT*, December 31, 1952; *Rosenberg* SDNY, Hearing transcript, December 30, 1952 (hereinafter cited as "RT 1952").

18. RT 1952, 94; Lehman, "Two Terrible Years," 88.

19. *United States v. Rosenberg*, 109 F. Supp. 108 (S.D.N.Y. 1953); Meeropol, *Rosenberg Letters*, 550 (quoting letter from Ethel to Bloch, January 9, 1953).

20. Don Olesen, "Reds Throw Frenzy over Rosenbergs," *WP*, January 11, 1953; Fineberg, *Rosenberg Case*, 99 (quoting Einstein letter), 107; Neville, *Press*, 100–104.

21. Clune, *Executing the Rosenbergs*, 58 (quoting Pius XII statement); Zion, *Autobiography*, 76–77; Francis Spellman Address, October 23, 1953, box 23, folder 3, IRKP.

22. FBI memos, William E. Foley to Charles B. Murray, December 31, 1952, and January 2, 1953; FBI memo, W. V. Cleveland to A. H. Belmont, January 27, 1953, reprinted in *Hearings Before the Subcommittee on Criminal Justice, Committee on the Judiciary, House of Representatives, December 9, 1982* ("1982 Rosenberg Hrg."), 2399; RT 1952, 65; "Spies Granted Stay; Fate Up to President," *WP*, January 7, 1953; Edward T. Folliard, "Rosenbergs Must Die for Spying, Ike Says," *NYT*, February 12, 1953; Rhodes, *Dark Sun*, 520–21 (quoting Eisenhower letter); Clune, *Executing the Rosenbergs*, 78–79.

23. William R. Conklin, "Pressure Growing to Save Atom Spies," *NYT*, February 14, 1953; "Rosenbergs Given 3 More Weeks of Life," *WP*, February 17, 1953; Meeropol, *Rosenberg Letters*, 607.

24. FBI memos, February 24 to June 16, 1953.

25. Walter Arm, "Rosenbergs Get New Death Stay for Last Plea to Supreme Court," *NYHT*, February 18, 1953; William R. Conklin, "Rosenbergs Obtain Stay of Execution," *NYT*, February 18, 1953; Parrish, "Cold War Justice," 822

(quoting Hand); Radosh and Milton, *Rosenberg File*, 344–45; FBI memo, Belmont to Hoover, February 19, 1953, NARA NY RF, box 10, folder 9.

26. Parrish, "Cold War Justice," 822–25; FBI memo, Belmont to Ladd, June 3, 1953; "Judge's Home Guarded by Cops," *New York Journal American*, May 26, 1953; Edward Ranzal, "Rosenbergs' Death Set for Mid-June," *NYT*, May 30, 1953; FBI memo, Hoover to Tolson et al., May 8, 1953, reprinted in 1982 Rosenberg Hrg. 2403. For a history of the Rosenberg case in the Supreme Court see Sharlitt, *Fatal Error*.

27. Edward Ranzal, "Rosenbergs Lose in New Court Plea," *NYT*, June 2, 1953; Radosh and Milton, *Rosenberg File*, 387–88; Sharlitt, *Fatal Error*, 38–40; Fyke Farmer, "Good Will Mission," *WP*, December 19, 1948; Drew Pearson, "The Washington Merry-Go-Round," *WP*, October 20, 1945; E. Thomas Wood, "Nashville Now and Then: A Lawyer's Last Gamble," *Nashville Post*, June 17, 2007; "Volunteers Cited Key Legal Points," *NYT*, June 18, 1953; Schnier and Schnier, *Invitation*, 210–12; Radosh and Milton, *Rosenberg File*, 361–72; Parrish, "Cold War Justice," 828–29; FBI memo, Hoover to Brownell, June 9, 1953; "Rosenbergs Denied a New Trial or Stay," *NYT*, June 9, 1953; Text of IRK ruling, June 8, 1953, OFWA; Neville, *Press*, 123 (quoting Urey).

28. Fineberg, *Rosenberg Case*, 108–9; *Trial by Treason*, 11, 42; "Rosenberg Rally Hears New Story," *NYT*, May 4, 1953; "Justice and Propaganda," *WP*, May 28, 1953; Clune, *Executing the Rosenbergs*, 110–11; R. Buckman, "Rosenberg Plea," *Jewish Advocate*, June 11, 1953; Radosh and Milton, *Rosenberg File*, 373–78; Miller, "*The Crucible* and the Execution," 71. Lee Harvey Oswald's receipt of a Rosenberg leaflet in New York appears in Priscilla Johnson McMillan, *Marina and Lee* (New York: Harper & Row, 1977), 76.

29. FBI memos, Belmont to Ladd, June 2–4, 1953; FBI memo, Hoover to Tolson et al., June 3, 1953; "Home of A-Spy Judge Guarded after Threat," *NYP*, June 7, 1953; Roiphe, *1185 Park*, 177; Robert Kaufman oration at Wilbraham Academy, January 20, 1958, OFWA.

30. Bennett, *I Chose Prison*, 170–76; Bennett memo to Brownell, June 5, 1953; Meeropol, *Rosenberg Letters*, 674–75, 679–80.

31. Sharlitt, *Fatal Error*, 42–45; Paul P. Kennedy, "Rosenberg Ruling Likely Tomorrow," *NYT*, June 14, 1953; Sand interview; Radosh and Milton, *Rosenberg File*, 393.

32. Sharlitt, *Fatal Error*, 44–45; FBI memo, Belmont to Ladd, June 15, 1953, NARA NY RF, box 10, folder 9.

33. Sharlitt, *Fatal Error*, 54; Parrish, "Cold War Justice," 832; Jack Steele, "Rosenberg Stay Denied, Douglas Gets Last Plea," *NYHT*, June 16, 1953.

34. Meeropol, *Rosenberg Letters*, 697–99; Clune, *Executing the Rosenbergs*, 115.

35. Sharlitt, *Fatal Error*, 61–70, 119–20; Parrish, "Cold War Justice," 835–36; Douglas, *Court Years*, 81; FBI memo, Belmont to Ladd, June 17, 1953, NARA NY RF, box 10, folder 9; *Rosenberg v. United States*, 346 U.S. 273; "Judge Kaufman's Home Is Guarded," *NYHT*, June 18, 1953; Joseph Paull, "Fate of 2 Sealed in Final Hour; Justices Disclaim Indorsing 'Doom,'" *WP*, June 20, 1953. Stern, then solicitor general, has argued that the Vinson-Jackson-Brownell meeting was proper because Brownell only asked Vinson "to convene the Court the next day,

not to decide anything or set aside Justice Douglas's order on his own," Stern, "Rosenberg Case in Perspective," 83, but others have disagreed. See, e.g., Snyder, *Taking Great Cases*, 935, n. 171.

36. Meeropol, *Rosenberg Letters*, 705–9 (quoting clemency request, June 16, 1953); "Execution of the Rosenbergs," *Guardian*, June 20, 1953 (quoting Eisenhower clemency denial).

37. George Trow, "High Court Ruling Today Decides on Life or Death for Rosenbergs," *NYP*, June 19, 1953; Sharlitt, *Fatal Error*, 132–43; "Kaufman Rejects 11th-Hour Appeal," *NYT*, June 20, 1953; Roberts, *Brother*, 11.

38. Sand interview; Radosh and Milton, *Rosenberg File*, 416–17; Roberts, *Brother*, 17–18, 438.

39. "5,000 Rally at Union Square for Spies," *NYHT*, June 20, 1953; "White House Pickets Sob and Cheer," *NYHT*, June 20, 1953; Miller, "*The Crucible* and the Execution," 71; Marilyn Berger, "Arthur Miller, a Voice of Conscience in the American Theater, Dies at 89," *NYT*, February 12, 2005; *Trial by Treason*, 57; FBI memo, Belmont to Ladd, June 15, 1953; FBI memo, Hennrich to Belmont, June 18, 1953; Root, *Betrayers*, 280.

8. Beaten by the Harvards

1. IRK to Irwin Rosenberg, June 26, 1953, box 128, folder 17, IRKP; IRK to Clark, February 4, 1954, TCCP-UT, box B69; IRK to Hoover, June 24, 1953; FBI memo, Belmont to Ladd, June 23, 1953.

2. Alan M. Dershowitz, "Rosenbergs Were Guilty—and Framed," *LAT*, July 19, 1995. Dershowitz repeated the claim during Ivy Meeropol's documentary on Roy Cohn, *Bully. Coward. Victim.*

3. FBI memo, Belmont to Ladd, June 12, 1953; FBI memo, Laughlin to Belmont, June 29, 1953; FBI memo, Belmont to Ladd, November 13, 1953; FBI memo, Nichols to Tolson, September 22, 1954; FBI memo, Nichols to Tolson, December 31, 1954; FBI memo, Legat. London to Hoover, July 24, 1961; FBI memo, SAC Miami to Hoover, February 7, 1963; Kaufman to Nichols, June 5, 1957.

4. IRK to Hoover, July 15, 1954; IRK to Hoover, November 8, 1957; IRK to Hoover, November 14, 1957; IRK to Nichols, March 4, 1957; FBI memo, Legal Attaché Havana to Hoover, January 8, 1957; FBI memo, Nease to Tolson, March 28, 1958; FBI memo, Malone to Tamm, April 8, 1958.

5. FBI memo, Nichols to Tolson, December 31, 1953; "Sarnoff and the FBI," *New Hampshire Sunday News*, June 8, 1958; IRK to Hoover, June 20, 1958; Hoover to IRK, June 26, 1958.

6. "Spies Were Cheated, Law Students Hold," *NYT*, February 18, 1954; IRK to A. H. Sulzberger, March 9, 1954, box 36, file 26, Arthur Hays Sulzberger Papers, NYTP; FBI memo, Tolson to Nichols, November 2, 1953; Roberts, *Brother*, 446; Norman S. Beier and Leonard B. Sand, *The Rosenberg Case: History and Hysteria*, 40 A.B.A. J. 1046 (Dec. 1954); Norman Beier interview, February 22, 2005; FBI memo, Jones to Nichols, November 21, 1958; FBI memo, Nichols to Tolson, July 21, 1955.

7. Wexley, *Judgment*, 584, 591, 594. Regarding threatening letters to IRK see FBI memo, Nichols to Tolson, April 20, 1955; FBI memos, April 13–18, 1956; and FBI memos, October 29, 1956, to November 15, 1956. Discussion regarding Bishop's book appears in multiple FBI memos and correspondence from 1956 to 1960. The suggested approach to Rebecca West appears in FBI memo, DeLoach to Mohr, January 6, 1965. Benjamin F. Pollack, memo, "'The Judgment of Julius and Ethel Rosenberg' by John Wexley," November 7, 1957, 2, 73–76, OFWA; Bill Davidson, "Exclusive: The Atomic Bomb and Those Who Stole It," *Look*, October 29, 1957; IRK to Brownell, October 15, 1957, NARA NY RF, box 10, folder 9.

8. FBI memos, Hendrick to Belmont, May 8 and 16, 1956, NARA NY RF, box 10, folder 9; *United States v. Sobell*, 142 F. Supp. 515 (S.D.N.Y. 1956).

9. IRK, *Representation by Counsel, a Threatened Right*, 40 A.B.A. J. 299 (Apr. 1954); IRK speech to Federation of Bar Associations of the Sixth Judicial District, September 11, 1954, box 28, folder 6, IRKP; "The Defense of Unpopular Clients," *NYLJ*, June 2, 1958 (reprinting IRK address); IRK, "A Judge Looks at Law Enforcement," June 6, 1957, OFWA.

10. Robert Haft interview, April 27, 2016.

11. IRK to Richard Nixon, September 1, 1955, "Kaufman, Irving R., The Hon.," General Correspondence 1946–1963, RMNP.

12. *United States ex rel. Mezei v. Shaughnessy*, 101 F. Supp. 66, 68–71 (S.D.N.Y. 1951); Richard A. Serrano, "Detained, without Details," *LAT*, November 1, 2003; Judith Crist, "Alien Faces Life Sentence on Ellis Island," *NYHT*, April 23, 1953.

13. George Lardner Jr., "50s Memos Illustrate Rehnquist Consistency," *WP*, July 20, 1986; *Shaughnessy v. United States ex rel. Mezei*, 345 U.S. 206 (1953).

14. "Man without a Country," *NYHT*, April 24, 1953; "Opening the Door," *NYT*, April 24, 1953; "Barred Alien's Case Stated," *NYT*, January 1, 1954; Crist, "Alien Faces"; Kalman Seigel, "Stateless, He Faces Life on Ellis Island," *NYT*, April 23, 1953; "Alien, Long Held, Freed," *NYT*, August 12, 1954.

15. Oliver Pilat, "The Judge in the A-Spy Case," *NYP*, January 11, 1953.

16. FBI memo, Nichols to Tolson, July 14, 1953.

17. "Two First-Rate Judges," *NYHT*, May 6, 1955; "Candidate for Promotion," *New York Mirror*, May 9, 1955; "The Appeals Court Vacancies," *NYWT*, February 1, 1955; FBI memo, Nichols to Tolson, February 3, 1955.

18. FBI memos, Nichols to Tolson, January 17, 18, and 23, 1957; "Sen. Bridges, GOP Stalwart," *WP*, November 27, 1961; Anthony Lewis, "Kaufman Slated for Higher Bench," *NYT*, March 24, 1958; IRK to Bridges, May 13, 1955, box 43, folder 128, HSBP; Walsh, *Gift of Insecurity*, 174 (Rosenstiel-Styles connection); "Jacob Javits Dies in Florida at 81," *NYT*, March 8, 1986; Javits intraoffice memo, January 30, 1957, box 7, folder "Judgeships 1957–59," Series 9, Subseries 3, JKJP; "Program Offered to Cut Court Jams," *NYT*, January 7, 1957; FBI memo, Nichols to Tolson, January 23, 1957.

19. Weinberg telegram to Eisenhower, March 12, 1957, box 321, folder OF-100-B2, WHOF, OF, Eisenhower Lib.; Klutznick telegram to Javits (undated), Klein to Eisenhower, February 6, 1957, and Klein to Javits, February 5, 1957,

box 7, folder "Judgeships 1957–59," Series 9, Subseries 3, JKJP; James Barron, "Julius Klein, Retired General; Helped Victims of the Holocaust," *NYT*, April 9, 1984.

20. Dorsen, *Henry Friendly*, 73–74; "Big U.S. Court Job Hotly Contested," *NYT*, February 18, 1957; Brownell to Weinberg, March 13, 1957, box 321, folder OF-100-B2, WHOF, OF, Eisenhower Lib.

21. "Kaufman Slated"; IRK to Javits, December 23, 1957 (including Clark to IRK, December 16 and 20, 1957), box 7, folder "Judgeships 1957–59," Series 9, Subseries 3, JKJP; Martin Arnold, "Medina Is Retiring to 'Sleep Late,'" *NYT*, February 19, 1958; Kenneth Keating to Schafer, April 11, 1959, box 323, folder 1, Series 2, KBKP; "Old Rough-on-Reds," *NYDN*, March 25, 1958.

22. "Judge Kaufman's Rise," *New Republic*, April 7, 1958; IRK to Hoover, May 2, 1958.

23. Murphy, *Brandeis/Frankfurter Connection*, 330–31; Frankfurter to Hand, January 25, 1958, box 105D, folder 23, LHP; Dorsen, *Henry Friendly*, 74; Frankfurter to Brownell, January 14, 1957, box 192, folder 3, HJFP.

24. This discussion of Friendly's life is based on Dorsen, *Henry Friendly*, 1–70, and "From Clerk to Judge, Henry Jacob Friendly," *NYT*, March 11, 1959.

25. Hand to Frankfurter, December 30, 1954, box 192, folder 3, HJFP; Frankfurter to Brownell, January 14, 1957, box 192, folder 3, HJFP; Frankfurter to Brownell, February 18, 1957, box 30, reels 17–18, "Brownell," FFP; Hand to Frankfurter, February 18, 1957, box 105D, folder 22, LHP.

26. Friendly to George Ball, undated, box 192, folder 3, HJFP; Hand to Frankfurter, January 19 and 22, 1958, box 105D, folder 23, LHP.

27. Frankfurter to Hand, February 13, 1958, box 105D, folder 23, LHP; Frankfurter to Rogers, January 28, 1958, box 97, reels 59–60, "Rogers," FFP; Frankfurter to Burlingham, January 6, 1958, box 5, folder 17, CCBP.

28. Correspondence to and from Friendly and others supporting his candidacy appears in box 192, folder 3, HJFP; "City Lawyer Gets Backing as Judge," *NYT*, January 16, 1959; Hand to Eisenhower, January 22, 1959, box 321, folder OF-100-B2(2), WHOF, OF, Eisenhower Lib.; Edward Ranzal, "Politics Strains Courts," *NYT*, February 8, 1959; Dorsen, *Henry Friendly*, 75.

29. Dorsen, *Henry Friendly*, 75; "Hunt Solution on Promotion for Kaufman," *NYWT*, February 13, 1959; "Politics as Usual," *NYWT*, February 13, 1959; Roger Stuart, "Senator Blasts Kaufman Delay," *NYWT*, February 19, 1959; "Partisans at Work," *NYWT*, February 19, 1959; Dodd to Eisenhower, March 4, 1959, box 60, Series 9, Subseries 1, JKJP; Friendly to Perry, box 192, folder 3, March 9, 1959, HJFP.

30. Friendly to Hand, March 11, 1959, box 88, folder 19, LHP; "Friendly Is Recommended for Judge Medina's Seat," *NYHT*, March 5, 1959; Frankfurter to Burlingham, March 11, 1959, box 5, folder 17, CCBP; Hand to Frankfurter, March 21, 1959, box 105D, folder 24, LHP.

31. IRK to Friendly, March 16, 1959, box 43, folder 128, HSBP; IRK to Hand, April 7, 1959, box 91, folder 26, LHP.

32. Jim Bishop, "The Judge Who Never Wavered," *NYJA*, March 24, 1959; IRK to Bridges, March 19, 1959, box 43, folder 128, HSBP; Nixon to W. R.

Hearst Jr., April 14, 1959, "Kaufman, Irving R., The Hon.," General Correspondence 1946–1963, RMNP.

33. Dorsen, *Henry Friendly*, 77.

9. Apalachin and the Little Rock of the North

1. Alexis de Tocqueville, *Democracy in America*, Everyman's Library (New York: Knopf, 1994), 280 ("Scarcely any political question arises in the United States that is not resolved, sooner or later, into a judicial question").

2. *Bonanno* SDNY, Trial Transcript (hereinafter cited as "BT") 2114–15; Jack Kelly, "How America Met the Mob," *American Heritage*, July–August, 2000, 79; Croswell quoted in "65 Hoodlums Seized in a Raid and Run Out of Upstate Village," *NYT*, November 15, 1957.

3. "Urbane Crime Buster, Sgt. Edgar DeWitt Croswell," *NYT*, November 3, 1959; Milton R. Wessel, "How We Bagged the Mafia," *Saturday Evening Post*, July 16, 1960, 20; Kelly, "How America Met," 76–82; Edgar D. Croswell, "Trooper's Own Story," *New York Mirror*, November 24, 1957; Hortis, *Mob and the City*, 256; "Police Eyes on Barbara for 25 Years," *NYHT*, November 24, 1957; Carl J. Pelleck, "The Lonesome Princess of Apalachin," *NYP*, November 17, 1957; "65 Hoodlums Seized in a Raid and Run Out of Upstate Village," *NYT*, November 15, 1957; BT 683–1020, 2114–15, 2130–2212.

4. Irving Lieberman, "The Mobsters Meet—and Cops Fear a Brand New Murder," *NYP*, November 17, 1957; "Who's Who in Upstate Roundup," *NYP*, November 17, 1957; Richard C. Wald, "Careers of Roundup Figures," *NYHT*, November 16, 1957; Hortis, *Mob and the City*, 258–67; *Bonanno* SDNY, Milton Wessel Notice of Motion and Affidavit, June 4, 1959, 2; Wessel, "How We Bagged," 21; Reppetto, *Bringing Down the Mob*, 31–33; "The Invisible Government," *NYHT*, November 17, 1957; Kelly, "How America Met," 84–85.

5. IRK, *The Apalachin Trial: Further Observations on Pre-trial in Criminal Cases*, 44 J. Am. Judicature Soc. 53 (Aug. 1960); *Bonanno* SDNY, Magliocco Motion, June 4, 1959, 5; *United States v. Bonanno*, 177 F. Supp. 106 (S.D.N.Y. 1959); IRK to Olney, November 16, 1964, box 34, folder 10, IRKP; *Bonanno* SDNY, Pretrial Hrg., 6869–72; IRK address to Kansas City Bar Association, May 1, 1963, OFWA; *Bonanno* SDNY, IRK Mem. Op., October 15, 1959.

6. BT 2250–95; *United States v. Bonanno*, 180 F. Supp. 71 (S.D.N.Y. 1960); "Arrest for Questioning," *WP*, December 5, 1959.

7. FBI memo, Nichols to Tolson, June 4, 1957; Hoover to IRK, June 20, 1957; Nichols to IRK, June 20 and 26, 1957; IRK to Hoover, September 18, 1957.

8. BT.

9. BT 683–898, 1880, 2249, 4272, 5771–988; Charles Stillman interview, August 3, 2018 ("Stillman interview 2").

10. Charles Stillman interview, November 29, 2006; Charles Stillman interview 2; Howard Weinreich interview, April 14, 2016; Donald Zoeller interview, April 20, 2016.

11. "20 Apalachin Men Guilty of Plot to Block Justice, U.S. Hails 'Landmark' Case," *NYT*, December 19, 1959; "20 Apalachin Hoods Guilty," *New York*

Mirror, December 18, 1959; BT 6015-94; "The Apalachin Conspiracy," *Time*, December 28, 1959; "Landmark in the War on Crime," *NYHT*, December 20, 1959; "Apalachin's Mob Is In and Its Secret Is Out," *Life*, January 25, 1960; Gerard L. Goettel, "Why the Crime Syndicate Can't Be Touched," *Harper's*, November 1960, 35; Walsh, *Gift of Insecurity*, 166; Smith, *Mafia Mystique*, 201–3; Ronald W. May, "Organized Crime and Disorganized Cops," *Nation*, June 27, 1959, 568.

12. 106 Cong. Rec. S7860 (daily ed. April 21, 1960) (statement of Sen. Keating); IRK to John Biggs, April 21, 1960, box 26, folder 4, IRKP.

13. *United States v. Bufalino*, 285 F.2d 408 (2d Cir. 1960); FBI memo, SAC Dallas to Hoover, July 11, 1961.

14. "Startling Reversal," *NYWT*, November 30, 1960; Nathan Lewin, "Memories of Judge J. Edward Lumbard Jr.," *NYLJ*, June 24, 1999; IRK to Will Shafroth, December 1, 1960, box 129, folder 11, IRKP.

15. Salerno and Tompkins, *Crime Confederation*, 307–18; Reppetto, *Bringing Down the Mob*, 67–85.

16. "Foe of Northern Bias, Paul Burgess Zuber," *NYT*, February 26, 1962; Walter D. Littell, "Segregation in the North—Suave," *NYHT*, February 11, 1962; Marya Mannes, "School Trouble in Harlem," *Reporter*, February 5, 1959.

17. Paul Zuber, "The Importance of Being a Negro," *NYAN*, July 21, 1962; "Hits Board on Harlem Schools," *NYAN*, June 16, 1956; "School Bias Heading for Legislature," *NYAN*, November 24, 1956; Joel Seldin, "Urge Action on School Integration," *NYHT*, July 12, 1957; "New York School Case Off Again," *NYAN*, October 19, 1957; Benjamin Fine, "Negro Sues City on School Zoning," *NYT*, July 18, 1957.

18. Fine, "Negro Sues City"; "Young Upstart," *NYAN*, August 24, 1957; Sara Slack, "Harlem Parents Still on Strike," *NYAN*, September 20, 1958; Lawrence O'Kane, "Harlem Parents Move to Sue City," *NYT*, October 15, 1958; Mannes, "School Trouble," 15; Sugrue, *Sweet Land of Liberty*, 163–90; *In re Skipwith*, 180 N.Y.S.2d 852 (Dom. Rel. Ct. 1958); Sara Slack, "Boycott Parents to Sue on Schools," *NYAN*, January 10, 1959; James J. Morisseau, "Harlem Set for Boycott of Schools," *NYHT*, September 11, 1959; "23 Harlem Pupils' Boycott Is Settled by Compromise," *NYHT*, March 3, 1960; Lomax, *Negro Revolt*, 158.

19. Guttman, "Division and Diversity," 9–11; Mel Elfin, "Why Pick on New Rochelle?," *Reporter*, December 8, 1960, 28.

20. Elfin, "Why Pick," 28; "Willie Mays Buys Westchester Home," *NYT*, May 28, 1960, 1; Guttman, "Division and Diversity," 237–38; interview with Henrietta Mills, in Forstall, "Voices and Profiles," vol. 2, p. 6. Two New Rochelle residents are quoted in Guttman, "Division and Diversity," 244, 310, and Reid is quoted from an oral history recorded in "Reflections"; Marilyn Littman interview, October 24, 2018.

21. Guttman, "Division and Diversity," 255–59, 286, 291–92; "Segregation Out in 1885, Lions Told," *NRSS*, February 17, 1961; "Lincoln Protest Heard by Board," *NRSS*, December 8, 1948; Florence D. Shelley, "The Leadership Role of School Officials in Integration," in Dodson, *Crisis*, 31; *Taylor* SDNY, Trial Transcript (hereinafter cited as "TT") 371 (quoting 1948 Lyon report); Keith Wheeler, "Ordeal by Integration," *Life*, May 6, 1966, 96.

22. Guttman, "Division and Diversity," 301–24; TT 416, 745, 768–69, 786–90; *Taylor v. Bd. of Education of the City School Dist. of the City of New Rochelle,* 191 F. Supp. 181, 189 (S.D.N.Y. 1961); Virginia Clair, "2-Day Protest Ends at Lincoln School," *NRSS,* October 7, 1959; "Ministers Alliance Supports Lincoln School Protestation," *NRSS,* October 13, 1959; "Reflections," Reid oral history. For sometimes conflicted Black attitudes toward school integration in the North see Burkholder, *African American Dilemma,* 85–128.

23. Kimberly Atkins, "Quest for Justice," *White Plains Journal News,* May 16, 2004; Merrill Folsom, "Negro Pupil Shift Balked in Suburb," *NYT,* September 15, 1960; Bob Meadows, "The Freeing of Lincoln," *NRSS,* March 8, 1993; Merrill Folsom, "Negro Principal Rebuffs Negroes," *NYT,* September 16, 1960.

24. Merrill Folsom, "New Rochelle Quashes School Sitdown by Negroes," *NYT,* September 22, 1960; "Parents Try to Enroll 14 at Roosevelt," *NRSS,* October 25, 1960; *Taylor* SDNY, Hearing transcript, October 27, 1960, 16; Merrill Folsom, "School Sitdown Divides Negroes," *NYT,* September 29, 1960; Merrill Folsom, "2 of NAACP Quit in New Rochelle," *NYT,* October 6, 1960; Elfin, "Why Pick," 29; Sugrue, *Sweet Land of Liberty,* 193–94; Guttman, "Division and Diversity," 348–54; Atkins, "Quest for Justice."

25. Elfin, "Why Pick," 30; Edward Ranzal, "Bias Suit Is Filed on New Rochelle," *NYT,* October 21, 1960; Wheeler, "Ordeal by Integration," 99.

26. *Taylor* SDNY, Plaintiff's Motion to Show Cause, Zuber Affidavit, October 19, 1960, 2–4; Kaplan, *Segregation Litigation,* 10.

27. *Taylor* SDNY, Hearing transcript, October 27, 1960, 29–30, 34, 53; *Taylor* SDNY, Hearing transcript, November 21, 1960, 22.

28. TT 1–60, 10–18, 113–55, 232–82, 863, 78–112, 283–396, 397–440, 485–668, 539, 547, 561, 579, 631–32, 634, 640.

29. TT 710–58, 818–22; *Taylor,* 191 F. Supp. at 186.

30. TT 857–71, 894, 1260.

31. TT 922–1033, 950–52, 993, 1001, 1022, 1053–99, 1220.

32. TT 554–58, 1100–60, 1147, 1155–56.

33. TT 1387–1420, 1333–38, 1399.

34. Marc Cherno interview, January 25, 2007; Charles Stillman interview 2, August 3, 2018; "Zuber Welcomes Lincoln Appeal," *NRSS,* January 30, 1961.

35. *Taylor,* 191 F. Supp. at 183–98. Although his decision made clear that the board deliberately discriminated through gerrymandering and other measures, later descriptions and tributes erroneously referred to the case as involving de facto segregation. Kaufman himself made this error in a *New York Times* piece he authored, describing the case as posing the question "whether a school system might be guilty of de facto segregation." IRK, "What Did the Founding Fathers Intend?," *NYT,* February 23, 1986.

36. Al Nall, "Negroes Win New Rochelle School Suit," *NYAN,* January 28, 1961; Lewis Lapham, "New Rochelle Desegregation Ordered," *NYHT,* January 25, 1961; "Negroes Rejoice in New Rochelle," *NYT,* January 26, 1961.

37. "What's Sauce for the Goose," *NYDN,* January 26, 1961; "Northern Desegregation," *New York Daily Mirror,* January 26, 1961; "Segregation in the North," *Boston Globe,* January 26, 1961; "New Rochelle's Case Is a Special One,"

Louisville Courier-Journal, January 28, 1961; "A Decision to Fear, Not Cheer," Fort Myers News-Press, February–March, 1961.

38. "Board Doesn't Plan Parley on Lincoln," *NRSS*, January 27, 1961; "New Rochelle Decision Seen Affecting All North," *WP*, January 26, 1961; "Too Important for One Man to Decide," *NRSS*, February 1, 1961; "Kaufman's Decision Left No Room for Any Doubt," *NRSS*, February 1, 1961; "School Board Delays on Appeal," February 2, 1961; Denslow Dade, "New Rochelle Negroes Press for Integration," *NYHT*, February 3, 1961; Virginia Clair, "School Board Proceeding on Lincoln Case Appeal," *NRSS*, February 8, 1961; "Integration Urged for New Rochelle," *NYT*, February 7, 1961.

39. Normand Poirier, "New Rochelle Negroes Planning School Protest," *NYP*, February 9, 1961; "Lincoln 'Stay-Out' Protest Keeps 105 from Classes," *NRSS*, February 10, 1961; "Westchester Fight on Bias Is Planned," *NYT*, February 13, 1961; "Lincoln Issue Hearing Date Is Postponed," *NRSS*, February 15, 1961; "Dr. Clish Denies Questioning of Lincoln Pupils Unduly," *NRSS*, February 18, 1961; "Columbians Accuse Zuber of Agitation," *NRSS*, February 27, 1961; "How Could New Rochelle Created [*sic*] Such Ill Feeling," *NRSS*, February 21, 1961; "Lincoln Decision Backers to Tell Judge of Slurs," *NRSS*, March 2, 1961; "Zuber Vows More Jimcrow School Cases," *NYAN*, February 18, 1961. The threats to Kaufman appear in FBI memos from 1961.

40. Edward Ranzal, "Both Sides Chided in New Rochelle," *NYT*, March 8, 1961; Virginia Clair, "Lincoln Plan Delay Pushed," *NRSS*, March 8, 1961; *Taylor* SDNY, "Statement, Plan, Request for Stay," May 2, 1961; Guttman, "Division and Diversity," 379; *Taylor* SDNY, Hearing transcript, May 10, 1961, 28–54, 82, 108, 119, 191, 212.

41. Edward Ranzal, "Assents to Request by Judge Kaufman to File Brief in Segregation Case," *NYT*, May 16, 1961; Edward Ranzal, "U.S. Submits Integration Guide for New Rochelle School Board," *NYT*, May 25, 1961; *Taylor* SDNY, Critical Analysis of the Proposed Plan of Majority of the Board of Education and Proposed Plan of Minority Members, May 2, 1961.

42. *Taylor v. Bd. of Education of the City School Dist. of the City of New Rochelle*, 195 F. Supp. 231 (S.D.N.Y. 1961).

43. "Novelty of Lincoln Case Demands Appeal—Rukeyser," *NRSS*, June 1, 1961; Virginia Clair, "School Board Begins to Obey," *NRSS*, June 2, 1961; "Why Board of Education Must Appeal," *NRSS*, June 2, 1961; *Taylor* SDNY, Hearing transcript, June 26, 1961.

44. *Taylor v. Bd. of Education of the City School Dist. of the City of New Rochelle*, 294 F.2d 36 (2d Cir. 1961).

45. Littell, "Segregation in the North"; Sugrue, *Sweet Land of Liberty*, 452–53 (quoting Zuber in Chicago); Wheeler, "Ordeal by Integration," 96–97; Lomax, *Negro Revolt*, 157–62.

46. "Englewood—Sit-In by 100 Parents," *NYHT*, February 2, 1962; "Englewood: A Good Town in Conflict over Color and Conscience," *NYHT*, February 6, 1962; "The Background and the Future," *NYHT*, August 19, 1962; Sarah Slack, "The Englewood Victory and the Next Step," *NYAN*, November 23, 1963; "Harlem Boy Wins an Important Battle," *NYHT*, February 10, 1962.

47. Lomax, *Negro Revolt*, 159–60; "Zuber to Run in Harlem in Fall against Powell," *NYHT*, April 29, 1962; "Zuber to Give Up Role in Integration Campaigns," *NYT*, May 18, 1963; "Please, No, Paul," *NYAN*, May 25, 1963.

48. *Taylor* SDNY, Transcript, June 24, 1963, 10–11; Sarah Slack, "Zuber's Daughter Sues," *NYAN*, September 28, 1963; "Zuber's Hat in the Ring," *NYAN*, November 16, 1963; "Court Censures Paul Zuber for His Actions," *NYAN*, July 2, 1966; Chester West, "Paul Zuber Claims Jim Crow behind His Suspension," *NYAN*, September 20, 1969; "Policeman Sues Lawyer, Wins," *NYHT*, March 9, 1961; "Friends Rally to Zuber," *NYAN*, January 11, 1969.

49. "Paul Zuber Named Professor at RPI," *NYAN*, February 7, 1970; "Whatever Happened to Paul Zuber?," *NYAN*, June 4, 1975; Susan Retsky, "Desegregation Landmark," *NRSS*, May 25, 1986.

50. Burkholder, *African American Dilemma*, 85–128; Purnell and Theoharis, *Strange Careers*, 23–24. While Kaufman's ruling was the first by a federal court, at least one state court had already ordered school integration to comply with state nondiscrimination law. See *Hedgepeth v. Bd. of Educ. of City of Trenton*, 35 A.2d 622 (N.J. 1944).

51. White, *Here Is New York*, 43; James Morisseau, "School Desegregation Moves North with N.Y. Its First Battleground," *NYHT*, October 8, 1961; Alex Poinsett, "School Segregation Up North," *Ebony*, June, 62, 89, 90.

52. Sugrue, *Sweet Land of Liberty*, 198–99, 459–64; "The Facts of De Facto," *Time*, August 2, 1963; Burkholder, *African American Dilemma*, 117; "Should All Northern Schools Be Integrated?," *Time*, September 7, 1963.

53. New York State Education Department, "Districts" page, https://data.nysed.gov/profile.php?instid=800000035159, last accessed November 18, 2018. James Feron, "New Rochelle Recalls Landmark Bias Ruling," *NYT*, June 1, 1986.

10. Elevation and Descent

1. IRK to Clark, May 24 and June 24, 1960, box 69, TCCP-UT.

2. Anthony Lewis, "Congress Passes Judgeships Bill," *NYT*, May 5, 1961; IRK, *New Remedies for the Next Century of Judicial Reform: Time as the Greatest Innovator*, 57 FORDHAM L. REV. 253, 257–61 (November 1988).

3. "Judge Hand Gives Kaufman Backing," *NYT*, June 18, 1961 (reprinting Hand letter); IRK to Hand, May 25, 1961, box 9, folder 26, LHP; Joseph Dolan to Dorothy Davies, November 9, 1961, "Kaufman, Irving R." folder, John Macy Files, Johnson Lib.

4. "Thurgood Marshall Slated to Get Circuit Court Post," *NYT*, September 14, 1961; "Kennedy Will Elevate Judge Irving Kaufman," *NYHT*, September 14, 1961; Senate Committee on the Judiciary, Sen. 87B-A3, box 39, folder: Kaufman, 87th Cong., N-203; FBI memo, Malone to Mohr, September 19, 1961; IRK to Brownell, September 17, 1970, box 73, folder 9, IRKP.

5. "Dignitaries See Judge Kaufman Seated on Appeals Court Here," *NYT*, September 30, 1961; Schick, *Learned Hand's Court*, 67; FBI memo, Malone to Mohr, September 14, 1961.

6. Goldman, *Picking Federal Judges*, 163–73 (Katzenbach quoted at 163).
7. IRK to Hoover, October 10, 1962.
8. Sabin, *Public Citizens*, 47, 66; Mailer, *Some Honorable Men*, 273.
9. Brennan, *Constitutional Adjudication*, 563.
10. IRK, "The Supreme Court and Its Critics," *Atlantic*, December 1963, 47.
11. The four Jewish judges on the Second Circuit before Kaufman were Julian Mack (intermittently between 1929 and 1940), Julius Mayer (1921–24), Frank (1941–57), and Friendly (1959–86).
12. John P. Frank, "The Top U.S. Commercial Court," *Fortune*, January 1951, 92 ("ablest group of U.S. judges"); Charles Wyzanski, *Augustus Noble Hand*, 61 Harv. L. Rev. 573 (1948) ("ablest court now sitting"); Llewellyn, *Common Law Tradition*, 48 ("most distinguished and admired bench in the United States").
13. Morris, *Federal Justice*, 174–75; *Conversation with J. Edward Lumbard*, 96; Arnold H. Lubasch, "New Federal Judges Likely to Maintain Court's Tenor," *NYT*, July 19, 1982.
14. Schick, *Learned Hand's Court*, 73–74; *Conversation with J. Edward Lumbard*, 66; IRK to Sol Rubin, June 10, 1963, box 35, folder 3, IRKP.
15. Swan's note appears in Rifkind, *One Man's World*, 2:759.
16. Jack Auspitz interview, October 19, 2016; Bartley Deamer interview, February 16, 2017; Dorsen, *Henry Friendly*, 99, 120; Gunther, *Learned Hand*, 289; Robert Gorman interview, April 12, 2016; Bruce Kraus interview, March 6, 2019; Robert Winter interview, April 13, 2016; Michael Rosen interview, April 28, 2016; Robert L. Freedman interview, April 11, 2016; Richard Abt interview, February 13, 2017.
17. Freedman interview; José Cabranes interview, December 9, 2019; Lawrence W. Pierce, *Appellate Advocacy: Some Reflections from the Bench*, 61 Fordham L. Rev. 829, 837–38 (March 1993); Jon O. Newman interview, May 17, 2016.
18. Jon Lindsey interview, March 17, 2020; Auspitz interview; Jerrold Ganzfried interview, May 3, 2017; Dan Kelly interview, December 20, 2019; IRK to Murrah, April 27, 1964, box 63, folder 2, IRKP; Michael Tabak interview, March 24, 2020; Arthur Amron interview, October 1, 2020; Richard Friedman interview, March 4 and 27, 2019; Rosen interview; Abt interview; Andrew Klein interview, October 29, 2020; Gerald Rokoff interview, February 28, 2020; Tom Dahdouh interview, October 9, 2020; IRK chambers instructions, July 1985, box 36, folder 10, IRKP; Adam Eilenberg interview, March 30, 2020; Peter Kreindler interview, February 7, 2016; Deamer interview; Wendy Leibowitz interview, October 5, 2020; Dorsen, *Henry Friendly*, 106; Freedman interview; Gorman interview; Winter interview; "PMH" Memo to IRK and IRK response, undated, box 71, folder 4, IRKP; Mulligan, *Mulligan's Law*, 66.
19. Rosalind Rosenberg interview, April 26, 2017; Maxine Berman interview, September 11, 2018; John Kaufman interview, June 7, 2016; John and Steven Kaufman interview, October 18, 2016; John Kaufman and Jane Fishman interview, January 22, 2022.
20. John Kaufman interview.
21. *Taylor*, SDNY, Trial Transcript, 1095; Maier, *Newhouse*, 28, 36, 39.

22. Robert Kaufman to IRK, March 8, 1961, OFWA; Robert and Richard Kaufman telegraph to IRK, undated, box 26, folder 13, IRKP.

23. IRK to Clark, September 7, 1954, TCCP-UT box B69; IRK to Hoover, January 28, 1958; John and Seven Kaufman interview; John Kaufman and Jane Fishman interview.

24. Robert Kaufman to IRK, March 8, 1961, OFWA; Berman interview; John Kaufman interview; Roger Kaufman interview, September 28, 2016.

25. IRK to Doris Rosenberg, June 22, 1966, box 128, folder 17, IRKP; Berman interview; David du Pont interview, April 3, 2020.

26. Berman interview; Jason Horowitz, "For Donald Trump, Lessons from a Brother's Suffering," *NYT*, January 2, 2016.

27. Berman interview; Rosalind Rosenberg interview; John Kaufman and Jane Fishman interview.

28. FBI memo, Malone to Mohr, September 25, 1962; FBI memo, Malone to Mohr, October 1, 1962.

29. Rosalind Rosenberg interview; Berman interview.

11. The Forgotten Man

1. FBI memo, Malone to Mohr, June 8, 1962; IRK to Hoover, June 26, 1962; Hoover to IRK, June 28, 1962; IRK to Hoover, March 13, 1963; IRK to Hoover, December 16, 1963; Jack Auspitz interview, October 19, 2016.

2. *Seeger* 2d Cir., Defendant-Appellant's Brief, 10–14, Appendix 280a; *U.S. v. Seeger*, 303 F.2d 478, 485 (2d Cir. 1962); *U.S. v. Tribote*, 297 F.2d 598, 604 (2d Cir. 1961); "Court Throws Out Contempt Case against Folk Singer Pete Seeger," *WP*, May 19, 1962; Jon Pareles, "Pete Seeger, Champion of Folk Music and Social Change, Dies at 94," *NYT*, January 28, 2014.

3. *U.S. v. Como*, 340 F.2d 891 (2d Cir. 1965); *U.S. v. Middleton*, 344 F.2d 78 (2d Cir. 1965); *U.S. v. Dehar*, 388 F.2d 430 (2d Cir. 1968); *U.S. v. Mancuso*, 420 F.2d 556 (2d Cir. 1970); *U.S. v. Harary*, 457 F.2d 471 (2d Cir. 1972); *U.S. v. Guerra*, 334 F.2d 138, 147 (2d Cir. 1964); *U.S. v. Russ*, 362 F.2d 843, 845 (2d Cir. 1966).

4. *U.S. v. Drummond*, 354 F.2d 132 (2d Cir. 1965).

5. Dershowitz, *Best Defense*, 3–16; Roy Bongartz, "Superjew," *Esquire*, August 1970, 110; Leon Wieseltier, "The Demon of the Jews," *New Republic*, November 10, 1985, 24; "The Jewish Vigilantes," *Newsweek*, January 12, 1970, 35; "The Private Jewish War on Russia," *Time*, January 25, 1971, 24; "Armed Summer Camp," *Time*, August 30, 1971, 23; "Violence Is Not Un-Jewish," *Newsweek*, January 25, 1971, 32.

6. Tad Szulc, "Shots at Soviet Mission Stir Bitter Debates in the U.N.," *NYT*, October 22, 1971; "3 in Jewish Defense League Halt Soviet Pianist Here," *NYT*, November 11, 1985; Murray Schumach, "Jewish Defense League Plays Grim Game with the Russians," *NYT*, January 13, 1971; "Youth Seized in Firing at Soviet Mission," *NYT*, October 22, 1971.

7. Dershowitz, *Best Defense*, 16–72, 73–75.

8. *U.S. v. Huss*, 482 F.2d 38, 47–52 (2d Cir. 1973). The later wiretapping decisions are *U.S. v. Marion*, 535 F.2d 697 (2d Cir. 1976), and *U.S. v. Gigante*, 538 F.2d 502 (2d Cir. 1976).

9. *Freeman* 2d Cir., Brief and Appendix for Defendant-Appellant, 8–12; *U.S. v. Freeman*, 357 F.2d 606, 609–10 (2d Cir. 1966).

10. *U.S. v. Currens*, 290 F.2d 751, 764 (3d Cir. 1961); John L. Moore, *M'Naghten Is Dead—or Is It?*, 3 Hous. L. Rev. 58, 62–64, Appendices A–B (1965); *Freeman*, 357 F.2d at 616–18; Benjamin Cardozo, *What Medicine Can Do for Law*, abstracted in 2 Current Legal Thought 1 (1936); *Currens*, 290 F.2d at 765–66 (quoting Cardozo and Frankfurter).

11. William Hellerstein interview, April 25, 2019.

12. John Kaufman interview, June 7, 2016; IRK to Nichols, April 12, 1956; IRK, "20 Years on the Federal Court," box 116, folder 10, IRKP; Hellerstein interview.

13. *Freeman*, 357 F.2d at 618–20, 620–25.

14. Edward Ranzal, "U.S. Appeals Court Liberalizes Method for Defining Sanity," *NYT*, March 1, 1966; "Doing In M'Naghten," *Time*, March 11, 1966; "Court Upsets M'Naghten Insanity Rule," *LAT*, March 1, 1966; Herbert Weschler to IRK, March 2, 1966, box 39, folder 3, IRKP; *U.S. v. Brawner*, 471 F.2d 969 (D.C. Cir. 1972) (other circuits adopted ALI § 4.01); Warren Burger to IRK, March 11, 1966, and IRK to Burger, March 15, 1966, box 76, folder 1, IRKP.

15. *Fay v. Noia*, 372 U.S. 391 (1963); *Townsend v. Sain*, 372 U.S. 293 (1963); IRK, "The Uncertain Criminal Law: Rights, Wrongs and Doubts," *Atlantic Monthly*, January 1965, 61–62. For discussions of the Warren Court's criminal procedure and habeas jurisprudence see Yale Kamisar, "The Warren Court and Criminal Justice," in Schwartz, *Warren Court*, 116–58; White, *Earl Warren*, 263–78; Cray, *Chief Justice*, 366–78, 403–6, 455–68; and Powe, *Warren Court and American Politics*, 379–411.

16. Robert E. Baker, "Presidential Campaigning: Union Cheers Johnson on Medicare; Big Dixie Crowds Greet Goldwater," *WP*, September 16, 1964; "Warren Speech Hits on Court Criticism," *WP*, February 9, 1965; Bennett, *I Chose Prison*, 9 (quoting Warren); "Earl Warren Dies at 83; Chief Justice for 16 Years," *LAT*, July 10, 1974; Cray, *Chief Justice*, 322.

17. *McGrath v. LaVallee*, 319 F.2d 308, 315, 318 (2d Cir. 1963); *Durocher v. LaVallee*, 330 F.2d 303, 313, 315 (2d Cir. 1965); "Court Ruling May Free Thousands of Convicts," *NYT*, March 28, 1964.

18. *Ross v. McMann*, 409 F.2d 1016.

19. *Marcelin v. Mancusi*, 462 F.2d 36, 48 (Kaufman, J., dissenting); *Ross*, 409 F.2d at 1028. Other habeas cases that fit this mold include *Smith v. McMann*, 417 F.2d 648 (2d Cir. 1969), and *Vanderhorst v. LaVallee*, 417 F.2d 411 (2d Cir. 1969), though exceptions to Kaufman's siding with the petitioner in more significant habeas cases include *Angelet v. Fay*, 333, F.2d 12 (2d Cir. 1964), *aff'd*, 381 U.S. 618 (1965), and *Stovall v. Denno*, 355 F.2d 731 (2d Cir. 1966). IRK, *Reform in Criminal Law: Have the Lawyers Lagged Behind?*, N.Y. State Bar Journal (June 1965), 217, 224; *Cruz v. Ward*, 558 F.2d 658, 667 (2d Cir. 1977).

20. *Schuster I* 2d Cir., Minutes of Proceedings at Dannemora, N.Y., May 11, 1963, 19–20; *Schuster v. Herold*, 410 F.2d 1071, 1073–74 (2d Cir. 1969); "Alimony Debtor Slays Wife and Wounds Lawyer," *NYHT*, May 3, 1931; "Tap Dancer Kills Estranged Wife," *WP*, May 3, 1931.

21. "Sing Sing Prisoners Stage Minstrel Show," *NYHT*, December 13, 1931; *Schuster I* 2d Cir., Proceedings at Dannemora, May 11, 1963, 18–19, Application for Writ of Habeas Corpus, July 13, 1965, 22–23.

22. *Schuster I* 2d Cir., Hearing, July 12, 1967, 46–47, 52, 96–97, Petition to Hon. Edmund Port, 1967, 9–10, Brief to U.S. Court of Appeals, June 3, 1966, 20–21; *Schuster II* 2d Cir., Petitioner's Brief, May 21, 75, 29; *Dennison v. State*, 267 N.Y.S.2d 920 (Ct. Claims 1966).

23. *Schuster I* 2d Cir., Proceedings at Dannemora, May 11, 1963, 25, Hearing, July 12, 1967, 85–96.

24. *Schuster*, 410 F.2d at 1077–94.

25. Auspitz interview; IRK to A. O. Sulzberger, April 28, 1969, OFWA; *Matthews v. Hardy*, 420 F.2d 607, 611 (D.C. Cir. 1970); Elizabeth Alexander, *The New Prison Administrators and the Court: New Directions in Prison Law*, 56 Tex. L. Rev. 963, 985 (1978).

26. *Schuster v. Vincent*, 524 F.2d 153, 154–55 (2d Cir. 1975); *Schuster II* 2d Cir., Spiegel Affidavit, June 21, 1974, Exh. C, Parole Hearing, May 20–23, 1974.

27. Michael Tabak interview, March 24, 2020; *Schuster*, 524 F.2d at 154–61.

28. "Court Orders State to Free Prisoner after 44 Years, 31 in Insane Asylum," *NYT*, September 24, 1975, 88; "Sentenced in 1931, Inmate, 70, Is Free," *NYT*, September 26, 1975.

29. *Attica*, xi, xvi–xxi, 18–19, 31–72; Thompson, *Blood in the Water*, 5–17, 278–86.

30. *Wright v. McMann*, 387 F.2d 519 (2d Cir. 1967); *Sostre v. McGinnis*, 442 F.2d 178 (2d Cir. 1971).

31. IRK, *Prison: A Judge's Dilemma*, 41 Fordham L. Rev. 495, 504, 510, 511 (1973); "Judges and Jailbirds," *NYDN*, November 26, 1972; Harold Sager to IRK, December 5, 1972, box 106, folder 6, IRKP.

32. *Cruz*, 558 F.2d at 663–67; *Todaro v. Ward*, 565 F.2d 48 (2d Cir. 1977).

33. *Haymes v. Montanye*, 505 F.2d 977, 980 (2d Cir. 1974); *Gilliard*, 557 F.2d at 359–60.

34. *Wolfish v. Levi*, 573 F.2d 118 (1978).

35. "Report of the Committee on the Operation of the Jury System," March 30, 1967, box 56, folder 6, IRKP; IRK, *The Judges and Jurors: Recent Developments in Selection of Jurors and Fair Trial–Free Press*, 41 U. Colo. L. Rev. 179 (1969); Robert Freedman interview, April 11, 2016; Hearings Before Senate Committee on the Judiciary, Subcommittee on Improvements in Judicial Machinery of the U.S., 90th Cong., 269–70 (May 2, 1967) (testimony of IRK); Fred P. Graham, "Random Selection of U.S. Juries Voted," *NYT*, March 16, 1968; Marvin Smilon, "The Jury Doors Are About to Open Wider," *NYP*, November 12, 1968; Drew McKillips, "Kaufman Jury Plan Accepted," *Honolulu Advertiser*, July 31, 1968; Walter Gerwin to Rowland Kirks, October 2, 1970, box 54, folder 5, IRKP.

36. IRK, press release, "Announcement of Formation of Committee on Sentencing Practices, July 5, 1973, box 64, folder 3, IRKP; Lesley Oelsner, "U.S. Courts Acting to End Disparity in Prison Terms," *NYT*, July 5, 1973; IRK, press releases, March 17, 1976, and December 23, 1979, box 64, folder 3, IRKP;

Arnold H. Lubasch, "U.S. 2d Circuit Court Issues Plan to Lessen Sentencing Disparities," *NYT*, December 23, 1979.

37. *Gesicki v. Oswald*, 336 F. Supp. 371, 378 (S.D.N.Y. 1971); "Wayward Winners," *Time*, January 10, 1972, 65; *U.S. v. Preiser*, 506 F.2d 1115 (2d Cir. 1974).

38. "27 Are Appointed to Justice Panel," *NYT*, July 26, 1971; IRK Remarks at Opening Meeting of Commission, "Juvenile Justice Standards Project: The Child Is Father to the Man," May 18, 1973, box 92, folder 1, IRKP; Lesley Oelsner, "Juvenile Justice Is Target of Drive," *NYT*, May 19, 1973; IRK, *Of Juvenile Justice and Injustice*, ABA J., June 1976, 730; Report to ABA House of Delegates, February 1978, box 91, folder 6, IRKP.

39. For a description of the standards see IRK, *Of Juvenile Justice*; Merril Sobie and John D. Elliott, *The IJA-ABA Juvenile Justice Standards*, Crim. Justice, Fall 2014, 24. IRK to John H. Lashley, April 1, 1976, box 90, folder 7, IRKP; Marcia Chambers, "Radical Changes Urged in Dealing with Youth Crime," *NYT*, November 30, 1975; IRK, "Juvenile Justice: A Plea for Reform," *NYT Magazine*, October 14, 1979.

40. IRK Opening Remarks, Seventh Meeting, IJA-ABA Joint Commission on Juvenile Justice Standards, January 25, 1976, 3, box 92, folder 5, IRKP; IRK Remarks, ABA House of Delegates, February 13, 1978, box 92, folder 6, IRKP; Council on Juvenile Court Judges, Resolution #8, box 92, folder 5, IRKP; Scott Slonim, *ABA Delegates Defer "Runaways" Proposal*, ABA J., March 1980; Linda Greenhouse, "Bar Association Again Backs Ban on Television and Radio in Court," *NYT*, February 13, 1979.

41. Sobie and Elliott, *IJA-ABA Juvenile Justice Standards*, 25.

12. Hippieland

1. Rifkind, *One Man's World*, vol. 1 (Address to Lawyer's Division of American Jewish Committee, November 18, 1969), 211–15.

2. IRK to Robert Moses, June 4, 1968, box 126, folder 10, IRKP; IRK to Grace Mayes, April 7, 1971, box 125, folder 2, IRKP.

3. Daniel Seeger, "Check Box Yes, Check Box No," in Irons, *Courage of their Convictions*, 167–73; Cherie Roberts, "Quaker Universalist Fellowship Interview with Daniel A. Seeger," *Quaker Universalist Voice*, November 11, 2013, https://universalistfriends.org/library/interview-with-daniel-seeger; *United States v. Seeger*, 326 F.2d 846, 848, 852–55 (2d Cir. 1964). The phrase "skeptical generation," so apt for the 1960s, was actually borrowed from an opinion by Augustus Hand considering conscientious objection in the 1940s: *United States v. Kauten*, 133 F.2d 703, 708 (2d Cir. 1943).

4. John Biggs to IRK, January 23, 1964, box 75, folder 9, IRKP; Edward Ranzal, "Part of Draft Act Is Upset by Court," *NYT*, January 21, 1964; "Respect for Conscience," *NYT*, January 26, 1964; "Judge Kaufman to Get Award from Unitarians," *NYT*, March 3, 1964; Seeger, "Check Box Yes," in Irons, *Courage of Their Convictions*, 173–75; *U.S. v. Seeger*, 380 U.S. 163,184 (1965); 50 U.S.C. § 3806(j); "Conscientious Objectors," Selective Service System website, accessed December 2, 2021, www.sss.gov/conscientious-objectors/.

5. Ferber and Lynd, *Resistance*, 33–34; Daniel A. Seeger, "An AFSC Defense of the Rights of Conscience," *Friends Journal*, October 1, 2017, www.friendsjournal.org/conscientious-objection-seeger/; Kohn, *Jailed for Peace*, 92–93.

6. *United States v. Bornemann*, 424 F.2d 1343 (2d Cir. 1970); *United States v. Holmes*, 426 F.2d 915 (2d Cir. 19700), *vacated following Ehlert v. United States*, 402 U.S. 99 (1971); *United States v. Aull*, 469 F.2d 151, 154–55 (2d Cir., IRK dissenting); *Hammond v. Lenfest*, 398 F.2d 705 (2d Cir. 1968).

7. *James* 2d Cir., Plaintiff-Appellant's Appendix, 47a–49a (James Affidavit); *Charles James v. Board of Education of Central District No. 1 of Towns of Addison*, 461 F.2d 566, 568 (2d Cir. 1972); Richard Harris, "Annals of Law: A Scrap of Black Cloth—I," *New Yorker*, June 17, 1974, 37; Richard Harris, "Annals of Law: A Scrap of Black Cloth—II," *New Yorker*, June 24, 1974; Jonathan Kandell, "Antiwar Teacher Savors Vindication," *NYT*, May 26, 1972; Burt Neuborne interview, June 12, 2019.

8. *Russo* 2d Cir., Plaintiff-Appellant's Appendix 91a, 342a–43a, 367a; *Russo v. Central School Dist. No. 1, Towns of Rush et al.*, 469 F.2d 623 (2d Cir. 1972); Mary Breasted, "A Teacher's Right to Shun Pledge to the Flag," *NYT*, February 18, 1974.

9. *Tinker v. Des Moines Independent Community School Dist.*, 393 U.S. 503 (1969); *West Virginia State Bd. of Education v. Barnette*, 319 U.S. 624 (1943).

10. Neuborne interview; *Russo* 2d Cir., Appellees' Brief.

11. Neuborne interview; Harris, "Scrap of Black Cloth—II," 67.

12. *James*; *Russo*; Ruth Bader Ginsburg to IRK, February 20, 1973, box 78, folder 9, IRKP.

13. Kandell, "Antiwar Teacher"; Neuborne interview; Breasted, "Teacher's Right"; Carron J. Phillips, "Susan Russo's Court Case on the "Pledge of Allegiance" Is Still Relevant in the Age of Colin Kaepernick," *NYDN*, January 20, 2018.

14. *Orlando v. Laird*, 443 F.2d 1039 (2d Cir. 1971); *DaCosta v. Laird*, 471 F.2d 1146 (2d Cir. 1971); Belknap, *American Political Trials*, 116; Burt Neuborne, "I Fought the Imperial Presidency, and the Imperial Presidency Won," September 27, 2019, aclu.org/issues/national-security/i-fought-imperial-presidency-and-imperial-presidency-won.

15. FBI BR 1947; Jeremiah Horrigan, "I Was Ready to Go to Prison for My Anti-war Beliefs, Then One Man Changed My Life," *Narratively Memoir*, May 23, 2016, https://narratively.com/i-was-ready-to-go-to-prison-for-my-anti-war-beliefs-then-one-man-changed-my-life (quoting Judge Curtin); *Lawton v. Tarr*, 327 F. Supp. 670 (E.D.N.C. 1971) (James Craven speech); IRK, *The Anatomy of Decisionmaking*, 53 Fordham L. Rev. 1, 17 (Oct. 1984).

16. Charles Stillman interview, November 29, 2006; Robert Winter interview, April 13, 2016; Warren Olney memo to All Judges, June 26, 1963, box 104, folder 2, IRKP; Maxine Berman interview, September 11, 2018; Dodd to IRK, August 7 and 11, 1964, September 1, 1964, October 23, 1964, November 5 and 13, 1964, Series I, "Kaufman, Irving R., 1959," TJDP; John Kaufman interview, June 7, 2016.

17. "Bar of Mississippi Scored by Kaufman," *NYT*, October 17, 1962.

18. Sugrue, *Sweet Land of Liberty*, 464–65; *Norwalk* 2d Cir., Plaintiffs-Appellants' Brief, 13, 18; *Norwalk CORE v. Norwalk Bd. of Education*, 298 F. Supp. 213 (D. Conn. 1969); *Norwalk CORE v. Norwalk Bd. of Education*, 423 F.2d 121, 126 (2d Cir. 1970); "CORE Challenges NAACP to Debate," *Hartford Courant*, March 7, 1970.

19. *Kirkland v. N.Y. State Dept. of Correctional Services*, 531 F.2d 5 (2d Cir. 1975); IRK Address, "State of the Judicial Business in the Second Circuit," September 10, 1976, box 141, folder 6, IRKP.

20. Dan Kelly interview, December 20, 2019; Bruce Kraus interview, March 6, 2019.

21. Lyndon Johnson, "State of the Union Address," *WP*, January 9, 1964; "Address by Attorney General Robert F. Kennedy, University of Chicago Law School, Chicago, Illinois, Law Day, May 1, 1964," www.justice.gov/sites/default/files/ag/legacy/2011/01/20/05-01-1964.pdf; "Our History," Legal Services Corporation website, accessed December 2, 2021, www.lsc.gov/about-lsc/who-we-are/history; *Discriminations against the Poor and the Fourteenth Amendment*, 81 HARV. L. REV. 435 (1967); Reich, *New Property*.

22. For a discussion of the Supreme Court decisions concerning fees and due process for poor people see Sunstein, *Second Bill of Rights*, 156–62. Clark's and Harlan's dissents appear in *Douglas v. California*, 372 U.S. 353 (1963).

23. *Bynum v. Conn. Commission on Forfeited Rights*, 410 F.2d 173 (2d Cir. 1969); *Male v. Crossroads Associates*, 469 F.2d 616 (2d Cir. 1972).

24. *Johnson v. N.Y. State Educ. Dept.*, 449 F.2d 871 (2d Cir. 1971) (IRK dissenting); *Johnson v. N.Y. State Educ. Dept.*, 409 U.S. 75 (1972) (Marshall, J., concurring). For a list of decisions reaching similar conclusions in public school financing cases as of 1972 see Note, *A Statistical Analysis of the School Finance Decisions: On Winning Battles and Losing Wars*, 81 YALE L. J. 1303 n. 2 (1972).

25. *Snell v. Wyman*, 281 F. Supp. 853 (S.D.N.Y. 1968).

26. IRK, "Philosophy of Judicial Administration," *NYLJ*, September 9, 1968.

27. *Boutilier* 2d Cir., Respondent's Brief, Record of Sworn Statement, January 13, 1964, 12a–21a; *Boutilier v. INS*, 363 F.2d 488, 490–92 (2d Cir. 1966).

28. "The Case of the Elusive Euphemism," *Time*, July 22, 1966, 49; Webster Schott, "Civil Rights and the Homosexual: A 4-Million Minority Asks for Equal Rights," *NYT Magazine*, November 12, 1967, 44; "A Minority's Plea: U.S. Homosexuals Gain in Trying to Persuade Society to Accept Them," *WSJ*, July 17, 1968; Murdoch and Price, *Courting Justice*, 34–39; Stein, "All the Immigrants Are Straight," 49–50; *Boutilier* 2d Cir., Brief and Appendix for Petitioner's, Report of Montague Ullman, March 30, 1965, 18a–19a.

29. *Boutilier* 2d Cir., Brief and Appendix for Petitioner; James Greilsheimer interview, May 28, 2019. Professor Marc Stein, who has written extensively about *Boutilier*, maintains that Freedman's and amici's arguments reflected "a profound ambivalence about homosexuality" and mirrored those she had asserted in earlier cases on behalf of accused communists. Stein, "All the Immigrants Are Straight," 65–69. See also Stein, "Sexual Revolution," 527.

30. *Boutilier*, 363 F.2d at 482–99; "Are Homosexuals Psychopaths?," *Playboy*, July 1967, 135.

31. William N. Eskridge, *Dynamic Statutory Interpretation* (Cambridge, MA: Harvard University Press, 1994), 62–66.

32. *Boutilier v. INS*, 387 U.S. 118, 125, 128 (1967).

33. Eskridge, *Gaylaw*, 133; Murdoch and Price, *Courting Justice*, 117–19, 134; Marc Stein, "Forgetting and Remembering a Deported Alien," History News Network, August 8, 2005, www.historynewsnetwork.org/article/1769; Stein, "All the Immigrants," 51–68; Stein, "Sexual Revolution," 534 (quoting letter from Boutilier's niece).

34. Agis Salpukas, "Freed Poet Hails Michigan Ruling," *NYT*, March 12, 1972; Agis Salpukas, "15,000 Attend Michigan U. Rally to Protest Jailing of Radical Poet," *NYT*, December 12, 1971; John Lennon, "John Sinclair," track 8 on *Some Time in New York City*, Apple Records, 1972. Copies of FBI memos concerning the Sinclair concert appear in Wiener, *Gimme Some Truth*, 110–21.

35. FBI memos and correspondence, 1972, reprinted in Wiener, *Gimme Some Truth*, 137–51, 238–41.

36. Wiener, *Gimme Some Truth*, 3–4 (Thurmond letter); Pete Hamill, "Long Night's Journey into Day: A Conversation with John Lennon," *Rolling Stone*, June 5, 1975, 73; Wiener, *Come Together*, 227; Wildes, *John Lennon vs. the USA*, 64–65, 95 (quoting Bob Dylan letter); Stephen Isaacs, "Ballad of John and Yoko: They'll Hear the News Today," *WP*, May 12, 1972; "Love It and Leave It," *NYT*, May 2, 1972; "The Lennons: Where Is the Threat?," *LAT*, May 23, 1972; *Lennon* 2d Cir., Petitioner's Appendix, 178–99.

37. *Lennon* 2d Cir., Petitioner's Appendix, 133; Laurie Johnston, "Lennon Sees a Wide Impact in Ouster," *NYT*, April 3, 1973; Lisa Robinson, "John Lennon Interview," *Hit Parade*, December 1975, www.beatlesinterviews.org/db1975.1200.beatles.html; Wiener, *Come Together*, 276; Wildes, *John Lennon vs. the USA*, 130–31; Grace Lichtenstein, "U.S. Orders Lennon Out," *NYT*, March 24, 1973.

38. Jack Auspitz interview, October 19, 2016; Johnston, "Lennon Sees"; Wildes, *John Lennon vs. the USA*, 145–88; IRK to Doris Rosenberg, June 23, 1964, box 128, folder 17, IRKP; Jon Lindsey interview, March 17, 2020; Brian Schwartz email, August 23, 2020.

39. *Lennon v. INS*, 527 F.2d 187 (2d Cir. 1975).

40. Arnold Lubasch, "Deportation of Lennon Barred by Court of Appeals," *NYT*, October 8, 1975; Wildes, *John Lennon vs. the USA*, 197; Leslie Maitland, "John Lennon Wins His Residency in U.S.," *NYT*, July 28, 1976; Lindsey interview.

13. The Most Cherished Tenet

1. Goodale, *Fighting for the Press*, 79–122; Rudenstine, *Day the Presses Stopped*, 15–47; *U.S. v. New York Times Co.*, 328 F. Supp. 324 (S.D.N.Y. 1971).

2. *New York Times*, 328 F. Supp. at 331; Oakes, *Judge Gurfein*; Sanford J. Ungar, "Decisions of Two Men Become Law of the Land," *WP*, July 4, 1971.

3. Ungar, *Papers*, 169; Rudenstine, *Day the Presses Stopped*, 180–81; "Court Denies U.S. an Injunction to Block Times Vietnam Series, Appeals Judge Continues Stay," *NYT*, June 20, 1971 (reproducing IRK order); Floyd

Abrams interview, December 20, 2019; James Goodale interview, November 19, 2019.

4. "Memorandum of IRK," undated, box 56, folder "USA v. New York Times, No. 71-1617, June 22, 1971," HJFP ("Friendly PP File"); Ungar, *Papers*, 205–6.

5. Rudenstine, *Day the Presses Stopped*, 217–27; Abrams, *Speaking Freely*, 16.

6. Oakes, *Judge Gurfein*, 3; Fred P. Graham, "Times Case Heard, Restraint Extended; U.S. Action Halts a Boston Globe Series," *NYT*, June 23, 1971; *PP* 2d Cir., Transcript of Oral Argument and "In Camera Proceedings," June 22, 1971; Alexander M. Bickel, "The Rosenberg Affair," *Commentary*, January 1966, 69; Rudenstine, *Day the Presses Stopped*, 231–33; Abrams, *Speaking Freely*, 34.

7. Goodale, *Fighting for the Press*; Goodale interview; Dorsen, *Henry Friendly*, 158–60.

8. Ungar, *Papers*, 205–6; Salisbury, *Without Fear or Favor*, 320; "Memorandum of IRK," June 23, 1971, Friendly PP File.

9. Judges' memos, Friendly PP File; *U.S. v. New York Times Co.*, 444 F.2d 544 (2d Cir. 1971); Ungar, "Decisions of Two Men"; Ungar, *Papers*, 205–7; Oakes, *Judge Gurfein*, 13.

10. *New York Times Co. v. U.S.*, 403 U.S. 713 (1971); Abrams, *Speaking Freely*, 58–59; Goodale, *Fighting for the Press*, 167–69. Federal courts have issued "gag orders" limiting certain speech in advance of criminal trials in order to preserve their fairness, as well as orders limiting the dissemination of intellectual property, but these are viewed differently from classic prior restraints despite their limiting effect on prospective speech.

11. Dorsen, *Henry Friendly*, 421–22 n. 102.

12. *Branzburg v. Hayes*, 408 U.S. 665 (1972).

13. Norris Vitchek as told to Alfred Balk, "Confessions of a Block-Buster," *Saturday Evening Post*, July 14, 1962; *Baker v. F&F Investment*, 470 F.2d 778 (2d Cir. 1972).

14. James T. Wooten, "How a Supersoldier Was Fired from His Command," *NYT Magazine*, September 5, 1971; James T. Wooten, "Army Officers' Accuser Anthony Bernard Herbert," *NYT*, March 13, 1971; Michael Getler and Peter Braestrup, "Army Clears Colonel Who Charged Coverup," *WP*, October 9, 1971; Transcript of *Sixty Minutes*, season 5, episode 10, "The Selling of Col. Herbert," aired February 4, 1973, on CBS, in *Herbert* 2d Cir., Joint Appendix 51a (hereinafter cited as "Selling"); Peter Braestrup, "A Soldier's Tale," *WP*, February 18, 1973; Herbert and Wooten, *Soldier*, 257, 300, 328, 357–58, 396.

15. Wooten, "How a Supersoldier"; Donald Jackson, "Confessions of 'The Winter Soldiers,'" *Life*, July 9, 1971, 23; "Selling" (quoting Dick Cavett); "The Army on Trial," *NYT*, September 5, 1971; "The Herbert Case," *NYT*, October 26, 1971; "Retirement under Pressure," *NYT*, November 11, 1971; Herbert and Wooten, *Soldier*, 301; "Anarv Ex-Soldier Cries 'Fowl,'" *LAT*, June 14, 1972.

16. Barry Lando, "The Herbert Affair," *Atlantic Monthly*, May 1973, 76; "Selling"; James Lardner, "Up against the Wallace: After Ten Years, the Hard Edge of '60 Minutes' Is, If Anything, Harder," *WP*, September 18, 1977.

17. *Herbert v. Lando*, 568 F.2d 974 (2d Cir. 1977); *Herbert* 2d Cir., Brief of Defendant-Appellants Barry Lando, Mike Wallace, and CBS, 4–5, 10–32.

18. "The Limits of Libel," *NYT*, November 10, 1977; "A Good Decision on Libel," *WP*, November 9, 1977; Abrams interview.

19. *Herbert v. Lando*, 441 U.S. 153 (1979).

20. IRK, "Blunting the Court's Sword against Press," *Editor & Publisher*, June 2, 1979, 96. For a list of state laws establishing reporters' privileges see *U.S. v. Sterling*, 724 F.3d 482, 532 (4th Cir. 2013) (Gregory, J., dissenting); see also Christina Koningisor, *The De Facto Reporters' Privilege*, 127 Yale L. J. 1176, 1201–5 (March 2018).

21. Deborah Nelson and Nick Turse, "A Tortured Past: Documents Show Troops Who Reported Abuse in Vietnam Were Discredited Even as the Military Was Finding Evidence of Worse," *LAT*, August 20, 2006.

22. *Edwards v. Nat'l Audubon Society*, 556 F.2d 113, 115, 122 (2d Cir. 1977); Rodney A. Smolla, *Law of Defamation*, § 4:100 (Eagan, MN: Thomson Reuters, 2019); IRK, "Press, Privacy and Malice: Reflections on New York v. Sullivan," *New York State Bar Association Journal*, July 1984, 10, 14–15; IRK, "Congress Should Preempt Libel Field, Set Remedies," *LAT*, August 23, 1985; IRK, "The Creative Process and Libel," *NYT Magazine*, April 5, 1987.

23. *Harper & Row, Publishers, Inc. v. Nation Enter.*, 723 F.2d 195 (2d Cir. 1983), *rev'd*, 471 U.S. 539 (1985).

24. *FEC v. Central Long Island Tax Reform Immediately*, 616 F.2d 45, 54 (2d Cir. 1980) (IRK concurring); *FEC v. Hall-Tyner Election Campaign Comm.*, 678 F.2d 416, 420 (2d Cir. 1982); IRK to Hoover, November 4, 1957; *Republican Party of the State of Connecticut v. Tashjian*, 770 F.2d 265 (2d Cir. 1985), *aff'd*, 479 U.S. 208 (1986).

25. *Wolin v. Port of New York Auth.*, 392 F.2d 83 (2d Cir. 1968); *Council of Greenburgh Civic Ass'n v. U.S. Postal Serv.*, 586 F.2d 935 (2d Cir. 1978) (IRK, concurring); *U.S. Postal Serv. v. Council of Greenburgh Civic Ass'n*, 453 U.S. 114 (1981).

26. *Eisner v. Stamford Bd. of Educ.*, 440 F.3d 803 (2d Cir. 1971); *Thomas v. Bd. of Educ., Granville Central School Dist.*, 607 F.2d 1043, 1045 (2d Cir. 1979); IRK voting memo, *Mareno v. Walker*, March 14, 1980, OFWA.

27. *U.S. v. Dellapia*, 433 F.2d 1252, 1253–54, 1258–59 (2d Cir. 1970); *Dellapia* 2d Cir., Appellant's Appendix 33a–36a, Appellant's Brief, Petition of the U.S. for Rehearing or, in the Alternative, for Rehearing En Banc; Bartley Deamer interview, February 16, 2017.

28. Abrams interview; Second Circuit judge interview (anonymous); Jon O. Newman interview, May 17, 2016.

29. Newman interview; "Professor's Alleged C.I.A. Ties Stir Controversy at Brooklyn College," *NYT*, January 9, 1977; "Teacher Awarded $580,000; Talk to C.I.A. Barred Tenure," *NYT*, May 19, 1979; *Selzer v. Fleisher*, 629 F.2d 809, 814–17 (2d Cir. 1980) (IRK, concurring in part and dissenting in part).

30. IRK to Sidney Hook, September 20, 1965, box 155, folder 8, SHP; Sidney Hook, "Echoes of the Rosenberg Case: An Autobiographical Postscript," *American Spectator*, January 1989, 18.

31. Lee Levine interview, February 28, 2019.

32. IRK to Arthur Hays Sulzberger, September 19, 1951, March 9, 1954, January 12, 1956, and April 26, 1961, A. H. Sulzberger papers, box 36, folder

26, NYTP; Jack Auspitz interview, October 19, 2016; Goodale interview; IRK to Donald Newhouse, December 7, 1982, box 127, folder 7, IRKP; Max Frankel email, May 25, 2016; guest list for IRK dinner for Lord Chief Justice Widgery, April 29, 1976, box 130, folder 10, IRKP.

33. Fred P. Graham, "U.S. Judges Propose Eased Press Code," *NYT*, February 29, 1968; "'Satisfactory Accommodation,'" *NYT*, March 8, 1968; "Insuring Fair Trial," *NYT*, September 25, 1968; "Report of the Committee on the Operation of the Jury System on the 'Free Press–Fair Trial' Issue," 45 F.R.D. 391 (1969); IRK, *The Judges and Jurors: Recent Developments in Selection of Jurors and Fair Trial-Free Press*, 41 U. Colo. L. Rev. 179, 188–99 (1969).

34. Tom Goldstein interview, December 9, 2019; Craig Whitney interview, May 25, 2016; Max Frankel email, May 27, 2016; Linda Greenhouse interview, November 12, 2019.

35. Goldstein, *News at Any Cost*, 198; Goldstein interview.

36. Rod Townley, "A Specter Is Haunting Irving Kaufman," *Juris Doctor*, November 1977, 17, 20; Goldstein, *News at Any Cost*, 199; Dorothy Rabinowitz to A. M. Rosenthal, November 3, 1977, A. M. Rosenthal Papers, box 22, folder 24, NYTP; Jerry Menikoff interview, December 16, 2019.

37. Goldstein, *News at Any Cost*, 198.

38. Greenhouse interview; Linda Greenhouse, "A Judge Who Likes Action," *NYT*, July 29, 1983; Peter Millones memo to A. M. Rosenthal, August 3, 1983, and IRK to Millones, August 2, 1983, A. M. Rosenthal Papers, box 22, folder 24, NYTP.

39. Frankel email, May 25, 2016; Goldstein, *News at Any Cost*, 197; Richard Friedman interview, March 4 and 27, 2019; IRK to A. M. Rosenthal, August 21, 1981, A. M. Rosenthal Papers, box 22, folder 24, NYTP.

40. A. O. Sulzberger to publishers, October 1, 1980, box 51, folder 5, IRKP; A. O. Sulzberger to IRK, October 22, 1980, box 51, folder 6, IRKP; "LCC" memo to IRK regarding contribution to IJA, undated, IRKP box 74, folder 5; IRK to A. O. Sulzberger, July 27, 1990, box 74, folder 6, IRKP; IRK to A. O. Sulzberger, February 4, 1991, box 74, folder 7, IRKP.

41. Steven Flanders, "Kaufman, Irving R.," in Newman, *Yale Biographical Dictionary*, 309; Robert Mintz interview, September 23, 2020; *Almanac of the Federal Judiciary*, vol. 2 (New York: Prentice-Hall Law & Business 1990), 14. Correspondence with and about the reader who wrote the *Times* about Kaufman appears in A. M. Rosenthal Papers, box 22, folder 24, NYTP.

42. 28 U.S.C. § 455; Lesley Oelsner, "Panel Urges Strict Ethics Code for Judges," *NYT*, June 8, 1972; IRK to Elbert Tuttle and Edward Tamm, January 25, 1974, 3–4, box 46, folder 1, IRKP; IRK, *Lions or Jackals: The Function of a Code of Judicial Ethics*, 35 Law & Contemp. Prob. 3, 5 (1970); Goldstein interview.

43. Goodale interview; Frankel email, May 27, 2016.

44. Goldstein, *News at Any Cost*, 195; Goldstein interview; Greenhouse interview.

45. Tom Goldstein, "Kaufman Opposes Court Cutbacks," *NYT*, April 30, 1976; *Guide on Federal Courts Planned, NYT*, February 9, 1980; Robert McG. Thomas, "Kaufman Gives His Reflections on Court Work," *NYT*, November 4,

1979; IRK to A. M. Rosenthal, June 1, 1979, A. M. Rosenthal Papers, box 22, folder 24, NYTP; Jonathan Friendly, "20 Years after Key Libel Ruling, Debate Goes On," *NYT*, March 9, 1984; IRK to Robert Erburu, July 20, 1982, box 48, folder 5, IRKP.

46. Sidney E. Zion, *Judiciary Scored for Obfuscation*, December 22, 1968; IRK, "Judges Must Speak Out," *NYT*, January 30, 1982; IRK Memo to Steve Flanders, "Newsletter Article on Senior States," undated, box 124, folder 1, IRKP; IRK, "Helping the Public Understand and Accept Judicial Decisions," *American Bar Association Journal*, November 1977, 1567; Whitney interview. For IRK's relation to Robert Erburu see IRK to Erburu, April 28, 1982, box 48, folder 4, IRKP.

47. Goodale interview.

48. Marilyn Berger, "Judge Irving Kaufman, of Rosenberg Spy Trial and Free Press Rulings, Dies at 81," *NYT*, February 3, 1992; Greenhouse interview.

14. Annus Horribilis

1. J. Edgar Hoover to Lyndon Johnson, telephone conversation, November 17, 1964, Conversation #6385, Johnson Lib., www.discoverlbj.org/item/tel-06385.

2. FBI memo, C. D. DeLoach to Mohr, January 6, 1965.

3. Ted Sorenson memo to John F. Kennedy, "Names Deserving of Consideration for Court Vacancy," March 21, 1962, President's Office Files, Agencies, Departments and Supreme Court, Digital Identifier JFKPOF-088a-011-p0001, JFKP, https://www.jfklibrary.org/asset-viewer/archives/JFKPOF/088a/JFKPOF-088a-011; Nicholas Katzenbach Oral History Interview–JFK #1, November 16, 1964, 55–69, Digital Identifier JFKOH-NDK-01, JFK Lib., https://www.jfklibrary.org/asset-viewer/archives/JFKOH/Katzenbach%2C%20Nicholas%20deB/JFKOH-NDK-01/JFKOH-NDK-01 (hereinafter cited as "Katzenbach Oral History"); Robert F. Kennedy Oral History, December 4, 1964, 410–13, JFK Lib. (hereinafter cited as "RFK Oral History"); Schlesinger, *Robert Kennedy*, 377–79; Hutchison, *Man Who Once Was Whizzer White*, 310–21; Yalof, *Pursuit of Justices*, 74–78.

4. FBI memo, Malone to Mohr, May 16, 1962.

5. "Longer Rest Set for Frankfurter," *NYT*, May 1, 1962; Katzenbach Oral History, 66–67, 71; RFK Oral History, 410–14; Schlesinger, *Robert Kennedy*, 379 (quoting RFK memo: "The President said that Mike Feldman [of the White House staff] indicated clearly that the various Jewish organizations would be upset if this appointment did not go to a person of the Jewish faith"); Stebenne, *Arthur J. Goldberg*, 309–10; Yalof, *Pursuit of Justices*, 80–81. Correspondence between IRK, Dolan, Kenneth O'Donnell, and RFK reflecting IRK's desire to meet JFK and later RFK was provided to the author by the Kennedy Library without specification as to the documents' location in library collections.

6. Yalof, *Pursuit of Justices*, 81–86; Murphy, *Fortas*, 174–76.

7. Thomas Dodd to Johnson, July 23, 1965, John Macy Files, "Kaufman, Irving R." folder, Johnson Lib.; Dodd to Valenti, August 7, 1964, Gen FG File, box 505, Johnson Lib.; Weisl to Johnson, July 23, 1965, FG 535, "Supreme Court of the U.S. 3/25/65–3/19/66," box 359, Johnson Lib.

8. Ramsey Clark to Johnson, telephone conversation, July 23, 1965, 4:25 p.m., Conversation #8381, Johnson Lib.

9. Katzenbach to Johnson, July 22, 1965, WH Central File, box 360, folder FG 535/A "11/23/65-6/16/67," Johnson Lib.; Johnson draft reply to Ed Weisl prepared by Katzenbach re Chairman of the Commission on Law Enforcement and Administration of Justice, March 1965, John Macy Files, "Kaufman, Irving R." folder, Johnson Lib.; Tom Clark to IRK, October 21, 1964, box B69, TCCPUT; Tom Clark Oral History Interview, October 7, 1969, 15, Johnson Lib., www.discoverlbj.org/item/oh-clarkt-19691007-1-73-15; Yalof, *Pursuit of Justices*, 83–85.

10. Yalof, *Pursuit of Justices*, 90–94; James Eastland to Johnson, telephone conversation, June 23, 1968, 9:09 a.m., Conversation #13136, Johnson Lib. (discussing Thornberry).

11. "John N. Mitchell Dies at 75, Major Figure in Watergate," *NYT*, November 10, 1988; Dean, *Rehnquist Choice*, 73 (Nixon-Mitchell conversation), 147–48 (Nixon-Buchanan conversation).

12. Research at the Nixon Presidential Library failed to locate the Mitchell list(s) of 100 or 150 possible nominees. See Abraham, *Justices, Presidents and Senators*, 262 ("master list of some 100 names"); John L. Steele, "Haynesworth v. the U.S. Senate (1969)," *Fortune*, March 1970, 90, 91 ("a list of 150 names"); Dean, *Rehnquist Choice*, 13, 294 n. 42 (Dean unable to find Mitchell lists). One smaller list of thirty-nine names prepared by White House aide David R. Young excluded IRK. *See* David R. Young, "Memorandum for the Record, Prospective Supreme Court Nominees," WH Special Files, Staff Member and Office Files, Young Collection, box 17, folder "Supreme Court Nomination," Nixon Lib. Regarding specific potential nominees see Abraham, *Justices, Presidents and Senators*, 262 (Arlin Adams); Dean, *Rehnquist Choice*, 34 (Specter), 202–26 (Mulligan); Yalof, *Pursuit of Justices*, 103, 118 (Friendly, Mentschikoff), 250 n. 110; Dorsen, *Henry Friendly*, 136 (Friendly). Regarding Nixon on integration see Dean, *Rehnquist Choice*, 77. Regarding IRK see Walter Trohan, "Report from Washington," *CT*, June 6, 1969; Anthony Ripley, "New Yorker May Direct Watergate Investigation," *NYT*, June 6, 1973.

13. Linda Charlton, "A Friend of Nixon Linked to Offer," *NYT*, June 6, 1974.

14. Kreindler interview, February 14, 2016. On Burger's self-promotion see Yalof, *Pursuit of Justices*, 99–104; Dean, *Rehnquist Choice*, 12.

15. Kutler, *Wars of Watergate*, 329–30; Ripley, "New Yorker May Direct"; "Kaufman Says Code Bars Sitting Judge as Prosecutor," *NYT*, May 9, 1973; boxes I:197–98, folders "Memoranda of Conversations, General, 1973 Apr.-May 11," and "Memoranda of Conversations, General, May 12-Nov., undated," and boxes I:223–24, folders "Search for Special Prosecutor," ELRP.

16. IRK remarks, NYU dinner, June 4, 1973, box 140, folder 3, IRKP.

17. Regarding the 1975 vacancy see Abraham, *Justices, Presidents and Senators*, 275; Yalof, *Pursuit of Justices*, 126–30; Douglas P. Bennett memo to Ford through Richard B. Cheney, undated, box 11, folder "Supreme Court Nomination—Background on Recommended Candidates," Richard B. Cheney files, Ford Lib. Ford's age limit excluded sitting judges younger than Kaufman. See Edward Levi Memo to Ford, November 10, 1975, 2, box 11, folder "Supreme Court Nomination—Letters to the President," Richard B. Cheney files, Ford Lib.

18. C. S. Lewis, "Learning in War-Time," reprinted in C. S. Lewis, *The Weight of Glory* (New York: HarperOne, 2001), 60–61.

19. George Pratt interview, April 8, 2016.

20. FBI memo, C. D. DeLoach to Mohr, December 21, 1962; *United States v. Sobell*, 314 F.2d 314 (2d Cir. 1963); FBI memo, M. A. Jones to DeLoach, March 24, 1965; FBI memo, [redacted] to Hoover, April 11, 1966; FBI memo, W. A. Branigan to W. C. Sullivan and Hoover, April 14, 1966; Edward Ranzal, "Sobell, Spy, Freed by Circuit Court," *NYT*, January 15, 1969.

21. IRK to Sidney Hook, September 20, 1965, box 155, folder 8, SHP; Sidney Hook, "Echoes of the Rosenberg Case: An Autobiographical Postscript," *American Spectator*, January 1989, 18; FBI memo, W. C. Sullivan to Belmont, October 16, 1965, and Addendum from C. D. DeLoach, October 18, 1965.

22. Nathan Glazer, "Dissenting Opinion," *NYT*, September 5, 1965; Alexander M. Bickel, "The Rosenberg Affair," *Commentary*, January 1966, 69.

23. Freed, *Inquest*, 18; Julius Novick, "'The U.S. v. the Rosenbergs,'" *NYT*, April 20, 1969; Beatrice Berg, "'Inquest': Its Author Speaks for It," *NYT*, May 3, 1970; Allen Weinstein, "Agit-prop and the Rosenbergs," *Commentary*, July 1970, 18.

24. FBI memo, W. M. Felt to Tolson, May 8, 1970; FBI memo, Hoover to Tolson et al., April 29, 1969; FBI teletype, April 30, 1969; Hoover to IRK, May 2, 1969; FBI memo, Hoover to Mitchell, May 2, 1969.

25. Carl M. Loeb to IRK, May 15, 1974, and IRK to Loeb, May 17, 1974, box 125, folder 15, IRKP; IRK to Morris B. Abram, September 18, 1985, box 117, folder 9, IRKP.

26. Simon Rifkind, "Letter to the Editor: Guilt of the Rosenbergs," *NYT*, May 18, 1969; Berg, "'Inquest.'"

27. D. Keith Mano, "The Rosenberg Kids," *National Review*, August 6, 1976; "Vigil Marks Anniversary of Rosenbergs' Execution," *NYT*, June 20, 1969.

28. FBI memo, SAC Los Angeles to Hoover, November 5, 1969; Hoover to IRK, March 21, 1972; FBI memo, SAC Los Angeles to Hoover, March 16, 1972; Hoover to IRK, April 5, 1972; Nizer, *Implosion Conspiracy*, 525–27.

29. Robert Meeropol, *Execution in the Family*, 115–27; Meeropol and Meeropol, *We Are Your Sons*, 315–16; Ted Morgan, "The Rosenberg Jury," *Esquire*, May 1975, 106–7; Robert Reinhold, "2 Rosenberg Sons Try to Vindicate Executed Parents," *NYT*, March 10, 1974; Sid Moody, "Sons Campaigning to Vindicate Rosenbergs," *LAT*, March 10, 1974.

30. Doctorow, *Book of Daniel*, 185; Garry Abrams, "E. L. Doctorow in Defense of 'Daniel,'" *LAT*, November 3, 1983; Cecil Smith, "Kramer's Judgment: Designed to Provoke," *LAT*, January 22, 1974; John Carmody, "The Rosenbergs, a Point of View," *WP*, February 25, 1974; FBI memo, [unknown] to Clarence Kelley, September 12, 1973; FBI memo, Heim to Franck, February 27, 1974; Simon Rifkind, "TV Turns Soviet Spies into U.S. Folk Heroes," *TV Guide*, March 16, 1974; Goldstein, *Unquiet Death*, unpaginated.

31. Will Lissner, "Review Is Sought in Rosenberg Case," *NYT*, May 12, 1974; "The Hundred Years' War against Judge Kaufman," *National Review*, October 24, 1986; "Some Basic Facts in the Rosenberg-Sobell Case" (listing committee

"sponsors"), reprinted in Hearings Before the Subcommittee on Criminal Justice, Committee on the Judiciary, House of Representatives, December 9, 1982 (hereinafter cited as "1982 Rosenberg Hrg."), 2454; Robert Meeropol interview, March 18, 2020; "2,800 Begin Drive for Rosenbergs," *NYT*, June 18, 1974; Robert Meeropol, *Execution in the Family*, 128; Morgan, "Rosenberg Jury," 105; Allen G. Schwartz, "The Rosenbergs' Trial: Some Considerations about Justice," *NYT*, June 19, 1974.

32. John Mullane, "Legal Aid Lawyers Sum It Up," *NYP*, May 3, 1974; IRK to Arthur L. Liman, May 10, 1974, box 125, folder 11, IRKP; FBI memo, SAC New York to Kelley, May 4, 1975; draft of IRK speech re Learned Hand medal, [undated] 1974, box 74, folder 3, IRKP; IRK note to Lumbard, undated [April 1974], box 63, folder 5, IRKP.

33. Robert Meeropol, *Execution in the Family*, 128–39; Michael Meeropol, *We Are Your Sons*, 2nd ed., 366–69; Jerrold K. Footlick, "The Rosenbergs Retried," *Newsweek*, May 19, 1975, 54.

34. Robert Meeropol interview.

35. Simon Rifkind, "Rosenbergs: The Untainted Verdict," *NYT*, July 14, 1974; Simon Rifkind, "The New Rosenberg Myths," *LAT*, August 25, 1974; Simon Rifkind, "Atom Spies 'Fairly Tried and Convicted,'" *Honolulu Advertiser*, September 5, 1974; Carol Kramer, "Rosenbergs' 'Trial' Goes on after 23 Years," *CT*, December 30, 1974; Ron Shaffer, "Rosenberg Defenders March Again," *WP*, June 20, 1975; Lawrence Christon, "The Rosenberg Rally: Tear Gas and Darrow," *LAT*, February 7, 1975.

36. David Alexander to IRK, January 6, 1975, and IRK to Alexander, January 22, 1975, box 141, folder 3, IRKP; IRK, "A Free Speech for the Class of '75," *NYT Magazine*, June 8, 1975; Letters, *NYT Magazine*, July 20, 1975.

37. Meeropol and Meeropol, *We Are Your Sons*, 2nd ed., 369; Zirin, *Mother Court*, 90–92; Michael Meeropol interview, March 19, 2020; Gerald Rokoff interview, February 28, 2020.

38. "City Bar Leaders Defend Kaufman," *NYLJ*, June 23, 1975; Barbara Campbell, "Bar Group Decries Attacks on Judge in Rosenbergs Case," *NYT*, June 21, 1975; William Claiborne, "ABA Panel Created to Defend Judge in Rosenberg Case," *WP*, January 9, 1976; Robert W. Meserve to IRK, January 18, 1984, and IRK to Meserve, January 23, 1984, box 128, folder 15, IRKP.

39. Robert Meeropol interview; Meeropol, *Execution in the Family*, 139–41; Meeropol and Meeropol, *We Are Your Sons*, 2nd ed., 370–71. For discussions of the struggle to gain access to the FBI's Rosenberg case records see "Freeing the Rosenberg Files," *WP*, November 21, 1975; Allen Weinstein, "The Hiss and Rosenberg Files," *New Republic*, February 14, 1976; Weinstein, "Open Season on 'Open Government,'" *NYT Magazine*, June 10, 1979.

40. Michael Meeropol interview.

41. National Committee to Reopen the Rosenberg Case, "The Kaufman Papers," undated, OFWA.

42. Peter Kihss, "Rosenberg Lawyers Alleging Judicial Impropriety in Case," *NYT*, June 11, 1976; Marshall Perlin to IRK, June 10, 1976 (enclosing Meeropols' press release), box 130, folder 1, IRKP; William Chapman, "Rosenberg

Trial Judge Criticized," *WP*, July 28, 1976; Meeropol and Meeropol, *We Are Your Sons*, 2nd ed., 366; Nat Hentoff, "The Rosenberg Children Nail the Judge Who Made Them Orphans," *Village Voice*, September 20, 1976, 25, 29.

43. Andrew L. Kaufman, *In Memoriam: Vern Countryman*, 113 Harv. L. Rev. 1071 (March 2000); "HLS' Vern Countryman Dies," *Harvard University Gazette*, May 13, 1999; Vern Countryman to James O. Eastland, September 20, 1976, box 155, folder 8, SHP; Rod Townley, "A Specter Is Haunting Irving Kaufman," *Juris Doctor*, November 1977, 24.

44. Tom Goldstein, "Issue over the Rosenberg Case Brings Debate on Role of Judges," *NYT*, March 18, 1977; Arnold Forster to Edward J. Ennis, October 1, 1976, box 155, folder 8, SHP; "Invitation to a Vendetta," *NYT*, March 20, 1977; "They Should Be Ashamed," *NYDN*, March 27, 1977.

45. Vern Countryman, "Out, Damned Spot," *New Republic*, October 8, 1977, 15; Townley, "Specter Is Haunting," 24.

46. Coover, *Public Burning*, 22, 427.

47. "An Open Letter to Judge Irving R. Kaufman," *NYT*, June 19, 1977; Meeropol and Meeropol, *We Are Your Sons*, 2nd ed., 386–87.

48. IRK to Rosenthal, July 24, 1984, A. M. Rosenthal Papers, box 22, folder 24, NYTP; IRK to John Biggs Jr., December 20, 1976, box 26, folder 4, IRKP; Arthur Allen Leff, letter to the editor, *NYT*, March 27, 1977; Robert A. Gorman to Howard Lesnick, November 17, 1976, box 155, folder 8, SHP; Arnold Bauman, letter to the editor, *NYT*, April 17, 1977; Rifkind to Countryman, September 6, 1976, box 155, folder 8, SHP; Lewis F. Powell remarks, April 27, 1977, box 79, folder 17, IRKP.

49. Marilyn Berger, "Judge Irving Kaufman, of Rosenberg Spy Trial and Free Press Rulings, Dies at 81," *NYT*, February 3, 1992, IRKP; Floyd Abrams interview, December 20, 2019; Peter Vaira interview, January 21, 2020; Jack Auspitz interview, October 19, 2016.

50. IRK to Henry J. Taylor, January 11, 1977, box 129, folder 16, IRKP; IRK to Burger, January 22, 1976, box 76, folder 3, IRKP; IRK to Burger, December 9, 1977, box 76, folder 4, IRKP; IRK to Biggs, December 20, 1976, box 24, folder 4, IRKP; Dan Kelly interview, December 20, 2019.

51. Maxine Berman interview, September 11, 2018; John Kaufman interview, June 7, 2016; John and Steven Kaufman interview, October 18, 2016.

52. Berman interview; John Kaufman interview; John and Steven Kaufman interview; IRK to Thomas J. MacBride, March 24, 1981, box 47, folder 5, IRKP; IRK to Armand Deutsch, July 13, 1983, box 49, folder 3, IRKP; IRK to Edward Lasker, July 13, 1983, box 49, folder 3, IRKP; FBI memo, Legat. Rome to Hoover, July 14, 1969; IRK to Bernard G. Segal, May 8, 1970, box 37, folder 2; IRK to John Hanbridge, November 17, 1982, box 130, folder 7, IRKP.

53. Materials relating to the Anglo-American exchanges appear in box 39, folders 4–7, and box 50, folders 5–6, IRKP. IRK to Robert J. Kelleher, May 27, 1980, box 79, folder 4, IRKP.

54. Berman interview; John Kaufman interview; John and Steven Kaufman interview; James Goodale interview, November 19, 2019; Adam Eilenberg interview, March 30, 2020; "White House Guests," *WP*, October 3, 1968; "Dinner Honoring the Federal Judiciary and Guest List," November 20, 1975, WH

Subject File, box 3, folder 503 (November 1, 1975–November 30, 1975), Ford Lib.; IRK acceptance of Ford invitation, November 24, 1975, OFWA.

55. FBI memo, John Malone to Hoover, April 5, 1966; FBI memo, M. A. Jones to "Mr. Bishop," May 31, 1972; FBI memo, ADIC New York (80-917) to Kelly, November 15, 1972.

56. FBI memo, "Legal Counsel" to Kelly, April 25, 1977; FBI memo, Kelly to Hold, Adams, McDermott, April 14, 1977; FBI memo, Kelly to Griffin Bell, June 30, 1977.

57. John and Steven Kaufman interview; IRK note to HRK, undated, OFWA; Spence Toll interview, December 4, 2006; Donald Zoeller interview, April 20, 2016; Richard Abt interview, February 13, 2017; Kelly interview; Jerry Menikof interview, December 16, 2019.

58. IRK to Ramsey Clark, January 29, 1965, box 71, folder 5, IRKP; Berman interview; David du Pont interview, April 3, 2020; John and Steven Kaufman interview.

59. John Kaufman interview; John and Steven Kaufman interview; Rosalind Rosenberg interview, April 27, 2017; Auspitz interview.

60. Berman interview; du Pont interview; John Kaufman and Jane Fishman interview, January 22, 2022.

61. John and Steven Kaufman interview; Kelly interview.

62. IRK to Lord and Lady Widgery, box 130, folder 10, IRKP; IRK to Robert J. Kelleher, June 30, 1977, box 79, folder 4, IRKP.

63. IRK to David B. du Pont, November 11, 1977, box 120, folder 8, IRKP; Rosenberg interview; Tom Dahdouh interview, October 9, 2020.

64. Berman interview.

65. John Kaufman interview; John and Steven Kaufman interview; Rosenberg interview; Daphna Boros interview, December 29, 2020.

66. John Kaufman interview; John and Steven Kaufman interview; Jean Steele to IRK, June 29, 1983, and IRK to Steele, August 2, 1983, box 129, folder 15, IRKP.

67. Menikoff interview; Michael Meeropol interview.

68. Robert W. Meserve to IRK, January 18, 1984, box 128, folder 15, IRKP; minutes of the American Bar Association Board of Governors, October 1969–January 1992 \ 1977 \ American Bar Center Chicago, October 13–14, 1977, 1905–6, and July 11, 1977, 1970, and October 14–15, 1976, 2099–2100, OFWA.

69. Townley, "Specter Is Haunting," 24; Meeropol and Meeropol, *We Are Your Sons*, 2nd ed., 385; Meeropol, *Execution in the Family*, 149–51.

70. Sol Stern and Ronald Radosh, "The Deceits of the Rosenberg Case," *WP*, June 17, 1979; Sol Stern and Ronald Radosh, "The Hidden Rosenberg Case," *New Republic*, June 23, 1979, 13; Sol Stern and Ronald Radosh, letter to the editor, "The Need to Reopen the Rosenberg Case for Public Scrutiny," *NYT*, July 26, 1979; Radosh and Milton, *Rosenberg File*.

71. Walter Goodman, "For a Spirited Audience at Town Hall, 'The Rosenberg File' Remains Open," *NYT*, October 22, 1983; 1982 Rosenberg Hrg.

72. Zion, *Autobiography*, 64–66; von Hoffman, *Citizen Cohn*; Sidney Zion, "Roy Stories: Roy Cohn Speaks from beyond the Grave," *New York*, February 22, 1988, 41.

73. Associated Press report, untitled, November 1976, OFWA.

15. Some Form of Justice

1. White, *Breaking Silence*, 5–7; Harrison Smith, "Joel Filártiga, Paraguayan Doctor Who Battled Stroessner Dictatorship, Dies at 86," *WP*, July 9, 2019.

2. White, *Breaking Silence*, xx, 12.

3. Richard Alan White, "Paraguay: Latin America's Neglected Chamber of Horrors," *WP*, May 28, 1978; Ben S. Stephasky, *Report of the Commission of Enquiry into Human Rights in Paraguay of the International League of Human Rights*, September 1976; United States Institute of Peace, *Truth Commission: Paraguay*, June 1, 2004, Findings, www.usip.org/publications/2004/06/truth-commission-paraguay.

4. *Filártiga v. Peña-Irala*, 79 Civ. 917 (S.D.N.Y.), Hearing, February 12, 1982, in Aceves, *Anatomy of Torture* (hereinafter cited as "Filártiga Damages Hrg."), 626–27, 633; Kenneth Clark, "Murder in Paraguay," *CT*, April 18, 1991; *Making of Filártiga*, 258 (remarks of Robert White).

5. White, *Breaking Silence*, 14; Filártiga Damages Hrg., 628.

6. White, *Breaking Silence*, 10–11, 35–37; Filártiga Damages Hrg., 619–20; Aceves, *Anatomy of Torture*, 18–19 (quoting Plaintiff's Post-trial Memorandum of Law and Facts, 3–4).

7. White, *Breaking Silence*, 19–20.

8. Aceves, *Anatomy of Torture*, 20–22; *Filártiga* SDNY, José Lugo Affidavit; White, *Breaking Silence*, 19–21, 44–47, 98–100, 113–14, 143, 188; Filártiga Damages Hrg., 622–23, 632–33. For the historical background to the Alien Tort Statute see *Sosa v. Alvarez-Machain*, 542 U.S. 692, 716–17 (2004).

9. White, *Breaking Silence*, 74, 138, 141–46, 151, 164–66, 178.

10. Aceves, *Anatomy of Torture*, 28–29, 617 (quoting Dolly Filártiga); White, *Breaking Silence*, 183; Selwyn Raab, "Paraguayan Alien Tied to Murders in Native Land," *NYT*, April 5, 1979; Carla Hall, "In Paraguay, a Death in the Family," *WP*, March 25, 1982.

11. White, *Breaking Silence*, 191–211; Aceves, *Anatomy of Torture*, 30–31; *Making of Filártiga*, 252 (remarks of Peter Weiss).

12. Peter Weiss interview, February 25, 2019; 28 U.S.C. § 1350.

13. White, *Breaking Silence*, 214–21; Selwyn Raab, "U.S. Judge Rules Peña Can be Sued Here over Slaying in Paraguay," *NYT*, April 10, 1979; *Making of Filártiga*, 252.

14. Weiss interview; *Making of Filártiga*, 253; White, *Breaking Silence*, 220; *ITT v. Vencap, Ltd.*, 519 F.2d 1001, 1015 (2d Cir. 1975); *Dreyfus v. Von Finck*, 534 F.2d 24, 30–31 (2d Cir. 1976).

15. *Making of Filártiga*, 255; *Filártiga* 2d Cir., Appellant's Brief; *id.* (quoting Emerich de Vattel, *The Law of Nations* §§ 232–33 (1849)); *id.*, Appellee's Brief.

16. Weiss interview; White, *Breaking Silence*, 244.

17. *Filártiga* 2d Cir., Transcript of Oral Argument.

18. Weiss interview; White, *Breaking Silence*, 248–49; *Making of Filártiga*, 256 (remarks of Rhonda Copelon).

19. Bruce Kraus interview, March 6, 2019; Harold Hongju Koh, "*Filártiga v. Peña-Irala*: Judicial Internalization into Domestic Law of the Customary

International Law Norm Against Torture," in Noyes, Dickinson, and Janis, *International Law Stories*, 50–51.

20. Kraus interview; Aceves, *Anatomy of Torture*, 41–51; *Making of Filártiga*, 260–61 (remarks of John Huerta); *Filártiga* 2d Cir., Memorandum for the United States as Amicus Curiae; White, *Breaking Silence*, 252.

21. *Filártiga v. Peña-Irala*, 630 F.2d 876 (2d Cir. 1980).

22. IRK, *Eulogy for Murray Gurfein*, 2 CARDOZO L. REV. 1 (1980).

23. IRK, "A Legal Remedy for International Torture?," *NYT Magazine*, November 9, 1980; Kraus interview; White, *Breaking Silence*, 257–58.

24. "Foreign Torture, American Justice," *NYT*, August 20, 1980; Hall, "In Paraguay"; "Brooklyn Judge Rules on Killing in Paraguay," *NYT*, January 15, 1984.

25. Aceves, *Anatomy of Torture*, 91–143; Neil A. Lewis, "At the Bar; Suing Dictators (and Similar Types) Here for Violations Committed Elsewhere," *NYT*, March 3, 1995; John Sullivan, "The World; American Justice Tackles Rights Issues Abroad," *NYT*, September 3, 2000; Joseph Berger, "After Scars of Holocaust, Fresh Pain over Money," *NYT*, May 8, 2005.

26. Bill Miller and Christine Haughey, "War Crimes Trials Find a U.S. Home, Bosnian Women Sue under a 1789 Law," *WP*, August 9, 2000; *Making of Filártiga*, 276–77 (remarks of Sandra Coliver); Koh, "Judicial Internalization," in Noyes, Dickinson, and Janis, *International Law Stories*, 60, 65–72; Smith, "Joel Filártiga" (quoting John Bellinger); Remarks of James Oakes, Second Circuit Judicial Conference, June 2, 1992, OFWA.

27. *Making of Filártiga*, 258 (remarks of Robert White); White, *Breaking Silence*, 285; Larry Rohter, "Dramatizing a Family That Took on Dictatorship," *NYT*, April 18, 1991.

16. Keep the Beacon Burning

1. Arnold H. Lubasch, "Dinner for Kaufman to Mark His 30 Years on the Federal Bench," *NYT*, April 10, 1980; Peter M. Brown, memo re IRK dinner, and IRK to Brownell, April 11, 1980, box 90, folder K, HBP; Mulligan, *Mulligan's Law*, 107–8; Ken Plevan interview, November 22, 2019.

2. Jerry Menikoff interview, December 16, 2019; Richard Friedman interview, March 4 and 27, 2019; Dorsen, *Henry Friendly*, 120–21; IRK to Burger, April 18, 1986, box 35, folder 1, IRKP; Wilfred Feinberg, *The Office of Chief Judge of a Federal Court of Appeals*, 53 FORDHAM L. REV. 369 (1984).

3. Wilfred Feinberg, *Office of Chief Judge*, 385; Jon O. Newman interview, May 17, 2016; minutes, Special Session of the US Court of Appeals for the Second Circuit, June 26, 1978, 24, box 43, folder 9, IRKP; George Pratt interview, April 8, 2016; Tom Goldstein, "U.S. Judges Here Reject Rules for Trial Lawyers," *NYT*, December 21, 1975; Arnold H. Lubasch, "Kaufman Assails Judge's Criticism," *NYT*, January 11, 1976; "New Criticism Is Directed at Nation's Judicial System," *NYLJ*, August 12, 1970; IRK, "Courts and Parajudges," *NYT*, January 29, 1972; IRK, *Judicial Reform in the Next Century*, 29 STANFORD L.

Rev. 1 (1976); IRK press release, "State of the Circuit Address," August 9, 1977, box 106, folder 5, IRKP; Tom Goldstein, "U.S. Judge Decries Rise in Civil Suits, Slowness and Cost," *NYT*, September 10, 1977; Erwin Griswold to IRK, January 21, 1985, box, 123, folder 10, IRKP.

4. Linda Greenhouse interview, November 12, 2019; Kenneth Feinberg interview, January 17, 2020.

5. Greenhouse interview; "A Judge Who Likes Action," *NYT*, July 29, 1983; IRK to Millones, August 2, 1983, A. M. Rosenthal Papers, box 22, folder 24, NYTP.

6. Greenhouse interview; IRK memo to Wilfred Feinberg, April 15, 1982, box 78, folder 1, IRKP. IRK's use of the title "Chief Judge Emeritus" appears in IRK, *Fair Pay and Judicial Independence*, 64 Judicature 434 (May 1981), and in a typed addition to his form letterhead. Pratt interview.

7. Roland Evans and Robert Novak, "Justice Dept. Holding Cocked Pistol against Dodd in Tax-Evasion Case," *WP*, November 27, 1969.

8. Drew Pearson and Jack Anderson, "Mideast Crisis Rallies Aid for Dodd," *WP*, June 9, 1967; Drew Pearson, "Memo for Jack Anderson," May 29, 1967, OFWA; Edward J. McLaughlin to IRK, February 12, 1971, box 129, folder 2, IRKP; IRK to John H. Hughes, January 29, 1971, box 129, folder 2, IRKP; von Hoffman, *Citizen Cohn*, 459.

9. Burger to IRK, October 23, 1979, box 76, folder 6, IRKP.

10. IRK reports, memos, and correspondence on the commission and the effort to raise judicial salaries appear in boxes 46–53, IRKP. "Kaufman Criticizes Judge-Ouster Plan," *NYT*, November 6, 1978; "Surviving Justice," *NYT*, January 10, 1983; Stuart Taylor, "Federal Panel Urged to Endorse $95,000 Salary for District Judges," *NYT*, November 8, 1980; *Hearings Before the Quadrennial Pay Commission Task Force of the House Committee on Post Office and Civil Service*, 97th Cong. 159–60 (February 17, 18, 24, 25, and March 11, 1981) (statement of Ralph Nader), in box 53, folder 2, IRKP; Irving Shapiro to Harold Tyler, December 3, 1980, box 47, folder 3, IRKP (attaching Chamber of Commerce press release); Burger to IRK, February 24, 1983, box 49, folder 2, IRKP; Wilfred Feinberg note to IRK, December 29, 1980, box 51, folder 7, IRKP (attaching *NYDN* column); IRK to Alfred R. Stern, December 3, 1982, box 126, folder 9, IRKP.

11. Correspondence to IRK from colleagues regarding the judicial branch committee appears in boxes 47–49, IRKP. IRK to James Oakes, August 20, 1981, box 48, folder 2, IRKP; IRK to Sterry Waterman, March 9, 1981, box 47, folder 5, IRKP.

12. Anthony R. Dolan, in Griffin and Colucci, *Rogue Town*, foreword; Dolan email, February 6, 2020; "Text of President's Speech on Drive against Crime," *NYT*, October 15, 1982.

13. "Crime Panel Possibility," *NYT*, October 22, 1982; Leslie Maitland Werner, "President Chooses 20 as Members of Organized Crime Commission," *NYT*, July 29, 1983; Dolan memo to Donald T. Regan, October 1, 1985, WH Office of Records Management (hereinafter cited as "WHORM"), Subject File, box 101, FG006-01, 347613–354899, Reagan Lib. Regarding Dolan and the

commission see James Harmon interview, January 31, 2020; Leslie Maitland Werner, "Crime Commission Bogs Down in Power Struggle," *NYT*, October 7, 1983. Regarding IRK's expected assumption of senior status see Peter Vaira interview, January 21, 2020. IRK to Burger, May 9, 1983, box 49, folder 3, IRKP.

14. Ronald J. Ostrow, "Judge's Refusal to Sign President's Crime Panel Pact Creates a Dilemma," *LAT*, December 14, 1983; Memo from Fred Fielding to Aram Bakshian, July 27, 1983, WHORM Subject File, FG 393, folder 073514, Reagan Lib.; *In re Subpoena of . . . Lorenzo Scaduto*, 763 F.2d 1191 (11th Cir. 1985); Vaira interview; Mary Thornton, "Crime Panel Director Resigns in Conflict with Chief," *WP*, October 1, 1983; Leslie Maitland Werner, "Kaufman Declines to Sign Secrecy Pact as Crime Unit Head," *NYT*, December 3, 1983; Ostrow, "Judge's Refusal"; "Judge Who Likes Action"; Werner, "Crime Commission Bogs Down."

15. Ronald J. Ostrow, "Organized Crime Panel to Hold First Meetings," *LAT*, November 22, 1983; Samuel Skinner interview, January 30, 2020; Harmon interview.

16. PCOC Records of Hearings II, III, V, March 14, 1984, October 23–25, 1984, February 20–21, 1985; Leslie Maitland Werner, "U.S. Crime Panel Seeks New Laws to Halt the Laundering of Money," *NYT*, October 31, 1984; Ed Magnuson and Kenneth W. Banta, "Triads and the Yakuza," *Time*, November 4, 1984; Michael S. Serrill, "The Mob Lawyer," *Time*, March 25, 1985; Ronald Koziol and John O'Brien, "Teamsters Boss Testifies in a Symphony of the 5th," *CT*, April 24, 1985.

17. Leslie Maitland Werner, "Inquiry on Crime, a Year Old, Has Little to Show," *NYT*, July 31, 1984; Ronald J. Ostrow and Robert L. Jackson, "Critics Accuse Crime Panel of Assault on Civil Liberties," *LAT*, November 23, 1984.

18. Andy Pasztor, "Anti-drug Report Seeks United Effort by U.S. Agencies," *WSJ*, March 4, 1986; PCOC Report: *America's Habit: Drug Abuse, Drug Trafficking, and Organized Crime*, March 1986, 483–85; Joel Brinkley, "Panel Members Say They Weren't Given Final Crime Report," *NYT*, March 6, 1986; Ronald J. Ostrow, "Crime Panel Member Scores Drug Tests," *LAT*, March 6, 1986; "The Mob Commission Moves On," *NYT*, March 8, 1986; PCOC Report: *The Edge: Organized Crime, Business, and Labor Unions*, March 1986; Kenneth B. Noble, "Crime Panel Urges Broad U.S. Attack on Teamsters," *NYT*, March 7, 1986.

19. PCOC Report: *The Impact: Organized Crime Today*, April 1986, 173–79, 425; Skinner interview; Phillip Shenon, "U.S. Crime Panel: Discord to the End," *NYT*, April 4, 1986.

20. 18 U.S.C. § 1956; Harmon interview; Judith Haverman, "Reagan Signs Antidrug Bill," *WP*, October 28, 1986; Jacobs, *Mobsters, Unions and Feds*, 138–60, 203–37; Sean Gardiner, "Mob's Hold on Unions Isn't What It Used to Be," *WSJ*, March 4, 1986.

21. Harmon interview; Shenon, "Discord"; Philip Shenon, "Crime Panel Issues Its Final Report," *NYT*, April 2, 1986.

22. William R. Greer, "Judge Kaufman Terms Crime Role a Duty," *NYT*, June 23, 1985; IRK, "Judges Must Speak Out," *NYT*, January 30, 1982; IRK to Mrs. Irwin Rosenberg, June 21, 1984, box 128, folder 18, IRKP.

23. Bartley Deamer interview, February 16, 2017; IRK to Burger, November 18, 1971, box 76, folder 2, IRKP; IRK to Burger, December 14, 1976, box 76, folder 2, IRKP; IRK note to Burger, March 22, 1978, box 76, folder 4, IRKP; IRK note to Burger, July 24, 1972, box 76, folder 2, IRKP.

24. Arnold H. Lubasch, "Dinner for Kaufman to Mark His 30 Years on the Federal Bench," NYT, April 10, 1980; IRK, "Helping the Public Understand and Accept Judicial Decisions," *American Bar Association Journal*, November 1977, 1567, 1569.

25. Graetz and Greenhouse, *Burger Court*, 14; Keck, *Most Activist Supreme Court*; Abrams Chayes, *Public Law Litigation and the Burger Court*, 96 Harv. L. Rev. 4, 7 (Nov. 1982).

26. *McMann v. Richardson*, 397 U.S. 759 (1970); National Registry of Exonerations Report, *Innocents Who Plead Guilty*, November 24, 2015, www.law.umich.edu/special/exoneration/Documents/NRE.Guilty.Plea.Article1.pdf.

27. *Montanye v. Haymes*, 427 U.S. 236 (1976); *Meachum v. Fano*, 427 U.S. 215 (1976); Max Friedman interview, November 25, 2019; *Bell v. Wolfish*, 441 U.S. 520, 540, 562 (1979); *O'Lone v. Estate of Shabazz*, 482 U.S. 342, 358–59 (1987) (Brennan, J., dissenting); Herman Schwartz, "The Burger Court and the Prisoner," in Schwartz, *Burger Years*.

28. Steven V. Roberts, "High U.S. Officials Express Outrage, Asking for New Laws on Insanity Plea," NYT, June 23, 1982; IRK, "The Insanity Plea on Trial," *NYT Magazine*, August 8, 1982; 18 U.S.C. § 17; Leslie Maitland Werner, "Judicial Nominee's Rejection Assailed," NYT, April 2, 1985.

29. *Keyes v. School Dist. No. 1, Denver, CO*, 413 U.S. 189, 204–13 (1973); Sugrue, *Sweet Land of Liberty*, 478–80; Delmont, *Why Busing Failed*, 5, 211; *Milliken v. Bradley*, 418 U.S. 717 (1974); *Oklahoma v. Dowell*, 498 U.S. 237 (1991); *Freeman v. Pitts*, 503 U.S. 467 (1992); *Parents Involved in Community Schools v. Seattle School Dist. No. 1*, 551 U.S. 701, 731, 747–48 (2005); Orfield and Frankenberg, *Brown at 60*, 39–40; Laura Meckler and Kate Rabinowitz, "The Lines That Divide: School District Boundaries Often Stymie Integration," WP, December 16, 2019; Laura Meckler and Kate Rabinowitz, "The Changing Face of School Integration," WP, September 12, 2019.

30. *Johnson v. N.Y. State Educ. Dept.*, 449 F.2d 871 (2d Cir. 1971); *San Antonio Indep. School Dist. v. Rodriguez*, 411 U.S. 1, 55 (1973).

31. *Sosa v. Alvarez-Machain*, 542 U.S. 692 (2004); *Kiobel v. Royal Dutch Petroleum Co.*, 569 U.S. 108 (2013); *Jesner v. Arab Bank, PLC*, 138 S. Ct. 1386 (2018); *Nestle USA, Inc. v. Doe*, 141 S. Ct. 1931 (2021); Peter Weiss interview, February 25, 2019; Peter Weiss email, April 1, 2019.

32. *United States v. Gantzer*, 810 F.2d 349 (2d Cir. 1987); *McConnell v. FEC*, 540 U.S. 93 (2003); *Randall v. Sorrell*, 548 U.S. 230 (2006); *Citizens United v. FEC*, 558 U.S. 310 (2010); *Mahanoy Area School Dist. v. B.L. by and through Levy*, 141 S. Ct. 2038 (2021); *Carroll v. Blinken*, 957 F.2d 991 (2d Cir. 1992); *Bd. of Regents, U. Wisconsin System v. Southworth*, 529 U.S. 217 (2000).

33. *Brandon v. Bd. of Ed. of Guilderland Cent. School Dist.*, 635 F.2d 971, 973, 978 (1980); Arnold H. Lubasch, "Court Uphold Ban on School Prayers," NYT, November 18, 1980; *Bd. of Ed. of Westside Community Schools v. Mergens*, 496 U.S.

226 (1990); Leonard Garth to IRK, June 13, 1990, and IRK to Garth, June 22, 1990, box 78, folder 12, IRKP.

34. *Int'l Society for Krishna Consciousness, Inc. v. Barber*, 650 F.2d 430, 447 (2d Cir. 1981), *abrogated by*, 452 U.S. 640 (1981); IRK note, undated, box 76, folder 6, IRKP.

35. IRK, "A Tribute to Chief Justice Burger," June 20, 1986, box 76, folder 6, IRKP; IRK to Burger, May 5, 1986, box 76, folder 6, IRKP.

36. "Reagan Assails High Court, Says New Justices Needed," WP, February 22, 1980; "Excerpts from Attorney General's Remarks on Plans of Justice Department," NYT, October 30, 1981; Stuart Taylor, "The Attorney General and Rulings of Federal Courts," NYT, October 31, 1981.

37. IRK, "Charting a Judicial Pedigree," NYT, January 24, 1981; IRK to Reagan, January 30, 1981, box 128, folder 12, IRKP.

38. Linda Greenhouse, "Busing Bill Backed by Administration," NYT, May 7, 1982; Mark Agrast, *Judge Roberts and the Court-Stripping Movement*, Center for American Progress, September 2, 2005, americanprogress.org/issues/courts/news/2005/09/02/1622/judge-roberts-and-the-court-stripping-movement; IRK, "Congress v. the Court," *NYT Magazine*, September 20, 1981.

39. IRK, "Keeping Politics Out of the Court," *NYT Magazine*, December 9, 1984.

40. IRK, *The Anatomy of Decisionmaking*, 53 Fordham L. Rev. 1 (Oct. 1984); David E. Sanger, "Kaufman Defends Using Laws' Intent," NYT, December 30, 1984; Rosenthal memo to Edward Klein, July 24, 1984, A. M. Rosenthal Papers, box 22, folder 24, NYTP; *Tales Out of Court*, WSJ, January 14, 1985.

41. Edwin Meese III, *Construing the Constitution*, 19 U.C. Davis L. Rev. 22, 25, 29 (1985). For descriptions of originalism more generally see Keck 115–19, 151–60; Segall, *Originalism as Faith*, 56–65; Robert H. Bork, "The Case against Political Judging," *National Review*, December 8, 1989, 23, 24; Antonin Scalia, *Originalism: The Lesser Evil*, 57 Cincinnati L. Rev. 849, 857 (1989).

42. *Evans v. Lynn*, 537 F.2d 571 610 (2d Cir. 1975) (IRK, dissenting).

43. IRK notes, undated, box 116, folder 10, IRKP; IRK, "Statement in Connection with Assuming Duties of Chief Judge of the U.S. Court of Appeals on May 28, 1973," box 118, folder 1, IRKP; IRK, "By and Large, We Succeed," *Time*, May 5, 1980; IRK to Charles L. Brieant, March 11, 1986, box 74, folder 14, IRKP.

44. IRK, "What Did the Founding Fathers Intend?," *NYT Magazine*, February 23, 1986.

45. IRK, "No Way to Interpret the Constitution," NYT, January 2, 1987.

46. IRK to Meese, May 2, 1986, and Meese note to IRK, January 19, 1988, box 619, folder K11 "Kaufman, Irving R. (1986)," EMP.

47. IRK remarks at dinner inaugurating Kaufman Fellowships, January 27, 1990, box 124, folder 2, IRKP.

48. Dorsen, *Henry Friendly*, 358; Newman interview.

49. IRK memo to file, October 6, 1989, box 123, folder 16, IRKP; Rifkin to Arthur Krim, March 19, 1981, box 128, folder 15, IRKP; José Cabranes interview, December 9, 2019.

50. Correspondence and memoranda related to Annenberg's gift appear in box 116, folder 9, and box 123, folder 16, IRKP. See also Paul Tarr, "Clark Announces $1 Million Endowment; Defends Public Interest Reorganization," *Harvard Law Record*, October 20, 1989; Susan B. Glasser and Tara A. Nyak, "Law School Gets $1M for Public Service," *Harvard Crimson*, October 11, 1989.

51. IRK note to Rifkind, September 17, 1979, box 128, folder 14, IRKP; memo to Carter from Stu Eizenstat, Steve Simmons, and Frank White, "Bell Memo on Reception for Judges and Lawyers," January 31, 1979, WH Central File–Name File Collection, Carter Lib.; letter re IRK and Medal of Freedom, undated, box 619, folder K11 "Kaufman, Irving R. (1986)," EMP.

52. IRK to Meese, May 2, 1986, box 619, folder K11, "Kaufman, Irving R. (1986)," EMP; Arthur B. Culvahouse memos to Rhett Dawson, April 9, 1987, and Frederick Ryan, September 17, 1987, WHORM, Subject File, MA020, Reagan Lib.; Reagan to IRK, July 1, 1987, box 126, folder 5, IRKP.

53. Ruth Marcus and David Hoffman, "U.S. Judge Retires, Gets Reagan Award," *WP*, September 19, 1987; subject interview [anonymous], October 7, 2020; Andrew Klein interview, October 29, 2020; Tom Dahdouh interview, October 9, 2020.

54. Ernest P. Ferguson, "Knighthood in America," *Baltimore Sun*, October 11, 1987; Ruth Marcus and David Hoffman, "Honoring Burger: Not Today," *WP*, October 7, 1987.

55. IRK to Kenneth Duberstein, December 14, 1987, box 126, folder 5, IRKP; "Remarks by the President at Medal of Freedom Ceremony," box 126, folder 7, IRKP. IRK's Medal of Freedom ceremony is on YouTube at youtube.com/watch?v=aPc6pjXjEWo.

Epilogue

1. HRK card to IRK, June 21, 1991, OFWA.

2. Richard Abt interview, February 13, 2017.

3. Patrick Hanlon to Susan Estrich, May 23, 1977, box 123, folder 14, IRKP; IRK to Philip Heyman, March 29, 1982, box 124, folder 9, IRKP; Andrew Klein interview, October 29, 2020; "Law Clerks Wanted," *National Law Journal*, November 17, 1986.

4. IRK memo to Walter Mansfield, June 1, 1981, box 43, folder 3, IRKP; IRK to William Guste, May 6, 1985, box 123, folder 10, IRKP; IRK memo to Wilfred Feinberg, April 14, 1982, box 78, folder 1, IRKP; Wendy Leibowitz interview, October 5, 2020; Julian Bach to IRK, May 28, 1982, and IRK to Bach, June 1, 1982, box 119, folder 3, IRKP.

5. Daphna Boros memo, August 5, 1991, OFWA.

6. Klein interview; Tom Dahdouh interview, October 9, 2020.

7. Bruce Kraus interview, March 6, 2019; Daphna Boros interview, December 29, 2020.

8. Kevin Merida, "The Seniority of Strom Thurmond," *WP*, April 26, 2001; Amanda Robert, "Benching Judges: Knowing When It's Time to Hang Up the Robe," *American Bar Association Journal*, December-January 2020–21, 54; IRK, *Chilling Judicial Independence*, 88 YALE L. J. 681, 709 (1979).

9. John Kaufman and Jane Fishman interview, January 22, 2022.

10. Jerome Frank, *Law and the Modern Mind* (New York: Brentano's 1930), 114; Norman Dorsen and Christopher L. Eisgruber, *Judicial Biography Symposium—Preface*, 70 N.Y.U. L. Rev. 485 (June 1995); IRK, *The Anatomy of Decisionmaking*, 53 Fordham L. Rev. 1, 20 (Oct. 1984).

11. IRK statement upon assuming chief judgeship, May 28, 1973, box 118, folder 1, IRKP (quoting Cardozo, *Judicial Process*, 137).

12. Stern and Wermiel, *Justice Brennan*, 234 (quoting Bickel).

13. Sidney Hook, "Echoes of the Rosenberg Case: An Autobiographical Postscript," *American Spectator*, January 1989, 18; Linda Greenhouse interview, November 12, 2019; White, *Breaking Silence*, 257–58.

14. IRK, "A Free Speech for the Class of '75," *NYT Magazine*, June 8, 1975.

15. IRK "Draft-Extemporaneous Remarks," undated, box 29, folder 4, IRKP.

16. IRK, *Anatomy*, 15; Michael Tabak interview, March 24, 2020; IRK, *Judicial Review of Agency Action: A Judge's Unburdening*, 45 N.Y.U. L. Rev. 201 (1970).

17. Thomas Healy, "The Unlikely Birth of Free Speech," *NYT*, November 9, 2019; Piero Calamandrei, *Eulogy of Judges* (Clark, NJ: Lawbook Exchange, 2008), 62.

18. Ruth Bader Ginsburg, "Remarks for Touro Synagogue (Newport, Rhode Island) Celebration of the 350th Anniversary of Jews in America," August 22, 2004, www.supremecourt.gov/publicinfo/speeches/viewspeech/sp_08-22-04; Arthur Amron interview, October 1, 2020. For a discussion of Jewish American judges in the twentieth century see Jeffrey B. Morris, "The American Jewish Judge: An Appraisal on the Occasion of the Bicentennial," *Jewish Social Studies* 38, no. 3–4 (Summer–Autumn 1976): 195–223.

19. Millones memo to Rosenthal, August 3, 1983, A. M. Rosenthal Papers, box 22, folder 24 NYTP; Zion, *Autobiography*, 61–62.

20. "A Judge Who Likes Action," *NYT*, July 29, 1983.

21. George Pratt interview, April 8, 2016; IRK to Ernest Friesen, November 21, 1969, box 34, folder 10, IRKP; Robert Gorman interview, April 12, 2016; Carol Lam interview, November 6, 2020.

22. "Price of Justice Is Toil, Effort, Judge Declares," *L.A. Examiner*, August 27, 1958.

23. Adam Eilenberg interview, March 30, 2021; Neal Karlen, *The Story of Yiddish: How a Mish-Mosh of Languages Saved the Jews* (New York: William Morrow, 2008), 1383–39.

24. IRK, *Anatomy*, 2, 16.

Bibliography

Abraham, Henry J. *Justices, Presidents and Senators: A History of the U.S. Supreme Court Appointments from Washington to Clinton*. New York: Rowman & Littlefield, 1999.

Abrams, Floyd. *Speaking Freely: Trials of the First Amendment*. New York: Viking, 2005.

Aceves, William J. *The Anatomy of Torture: A Documentary History of Filartiga v. Pena-Irala*. Boston: Martinus Nijhoff, 2007.

Allen, Oliver. *The Tiger: The Rise and Fall of Tammany Hall*. Boston: Da Capo, 1993.

Altman, James M. *Considering the A.B.A.'s 1908 Canons of Ethics*, 2008 PROF. LAW 235 (2008).

American Bar Association. *Canons of Judicial Ethics*. 1924. americanbar.org/content/dam/aba/administrative/professional_responsibility/pic_migrated/1924_canons.pdf. Accessed November 12, 2021.

Attica: The Official Report of the New York States Special Commission on Attica. New York: Praeger, 1972.

Belknap, Michael, ed. *American Political Trials*. Westport, CT: Greenwood, 1981.

——. *Cold War Political Justice: The Smith Act, the Communist Party, and American Civil Liberties*. Westport, CT: Praeger, 1977.

Bell, Jonathan. *The Liberal State on Trial: The Cold War and Politics in the Truman Years*. New York: Columbia University Press, 2004.

Bennett, James. *I Chose Prison*. New York: Knopf, 1970.

Berle, Milton, and Haskel Frankel. *Milton Berle: An Autobiography*. New York: Applause, 1974.

Bickel, Alexander M. "The Rosenberg Affair." *Commentary*, January 1966.

Birmingham, Stephen. *"The Rest of Us": The Rise of America's Eastern European Jews*. Boston: Little, Brown, 1984.

Brands, H. W. *The Strange Death of American Liberalism*. New Haven, CT: Yale University Press, 2001.

Brennan, Sheila M. *Popular Images of American Women in the 1950s and Their Impact on Ethel Rosenberg's Trial and Conviction*, 14 WOMEN'S RTS. L. REP. 43 (Winter 1992).

Brennan, William. *Constitutional Adjudication*, 40 NOTRE DAME LAWYER 559 (August 1965).

Brief, Richard P., ed. *Accountancy in Transition*. New York: Garland, 1982.

Burak, H. Paul. *History of the United States District Court for the Southern District of New York*. New York: Federal Bar Association of New York, New Jersey and Connecticut, 1962.

Burkholder, Zoe. *An African American Dilemma: A History of School Integration and Civil Rights in the North*. New York: Oxford University Press, 2021.

Cahan, Abraham. *The Rise of David Levinsky*. Harper & Bros., 1917. Reprint, with introduction and notes by Jules Chametzky, New York: Penguin Books, 1993.

Cardozo, Benjamin. *The Nature of the Judicial Process*. New Haven, CT: Yale University Press, 1921. Reprint, Mineola, NY: Dover, 2005.

Clune, Lori. *Executing the Rosenbergs: Death and Diplomacy in a Cold War World*. New York: Oxford University Press, 2016.

Considine, Bob. *It's All News to Me*. New York: Meredith, 1967.

A Conversation with J. Edward Lumbard: An Oral History Project of Columbia University and the New York Bar Foundation. Albany: Charles Evans Hughes, 1980.

Coover, Robert. *A Public Burning*. New York: Viking, 1977.

Cray, Ed. *Chief Justice: A Biography of Earl Warren*. New York: Simon & Schuster, 1997.

Daniel, Hawthorne. *Judge Medina*. New York: Wilfred Funk, 1952.

Dean, John W. *The Rehnquist Choice: The Untold Story of the Nixon Appointment That Redefined the Supreme Court*. New York: Free Press, 2001.

Delmont, Matthew F. *Why Busing Failed: Race, Media, and the National Resistance to School Desegregation*. Los Angeles: University of California Press, 2016.

Dershowitz, Alan M. *The Best Defense*. New York: Random House, 1982.

Dillard, Irving, ed. *The Spirit of Liberty: Papers and Addresses of Learned Hand*. New York: Vintage, 1959.

Doctorow, E. L. *The Book of Daniel*. New York: Random House, 1971.

Dodson, Dan W., ed. *Crisis in the Public Schools: Racial Segregation, Northern Style*. New York: Council for American Unity, 1965.

Dorsen, David. *Henry Friendly: Greatest Judge of His Era*. Cambridge, MA: Belknap Press of Harvard University Press, 2012.

Douglas, William O. *The Court Years: 1939–1975*. New York: Random House, 1980.

Drinker, Henry S. *Legal Ethics*. New York: Columbia University Press, 1953.

Eskridge, William N. *Gaylaw: Challenging the Apartheid of the Closet*. Cambridge, MA: Harvard University Press, 1999.

Federal Bar Council (Patricia A. McGowan and Michael P. Zeig, eds.). *Courthouses of the Second Circuit: Their Architecture, History, and Stories*. New York: Avanthus, 2015.

Ferber, Michael, and Staughton Lynd. *The Resistance*. Boston: Beacon, 1971.

Fineberg, S. Andhil. *The Rosenberg Case: Fact and Fiction*. New York: Oceana, 1953.

Forstall, Marion. "Voices and Profiles of New Rochelle's Rich and Colorful History." Unpublished oral histories, New Rochelle Public Library, 1980.

Fox, Stephen. *Transatlantic: Samuel Cunard, Isambard Brunel, and the Great Atlantic Steamships*. New York: HarperCollins, 2003.

Frank, Jerome. *Courts on Trial: Myth and Reality in American Justice*. Princeton, NJ: Princeton University Press, 1950.

———. *Law and the Modern Mind*. New York: Brentano's, 1930.

Freed, Donald. *Inquest*. New York: Hill & Wang, 1969.

Fried, Albert, ed. *McCarthyism: The Great American Red Scare; A Documentary History*. New York: Oxford University Press, 1997.

Fried, Richard M. *Nightmare in Red: The McCarthy Era in Perspective*. New York: Oxford University Press, 1990.

Gannon, Robert I. *Up to the Present: The Story of Fordham*. New York: Doubleday, 1967.

Gentry, Curt. *J. Edgar Hoover: The Man and the Secrets*. New York: W. W. Norton, 1991.

Gillon, Steven M. *Politics and Vision: The ADA and American Liberalism, 1947–1985*. New York: Oxford University Press, 1987.

Goldman, Sheldon. *Picking Federal Judges: Lower Court Selection from Roosevelt through Reagan*. New Haven, CT: Yale University Press, 1997.

Goldstein, Alvin H. *The Unquiet Death of Julius and Ethel Rosenberg*. New York: Lawrence Hill, 1975.

Goldstein, Tom. *The News at Any Cost: How Journalists Compromise Their Ethics to Shape the News*. New York: Simon & Schuster, 1985.

Goodale, James C. *Fighting for the Press: The Inside Story of the Pentagon Papers and Other Battles*. New York: CUNY Journalism, 2013.

Gould, Milton. *The Witness Who Spoke with God*. New York: Viking, 1979.

Graetz, Michael J., and Linda Greenhouse. *The Burger Court and the Rise of the Judicial Right*. New York: Simon & Schuster, 2016.

Griffin, Dennis N., and Vito Colucci Jr. *Rogue Town*. Las Vegas: Houdini, 2013.

Gronlund, Mimi Clark. *Supreme Court Justice Tom C. Clark: A Life of Service*. Austin: University of Texas Press, 2010.

Gunther, Gerald. *Learned Hand: The Man and the Judge*. New York: Knopf, 1994.

Gurock, Jeffrey S. *Jews in Gotham: New York Jews in a Changing City, 1920–2010*. New York: NYU Press, 2012.

——. *The Jews of Harlem: The Rise, Decline, and Revival of a Jewish Community*. New York: NYU Press, 2016.

——. *When Harlem Was Jewish, 1870–1930*. New York: Columbia University Press, 1979.

Guttman, Gail Kaplan. "Division and Diversity: Community Transition in Postwar America, 1945–1970; New Rochelle, New York, a Case Study." PhD diss., Columbia University, 2001.

Haynes, John Earl, and Harvey Klehr. *In Denial: Historians, Communism and Espionage*. San Francisco: Encounter Books, 2003.

——. *Venona: Decoding Soviet Espionage in America*. New Haven, CT: Yale University Press, 1999.

Herbert, Anthony, and James T. Wooten. *Soldier*. New York: Holt, Rinehart and Winston, 1973.

Hindus, Milton. *The Old East Side: An Anthology*. Philadelphia: Jewish Publication Society of America, 1969.

Hortis, C. Alexander. *The Mob and the City: The Hidden History of How the Mob Captured New York*. Amherst, NY: Prometheus Books, 2014.

Howe, Irving. *World of Our Fathers: The Journey of the East European Jews to America and the Life They Found and Made*. New York: Harcourt Brace Jovanovich, 1976.

Howe, Irving, and Kenneth Libo. *How We Lived: A Documentary History of Immigrant Jews in America*. New York: Richard Marek, 1979.

Hutchison, Dennis J. *The Man Who Once Was Whizzer White: A Portrait of Justice Byron R. White*. New York: Free Press, 1998.

Irons, Peter. *The Courage of Their Convictions*. New York: Free Press, 1988.

Jacobs, James B. *Mobsters, Unions, and Feds*. New York: NYU Press, 2004.

Kaczorowski, Robert. *Fordham University School of Law: A History*. New York: Fordham University Press, 2012.

Kaplan, John. *Segregation Litigation and the Schools—Part I: The New Rochelle Experience*, 58 NW U. L. Rev. 1 (March–April 1963).

Katz, Myrna, and Harvey Frommer. *It Happened in the Catskills*. New York: Harcourt Brace Jovanovich, 1991.

Kazin, Alfred. *A Walker in the City*. New York: MJF Books, 1951.

Keats, Charles. *Magnificent Masquerade*. New York: Funk & Wagnalls, 1964.

Keck, Thomas M. *The Most Activist Supreme Court in History: The Road to Modern Judicial Conservatism*. Chicago: University of Chicago Press, 2004.

Kennett, Lee. *G.I.: The American Soldier in World War II*. New York: Scribner, 1987.

Kisseloff, Jeff. *You Must Remember This: An Oral History of Manhattan from the 1890s to World War II*. New York: Harcourt Brace Jovanovich, 1989.

Knox, John C. *A Judge Comes of Age*. New York: Charles Scribner's Sons, 1941.

Kobrick, Jake. *The Rosenberg Trial*. Washington, DC: Federal Judicial Center, 2013.

Kohn, Steven M. *Jailed for Peace: The History of American Draft Law Violators, 1658–1985*. Westport, CT: Greenwood, 1986.

Kutler, Stanley I. *The American Inquisition: Justice and Injustice in the Cold War*. New York: Hill & Wang, 1982.

——. *The Wars of Watergate: The Last Crisis of Richard Nixon*. New York: Knopf, 1990.

LaCerra, Charles. *Franklin Delano Roosevelt and Tammany Hall of New York*. New York: University Press of America, 1997.

Lamphere, Robert J., and Tom Shachtman. *The FBI-KGB War: A Special Agent's Story*. Macon, GA: Mercer University Press, 1995.

Lederhendler, Eli. *New York Jews and the Decline of Urban Ethnicity*. Syracuse, NY: Syracuse University Press, 2001.

Lerner, Max. *The Unfinished Country*. New York: Simon & Schuster, 1959.

Llewellyn, Karl. *The Common Law Tradition*. Boston: Little, Brown, 1960.

Lomax, Louis E. *The Negro Revolt*. New York: Harper & Row, 1962.

Lynch, Geoffrey. *Manhattan Classic: New York's Finest Prewar Apartments*. New York: Princeton Architectural Press, 2014.

Maier, Thomas. *Newhouse: All the Glitter, Power, and Glory of America's Richest Media Empire and the Secretive Man behind It*. New York: Johnson Books, 1997.

Mailer, Norman. *Some Honorable Men: Political Conventions, 1960–1972*. Boston: Little, Brown, 1976.

The Making of Filártiga v. Peña: The Alien Tort Claims Act after Twenty-Five Years, Symposium, 9 N.Y. City L. Rev. 249 (Summer 2006).

Manz, William H., ed. *Civil Liberties in Wartime: Legislative Histories of the Espionage Act of 1917 and the Sedition Act of 1918*. Buffalo, NY: Hein, 2007.

Martineau, Robert J. *Enforcement of the Code of Judicial Conduct*, 1972 Utah L. Rev. 410 (1972).

Mayer, Martin. *Emory Buckner*. New York: Harper & Row, 1968.

McCullough, David. *Truman*. New York: Simon & Schuster, 1992.

Meeker, Richard H. *Newspaperman S. I. Newhouse and the Business of News*. New York: Ticknor & Fields, 1983.

Meeropol, Michael, ed. *The Rosenberg Letters: A Complete Edition of the Prison Correspondence of Julius and Ethel Rosenberg*. New York: Garland, 1994.

Meeropol, Robert. *An Execution in the Family: One Son's Journey*. New York: St. Martin's, 2003.

Meeropol, Robert, and Michael Meeropol. *We Are Your Sons: The Legacy of Ethel and Julius Rosenberg*. Boston: Houghton Mifflin, 1975.

——. *We Are Your Sons: The Legacy of Ethel and Julius Rosenberg*. 2nd ed. Urbana: University of Illinois Press, 1986.

Metzker, Isaac. *A Bintel Brief: Sixty Years of Letters from the Lower East Side to the* Jewish Daily Forward. New York: Schocken Books, 1971.

Miller, Arthur. "*The Crucible* and the Execution: A Memoir." *Rethinking Marxism: A Journal of Economics, Culture and Society* 2, no. 3 (Fall 1989).

Mitenbuler, Reid. *Bourbon Empire: The Past and Future of America's Whiskey*. New York: Viking, 2015.

Moore, Deborah Dash. "Reconsidering the Rosenbergs: Symbol and Substance in Second Generation American Jewish Consciousness." *Journal of American Ethnic History* 8, no. 1 (Fall 1988): 21–37.

Morris, Jeffrey B. "The American Jewish Judge: An Appraisal on the Occasion of the Bicentennial." *Jewish Social Studies* 38, no. 3/4 (Summer–Autumn 1976): 195–223.

——. *Federal Justice in the Second Circuit*. New York: Second Circuit Historical Committee, 1987.

Moskowitz, Miriam. *Phantom Spies, Phantom Justice: How I Survived McCarthyism and My Prosecution That Was the Rehearsal for the Rosenberg Trial*. Seattle: Justice Institute, 2012.

Mulligan, William. *Mulligan's Law: The Wit and Wisdom of William Hughes Mulligan*. New York: Fordham University Press, 1997.

Murdoch, Joyce, and Deb Price. *Courting Justice: Gay Men and Lesbians v. the Supreme Court*. New York: Basic Books, 2001.

Murphy, Bruce Allen. *The Brandeis/Frankfurter Connection: The Secret Political Activities of Two Supreme Court Justices*. New York: Oxford University Press, 1982.

——. *Fortas: The Rise and Ruin of a Supreme Court Justice*. New York: William Morrow, 1988.

Neville, John F. *The Press, the Rosenbergs, and the Cold War*. Westport, CT: Praeger, 1995.

Newman, Roger K., ed. *The Yale Biographical Dictionary of American Law*. New Haven, CT: Yale University Press, 2009.

Nizer, Louis. *The Implosion Conspiracy*. New York: Doubleday, 1973.

NOVA: Secrets, Lies, and Atomic Spies. Season 29, episode 13. February 5, 2002. PBS.

Noyes, John E., Laura A. Dickinson, and Mark W. Janis, eds. *International Law Stories*. Eagan, MN: Foundation, 2007.

Oakes, James L. *Judge Gurfein and the Pentagon Papers*, 2 CARDOZO L. REV. 5 (1980).

Olmsted, Kathryn S. "Blond Queens, Red Spiders, and Neurotic Old Maids: Gender and Espionage in the Early Cold War." *Intelligence and National Security* 19, no. 1 (Spring 2004).

Orfield, Gary, and Erica Frankenberg, with Jongyeon Ea and John Kuscera. "Brown at 60: Great Progress, a Long Retreat and an Uncertain Future." Civil Rights Project, May 15, 2014. https://civilrightsproject.ucla.edu/research/k-12-education/integration-and-diversity/brown-at-60-great-progress-a-long-retreat-and-an-uncertain-future.

Parrish, Michael E. "Cold War Justice: The Supreme Court and the Rosenbergs." *American Historical Review* 82, no. 4 (1977): 805–42.

Pearce, Russell G. *Rediscovering the Republican Origins of the Legal Ethics Codes*, 6 GEO. J. LEGAL ETHICS 241 (1992).

Pelisson, Gerard J., and James A. Garvey III. *The Castle on the Parkway: The Story of New York City's DeWitt Clinton High School and Its Extraordinary Influence on American Life*. Scarsdale, NY: Hutch, 2009.

Pilat, Oliver. *The Atom Spies*. New York: G. P. Putnam's Sons, 1952.

Powe, Lucas. *The Warren Court and American Politics*. Cambridge, MA: Harvard University Press, 2000.

Purnell, Brian, and Jeanne Theoharis, eds. *The Strange Careers of Jim Crow North: Segregation and Struggle outside of the South*. New York: NYU Press, 2019.

Radosh, Ronald, and Joyce Milton. *The Rosenberg File*. New York: Holt, Rinehart and Winston, 1983.

"Reflections: 50 Year Retrospective of the Lincoln School Decision Oral History Project." Unpublished oral histories. New Rochelle (NY) Public Library, 2010.

Reich, Charles. *The New Property*, 73 YALE L.J. 733 (1964).

Reiss, Marcia. *Lost New York*. New York: Pavilion Books, 2011.

Reppetto, Thomas. *American Mafia: A History of Its Rise to Power*. New York: MJF Books, 2004.

———. *Bringing Down the Mob: The War against the American Mafia*. New York: Henry Holt, 2006.

Rhodes, Richard. *Dark Sun: The Making of the Hydrogen Bomb*. New York: Simon & Schuster, 1995.

Rifkind, Simon. *One Man's World: Selected Works of Simon H. Rifkind*. 3 vols. New York: Keens, 1989.

Riis, Jacob. *How the Other Half Lives: Studies among the Tenements of New York*. New York: Scribner's, 1914.

Roberts, Sam. *The Brother: The Untold Story of the Rosenberg Case*. New York: Simon & Schuster Paperbacks, 2014.

Roiphe, Anne. *1185 Park Avenue*. New York: Touchstone, 1999.

Root, Jonathan. *The Betrayers*. London: Secker & Warburg, 1963.

The Rosenberg Case: Some Reflections on Federal Criminal Law, 54 COLUM. L. REV. 219 (Feb. 1954).

Rudenstine, David. *The Day the Presses Stopped: A History of the Pentagon Papers Case*. Berkeley: University of California Press, 1996.

Sabin, Paul. *Public Citizens: The Attack on Big Government and the Remaking of American Liberalism*. New York: W. W. Norton, 2021.

Salerno, Ralph, and John S. Tompkins. *The Crime Confederation: Cosa Nostra and Allied Operations in Organized Crime*. New York: Doubleday, 1969.

Salisbury, Harrison E. *Without Fear or Favor: The* New York Times *and Its Times*. New York: Times Books, 1980.

Schick, Marvin. *Learned Hand's Court*. Baltimore: Johns Hopkins University Press, 1970.

Schlesinger, Arthur M., Jr. *Robert Kennedy and His Times*. Boston: Houghton Mifflin, 1978.

———. *The Vital Center: The Politics of Freedom*. Boston: Houghton Mifflin, 1949. Reprint, with introduction by author, New York: Da Capo, 1988.

Schneir, Walter. *Final Verdict: What Really Happened in the Rosenberg Case*. New York: Melville House, 2010.

Schneir, Walter, and Miriam Schneir. *Invitation to an Inquest*. New York: Pantheon Books, 1983.

Schriftgiesser, Kirk. *The Lobbyists: The Art and Business of Influencing Lawmakers*. Boston: Little, Brown, 1951.

Schroth, Raymond A. *Fordham: A History and a Memoir*. New York: Fordham University Press, 2008.

Schwartz, Bernard, ed. *The Warren Court: A Retrospective*. New York: Oxford University Press, 1996.

Schwartz, Herman, ed. *The Burger Years*. New York: Viking, 1987.

Sebba, Anne. *Ethel Rosenberg*. New York: St. Martin's, 2021.

Segall, Eric J. *Originalism as Faith*. Cambridge: Cambridge University Press, 2018.

Sharlitt, Joseph H. *Fatal Error: The Miscarriage of Justice That Sealed the Rosenbergs' Fate*. New York: Scribners, 1989.

Sharswood, George. *An Essay on Professional Ethics*. 5th ed. (1884). Reprint, Littleton, CO: Fred B. Rothman, 1993.

Shelley, Thomas. *Fordham: A History of the Jesuit University of New York, 1841–2003*. New York: Fordham University Press, 2016.

Smith, Dwight C. *The Mafia Mystique*. New York: Basic Books, 1975.

Smith, Richard Norton. *Thomas E. Dewey and His Times*. New York: Simon & Schuster, 1982.

Snyder, Brad. *Taking Great Cases: Lessons from the "Rosenberg" Case*, 63 VAND. L. REV. 885 (2019).

Sobell, Morton. *On Doing Time*. New York: Scribners, 1974.

Sorin, Gerald. *Irving Howe: A Life of Passionate Dissent*. New York: NYU Press, 2002.

Stebenne, David. *Arthur J. Goldberg: New Deal Liberal*. New York: Oxford University Press, 1996.

Stein, Marc. "All the Immigrants Are Straight, All the Homosexuals Are Citizens, but Some of Us Are Queer Aliens: Genealogies of Legal Strategy in *Boutilier v. INS*." *Journal of American Ethnic History* 29, no. 4 (Summer 2010): 45–77.

——. "*Boutilier* and the U.S. Supreme Court's Sexual Revolution." *Law and History Review* 23, no. 3 (Fall 2005): 491–536.

Stern, Robert. "The Rosenberg Case in Perspective—Its Present Significance." *Journal of Supreme Court History* (1990): 79–92.

Stern, Seth, and Wermeil, Stephen. *Justice Brennan: Liberal Champion*. New York: Houghton Mifflin Harcourt, 2010.

Strub, Whitney. *Obscenity Rules,* Roth v. United States *and the Long Struggle over Sexual Expression*. Lawrence: University Press of Kansas, 2013.

Sugrue, Thomas J. *Sweet Land of Liberty: The Forgotten Struggle for Civil Rights in the North*. New York: Random House, 2008.

Sunstein, Cass. *The Second Bill of Rights: FDR's Unfinished Revolution and Why We Need It More Than Ever*. New York: Basic Books, 2004.

Thompson, Heather Ann. *Blood in the Water: The Attica Prison Uprising of 1971 and Its Legacy*. New York: Pantheon Books, 2016.

To Secure These Rights. Report of the President's Committee on Civil Rights. October 29, 1947. www.trumanlibrary.gov/library/to-secure-these-rights.

Truman, Harry S. *1946–1952: Years of Trial and Hope*. New York: Time, 1956.

225 Years (1789–2014): The United States Attorneys for the Southern District of New York. New York: Committee for the Bicentennial Celebration (1789–1989) of the United States Attorneys (Southern District of New York), 2014.

Ungar, Sanford J. *The Papers and the Papers: An Account of the Political Battle over the Pentagon Papers*. New York: Dutton, 1972.

von Hoffman, Nicholas. *Citizen Cohn: The Scandalous Life and Times of Roy Cohn, Lawyer, Fixer, Destroyer*. Boston: Abacus, 1988.

Walsh, Lawrence A. *The Gift of Insecurity: A Lawyer's Life*. Chicago: American Bar Association, 2003.

Wasserstein, Bernard. *On The Eve: The Jews of Europe before the Second World War*. New York: Simon & Schuster, 2012.

Wexley, John. *The Judgment of Julius and Ethel Rosenberg*. New York: Cameron & Kahn, 1955.

White, E. B. *Here Is New York*. New York: Harper & Bros., 1949.

White, G. Edward. *Earl Warren: A Public Life*. New York: Oxford University Press, 1982.

White, Richard Alan. *Breaking Silence: The Case That Changed the Face of Human Rights*. Washington, DC: Georgetown University Press, 2004.

Wiener, Jon. *Come Together*. New York: Random House, 1984.

——. *Gimme Some Truth: The John Lennon FBI Files*. Berkeley: University of California Press, 1999.

Wildes, Leon. *John Lennon vs. the USA: The Inside Story of the Most Bitterly Contested and Influential Deportation Case in United States History*. Chicago: American Bar Association, 2016.

Winter-Berger, Robert N. *The Washington Pay-Off: An Insider's View of Corruption in Government*. Secaucus, NJ: Lyle Stuart, 1972.

Wohl, Alexander. *Father, Son, and Constitution: How Justice Tom Clark and Attorney General Ramsey Clark Shaped American Democracy*. Lawrence: University Press of Kansas, 2013.

Yalof, David Alistair. *Pursuit of Justices: Presidential Politics and the Selection of Supreme Court Nominees*. Chicago: University of Chicago Press, 1999.

You and the Atomic Bomb: What to Do in Case of Atomic Attack. New York: New York State Civil Defense Commission, 1950.

Zion, Sidney. *The Autobiography of Roy Cohn*. New York: St. Martin's, 1988.

Zirin, James D. *The Mother Court: Tales of Cases That Mattered in America's Greatest Trial Court*. Chicago: American Bar Association, 2014.

Index